Thanks to God, my wife Denise, my colleagues, and my students. All continue to be a source of inspiration and support.

BRIEF CONTENTS

CONTENTS

From scandals in corporate ethics to the business effects of 9/11, the challenge to lead an organization has never been more demanding. Managers at all levels must understand how a company's departments and processes "fit" together to comprise a successful firm. This text draws from all functional areas of business and presents a cohesive strategic management model from a top-level strategic perspective. It is most useful for students with backgrounds in related fields such as management, marketing, finance, accounting, and economics.

Three key characteristics of this text distinguish it from other books on strategic management. First, the text is organized sequentially around the strategic management process.

- Foundations (Chapters 1–2)
- External Environment (Chapters 3–4)
- Internal Environment (Chapter 5)
- Fundamentals of Strategy (Chapters 6–8)
- Strategy Formulation (Chapter 9)
- Strategy Execution (Chapter 10–11)
- Strategic Control (Chapter 12)
- Case Studies

Current issues such as corporate ethics, terrorism, global strategies, and e-commerce are not relegated to distinct chapters, but are instead considered via their relationships to various steps in the strategic management process. This text adopts the view that such special topics should not be treated as independent entities, but rather as component parts of the ongoing strategic management effort.

Second, strategic analysis of a firm (i.e., a case analysis) is viewed as inseparable from the concepts presented in the chapters. As such, the twenty-five key questions that should be answered as part of a strategic analysis are presented in "boxes" throughout the text alongside the relevant theory.

Finally, the text is very readable. It provides a comprehensive presentation of current strategic management thinking in a clear and succinct format. This approach enables the professor to cover the entire book in a typical capstone business course while retaining valuable course time for case projects, simulations, discussion of real-time strategic issues, and other activities.

What's New in This Edition

The strategic management model presented in the third edition of the text remains relatively unchanged, with only minor enhancements. The integration of new concepts and the enhancement of existing ones can be seen throughout the chapters, from a discussion of Thomas Friedman's flat world in Chapter 2 to expanded coverage of crisis management in Chapter 12.

The third edition contains two additional chapters, twelve in total. The topics covered in the first chapter of the second edition—fundamentals of strategic management—have been expanded to cover two chapters. Chapter 2—the strategy landscape—provides detailed discussions on key trends and issues that are changing how organizations compete and how strategic decisions are made. Topics such as outsourcing, offshoring, commoditization, mass customization, and the effects of the Internet are addressed in the second chapter.

The single chapter on strategy execution in the second edition has been expanded into two chapters in the third edition. First, Chapter 10 focuses on structural concerns, then Chapter 11 emphasizes organizational culture and strategic leadership.

The material presented for each real-time case has been updated and reorganized, with a complete citation and a brief synopsis for each key article referenced. Links to sources of information to support a case study are constantly updated and can still be found at www.jparnell.com/text/researchlinks.htm.

In addition to updated real-time cases, this edition includes twelve traditional, full-length cases. Some of these can be easily updated, but others feature small, private, and international enterprises whereby outside information may not be readily available. These cases can be used for term projects or daily discussions, giving instructors a broader range of assignment options.

Online and in Print

Strategic Management: Theory and Practice, Third Edition, is available online as well as in print. The online version demonstrates how the interactive media components of the text enhance presentation and understand. For example, consider the following:

- Animated illustrations help clarify concepts and bring them to life.
- Chapter quizzes test students' knowledge of various topics and provide immediate feedback.
- Clickable glossary terms provide immediate definitions of key concepts.
- References and footnotes "pop up" with a click.
- Highlighting capabilities allow students to emphasize main ideas. They can also add personal notes in the margin.
- The search function allows students to quickly locate discussions of specific topics throughout the text.
- An interactive study guide at the end of each chapter provides tools for learning, such as interactive key-term matching and the ability to review customized content in one place.

Students may choose to use only the online version of the text or both the online and print versions together. This gives them the flexibility to choose which combination of resources works best for them. To assist those who use the online and print version together, the primary heads and subheads in each chapter are numbered the same. For example, the first primary head in Chapter 1 is labeled 1-1, the second primary head in this chapter is labeled 1-2, and so on. The subheads build from the designation of their corresponding primary head: 1-1a, 1-1b, and so on. This numbering system is designed to make moving between the online and print versions as seamless as possible.

Finally, next to a number of figures and exhibits in the print version of the text you will see an icon similar to those below. The icon indicates that this figure or exhibit in the online edition is interactive in a way that applies, illustrates, or reinforces the concept.

Ancillaries

Thomson Custom Solutions is pleased to offer a robust suite of supplemental materials for instructors using its textbooks. These ancillaries include a Test Bank, PowerPoint® slides, and Instructor's Manual, all constructed by the author himself.

The Test Bank for this book includes over 1,000 carefully constructed questions in a wide range of difficulty levels, including true or false, multiple-choice, short answer, and essay questions. The Test Bank offers not only the correct answer for each question, but also a rationale or explanation for the correct answer and a chapter reference where materials addressing the question content can be found. This Test Bank comes with ExamViewPro® software for easily creating customized or multiple versions of a test, and includes the option of editing or adding to the existing question bank.

A set of over 250 PowerPoint slides is available for this text. This is designed to provide instructors with comprehensive visual aids for each chapter in the book. These slides include outlines of each chapter, highlighting important terms, concepts, and discussion points. The Instructor's Manual for this book offers suggested syllabi for ten- and fifteen-week terms, learning objectives, lesson plans, lecture outlines and notes, answers to discussion questions, critical thinking questions, and additional Web resources for each chapter.

About Atomic Dog

Atomic Dog is faithfully dedicated to meeting the needs of today's faculty and students, offering a unique and clear alternative to the traditional textbook. Breaking down textbooks and study tools into their basic "atomic parts," we then recombine them and utilize rich digital media to create a "new breed" of textbook.

This blend of online content, interactive multimedia, and print creates unprecedented adaptability to meet different educational settings and individual learning styles. As part of Thomson Custom Solutions, we offer even greater flexibility and resources in creating a learning solution tailor-fit to your course.

Atomic Dog is loyally dedicated to our customers and our environment, adhering to three key tenets.

Focus on essential and quality content: We are proud to work with our authors to deliver a high-quality textbook at a lower cost. We focus on the essential information and resources students need and present them in an efficient but student-friendly format.

Value and choice for students: Our products are a great value and provide students with more choices in "what and how" they buy—often at savings of 30 to 40 percent less than traditional textbooks. Students who choose the online edition may see even greater savings compared to a print textbook. Faculty play an important and willing role—working with us to keep costs low for their students by evaluating texts and supplementary materials online.

Reducing our environmental "paw-print": Atomic Dog is working to reduce its impact on our environment in several ways. Our textbooks and marketing materials are all printed on recycled paper. We encourage faculty to review text materials online instead of requesting a print review copy. Students who buy the online edition do their part by going paperless and eliminating the need for additional packaging or shipping. Atomic Dog will continue to explore new ways to reduce our "paw-print" in the environment and hope you will join us in these efforts.

Atomic Dog is dedicated to faithfully serving the needs of faculty and students—providing a learning tool that helps make the connection. We hope that after you try our texts, Atomic Dog—like other great dogs—will become your faithful companion.

Reviewers

The author would like to thank the following individuals for reviewing the text.

Woodrow D. Richardson, Ball State University

Ralph R. Braithwaite, University of Connecticut

Acknowledgments

I am indebted to Sarah Blasco, Victoria Putman, and the entire Atomic Dog team for their commitment to excellence and their continued support of this textbook. I am also grateful to the adopters of previous editions whose comments and suggestions have fostered continuous improvement in this edition.

Dr. John A. Parnell currently serves as the William Henry Belk Distinguished Professor of Management at the University of North Carolina at Pembroke. He completed the B.S.B.A., M.B.A., and M.A.Ed. degree from East Carolina University, the Ed.D. degree from Campbell University, and the Ph.D. degree from The University of Memphis. His academic career includes a number of institutions, including service as Professor and Head of the Department of Marketing & Management at Texas A&M University-Commerce. He received the H.M. Lafferty Distinguished Faculty Award at A&M-Commerce in 2002 and the Adolph Dial Award for Scholarly & Creative Activity at UNC-Pembroke in 2005.

Dr. Parnell is a recognized authority in the field, having published more than 200 articles, cases, proceedings, books, and book chapters in strategic management and related fields. He serves on numerous academic journal editorial boards and consults with select firms in the area of strategic planning. He has also appeared frequently as a guest to discuss issues related to business and competitiveness on Sirius Satellite Radio's Andrew Wilkow Show.

Dr. Parnell has lectured at institutions abroad, including Instituto Tecnologico Y De Estudios Superiores De Monterrey-Campus Estado de Mexico (ITESM-CEM), Chung Yuan Christian University in Taiwan, and China University of Geosciences in Beijing. He also served as a Fulbright Scholar in Cairo, Egypt, in 1995.

Fundamentals of Strategic Management

1

Chapter Outline

Today's business world is global, Internet driven, and obsessed with speed. The challenges it creates for strategic managers are often complex, ambiguous, and unstructured. Add to this the constant allegations of top management wrongdoings, ethical blunders, and skyrocketing executive compensation, and it is easy to see why firm leaders are under greater pressure than ever to respond to strategic problems quickly, decisively, and responsibly. Hence, the need for effective strategic management has never been more pronounced than it is today. This text presents a framework for addressing these immediate strategic challenges.

This chapter introduces the notion of strategic management, highlights its importance, and presents a five-step process for strategically analyzing an organization. The remaining chapters expand on the various steps in the process, with special emphasis on their application to ongoing enterprises.

1-1 What Is Strategic Management?

Strategy refers to top management's plans to develop and sustain **competitive advantage**—a state whereby a firm's successful strategies cannot be easily duplicated by its competitors[1]—so that the organization's mission is fulfilled.[2] Following this definition, it is assumed that an organization has a plan, its competitive advantage is understood, and that its members understand the reason for its existence. These assumptions may appear self-evident, but many strategic problems can be traced to fundamental misunderstandings associated with defining the strategy. Debates over the nature of the organization's competitive advantage, its mission, and whether a strategic plan is really needed can be widespread.[3] Comments such as "We're too busy to focus on developing a strategy" or "I'm not exactly sure what my company is really trying to accomplish" can be overheard in many organizations.

Strategic management is a broader term than *strategy* and is a process that includes top management's analysis of the environment in which the organization operates prior to formulating a strategy, as well as the plan for implementation and control of the strategy. The difference between a strategy and the strategic management process is that the latter includes considering what must be done before a strategy is formulated through assessing the success of an implemented strategy. The strategic management process can be summarized in five steps, each of which is discussed in greater detail in subsequent chapters of the book (see Figure 1-1).[4]

1. **External analysis:** Analyze the opportunities and threats or constraints that exist in the organization's external environment, including industry and macroenvironmental forces.
2. **Internal analysis:** Analyze the organization's strengths and weaknesses in its internal environment. Consider the appropriateness of its mission.
3. **Strategy formulation:** Formulate strategies that build and sustain competitive advantage by matching the organization's strengths and weaknesses with the environment's opportunities and threats.
4. **Strategy execution:** Implement the strategies that have been developed.
5. **Strategic control:** Measure success and make corrections when the strategies are not producing the desired outcomes.

Is it necessary to address these steps sequentially? The answer depends on one's perspective. *Outsiders* analyzing a firm should apply a systematic approach that progresses through these steps in order. Doing so develops to a holistic understanding of the firm, its industry, and its strategic challenges.

Source: Comstock.com

Strategy

Top management's plans to attain outcomes consistent with the organization's mission and goals.

Competitive advantage

A state whereby a business unit's successful strategies cannot be easily duplicated by its competitors.

Strategic Management

The continuous process of assessing its external environment and its internal strengths and weaknesses, formulating and implementing strategies, and exerting strategic control to achieve success.

FIGURE 1-1 Organization of the Book

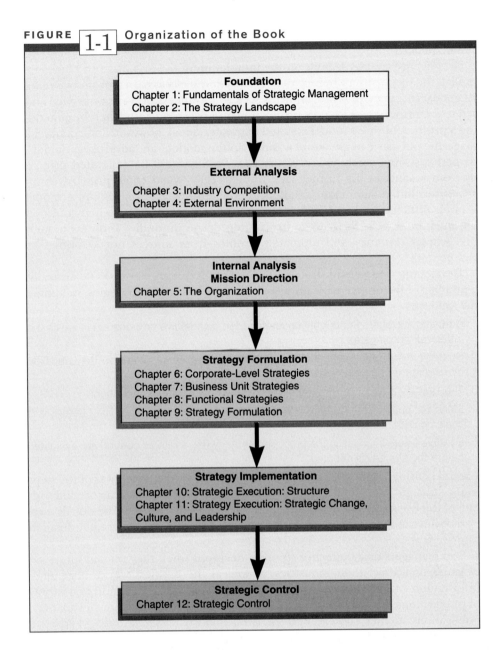

In organizations, however, strategies are being formulated, implemented, and controlled simultaneously while external and internal factors are being assessed and reassessed. In addition, changes in one stage of the strategic management process will inevitably affect other stages as well. After a planned strategy is implemented, for example, it often requires modification as conditions change. Hence, because these steps are so tightly intertwined, *insiders* treat all of the steps as a single integrated, ongoing process.[5]

Consider the strategic management process at a fast-food restaurant chain. At any given time, top managers are likely assessing changes in consumer taste preferences and food preparation, analyzing the activities of competitors, working to overcome firm weaknesses, controlling remnants of a strategy implemented several years ago, implementing a strategy formulated several months ago, and formulating strategic plans for the future. Although each of these activities can

Business Model

The economic mechanism by which a business hopes to sell its goods or services and generate a profit.

be linked to a distinct stage in the strategic management process, they occur simultaneously.

An effective strategy is built on the foundation of the organization's **business model,** the mechanism whereby the organization seeks to earn a profit by selling its goods. In a general sense, all firms seek to produce a product or service and sell it at a price higher than its production and overhead costs, thereby generating a profit. A business model is stated in greater detail, however. For example, a magazine publisher might adopt a "subscription model," an "advertising model," or perhaps some combination of the two. Profits would be generated primarily from readers in the former case whereas they would come primarily from advertisers in the latter case. Needless to say, identifying a firm's business model is rarely difficult at a basic level, but can become more complex when considering intricate details. Progressive firms often devise innovative business models that extract revenue—and ultimately profits—from sources not identified by competitors.

Developing a successful strategy for the firm is not an easy task. Realistically, a number of factors are typically associated with successful strategies, including the following:

1. Strategic managers thoroughly understand the competitive environment in which the organization competes.
2. Strategic managers understand the organization's resources and how they translate into strengths *and* weaknesses.
3. The strategy is consistent with the mission and goals of the organization.
4. Plans for putting the strategy into action are designed with specificity before it is implemented.
5. Possible future changes in the proposed strategy (i.e., strategic control) are evaluated before the strategy is adopted.

Careful consideration of these factors reinforces the interrelatedness of the steps in the strategic management process. Each factor is most closely associated with one of the five steps, yet they fit together like pieces of a puzzle. The details associated with the success factors—and others—will be discussed in greater detail in future chapters.

Top managers make effective strategic decisions when they remain informed of issues that affect their industries, as well as the business world in general. Information vital to effective strategic decision making can be found in a variety of publications. In addition to the business sections of most major newspapers, publications such as *Fortune, Business Week, Industry Standard, Strategy+Business,* and *Wall Street Journal* report on a wide variety of strategic management topics (see Table 1-1). Not only are these concepts of interest to top managers, but they are also a concern for employees, supervisors, and middle managers of all organizations. An appreciation of the organization's strategy helps all of its members relate their work assignments more closely to the direction of the organization.

Strategic management is not limited to for-profit organizations. Top managers of any organization, regardless of profit or nonprofit status, must understand the organization's environment and its capabilities and develop strategies to assist the enterprise in attaining its goals. Drexel University President Constantine Papadakis, for example, is widely considered to be a leading strategic thinker among university top executives. The innovative Greek immigrant promotes Drexel through aggressive marketing, while campaigning for an all-digital library without books. In many respects, he manages the university in the same way that other executives manage profit-seeking enterprises. Interestingly, his salary in 2005 was about $900,000 per year—not including

TABLE 1-1   **Select Online Sources of Business Strategy News**

Publication	Contact Information
Business Week	www.businessweek.com
E-Commerce Times	www.ecommercetimes.com
Economist	www.economist.com (payment required for full access)
Fast Company	www.fastcompany.com
Forbes	www.forbes.com
Fortune	www.fortune.com
Industry Standard	www.thestandard.com(e-commerce)
Strategy+Business	www.strategy-business.com (payment required for full access)
Wall Street Journal	http://wsj.com (payment required for full access)

income from outside sources—making him one of the highest paid university presidents in the country.[6]

1-1a Intended and Realized Strategies

A critical challenge facing organizations is the reality that strategies are not always implemented as originally planned. Henry Mintzberg introduced two terms to help clarify the shift that often occurs between the time a strategy is formulated and the time it is implemented. An **intended strategy,** that which management originally planned, may be realized just as it was planned, in a modified form, or even in an entirely different form. Occasionally, the strategy that management intends is actually realized, but the intended strategy and the **realized strategy,** which is what management actually implements, usually differ.[7] Hence, the original strategy may be realized with desirable or undesirable results, or it may be modified as changes in the firm or the environment become known.

> **Intended Strategy**
>
> The original strategy top management plans and intends to implement.

> **Realized Strategy**
>
> The strategy top management actually implements.

The gap between the intended and realized strategies usually results from unforeseen environmental or organizational events, better information that was not available when the strategy was formulated, or an improvement in top management's ability to assess its environment. Although it is important for managers to formulate responsible strategies based on a realistic and thorough assessment of the firm and its environment, things invariably change along the way. Hence, it is common for such a gap to exist, creating the need for constant strategic action if a firm is to stay on course. Instead of resisting modest strategic changes when new information is discovered, managers should search for new information and be willing to make such changes when necessary. This activity is part of strategic control, the final step in the strategic management process.

1-1b Scientific and Artistic Perspectives on Strategic Management

Top executives should take one of two different perspectives on the approach to strategic management. Most strategy scholars have endorsed a *scientific perspective,* whereby strategic managers are encouraged to systematically assess the firm's external environment and evaluate the pros and cons of myriad alternatives before formulating strategy. The business environment is seen as largely objective, analyzable, and at least somewhat predictable. As such, strategic managers should follow a systematic process of environmental, competitive, and internal analysis and build the organization's strategy on this foundation.

According to this perspective, strategic managers should be trained, highly skilled analytical thinkers capable of digesting a myriad of objective data and translating it into a desired direction for the firm. "Strategy scientists" tend to minimize or reject altogether the role of imagination and creativity in the strategy process, and are not generally receptive to alternatives that emerge from any process other than a comprehensive, analytical approach.

Others, however, have a different view. According to the *artistic perspective* on strategy, the lack of environmental predictability and the fast pace of change render elaborate strategy planning as suspect at best. Instead, strategists should incorporate large doses of creativity and intuition in order to design a comprehensive strategy for the firm.[8] Mintzberg's notion of a craftsman—encompassing individual skill, dedication, and perfection through mastery of detail—embodies the artistic model. The strategy artist senses the state of the organization, interprets its subtleties, and seeks to mold its strategy like a potter molds clay. The artist visualizes the outcomes associated with various alternatives and ultimately charts a course based on holistic thinking, intuition, and imagination.[9] "Strategy artists" may even view strategic planning exercises as time poorly spent and may not be as likely as those in the science school to make the effort necessary to maximize the value of a formal planning process.[10]

This text acknowledges the validity of the artistic perspective but emphasizes the scientific view. Creativity and innovation are important and encouraged, but are most likely to translate into organizational success when they occur as part of a comprehensive approach to strategic management. Nonetheless, the type of formal, systematic strategic planning proposed in this text is not without its critics. Some charge that such models are too complex to apply, or that they apply only to businesses in highly certain environments.[11] Others emphasize that the stages in the process are so closely interrelated and that considering them as independent steps may be counterproductive. Still others, such as Mintzberg, argue that planning models stifle the creativity and imagination that is central to formulating an effective strategy.[12] Although these views have merit, the comprehensive, systematic model proposed herein is presented as a proper foundation for understanding the strategic management process. It does not, however, preclude the application of other approaches.

1-2 Influence on Strategic Management

The roots of the strategic management field can be traced to the 1950s when the discipline was originally called "business policy." Today, strategic management is an eclectic field, drawing upon a variety of theoretical frameworks. Three prominent perspectives are summarized in Table 1-2 and discussed in this section.

TABLE 1-2 Theoretical Perspectives on Firm Performance

Theoretical Perspective	Primary Influence on Firm Performance	How Perspective Is Applied to the Case Analysis
Industrial organization (IO) theory	Structure of the industry	Industry analysis portion of the external environment
Resource-based theory	Firm's unique combination of strategic resources	Analysis of internal strengths and weaknesses
Contingency theory	Fit between the firm and its external environment	Strengths, weaknesses, opportunities, and threats (SWOT) analysis and SW/OT matrix

Industrial organization (IO), a branch of microeconomics, emphasizes the *influence of the industry environment* upon the firm. The central tenet of industrial organization theory is the notion that a firm must adapt to influences in its industry to survive and prosper; thus, its financial performance is primarily determined by the success of the industry in which it competes. Industries with favorable structures offer the greatest opportunity for firm profitability.[13] Following this perspective, it is more important for a firm to choose the correct industry within which to compete than to determine *how* to compete within a given industry. Recent research has supported the notion that industry factors tend to play a dominant role in the performance of most firms, except for those that are the notable industry leaders or losers.[14]

IO assumes that an organization's performance and ultimate survival depend on its ability to *adapt* to industry forces over which it has little or no control. According to IO, strategic managers should seek to understand the nature of the industry and formulate strategies that feed off the industry's characteristics.[15] Because IO focuses on industry forces alone, strategies, resources, and competencies are assumed to be fairly similar among competitors within a given industry. If one firm deviates from the industry norm and implements a new, successful strategy, then other firms will rapidly mimic the higher performing firm by purchasing the resources, competencies, or management talent that have made the leading firm so profitable. Hence, although the IO perspective emphasizes the industry's influence on individual firms, it is also possible for firms to influence the strategy of rivals, and in some cases even modify the structure of the industry.[16]

Perhaps the opposite of the IO perspective, **resource-based theory** views performance primarily as a function of a firm's ability to utilize its resources.[17] Although environmental opportunities and threats are important, a firm's unique resources comprise the key variables that allow it to develop a **distinctive competence,** enabling the firm to distinguish itself from its rivals and create competitive advantage. "Resources" include all of a firm's tangible and intangible assets, such as capital, equipment, employees, knowledge, and information.[18] An organization's resources are directly linked to its capabilities, which can create value and ultimately lead to profitability for the firm. Hence, resource-based theory focuses primarily on individual firms rather than on the competitive environment.

If resources are to be used for **sustained competitive advantage**—a firm's ability to enjoy strategic benefits over an extended time—those resources must be valuable, rare, not subject to perfect imitation, and without strategically relevant substitutes.[19] Valuable resources are those that contribute significantly to the firm's effectiveness and efficiency. Rare resources are possessed by only a few competitors, and imperfectly imitable resources cannot be fully duplicated by rivals. Resources that have no strategically relevant substitutes enable the firm to operate in a manner that cannot be effectively imitated by others, and thereby sustain high performance.

According to **contingency theory,** the most profitable firms are likely to be those that develop a *beneficial fit* with their environment. In other words, a strategy is most likely to be successful when it is consistent with the organization's mission, its competitive environment, and its resources. Contingency theory represents a *middle ground* perspective that views organizational performance as the joint outcome of environmental forces and the firm's strategic actions. Firms can become proactive by choosing to operate in environments where opportunities and threats match their strengths and weaknesses.[20] Should the industry environment change in a way that is unfavorable to the firm, its top managers should consider leaving that industry and reallocating its resources to other, more favorable industries.

Industrial Organization (IO)

A view based in microeconomic theory which states that firm profitability is most closely associated with industry structure.

Resource-Based Theory

The perspective that views performance primarily as a function of a firm's ability to utilize its resources.

Distinctive Competence

Unique resources, skills, and capabilities that enable a firm to distinguish itself from its competitors and create competitive advantage.

Sustained Competitive Advantage

A firm's ability to enjoy strategic benefits over time.

Contingency Theory

A view which states that the most profitable firms are likely to be the ones that develop the best fit with their environment.

Each of these three perspectives has merit and has been incorporated into the strategic management process laid out in this text. The industrial organization view is seen in the industry analysis phase, most directly in Michael Porter's "five forces" model. Resource-based theory is applied directly to the internal analysis phase and the effort to identify an organization's resources that could lead to sustained competitive advantage. Contingency theory is seen in the strategic alternative generation phase, where alternatives are developed to improve the organization's fit with its environment. Hence, multiple perspectives are critical to a holistic understanding of strategic management.[21]

1-3 Strategic Decisions

How does one think and act strategically, and who makes the decisions? The answers to these questions vary across firms and may also be influenced by factors such as industry, age of the firm, and size of the organization. In general, however, strategic decisions are marked by four key distinctions.

1. They are based on a systematic, comprehensive analysis of internal attributes and factors external to the organization. Decisions that address only part of the organization—perhaps a single functional area—are usually not considered to be strategic decisions.

2. They are long term and future oriented, but are built on knowledge about the past and present. Scholars and managers do not always agree on what constitutes the "long term," but most agree that it can range anywhere from several years in duration to more than a decade.

3. They seek to capitalize on favorable situations outside the organization. In general, this means taking advantage of opportunities that exist for the firm, but it also includes taking measures to minimize the effects of external threats.

4. They involve choices. Although making win-win strategic decisions may be possible, most involve some degree of trade-off between alternatives, at least in the short run. For example, raising salaries to retain a skilled workforce can increase wages, and adding product features or enhancing quality can increase the cost of production. Such trade-offs, however, may diminish in the long run, as a more skilled, higher paid workforce may be more productive than a typical workforce, and sales of a higher quality product may increase, thereby raising sales and potentially profits. Decision makers must understand these complex relationships across the business spectrum.

Source: Comstock.com

Top Management Team

A team of top-level executives, headed by the CEO, all of whom play instrumental roles in the strategic management process.

Because of these distinctions, strategic decision making is generally reserved for the top executive and members of the **top management team.** The chief executive is the individual ultimately responsible (and generally *held* responsible) for the organization's strategic management, but this person rarely acts alone. Except in the smallest companies, the CEO relies on a *team* of top-level executives—including members of the board of directors, vice presidents, and various line and staff managers—all of whom play instrumental roles in strategically managing the firm. Generally speaking, the quality of strategic decisions improves dramatically when more than one capable executive participates in the process.[22]

The size of the team on which the top executive relies for strategic input and support can vary from firm to firm. Companies organized around functions such as marketing and production generally involve the heads of the functional departments in strategic decisions. Very large organizations often employ corporate-level strategic planning staffs and outside consultants to assist top executives in the process. The degree of involvement of top and middle managers in the strategic management process also depends on the personal philosophy of the CEO.[23]

Some chief executives are known for making quick decisions, whereas others have a reputation for involving a large number of top managers and others in the process.

Input to strategic decisions, however, need not be limited to members of the top management team. To the contrary, obtaining input from others throughout the organization, either directly or indirectly, can be quite beneficial. In fact, most strategic decisions result from the streams of inputs, decisions, and actions of many people. For example, an employee in a company's research and development department attends a trade show where vendors discuss a new product or production process idea that seems relevant to the company. The employee relates the idea to the next level manager who, in turn, modifies and passes it along to a higher level manager. Eventually, the organization's marketing and production managers discuss a version of the idea, and later present it to top management. The CEO ultimately decides to incorporate the idea into the ongoing strategic planning process. This example illustrates the indirect involvement of individuals throughout the organization in the strategic management process. Top management is ultimately responsible for the final decision, but this decision is based on a culmination of the ideas, creativity, information, and analyses of others[24] (see Strategy at Work 1-1).

Ethics and social responsibility are also key concerns in strategic decision making. Simply stated, the moral components and social outcomes associated with a strategic decision, such as the effects of closing an existing production facility in search of lower costs abroad, should be considered alongside economic concerns. These issues are discussed in greater detail in Chapters 6 through 9 under the umbrella of strategy formulation (see Case Analysis 1-1).

STRATEGY AT WORK 1-1

Strategic Decisions

Strategic decisions, by their nature, may be characterized by considerable risk and uncertainty. Unpredictable environmental changes can quickly threaten well-conceived plans. Most strategic decision makers clearly recognize this danger and learn to adapt. Here are two examples.

1. Like all aircarriers, American Airlines faces a number of challenges: international terrorism, steadily rising costs, unstable national economies, uncertain volumes of domestic traffic, and protectionist threats to international traffic. In the face of these threats, CEO Robert Crandall suggests that senior managers rarely know the outcomes of these situations anyway and should be accustomed to dealing with the uncertainty associated with critical strategic decisions.

2. Bernard Food Industries Inc. is a fifty-three-year-old family-held business of more than 1,500 sugar-free, low-fat, and low-calorie food products. At first, the company sold most of its products to hospitals, nursing homes, and other such institutions. In 1996, however, Steve Bernard, the founder's son, decided to expand the market. Although only a handful of companies were marketing such products at that time, Bernard viewed the Web as the future. The firm's online subsidiary, eDietShop (www.diet-shop.com) performed extremely well and quintupled retail sales in the first two years and has continued to grow, developing into one of its industry's leaders by the mid-2000s. As Bernard put it, "We didn't turn to the Web because other people were doing it but because we knew where we wanted our business to go."

Sources: S. Forster, "Online Brokerage Firms Adopt a 'Bricks-and-Clicks' Strategy," Wall Street Journal Interactive Edition, 6 February 2001; Anonymous, "Taming the Techno Beast—Technology Is Running Wild. Learn to Manage Change, or You'll Get Eaten Alive," Business Week, Technology section, 8 June 2000; P. Wright, M. Kroll, and J. A. Parnell, Strategic Management: Concepts (Upper Saddle River, NJ: Prentice Hall, 1998); W. M. Carley, "GE and Pratt Agree to Build Engine for Boeing Jumbo Jet," Wall Street Journal Interactive Edition, 9 May 1996; J. Cole and C. S. Smith, "Boeing Loses Contest to Become China's Partner in Building Plane," Wall Street Journal Interactive Edition, 2 May 1996.

Case Analysis 1-1

Step 1: Introduction of the Organization

The first step in the case analysis process is to develop familiarity with the organization, a basic task not directly related to a specific theory or set of concepts presented in this chapter. Analyzing an ongoing enterprise begins with a general introduction and understanding of the company. When was the organization founded, why, and by whom? Is any unusual history associated with the organization? Is it privately or publicly held? What is the company's mission? Has the mission changed since its inception?

It is also important at this point to identify the business model on which the organization's success is predicated. In other words, what is the basic profit-generating idea behind the company? Determining this information is simple for some companies (Ford, for example, hopes to sell cars and offer consumer financing at a profit) but may be complicated for others where revenue streams and competitive advantage are more difficult to identify.

1-4 Summary

Top managers face more complex strategic challenges today than ever before. Strategic management involves analysis of an organization's external and internal environments, formulation and implementation of its strategic plan, and strategic control. These steps in the process are interrelated and typically done simultaneously in many firms.

A firm's intended strategy often requires modification before it has been fully implemented due to changes in environmental and/or organizational conditions. Because these changes are often difficult to predict, substantial changes in the environment may transform an organization's realized strategy into one that is quite different from its intended strategy.

The strategic management field has been influenced by such perspectives as industrial organization theory, resource-based theory, and contingency theory. Although they are based on widely varied assumptions about what leads to high performance, each of these perspectives has merit and contributes to an overall understanding of the field.

Strategy formulation is the direct responsibility of the CEO, who also relies on a team of other individuals, including the board of directors, vice presidents, and various managers. In its final form, a strategic decision is crafted from the streams of inputs, decisions, and actions of the entire top management team.

Key Terms

business model	industrial organization	strategic management
competitive advantage	intended strategy	strategy
contingency theory	realized strategy	sustained competitive advantage
distinctive competence	resource-based theory	top management team

Review Questions and Exercises

1. Is it necessary that the five steps in the strategic management process be performed sequentially? Why or why not?

2. What is the difference between an intended strategy and a realized strategy? Why is this distinction important?

3. How have outside perspectives influenced the development of the strategic management field?

4. Does the CEO *alone* make the strategic decisions for an organization? Explain.

Practice Quiz

True or False

1. A strategy seeks to develop and sustain competitive advantage.

2. Strategic management refers to formulating successful strategies for an organization.

3. Each step in the strategic management process is independent so that changes in one step will not substantially affect other steps.

4. The intended strategy and the realized strategy can never be the same.

5. Whereas industrial organization theory emphasizes the influence of industry factors of firm performance, resource-based theory emphasizes the role of firm factors.

6. Strategic decisions are made solely by and are ultimately the responsibility of the chief executive alone.

Multiple Choice

7. Strategies are formulated in the strategic management stage that occurs immediately after
   A. the assessment of internal strengths and weaknesses.
   B. implementation of the strategy.
   C. control of the strategy.
   D. none of the above

8. The strategy originally planned by top management is called the
   A. grand strategy.
   B. realized strategy.
   C. emergent strategy.
   D. none of the above

9. The notion that successful firms tend to be the ones that adapt to influences in their industries is based on
   A. industrial organization theory.
   B. resource-based theory.
   C. contingency theory.
   D. none of the above

10. The notion of distinctive competence is consistent with
   A. industrial organization theory.
   B. resource-based theory.
   C. contingency theory.
   D. none of the above

11. In order to contribute to sustained competitive advantage, firm resources should be
   A. valuable and rare.
   B. not subject to perfect imitation.
   C. without strategically relevant resources.
   D. all of the above.

12. Which of the following is not a characteristic of strategic decisions?
   A. They are long term in nature.
   B. They involve choices.
   C. They do not involve trade-offs.
   D. All of the above are characteristics of strategic decisions.

Notes

1. I. M. Cockburn, R. M. Henderson, and S. Stern, "Untangling the Origins of Competitive Advantage," *Strategic Management Journal* 21 (2000): 1123–1145.

2. P. Wright, M. Kroll, and J. A. Parnell, *Strategic Management: Concepts* (Upper Saddle River, NJ: Prentice Hall, 1998).

3. D. C. Hambrick and J. W. Fredrickson, "Are You Sure You Have a Strategy?" *Academy of Management Executive* 15 (2001): 48–59.

4. Based on Wright et al., *Strategic Management*.

5. A. E. Singer, "Strategy as Moral Philosophy," *Strategic Management Journal* 15 (1994): 191–213.

6. B. Wysocki, Jr., "How Dr. Papadakis Runs a University Like a Company," *Wall Street Journal* (23 February 2005): A1; P. Fain, "High Pay Makes Headlines," *Chronicle of Higher Education Online Edition* (24 November 2006).

7. H. Mintzberg, "Opening Up the Definition of Strategy," in J. B. Quinn, H. Mintzberg, and R. M. James, eds., *The Strategy Process* (Englewood Cliffs, NJ: Prentice Hall, 1988), 14–15.

8. C. M. Ford and D. M. Gioia, "Factors Influencing Creativity in the Domain of Managerial Decision Making," *Journal of Management* 26 (2001): 705–732.

9. H. Mintzberg, "Crafting Strategy," *Harvard Business Review* 65(4) (1987): 66–75.

10. G. Hamel, "Strategy as Revolution," *Harvard Business Review* 74(4) (1996): 69–82; B. Huffman, "What Makes a Strategy Brilliant?" *Business Horizons* 44(4) (2001): 13–20.

11. H. Courtney, J. Kirkland, and P. Viguerie, "Strategy Under Uncertainty," *Harvard Business Review* (November–December 1997): 67–79.

12. Hamel, "Strategy as Revolution"; B. Huffman, "What Makes a Strategy Brilliant?"

13. M. E. Porter, "The Contributions of Industrial Organization to Strategic Management," *Academy of Management Review* 6 (1981): 609–620.

14. G. Hawawini, V. Subramanian, and P. Verdin, "Is Performance Driven by Industry- or Firm-Specific Factors? A New Look at the Evidence," *Strategic Management Journal* 24 (2003): 1–16.

15. J. S. Bain, *Industrial Organization* (New York: Wiley, 1968); F. M. Scherer and D. Ross, *Industrial Market Structure and Economic Performance* (Boston: Houghton-Mifflin, 1990).

16. A. Seth and H. Thomas, "Theories of the Firm: Implications for Strategy Research," *Journal of Management Studies* 31 (1994): 165–191; J. B. Barney, "Strategic Factor Markets: Expectations, Luck, and Business Strategy," *Management Science* 42 (1986): 1231–1241.

17. It has been argued that the resource-based perspective does not qualify as an academic theory. For details on this exchange, see R. L. Priem and J. E. Butler, "Is the Resource-Based 'View' a Useful Perspective for Strategic Management Research," *Academy of Management Review* 26 (2001): 22–40; J. B. Barney, "Is the Resource-Based 'View' a Useful Perspective for Strategic Management Research? Yes," *Academy of Management Review* 26 (2001): 41–56.

18. J. B. Barney, "Looking Inside for Competitive Advantage," *Academy of Management Executive* 19 (1995): 49–61.

19. S. L. Berman, J. Down, and C. W. L. Hill, "Tacit Knowledge as a Source of Competitive Advantage in the National Basketball Association," *Academy of Management Journal* 45 (2002): 13–32.

20. E. J. Zajac, M. S. Kraatz, and R. K. F. Bresser, "Modeling the Dynamics of Strategic Fit: A Normative Approach to Strategic Change," *Strategic Management Journal* 21 (2000): 429–453.

21. C. A. Lengnick-Hall and J. A. Wolff, "Similarities and Contradictions in the Core Logic of Three Strategy Research Streams," *Strategic Management Journal* 20 (1999): 1109–1132; O. E. Williamson, "Strategy Research: Governance and Competence Perspectives," *Strategic Management Journal* 20 (1999): 1087–1108.

22. T. K. Das and B. Teng, "Cognitive Biases and Strategic Decision Processes: An Integrative Perspective," *Journal of Management Studies* 36 (1999): 757–778; M. A. Carpenter, "The Implications of Strategy and Social Context for the Relationship Between Top Team Management Heterogeneity and Firm Performance," *Strategic Management Journal* 23 (2002): 275–284.

23. A. J. Hillman and M. A. Hitt, "Corporate Political Strategy Formulation: A Model of Approach, Participation, and Strategy Decisions," *Academy of Management Review* 24 (1999): 825–842.

24. Wright et al., *Strategic Management*.

Insight from *strategy+business*

Southwest Airline's Herb Kelleher is widely viewed as an effective organizational leader and strategic thinker. Under his leadership, the low-cost airline recorded thirty consecutive years of profits, a feat unmatched in the industry. Kelleher provides insight into his philosophy and perspectives on strategy and success in this chapter's strategy+business reading.

Herb Kelleher: The Thought Leader Interview

The cofounder and chairman of Southwest Airlines tells why a firm's people are everything.

By Chuck Lucier

The airline industry is a tough place to make a buck: too many competitors, price-sensitive customers, high capital intensity, boom-or-bust cyclicality, powerful suppliers, and often intransigent unions. Nevertheless, Herb Kelleher, the cofounder and chairman of Southwest Airlines, created the sort of value that any company leader would envy.

From its start in 1971, Southwest has grown into the fourth-largest airline in the United States, with 30 consecutive years of profitability, in an industry in which no other company has been profitable for even five straight years. Total shareholder returns during that period were almost double the returns for the S&P 500. Southwest has managed to accrue a market capitalization larger than that of the rest of the American airlines combined. Major competitors have tried to imitate Southwest with clones. Many entrepreneurial startups in the United States and Europe, including JetBlue and Ryanair, cite Southwest as their inspiration.

Southwest's achievements are widely attributed to its relentless focus. From the start, Southwest's strategy has been to draw travelers not from other airlines, but from cars, buses, and trains, by providing them the least expensive and fastest service available. To support the strategy, the company determined to fly only one type of airplane, the Boeing 737, and to substitute linear flying for the hub-and-spoke model that has prevailed in the industry. But at the center of Southwest's success are its culture and employees. "Your spirit," says Mr. Kelleher, a man fabled for his willingness to party hard with his staff, is "the most powerful thing of all."

In recognition of the inspiration he provides all who study and practice strategy, for his contributions in redefining how companies think about strategy, and for his achievements in redefining an industry, in November 2003 Mr. Kelleher was granted the Lifetime Achievement Award by the Strategic Management Society (SMS), the prestigious global association of academic and corporate strategists.

At the SMS annual meeting in Baltimore, Md., where Mr. Kelleher accepted the award, *strategy+ business* contributing editor and "Breakthrough Thoughts" co-columnist Chuck Lucier led a spirited public conversation with Mr. Kelleher about Southwest's success.

S+B: Let's start with some words from your award. You made an "audacious commitment" to putting employees first, customers second, and shareholders third. How did you get away with that for 20 years?

KELLEHER: When I started out, business school professors liked to pose a conundrum: Which do you put first, your employees, your customers, or your shareholders? As if that were an unanswerable question. My answer was very easy: You put your employees first. If you truly treat your employees that way, they will treat your customers well, your customers will come back, and that's what makes your shareholders happy. So there is no constituency at war with any other constituency. Ultimately, it's shareholder value that you're producing.

S+B: A dollar invested at Southwest's 1972 initial public offering is worth $1,400 today. Does that come solely from putting your employees first?

KELLEHER: We have been successful because we've had a simple strategy. Our people have bought into it.

Source: Reprinted with permission from *strategy+business*, the award-winning management quarterly published by Booz Allen Hamilton. http://www.strategy-business.com.

Our people fully understand it. We have had to have extreme discipline in not departing from the strategy.

We basically said to our people, there are three things that we're interested in. The lowest costs in the industry – that can't hurt you, having the lowest costs. The best customer service – that's a very important element of value. We said beyond that we're interested in intangibles – a spiritual infusion – because they are the hardest things for your competitors to replicate. The tangible things your competitors can go out and buy. But they can't buy your spirit. So it's the most powerful thing of all.

S+B: Not to deny the importance of intangibles, but what's the source of Southwest's cost advantage?

KELLEHER: The cost advantage is very important because we started out with a philosophy that we were going to charge low fares, come hell or high water. We were going to enable more people to fly. It didn't matter whether we had competition or not. In other words, we just said we're a different type of cat. When we get a load factor that gets into the 70 or 75 percent range over an appreciable period of time, we don't increase fares. We add flights and put additional seats in. So if you come from that basic position, that this is what you are, then of course you have to have low costs.

Now, how do you get low costs? Through a lot of things, including the inspiration that you give your people, their productivity, the fact that they feel that they're doing something that is really significant and that they enjoy. If you take all of Southwest's compensation together – wage rates, profit sharing, the full 401(k) match, the stock options that our people have – Southwest employees are the most highly compensated people in the airline industry. One of our pilots just retired with $8 million in his profit-sharing account. Now, you have to do well to produce that.

Meeting Life's Needs

S+B: A compensation scheme based on stock is great when the company is doing well. But when the stock doesn't do well, you can have a motivation problem.

KELLEHER: Absolutely, that is a risk. So we don't just give people stock options. We have an educational team that goes around and explains to them what stock options are, how they work, the fact that it's a longer-term investment. From 1990 to 1994, the airline industry as a whole lost $13 billion. Southwest Airlines was profitable during that entire time, but our stock was

battered. Eighty-four percent of our employees continued with Southwest Airlines stock during that four-year period. That's the kind of confidence and faith that you have to engender, so people have a longer-term view, and they're not trying to outplay the market every day.

S+B: Virtually all of the major U.S. airlines have tried to copy you at some point. None of them has come remotely close. What's so hard? It looks like it ought to be a pretty simple model.

KELLEHER: We've had many airlines that professed that they were going to be low-fare carriers. There's only one problem: They had high costs. You can do that, but Chapter 11 is your destiny.

I think the difficulty for them is the cultural aspect of it. That cannot be duplicated. One of the things that demonstrates the power of people is when the United Shuttle took out after us in Oakland. They had all the advantages. I mean, they had first-class seats for those who don't want to fly anything but first class. They had a global frequent flyer program, which we did not have. They probably spent $25 million or $30 million on their advertising campaign. I probably have something like a thousand letters at my office that tell you why they finally receded from Oakland. Those letters say, "Herb, I tried them, but I just like your people more, so I'm back." Don't ever doubt, in the customer service business, the importance of people and their attitudes.

S+B: So now we're back to the intangibles – the "spirit" competitors can't go buy. How does a company create a culture like that?

KELLEHER: We used to have a corporate day. Companies would come in from around the world and they were interested in how we hired, trained, that sort of thing. Then we'd say, "Treat your people well and they'll treat you well," and then they'd go home disappointed. It was too simple.

S+B: Or too hard.

KELLEHER: Or too hard – because it's a vast mosaic with thousands of little pieces that you have to keep putting in place every day. It's not a programmatic thing. It can't be. It has to come from the heart, not the head. If it's programmatic, everybody will know that and say, "Hell, they're not sincere; they don't really care, they're just telling us that they care." It has to be a continuous stream of one-on-one communication, not like you sit down and say, "Boy, communication is pretty important.

Let's really communicate for the next six months and then move on to what's really significant. It has to be part of your fabric; it has to be something that you do really as a product of your soul.

I'll give you an illustration of why this works, if I might. When the industry was deregulated. I sat down with our very, very creative advertising agency, GSD&M, from Austin. (We call them "Greed, Sex, Drugs, and Money.") They said, "Okay, now we have deregulation, Herb. Airlines can fly wherever they want to. What's different about Southwest Airlines?" I said, "Our people are different." That's where the "Spirit of Southwest" campaign was born. That could have been a huge risk because we were telling the world on television, radio, newspapers that our people are different and they're better and they're special and they welcome customers. We ran that campaign for probably six or seven years and never had anybody write in and say, "You're wrong. Your people are not special." Which I think demonstrates that they are.

S+B: Is that why Southwest flight attendants sing?

KELLEHER: Southwest flight attendants sing because they want to. We don't program our flight attendant training to teach people to sing or tell jokes. What we say is, "If that is your basic personality, feel free to go ahead and do it." We're not trying to train you to be anything different from what you really are. If singing buoys up your heart, makes you feel good, go ahead and do it. We have tried to say to our people, "You don't have to put on a mask, you don't have to be an automaton when you come to work. You can just be yourself." Wasn't it Robert Frost who said, "Isn't it a shame that people's minds work furiously until they get to work?" Well, that's because they feel that they become artificial and constrained by the workplace.

S+B: One of your values in the mission statement is humility as a corporation. With all of your wonderful results, is Southwest *really* humble?

KELLEHER: No question. I constantly have warned our people over the years that, as we became bigger and more successful, our primary potential enemy was ourselves, not our competitors. Getting cocky, getting complacent, thinking that the world was our oyster, disregarding our competitors, both new and old. I think humility is very important in keeping your eye on the carrot, keeping focused outwardly instead of inwardly,

and knowing when you have to change. An investor in the airline industry some years ago that I was talking to said, "Southwest Airlines is the most humble and disciplined airline that I deal with." I said, "The two go together."

S+B: Why do they go together?

KELLEHER: Because you can't really be disciplined in what you do unless you are humble and open-minded. Humility breeds open-mindedness – and really, what we try to do is establish a clear and simple set of values that we understand. That simplifies things; that expedites things. It enables the extreme discipline I mentioned in describing our strategy. When an issue comes up, we don't say we're going to study it for two and a half years. We just say, "Southwest Airlines doesn't do that. Maybe somebody else does, but we don't." It greatly facilitates the operation of the company.

For example, we bought Morris Air. They were a Salt Lake City carrier with only about 14 or 16 airplanes. We were much larger. When we paid a visit to their headquarters, I told our people, "When you get there, shut up. You can ask questions. But you cannot lecture. You cannot tell people the way they ought to do things. You know why? Because we're on a learning expedition. Let the Morris Air people tell us. They're new, they're young, they're fresh, they're untrammeled. Let them tell us the ideas that they have." And we got some fabulous ideas as a consequence of it, and basically *that's* the value of humility.

Growth and Change

S+B: You've grown from a few people to more than 34,000. How much did growth change the way you manage Southwest?

KELLEHER: It didn't really. Your tactics change, but your basic strategy does not. Our mission statement is eternal. Our mission statement deals solely with people. That never changes – in any way, shape, or form. The focus of Southwest Airlines has always been on its people, regardless of how large we grew. Everybody would keep saying to me, "Wait until you get to a thousand, wait until you get to 5,000, wait until you get to 10,000" – as if there was some bright line when you go over from the humanistic and entrepreneurial into the totally managerial. There is no such line in dealing with your people. Making them happy with what they're doing, making them proud of what they're doing, putting them in a position where they're telling their grandchildren that Southwest Airlines gave me a greater reach than I ever would have had by myself — that continues to be effective whether you've got 5,000, 15,000, or 35,000.

One of the things that we do is continue to emphasize that we value our people as people, not just as workers. Any event that you have in your life that is celebratory in nature or brings grief you hear from Southwest Airlines. If you lose a relative, you hear from us. If you're out sick with a serious illness, you hear from us, and I mean by telephone, by letter, by remembrances from us. If you have a baby, you hear from us. What we're trying to say to our people is, "Hey, wait a second, we value you as a total person, not just between eight and five."

S+B: A lot of things are changing in the industry that might undermine the strategy you have followed for a long time. For example, you're doing transcontinental flights. Does that require big changes in what you do?

KELLEHER: No. I'll tell you, that was an interesting exercise because basically we've always tried to be empiricists and not theorize about what people want. When we started flying longer haul, even our own people would say, "Herb, you've got to have meals." We've got to do this and we've got to do that. I said, "I'm not sure, but let's just start flying and see." Well, here are these people from Nashville who want to fly to Los Angeles. It costs them $1,200 less round trip, which gives them a lot of money to buy a dinner at Chasen's, and they save two hours of their time because they don't go through a hub. You think they care whether we have airline meals?

That's another thing that we tried to do over the years: ready, fire, aim. In our business, where capital assets travel at over 500 miles an hour, you don't have a lot of time to fool around with aiming, because by the time you're finished aiming, somebody else will already be there. So get out there, do it, and clean up the mistakes afterward.

S+B: You're being honored today as a "lifetime strategist." Did you have a vision for the whole thing? Thirty-five years ago, did you write, "We're going to become the largest airline with the lowest cost"?

KELLEHER: Oh, no. We didn't write it down because when you write things down you confine yourself. That's why we have never used the fancy titles for empowerment, total quality, etc. Every time you talk jargon you find that people assume that they have the same thing in mind when they really don't. We don't apply labels to things because they prevent you from thinking expansively.

Basically what we said 35 years ago was that Texas was captive: Braniff had a monopoly among the larger cities; Trans Texas had a monopoly among the smaller cities. The fares were very high. Because the short-haul passenger was merely an addendum to long-haul service, the short-haul passenger was being totally neglected. In other words, flights from San Antonio to Dallas were scheduled in terms of what your arrival was in Seattle or Paris. It looked like an opportunity to do something a lot better: provide higher-quality air service at lower fares.

One of the things that people, I think, didn't understand is that we started out saying we're going to give you more for less, not less for less. We're going to give you new airplanes, not old airplanes. We're going to give you the best on-time performance. We're going to give you the people who are most hospitable.

We've never done the long-range planning that is customary in many businesses. When planning became big in the airline community, one of the analysts came up to me and said, "Herb, I understand you don't have a plan." I said that we have the most unusual plan in the industry: Doing things. That's our plan. What we do by way of strategic planning is we define ourselves and then we redefine ourselves.

S+B: There's a big market opportunity in Europe. Haven't you missed the boat there?

KELLEHER: It wasn't a boat that we ever wanted to get on. It's just way beyond our competence. International service has lots of complications. You're dealing with different cultures. You're dealing with currency exchanges. Compared with going into Raleigh-Durham and operating at 84.3 percent load factor on opening day, it's much more complex. We would have to vary our fleet.

We have had most of the European carriers coming to Southwest Airlines and saying, "We have to be competitive for the first time in a long time. What should we do?" We said, "First of all, find out what your customers want. Basically, you have dictated to your customers. Would they prefer to give up the babysitting service in Frankfurt in order to get a $15 reduction in fares?" The startups in Europe like Ryanair also asked our opinion about what they could do and how they could do it.

It was interesting because 15 or 20 years ago there was the assumption that Southwest Airlines could succeed with things in the United States that Europeans would not accept in Europe. I said that's exactly what everybody told me when Southwest started: that people in the U.S. would not accept it. Well, you have to educate people as to the value of what you're providing. Obviously Ryanair and easyJet are very successful. I think you'll see more and more of that kind of activity not only on the continent but also in Central America, South America, and Asia.

Boards and CEOs

S+B: I'd like to get your views on some cross-industry issues. How much has the CEO's job changed in the last 20 years? How much do you think it will change in the future?

KELLEHER: I think the CEO's job has changed a lot in the last 20 years. I don't say that it's necessarily for the better or the worse, but there has been a significant change. I think that CEOs of substantial companies have now become public figures, whether they want to be or not. You might as well acknowledge that. With all the media coverage of companies, you're going to be in the limelight. You're going to have to be able to respond to the media. You're going to have to be able to address the public. That's different.

Also, of course, as we've gotten more complex in America, we have become more regulated. So you spend a lot more of your time dealing with various governmental agencies than you did in the past. When I started practicing law, I would estimate that 5 percent of our total practice involved some kind of interface with the government in one of its myriad forms – local, state, or national. When I stopped practicing law, it was about 60 percent. I think that's just a manifestation of what's happened in business – that the regulatory aspects of it are now much more important than they used to be, and you have to know how to deal with those because that is a fact of life.

S+B: What about the relationship with the board? With changes in governance, Sarbanes-Oxley, and so forth, how is that going to shift?

KELLEHER: That's not really a problem. If you were running your company right, if you weren't trying to deceive someone, if you were basically making judgments that were intended to tell the public as closely as you could exactly what your earnings were, then Sarbanes-Oxley and the New York Stock Exchange regulations are just minor addenda to what you're already doing. It may take

you a little more time. It may cost you a little more money to comply. But it's not unduly burdensome.

The primary thing I'm concerned about is that the new compliance focus distracts your board of directors, and this is relatively new. When you see that your board is now spending three hours focusing on regulatory issues and a half hour on the company's business and what it plans to do, you have the feeling that perhaps it's taking people away from focusing on results and achievement, at least on an interim basis.

Another thing that concerns me is the impact on internal controls. I've asked several heads of big accounting concerns, "What's going to be your criteria of what's material and immaterial?" Business judgment has to enter into it. Years ago, our internal audit department concluded that some passengers were defrauding us. So audit went out and bought a $300,000 system and hired two people to operate and maintain it. So I asked them, "How much are we losing here?" They said $18,000. I said, "Let them steal $18,000. We're spending $65,000 a year to keep people from stealing $18,000."

It reminds me of a fellow who owned a chain of theaters in Texas. He had a manager of 17 years standing, and went in and fired him one day. The guy says, "After 17 years and this enormous success that we have had, how can you fire me?" The owner said, "Well, for the first 15 years you were stealing $800 a month, and you were worth that. But lately you've been stealing $1,200 a month, and you're not worth that." So I hope we don't just surrender business judgment and say that every little thing that goes awry from the accounting standpoint is as important as every other thing that might go awry. That concerns me a little bit.

S+B: I think boards play two very different roles. On the one hand, they play the role of cop: "Boy, this thing is out of control, it's not working very well. We need to find a new CEO." On the other hand, they help management by offering advice and counsel and by playing a sounding-board role. Are we in danger of losing the sounding-board role?

KELLEHER: I'm concerned about that. It's not that I rebel against any of the changes that have been made, because I think in and of themselves they are salutary and not particularly burdensome. But I am a little bit worried about the psychological reaction to them. I was talking to a CEO in Dallas probably a month ago and he said, "I formulated a new strategic paper. It proposes that my company go into another business. I've been trying to present it to the board during the last two meetings, but we were so preoccupied with compliance issues and fear of noncompliance that I haven't been able to present it to the board."

Training Entrepreneurs

S+B: You funded the Herb Kelleher Center for Entrepreneurship at the University of Texas. Why?

KELLEHER: Because I think it's very important to Texas and to our country that we preserve our entrepreneurial spirit. As you get bigger and things get more complex, I think there is more of a tendency to get mired in the details, to get mired in the bureaucratic aspects of things and the hierarchical aspects of things. One of the things I always tried to do was to keep the entrepreneurial spirit alive at Southwest Airlines, even as we grew bigger and more complex. That's where the job creation is coming from. It's from the small businesses, not big businesses.

S+B: What would you like business schools to be doing better?

KELLEHER: By and large, our business schools, at least in the United States, are doing a far better job today than perhaps they were doing 30 years ago. Now, business schools are actually talking about entrepreneurship, perhaps kindling that spark in their students. They're focusing more on dealing with employees and how you achieve good relationships with your employees. They teach more about customer service and how to do customer service. They've gotten away from pure financial analysis and planning, to some extent, which I think is very important if you're going to have a well-rounded CEO.

S+B: What advice would you give brand-new CEOs if they wanted to have the kind of success you've had?

KELLEHER: First of all, they have to focus intently upon what's important and what's unimportant, not be trapped in bureaucracy and hierarchy. Be results- and mission-oriented. Keep it as simple as they possibly can, so that the values and the destination of the organization are well understood by all the people that are part of it so that they can feel that they are truly participants in it. I don't know whether it was Calvin Coolidge or Bianca Jagger who said — they're both thin, that's why I get them confused — "the business of business is business." We've always said, "The business of business is people."

Chuck Lucier (lchuck@chucklucier.com) senior vice president emeritus of Booz Allen Hamilton. He is currently writing a book and consulting on strategy and knowledge issues with selected clients. For Mr. Lucier's latest publications, see www.chucklucier.com.

The Strategy Landscape 2

Chapter Outline

The world is flat. *New York Times* foreign affairs correspondent Thomas Friedman's 2005 bestseller presents his spin on a phenomenon that has changed the world forever: globalization. In *The World Is Flat*, Friedman argues that the period of American world economic domination has ended because changes during the last two decades have leveled or "flattened" the economic playing field for those in other countries, most notably India and China.[1]

The dot-com boom and subsequent bust around the turn of the century contributed significantly to the emergence of Friedman's "flat world." During the bubble, telecommunications companies were replete with cash and invested hundreds of millions of dollars to lay fiber-optic cables across the ocean floors, cables that currently and inexpensively connect countries such as India and China to the United States. The dot-com bust resulted in significant stock market losses, forcing companies to cut spending wherever possible. Hence, many turned to opportunities for cost-cutting created by the fiber-optic cables and began to offshore jobs as a means of addressing a new economic reality. As Indian entrepreneur Jerry Rao explained, any work that can be digitized and moved from one location to another will be moved. Indeed, approximately half a million U.S. Internal Revenue Service (IRS) tax returns are actually completed by accountants in India each year.[2]

The notion of a level economic playing field creates a number of challenges for Western firms and societies, one of which is the debate over free trade. Supporters contend that a flatter world is here to stay and that efforts to thwart it will only stifle growth in economic powers such as the United States, an argument Friedman echoes. Proponents charge that the unbridled global trade drives down wages and will ultimately result in a reduced standard of living in developed nations.

One thing is clear. The effects of globalization have altered the world in dramatic ways over the past two decades, and these effects are especially clear in the business world. From a strategic management perspective, many traditional approaches to managing a firm remain valid, but must be considered in light of these changes. This chapter highlights key trends that have altered how progressive firms today should be managed.

2-1 Outsourcing and Offshoring

Outsourcing

Contracting out a firm's noncore, nonrevenue-producing activities to other organizations primarily (but not always) to reduce costs.

Outsourcing involves contracting out a firm's noncore, nonrevenue-producing activities to other organizations primarily (but not always) to reduce costs. This method has become more widespread in the United States in recent years. Many consumers and activists have become increasingly concerned about trade deficits with other nations and job losses that occur when a firm moves a production facility abroad or a retailer stocks its shelves with imported products.[3] A number of American firms have closed production facilities in the United States and opened new ones in Mexico, China, India, and other countries where labor costs are substantially lower and regulations are less inhibitive.[4]

The facts are compelling. The U.S. trade deficit grew 6.5 percent to $763 billion in 2006, with China responsible for $233 billion of the gap.[5] Chinese firms export large quantities of everything from apparel to electronics to the United States. When world garment quotas expired in 2005, China's lead in apparel exports increased even further.[6] Hence, outsourcing—specifically to China—is a sensitive issue among a number of politicians and business leaders.

Another key beneficiary of the outsourcing trend is India. General Electric's Jack Welch was instrumental in one of the earliest partnerships with India. Welch first met with the Indian government in 1989, and GE formed a joint venture to develop and market medical equipment with Wipro Ltd. in 1990. By the mid-1990s, much of GE's software development and maintenance activities had been shifted to Indian companies. GE Capital Services (Gecis) established the first international call center in India in 1999. GE sold 60 percent of Gecis for $500 million in 2004, freeing it to compete against IBM, Accenture, and Indian firms.[7] In 2005, India received more than $17 billion from foreign corporations outsourcing a variety of jobs to the emerging Asian country.[8]

Some analysts suggest that wage differences between the United States and countries such as China and India could spark increased global outsourcing in a broad array of professional and technical fields, such as architecture, accounting, and even law.[9] The outsourcing of legal jobs from the United States—especially to India—has also risen in recent years and approached thirty thousand jobs abroad in 2007. The argument is simple. According to one analyst, developing a particular legal database for contracts might cost about $60,000 in the United States, compared to only $5,000 in India.[10]

Chinese firms have begun to compete for many of the IT outsourcing contracts that U.S. firms originally awarded to companies in India. Consulting firm A. T. Kearney still ranks India highest among outsourcing countries based on financial structure, business environment, and people skills and availability. India is followed by China, Malaysia, and the Czech Republic. However, Kearney believes China can catch India as it improves its accounting, financial, and IT skills, but probably not until the early 2010s.[11]

Although outsourcing offers opportunities for firms throughout the world, it presents challenges as well. Consider the automobile industry in China. In 2005, Daimler-Chrysler and Honda launched an effort to build inexpensive cars in China and export them to parts of the developed world, including the United States.[12] In 2006, General Motors unveiled the Cadillac SLS in Beijing in an effort to capitalize on a luxury car market in China that skyrocketed from about 10,000 cars in 2004 to about 125,000 in 2007.[13] However, beneficiaries of American outsourcing efforts are experiencing some difficulties as well. As sales of cars in China skyrocketed in the past decade, Chinese automobile manufacturers began to experience many of the problems common to producers in other parts of the world: excess capacity, intense price competition, and declining profits.

When implemented properly, outsourcing can cut costs, improve performance, and refocus the core business. Many outsourcing efforts fail, however, due to unforeseen hidden costs, loss of control of the outsourced activity, or simply outsourcing activities that should not be outsourced.[14] For example, Cincinnati's Standard Textile experienced a number of problems when it opened its first factory in northern China in 2005. The heating did not work for two weeks, causing more than an inconvenience for workers whose job is to separate thousands of fine cotton threads. Custom-made parts ordered from Chinese suppliers did not meet specifications. Early on, Chinese authorities hiked electric charges for the plant by 18 percent.[15]

Cost savings aside, excessive outsourcing can leave a firm in a compromised position. When an organization no longer performs key activities, it loses expertise and can find itself at the mercy of suppliers. When a company's resource strengths erode, the available array of strategic options becomes much more limited. Reevaluating suppliers and changing them when necessary is a proactive means of managing this downside.[16]

Politicians have also kept a careful watch on outsourcing trends. Growing concern in the 2000s over the flood of inexpensive textile products from China resulted in agreements in 2005 and 2006 to curb exports to Europe and the

United States. In response, the Chinese government offered preferential treatment to firms producing higher priced items when calculating the volume of their exports, thereby encouraging them to develop and produce higher quality, premium products.[17]

Offshoring

Relocating some or all of a firm's manufacturing or other business processes to another country, typically to reduce costs.

Offshoring means relocating some or all of a firm's manufacturing or other business processes to another country, typically to reduce costs. This method is similar to outsourcing, but enables the firm to retain control of the operations abroad instead of relinquishing them to other firms. A key incentive for outsourcing and offshoring—cost containment—is the same, however.

The globalization effect that has fostered an increase in outsourcing and offshoring has also had other effects that are not as easy to identify. As Ford and General Motors eliminated jobs in Detroit in the mid-2000s and continued production overseas, Asian manufacturers and their top-tier suppliers were expanding operations in the United States, particularly in the South. In 2003, for example, Toyota affiliate Denso Corporation opened a new auto air-conditioning plant in rural Osceola, Arkansas—a town of nine thousand that had suffered greatly from the outsourcing of textile jobs in the previous decade. Hence, Asian company success in the United States can bode well for local suppliers, especially when shipping components in from abroad can be too costly.[18]

Interestingly, Ford's recent "Red, White, and Bold" advertising campaign encouraged Americans to be patriotic and purchase a Ford Mustang instead of an "imported" vehicle. However, 2006 data from the U.S. National Highway Traffic Safety Administration showed that only 65 percent of the parts for the 2005 Mustang came from the United States or Canada, compared to 90 percent of the parts for the 2005 Toyota Sienna, a vehicle built in Indiana. Many vehicles produced by other Asian carmakers such as Honda and Nissan are also built in the United States with predominantly local parts.[19] Hence, while outsourcing and offshoring remain vibrant topics in American political debates, it has become increasingly difficult to distinguish "local" products from "imported" ones.

Rising health care costs have created incentives for many firms to outsource or offshore their production, most notably in the United States where employers often pay a significant portion of employee health insurance premiums and where such costs are rising an average of 15 percent per year. Union Pacific, for example, has stopped hiring smokers in states where it is legal to do so. Publisher Gannett began adding fifty dollars to premiums of smokers who do not participate in a smoking cessation program. The issue became even more pronounced in late 2005 when a draft of an internal Wal-Mart memo proposed that the retailer cut costs by discouraging "unhealthy" people from applying for jobs. The memo proposed adding physical activity to all jobs—such as requiring cashiers to collect shopping carts—so that those not able to perform the tasks would be less likely to apply.[20]

Health care costs at General Motors approached $6 billion in 2005, prompting the giant automaker to consider asking its hourly employees to pay more of their own expenses, a move that always meets stiff resistance when union negotiations begin. Like many other firms, GM has broadened its efforts to encourage healthy living by discouraging unhealthy habits and adding gym facilities at some of its production plants.[21] Hence, all firms—especially large ones based in the United States—are challenged to cover these expenses or consider shifting production to countries where costs are lower or health care is provided through government agencies.

The debate over outsourcing and offshoring is complex and can take on a new tack when companies outsource business activities that are politically sensitive or have safety concerns. In 2005, for example, JetBlue flew a number of its Airbus

A320 jets to El Salvador for maintenance. In the same year, about half of U.S. carrier heavy-overhaul work was performed outside of the United States.[22] As emerging nations develop, however, their firms may find it useful to outsource certain activities to more developed nations. In 2004, for example, Indian telephone giant Bharti Tele-Ventures outsourced hundreds of millions of dollars of work to Western firms. Most of Bharti's information technology services, including billing and internal e-mail systems, were contracted to IBM.[23]

Although conventional wisdom is that the wages of unskilled workers decline when firms pursue cheaper labor abroad, some have suggested that global outsourcing and offshoring can have a positive effect on both wages and economic development in the richer nation. According to economist Anthony Venables, an industry in a richer nation may rely on local inputs such as specialized workers that are not available to its competitors in new foreign markets. The proximity to these inputs can create a substantial advantage in the new market, boosting productivity throughout the industry and enabling the firms to pay higher wages.[24]

The outsourcing/offshoring debate can also be difficult to resolve because of differences in regulatory environments and the complexity of relationships among firms across borders. A lack of data is also a key concern. Chinese officials, for example, compute trade deficits differently from their American counterparts and always calculate lower figures. In India, the number of information technology professionals who provide services to offshore customers rose from about 276,000 in 2002 to over 500,000 in 2004. Exports of private U.S. services to India are likely to reach $10 billion by 2010. Hence, it is difficult to determine the extent to which such an exchange is beneficial to both nations from a trade perspective.[25]

Some firms have attempted to avoid the outsourcing controversy, as is the case with the "Big Three" U.S. auto producers. Because union contracts prevent global outsourcing under certain conditions, the automakers simply pressure suppliers to outsource.[26] In addition, a number of firms have become more sensitive to this issue. In 2004, for example, E-Loan announced that customers would be given a choice about whether loan applications will be processed in Delhi or Dallas, with the latter taking as much as two days longer.[27]

Interestingly, the assumption that outsourcing always refers to firms in developed nations seeking labor from emerging economies is not always true. Following the layoff of a large number of airline pilots in the mid-2000s, many American pilots departed U.S.-based carriers for airlines in China, India, Southeast Asia, and the Middle East. Pilots who faced a glut in the United States found a shortage of experienced pilots in most parts of the world. Many have secured attractive compensation and benefits in their new positions in other countries.[28]

In sum, outsourcing and offshoring offer intriguing options to strategic managers. In an increasingly competitive global marketplace, firms must take steps to minimize costs and improve efficiency. These steps may not be taken without political or buyer repercussions in the home market, however, as recent developments in the United States illustrate.

2-2 Commoditization and Mass Customization

Two key trends of the 1990s and 2000s have changed the context of strategic management. From a strategy perspective, **commoditization** refers to the increasing difficulty firms have in distinguishing their products and services from those of their rivals. Rapid advances in technology have created numerous opportunities for firms to

Commoditization
The increasing difficulty that firms have in distinguishing their products and services from those of their rivals.

differentiate their products from those of their competitors – differentiation that can exceed the needs of buyers and even confuse them. Buyers become inundated with an excessive number of options and little time to investigate or comprehend most of them. In an effort to simplify their choices, buyers view products as commodities and tend to reduce purchase decisions to a few key factors, such as a major product feature, reliability, or convenience. If buyers are unable to readily distinguish among the competitors along these factors, they may view the product as a commodity and base their final purchase decision on price. Hence, while firms may be doing all they can to set themselves and their products apart from the competition, customers may not see them quite as distinguishable.

Commoditization can create serious problems for firms that end up spending more to enhance product features only to be met with buyers who are inexorably price conscious. In a relatively short time, for example, digital cameras have overtaken film cameras as the product of choice. Whereas most film cameras had only a limited number of options, digital cameras can be complex to evaluate and many come with thick manuals describing all of the features and controls. Although camera aficionados appreciate the bells and whistles, many consumers may be confused by such features or simply may not wish to invest much time into learning how to use what they perceive as a low-involvement product. Unless camera producers or retailers can break through this confusion, such buyers may limit their product consideration set on the basis of only one or two key features such as brand, size, or the number of megapixels, and then base a final purchase decision on price.

Mass Customization

The ability to individualize product and service offerings to meet specific buyer needs.

A second trend, **mass customization,** refers to the ability to individualize product and service offerings to meet specific buyer needs. Like commoditization, its prominence has also been fostered by advances in technology. It occurs, for example, when Amazon.com suggests top-selling books for customers at its Web site based on previous product searches or purchases. In this way, Amazon.com takes a commodity—the same product that could be readily purchased as other retailers—and customizes its presentation to individual consumers.

Economies of Scale

The decline in unit costs of a product or service that occurs as the absolute volume of production increases.

Mass customization is important because it enables firms to personalize offerings while building **economies of scale,** which is the decline in unit costs of a product or service that occurs as the absolute volume of production increases. In a general sense, customization and economies of scale are inversely related. Scale economies develop when a firm produces a large quantity of a product, thereby eliminating its ability to satisfy individual needs with specialized products. Although not easy to achieve, mass customization—via technology and creative approaches—enables firms to achieve both customization and economies of scale.

Commoditization and mass customization are related to some extent. In some respects, technology enabling mass customization can enable firms to combat encroaching commoditization. When both trends are considered in concert, it becomes clear that successful firms must find a way to cut through all of the confusion and reach buyers in meaningful, personalized ways while maintaining production efficiencies.

2-3 Strategy and the Internet

It is difficult to understand strategic management today without considering how the field has been changed by the emergence of the Internet in recent years. Initial Internet growth occurred in the most developed nations, but now the rest of the world is catching up. China passed the 100 million mark in Internet users in 2005, 60 percent of which are male and 71 percent of which are under thirty years of age.[29]

The Internet has provided a new channel of distribution, a more efficient means of gathering and disseminating strategic information, and a new way of communicating with customers. In the early years of its inception, economic activity on the Web was dominated by "e-businesses" whose success and failure was almost solely dependent on the Internet. Today, most large, traditional firms—including such giants as Wal-Mart and General Electric—are utilizing the Internet to track customers, increase sales, and enhance visibility.[30]

Source: Ablestock.com

A key fundamental strategic change, however, concerns the dramatic shifts in organizational structure and their influences on viable business models. Put simply, many organizations are modifying their business models to augment their revenues through sources other than sales. As John Magretta put it, "A good business model begins with an insight into human motivations and ends in a rich stream of profits."[31]

The Internet has unleashed a number of alternative business models, some successful and some not. Consider the business model of one short-lived dot-com. By early 2001, Cyberrebate had become a popular Web site, offering rebates with every product, some for the full purchase price. Critics charged that such a business could not sustain itself by giving away merchandise. However, a small percentage of customers (less than 10 percent, according to CEO Joel Granik) failed to collect their rebates for merchandise typically priced several times the retail level, and many others converted to products whose rebates constituted only part of the purchase prices.[32] Time will determine the viability of such alternative business models. In Cyberrebate's case, the company filed for Chapter 11 bankruptcy protection in May 2001.[33]

Critics have challenged the notion that "new business models" are needed to compete in the "new economy." Michael Porter noted that "many of the pioneers of Internet business . . . have competed in ways that violate nearly every precept of good strategy . . . By ignoring strategy, many companies have undermined the structure of their industries . . . and reduced the likelihood that they or anyone else will gain a competitive advantage."[34] In essence, Porter and others have argued that the market forces that governed the traditional economy have not disappeared in the Internet economy; hence, many of the dot-coms that failed in 2000 did not succeed because they discarded these rules, set out to write their own, and built "bad business models."

Interestingly, the success or failure of a business model may be a function of factors such as time, technology, or problems with execution, not the quality of the idea itself. As such, some business models may not prove successful at first, but with minor changes may become successful in a future period. For example, the concept of purchasing groceries online was originally unsuccessful, due to such factors as Web design, inefficient warehousing, and relatively high prices. By the mid-2000s, improvements in these areas, as well as technological advances and a more Internet-savvy consumer, sparked a turnaround among online grocers. The original model has now been enhanced and is yielding positive results.[35]

The failure of many dot-coms notwithstanding, the Internet has spawned a key change in the structure of business. During the past two decades, organizations have engaged in a process economists refer to as "disaggregation and reaggregation."[36] The economic basis for this transformation was proposed by Nobel Laureate Ronald Coase in what is called *Coase's law.* A firm will tend to expand until the costs of organizing an extra transaction within the firm become equal to the costs of carrying out the same transaction on the open market.[37] In other words, large firms exist because they can perform most tasks—raw material procurement, production, human resource management, sales, and so forth—more efficiently than they would otherwise be performed if they were outsourced to the open market.

Recent advances in Internet and related technologies, however, coupled with rapid economic development in parts of Asia and Eastern Europe, have enabled firms to reorganize work processes and improve efficiency. As a result, it is much easier now than ever before to share and exchange information, and to "farm out" specific tasks to the most efficient parties across the globe. Today, more than a quarter of a million Indians manage call centers and perform telemarketing functions primarily for firms in the United States because they can perform the tasks—with the assistance of technology—more efficiently than their American counterparts. This fast growing service industry in India was virtually nonexistent just a decade ago.[38]

Partnership

A contractual relationship with an enterprise outside the organization.

As a result of this change, many progressive firms have placed less emphasis on performing all of the required activities themselves and have formed **partnerships,** or contractual relationships with enterprises outside the organization, to manage many of the functions that were previously handled in-house. Whereas *outsourcing* refers to specific agreements associated with a single task, *partnering* implies a longer term commitment associated with complex activities.

World Wide Web (WWW)

The vast assortment of computers on the Internet that support hypertext.

It is difficult to overstate the effects that disaggregation and reaggregation have had on business enterprises, and more specifically, the effort to manage them strategically. In many respects, a partner can be viewed as an extension of the organization. Partner capabilities and limitations are fast becoming as important as internal strengths and weaknesses. Although these changes are more pronounced in some markets than in others, the development of the Internet economy has significantly changed the nature of business in all industries. Although the strategic management process described herein is applicable to almost any organization, most successful companies have already developed a substantial presence on the Internet (see Strategy at Work 2-1).

S T R A T E G Y   A T   W O R K   2 - 1

Strategy, the Internet, and Its Nomenclature

Perhaps the greatest technological influence on strategic management in the late twentieth century was the widespread dissemination of the Internet. The *Internet* is an intricate, interconnected assortment of computer networks capable of encoding and decoding specialized computer *protocols*, or specifications of how information is exchanged. The Internet infrastructure consists of several key components. The *backbone* refers to the high-speed telecommunication lines used to connect the various computers in the system. *Bandwidth* refers to a telecommunication line's capacity to transmit data. *Routers* are digital switches (i.e., dedicated computers) that organize and route Internet traffic throughout the backbone. The bandwidth enhancement forecast for the first decade of the twenty-first century will speed up the transfer of data across the Internet.

Point of presence (POP) refers to a point of access to the Internet. Individuals typically gain access to the

Internet by means of an *Internet Service Provider's (ISP's)* POP. Large organizations are typically connected to the Internet by integrating their hardware into a *local area network (LAN)* server and linking it directly to the Web. Such organizations often construct hardware and software *firewalls* to restrict access between users within and outside the LAN.

The **World Wide Web (WWW)** is the vast assortment of computers on the Internet that support *hypertext*, a form of text that allows for the proper encoding and decoding of material on the Web. *HyperText Markup Language (HTML)* is the "common denominator" that allows documents to be linked contextually. Software such as Netscape Composer and Microsoft Front Page has simplified the Web page development process by eliminating the need to program in HTML code.

2-4 Strategic Dimensions of the Internet

In addition to the movement toward disaggregation and reaggregation, the Internet has a number of characteristics closely associated with the strategic management process, the effects of which typically vary among industries. Five key interrelated strategic factors are discussed in this section.

Source: Ablestock.com

2-4a Movement toward Information Symmetry

Information symmetry occurs when all parties to a transaction share the same information concerning that transaction. Information symmetry is an underlying assumption of the economics-based models of "pure competition." **Information asymmetry,** when one party to a transaction has information that another does not, is the primary reason why many markets are less competitive than they otherwise would be. Firms have a distinct advantage when they possess information not available to their prospective buyers. On the other hand, buyers gain an advantage when they obtain access to this information.

Businesses often seek to promote information asymmetry and utilize the information edge to their own advantage. Automobile retailers, for example, rarely post their absolute bottom-line prices on their vehicles. Consumers are generally left to haggle with a number of dealers to estimate the true wholesale cost of the vehicle and the value of various options and accessories. The lack of consumer knowledge, as well as the lack of time and expertise required to obtain the information desired, results in higher selling prices for many of the retailers.

Following this example, the Internet provides a wealth of information to educate consumers. Independent vehicle test results, retailer Web sites, wholesale costs for new vehicles, and estimated trade-in values are only a few mouse clicks away. Some consumers may end up purchasing a vehicle from a sponsor of an informational site, and even educated consumers who do not complete part or all of the transaction process online will likely force their traditional retailer of choice to negotiate in a more competitive manner. Hence, this shift toward information symmetry is ultimately a detriment for firms and beneficial for buyers.

Information Symmetry
When all parties to a transaction share the same information concerning that transaction.

Information Asymmetry
When one party to a transaction has information that another does not.

2-4b Internet as Distribution Channel

The Internet acts as a distribution channel for nontangible goods and services. Consumers can purchase items such as airline tickets, insurance, stocks, and computer software online without the necessity of physical delivery. For largely tangible goods and services, businesses can often distribute the "intangible portion" online, such as product and warranty information. When physical distribution can be replaced completely or in part by electronic distribution, transactions are likely to occur more rapidly and at lower costs.

2-4c Speed

The Internet offers numerous opportunities to improve the speed of the actual transaction, as well as the process that leads up to and follows it. Consumers and businesses alike can research information twenty-four hours a day. Orders placed online may be processed immediately. Software engineers in the United States can work on projects during the day and then pass their work along to their counterparts in India who can continue work while the Americans sleep. The pace of business has increased and has been accompanied by heightened expectations for speed by consumers.

2-4d Interactivity

The Internet provides extensive opportunities for interactivity that would otherwise not be available. Consumers can discuss their experiences with products and services on bulletin boards or in chat rooms. Firms can readily exchange information with trade associations that represent their industries. Users can share files with relative ease. Rumors and bad news can and will spread rapidly.

2-4e Potential for Cost Reductions and Cost Shifting

The Internet provides many businesses with opportunities to minimize their costs—both fixed and variable—and thereby enhance flexibility. Information can be distributed to thousands or millions of recipients without either the expense associated with the mail system or the equipment required to do so. The virtual storefront, for example, does not necessarily require an actual facility and may reduce transaction costs through automated online ordering systems, although this is not always the case.

2-5 Forms of Electronic Commerce

Electronic commerce activities can be classified into five basic categories by identifying businesses and consumers as initiators and recipients of the offer (see Figure 2-1). Business-to-business and business-to-consumer categories account for most global e-commerce activity. Businesses are commonly involved in more than one of these segments simultaneously and/or involved in both electronic (i.e., "clicks") and traditional (i.e., "bricks") forms of commerce, often referred to as **clicks and bricks.** It is widely believed that successful retail firms of the future will likely be the ones that adopted this combination approach.

2-5a Business-to-Business Segment

Business-to-business (B2B) is the largest classification of Internet business, with global transactions estimated to be $6.8 trillion in 2007.[39] Because the Internet reduces transaction costs (costs associated with searching for suppliers, negotiating terms, etc.), the Internet provides exceptional opportunities for streamlining business-to-business operations. B2B is widely used as a means of increasing the efficiency of transactions. B2B firms seek to profit on the transactions among firms. Many consumers are unaware of the size of B2B relative to other forms.

Interestingly, the B2B segment experienced some turbulence in the early 2000s. Only about one-third of the more than two thousand new B2B start-ups in 2000 and 2001 survived into 2003. During this time, traditional brick-and-mortar

Clicks and Bricks

The simultaneous application of both electronic ("clicks") and traditional ("bricks") forms of commerce.

Business-to-Business (B2B)

The segment of electronic commerce whereby businesses utilize the Internet to solicit transactions from each other.

FIGURE | 2-1 | E-Commerce Matrix

		Offer Recipient		
		Business	**Consumer**	**Government**
Offer Initiator	**Business**	Business-to-Business (B2B)	Business-to-Consumer (B2C)	Business-to-Government (B2G)
	Consumer	Customer-to-Business (C2B)	Customer-to-Consumer (C2C)	

firms launched their own B2B initiatives to retain the transaction fees that otherwise would have been secured by the start-ups from the $482 billion spent on B2B transactions in the United States.[40]

2-5b Business-to-Consumer Segment

The **business-to-consumer (B2C)** segment is the second largest and fastest growing segment, including such competitors as Amazon.com and 1800flowers.com. Often referred to as **e-tailing,** B2C successes are often associated with advances in consumer acceptance of the Internet as a retail alternative. Global B2C transactions were estimated to be $240 billion in 2007.[41]

B2C offers retailers certain advantages over traditional forms of retailing, one of which is the potential for a larger average transaction. For example, when consumers read the description of a book at Amazon.com, they also see what others who ordered the same book also purchased, resulting in opportunities for increased business.

B2C can reduce transaction costs by eliminating the need for much of the overhead associated with traditional retailing; however, it is easy to overestimate the extent to which overhead can be reduced. Many analysts believe that the "dot-com debacle" of 2000 and 2001, during which time a number of Internet businesses filed for bankruptcy, was due to expected efficiencies and overhead reductions that never fully materialized.

B2C can offer exceptional convenience for consumers by enabling them to search large catalogs in only a few seconds, build an order over several days, and configure various products and view actual prices. "Frequently Asked Questions" (FAQ) pages can provide customers with clear, accurate answers to their most common questions instantaneously and at virtually no cost to the business. Most studies suggest, however, that the vast majority of potential customers who select items for purchase abandon the site before completing the purchase, creating an interesting challenge for strategic managers at e-tailers.

The challenges associated with a successful e-tailing operation are simple to identify, yet difficult to resolve. Simply stated, e-tailers must persuade consumers to frequent their sites, stay there long enough to evaluate the offerings (i.e., e-tailers must create a site high in "stickiness"), and complete their purchases. Needless to say, e-tailers must be able to fulfill these orders as advertised.

2-5c Business-to-Government Segment

The segment of electronic commerce whereby businesses utilize the Internet to solicit transactions from government entities is known as **business-to-government (B2G).** This segment has emerged as government agencies have realized that purchases can be handled efficiently when facilitated by the Internet. Global B2G expenditures were estimated to be approximately $7 to $8 billion in 2007.[42]

2-5d Consumer-to-Consumer Segment

The **consumer-to-consumer (C2C)** segment involves utilization of the Internet as a facilitator of transactions involving only consumers. Because transaction costs can be quite high, intermediaries such as eBay are often required to manage the exchange of information and Paypal to facilitate payments. Many C2C businesses were established solely to take advantage of technological advantages of the Internet and/or to meet consumer needs specifically created by the existence of the Internet. Although companies such as eBay are widely recognized, the C2C category is tiny relative to B2B and B2C.

Business-to-Consumer (B2C)
The segment of electronic commerce whereby businesses utilize the Internet to solicit transactions from consumers, also known as *e-tailing.*

E-tailing
Another term for *business-to-consumer (B2C).*

Business-to-Government (B2G)
The segment of electronic commerce whereby businesses utilize the Internet to solicit transactions from government entities.

Consumer-to-Consumer (C2C)
The segment of electronic commerce whereby consumers utilize the Internet to solicit transactions from each other.

2-5e Consumer-to-Business Segment

Consumer-to-Business (C2B)

The segment of electronic commerce whereby consumers utilize the Internet to solicit transactions from businesses.

In the **consumer-to-business (C2B)** segment, consumers generate the offer and businesses accept or decline it. This form of electronic commerce is the least developed of the four and includes competitors such as Priceline.com. Under the Priceline "reverse auction" model, consumers name their prices for goods and services such as airline tickets, hotel rooms, and long-distance phone service, and businesses are free to accept or reject them. Unlike traditional models, the reverse auction allows for price discrimination, because any given buyer does not know how much other buyers are paying for the same good or service.[43] Like C2C, the C2B category is tiny when compared to B2B and B2C.

2-6 Summary

The Internet has had a profound effect on the field of strategic management. It increases access to information for all parties involved in a transaction, acts as a distribution channel for nontangible goods and services, can improve transaction speed, offers opportunities for interactivity among participation in business transactions, and presents potential for cost reductions and cost shifting. Business-to-business (B2B) and business-to-consumer (B2C) segments are the two largest classifications of Internet-based business.

Key Terms

business-to-business

business-to-consumer

business-to-government

clicks and bricks

commoditization

consumer-to-business

consumer-to-consumer

economies of scale

e-tailing

information asymmetry

information symmetry

mass customization

offshoring

outsourcing

partnership

World Wide Web

Review Questions and Exercises

1. What is Friedman's thesis in his book, *The World Is Flat*?

2. What is the difference between outsourcing and offshoring?

3. What is the difference between commoditization and mass customization?

4. Has the advent of the Internet created new business models?

5. How has the development of the Internet affected the strategic management field?

6. What are the five categories of electronic commerce? Provide examples of each.

Practice Quiz

True or False

1. In *The World Is Flat*, Thomas Friedman argues that recent global and technological changes have increased the world dominance of Western powers such as the United States.

2. Outsourcing refers to contracting out a firm's non-core, nonrevenue-producing activities to other organizations primarily to reduce costs.

3. Mass customization refers to a process whereby firms are having a more difficult time distinguishing their products and services from those of their rivals.

4. The widespread application of the Internet has increased information asymmetry.

5. The fastest growing segment of Internet business is business-to-business (B2B).

6. The largest segment of Internet business is business-to-consumer (B2C).

Multiple Choice

7. Contracting out a firm's noncore, nonrevenue-producing activities to other organizations primarily to reduce costs is known as
   A. outsourcing.
   B. offshoring.
   C. mass customization.
   D. commoditization.

8. A process whereby firms are having a more difficult time distinguishing their products and services from those of their rivals is known as
   A. outsourcing.
   B. offshoring.
   C. mass customization.
   D. commoditization.

9. The ability to individualize product and service offerings to meet specific buyer needs is known as
   A. outsourcing.
   B. offshoring.
   C. mass customization.
   D. commoditization.

10. The phenomenon of "disaggregation and reaggregation" has led to an increased emphasis on
    A. outsourcing.
    B. partnerships.
    C. the Internet.
    D. all of the above

11. The state whereby one party has information that another does not is called
    A. information symmetry.
    B. offshoring.
    C. knowledge redistribution.
    D. customization.

12. E-tailing is synonymous with which category of e-commerce?
    A. business-to-business
    B. business-to-consumer
    C. consumer-to-business
    D. consumer-to-consumer

Notes

1. T. L. Friedman, *The World Is Flat* (New York: Farrar, Straus and Giroux, 2005).

2. Ibid.

3. C. Ansberry and T. Aeppel, "Surviving the Onslaught," *Wall Street Journal* (6 October 2003): B1, B6.

4. J. Dean, "Long a Low-Tech Power, China Sets Its Sight on Chip Making," *Wall Street Journal* (17 February 2004): A1, A16; D. Morse, "In North Carolina, Furniture Makers Try to Stay Alive," *Wall Street Journal* (20 February 2004): A1, A6; D. Luhnow, "As Jobs Move East, Plants in Mexico Retool to Compete," *Wall Street Journal* (5 March 2004): A1, A8; J. Millman, "Blueprint for Outsourcing," *Wall Street Journal* (3 March 2004): B1, B4.

5. E. Price, "Trade Gap Widens, Yet Outlook Is Upbeat," *Wall Street Journal* (14 February 2007): A2.

6. R. Buckman, "Apparel's Loose Thread," *Wall Street Journal* (22 March 2004): B1, B8.

7. J. Solomon and K. Kranhold, "In India's Outsourcing Boom, GE Played a Starring Role," *Wall Street Journal* (23 March 2005): A1, A12.

8. Ibid.

9. K. Maher, "Next on the Outsourcing List," *Wall Street Journal* (23 March 2004): B1, B8.

10. E. Bellman and N. Koppel, "More U.S. Legal Work Moves to India's Low-Cost Lawyers," *Wall Street Journal* (28 September 2005): B1, B2.

11. L. Yuan, "Chinese Companies Vie for a Role in U.S. IT Outsourcing," *Wall Street Journal* (5 April 2005): B1, B8.

12. N. Boudette, J. Sapsford, and P. Wonacott, "Cars Made in China Are Headed to the West," *Wall Street Journal* (22 April 2005): B1, B2.

13. G. Fairclough, "Chinese Cadillac Offers a Glimpse of GM's Future," *Wall Street Journal* (17 November 2006): B1, B4.

14. J. Barthelemy, "The Seven Deadly Sins of Outsourcing," *Academy of Management Executive* 17(2) (2003): 87–98.

15. M. Fong, "Woven in China," *Wall Street Journal* (11 April 2005): B1, B4.

16. Barthelemy, "The Seven Deadly Sins."

17. M. Fong, "Building a Better Bra," *Wall Street Journal* (9 November 2005): B1, B2.

18. N. Shirouzu, "As Detroit Slashed Car Jobs, Southern Towns Pick Up Slack," *Wall Street Journal* (1 February 2006): A1, A12.

19. J. Sapsford and N. Shirouzu, "Mom, Apple Pie, and . . . Toyota?" *Wall Street Journal* (11 May 2006): B1, B2.

20. A. Zimmerman, R. G. Matthews, and K. Hudson, "Can Employers Alter Hiring Practices to Cut Health Costs?" *Wall Street Journal* (27 October 2005): B1, B4.

21. L. Hawkins, Jr., "As GM Battles Surging Costs, Workers' Health Becomes Issue," *Wall Street Journal* (7 April 2005): A1, A11.

22. S. Carey & A. Frangos, "Airlines, Facing Cost Pressure, Outsource Crucial Safety Tasks," *Wall Street Journal* (21 January 2005): A1, A5.

23. R. Buckman, "Outsourcing with a Twist," *Wall Street Journal* (18 January 2005): B1, B4.

24. G. Ip, "Offshore Outsourcing Finds Fans at Fed Forum," *Wall Street Journal* (28 August 2005): A2.

25. J. E. Hilsenrath, "Behind Outsourcing Debate: Surprisingly Few Hard Numbers," *Wall Street Journal* (12 April 2004): A1, A12; K. Parthasarathi, "Keep Outsourcing Blues out of U.S. Election Politics," *Hindu Business Line* (25 August 2004).

26. N. Shirouzu, "Big Three's Outsourcing Plan: Make Parts Suppliers Do It," *Wall Street Journal* (10 June 2004): A1, A6.

27. J. Drucker and K. Brown, "Latest Wrinkle in Jobs Fight: Letting Customers Choose Where Their Work Is Done," *Wall Street Journal* (9 March 2004): B1, B3.

28. S. Carey, B. Stanley, and J. Larkin, "With Jobs Scarce, U.S. Pilots Sign on at Foreign Airlines," *Wall Street Journal* (5 May 2006): A1, A13.

29. M. Mangalindan, "In a Challenging China Market, Ebay Confronts a Big New Rival," *Wall Street Journal* (12 August 2005): A1, A6.

30. N. Wingfield, "E-tailing Comes of Age," *Wall Street Journal* (8 December 2003): B1, B7.

31. J. Magretta, "Why Business Models Matter," *Harvard Business Review* 80(5) (2002): 3.

32. P. Edmonston, "One Web Retailer's Watchword: 'Free after Rebate,'" *Wall Street Journal* (5 March 2001): B1, B5.

33. P. Edmonston, "Free-with-Rebate Costs Web Buyers Some Big Bucks," *Wall Street Journal* (18 May 2001): B1, B4.

34. M. E. Porter, "Strategy and the Internet," *Harvard Business Review* 79(3) (2001): 72.

35. K. McLaughlin, "Back from the Dead: Buying Groceries Online," *Wall Street Journal* (25 February 2003): D1–D2.

36. T. Malone and R. J. Laubaucher, "The Dawn of the E-Lance Economy," *Harvard Business Review* 76(5) (1998): 144–152; D. Tapscott, D. Ticoll, and A. Lowy, *Digital Capital: Harnessing the Power of Business Webs* (Boston: Harvard Business School Press, 2000).

37. R. Coase, *The Firm, The Market, and The Law* (Chicago: University of Chicago Press, 1990).

38. Friedman, *The World Is Flat.*

39. N. L. Karmakar, "E-Business for Creating Wealth: The Hype or Reality," paper presented at the 2005 Information Technology in Business Conference, St. Petersburg, Russia.

40. J. Angwin, "Renaissance in Cyberspace," *Wall Street Journal* (20 November 2003): B1.

41. Karmakar, "E-Business for Creating Wealth."

42. Ibid.

43. A. Cortese, "E-Commerce: Good-Bye to Fixed Pricing?" *Business Week* (4 May 1998), www.businessweek.com/1998/18/b3576023.htm.

Insight from *strategy+business*

The Internet's influence on business models is undeniable, but not all firms have leveraged the Web successfully. This chapter's strategy + business reading examines the underlying economics that explains why some e-tailing ventures are successful and others are not.

The Hidden Costs of Clicks

Internet retailers are finally learning why books and luggage make money online—whereas shoes and toys do not.

By Tim Laseter, Elliot Rabinovich, and Angela Huang

Bags.com ranks as one of the more notable successes among Internet retailers. The leading online purveyor of luggage, eBags generates more than $38 million in revenue a year and has been consistently profitable since its founding in 1998, in the heyday of the Internet bubble. Operating with minimal inventory thanks to direct "drop shipments" from manufacturers to end customers, eBags could be the model for the future of commerce.

But that model is still developing. EBags continues to expand and adapt its business. In 2004, the online retailer, which is based in Greenwood Village, Colo., acquired Shoedini.com, a seller of dress shoes for men and women, and renamed it 6pm.com. Having expanded from its original focus on luggage into backpacks, handbags, and other accessories, eBags considered shoes the next logical category for marketing synergies. Yet, despite the clear marketing logic, selling shoes online turned out to be more complicated than selling the other product lines.

The issue, as eBags discovered and as many online vendors have yet to understand, highlights the fundamental operational challenges of Internet retailing. It centers on a concept common in the businessto-business realm but rarely employed in a business-to-consumer context: cost-to-serve. Defined as the total supply chain cost from origin to destination, cost-to-serve incorporates such factors as inventory stocking, packaging, shipping, and returns processing. This metric also helps to explain why some of the early high-flying "e-tailers," such as eToys and Webvan, failed miserably.

In the eBags example, the cost of serving shoe customers is far higher than the cost of serving luggage customers. The Shoedini acquisition more than doubled the number of SKUs that eBags handled, and the complexity of managing the inventory exploded. Most bags come in two variations—usually different colors. But a shoe style comes in several colors and many sizes; there can be 30 or more variations of a single model.

Bags, furthermore, come in boxes that manufacturers use for shipping via small-package delivery to a fragmented base of mostly mom-and-pop retail customers. But shoes ship to retailers in bulk packaging rather than in individual boxes. When 6pm.com sells a pair of dress loafers direct to a consumer, the manufacturer thus has to incur extra shipping and handling costs to repackage and ship the shoes.

Most important, shoes have a short product life cycle—typically three to six months—and suffer from a high return rate. (Some customers order two pairs at a time, planning to return the pair that doesn't fit.) Luggage life cycles can last six years, and return rates are minimal. For eBags, this means that although shoes and luggage command similar gross margins, shoes carry a much higher cost-to-serve, and selling them online thus requires a different business model.

Understanding the cost-to-serve dynamics is more important than ever as online retailing continues its growth spurt. More than a third of U.S. households now shop online, according to a September 2005 report from Forrester Research, and annual sales of physical goods are expected to hit $100 billion for the year.

Over the second decade of online retailing, the companies that truly grasp the drivers of cost-to-serve at the level of individual items and individual customers will unlock the full value-creating potential of online retailing as an alternative to—and complement of—traditional retailing.

Trial and Error

Back at the dawn of online retailing, highflyers like Value America (an online "department store") and Webvan (an

Internet-based delivery service that focused its offerings on grocery items) did not comprehend the operational cost implications of their business models. Value America started with a virtual inventory model supposedly applicable to any branded product. Although its initial offering, computer hardware, sold well, shipping and handling costs for lower-value goods proved prohibitive, and an unmanageable flood of returns ultimately sank the company in August 2000. Less than a year later, in July 2001, Webvan declared bankruptcy after concluding that it would never turn a profit, despite its state-of-the-art supply chain with a hub-and-spoke network of delivery cross-docks and highly automated distribution centers. (The flaws in its economic model were highlighted in a Booz Allen Hamilton study more than a year before its collapse. See "The Last Mile to Nowhere: Flaws & Fallacies in Internet Home-Delivery Schemes," by Tim Laseter, Pat Houston, Anne Chung, Silas Byrne, Martha Turner, and Anand Devendran, s+b, Third Quarter 2000.)

Even Amazon.com did not fully appreciate all the factors driving its cost-to-serve. When Jeff Bezos opened his Internet store in 1995, he started with books, reasoning that it would be easier to offer the millions of titles in print online than through a traditional mail-order catalog. Although Mr. Bezos may not have fully grasped all of the inefficiencies inherent in the book industry, he saw that his model could minimize inventory risk — a significant problem in book retailing. Unlike other manufacturers, publishers take back all unsold copies of their product. Up to 30 percent of trade books ship back to the publisher at enormous cost to everyone: to the publisher, who refunds the payment to the retailer; to the retailer, who pays for shipping and restocking; and indirectly to the consumer. Amazon's online model minimizes the inherent inefficiency of placing potentially unsellable titles on thousands of retail bookshelves by relying instead on a relatively small inventory to support a "virtual bookshelf." If Amazon returns fewer books than a bricks-and-mortar retailer, it should be able to negotiate lower prices from the publishers (reflecting its lower cost-to-serve as a customer of the publisher). Amazon can then pass along those savings through lower prices to the consumer.

Although books worked for Amazon, toys were a different matter. As Jeff Bezos learned, the toy supply chain comes with a much higher cost-to-serve. Toys are more seasonal than books and demand for them is far less predictable. Magnifying those challenges, most toys are made in Asia, and the replenishment cycle can easily outlast the actual selling season. That means merchandisers must accurately predict which toys will be hits and then buy enough inventory for the whole season; Amazon therefore gained no benefit from its "virtual shelves." Guessing too conservatively results in missed sales, and guessing too optimistically leads to write-offs because toy manufacturers do not typically accept returns of unsold goods. Without any toy merchandising expertise, Amazon guessed wrong for the 1999 holiday season and wrote off $39 million in excess toy inventory in early 2000, having sold only $95 million worth of toys.

Furthermore, conventional toy retailers enjoy advantages that traditional booksellers don't. Unlike Barnes & Noble, Wal-Mart and Toys "R" Us ship multiple truckloads of goods to each store weekly, which puts their transportation costs far below the cost of shipping individual toys to consumers. Recognizing these differences, Amazon gladly partnered with Toys "R" Us in 2000, shifting the inventory risk to the experts but leveraging the additional product lines to lower its own shipping cost for multi-item orders.

Nonetheless, the two partners had a falling-out in 2004, with dueling lawsuits in the New Jersey court system. This denouement suggests that the cost-to-serve for online toy retailing produced a financial model that would not support the two parties' aspirations adequately.

Channels and Brands

Although successful online retailing depends on a variety of factors, the cost-to-serve of a particular product category can explain much of the variance in the penetration rates of Internet sales. For example, according to the United States Census Bureau, in 2002 (the latest data available), 44 percent of retail sales of computer hardware and software took place via the Internet. Certainly tech-savvy computer buyers are more likely than the general population to shop online. But equally important, the high value-to-weight ratio of computers—especially as laptops become more popular—minimizes the importance of transportation cost and makes the category a low-cost-to-serve option over the Internet.

Cost-to-serve factors like inventory, packaging, shipping, and returns help explain why online sales of books outstrip online sales of other kinds of merchandise. E-commerce accounts for nearly 13 percent of the total bookstore and newsstand sales in the United States $15 billion in 2002 (the latest year available from the U.S. Census Bureau)—and the same portion of the $21 billion market for office equipment and supplies. By contrast, the Internet accounted for just 2.7 percent of the $92 billion in U.S. sales of furniture and home furnishings.

Or consider the largest retail category, food and beverages. Online sales accounted for only two-tenths of 1 percent of the $450 billion U.S. food and beverage retail sales total in 2002. As Webvan (and many investors) learned, targeting a huge market does not guarantee success if the cost-to-serve economics don't work.

Future growth in e-commerce will likely come from continued modification of existing supply chains rather than wholesale replacement. For example, despite the generally low level of Internet sales in furniture and housewares, Williams-Sonoma has achieved great success online. The company, which operates a mix of retail, catalog, and Internet channels under its eponymous store brand as well as the Pottery Barn and Hold Everything brands (among others), sold $3.1 billion in fiscal 2005—52 percent through its traditional retail stores and 48 percent through its two direct-to-consumer channels. At $3.3 million in annual sales for its average kitchenware store, Williams-Sonoma doesn't gain any significant transportation economies in shipping to its stores rather than directly to its customers. Ultimately, the company can maximize profits by assigning items to channels and brands to reach consumers at the lowest cost-to-serve.

Circuit City's Opportunity

Rather than minimizing the cost-to-serve across channels, traditional retailers often put their most popular items on their Web site. Although such an approach sounds logical, the reverse would typically work better. Traditional store-based retailing requires turning inventory quickly to justify expensive floor space. Slow-moving inventory—especially products with a high risk of obsolescence—can benefit from the centralized inventory pooling of online retailing. And if the product commands a high value-to-weight ratio, the cost penalty from direct-to-consumer shipping is minimal.

Circuit City, the "big box" consumer electronics and small appliances retailer, has an opportunity to minimize its cost-to-serve by making smart use of its many service options: in-store shopping, in-store or online ordering with delivery from the store, online ordering with store pickup, and online ordering with direct home delivery. Consumer electronics is a category currently underexploited by e-commerce. In 2002, only 2.5 percent of electronics and appliances sales went through online channels despite the fact that many electronic goods share the high value-to-weight ratio of computer hardware and software. Finding the optimal cost-to-serve for each product and customer category would give Circuit City a competitive advantage over pure-play online retailers or less aggressive traditional competitors.

Circuit City operates a network of nine regional distribution centers to serve its 621 domestic stores. With average weekly sales of more than $300,000 per store, Circuit City generates overall cost savings from its transportation network scale. But the relative importance of this bulk shipping network varies by product.

Consider the Hitachi 65" HDTV Display recently offered at $1,299. It weighs 324 pounds and measures 5-feet-by-5-feet with a 28-inch depth. Shipment of such a bulky item through the company's full-truckload distribution network offers significant savings over a small-package shipment directly to a consumer's home via UPS. But, with relatively low unit sales and a short product life cycle, inventory held at the store represents a high cost and big risk. Circuit City might benefit from keeping a minimum inventory of this item at the store—even just a display model—and having customers order it online for in-store pickup after the next delivery from the regional distribution network.

A pure online offering might work best for the Sony HDV camcorder. Priced at around $1,999, it is the most expensive model among the 60-plus camcorders that Circuit City sells, and it costs three to five times the price of the most popular models. As with the Hitachi HDTV, low unit sales of the Sony HDV camcorder may not justify stocking the item at the store because of the high inventory-carrying cost and risk of obsolescence. But unlike the Hitachi HDTV, the camcorder weighs very little—less than two pounds—and, accordingly, Circuit City's distribution network provides little transportation cost savings. Rather than stocking it at each of the nine regional distribution centers, Circuit City could gain further savings by pooling the inventory in a single national distribution center and shipping directly to customers' homes, minimizing the cost-to-serve for Circuit City as well as for the customer.

For each combination of customer and merchandise, there is an optimal cost-to-serve option among the different delivery choices: store inventory, store delivery, in-store pickup, and direct delivery. For customers living far from a store, for example, even for bulky products like the HDTV, the benefits of routing the goods through a regional distribution center (such as that maintained by Circuit City) may be offset by the extra costs of a two-step distribution cycle, compared to the simplicity of direct home delivery. Finding the optimal cost-to-serve at the levels of customer and item may be challenging, but it will be rewarding.

Even pure-play online retailers should consider the cost-to-serve in their pricing. Despite having the ability to customize Web pages to each individual, few companies fully leverage the potential to price products to reflect the different underlying costs. For example, eBags offers special pricing for bulk purchases for corporate sales, but it does not attempt to adjust shipping costs on the basis of a customer's geographic location. Such fine-tuned pricing could potentially increase the company's profitability. That's the kind of detail that retailers will have to consider as they grow their online businesses.

Accounting for Intangibles

Cost-to-serve in online retailing includes such factors as the expenses associated with inventory, transportation, and replication of the existing offerings of traditional retailers. But to get a truer sense of cost-to-serve, it should also take into account intangible costs to the customer. Consider the current approach to furniture retailing, one of the least customer-friendly supply chains in retailing.

Because there are so many manufacturers offering so many styles in so many woods, finishes, and fabrics, most furniture retailers display a limited selection of goods. Customers place their orders and then wait for the couch, table, or chair to be manufactured, shipped to the retailer, and finally delivered to their homes. The whole process regularly takes 12 or more weeks—a cost in "pain and suffering" that falls squarely on the customers.

Early attempts to improve on the furniture retailing process via the Internet proved daunting. Living.com and Furniture.com, two failed Web retailers, focused on the "consumer experience" by investing in technology to allow shoppers to visualize the furniture in virtual mockups of their home. These companies' supply chains—which, like Amazon's, depended on outside delivery services—proved untenable. The challenge of scheduling precisely timed home deliveries, something Amazon's products typically do not demand, proved to be beyond the ability of these nascent furniture retailers. Moreover, products often arrived damaged or unacceptable for some other reason, resulting in return rates of up to 35 percent of sales. Despite good efforts, the "virtual" model failed in the furniture category.

The Amazon online model doesn't work for furniture sellers. It would be better for them to emulate the automotive industry. The big opportunity online for furniture retailers may lie not in eliminating storefronts, but in dramatically reducing the lead times in the order-to-delivery cycle. Car dealers resolve the choice challenge by sharing inventory information among dealerships and exchanging vehicles to better meet a particular customer's desires. Roughly half of the vehicles sold by a typical dealership come from such an exchange; the other half come from the dealer's own inventory on the lot. Similarly, with furniture, customers could check the "look and feel" of a display model, and the retailer would then locate the desired inventory at another store or at a centralized stock pool with delivery in days, not weeks. Such a business model would leverage the Internet's information-sharing power to lower the "cost" of long lead times without incurring an undue level of inventory investment.

In the end, future success for retailers of furniture, electronics, luggage—any sort of retailers—won't be a matter of expanding standard offerings to the burgeoning Internet channel or replicating existing online models. Despite the obvious marketing synergies, toys present different challenges from books, and shoes different challenges from luggage. Smart retailers will take a closer look at the costs of bringing each item to each consumer the cost-to-serve—to decide how to merchandise their offerings and ultimately grow their business by applying the right retail model at the right time.

Tim Laseter (lasetert@darden.virginia.edu) serves on the faculty of the Darden Graduate School of Business at the University of Virginia. Author of *Balanced Sourcing: Cooperation and Competition in Supplier Relationships* (Jossey-Bass, 1998) and formerly a vice president with Booz Allen Hamilton, he has more than 20 years of experience in operations strategy and supply chain management.

Elliot Rabinovich (elliot.rabinovich@asu.edu), a faculty member at the W.P. Carey School of Business at Arizona State University, is an expert on Internet retailing and supply chain management. He is the coauthor of *Logistics and the Extended Enterprise:* Benchmarks and Best Practices for the Manufacturing Professional (John Wiley & Sons, 1999).

Angela Huang (huang_angela@bah.com), formerly a financial analyst at the Reserve Bank of New Zealand, is an associate in Booz Allen Hamilton's Cleveland office. She works with clients on operational challenges, including retail supply chain issues.

Industry Competition

3

Chapter Outline

This chapter marks the beginning of the strategic management process and is one of two that considers the external environment. At this point it is appropriate to focus on factors *external* to the organization and to view firm performance from an industrial organization perspective. *Internal* factors are considered later in the process and in future chapters.

Each business operates among a group of companies that produces competing products or services known as an **industry.** The concept of an industry is a simple one, but it is often confused in everyday conversations. The term *industry* does not refer to a single company or specific firms in general. For example, in the statement, "A new industry is moving to the community," the word *industry* should be replaced by *company* or *firm.*

Industry

A group of competitors that produce similar products or services.

Although usually differences exist among competitors, each industry has its own set of combat rules governing such issues as product quality, pricing, and distribution. This is especially true for industries that contain a large number of firms offering standardized products and services. Most competitors—but not all—follow the rules. For example, most service stations in the United States generally offer regular unleaded, midgrade, and premium unleaded gasoline at prices that do not differ substantially from those at nearby stations. Breaking the so-called rules and charting a different strategic course might be possible, but may not be desirable. As such, it is important for strategic managers to understand the structure of the industry(s) in which their firms operate before deciding how to compete successfully.

Defining a firm's industry is not always an easy task. In a perfect world, each firm would operate in one clearly defined industry; however, many firms compete in multiple industries, and strategic managers in similar firms often differ in their conceptualizations of the industry environment. In addition, some companies have utilized the Internet to redefine industries or even invent new ones, such as eBay's online auction or Priceline's travel businesses. As a result, the process of industry definition and analysis can be especially challenging when Internet competition is considered.[1]

Numerous outside sources can assist a strategic manager in determining "where to draw the industry lines" (i.e., determining which competitors are in the industry, which are not, and why). Government classification systems, such as the Standardized Industrial Classification (SIC), as well as distinctions made by trade journals and business analysts may be helpful. In 1997, the U.S. Census Bureau replaced the SIC system with the North American Industry Classification System (NAICS), an alternative system designed to facilitate comparisons of business activities across North America. Astute managers assess all of these sources, however, and add their own rigorous and systematic analysis of the competition when defining the industry.

Numerous descriptive factors can be used when drawing the industry lines. In the case of McDonald's, for example, attributes such as speed of service, types of products, prices of products, and level of service may be useful. Hence, one might define McDonald's industry as consisting of restaurants offering easy to consume, moderately priced food products rapidly and in a limited service environment. Broad terms such as "fast food" are often used to describe such industries, but doing so does not eliminate the need for a clear, tight definition.

Some factors are usually not helpful when defining an industry, however, such as those directly associated with strategy and firm size. For example, it is not a good idea to exclude a "fast-food" restaurant in McDonald's industry because it is not part of a large chain or because it emphasizes low-priced food. Rather, these factors explain how such a restaurant might be positioned vis-à-vis to McDonald's, a concept discussed in greater detail in Chapter 7.

The concept of primary and secondary industries may also be a useful tool in defining an industry. A primary industry may be conceptualized as a group of close competitors, whereas a secondary industry includes less direct competition. When one analyzes a firm's competition, the primary industry is loosely considered to be "the industry," whereas the secondary industry is presented as a means of adding clarity to the analysis. For example, McDonald's primary industry includes such competitors as Burger King and Wendy's, whereas its secondary industry might also include restaurants that do not emphasize hamburgers and offer more traditional restaurant seating such as Pizza Hut and Denny's. The distinction between primary and secondary industry may be based on objective criteria such as price, similarity of products, or location, but is ultimately a subjective call.

Once the industry is defined, it is important to identify the **market share,** which is a competitor's share of the total industry sales, for the firm and its key rivals. Unless stated otherwise, market share calculations are usually based on total sales revenues of the firms in an industry rather than units produced or sold by the individual firms. This information is often available from public sources, especially when there is a high level of agreement as to how an industry should be defined.

When market share is not available or substantial differences exist in industry definitions, however, **relative market share,** or a firm's share of industry sales when only the firm and its key competitors are considered, can serve as a useful substitute. Consider low-end discount retailer Dollar Tree as an example and assume that the only available market share data considers Dollar Tree to be part of the broadly defined discount department store industry. If a more narrow industry definition is proposed—perhaps one limited to deep discount retailers— new market share calculations will be necessary. In addition, it becomes quite complicated when one attempts to include the multitude of mom-and-pop dis-counters in the calculations. In this situation, computing relative market shares that consider Dollar Tree and its major competitors can be useful. Assume for the sake of this example that four major competitors are identified in this industry— Dollar General, Family Dollar, Dollar Tree, and Fred's—with annual sales of $6 billion, $5 billion, $2 billion, and $1 billion, respectively. Relative market share would be calculated on the basis of a total market size of $14 billion (i.e., 6 + 5 + 2 + 1). In this example, relative market shares for the competitors are 43 percent, 36 percent, 14 percent, and 7 percent, respectively. From a practical standpoint, calculating relative market share can be appropriate when external data sources are limited.

A firm's market share can also become quite complex as various industry or market restrictions are added. Unfortunately, the precise market share informa-tion most useful to a firm may be based on a set of industry factors so com-plex that computing it becomes an arduous task. In a recent analysis, the Mintel International Group set out to identify the size of the "healthy snack" market in the United States, a task complicated by the fact that many products such as cheese, yogurt, and cereal are eaten as snacks in some but not all instances.[2] To overcome this barrier, analysts computed a total for the healthy snack market by adding only the proportion of each food category consumed as a healthy snack. In other words, 100 percent of the total sales of products such as popcorn and trail mix—foods consumed as "healthy snacks" 100 percent of the time—were included in the total. In contrast, only 40 percent of cheese consumption, 61 per-cent of yogurt consumption, and 21 percent of cereal consumption were included

Market Share

The percentage of total market sales attributed to one competitor (i.e., firm sales divided by total market sales).

Relative Market Share

A firm's share of industry sales when only the firm and its key competitors are considered (i.e., firm sales divided by total sales of a select group firms in the industry).

Step 2: Identification of the Industry and the Competitors

After the organization has been introduced, its industry must be specifically identified. This process can be either relatively simple or difficult. For example, most would agree that Kroger is in the "grocery store industry," and its competition comes primarily from other grocery stores. However, not all decisions are simple. For example, should Wal-Mart be classified in the department store industry (competing with upscale mall-oriented stores) or in the discount retail industry (competing with low-end retailers such as Family Dollar)? Is Taco Bell in the fast-food industry or in the broader restaurant industry? To further complicate matters, many corporations are diversified and compete in a number of different industries. For example, Anheuser Busch operates breweries and theme parks. In cases in which multiple business units are competing in different industries, one needs to identify multiple industries. Market shares or relative market shares for the firm and its key competitors—based on the best available data—should also be identified. It is important to clarify industry definition at the outset so that the macroenvironmental forces that affect it can be realistically assessed. In addition, a firm's relative strengths and weaknesses can be classified as such only when compared to other companies in the industry.

in the total. Although this approach is reasonable and can be quite useful, it can only be calculated when one has access to data that may not be readily available. Hence, analysts must use the best data available to describe the relative market positions of the competitors in a given industry (see Case Analysis 3-1).

3-1 Industry Life Cycle Stages

Industry Life Cycle

The stages (introduction, growth, shakeout, maturity, and decline) through which industries often pass.

Like firms, industries develop and evolve over time. Not only might the group of competitors within a firm's industry change constantly, but also the nature and structure of the industry can change as it matures and its markets become better defined. An industry's developmental stage influences the nature of competition and potential profitability among competitors.[3] In theory, each industry passes through five distinct phases of an **industry life cycle** (see Figure 3-1).

A young industry that is beginning to form is considered to be in the *introduction stage.* Demand for the industry's outputs is low at this time because product and/or service awareness is still developing. Virtually all purchasers are first-time buyers and tend to be affluent, risk tolerant, and innovative. Technology is a key concern in this stage because businesses often seek ways to improve production and distribution efficiencies as they learn more about their markets.

Normally, after key technological issues are addressed and customer demand begins to rise, the industry enters the *growth stage.* Growth continues but tends to slow as the market demand approaches saturation. Fewer first-time buyers remain, and most purchases tend to be upgrades or replacements. Many competitors are

FIGURE 3-1 The Industry Life Cycle

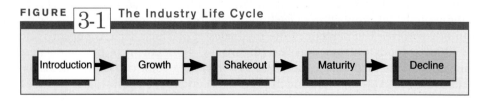

profitable, but available funds may be heavily invested into new facilities or technologies. Some of the industry's weaker competitors may go out of business in this stage.

Shakeout occurs when industry growth is no longer rapid enough to support the increasing number of competitors in the industry. As a result, a firm's growth is contingent on its resources and competitive positioning instead of a high growth rate within the industry. Marginal competitors are forced out, and a small number of industry leaders may emerge.

Maturity is reached when the market demand for the industry's outputs is completely saturated. Virtually all purchases are upgrades or replacements, and industry growth may be low, nonexistent, or even negative. Industry standards for quality and service have been established, and customer expectations tend to be more consistent than in previous stages. The U.S. automobile industry is a classic example of a mature industry. Firms in mature industries often seek new uses for their products or services or pursue new markets, often through global expansion.

The *decline stage* occurs when demand for an industry's products and services decreases and often begins when consumers turn to more convenient, safer, or higher quality offerings from firms in substitute industries. Some firms may divest their business units in this stage, whereas others may seek to "reinvent themselves" and pursue a new wave of growth associated with a similar product or service.

A number of external factors can facilitate movement along the industry life cycle. When oil prices spiked in 2005, for example, firms in oil-intensive industries such as airlines and carmakers began to feel the squeeze.[4] When an industry is mature, however, firms are often better able to withstand such pressures and survive.

Although the life cycle model is useful for analysis, identifying an industry's precise position is often difficult, and not all industries follow these exact stages or at predictable intervals.[5] For example, the U.S. railroad industry did not reach maturity for many decades and extended over a hundred years before entering decline, whereas the personal computer industry began to show signs of maturity after only seven years. In addition, following an industry's decline, changes in the macroenvironment may revitalize new growth. For example, the bicycle industry fell into decline some years ago when the automobile gained popularity but has now been rejuvenated by society's interest in health and physical fitness.

3-2 Industry Structure

Factors associated with industry structure have been found to play a dominant role in the performance of many companies, with the exception of those that are its notable leaders or failures.[6] As such, one needs to understand these factors at the outset before delving into the characteristics of a specific firm. Michael Porter, a leading authority on industry analysis, proposed a systematic means of analyzing the potential profitability of firms in an industry known as Porter's "five forces" model. According to Porter, an industry's overall profitability, which is the combined profits of all competitors, depends on five basic competitive forces, the relative weights of which vary by industry (see Figure 3-2).

1. Intensity of rivalry among incumbent firms
2. Threat of new competitors entering the industry
3. Threat of substitute products or services
4. Bargaining power of buyers
5. Bargaining power of suppliers

FIGURE 3-2 Porter's Five Forces Model

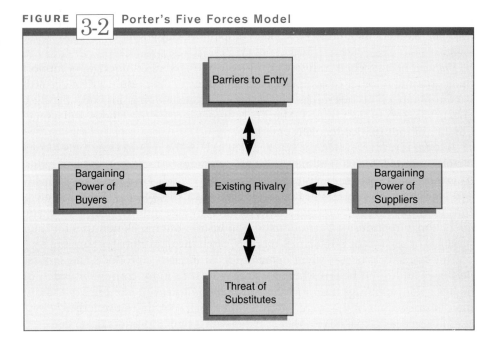

These five factors combine to form the industry structure and suggest (but do not guarantee) profitability prospects for firms that operate in the industry. Each of the factors is discussed in greater detail in sections 3-3 through 3-7.

3-3 Intensity of Rivalry among Incumbent Firms

Competition intensifies when a firm identifies the opportunity to improve its position or senses competitive pressure from other businesses in its industry, which can result in price wars, advertising battles, new product introductions or modifications, and even increased customer service or warranties.[7] Rivalry can be intense in some industries. For example, a battle wages in the U.S. real-estate industry, where traditional brokers who earn a commission of 5 to 6 percent are being challenged by discount brokers who charge sellers substantially lower fees. Agents for the buyer and seller typically split commissions, which usually fall in the $7,000 range for both agents when a home sells for $250,000. Discount brokers argue that the primary service provided by the seller's agent is listing the home in a multiple listing service (MLS) database, the primary tool used by most buyers and their agents to peruse available properties. Discount brokers provide sellers with a MLS listing for a flat fee in a number of markets, sometimes less than $1,000. Traditional brokers are angry, however, and argue that discount brokers simply do not provide the full array of services available at a so-called full-service broker. Traditional brokers dominate the industry, accounting for 98 percent of all sales in 2005. They often control the local MLS databases, and many discount brokers charge that they are not provided equal access to list their properties.[8] Hence, rivalry in this industry—especially between full-service and discount brokers—remains quite intense.

Competitive intensity often evolves over time and depends on a number of interacting factors, as discussed in sections 3-3a through 3-3h. Factors should be assessed independently and then integrated into an overall perspective.

3-3a Concentration of Competitors

The number of companies in the industry and their relative sizes or power levels influence an industry's intensity of rivalry. Industries with few firms tend to be less competitive, but those with many firms that are roughly equivalent in size and power tend to be more competitive, as each firm fights for dominance. Competition is also likely to be intense in industries with large numbers of firms because some of those companies may believe that they can make competitive moves without being noticed.[9]

3-3b High Fixed or Storage Costs

When firms have unused productive capacity, they often cut prices in an effort to increase production and move toward full capacity. The degree to which prices (and profits) can fall under such conditions is a function of the firms' cost structures. Those with high fixed costs are most likely to cut prices when excess capacity exists, because they must operate near capacity to be able to spread their overhead over more units of production.

The U.S. airline industry experiences this problem periodically, as losses generally result from planes that are flying substantially less than full or those that are not flying at all. This dynamic often results in last-minute fare specials in an effort to fill seats that would otherwise fly vacant. During the difficult times for U.S. airlines immediately following the 9/11 terrorist attacks, frequent price wars were often initiated by low-cost airlines such as JetBlue, Southwest, and AirTran.[10] Interestingly, airlines filled 73.4 percent of their seats in 2003 compared to only 63.5 percent a decade earlier.[11]

3-3c Slow Industry Growth

Firms in industries that grow slowly are more likely to be highly competitive than companies in fast growing industries. In slow-growth industries, one firm's increase in market share must come primarily at the expense of other firms' shares. Competitors often attend more to the actions of their rivals than to consumer tastes and trends when formulating strategies.

Slow industry growth can be caused by a sluggish economy, as was the case for vehicles during the early 2000s. As a result, manufacturers began to emphasize value by enhancing features and cutting costs. Ford, DaimlerChrysler, Nissan, Toyota, and others began to produce slightly larger trucks with additional features, while trimming prices. Producers also began to develop lower priced luxury cars in a fierce battle for sales.[12]

Slow industry growth—and even declines—are frequently caused by shifts in consumer demand patterns. For example, per capita consumption of carbonated soft drinks in the United States fell from its peak of fifty-four gallons in 1997 to approximately fifty-two gallons by 2004. During this same period, annual world growth declined from 9 percent to 4 percent as consumption of fruit juices, energy drinks, bottled water, and other noncarbonated beverages continued to rise. Coca-Cola and PepsiCo acquired or developed a number of noncarbonated brands during this time in efforts to counter the sluggish growth prospects in soft drinks. Interestingly, these rivals now appear to have modified their industry definitions from a narrow "soft drink" focus to a broader perspective including noncarbonated beverages.[13]

3-3d Lack of Differentiation or Low Switching Costs

The more similar the offerings among competitors, the more likely customers are to shift from one to another. As a result, such firms tend to engage in price competition. **Switching costs** are one-time costs that buyers incur when they switch from one company's products or services to another. When switching costs are low, firms are under considerable pressure to satisfy customers who can easily switch competitors at any time. When products or services are less differentiated, purchase decisions are based on price and service considerations, resulting in greater competition.

Interestingly, firms often seek to create switching costs in efforts to encourage customer loyalty. Internet Service Provider (ISP) America Online, for example, encourages users to obtain and use AOL e-mail accounts. Historically, these accounts were eliminated if the AOL customer switched to another ISP. Free e-mail accounts with Yahoo and other providers proliferated in the mid-2000s, however. As a result, AOL loosened this restriction in 2006, suggesting that most consumers no longer see the loss of an e-mail account as a major factor when considering a switch to another ISP (see Strategy at Work 3-1). Frequent flier programs also reward fliers who fly with one or a limited number of airlines. The Southwest Airlines generous program rewards only customers who complete a given number of flights within a twelve-month period, thereby effectively raising the costs of switching to another airline.

The cellular telephone industry in the United States benefited from key switching costs for a number of years. Until regulations changed in late 2003, consumers who switched providers were not able to keep their telephone numbers. Hence, many consumers were reluctant to change due to the hassle associated with alerting friends and business associates of the new number. Today, however, "number portability" greatly reduces switching costs, allowing consumers to retain their original telephone number when they switch providers.[14]

3-3e Capacity Augmented in Large Increments

When production can be easily added one increment at a time, overcapacity is not a major concern. If economies of scale or other factors dictate that

Switching Costs

One-time costs that buyers of an industry's outputs incur as they switch from one company's products or services to another's.

Rivalry and Cooperation in Internet Services

Amidst a flurry of copromotion agreements between retailers and Internet brands, Microsoft and Best Buy embarked on a strategic alliance that includes Internet, broadcasting, and in-store promotional projects. Microsoft utilizes the new agreement to expand its distribution and increase subscribers to its Internet services. The agreement also displays and promotes the Best Buy logo and BestBuy.com links at Microsoft's Web sites and broadcasting properties, including the Expedia.com travel service, Microsoft's e-mail services, Hotmail, WebTV Network, the new MSN eShop online, and MSNBC. In return, Best Buy became a major advertiser with Microsoft's Internet and broadcast properties.

Wal-Mart and America Online (AOL) have also teamed up to drive traffic to Wal-Mart's Web site and introduce millions of customers to the AOL brand. AOL is most interested in the in-store promotion of its online service in more than four thousand Wal-Mart stores in the United States, in return for promoting Wal-Mart's online store to its 18 million subscribers. Under the agreement, AOL also provides Web design assistance to the nation's largest retailer.

Sources: R. Spiegel, "Microsoft and Best Buy Join Alliance Frenzy," E-Commerce Times, 16 December, 1999; C. Dembeck, "Wal-Mart Looking to AOL for E-Commerce Boost," E-Commerce Times, 13 December, 1999; C. Dembeck, "Yahoo! and Kmart Forge Alliance to Counter AOL," E-Commerce Times, 14 December 1999.

production be augmented in large blocks, however, then capacity additions may lead to temporary overcapacity in the industry, and firms may cut prices to clear inventories. Airlines and hotels, for example, usually must acquire additional capacity in large increments because it is not feasible to add a few airline seats or hotel rooms as demand warrants. When additional blocks of seats or rooms become available, firms are under intense pressure to cover the additional costs by filling them.

3-3f Diversity of Competitors

Companies that are diverse in their origins, cultures, and strategies often have different goals and means of competition. Such firms may have a difficult time agreeing on a set of combat rules. As such, industries with global competitors or with entrepreneurial owner-operators tend to be diverse and particularly competitive. Internet businesses often change the rules for competition by emphasizing alternative sources of revenue, different channels of distribution, or a new business model. This diversity can sharply increase rivalry.

3-3g High Strategic Stakes

Competitive rivalry is likely to be high if firms also have high stakes in achieving success in a particular industry. For instance, many strong, traditional companies cannot afford to fail in their Web-based ventures if their strategic managers believe a Web presence is necessary even if it is not profitable. These desires can often lead a firm to sacrifice profitability.

3-3h High Exit Barriers

Exit barriers are economic, strategic, or emotional factors that keep companies from leaving an industry even though they are not profitable or may even be losing money. Examples of exit barriers include fixed assets that have no alternative uses, labor agreements that cannot be renegotiated, strategic partnerships among business units within the same firm, management's unwillingness to leave an industry because of pride, and governmental pressure to continue operations to avoid adverse economic effects in a geographic region.[15] When substantial exit barriers exist, firms choose to compete as a "lesser of two evils," a practice that can drive down the profitability of competitors as well.

3-4 Threat of Entry

An industry's productive capacity expands when new competitors enter. Unless the market is growing rapidly, new entrants intensify the fight for market share, thus lowering prices and, ultimately, industry profitability. When large, established firms control an industry, new entrants are often pelted with retaliation when they establish their operations or begin to promote their products aggressively. For example, when Dr. Pepper launched Like Cola directly against Coke and Pepsi, an effort to make inroads into the cola segment of the soft drink market, the two major competitors responded with strong promotional campaigns to thwart the effort. If prospective entrants anticipate this kind of response, they are less likely to enter the industry in the first place. As such, entry into an industry may well be deterred if the potential entering firm expects existing competitors to respond forcefully. Retaliation may occur if incumbent firms are committed to remaining in the industry or have sufficient cash and productive capacity to meet anticipated customer demand in the future.[16]

Barriers to Entry

Obstacles to entering an industry, including economies of scale, brand identity and product differentiation, capital requirements, switching costs, access to distribution channels, cost disadvantages independent of size, and government policy.

The likelihood that new firms will enter an industry is also contingent on the extent to which **barriers to entry** have been erected—often by existing competitors—to keep out prospective newcomers.[17] From a global perspective, many barriers have declined, as firms in countries such as India and China make use of technology—and specifically a developing global fiber-optic network—to gain access to industries in the West. For example, as many as half a million IRS tax returns are prepared annually in India. Hence, barriers are always changing as technology, political influences, and business practices also change.[18]

The seven major barriers (obstacles) to entry are described in sections 3-4a through 3-4g (see also Strategy at Work 3-2). As with intensity of rivalry, they should be assessed independently and then integrated into an overall perspective on entry barriers.

3-4a Economies of Scale

Economies of scale refer to the decline in unit costs of a product or service that occurs as the absolute volume of production increases. Scale economies occur when increased production drives down costs and can result from a variety of factors, most namely high firm specialization and expertise, volume purchase discounts, and a firm's expansion into activities once performed at higher costs by suppliers or buyers. Substantial economies of scale deter new entrants by forcing them either to enter an industry at a large scale—a costly course of action that risks a strong reaction from existing firms—or to suffer substantial cost disadvantages associated with a small-scale operation. For example, a new automobile manufacturer must accept higher per-unit costs as a result of the massive investment required to establish a production facility unless a large volume of vehicles can be produced at the outset.

3-4b Brand Identity and Product Differentiation

Established firms may enjoy strong brand identification and customer loyalties that are based on *actual or perceived* product or service differences. Typically, new entrants must incur substantial marketing and other costs over an extended time to overcome this barrier. Differentiation is particularly important among products

S T R A T E G Y   A T   W O R K   3 - 2

Creating Barriers to Entry in the Airline Industry

U.S. airline deregulation in 1978 was intended to encourage new start-up ventures and to foster competition. For a while, it seemed to be working; new companies such as Southwest Airlines and AirTran helped to lower ticket prices significantly. Over time, however, the major airlines have succeeded in erecting enormous barriers to entry, such as the following:

1. The global alliances that exist among major world carriers result in substantial control over hubs and passenger-loading gates at large airports, where such carriers already typically hold twenty- to forty-year leases. In addition, most airlines have a large number of U.S. hub airports, a feeder system to those hubs, and international routes that tie into the hubs. Such systems take decades and hundreds of millions of dollars to acquire.

2. Major airlines own the computer reservation systems, negotiate commission arrangements with travel agents for bringing business to them, and charge small carriers hefty fees for tickets sold through these systems. By operating their own Web sites, U.S. airlines have been able to eliminate the commission fees paid for domestic bookings.

3. All major carriers operate frequent flier programs that encourage passengers to avoid switching airlines. Many of the programs expire when a passenger does not fly on the airline after a specific period of time, often three years.

4. Airline computer-pricing systems enable them to selectively offer low fares on certain seats and to certain destinations (often purchased well in advance or at the last minute), thereby countering a start-up airline's pricing edge.

5. The dominant major carriers are willing to match or beat the ticket prices of smaller, niche airlines, and often respond to price changes within hours. Most are capable of absorbing some degree of losses until weaker competitors are driven out of business.

These barriers are designed to keep control of the airline industry's best routes and markets in the hands of a few carriers, even after two decades of deregulation. As such, newly formed carriers are often limited to less desirable routes. Although many upstarts fail in their first year or two of operation, others such as Southwest, AirTran, and JetBlue have been successful and are filling viable niches in the industry. Interestingly, the airline industry fallout from the events of 9/11 were felt the most by established competitors such as USAir and United Airlines.

Sources: T. A. Hemphill, "Airline Marketing Alliances and U.S. Competition Policy: Does the Consumer Benefit?" Business Horizons, *March 2000; P. A. Greenberg, "Southwest Airlines Projects $1B in Online Sales,"* E-Commerce Times, *8 December 2000; P. A. Greenberg and M. Hillebrand, "Airlines Band Together to Launch Travel Site,"* E-Commerce Times, *8 December 2000; P. A. Greenberg, "Six Major Airlines to Form B2B Exchange,"* E-Commerce Times, *8 December 2000; P. Wright, M. Kroll, and J. A. Parnell,* Strategic Management: Concepts *(Upper Saddle River, NJ: Prentice Hall, 1998); S. McCartney, "Conditions Are Ideal for Starting an Airline, and Many Are Doing It,"* Wall Street Journal, *1 April 1996, A1, A7; "Boeing 1st-Quarter Profit Off 34%,"* L.A. Times Wire Services, *30 April 1996; A. L. Velocci, Jr., "USAir Defends Aggressive Pricing,"* Aviation Week & Space Technology, *21 August 1995, 28; T. K. Smith, "Why Air Travel Doesn't Work,"* Fortune, *3 April 1995, 42–49.*

and services where the risks associated with switching to a competitive product or service are perceived to be high, such as over-the-counter drugs, insurance, and baby-care products.

3-4c Capital Requirements

Generally speaking, higher entry costs tend to restrict new competitors and ultimately increase industry profitability.[19] Large initial financial expenditures may be necessary for production, facility construction, research and development, advertising, customer credit, and inventories. Some years ago, Xerox cleverly created a capital barrier by offering to lease, not just sell, its copiers. As a result, new entrants were faced with the task of generating large sums of cash to finance the leased copiers.[20]

3-4d Switching Costs

Switching costs are the upfront costs that buyers of one firm's products may incur if they switch to those of a competitor. If these costs are high, buyers may need to test the new product first, make modifications in existing operations to accommodate the change, or even negotiate new purchase contracts. When switching costs are low—typically the case when consumers try a new grocery store—change may not be difficult. When switching costs are high, however, customers may be reluctant to change. For example, for a number of years, Apple has had the unenviable task of convincing IBM-compatible customers not only that Apple produces a superior product, but also that switching from IBM to Apple justifies the cost and inconvenience associated with software and file incompatibility. In contrast, fast-food restaurants generally have little difficulty persuading consumers to switch from one restaurant to another at the introduction of a new product.

3-4e Access to Distribution Channels

In some industries, entering existing distribution channels requires a new firm to entice distributors through price breaks, cooperative advertising allowances, or sales promotions. Existing competitors may have distribution channel ties based on long-standing or even exclusive relationships, requiring the new entrant to create its own channels of distribution. For example, certain manufacturers and retailers have formed partnerships with FedEx or UPS to transport merchandise directly to their customers. As a distribution channel, the Internet may offer an alternative to companies unable to penetrate the existing channels.

3-4f Cost Advantages Independent of Size

Many firms enjoy cost advantages emanating from economies of scale. Existing competitors may have also developed cost advantages not related to firm size, however, that cannot be easily duplicated by newcomers. Such factors include patents or proprietary technology, favorable locations, superior human resources, and experience in the industry. For example, eBay's experience, reputation, and technological capability in online auctions have made it difficult for prospective firms to enter the industry. When such advantages exist for one or more existing competitors, prospective new entrants are usually hesitant to join the industry.

3-4g Government Policy

Governments often control entry to certain industries with licensing requirements or other regulations. For example, establishing a hospital, a nuclear power facility, or an airline cannot be done in most nations without meeting substantial regulatory requirements. Although firms generally oppose government attempts to regulate their activity, this is not always the case. Existing competitors often lobby legislators to enact policies that make entry into their industry a complicated or costly endeavor.

3-5 Pressure from Substitute Products

Substitute Products

Alternative offerings produced by firms in another industry that satisfy similar consumer needs.

Firms in one industry may be competing with firms in other industries that produce **substitute products,** offerings produced by firms in another industry that satisfy similar consumer needs but differ in specific characteristics. Note that products and services affected by a firm's competitors (i.e., companies in the same industry) do *not* represent substitutes for that firm. By definition, substitutes emanate from outside of a firm's industry.

Although they emanate from outside the industry, substitutes can limit the prices that firms can charge. For instance, low fares offered by airlines can place a ceiling on the long-distance bus fares that Greyhound can charge for similar routes. Hence, firms that operate in industries with few or no substitutes are more likely to be profitable.

3-6 Bargaining Power of Buyers

The buyers of an industry's outputs can lower that industry's profitability by bargaining for higher quality or more services and playing one firm against another. Levi Strauss discovered this when negotiating a sizeable contract with megaretailer Wal-Mart. The famous American jean-maker was forced to create a lower cost brand by overhauling production and distribution efforts.[21]

The following circumstances can raise the bargaining power of an industry's buyers.

1. Buyers are concentrated, or each one purchases a significant percentage of total industry sales. If a few buyers purchase a substantial proportion of an industry's sales, then they will wield considerable power over prices. This is especially prevalent in markets for components and raw materials.

2. The products that the buyers purchase represent a significant percentage of the buyers' costs. When this occurs, price will become more critical for buyers, who will shop for a favorable price and will purchase more selectively.

3. The products that the buyers purchase are standard or undifferentiated. In such cases, buyers are able to play one seller against another and initiate price wars.

4. Buyers face few switching costs and can freely change suppliers.

5. Buyers earn low profits, creating pressure for them to reduce their purchasing costs.

6. Buyers have the ability to engage in backward integration by becoming their own suppliers. Large automobile manufacturers, for example, use the threat of self-manufacture as a powerful bargaining lever.

7. The industry's product is relatively unimportant to the quality of the buyers' products or services. In contrast, when the quality of the buyers' products is greatly affected by what they purchase from the industry, the buyers are less likely to have significant power over the suppliers because quality and special features will be the most important characteristics.

8. Buyers have complete information. The more information buyers have regarding demand, actual market prices, and supplier costs, the greater their bargaining power. The advent of the Internet has increased the quantity and quality of information available to buyers in a number of industries.

3-7 Bargaining Power of Suppliers

The tug of war between an industry's rivals and their suppliers is similar to that between the rivals and their buyers. When suppliers to an industry wield collective power over the firms in the industry, they can siphon away a portion of excess profits that may be gleaned. Alternatively, when an industry's suppliers are weak, they may be expected frequently to cut prices, increase quality, and add services. This was the case among U.S. automakers during the 1990s and early 2000s. Marred by mounting financial losses, Detroit's "Big Three" producers constantly squeezed their suppliers for price concessions. By the mid to late 2000s, however, many of these suppliers found themselves in Chapter 11 bankruptcy while others had developed a profitable nonauto business. Hence, power shifted from the automakers in favor of the suppliers during this time, an unwelcome reality to struggling GM, Ford, and Chrysler.[22]

The struggle between U.S. service stations and their suppliers—big oil companies—is another interesting example. When the popularity of E85 ethanol—a mixture containing 85 percent ethanol and 15 percent gasoline—began to rise in the mid to late 2000s, many U.S. service stations were prohibited from carrying the alternative fuel. Oil companies that do not supply E85 lose sales every time a driver fills the tank with the ethanol mix. As a result, many prohibit their franchisees from carrying fuel from other producers. Service stations that are allowed to carry E85 are often required to dispense it from a pump on a separate island not under the main canopy—a costly endeavor. Because there are only a few major oil companies and thousands of service stations in the United States, the oil companies are able to wield most of the power.[23]

The conditions that make suppliers powerful are similar to those that affect buyers. Specifically, suppliers are powerful under the following circumstances.

1. The supplying industry is dominated by one or a few companies. Concentrated suppliers typically exert considerable control over prices, quality, and selling terms when selling to fragmented buyers.

2. There are no substitute products, weakening buyers in relation to their suppliers.

3. The buying industry is not a major customer of the suppliers. If a particular industry does not represent a significant percentage of the suppliers' sales, then the suppliers control the balance of power. If competitors in the industry comprise an important customer, however, suppliers tend to understand the interrelationships and are likely to consider the long-term viability of their counterparts—not just price—when making strategic decisions.

4. The suppliers pose a credible threat of forward integration by "becoming their own customers." If suppliers have the ability and resources to operate their own manufacturing facilities, distribution channels, or retail outlets, then they will possess considerable control over buyers.

5. The suppliers' products are differentiated or have built-in switching costs, thereby reducing the buyers' ability to play one supplier against another.

3-8 Limitations of Porter's Five Forces Model

Generally speaking, the five forces model is based on the assumptions of the industrial organization (IO) perspective on strategy, as opposed to the resource-based perspective. Although the model serves as a useful analytical tool, it has several key limitations. First, it assumes the existence of a clear, recognizable industry. As complexity associated with industry definition increases, the ability to draw coherent conclusions from the model diminishes. Likewise, the model addresses only the behavior of firms in an industry and does not account for the role of partnerships, a growing phenomenon in many industries. When firms work together, either overtly or covertly, they create complex relationships that are not easily incorporated into industry models.

Second, the model does not consider that some firms, most notably large ones, can often take steps to modify the industry structure, thereby increasing their prospects for profits. For example, large airlines have been known to lobby for hefty safety restrictions to create an entry barrier to potential upstarts. Mega-retailer Wal-Mart even employs its own team of lobbyists on Capitol Hill.

Third, the model assumes that industry factors, not firm resources, comprise the primary determinants of firm profit. This issue continues to be widely debated among both scholars and executives.[24] This limitation reflects the ongoing debate between IO theorists who emphasize Porter's model and resource-based theorists who emphasize firm-specific characteristics. The resource-based perspective is addressed later in the strategic management process.

Finally, a firm that competes in many countries typically must analyze and be concerned with multiple industry structures. The nature of industry competition in the international arena differs among nations, and may present challenges that are not present in a firm's host country.[25] One's definition of McDonald's industry may be limited to fast-food outlets in the United States, but may also include a host of sit-down restaurants when other countries are considered. Different industry definitions for a firm across borders can make the task of assessing industry structure quite complex.

These challenges notwithstanding, a thorough analysis of the industry via the five forces model is a critical first step in developing an understanding of competitive behavior within an industry.[26] In a general sense, Porter's five forces model provides insight into profit-seeking opportunities, as well as potential challenges, within an industry (see Case Analysis 3-2).

Case Analysis 3-2

Step 3: Potential Profitability of the Industry

Porter's five forces model should be applied to the industry environment, as identified in step 2, by examining threat of entry, rivalry among existing competitors, pressure from substitute products, and the bargaining power of buyers and suppliers. Each of the specific factors identified in the rivalry and new entrants sections (3-3 and 3-4) should be assessed individually. In addition, each of the five forces should be evaluated with regard to its positive, negative, or neutral effect on potential profitability in the industry. It is also useful to provide an overall assessment (considering the composite effect of all five forces) of potential profitability that identifies the industry as either profitable, unprofitable, or somewhere in between.

Step 4: Who Has Succeeded and Failed in the Industry, and Why? What Are the Critical Success Factors?

Every industry has recent winners and losers. To understand the **critical success factors (CSFs)**—factors that tend to be essential for success for most or all competitors within a given industry—one must identify the companies that are doing well and those that are doing poorly, and determine whether their performance levels appear to be associated with similar factors. For example, McDonald's, Burger King, and Taco Bell are successful players in the fast-food industry. In contrast, Rax and Hardee's have been noted for their subpar performance. Are any common factors partially responsible for the differences in performance? Consider that many analysts have noted that consistency and speed of service are critical success factors in the fast-food industry. Indeed, McDonald's, Burger King, and Taco Bell are all noted for their fast, consistent service, whereas Rax and Hardee's have struggled in this area.

A business may succeed even if it does not possess a key industry CSF; however, the *likelihood* of success is diminished greatly. Hence, strategies that do not shore up weaknesses in CSF areas should be considered carefully before being implemented.

Critical Success Factors (CSFs)

Factors that are generally prerequisites for success among most or all competitors in a given industry.

3-9 Summary

An industry is a group of companies that produce similar products or services. Michael Porter has identified five basic competitive industry forces that can ultimately influence profitability at the firm level: intensity of rivalry among incumbent firms in the industry, the threat of new entrants in the industry, the threat of substitute products or services, bargaining power of buyers of the industry's outputs, and bargaining power of suppliers to the industry. Firms tend to operate quite profitably in industries with high entry barriers, low intensity of competition among member firms, no substitute products, weak buyers, and weak suppliers. These relationships are tendencies, however, and do not mean that all firms will perform in a similar manner because of industry factors. Although Porter's model has its shortcomings, it represents an excellent starting point for positioning a business among its competitors.

Key Terms

barriers to entry	industry	relative market share
critical success factors	industry life cycle	substitute products
exit barriers	market share	switching costs

Review Questions and Exercises

1. Visit the Web sites of several major restaurant chains. Identify the industry(s) in which each one operates. Would you categorize them in the same industry or in different industries (fast food, family restaurants, etc.)? Why or why not?

2. Identify an industry that has low barriers to entry and one that has high barriers. Explain how the difference in entry barriers influences competitive behavior in the two industries.

3. Identify some businesses whose sales have been adversely affected by substitute products. Why has this occurred?

4. Identify an industry in which the suppliers have strong bargaining power and another industry in which the buyers have most of the bargaining power. How does this affect potential profitability in both industries?

Practice Quiz

True or False

1. Each firm operates in a single, distinct industry.

2. All industries follow the stages of the industry life cycle model.

3. The likelihood that new firms will enter an industry is contingent on the extent to which barriers to entry have been erected.

4. Higher capital requirements for entering an industry ultimately raise average profitability within that industry.

5. Substitute products are produced by competitors in the same industry.

6. A key limitation of Porter's five forces model is its reliance on resource-based theory.

Multiple Choice

7. Industry growth is no longer rapid enough to support a large number of competitors in which stage of industry growth?

    A. growth

    B. shakeout

    C. maturity

    D. decline

8. The intensity of rivalry among firms in an industry is dependent on which of the following?

   A. concentration of competitors

   B. high fixed or storage costs

   C. high exit barriers

   D. all of the above

9. The decline in unit costs of a product or service that occurs as the absolute volume of production increases is known as

   A. production effectiveness.

   B. effective operations management.

   C. economies of scale.

   D. technological analysis.

10. When switching costs are high,

    A. customers are less likely to try a new competitor.

    B. companies spend more on technology.

    C. companies seek new suppliers to reduce costs.

    D. none of the above

11. Which of the following is not a cost advantage independent of scale?

    A. proprietary technology

    B. favorable locations

    C. experience in the industry

    D. high volume of production

12. What is occurring when those who purchase an industry's goods and services exercise great control over pricing and other terms?

    A. high bargaining power of suppliers

    B. low bargaining power of suppliers

    C. balance of power among suppliers

    D. none of the above

Notes

1. M. E. Porter, "Strategy and the Internet," *Harvard Business Review* 29(3) (2001): 62–79; M. E. Porter, "Clusters and the New Economics of Competition," *Harvard Business Review* 76(6) (1998): 77–90.

2. P. Daniels, "The New Snack Pack," *Prepared Foods* (February 2006): 11–17.

3. C. W. Hofer, "Toward a Contingency Theory of Business Strategy," *Academy of Management Journal* 18 (1975): 784–810; G. Miles, C. C. Snow, and M. P. Sharfman, "Industry Variety and Performance," *Strategic Management Journal* 14 (1993): 163–177.

4. D. Michaels and M. Trottman, "Fuel May Propel Airline Shakeout," *Wall Street Journal* (7 September 2005): C1, C5.

5. T. Levitt, "Exploit the Product Life Cycle," *Harvard Business Review* 43(6) (1965): 81–94.

6. G. Hawawini, V. Subramanian, and P. Verdin, "Is Performance Driven by Industry- or Firm-Specific Factors? A New Look at the Evidence," *Strategic Management Journal* 24 (2003): 1–16.

7. J. R. Graham, "Bulletproof Your Business against Competitor Attacks," *Marketing News* (14 March 1994): 4–5; J. Hayes, "Casual Dining Contenders Storm 'Junior' Markets," *Nations' Restaurant News* (14 March 1994): 47–52.

8. J. R. Hagerty, "Discount Real-Estate Brokers Spark a War over Commissions," *Wall Street Journal* (12 October 2005): A1, A6.

9. See A. Taylor III, "Will Success Spoil Chrysler?" *Fortune* (10 January 1994): 88–92.

10. S. Carey and E. Perez, "Traveler's Dilemma: When To Fly the Cheap Seats," *Wall Street Journal* (22 July 2003): D1, D3.

11. S. McCartney, "A Middle-seat Manifesto," *Wall Street Journal* (3 December 2004): W1, W14.

12. L. Hawkins, Jr., "Trucks Get Bigger, Fancier and Cheaper, *Wall Street Journal* (2 October 2003): D1, D2; N. E. Boudette, "Volkswagen Stalls on Several Fronts after Luxury Drive," *Wall Street Journal* (8 May 2003): A1, A17.

13. C. Terhune and B. McKay, "Behind Coke's CEO Travails: A Long Struggle over Strategy," *Wall Street Journal* (4 May 2004): A1, A10.

14. J. Drucker, "How to Dump Your Cellphone Company," *Wall Street Journal* (18 November 2003): D1, D4.

15. P. Wright, M. Kroll, and J. A. Parnell, *Strategic Management:Concepts* (Upper Saddle River, NJ: Prentice Hall, 1998).

16. K. C. Robinson and P. P. McDougall, "Entry Barriers and New Venture Performance: A Comparision of Universal and Contingency Approaches," *Strategic Management Journal* 22 (2001): 659–685.

17. J. K. Han, N. Kim, and H. Kim, "Entry Barriers: A Dull-, One-, or Two-Edged Sword for Incumbents? Unraveling the Paradox from a Contingency Perspective," *Journal of Marketing* 65 (2001): 1–14.

18. T. L. Friedman, *The World Is Flat* (New York: Farrar, Straus and Giroux, 2005).

19. M. Pietz, "The Pro-Competitive Effect of Higher Entry Costs," *International Journal of Industrial Organization* 20 (2002): 353–364.

20. Wright et al., *Strategic Management*.

21. Corporate author, "In Bow to Retailers's New Clout, Levi Strauss Makes Alterations," *Wall Street Journal* (17 June 2004): A1, A15.

22. J. McCracken and P. Glader, "New Detroit Woe: Makers of Parts Won't Cut Prices," *Wall Street Journal* (20 March 2007): A1, A16.

23. L. Meckler, "Fill up with Ethanol? One Obstable Is Big Oil," *Wall Street Journal* (2 April 2007): A1, A14.

24. S. F. Slater and E. M. Olson, "A Fresh Look at Industry and Market Analysis," *Business Horizons* (January–February 2002): 15–22; Hawawini et al., "Is Performance Driven by Industry- or Firm-Specific Factors?"

25. Y. Li and S. Deng, "A Methodology for Competitive Advantage Analysis and Strategy Formulation: An Example in a Transitional Economy," *European Journal of Operational Research* 118 (1999): 259–270.

26. Porter, "Clusters and the New Economics of Competition"; Slater et al., "A Fresh Look at Industry Analysis."

READING 3 - 1

Insight from *strategy+business*

The airline industry has undergone remarkable changes during the past two decades, particularly after the 9/11 terrorist attacks. In this chapter's strategy+business reading, Hansson and associates challenge the wisdom of the business models employed by traditional airlines. They argue that the structure of the industry has changed and that astute airlines will tailor their approaches to the new reality.

Flight for Survival

A New Business Model for the Airline Industry

To pare down their colossal operating costs, giant U.S. and European carriers must restructure the hub-and-spoke system and eliminate complexity.

By Tom Hansson, Jürgen Ringbeck, and Markus Franke

Since the 1970s, traditional market leaders in industry after industry, saddled with complex, high-cost business models, have been under attack by companies with new, simpler ways to manage their operations and contain costs.

This scenario occurred in the steel industry when minimills took on traditional smelters; in automobile manufacturing when more standardized Japanese cars won out over customized U.S. vehicles; and in retailing when superstores overtook conventional grocery stores. In each instance, the established companies struggled, often in vain, to rationalize operations and still deliver products and services to satisfy customer desires, defend their market positions, and reestablish profitability.

The lesson is fundamental: As markets mature, incumbent companies that have developed sophisticated, but complex, business models face tremendous pressure to find less costly approaches that meet broad customer needs with minimal complexity in products and processes.

The trouble is, many companies – manufacturers and service providers alike – have increased the scope and variety of their products and services over the years by layering on new offerings to serve ever larger and more diverse customer bases. Although each individual business decision to enhance a product line or service can usually be justified on its own, the result often is a cost structure that is sustainable only if the principal competitors take a similar approach. More often than not,

though, as incumbents expand the breadth and depth of their offerings, leveraging their sophisticated business infrastructure, they are undermined by smaller, nimbler competitors that supply a more focused product, usually to a specific set of customers, at a substantially lower cost. In these situations, the incumbent may know that the cost of complexity is dragging it down, but finds changing its business model easier said than done.

No companies illustrate this dilemma more vividly than the large U.S. and European hub-and-spoke airlines. Their business model – essentially designed to seamlessly take anyone from anywhere to everywhere – was a great innovation. But this model is no longer competitively sustainable in its current form. Tied to massive physical infrastructure, complex fleets of aircraft, legacy information systems, and large labor pools, the major carriers in both regions now face a double whammy: some of the worst economic conditions in the industry's history, and low-cost carriers that dictate prices in large and growing parts of the market.

U.S. carriers lost more than $10 billion in 2002, according to the Air Transport Association, up from $8 billion in the disastrous year of 2001. Worldwide, losses topped $50 billion. Bankruptcies litter the industry. Sabena, Swissair, US Airways, United Air Lines, and Hawaiian Airlines have all sought protection from their creditors. Others are likely to follow. The need for a new, less complex business model among hub-and-spoke carriers is growing stronger with each boom and bust cycle.

EXHIBIT 1 Average Cost per Seat Mile (in 2000)

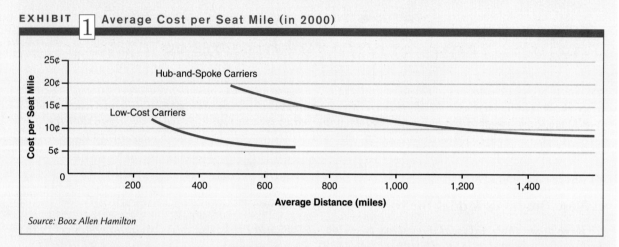

Source: Booz Allen Hamilton

In this article, we examine the significant downside of business complexity and provide a formula that would allow the airlines to simplify their operations, cut expenses, and compete with their low-cost competitors. It's not incremental change, but a fundamental overhaul.

Complexity Costs

While the major carriers face a future of red ink, low-cost carriers such as Southwest Airlines, JetBlue Airways, and Ryanair are prospering by exploiting a huge cost-of-operations advantage. Low-cost carriers spend seven to eight cents per seat mile to complete a 500- to 600-mile flight, according to our analysis. That's less than half of what it costs the typical hub-and-spoke carrier to fly a flight of the same duration and distance. (See Exhibit 1.)

It is easy to see how costs mount quickly in the hub-and-spoke airlines' intricate system of operations. Their business model is predicated on offering consumers a larger number of destinations, significant flexibility (ranging from last-minute seat reassignments and upgrades to complete itinerary and routing changes), and "frills" (e.g., specialty meals, private lounges, and in-flight entertainment). It is a model burdened by the built-in cost penalties of synchronized hub operations, with long aircraft turnaround times and slack built into schedules to increase connectivity by ensuring there is time for passengers and baggage to make connections. It's a system that implicitly accepts a slower business pace to accommodate continual change. In addition, the hub-and-spoke business model relies on highly sophisticated information systems and infrastructure to optimize its complex operations. By contrast, low-cost carriers have designed a focused, simple, highly productive business model around nonstop air travel to

and from medium- to high-density markets at a significantly lower price point.

We have analyzed the cost gap between large full-service airlines and low-cost carriers (LCCs) on both sides of the Atlantic, and the similarities are striking. On both continents, cost differences exist across the board; pilots, onboard services, sales and reservations, maintenance, aircraft ownership, ground handling. The low-cost carriers are not simply paying lower salaries or using cheaper airports, they are leveraging all resources much more effectively. In fact, the cost differential between the full-service and low-cost carriers is 2 to 1 for the same stage length and aircraft, even after adjustments for differences in pay scales, fuel prices, and seat density are made.

Surprisingly, only about 5 percent of this cost differential can be attributed to the extra amenities the hub-and-spoke carriers offer. Some 65 percent of the LCCs' cost advantage is the result of other production-model choices; another 15 percent comes from work rules and labor agreements; and 12 percent can be attributed to differences in balance-sheet structure and financial arrangements. (See Exhibit 2.)

Of the costs attributable to production-model differences, the largest contributing factors are business pace, process complexity, and ticket distribution. In fact, "no frills" and "full service" are misleading labels to describe the distinction between the two types of carriers. It is the relative simplicity or complexity of their operations that truly distinguishes them.

Most debilitating for the major carriers is the inability to overcome their cost burden with boom period pricing, as they did in the second half of the 1990s. As corporations tightened their belts and reduced the frequency of travel, business travelers, who have traditionally accounted for

EXHIBIT 2 Breakout of the Cost per Seat Mile Gap Between Full-Service and Low-Cost Carriers (in 2000)

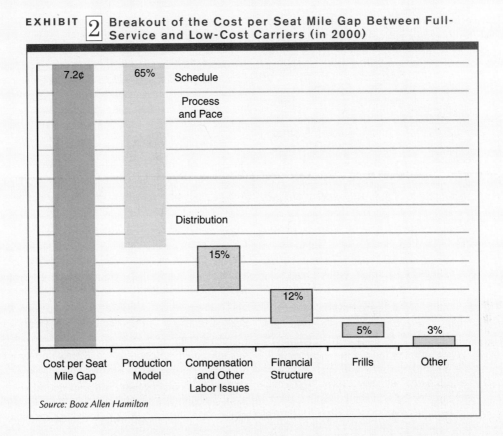

Source: Booz Allen Hamilton

as much as 60 percent of mainline airline revenues – and well over 100 percent of their profits – were no longer willing to pay the high fares they tolerated in the dot-com boom. Weakened by this fundamental change in customer choice as well as "industry leading" labor agreements and rising fuel prices, the U.S. hub-and-spoke airlines' cost per seat mile (CASM) rose above revenue per seat mile (RASM) by the third quarter 2000, a full year before the September 11 terrorist attack slashed air travel further. This eventually increased to an unprecedented cost-to-revenue gap of close to 2 cents per seat mile at the beginning of 2002 in the U.S.

That revenue outlook is likely to get worse. By our conservative estimates, low-cost carriers could potentially—and successfully – participate in more than 70 percent of the U.S. domestic market. Southwest Airlines typically prices 50 percent lower than large carriers in one- to two-hour nonstop markets. Even though traditional airlines have attracted a richer business mix than the low-cost carriers, they still stand to lose 25 to 35 percent price realization in those markets.

Recently, huh-and-spoke airlines have been trying to lower operating costs through new, less onerous labor agreements – American Airlines, United Air Lines, and US Airways have led the way in eking out pay concessions from their employees; negotiating better deals with intermediaries and financiers; eliminating discretionary costs; and, in some cases, smoothing out hub operations. Major carriers in the U.S. and Europe have also announced that they will add low-cost airline subsidiaries to their business portfolios to compete with the likes of Ryanair and Southwest Airlines.

A New Path

Many of these restructuring initiatives are clearly valuable and necessary, but they will likely not prove to be enough. Core airline operations need to become competitive with those of low-cost carriers, especially as LCC market penetration grows in the U.S. and makes inroads in Europe. The steps large carriers have taken so far do not address the fundamental productivity differences between themselves and the low-cost airlines. Traditional airlines will not achieve a competitive cost structure if they do not tackle the fundamental cost penalties associated with their business models. But they must do so without compromising the services, service quality, and coverage that distinguish them from their new rivals.

Although making such fundamental changes in a long-standing business model is difficult and risky, it is not without precedent. Successful change in other industries—such as manufacturing and financial services—provides important insights into the ways the burden and cost of complexity can be reduced. Not long ago, a major U.S.-based manufacturer of a highly engineered product realized that its policy of allowing extensive customization was increasing operating cost without delivering commensurate revenue benefits. Certain elements of this company's products required customization, but by a natural progression of complexity, customization had become an unintentional—and unnecessary—center-piece of the manufacturing process. Inventory, scheduling, delivery logistics, and the like were built around the ability to alter specifications quickly. The company's operational resources directed toward the most complicated features of manufacturing, rather than the simplest. And that was introducing significantly higher costs into its business model.

The manufacturer did an exhaustive study and found, to its surprise, that about 70 percent of the features in its products were never customized. The company introduced engineering controls to these less complicated aspects of the manufacturing process. By taking that step, the manufacturer was able to strategically apply complex systems—such as manufacturing resource planning, inventory, and expediting programs—to only the 30 percent of the design and plant processes that required customization. These segmented operations are called tailored business streams (TBS). Because of this action, which did not hamper service for those customers needing customization, the company is on course to slash 15 percent from its operational expense.

Large carriers must seriously consider three critical elements when restructuring the hub-and-spoke model and eliminating complexity from their business model.

- **Remove Scheduling Constraints.** At present, hub-and-spoke airlines generally schedule flights in a so-called wave system, which means that departures and arrivals are concentrated in peak periods to maximize effective passenger connections. However, the approach causes long aircraft turnarounds (to allow passengers and baggage to connect to their next flight), traffic congestion, and aircraft

downtime at the origin cities, resulting in low labor and aircraft utilization. This system, which is structured around the needs of the least profitable connecting passengers, also necessitates more complicated logistics and provides significantly lower yields—up to 45 percent less revenue per mile than for passengers traveling nonstop. Nevertheless, because of current pricing strategies and fleet structures, airlines rely on connecting passengers to fill seats that otherwise would be empty.

By redesigning the airline's network around the needs of nonstop passengers, and making connections a byproduct of the system as Southwest Airlines does, large carriers should be able to cut turnaround times by as much as half, increase aircraft utilization, reduce congestion, and significantly improve labor productivity. A large portion of manpower costs is driven by how long an aircraft is at the gate. Shorter turns would mean that pilots, flight attendants, baggage handlers, maintenance staff, and other personnel could be much more productive, and still in compliance with safety regulations. Moreover, with aircraft ready to take off more quickly, airlines could schedule more flights and provide more attractive timetables for nonstop passengers.

The trade-off between efficient operations and connectivity has to be evaluated carefully, however. Most likely the solution will involve "continuous" or "rolling" hubs, which would allow for more operationally efficient, continuous flight schedules throughout the day. The approach would be particularly suited for "mega-hubs," where the local "point-to-point" market is sufficiently large to support more frequent flights without relying as much on connecting traffic. Some airlines are already experimenting with rolling hubs. To fully realize the cost reduction opportunities created by this approach, and to justify the scheduling change, airlines will need to fundamentally alter airport operations, through such innovations as compressed turns and simplified baggage handling.

- **Implement Tailored Business Streams.** In other industries, such as manufacturing, complexity reduction has been achieved by applying a TBS approach. The basic principle is to segment operations into distinct business streams: Separate processes are created to handle routine and complex activities; capabilities and approaches are tailored to the inherent complexity of the chosen task and based on what customers are willing to pay. That often entails standardizing or "industrializing" the routine and stable processes, while segmenting and isolating the parts of the operation that are more complicated and variable.

By and large, the hub-and-spoke airlines have done exactly the opposite. Airlines have sophisticated, universally applicable processes for handling most, if not all, possible situations. It doesn't matter whether the passenger is on a simple one-hour flight or is traveling from one continent to another. This has added unnecessary costs to processes, and made them hard to automate and change, requiring massive retraining of personnel when a process is altered. If the airlines embraced TBS, simplified their policies, and streamlined their core processes to address the basic needs of the majority of customers, they could drastically reduce the number of activities performed at airports. Furthermore, they could automate many more of them, saving huge amounts of time and money. In this environment, the reservation and passenger-handling process would be designed so that passengers wouldn't need last-minute changes or long, multiple interactions with airline staff at the airport. Instead, travelers would be able to get to the gates faster.

At airports, dedicated processing staff would still deal with the small percentage of travelers who need to change itineraries, connect to a different airline, or request other special services. And customers who require extras (except for perhaps the most frequent flyers) would potentially pay for them in the ticket price or through a transaction fee. Efficiency improvements would be systemwide, cascading from reservations to front-line staff Overall, the product and experience would be better, and the organization would be much more efficient at delivering it.

- **Create Separate Business Systems for Distinct Customer Segments.** In simplifying their business model, large carriers have to be careful to retain the loyalty of their most profitable and frequent customers by providing more differentiated amenities, lounges, and services on the ground and in the air than they do today. This could mean separating both airport and onboard services into two (or more) classes, focused on either leisure or business passengers. Other industries' experiences suggest that mingling complex and simple operations, each of which has distinct objectives and missions, often increases costs and lowers service standards. This must be avoided: The goal is to offer a higher service level where it is needed, at a low operating cost. Besides providing more amenities, this approach would help create purer business streams that reflect the distinct needs of different customer segments.

It will be important for large carriers to retain the key service advantages they have over low-cost carriers, including destination breadth, superior loyalty programs, and select onboard amenities. At a minimum, this approach would enable greater product distinction than there is today. The objective is twofold: Change the business model to serve *all* customers better by providing a more efficient and less time-consuming experience; and provide dedicated services (and flexibility) to the customer segments prepared to pay for them.

These proposed restructuring elements are highly interdependent. If they're effectively coordinated, they will increase the pace of airline operations, reduce and isolate complexity, and increase service specialization—all results that are necessary for carriers to fly beyond the industry turbulence they're experiencing today. We estimate that by adopting these approaches, the major airlines would bring costs more in line with those of low-cost carriers, reducing their unit cost disadvantage for leisure travel by 70 to 80 percent.

It won't be easy to achieve. Any industry that undertakes such change faces the fear that not only will revenue premiums be lost, but costs will not fall commensurately. It is difficult to reduce fixed-cost structures. Existing infrastructure may be underutilized with the new business model, and the current aircraft base may not fit the new requirements. Another key challenge for airlines would be the potential drop in revenue in connecting markets. But they could make up this loss by using their lower cost base to stimulate market growth, and by offering viable new services that are not economically feasible at current cost levels.

The Horizon

To survive, major airlines have no choice but to change course. With a fundamentally lower cost structure, the large airlines would be far better positioned to become profitable, grow, and launch a marketplace offensive against low-cost carriers.

At this point, the outlook for the industry is highly uncertain. If the hub-and-spoke carriers stick to the current business model, and attempt to reduce costs within today's operational framework, they risk facing continued market share loss to LCCs, a round robin of bankruptcies, and a struggle for survival. The large U.S. airlines' early 1990s crisis was a cyclical, economy-based downturn. LCCs were not a major issue then. When the economy and their performance improved, the airlines largely ignored the threat posed by the lower-cost format. That inaction only hid the real emerging problem.

This time the crisis is again cyclical, but it is exacerbated by the presence of low-cost carriers. If the economic picture brightens significantly, it's possible that the large airlines will rebound, and that the fundamental business model problems will not be addressed. If that happens, the next cyclical crisis will be so much worse. In the U.S., the low-cost carriers could then dictate pricing in more than 70 percent of the domestic market, as opposed to the current 40 to 45 percent. At that point, a turnaround would be significantly more challenging than it is today.

Alternatively, if a few large carriers adopt the new business model that we suggest, the industry could be led by a couple of thriving carriers in the U.S. and Europe, with one to two random hubs each serving intercontinental and small community markets, a more differentiated service offering, and a number of centers of mass similar to those operated by Southwest Airlines.

The risk of inaction is much greater than the risk of change. The first traditional airline to apply a fundamentally new business model will reshape the industry's competitive landscape. The first prize that awaits the boldest flyers is significant, not just in terms of cost reduction, but also in considerable growth and future market leadership opportunities.

Resources

Tom Hansson, Jürgen Ringbeck, and Markus Franke. "Flight for Survival: A New Operating Model for Airlines," *s + b enews.* December 6, 2002; www.strategy-business.com/press/enewarticle/?art=19050189&pg=0

David Newkirk, Brad Corrodi, and Alison James. "Catching Travels on the Fly," *s + b*, Fourth Quarter 2001; www.strategy.-business.com/press/article/?art=24979&pg=0

Susan Carey and Scott McCartney; "United's Bid to Cut Labor Costs Could Force Rivals to Follow," *Wall Street Journal*, February 25, 2003; http://online.wsj.com/home/us

Darin Lee, "An Assessment of Some Recent Criticisms of the U.S. Airline Industry," *The Review of Network Economics*, March 2003; www.rnejournal.com/archives.html

Shawn Tully, "*Straighten Up and Fly Right*," Fortune, February 17, 2003; www.fortune.com

Tom Hansson (hansson_tom@bah.com) is a vice president in Booz Allen Hamilton's Los Angeles office. He focuses on strategy and operational restructuring in the airlines and travel arena.

Jürgen Ringbeck (ringbeck_jurgen@bah.com) is a vice president in Booz Allen Hamilton's Düsseldorf office. He focuses on strategy and transformation for companies in global transportation industries, such as airlines, tourism operators, postal and logistics companies, and railways.

Markus Franke (franke_markus@bah.com is a principal in Booz Allen Hamilton's Düsseldorf office. He focuses on strategy, network management, sales, and distribution in the airline, transportation, logistics, and rail industries.

External Environment

4

Chapter Outline

FIGURE 4-1   Macroenvironmental Forces

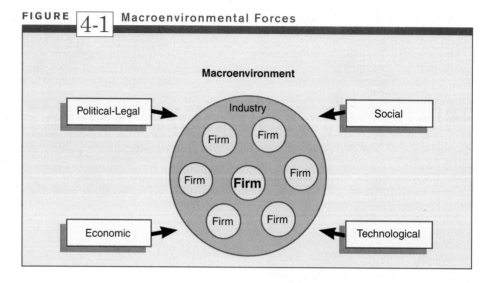

Macroenvironment

The general environment that affects all business firms in an industry and includes political-legal, economic, social, and technological forces.

PEST

An acronym referring to the analysis of the four macroenvironmental forces: Political-legal, Economic, Social, and Technological.

After the industry has been clearly defined and its prospects for profits identified, forces outside the industry should be considered. Constant changes in these forces present numerous opportunities and challenges to strategic managers. Hence, it is important to understand how these forces collectively influence the industry.

Every organization exists within a complex network of external forces. Together, these elements comprise the organization's **macroenvironment**. The four categories of macroenvironmental forces are political-legal, economic, social, and technological (see Figure 4-1). The analysis of macroenvironmental factors may be referenced as **PEST**, an acronym derived from the first letter of each of the four categories of forces. The effects of macroenvironmental forces on a firm's industry should be well understood before strategic options are evaluated.

4-1 Analysis of the Macroenvironment

Each macroenvironmental force embodies a number of key issues that vary across industries. Some issues are specific to a single force whereas others are related to more than one force. Automobile safety, for example, has political-legal (e.g., legislation requiring that safety standards be met), social (e.g., consumer demands for safe vehicles), and technological (e.g., innovations that may improve safety) dimensions. In such situations, one needs to understand how the various macroenvironmental forces combine to influence industry behavior and performance.

Firms operating in multiple markets may be affected in different manners by macroenvironmental forces in each market. For example, wide roads and relatively modest fuel taxes (i.e., political-legal factors), a culture that reinforces the automobile as a means of personal expression (i.e., a sociocultural factor), and a high standard of living (i.e., an economic factor) suggest higher demand for moderate to large vehicles in the United States. In contrast, narrow roads, higher fuel taxes, a view that a vehicle is more about transportation than about personal expression, and less disposable income suggest higher demand for smaller cars in Latin American countries. Hence, the application of Porter's model to firms operating in many different industry structures within a single nation or, most notably, many different nations can be quite cumbersome.

Although large organizations and trade associations often attempt to influence change in the macroenvironment, these forces are usually not under the direct control of business organizations. On occasion, a large, dominant firm such as Wal-Mart may be able to exert some degree of influence over one or more aspects of the macroenvironment. For example, the giant retailer's political action committee contributed about $1 million to candidates and parties in the United States in both 2003 and 2004.[1] However, this level of influence is not common because strategic managers typically seek to enable a firm to operate effectively within largely uncontrollable environmental constraints while capitalizing on the opportunities provided by its environment.

The key distinction here is strategic managers must first identify and analyze these national and global macroenvironmental forces and understand how each force affects the *industries* in which they operate before addressing firm-specific strategy concerns. Hence, understanding a force's broad effects should precede understanding its specific effects. Applications of these forces that are unique or specific to the firm are considered as opportunities and threats later in the strategic management process.

4-2 Political-Legal Forces

Political-legal forces include such factors as the outcomes of elections, legislation, and judicial court decisions, as well as the decisions rendered by various commissions and agencies at every level of government. Some regulations affect many or all organizations. When the Massachusetts state legislature passed a bill in 2006 to require that businesses provide health insurance for its workers, all firms operating in the state were affected.[2] When the U.S. Supreme Court ruled in 2007 that the Clean Air Act applies to car and truck carbon dioxide emissions, carmakers knew immediately that higher federal fuel economy standards were likely forthcoming.[3]

Industries are often affected by legislation and other political events specific to their line of business, however. Consider the following examples. The U.S. Highway Traffic Safety Administration constantly tests cars and trucks sold in the United States and pressures carmakers to improve safety performance.[4] Fuel economy standards can require that producers develop new vehicles or modify existing ones to meet average fuel economy targets, which can be a costly venture. When the Bush administration proposed higher minimum standards for fuel economy, analysts estimated that the industry would spend more than $6 billion to comply, adding $275 to the price tag of a large truck by 2011.[5]

Military conflicts can also influence how certain industries operate, especially those with tight global ties. For example, during the 2003 war in Iraq, many firms modified their promotional strategies, fearing that their television advertisements might be considered insensitive if aired alongside breaking coverage of the war. At the same time, others began to plan for meeting the anticipated future needs in Iraq for such products as cell phones, refrigerators, and automobiles. After the previous Iraqi regime was ousted in mid-2003, U.S. firms began to compete vigorously for lucrative reconstruction contracts.[6]

It is not safe to assume that firms always seek less regulation. In some instances, firm leaders prefer to operate within clear boundaries established by governments. In 2004, for example, Ford chief Bill Ford said he would support higher fuel taxes in exchange for incentives to produce more energy-efficient vehicles.[7] In another example, following the sharp declines in air travel in the United States, airlines on the verge of bankruptcy campaigned for and received $15 billion in government support in 2002 and an additional $2.9 billion in 2003.[8]

In more cases than not, however, regulation can prove costly for firms in an industry. When mad-cow disease—a rare disease of the brain passed through tainted meat—began to show up in the United Kingdom in early 2001, most of Europe responded by banning the import of British beef. Financial losses for the industry were staggering.[9] Beginning in 2005, U.S. packaged food manufacturers were required to disclose the amount of trans fats in the products they distribute through grocery stores.[10] As health advocates renewed attempts in that same year to secure governmental regulation, the U.S. food industry continued its long struggle to cut back on the use of salt. Critics warn of the link between salt and high blood pressure. Deeply ingrained in the food production process, however, salt is all but impossible to eliminate because of its many benefits. Salt is inexpensive, enhances the taste of myriad foods, and extends the shelf life of many foods.[11]

While most agree that regulations are necessary in many instances, they can be cumbersome. In 2006, the U.S. Food and Drug Administration (FDA) issued guidelines concerning when food companies can reference their products as "whole grain." Food companies can use the label if their products are made of rye, oats, popcorn, and wild rice, but not soybeans, chickpeas, and pearled barley. Use of terms such as "good source" and "excellent source" to describe the amount of whole grains included in a product are also subject to debate and FDA rulings.[12]

All societies have laws and regulations that affect business operations. A major shift in U.S. policy occurred in the late 1970s and the 1980s in favor of *deregulation,* eliminating a number of legal constraints in such industries as airlines, trucking, and banking; however, not all industries were deregulated. By 1990, a reversal of trade protectionism and strong governmental influence in business operations began to take place. In the United States, new economic policies reduced governmental influence in business operations by deregulating certain industries, lowering corporate taxes, and relaxing rules against mergers and acquisitions. This trend has continued into the twenty-first century, although not as forcefully as in the late 1990s. Table 4-1 summarizes some of the major laws in the United States.

Many broad regulations such as those listed in Table 4-1 affect multiple industries. Other regulations, however, are designed specifically for a single industry or category of firms. In 2005, for example, eighteen U.S. states implemented the Streamlined Sales Tax Project in an effort to remove obstacles preventing retailers from collecting sales taxes with online sales. Estimated potential taxes associated with Internet sales was more than $15 billion across the United States in 2003 and was expected to surpass $20 billion in 2008.[13]

Consider a second example. In 2006, a U.S. federal court ruled that cigarette manufacturers cannot use the adjectives "light" or "low tar" to describe their products. This ruling requires firms not only to rename some of their products, but also to reposition them and hope that smokers do not assume that other aspects of the cigarettes have been changed as well. Hence, familiar brands such as Altria's Marlboro Lights and Reynolds American's Camel Lights must be changed to accommodate the ruling.[14]

It is interesting to consider broad global trends toward regulation in recent decades. At the global level, the period from World War II to the late 1980s was marked by increased trade protection. Many countries protected their industries by imposing tariffs, import duties, and other restrictions. Import duties in many Latin American countries ranged from less than 40 percent to more than 100 percent,[15] but this trend was not limited to developing nations. Countries in Europe and Asia—and even the United States—have imposed import fees on a variety of products, including food, steel, and cars. In the 1980s, the United States also convinced Japanese manufacturers to voluntarily restrict exports of

TABLE $\boxed{4\text{-}1}$ Selected Examples of Government Regulation of Business in the United States

Legislation	Purpose
Sherman Antitrust Act (1890)	Prohibits monopoly or conspiracy in restraint of trade
Clayton Act (1914)	Forbids contracts that tie the sale of one product to the sale of another
Federal Trade Commission Act (1914)	Stops unfair methods of competition, including deceptive advertising, selling practices, and pricing
Webb-Pomerene Export Trade Act (1918)	Permits selected U.S. firms to form monopolies in order to compete with foreign firms
Fair Labor Standards Act (1938)	Sets minimum wage rates, regulations for overtime pay, and child labor laws
Antimerger Act (1950)	Makes the buying of competitors illegal when it lessens competition
Equal Pay (1963)	Prohibits discrimination in wages on the basis of gender when men and women are performing jobs requiring equal skill, effort, and responsibility under similar working conditions
Clean Air Act (1970)	Directs the Environmental Protection Agency to create emission standards for potential pollutants
Occupational Safety and Health Act (1970)	Requires employers to provide a hazard-free working environment
Consumer Product Safety Act (1972)	Sets standards on selected products, requires warning labels, and orders product recalls
Equal Employment Opportunity Act (1972)	Forbids discrimination in all areas of employer–employee relations
Magnuson-Moss Act (1975)	Requires accuracy in product warranties
Foreign Corrupt Practices Act (1978)	Outlaws direct payoffs and bribes of foreign governments or business officials
Americans with Disabilities Act (1992)	Protects those who are physically and mentally disabled from job discrimination
Family and Medical Leave Act (1993)	Offers workers up to twelve weeks of unpaid leave after childbirth or adoption, or to care for a seriously ill child, spouse, or parent
Food Quality Protection Act (1996)	Reduces the amount of carcinogenic pesticides allowed in foods
Pension Security Act (2002)	Gives workers more freedom to diversify their investments and greater access to quality investment advice concerning their 401(k) plans
CAN SPAM Act (2003)	Prescribes rules and penalties for e-mail "spammers," although enforcement is difficult

cars to the United States in lieu of a tariff. Interestingly, this particular tariff may be largely responsible for Japanese automobile manufacturers establishing a large number of production facilities in the United States, thereby blurring the concept of the "foreign car."

During this time, however, leaders from many nations recognized that all countries would likely benefit if trade barriers could be reduced across the board. After the end of World War II, twenty-three countries entered into the cooperative General Agreement on Tariffs and Trade (GATT), working to relax quota and import license requirements, introduce fairer customs evaluation methods,

TABLE 4-2   Major Regional Trade Agreements

Asia-Pacific Economic Cooperation (APEC)	Australia, Brunei, Canada, Chile, China, Hong Kong, Indonesia, Japan, Malaysia, Mexico, New Zealand, Papua New Guinea, Philippines, Singapore, South Korea, Taiwan, Thailand, United States
European Union (EU)	Austria, Belgium, Denmark, Finland, France, Germany, Greece, Ireland, Italy, Luxembourg, Netherlands, Portugal, Spain, Sweden, United Kingdom
North American Free Trade Agreement (NAFTA)	Canada, Mexico, United States
Asian Free Trade Area (AFTA)	Brunei, Indonesia, Malaysia, Philippines, Singapore, Thailand
Mercosur	Argentina, Bolivia, Brazil, Chile, Paraguay, Uruguay

and establish a common mechanism to resolve trade disputes. The World Trade Organization (WTO) and the International Monetary Fund (IMF) were also established at this time. By 1994, GATT membership had expanded to more than 110 nations when it was replaced by a new WTO. Today the WTO contains 147 members and continues to negotiate global trade agreements, although member nations must ratify the agreements before they become effective.

The move toward free marketing was also seen in Europe, where a number of nations banded together to develop a trade-free European community. Today, Europe is fast becoming a single market of 350 million consumers. The European Economic Area, as it is called, is the largest trading bloc on earth, accounting for more than 40 percent of the world's gross domestic product (GDP).[16]

Meanwhile, the United States, Canada, and Mexico established the North American Free Trade Agreement (NAFTA) to create its own strategic trading bloc. Many analysts believe that world business will eventually be divided into several such blocs, each providing preferred trading status to other nations within the bloc. Table 4-2 lists other important regional trade agreements.

This trend toward less regulation has even extended to the former Communist countries. As the nations of the former Soviet bloc in Eastern Europe overturned their governments, they began to open markets and to invite foreign investment.[17] The case of China is an interesting example to consider.

China is officially ruled by the Communist party, but its economic development policies have taken a distinctively free market approach since the late 1990s (see Case Analysis 4-1). In 2004, for example, McDonald's awarded its first franchise in China. The number of franchises awarded in China by McDonald's, Yum Brands (e.g., KFC), and others began to increase dramatically in early 2005 after Chinese officials introduced new guidelines concerning such issues as recruitment of entrepreneurs and property rights. These guidelines were required as a consideration of China's entry into the World Trade Organization. Previously, Western companies feared a loss of trade secrets and brands by offering franchises in China.[18] Regulation—or the lack thereof—always seems to be a key political and business issue, including the rather recently copyrighted products distributed electronically such as software, music, and movies.[19]

The political-legal environment can influence industries and firms in complex ways, especially when firms operate across borders. For example, Internet search firms Yahoo and Google must negotiate Chinese regulations in order to be successful there. The Chinese government believes that the Internet must be controlled to maintain social stability and thereby imposes strict censorship and

Case Analysis 4-1

Step 5: What Political-Legal Forces Affect the Industry?

The political-legal forces that affect the industry depend on the industry, but should include the effects that political and legal events will likely have on the industry in which the organization operates. Key issues include but are not limited to the following:

1. Legislation at all levels
2. Court judgments, as well as decisions rendered by various federal, state, and local agencies
3. Environmental regulations and enforcement of antitrust regulations
4. Tax laws
5. Consumer lending regulations
6. Outcomes of elections
7. International trade regulations and tariffs
8. Laws on hiring, firing, promotion, and pay
9. Political stability

   The focus at this point should be on the industry, not a specific firm. The application of the firm in question is discussed in the strengths, weaknesses, opportunities, and threats (SWOT) analysis in Chapter 9.

   As with the other macroenvironmental factors (discussed in sections 4-3 through 4-5), some political-legal forces affect different firms in the same industry in different manners, but one should first identify the key macroenvironmental factors affecting the industry, and then explain how they affect the overall industry. For example, stating that a particular industry will be affected by changes in tax laws is not sufficient. One should first elaborate by discussing specific changes, such as an increase in the investment tax credit, and then elaborate on how this change affects the industry as a whole. Although referencing individual firms in this section is acceptable, emphasis should be placed on the effects of political-legal and other macroenvironmental forces on the *entire* industry. Specifics concerning how these factors affect a particular organization should be elaborated in the section on opportunities and threats, later in the analysis.

   Researching political-legal forces, as well as other macroenvironmental forces, requires some digging and intuition, and a lot of reading. Rarely will one find a Web site that provides a comprehensive "macroenvironmental report" for a given firm or industry. When conducting research, it is often helpful to create four charts—one for each element in the macroenvironment—and add to it throughout the research process. One may locate direct and indirect references at the company home page and in various articles, but trade journals are often the best single source of information for reports on macroenvironmental issues. As many as two dozen (or more) different sources may be required to complete the analysis of the four macroenvironmental forces. It is rare that complete and thorough information can be found in only one or two sources.

   If a company competes in multiple industries (with multiple business units), one needs to analyze the major business units and industries. What constitutes "major" depends on the firm. For example, Ford Motor Company receives the majority of its revenues from automobile sales, but it also has a business unit that provides customer financing. With Ford, it would make the most sense to analyze its automobile business unit and not spend considerable time on the financial business unit. With other companies, however, determining which business unit or units are "major" may be more difficult. The key is to consider the relative contribution of each business unit to corporate revenues and profits. If questions remain, it is a good idea to present the professor with a list of the company's business units and each one's proportion of company revenues and profits, along with a proposal on how to proceed, and ask for guidance.

security laws. This control represents a distinct challenge for the search engines, whose purpose is to enable users to access the full spectrum of information available, not just what governments prefer users to see.[20]

Pollution is also becoming more of a challenge every day in China's capital, Beijing, where nearly a thousand new cars are added to the congestion every day. In 2006, China had about twenty-five vehicles for every thousand people—seven of which were cars—roughly the proportion common to the United States in 1915. This is expected to change markedly, however, with some analysts predicting an increase from 33 million vehicles in 2006 to more than 130 million by 2020.[21] Hence, automakers should anticipate increased regulations in the coming years to combat this growing problem.

Trade restrictions across borders will always exist to some extent, especially in politically sensitive areas. For example, the United States and other Western countries have banned the export of advanced technology in certain circumstances. The United States prohibits the export of certain electronic, nuclear, and defense-related products to many countries, particularly those believed to be involved in international terrorism. Many of these restrictions were revised and strengthened following the 9/11 terrorist attacks.[22]

4-3 Economic Forces

Economic forces significantly influence business operations, including growth or decline in gross domestic product and increases or decreases in economic indicators such as inflation, interest rates, and exchange rates. Other factors such as hikes in energy prices and health care costs and access to labor can also play a role. These changes can present both opportunities and threats to strategic managers, depending on the industry.

Although the focus here is on the effects of economic changes on an industry, some competitors may be hurt more than others. Hikes in fuel prices in mid-2005, for example, did not have the same effect on all airlines, although specific effects are difficult to determine because of other simultaneous environmental and competitive changes in the industry. Initially, weak players such as Delta seem to have been hit the hardest, whereas budget carriers such as Southwest and Ryanair may have been able to experience mild gains. As prices continued to rise, however, it became apparent that low-cost airlines were not going to suffer less than their traditional counterparts because fuel represents a higher percentage of running costs on short-haul flights such as those championed by budget carriers. Low-cost airlines hoped to spread these increased costs over more customers with higher occupancy rates, but this became more difficult because traditional airlines began to lower fares in 2006 in an effort to increase their own occupancy rates.[23]

Economic forces can also have interesting cross-border effects. Toymakers in the West suffered during the 2006 Christmas season when power and labor shortages in China limited production of projected top sellers.[24] Hence, analyzing the political environment should not necessarily be limited to a firm's host country.

Several classes of economic forces tend to have broad effects on industries. The four classes discussed in this section are gross domestic product, inflation rates, interest rates, and exchange rates.

4-3a Gross Domestic Product

Gross domestic product (GDP) refers to the value of a nation's annual total production of goods and services. GDP is a key area of concern for all firms, but can become quite complex for those heavily involved in global markets. Although clear relationships exist among the world's economies, they do not always rise and fall together. For example, while GDP levels in the West were stagnant during the late 1990s and early 2000s, China's GDP grew at a staggering pace and provided expansion opportunities for a number of Western firms.[25]

Consistent GDP growth generally produces a healthy economy fueled by increases in consumer spending. In contrast, however, a GDP decline signals lower consumer spending and decreased demand for goods and services. When GDP declines for two consecutive quarters, a nation's economy is generally considered to be in a **recession**, during which time competitive pressures can lower profits and increase business failure rates. Recessions do not threaten all industries equally, however. College and university enrollments often increase as undergraduate and graduate students seek to gain an advantage in a tight job market.[26] Likewise, "dollar" stores (i.e., those that price all products at one dollar) historically perform especially well during times of economic downturn.[27] Interestingly, after an extended growth surge, sales at dollar stores began to cool in 2004 and leveled off shortly thereafter. The dollar store industry appears to have entered the maturity stage of the industry life cycle. Such rivals as Family Dollar, Dollar Tree, Dollar General, Fred's, and 99 Cents Only can no longer anticipate increased earnings from sales growth.[28]

With dim prospects for rapid growth in the United States, certain dollar stores are moving abroad. California-based My Dollarstore operates only about fifty stores in the United States and holds a minuscule share of the market. It has expanded aggressively outside of the United States, however, and operates a couple hundred stores in Central America, Eastern Europe, and Southeast Asia where it faces less competition. My Dollarstores beat Wal-Mart to India, where it sells products for ninety-nine Indian rupees (about two dollars) and targets middle-class consumers.[29] The firm, though, must address a different set of macroenvironmental forces in each market it serves.

A recession can also create opportunities for businesses. The deluge of dot-com failures in 2000 and 2001, for example, increased the supply of technical personnel at a time when demand for workers in this area was not being met. As a result, many traditional businesses were able to procure sorely needed technical expertise as software engineers and others became leery of dot-com start-ups.[30] Unfortunately, it is difficult to forecast a recession in advance, and many recessions are identified only after they have bottomed out.

4-3b Inflation Rates

High inflation rates have a negative effect on most but not all businesses. High rates raise many of the costs of doing business, and continued inflation constricts the expansion plans of businesses and triggers governmental action designed

Gross Domestic Product (GDP)

The value of a nation's annual total production of goods and services.

Recession

A decline in a nation's GDP for two or more consecutive quarters.

Source: Ablestock.com

to slow economic growth. The U.S. Federal Reserve Board often raises its discount rate during inflationary periods to slow economic growth. Its counterparts in other developed nations typically follow suit, and in some cases precede Fed action.

An economic slowdown can have mixed effects on a particular industry as it affects interest rates. During a recession, for example, new car retailers tend to have a difficult time attracting prospective customers to their showrooms. However, slowdowns are often accompanied by central bank interest rate cuts, which in turn reduce both interest rates for consumers and bank costs that dealers must incur to finance their inventories. Hence, one needs to consider the composite impact that an economic factor may have on an industry, not only the single effect that may be most intuitive.

Like high interest rates, periods of inflation can present opportunities for some firms. For instance, oil companies may benefit during inflationary times if the prices of oil and gas rise faster than the costs of exploration, refinement, and transportation. Companies that mine or sell precious metals may also benefit during periods of inflation because such metals serve as inflation hedges for consumers.[31]

4-3c Interest Rates

Short- and long-term interest rates affect the demand for many products and services, especially big ticket items with costs that are financed over an extended time, such as automobiles, appliances, and even major home renovations or repairs. At the consumer level, low short-term interest rates, for instance, are particularly beneficial for retailers such as Wal-Mart and J.C. Penney because they also tend to lower rates on credit cards, thereby encouraging consumer spending. At the corporate level, interest rates also influence strategic decisions related to financing. High rates, for instance, tend to dampen business plans to raise funds to expand or to replace aging facilities. Lower rates, however, are more likely to spawn capital expenditures on expansion and development.

Interest rates are closely linked to inflation rates. The cost of borrowing can be high in developing countries, with annual interest rates sometimes exceeding 100 percent. These high interest rates are often accompanied and influenced by excessive rates of inflation, as was the case in parts of Latin America in the 1990s. In small nations such as Bolivia, annual inflation has been as high as 26,000 percent.[32] Even larger and more industrialized countries such as Brazil have recently experienced annual inflation rates of 2,700 percent.[33] Routine decisions such as pricing and costing become almost impossible to make under such conditions. In addition, high inflation rates cause the prices of goods and services to rise and become less competitive in international trade.

A real estate boom fueled by low interest rates as much as doubled home values in many U.S. markets between 2000 and 2005, but when rates began to rise, builders began to reassess their strategies to ride out an anticipated downturn. Market leader D. R. Horton sold over 50,000 homes in the United States in 2005 and still plans to reach the 100,000 mark by 2010 even if the economy shows a downturn. Horton and other leaders believe they can prosper through any economic cycle by squeezing suppliers for lower costs and taking market share from smaller rivals.[34] This remains to be seen, however.

4-3d Exchange Rates

Currency exchange rates can be influenced by international agreements, the coordinated economic policies of governments, and international economic conditions. When such conditions raise the value of the dollar, for example, U.S. firms find themselves at a competitive disadvantage internationally, as the prices of American-made goods rise in foreign markets. At the same time, American consumers may be inclined to purchase products that were produced abroad, which are less expensive than goods produced domestically.

When the dollar is strong, American manufacturers tend to locate more of their plants abroad and make purchases from foreign sources. However, when the dollar is weakens as it did in the mid-2000s, the financial incentive for American companies to purchase from foreign sources becomes more limited, and they tend to focus their activities more on the domestic markets.

Source: Ablestock.com

Currency exchange rates present challenges because of their dramatic and often unpredictable changes over time. For instance, the Mexican peso has been historically devalued relative to the world's major currencies once or twice every decade, reducing the profits of U.S. firms operating there. These rampant fluctuations began to subside in the late 1990s and early 2000s, but the future remains uncertain (see Case Analysis 4-2).

4-4　Social Forces

Social forces include such factors as societal values, trends, traditions, and religious practices. **Societal values** refer to concepts and beliefs that members of a society tend to hold in high esteem. In the United States and Canada, major values include individual freedom, fairness, free markets, and equality of opportunity. In a business sense, these values translate into an emphasis on entrepreneurship and the belief that one's success is limited only by one's ambition, energy, and ability. Interestingly, these values have attracted millions of immigrants to the United States and Canada during the past

Societal Values

Concepts and beliefs that members of a society tend to hold in high esteem.

Case Analysis 4-2

Step 6: What Economic Forces Affect the Industry?

Key economic forces that affect industry include but are not limited to the following:

1. GDP
2. Disposable personal income
3. Short- and long-term interest rates
4. Inflation
5. Exchange rates
6. Unemployment rate
7. Energy costs
8. Stage of the economic cycle
9. Monetary policy

As with other macroenvironmental forces, one needs to clarify specifically how these forces influence the industry in which the organization operates.

centuries in search of religious, economic, and political freedom, resulting in a business environment that is more vibrant than in countries that do not hold similar values.[35]

American consumers value convenience. Increases in costs and inconveniences associated with health care have created opportunities for retailers. In 2005, Wal-Mart, Target, and CVS began testing medical clinics in select stores, whereby consumers could pay between twenty-five and sixty dollars and receive fast access to basic medical services without an appointment. Costs are trimmed by staffing the clinics with nurse practitioners, who are permitted to treat patients and write prescriptions in most states.[36]

Societal trends can have a keen influence on the rise and fall of industries. Today, the average American is older, busier, better educated, less likely to be a member of the Caucasian race than in previous years, more bargain conscious, and more technologically astute and Internet savvy.[37] The latter trend has had a profound effect on the demand for personal computers and educational services, and has led firms operating in the broad middle-age market to modify their strategic approaches to include either younger or older adults. Cosmetics maker Avon, confronted with a shrinking clientele, launched a major effort in 2002 to expand its appeal to the trendier sixteen- to twenty-four-year-old market.[38] In 2005, Gap launched ten test stores designed to target boomer women (currently in their forties and fifties), a category that typically spends less on apparel than younger adults.[39] Retailers such as J.C. Penney, May Department Stores, and Sears have begun to open stand-alone locations to provide easier access to customers too busy to plan a day at the mall.[40]

Source: Comstock.com

Societal trends also include demographic changes that can dramatically affect business opportunities. For example, the U.S. baby boom, which lasted from 1945 through the mid-1960s, initially provided opportunities for businesses such as clothing, baby apparel and diaper manufacturers, private schools, and candy and snack makers. Later, as the baby boomers entered the job market, universities and businesses were blessed with a tremendous pool of applicants. As they have continued to age, the baby boomers have begun shopping at home more and are spending vast sums of money for health care needs, leisure activities, and vacation alternatives.[41] Further, this population segment may not be as brand loyal as previous generations of Americans and represents a key group of purchasers of goods and services on the Internet.[42]

Demographic changes have taken a toll on American Express. Long known for catering to older, more affluent executives, American Express is having a difficult time reaching members of a new generation to whom the prestige of having an AmEx card means little or nothing. Between 1984 and 2004, the number of credit cards in circulation in the United States rose from fewer than 200 million to over 600 million, and the number of debit cards grew from zero to over 200 million. In an effort to permeate the credit and debit card fog among young consumers, American Express even began offering unusual perks targeted to young prospective cardholders, such as free chocolate martinis and discounts at trendy nightspots.[43]

Societal trends present various opportunities and threats to businesses. For example, the health and fitness trend that emerged in the 1990s has spawned growth in manufacturers of fitness equipment, as well as producers of health drinks, while hurting certain businesses in less health-friendly industries such as tobacco and liquor. In 2002, Anheuser Busch launched Michelob Ultra, a low-carbohydrate beer, in an effort to tap the health-conscious market.[44] Also in 2002, PepsiCo announced it would attempt to increase its sales of healthy snacks, including baked and low-fat offerings, to 50 percent of its total snack food sales.[45]

Other consumer-related trends have been sparked by development of the Internet. In the early 2000s, a number of traditional retailers began to experience sales declines as more consumers shopped online. Online retail sales in the United States have risen rapidly in recent years. Purchases of big ticket items such as furniture and appliances have also grown as consumers have become more comfortable making large purchases via the Internet, creating opportunities for retailers such as Best Buy and Circuit City.[46]

Buyer behavior is a key concern, especially for retailers. Traditional department stores such as Sears, J.C. Penney, and Dillards suffered revenue declines in the late 1990s and early 2000s as a result of changes in consumer buying habits that favor discounters such as Target and Wal-Mart, and e-tailers such as Amazon. com. Department stores have responded by streamlining stores to facilitate faster service, modifying product lines to target specific consumer groups, and even increasing their reliance on private label brands.[47]

Increases in online sales have caused traditional retailers to develop new ways to attract prospective buyers to their stores. They discovered that many consumers were less likely to frequent a traditional retailer unless it also provided some form of entertainment value. Bass Pro Shops, for example, increased its store traffic substantially by including such amenities as a large fish tank, live bats, and even a rock-climbing wall. Mall developers began to include "activity zones" in their facilities for such attractions as skating and fitness centers. This trend of mixing retailing with entertainment is expected to continue in the coming years.[48]

Trends toward socially responsible manufacturing and waste management practices, as well as concerns for saving private wetlands from business development, should be noted as well.[49] Specifically, the last decade of the twentieth century witnessed a heightened interest in both consumer recycling and the production of recyclable products by manufacturers in the United States and other parts of the world. To address this shift, Norwegian recycling giant Tomra expanded to a couple hundred recycling kiosks in California in 2001. The cleaner, more accessible kiosks are designed to appeal to socially sensitive consumers who prefer not to deal with the inconveniences associated with the traditional recycling centers.[50] However, many analysts note that consumers are often unwilling to pay the higher prices typically associated with environmentally friendly products.[51]

The tragic events of 9/11 spawned social changes that affect a variety of industries. For example, concerns over air travel safety have greatly influenced everything from routes to marketing strategies of major airlines. Broadly speaking, Americans are more willing to accept inconveniences associated with their transactions if they believe that safety and security are heightened as a result. Studies also suggest that investment and personal life strategies have become more conservative and reflective as a result of the tragedy.[52] Even churches are taking notice, as the 25 percent increase in national attendance immediately following the events of 9/11 had all but disappeared by early 2002.[53]

Sections 4-4a and 4-4b develop in detail changes in two key social forces, eating habits and automobiles. These examples illustrate both the richness and the complexity of social change and how it affects firms. Section 4-4c elaborates on global concerns.

4-4a Case 1: Eating Habits

A key social force affecting several industries in the United States and worldwide is the changing of eating habits. One can argue that some firms in food-related industries have achieved success primarily on the basis of a single social force. Since its founding in 1980, Whole Foods Markets grew to 189 stores and $5.6 billion annual sales in twenty-five years as the largest U.S. organic and natural foods grocer. CEO John Mackey has demonstrated that the natural and organic food movement is not merely a fad, but one that is substantial enough to support a national grocer. Of course, Whole Foods Markets faces potential threats associated with this movement. If it declines, the grocer will most likely suffer. Alternatively, if it becomes mainstream, traditional grocers will continue to expand their natural and organic food product lines, increasing competition for the firm.[54]

Food producers understand the value of staying abreast of changes in consumer tastes, especially in terms of diet fads and health trends. While food sales have grown at a modest clip of about 2 percent annually, sales related to diet fads rise and fall rapidly, rewarding firms with the right array of products. In the mid-2000s, companies such as Nestle, Unilever, and Kraft began experimenting with special starches and fibers to create foods that make people feel full for a longer time. If successful, such products could lead to an overall reduction in food sales, creating an interesting conundrum for these companies.[55]

Interestingly, American consumers have been sending a mixed message of the celery stick and the double chocolate peanut swirl for the past decade, further complicating the task of identifying demand patterns for restaurants and packaged food producers alike. American and British women between the drinking age of twenty-one and twenty-four, for example, consumed 33 percent more alcoholic beverages in 2004 than they did just five years earlier, a trend likely connected to the fact that women are starting families later in life and therefore have more disposable income at this age.[56] Alcoholic beverage producers are responding with new alternatives targeted to the taste preferences of young women.

Responding to shifts in alcoholic beverage consumption patterns is not always easy, however. In late 2005, Anheuser Busch teamed up with notable Harvard epidemiologist Meir Stampfer to tout the potential medical benefits of beer consumptions. Stampfer cites studies suggesting that moderate consumption of alcohol may reduce the risk of heart attack, diabetes, and other ailments. Between 1995 and 2004, beer's share of the overall consumption of alcoholic beverages in the United States declined while wine's share increased. Although Anheuser Busch attributes some of this shift to the preference for beverages low in carbohydrates, the firm believes that a key factor is a misconception that moderate wine consumption can be healthy whereas moderate beer consumption is not.[57]

In the late 1990s and early 2000s, fast-food consumers began eating less at traditional giants such as Burger King, Pizza Hut, and Taco Bell, in favor of more healthy alternatives such as Subway and Panera Bread. Although competitors such as McDonald's have responded with more salads, expanded advertising campaigns, a rotation of temporary items, revamped dollar menus, and even credit card service, the company's "fried" image remains intact and sales increases have been difficult to muster.[58] In the fast-food business, rapid and effective adaptation to changes in taste can spell the difference between profit and loss. In the mid-2000s, tastes shifted from hamburgers and chicken to toasted sandwiches. Subway equipped its stores with high-tech ovens and began offering consumers the option of toasting their sandwiches. Rivals took similar measures as the sale of sandwiches grew at twice the pace of burgers.[59] Even as U.S. fast-food icons continue to expand abroad, restaurant chains from other parts of the world, such as Guatemala's Pollo Campero and Mexico's El Tizoncito, are expanding into the United States.[60]

During the past several years, many fast-food restaurants have been "supersizing" their meal combinations by adding extra fries and larger drinks, while at the same time expanding alternatives for items such as grilled chicken sandwiches and salads.[61] In 2004, Coca-Cola and PepsiCo began to emphasize smaller cans and bottles (at higher per-ounce prices),[62] while McDonald's introduced low-carb menu items.[63] Eating habits even changed markedly after the U.S.-led war with Iraq began as Americans consumed large quantities of high-calorie takeout food while watching war coverage on television.[64]

In early 2005, the U.S. government released a revised design of the *food pyramid,* a graphical depiction reflecting food choices the U.S. Dietary Guidelines Advisory Committee believe to be appropriate. Whether this attempt to communicate dietary guidelines more effectivly to consumers will be successful remains to be seen.[65] With the introduction and reported success of products such as the Hardee's Monster Thickburger with 107 fat grams and 1,418 calories, the extent to which many American consumers consider health factors when purchasing fast food is not clear.[66]

Traditionally, food in China has been viewed as something to be savored, not rushed. Only about 10 percent of business at fast-food restaurants in China is takeout. KFC (Yum Brands) opened its first drive-thru in China in 2002 and added a second in 2005, but response has been lackluster. McDonald's opened its first drive-thru in China in 2005 and partnered the following year with Sinopec, China's largest gasoline retailer, to build a large number of additional units in Sinopec service stations. With the faster pace of Chinese life and more cars on the road, McDonald's is banking on acceptance of the drive-thru concept (in Chinese, *De Lai Su,* which translates into "come and get it fast"). This move reflects an increased effort by McDonald's to tailor its offerings more to local tastes. Chicken outsells beef at McDonald's in China, where the fast-food giant blends the traditionally favorite Big Macs and fries with local favorites such as corn, spicy chicken wings, and triangle wraps (chicken or beef mixed with rice and vegetables in a tortilla-type wrapper).[67]

In late 2003, concern about obesity in developed nations such as the United States and the United Kingdom became more pronounced. Critics charge that sedentary lifestyles and unhealthy foods have led to increases in diabetes, heart disease, and other medical problems associated with obesity. Many charged that food processors and fast-food restaurants such as McDonald's have contributed to this phenomenon by encouraging individuals to consume larger quantities of unhealthy foods.[68] At the same time, however, a number of food producers and restaurants began catering to consumer interest in low-carbohydrate regiments as dieter concern shifted from fat content in foods to carbohydrate content. Unilever, for example, began promoting low-carb Skippy peanut butter, Wishbone dressing, and Ragu spaghetti sauce.[69]

4-4b Case 2: Automobiles

Social trends can drive consumer markets as, for example, in the automobile industry. The 1990s experienced the rise of sport utility vehicles (SUVs) on the American automotive landscape. By the end of the decade, SUVs were the vehicle of choice for many suburban families, and the minivan was passé. Auto manufacturers realized, however, that the new breed of SUV patrons was willing to give up some of the rugged features associated with the SUV in exchange for the additional space and softer ride associated with the minivan. As one GM executive put it, "The sport utility today is kind of becoming like the minivan, a family vehicle." In early 2001, Ford responded to the shift in consumer preferences by introducing a redesigned Explorer with three rows of seats, additional safety gadgets, and a softer ride.[70] By 2003, Ford, General Motors, and Nissan had begun to shift attention away from large SUVs to the hybrid vehicles they termed "crossovers" or "active lifestyle wagons."[71] Ford executives even called 2004 "the year of the car" in anticipation of a consumer move away from SUVs, trucks, and minivans.[72]

The evolution of the sport utility vehicle continued into the mid-2000s, as demand for traditional SUVs such as the Ford Explorer and the Chevrolet Tahoe leveled off in the United States. In 2005 and 2006, sales of crossover vehicles began to surpass those of SUVs in the United States. Crossovers are typically smaller and more fuel efficient than SUVs, but many grew wider and longer during this time, adding such features as a third row of seats, more cargo space, and greater towing capacity.[73] The 2006 models boasted designs that resembled a combination of SUV and sports car, station wagon, or mini van. Experts attributed the changes to both a greater interest in practicality and the reality of higher fuel prices.[74]

Spikes in fuel prices in the mid-2000s took a heavy toll on sales of fuel-inefficient vehicles, including SUVs. When gasoline prices in the United States approached three dollars per gallon, GM reported a sales decline of 24 percent over the same month in 2004, while Ford sales dropped 19.5 percent. Meanwhile, sales at Chrysler, which is less dependent on SUVs, rose 4 percent. Sales at Toyota, makers of more fuel-efficient vehicles, rose 10 percent during the same period, led by a 23 percent increase in sales of the gas-electric hybrid Prius.[75] Fuel prices eventually tapered off, but rose abruptly again the following year. By mid-2006, American automobile manufacturers and retailers were forced to respond with incentives worth thousands of dollars to move its less fuel-efficient vehicles from inventories.[76] In July 2006, sales at Toyota in the United States surpassed those of Ford for the first time.[77] In 2007, Chrysler announced plans to introduce its tiny, two-seat SmartForTwo in the United States in 2008. The SmartForTwo is only 106 inches long, compared to 150 inches for Toyota's subcompact Yaris and 202 inches for Chevrolet's Tahoe. Although the vehicle has enjoyed some success in Europe, serious questions remain about the viability of such a small car in the United States.[78]

Interestingly, however, the popularity of the SUV in the United States has been attacked on the grounds of another social force—environmental responsibility. Opponents charge that SUVs are simply too large and fuel inefficient, increasing the nation's dependence on external sources of oil and potentially compromising the nation's ability to broker a lasting peace in the oil-rich Middle East. Interestingly, some experts are predicting a decline in the SUV fervor during the mid-2000s.[79] Nonetheless, SUV manufacturers still face a daunting task of balancing environmental concerns and their desire to produce a vehicle still in demand.

Consider additional social changes related to automobile preferences. Led by European automakers, manufacturers began developing smaller premium vehicles for sale in the United States in the mid-2000s, a period during which demand for less-expensive, fuel-efficient, high-end cars is expected to rise.

Interestingly, the role of the "Big Three" American carmakers in the development of these vehicles has been indirect rather than direct, with primary activity coming from General Motor's Saab, Ford's Volvo, and DaimlerChrysler's Mercedes divisions.[80]

Following the 2005 hike in gasoline prices in the United States, GM and Ford began to promote their "flex-fuel" vehicles that can operate either on gasoline or E85, a mix of 15 percent gasoline and 85 percent ethanol. The automakers announced plans to produce 650,000 fuel-flex vehicles annually and push for more service stations that carry the alternative fuel. In 2005, approximately 5 million such vehicles—mostly GM and Ford products—were in operation in the United States, but E85 was not easy to find, especially outside of the Midwest. Not only are fuel-flex vehicles attractive to environmentally friendly consumers, but they also represent a competitive advantage for the giant American automakers. When GM and Ford launched a new focus in 2006, Nissan was the only Japanese carmaker with a compatible product on the market, a version of its large Titan pickup.[81]

4-4c Global Concerns

It is difficult to separate domestic social forces from global forces. Indeed, the analysis of social forces can be quite complex for firms operating in several countries.[82] Each of the world's nations has its own distinctive **culture**, its generally accepted values, traditions, and patterns of behavior. These cultural differences can interfere with the efforts of managers to understand and communicate with those in other societies. The unconscious reference to one's own cultural values as a standard of judgment—the **self-reference criterion**—has been suggested as the cause of many international business problems. Individuals, regardless of culture, become so accustomed to their own ways of looking at the world that they often cannot comprehend any significant deviation from their perspective. However, companies that can adjust to the culture of a host country can compete successfully.[83] For instance, by adapting to local tastes rather than rigidly adhering to those of its U.S. customers, Domino's has found profitable business overseas by selling tuna and sweet corn pizzas in Japan and prawn and pineapple pizzas to Australians.[84]

Progressive companies recognize that cross-cultural differences in norms and values require modifications in managerial behavior. For example, business negotiations may take months or even years in countries such as Egypt, China, Mexico, and much of Latin America. Until personal friendships and trust develop between the parties, negotiators are unwilling to commit themselves to major business transactions.[85] In addition, Japanese business executives invite and even expect their clients or suppliers to interact socially with them after working hours, for up to three or four hours an evening, several times a week. Westerners who decline to attend such social gatherings regularly may be unsuccessful in their negotiations because these social settings create a foundation for serious business relationships (see Case Analysis 4-3).

Societal trends can vary widely among nations, especially as they relate to other factors. For example, throughout the 1990s and early 2000s, smaller cars were the vehicles of choice in Europe, where roads are narrow, gasoline is heavily taxed, and fuel economy is a greater concern than in the United States. In contrast, U.S. consumers continued to demand relatively larger vehicles in a country where roads are wide, gasoline is much less expensive, and fuel consumption does not play as strong a role in the purchase decision.[86] Fashion in China also

Culture

A society's generally accepted values, traditions, and patterns of behavior.

Self-Reference Criterion

The unconscious reference to one's own cultural values as a standard of judgment.

Case Analysis 4-3

Step 7: What Social Forces Affect the Industry?

Key social forces that affect the industry include but are not limited to the following:

1. Societal traditions

2. Societal trends

3. Prevailing values

4. Consumer psychology

5. Society's expectations of business and consumer activism

6. Concern with quality of life

7. Expectations from the workplace

8. Religious trends and values

9. Population and demographics

10. Birth rates and life expectations

11. Women in the workforce

12. Health consciousness

13. Attitudes about career and family

As with other macroenvironmental forces, but especially with social forces, it is important to outline how each key force has affected the industry and organization to date, and to address how each will likely influence the industry in the future. For example, health consciousness and dual-career couples have spawned the demand for Healthy Choice microwavable dinners. Will these two social forces change in the upcoming years? If so, how?

---

illustrates how social trends vary across borders. In China, preferences reflect a mix of Asian, American, and European tastes.[87]

Societal traditions define societal practices that have often lasted for decades or even centuries, but changes can occur. For example, the celebration of Christmas in the Western Hemisphere provides significant financial opportunities for card companies, toy retailers, turkey processors, tree growers, mail-order catalog firms, and other related businesses. In fact, many retailers hope to break even during the year and generate their profits during the Christmas shopping season. The popularity of Christmas is increasing in China. Although Chinese celebrations are typically devoid of religious significance, opportunities have emerged for marketers and merchandisers seeking to cash in on the popularity of gifts, consumption, and Santa Claus.[88]

Strategic managers of U.S. corporations should remember that their firms have exceptionally high visibility because of their origins in the United States. As such, citizens of other countries may disrupt the business operations of U.S. corporations as a form of anti-American activity. Only two months after Euro Disneyland opened in France, many French citizens decried the venture. Hundreds of French farmers blocked entrances to the theme park with their tractors to express displeasure with cuts in European farm subsidies that had been encouraged by the United States, even though 90 percent of the food sold at the park was produced in France.[89]

4-5 Technological Forces

Technological forces include scientific improvements and innovations that create opportunities or threats for businesses. The rate of technological change varies considerably from one industry to another and can affect a firm's operations as well as its products and services. A number of businesses have used advances in computer technology such as computers, satellites, and fiber optics to perform their traditional tasks at lower costs and higher levels of customer satisfaction. Many analysts believe satellite radio for cars will revolutionize the automobile audio entertainment industry.[90]

Technological change can decimate existing businesses and even entire industries because it shifts demand from one product to another. Historical examples of such change include the shifts from vacuum tubes to transistors, steam locomotives to diesel and electric engines, fountain pens to ballpoints, propeller airplanes to jets, and typewriters to computers.[91] Internet icon Shawn Fanning spawned an "online music swapping" industry with his launch of Napster, a service whereby patrons could exchange music files via the Internet. Copyright and legal complications, however, forced a shutdown and sale of the business.[92]

Source: Comstock.com

The pace of adopting a technological change is not always easy to predict and can even be influenced by competing technologies. For example, high-definition radio technology became pervasive in the early 2000s and a couple hundred U.S. radio stations were broadcasting digital radio by the end of 2004. However, the first radios capable of using the new standard were originally priced as much as $1,000 at a time when demand for lower priced satellite radios was growing rapidly. Many analysts believe that digital radios will become commonplace by the late 2000s, but the specifics are difficult to predict.[93]

Advances in technology can substantially influence production costs associated with a product or service. Television manufacturer limitations in sizes of glass sheets they can handle, for example, kept prices for flat-screen televisions high throughout 2004 when many analysts had predicted production costs to drop.[94] Food and meat producers such as ConAgra Foods, Hormel Foods, and Perdue Farms are dunking prewrapped foods into tanks of pressurized water, a technique that enables vendors to keep deli meats in the pipeline for as long as one hundred days.[95]

Many retailers are beginning to utilize technology to better understand how buyers shop. Consumer research firm ShopperTrak RCT, for example, tracks shoppers nationwide using forty thousand hidden cameras in stores and shopping malls. The firm sells the data it collects to retailers, economists, and banks, all of which desire more insight into purchase trends.[96]

The widespread use of the Internet over the past decade is arguably the most pervasive technological force affecting business organizations since the dissemination of the personal computer (see Strategy at Work 4-1). The effects are most profound in select industries, such as brokerage houses, where online companies have demonstrated huge gains in the market, or the travel industry, where the number of flights, hotels, and travel packages booked over the past decade has skyrocketed. The Internet has also spawned the advent of online banking, a much less costly means of managing transactions. As such, by 2002, a number of major banks and creditors had begun encouraging customers to pay bills online by offering free software, elimination of fees, and even sweepstakes entries with each transaction.[97] Indeed, the Internet has had a major effect on virtually every industry in the developed world.

Leveraging Technological and Social Forces at Knight-Ridder and McClatchy

Founded in 1903, Knight-Ridder was originally a traditional print newspaper company, publishing such newspapers as the *Miami Herald* and the *Akron Beacon Journal*. It later purchased numerous newspapers including the *Detroit Free Press*, the *Philadelphia Inquirer*, and the *San Jose Mercury News*. Knight-Ridder was at one time the nation's second-largest newspaper publisher, with thirty-two daily newspapers in twenty-eight U.S. markets and a readership of 8.5 million daily and 12 million on Sundays. Like other U.S. newspapers, however, Knight-Ridder faced readership declines as consumers obtain information from other media outlets, most notably the Internet.

As the Internet developed, Knight-Ridder took advantage of technological innovations to expand its information network. The company's Internet operation, Knight-Ridder Digital, was created as a separate business unit in 2000 to create and maintain a variety of innovative online services, including Real Cities, a major national network of city and regional destination sites in fifty-eight U.S. markets. Knight-Ridder Digital was launched to provide local information on the Web, including regional searchable hubs, city resource Web sites, online newspapers, vertical channels, directories, online shopping, entertainment and recreation sources,

merchant storefront building, classified services and archives, and special interest Web sites. Knight-Ridder also acquired CareerBuilder Inc. and CareerPath.com Inc. to create a powerful local and national online recruitment network.

The company was also cognizant of changing social forces, successfully capitalizing on an opportunity provided by demographic changes in Miami several years ago. Observing the ever-increasing number of Cuban Americans in the Miami market, Knight-Ridder launched a Spanish-language paper, *El Nuevo Herald*, which immediately became a success and is now one of the largest of its kind in the United States.

Adjusting to these changes was not easy, however, and Knight-Ridder struggled to remain competitive. In 2006, rival McClatchy acquired Knight-Ridder and later sold some of its papers. Like Knight-Ridder, McClatchy also seeks to respond to changes in technology, working closely with Yahoo in a partnership that includes content sharing and cross-advertising.

Sources: P. Callahan, "Student Papers Are Resisting Gannett's Push onto Campuses," Wall Street Journal Interactive Edition, 21 February 2002; Knight-Ridder Corporate Web site, www.knightridder.com, accessed 14 March 2002; P. Wright, M. Kroll, and J. A. Parnell, Strategic Management: Concepts (Upper Saddle River, NJ: Prentice Hall, 1998).

Consider the airline industry. With the advent of the Internet, many consumers began to purchase their airline tickets online instead of utilizing the traditional intermediary, a travel agency. As airlines began investing in this much more efficient means of ticketing in the 1990s, they started to trim commissions paid to travel agencies for booking their flights. In 2003, the major U.S.-based airlines followed Delta's lead and eliminated commissions altogether for tickets sold in the United States, except where specially negotiated arrangements existed between the airline and the agency. Travel agencies have moved aggressively to the Internet and to expand volume. A number of agencies were dissolved during this period.[98]

Interestingly, Internet travel agencies such as Orbitz, Travelocity, and Expedia thrived during this time. These sites invest heavily in promotion and emphasize convenience, ease of use, and access to the "best deals." Unlike traditional travel agents, these online competitors aggressively target hotel reservations and have sparked feuds with large hotel chains that attempt to lure customers to their own Web sites for bookings. Hotel chains charge that online travel agents inflate room rates by as much as 30 percent, thereby discouraging potential customers and cutting into hotel profits. Online agents contend that they offer value to customers by increasing choices.[99]

On the consumer side, over 1.1 billion individuals have access to the Internet, most residing in the United States, Canada, Europe, or Asia. Reports also suggest that the majority of America's population shops online. Most online shoppers tend to be male, married, college educated, and between eighteen and forty years of age.[100] Online retail spending for 2007 exceeded $100 billion, growing at an average annual rate of about 24 percent.[101]

Technology has spawned major changes in the customer service arena. Many of the touch-tone consumer hotlines of the 1990s were replaced in the early 2000s by "virtual agents" that answer calls and use speech recognition technology to either resolve a question or transfer the customer to a "real person" who can. Studies suggest that these systems improve response time by as much as 40 percent. Whereas some consumers appreciate the increased speed and are enamored by many agents' use of accents and even flirtatious personalities, others feel awkward about "talking to a computer pretending to be a person." Interestingly, some U.S. companies have addressed this frustration by utilizing fewer technology-based systems and transferring incoming calls to their consumer hotlines and technical support centers directly to representatives in countries such as India, where labor costs are much lower.[102]

Technology also affects global business operations. For example, by 2003, 40 percent of the vehicles sold in Europe were powered by more fuel-efficient, cleaner, and more advanced diesel engines. In contrast, most transfer trucks in the United States consumed diesel fuel. Following renewed concerns over the political situation in the Middle East where much of the world's oil is produced, America's "Big Three" carmakers began to apply this technology to SUVs produced in the United States.[103]

Technology's effect on global business can also be viewed from a development perspective. For years, manufacturers in technologically advanced nations established operations in developing countries with low labor and raw material costs. These expansions have generally been welcomed because they bring financial resources, opportunities for workforce training and development, and the chance for the host country to acquire new technologies. In many cases, this interaction has benefited the developing country over the long term, most notably in the cases of emerging nations such as Mexico, Brazil, India, and China.[104]

Leaders in emerging nations are not always satisfied with the results of global business expansion, however, because anticipated economic and social benefits do not always materialize, such as specialized business development assistance, the establishment of research and development (R&D) facilities, and the hiring of locals in managerial and other professional positions.[105] On-the-job training notwithstanding, the overall long-term contribution to the host country is sometimes questioned by leaders in the developing nations (see Case Analysis 4-4).

Changes in technological and social forces often work together to influence an industry. In the last two decades, for example, the proliferation of segmented television networks and the emergence of the Internet have led to a decline in newspaper readership—particularly among younger readers—as busier professionals pursue information outlets in the "new media," including those facilitated by the Internet and talk radio. Many advertisers in newspaper classifieds have shifted to Internet sites or eBay. Daily newspaper readers in the United States peaked at 62.8 million in 1985 but declined to 54.6 million in 2005. As a result, many newspapers have launched targeted

Step 8: What Technological Forces Affect the Industry?

Key technological forces that affect the industry include but are not limited to the following:

1. Effect of the Internet
2. Scientific improvements
3. Inventions
4. Technology affecting production
5. Expenditures on research and development
6. Focus on R&D expenditures
7. Rate of new product introductions
8. Automation

youth-oriented publications and have begun to leverage the power of the Internet in an effort to regain readers.[106]

4-6 Environmental Scanning

Environmental Scanning

The systematic collection and analysis of information about relevant macroenvironmental trends.

Maintaining currency in macroenvironmental forces that affect one's firm can be a daunting task. **Environmental scanning** refers to the systematic collection and analysis of information about relevant macroenvironmental trends. Surveys of Fortune 500 firms generally indicate major payoffs associated with their environmental-scanning activities, including an increased general awareness of environmental changes, better strategic planning and decision making, greater effectiveness in governmental matters, and proper diversification and resource allocation decisions. However, the respondents often indicate that the results of their environmental analysis are typically too general or uncertain for specific interpretation.[107] Hence, the need for *effective* environmental scanning to produce relevant information is critical.[108]

Britain's leading retailer, Tesco, uses a "Clubcard" to collect data on its customers and tailor products and promotions specifically for individual customers. Tesco has leveraged this approach to increase its share of the grocery market in the United Kingdom to 31 percent in 2006, compared to 16 percent by Wal-Mart's Asda chain. Asda in the United Kingdom accounts for about 10 percent of Wal-Mart's overall revenues and almost half of its international sales. Tesco is using its knowledge of shoppers and customer preferences to combat Wal-Mart's emphasis on low prices.[109]

Some specialized firms presently offer environmental-scanning services to strategic managers by providing them with real-time searches of published material associated with their industries. Top managers at many smaller firms rely on publications such as the *Wall Street Journal* to remain abreast of changes that may affect their firms.

Top managers often have difficulty maintaining objectivity when they evaluate information because they selectively perceive their environment through the lens of their own experiences and organizational strategy. One study concluded

that the heads of financial institutions that emphasize cost minimization tend to focus their monitoring activities on competitors and regulators. By contrast, scanning activities in financial institutions that seek to differentiate themselves from their competitors are more likely to focus on opportunities for growth and customer satisfaction.[110]

Interestingly, environmental scanning often identifies relationships among key industry influences in two or more forces. For example, technological advances in the early to mid-2000s enabled manufacturers to produce hand-held devices for viewing DVDs at a price level suitable to a significant number of consumers. Interest in the product was further enhanced by heightened consumer interest in both DVDs and portable electronic products in general. When French firm Archos began producing such a product, however, it ignored an anticopying code found on a majority of prerecorded DVDs, enabling consumers to use the product to make illegal DVDs. Although there were no laws in place prohibiting Archos from ignoring the code, filmmakers began to exert political pressure to lobby for legislation to protect their copyrights.[111] Interestingly, this occurred at a time when Time Warner's HBO began to emphasize the sale of DVDs in addition to subscription fees as a means of enhancing revenues.[112]

Today, the main problem created by environmental scanning is often one of determining which available information warrants attention. For example, it is not uncommon for a major U.S. firm to be referenced in over a thousand news stories in a given week. For small organizations and for those competing in global markets, however, it may be difficult to obtain reliable information on environmental conditions and trends. In China, for example, research house Euromonitor International reported that 23 billion liters of soft drinks were consumed in 2002, whereas a Coca-Cola study concluded the level to be 39 billion liters. Discrepancies such as this create great difficulties for managers attempting to make informed strategic decisions.[113]

4-7 Summary

Four macroenvironmental forces affect every industry. Political-legal forces include various forms of legislation and judicial rulings, such as the decisions of various commissions and agencies at all levels of government. Economic forces include the effects of elements such as GDP, inflation, interest rates, and exchange rates. Social forces include traditions, values, societal trends, and a society's expectations of business. Technological forces include such factors as the Internet, as well as scientific improvements and innovations that affect firm operations and products and services in a given industry. Although each industry is affected by all four sets of macroenvironmental forces, the relative influence of the four forces can vary substantially by industry. Environmental scanning is the process of researching and analyzing macroenvironmental changes.

Key Terms

culture	macroenvironment	self-reference criterion
environmental scanning	PEST	societal values
gross domestic product	recession	

Review Questions and Exercises

1. Explain how changes in interest rates affect the automobile, home construction, and auto repair industries.

2. Give an example illustrating how social trends present both opportunities and threats to businesses in high-tech industries.

3. Give an example illustrating how the Internet has presented an opportunity or a threat to a particular industry or business organization.

4. Using your college or university as an example, explain how political-legal, economic, technological, and social forces have affected its operations over the past decade.

5. Select a large firm with which you are at least somewhat familiar. Utilize the search engines at www.findarticles.com and identify important macroenvironmental opportunities and threats for this company.

Practice Quiz

True or False

1. It is unusual for a single firm to influence a macroenvironmental force.

2. A decline in GDP negatively affects all industries.

3. In many respects, social forces are the drivers of consumer markets.

4. The expansion of a religion in an emerging country is an example of a social force.

5. Reading business publications can serve as a means of environmental scanning.

6. Environmental scanning can be difficult for large firms because of the availability of too much information.

Multiple Choice

7. The acronym referring to the analysis of macroenvironmental forces is
   A. WASP.
   B. PEST.
   C. STOP.
   D. SERCH.

8. At the global level, the period from World War II to the late 1980s was marked by
   A. an increase in trade protection.
   B. a decrease in trade protection.
   C. an absence of U.S. imports.
   D. none of the above

9. When the value of the U.S. dollar increases, U.S. firms
   A. compete at an advantage in foreign markets.
   B. compete at a disadvantage in foreign markets.
   C. tend to decrease exports to nations whose currencies are directly tied to the dollar.
   D. none of the above

10. Technological forces often
    A. decimate an entire industry.
    B. spawn new industries.
    C. vary substantially among industries.
    D. all of the above

11. Which of the following is *not* an example of a social force?
    A. trends
    B. values
    C. industrial change
    D. All of the above are examples.

12. When a recession occurs
    A. all industries benefit.
    B. some industries benefit.
    C. no industries benefit.
    D. none of the above

Notes

1. J. Cummings, "Wal-Mart Opens for Business in a Tough Market," *Wall Street Journal* (24 March 2004): A1, A15.

2. J. Hechinger and D. Armstrong, "Massachusetts Seeks to Mandate Health Coverage," *Wall Street Journal* (5 April 2006): A1, A15.

3. J. Bravin, "Court Rulings Could Hit Utilities, Auto Makers," *Wall Street Journal* (3 April 2007): A1, A9.

4. S. Power, "New Rollover Test Could Lead to Safer SUVs," *Wall Street Journal* (8 October 2003): D1, D7.

5. L. Meckler and K. Lundegaard, "New Fuel-Economy Rules Help the Biggest Truck Makers," *Wall Street Journal* (24 August 2005): B1, B2.

6. C. Cummins, "Business Mobilizes for Iraq," *Wall Street Journal* (24 March 2003): B1, B3; J. A. Trachtenberg and B. Steinberg, "Plan B for Marketers," *Wall Street Journal* (20 March 2003): B1, B3; N. King Jr., "The Race to Rebuild Iraq," *Wall Street Journal* (11 April 2003): B1, B3.

7. D. Roberts and J. Mackintosh, "Ford Chief Backs Higher Fuel Tax," *Financial Times* (8 April 2004): 1, 24.

8. D. Sevastopulo, "US Airlines 'Are On Life Support,'" *Financial Times* (2 October 2003): 15.

9. A. Higgins, "It's a Mad, Mad, Mad-Cow World," *Wall Street Journal* (12 March 2001): A13–A14.

10. S. Gray, "Pressure Mounts on Fast-food Chains to Remove Trans Fats," *Wall Street Journal* (14 December 2004): D1, D6.

11. S. Ellison, "Despite Big Health Concerns, Food Industry Can't Shake Salt," *Wall Street Journal* (25 February 2005): A1.

12. J. Zhang and S. Gray, "The Whole Truth about 'Whole Grain,'" *Wall Street Journal* (16 February 2006): D1, D8.

13. R. G. Matthews, "Some States Push to Collect Sales Tax from Internet Stores," *Wall Street Journal* (30 September 2005): B1, B4.

14. W. O'Connell, "From the Ashes of Defeat," *Wall Street Journal* (21 August 2006): B1, B4.

15. *International Financial Statistics Yearbook* (Washington, DC: International Monetary Fund, 1989).

16. C. Rapoport, "Europe Looks Ahead to Hard Choices," *Fortune* (14 December 1992): 145.

17. F. M. E. Raiszadeh, M. M. Helms, and M. C. Varner, "How Can Eastern Europe Help American Manufacturers?" *The International Executive* 35 (1993): 357–365.

18. S. Gray and G. A. Fowler, "China's New Entrepreneurs," *Wall Street Journal* (25 January 2005): B1, B4.

19. K. J. Delaney and C. Goldsmith, "Music Industry Targets Piracy by Europeans," *Wall Street Journal* (20 January 2004): B1, B2.

20. J. Dean and K. J. Delaney, "As Google Pushes into China, It Faces Clashes with Censors," *Wall Street Journal* (16 December 2005): A1, A12.

21. G. Farclough and S. Oster, "As China's Auto Market Booms, Leaders Clash over Heavy Toll," *Wall Street Journal* (13 June 2006): A1, A14.

22. "How September 11 Changed America," *Wall Street Journal* (8 March 2002): B1.

23. D. Michaels and M. Trottman, "Fuel May Propel Airline Shakeout," *Wall Street Journal* (7 September 2005): C1, C5; A. Johnson, "Low-Cost Airlines Raise Fares," *Wall Street Journal* (25 April 2006): D1, D3.

24. C. Binkley and N. Wingfield, "Trouble in Toyland," *Wall Street Journal* (20 November 2006): B1, B2.

25. M. Wolf, "Why Europe Was the Past, the US Is the Present and a China-Dominated Asia the Future of the Global Economy," *Financial Times* (22 September 2003): 13.

26. J. E. Hilsenrath, "America's Pricing Paradox," *Wall Street Journal* (16 May 2003): B1, B4.

27. C. Terhune, "In Modest Times, 'Dollar' Stores Remain Upbeat," *Wall Street Journal* (22 December 2000): B1.

28. K. Hudson, "Can the Dollar Stores Rebound?" *Wall Street Journal* (21 September 2005): C1, C4.

29. E. Bellman, "A Dollar Store's Rick Allure in India," *Wall Street Journal* (23 January 2007): B1, B14.

30. N. Harris, "Unemployed Dot-Commers Face Tough Job Market," *Wall Street Journal* (30 January 2001): B1.

31. P. Wright, M. Kroll, and J. A. Parnell, *Strategic Management: Concepts* (Upper Saddle River, NJ: Prentice Hall, 1998).

32. *International Financial Statistics Yearbook*, 35–52.

33. C. S. Manegold and M. Kepp, "Elegant Armed Robbery," *Newsweek* (2 April 1990): 30.

34. J. R. Hagerty and K. M. Dunham, "How Big U.S. Home Builders Plan to Ride out a Downturn," *Wall Street Journal* (30 November 2005): A1, A8.

35. Wright et al., *Strategic Management*.

36. J. Spencer, "Getting Your Health Care at Wal-Mart," *Wall Street Journal* (5 October 2005): D1, D5.

37. A. Zimmerman, "Behind the Dollar-store Boom: A Nation of Bargain Hunters," *Wall Street Journal* (13 December 2004): A1, A10.

38. S. Beatty, "Avon Is Set to Call on Teens," *Wall Street Journal* (17 October 2002): B1, B3.

39. A. Merrick, "Gap's Greatest Generation" *Wall Street Journal* (15 September 2004): B1, B3.

40. K. Stringer, "Abandoning the Mall," *Wall Street Journal* (24 March 2004): B1, B6.

41. K. J. Marchetti, "Customer Information Should Drive Retail Direct Mail," *Marketing News* (28 February 1994): 7.

42. S. Ratan, "Why Busters Hate Boomers," *Fortune* (4 October 1993): 56–69; B. W. Morgan, "It's the Myth of the '90s: The Value Customer," *Brandweek* (28 February 1994): 17.

43. R. Sidel, "American Express Tries to Find Its Place with a Younger Crowd," *Wall Street Journal* (22 September 2005): A1, A5.

44. C. Lawton, "Anheuser Tries Low-Carb Beer to Tap Diet Buzz," *Wall Street Journal* (13 September 2002): B1, B2.

45. B. McKay, "Pepsico Challenges Itself to Concoct Healthier Snacks," *Wall Street Journal* (23 September 2002): A1, A10.

46. M. Mangalindan, "Size Doesn't Matter Anymore in Online Purchases," *Wall Street Journal* (22 March 2006): D1, D4.

47. A. Merrick, J. A. Trachtenberg, and A. Zimmerman, "Department Stores Fight an Uphill Battle Just to Stay Relevant," *Wall Street Journal* (12 March 2002): A1.

48. D. Starkman, "Retail Riddle: Is Shopping Entertainment?" *Wall Street Journal* (22 January 2003): B1, B6.

49. J. Carlton, "Saving Private Wetlands," *Wall Street Journal* (13 November 2002): B1, B6.

50. J. Carlton, "Recycling Redefined," *Wall Street Journal* (6 March 2001): B1, B4

51. G. A. Fowler, "Green" Sales Pitch Isn't Helping to Move Products off the Shelf," *Wall Street Jounal* (6 March 2002): B1.

52. "How September 11 Changed America," *Wall Street Journal* (8 March 2002): B1.

53. K. McLaughlin, "The Religion Bubble: Churches Try to Recapture Their 9/11 Crowds," *Wall Street Journal* (11 September 2002): D1, D6.

54. S. Gray, "Natural Competitor: How Whole Foods CEO Mackey Intends to Stop Growth Slippage: Leadership on Salary of $1 a Year," *Wall Street Journal* (4 December 2006): B1, B3.

55. S. Ellison and D. Ball, "Slow to Spot Atkins, Food Firms Hunt for the Next Big Diet Fad," *Wall Street Journal* (16 February 2006): A1, A9.

56. B. Ball and V. O'Connell, "As Young Women Drink More, Alcohol Sales, Concerns Rise," *Wall Street Journal* (15 February 2006): A1, A14.

57. K. Hellier and S. Ellison, "Anheuser Wants World to Know Beer is Healthy," *Wall Street Journal* (9 December 2005): B1, B4.

58. S. Leung, "Fleeing from Fast Food," *Wall Street Journal* (11 November 2002): B1, B3; S. Leung and R. Lieber, "The New Menu Option at McDonald's: Plastic," *Wall Street Journal* (26 November 2002): D1, D2.

59. S. Gray, "Crunch Time in Fast Food," *Wall Street Journal* (26 August 2005): B1, B3.

60. T. Bouza and G. Sama, "America Adds Salsa to Its Burgers and Fries," *Wall Street Journal* (2 January 2003): A1, A12.

61. S. Ellison and B. Steinberg, "To Eat, Or Not to Eat," *Wall Street Journal* (20 June 2003): B1, B4.

62. B. McKay, "Downsize This!" *Wall Street Journal* (27 January 2004): B1, B5.

63. S. Leung, "McDonald's Makeover," *Wall Street Journal* (28 January 2004): B1, B10.

64. K. McLaughlin, "America's Wartime Diet: Finding Comfort in Cupcakes," *Wall Street Journal* (3 April 2003): D1, D2.

65. S. S. Munoz, "Rebuilding the Pyramid," *Wall Street Journal* (27 January 2005): B1, B3.

66. S. Gray, "For the Health-Unconscious, Era of Mammoth Burger Is Here," *Wall Street Journal* (27 January 2005): B1, B3.

67. G. Fairclough and G. A. Fowler, "Drive-Through Tips for China," *Wall Street Journal* (20 June 2006): B1, B9.

68. N. Buckley, "Have Fat, Will Sue," *Financial Times* (13-14 December 2003): W1-W2.

69. S. Ellison and D. Ball, "Now Low-Carb: Unilever's Skippy, Wishbone, Ragu," *Wall Street Journal* (14 January 2004): B1-B2.

70. J. B. White, G. L. White, and N. Shirouzu, "Drive for Lower Floors, Softer Rides Results in Domestic-Looking SUVs," *Wall Street Journal Interactive Edition* (4 January 2001).

71. J. Ball, "Detroit Revs Up the Wagon," *Wall Street Journal* (7 January 2003): B1, B3.

72. J. B. White, "Remaking the American Car," *Wall Street Journal* (23 October 2003): B1, B6.

73. K. Lundegaard, "A New Generation of SUVs," *Wall Street Journal* (10 January 2006): D1, D6.

74. N. Shirouzu and J. B. White, "The SUV Keeps on Evolving," *Wall Street Journal* (10 January 2005): B1, B5.

75. G. Chon, "Sales of SUVs Fall Sharply," *Wall Street Journal* (4 October 2005): D1, D5.

76. G. Chon, "Car Industry Brings Back Incentives," *Wall Street Journal* (2 May 2006): D1, D3.

77. C. Woodyard, "In a First, Toyota Outsells Ford," *USA Today* (2 August 2006): B1.

78. G. Chon and S. Power, "Can an Itsy-Bitsy Auto Survive in the Land of the SUV?" *Wall Street Journal* (9 January 2007): B1, B12.

79. "New TV Ads in US Link Gas-Guzzling SUVs to Terror Funding," *Dow Jones Newswire* (8 January 2003); J. Ball, "Detroit Worries Some Consumers Are Souring on Big SUVs," *Wall Street Journal* (8 January 2003): B1, B4.

80. N. E. Boudette and J. B. White, "Downsized Luxury: European Auto Makers Race to Win over Young Americans with Smaller Premium Models," *Wall Street Journal* (14 October 2003): B1, B7.

81. K. Lundegaard, "Ford, GM Make Big Push to Promote 'Flex-Fuel' Vehicles," *Wall Street Journal* (10 January 2006): B1, B8.

82. E. Weitz and Y. Shenhav, "A Longitudinal Analysis of Technical and Organizational Uncertainty in Management Theory," *Organization Studies* 21 (2000): 243–265.

83. Wright et al., *Strategic Management*.

84. M. J. Williams, "Rewriting the Export Rules," *Fortune* (23 April 1990): 89.

85. P. Wright, "Organizational Behavior in Islamic Firms," *Management International Review* 21(2) (1981): 86–94.

86. J. B. White and D. Gautier-Villars, "Little Cars, Lots of Tricks," *Wall Street Journal* (2 October 2002): B1, B3.

87. G. Kahn and A. Galloni, "Fashion's China Syndrome," *Wall Street Journal* (16 June 2003): B1, B5.

88. G. A. Fowler and J. Qin, "China's Yuletide Revolution," *Wall Street Journal* (22 December 2005): B1, B3; C. Dougherty, "Exporting Christmas," *Wall Street Journal* (23 December 2006): P1, P4.

89. "World Wire: French Protest Hits Euro Disney," *Wall Street Journal* (20 September 1993): A10.

90. G. L. White, "Satellite Radio Is Ready, but Cars That Can Accommodate It Aren't," *Wall Street Journal* (18 May 2001): B1.

91. Wright et al., *Strategic Management*.

92. N. Wingfield, "Napster Boy, Interrupted," *Wall Street Journal* (1 October 2002): B1, B3.

93. G. McWilliams, "Radio Goes Digital," *Wall Street Journal* (6 October 2004): D1, D11.

94. E. Ramstad, "I Want MY Flat T.V. Now!" *Wall Street Journal* (27 May 2004): B1, B4.

95. J. Adamy, "High-pressure Process Helps Keep Food Bacteria-free," *Wall Street Journal* (17 February 2005): B1, B7.

96. J. Pereira, "Spying on the Sales Floor," *Wall Street Journal* (21 December 2004): B1, B4.

97. M. Higgins, "Honest, the Check Is in the E-Mail," *Wall Street Journal* (4 September 2002): D1, D4.

98. N. Harris and S. Carey, "Delta Ends Commissions for Most Travel Agents," *Wall Street Journal Interactive Edition* (15 March 2002); J. Costello, "Travel Agents Blast Decision to Cut Commissions in U.S.," *Wall Street Journal Interactive Edition* (25 March 2002).

99. M. Garrahan, "Big Hotels Challenge Travel Websites," *Financial Times* (19 March 2004): 31.

100. Internetworldstats.com, "Internet Usage Statistics: The Big Picture," accessed June 14, 2007, http://www.internetworld-stats.com/stats.htm.

101. Comscore.com, "ComScore Networks Reports Total Non-Travel E-Commerce Spending Reaches $102 Billion in 2006; up 24 Percent Versus 2005," accessed June 14, 2007, http://www.comscore.com/press/release.asp?press=1166; Nua Internet Surveys, "Online Retail Spending to Soar in the U.S.," *Web Metro News & Internet Statistics*, accessed January 15, 2003, www.webmetro.com.

102. J. Spencer, "Virtual Phone Reps Replace the Old Touch-Tone Menus; Making Claire Less Irritating," *Wall Street Journal* (21 January 2002): D1, D4.

103. J. Ball, "Global Auto Makers Are Racing to Inject Diesel Into Mainstream," *Wall Street Journal* (28 July 2003): A1, A6.

104. B. Schofield, "Building-and-Rebuilding—A Global Company," *The McKinsey Quarterly* 2 (1994): 37–45; R. B. Reich, *The Next American Frontier* (New York: Times Books, 1983).

105. A. R. Negandhi, "Multinational Corporations and Host Governments' Relationships: Comparative Study of Conflict and Conflicting Issues," *Human Relations* 33 (1980): 534–535.

106. J. Angwin and J. Hagan, "As Market Shifts, Newspapers Try to Lure New, Young Readers," *Wall Street Journal* (22 March 2006): A1, A14.

107. K. Kumar, R. Subramanian, and K. Strandholm, "Competitive Strategy, Environmental Scanning, and Performance: A Context Specific Analysis of Their Relationship," *International Journal of Commerce & Management* 11 (2001): 1–33.

108. J. R. Groom and F. David, "Competitive Intelligence Activity among Small Firms," *SAM Advanced Management Journal* 66(1) (2001): 12–29.

109. C. Rohwedder, "No. 1 Retailer in Britain Uses 'Clubcard' to Thwart Wal-Mart," *Wall Street Journal* (6 June 2006): A1, A16.

110. D. F. Jennings and J. R. Lumpkin, "Insights between Environmental Scanning Activities and Porter's Generic Strategies: An Empirical Analysis," *Journal of Management* 18 (1992): 791–803.

111. K. J. Delaney, "Hand-Held Device for DVD Movies Raises Legal Issues," *Wall Street Journal* (7 January 2004): B1, B3.

112. J. Flint, "HBO's Next Business Model," *Wall Street Journal* (5 January 2004): B1, B6.

113. G. Kahn, "Chinese Puzzle: Spotty Consumer Data," *Wall Street Journal* (15 October 2003): B1, B10.

R E A D I N G   4 - 1

Insight from *strategy+business*

It is important for all firms to understand a key social force—how potential buyers make purchase decisions. Hirsh and associates examine the process by which cars are evaluated and purchased. They argue that the perceived value and performance levels associated with a brand ultimately govern the purchase decision.

Reality Is Perception: The Truth about Car Brands

Expensive advertising cannot compensate for weak brands and undifferentiated products.

By Evan Hirsh, Steve Hedlund, and Mark Schweizer

A strong car brand can create significant value in the automotive industry. The price consumers expect to pay for otherwise identical luxury vehicles can vary as much as $4,000, depending on the car's brand. For mass-market cars, brand helps determine which products a consumer considers buying. Furthermore, superior brands extend their halo across every model of vehicle within the brand. It's no surprise that most auto manufacturers make brand positioning and development a key item on their marketing agenda.

Yet despite intense interest in their power, automotive brands remain relatively poorly understood. Why do car brands have such value in a business that is clearly product driven? How do brands acquire their value? What causes their value to wax or wane over time?

Because of the prominent role that brand positioning and development play in many auto manufacturers' business strategies, we conducted extensive research and analysis to better understand how consumers think about car brands. Our analysis uses standard statistical techniques to distill multiple brand image attributes (drawn from Allison-Fisher International LLC surveys of car buyers) into a small set of underlying factors, which provide valuable insights into consumer brand perceptions. (See "Research Methodology," section at the end of the reading.)

Our research shows that consumers have a simple yet sophisticated understanding of what differentiates car brands. Notwithstanding automakers' attempts to distinguish their brands on the basis of lifestyle or emotional imagery, consumers evaluate brands in terms of their earned reputation for product excellence relative to their total ownership cost. Consumers' perceptions are based on their accumulated direct and indirect experience with the products that constitute those brands.

These perceptions are obviously not perfect. Some brands' reputations exceed or fall short of their demonstrable product attributes. But, as a rule, consumers' beliefs are accurate, stable, and relatively immune to manipulation. In contrast to the situation with other consumer goods, in which equity is created substantially through advertising, automotive brand perceptions change primarily through consistent and sustained changes in the underlying product portfolio.

Within this overarching conclusion, we were able to identify five central insights that are critical to understanding how, and to what extent, manufacturers can enhance and leverage the value of their brands.

1. **Virtually all of the difference in how consumers perceive competing brands can be explained by their relative performance against two holistic measures: product excellence and cost.**

Traditionally, car manufacturers have tried to measure their brands across a large number of image attributes, hoping to develop additional insights about brand differentiation. However, consumer perceptions of a brand's reputation are generally consistent across different measures of value. For example, consumers believe that manufacturers whose car lines have a reputation for luxury and prestige tend to produce cars that excel in many other areas, such as ride, handling, safety, and reliability. In fact, a brand's score on any one attribute tends to be so highly correlated with its score on another attribute that these scores can be integrated into one measure that represents a car line's propensity to create excellent products.

Consumers also have a sophisticated understanding of product cost. They recognize that vehicles differ not only in their initial purchase price, but also in their expected maintenance and operating costs, as well as their ultimate resale value. Together, these different types of expenditures determine the total cost to the consumer over the ownership cycle. As with the product excellence dimension, the various attributes that determine a brand's expected ownership costs can be integrated into a single measure of product cost.

These two holistic measures, product excellence and cost of ownership, account for 91 percent of the difference in how consumers perceive automotive brands. (See Exhibit 1.) In fact, these two holistic measures are comprehensive enough to predict the consumers' overall opinion of the brand with an extremely high degree of accuracy.

Of the remaining variation in consumer perceptions, roughly half (or 5 percent) is due to specific attributes such as "sporty." These secondary attributes are not highly correlated with other attributes and cannot be included in the holistic measure of product excellence. With the exception of a few outliers (for example, BMW, whose reputation rests in part on its sportiness), most brands tend to be relatively undifferentiated along these secondary attributes.

2. Consumers are not only elegantly simple in their view of automotive brands, they are acutely rational as well.

For the average consumer, a new car is second only to a new home in the size of the transaction, the length of the ownership cycle, and the potential to reaffirm and communicate an individual's sense of self-worth. Consequently, consumers spend a substantial amount of time evaluating their alternatives. In addition to their own firsthand experience, they consult a number of sources, from the anecdotal evidence of friends and family, to independent reviews by magazines, industry groups, and government agencies, to the manufacturers' marketing communications, including brochures, measured media, and owner events.

It's true that some brand reputations, particularly in the mass-market segment, don't keep lockstep pace with actual changes in the products. But in general, consumers are well informed, and their opinions accurately reflect the accumulated performance of the products that are the physical embodiment of those brands. For example, the cost-of-ownership brand measure is highly correlated with actual cost of ownership. Similarly, consumers' perceptions of a brand's reputation for durability, reliability, and workmanship (which are key constituents of the holistic product excellence measure) are highly correlated with the actual dependability of that brand's vehicles.

EXHIBIT 1   **Average Performance of Car Brands***

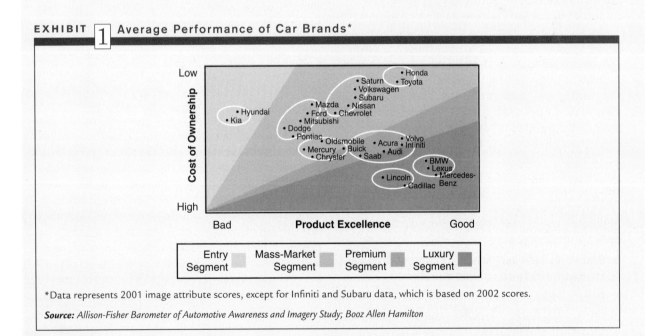

*Data represents 2001 image attribute scores, except for Infiniti and Subaru data, which is based on 2002 scores.

Source: *Allison-Fisher Barometer of Automotive Awareness and Imagery Study; Booz Allen Hamilton*

3. The relative magnitude of product excellence and low cost of ownership determines a brand's value proposition in the marketplace.

Consumers recognize that, in general, better products cost more. Consumers self-select an automotive segment on the basis of which attribute (cost of ownership or product excellence) they value more. Within a consumer's chosen segment, brands that deliver more of both attributes provide superior value to the consumer.

As a result, brands can differentiate themselves in two fundamental ways: by providing a different proportion of product excellence to cost of ownership (i.e., segment selection); and by providing more or less performance across both attributes (within the boundaries of the chosen segment). The result is a production function that's a classic trade-off between product excellence and cost of ownership, with the frontier defined by brands providing the most value in each segment.

It is possible to group brands using statistical clustering techniques, so that grouping definitions minimize the differences within clusters and maximize the differences between clusters. These clusters represent groupings of brands that consumers believe offer comparable *amounts* of product excellence and low cost of ownership. Consumers perceive that brands in a cluster offer a value proposition similar to those of other brands in the same cluster and materially different from those in different clusters.

This is not to argue that brands within the same cluster are identical. Brands can partially differentiate themselves on the basis of secondary attributes. BMW has carved a niche within the luxury segment based on its image as the "ultimate driving machine" that offers superior acceleration, turning, and handling. Likewise, Subaru has partially differentiated its reputation within the mass-market segment on the basis of the security of all-wheel drive.

Channel performance (e.g., dealership experience and product availability) can also be used to differentiate a brand. Saturn stands out for having good customer service and providing a pleasant buying experience. However, the majority of brands are not meaningfully differentiated on any basis other than product excellence and cost of ownership.

4. Brands in crowded, weakly positioned clusters tend to suffer from eroding margins.

Brands positioned closer to the lower left-hand corner of Exhibit 1 (i.e., those with higher cost of ownership and lower product excellence) offer less value to consumers.

Such brands naturally tend to achieve lower purchase consideration and hence volume. A large number of such brands within the mass-market segment are competitively disadvantaged relative to other brands within the same segment and relative to brands in neighboring segments, as Exhibit 1 shows.

For vehicle manufacturers with large capital investments, this situation is untenable. They must seek to improve at least one of the two holistic brand measures for their brands. Because improvement of a brand's product excellence is difficult to accomplish across an entire product portfolio and generally requires up to a decade, the only way for brands to improve their positioning quickly is to lower product prices and offer customers better cost of ownership.

By contrast, Honda and Toyota have clearly distanced themselves from the rest of the mass-market segment. In the consumer's mind, Honda and Toyota represent a combination of product excellence and cost of ownership that so far surpasses all other competitors that they operate along a different trade-off curve. While not yet in the same league, several other brands, such as Volkswagen, Saturn, and Subaru, have also separated themselves from the rest of the pack.

5. Brand positions tend to change relatively little over time.

Consumer perceptions are shaped in large part through accumulated product experience, both firsthand and indirect. Consumers also use a large number of objective sources of information to supplement their direct product experience (e.g., word of mouth, product reviews, and safety ratings). As a result, the perception-forming process is long and relatively immune to simple manipulation by the manufacturer, in contrast with most consumer goods, whose brand equity is created substantially through advertising.

Although marketing communications certainly play an important role in what consumers think, the only way to sustain meaningful change in automotive brand perceptions is with ongoing, consistent changes in the underlying product experience. Furthermore, since brand value is a function of performance relative to the brand's competition, significantly altering brand perceptions requires a manufacturer to systematically improve its entire product range faster than its competitors do.

Over the past two decades, most manufacturers have made concerted efforts to improve product quality, develop new features, and reduce costs. They have used various techniques, such as computer-aided design, system outsourcing, and component reuse, to speed up the product development cycle, reducing the time it takes to respond to competitors' innovations. As a result, it is increasingly difficult for manufacturers to improve their products continuously at a rate that outpaces the market.

Doing so requires a coordinated strategy and a concerted effort. In the late 1990s, Volkswagen deployed a steady stream of new products to significantly shift consumer perceptions of its brand. VW leveraged product and process technologies that had been developed for Audi in such areas as engine packaging, powertrain, chassis tuning, advanced material forming, and tight tolerance assembly. The result was a slate of products, including the Jetta, Passat, and New Beetle, that offered superior ride, handling, styling, and assembly quality at a reasonable cost. Furthermore, the migration of Audi process and product technologies to VW did not erode consumers' perceptions of the Audi brand. However, recent reports of cross-model quality problems (e.g., ignition coil faults) could serve as the reversal point of VW's recent brand improvement journey.

Like VW, the Hyundai and Kia brands have benefited from a sustained flow of new products that offer significantly improved quality, attractiveness, edgy styling (at times), and extremely low cost of ownership due to low sticker prices and extended warranty coverage. The resulting value proposition has not only increased these brands' unit volume, but also has radically changed consumers' perceptions of the brands. What is stunning is how much the Korean brands have improved in such a short time, especially in comparison with how long it took Toyota and Honda to shake their reputation for producing tin cans. If the Korean brands continue to improve their reputation for product excellence while maintaining their cost of ownership, they could leapfrog the Big Three mass market brands to join the cluster currently defined by VW, Nissan, and Saturn.

In contrast, the value of Saturn's brand has been deteriorating. Saturn was initially able to transfer consumers' satisfaction with the dealer experience to the product. Although Saturn still remains differentiated on the basis of its channel performance, the product has failed to satisfy consumers' expectations for quality, and the brand as a whole has experienced significant erosion.

Like Saturn, the Buick, Oldsmobile, and Mercury brands demonstrate the impact that a consistently weak product line has on brand value. In their heyday, Buick

and Oldsmobile represented the quintessential premium brands – steps above Chevrolet and only a notch or two below Cadillac. Several generations of product that were rebadged versions of mass-market vehicles, and the growth in market penetration of alternatives such as Volvo and, more recently, Audi, undermined the value position of the Buick, Oldsmobile, and Mercury brands.

Mercedes-Benz and BMW have both delivered significant improvements in cost of ownership over the past decade. In part, this was caused by direct pricing pressure from Japanese luxury brands (most notably Lexus). However, we believe a large portion of the difference is due to a change in product mix to include more entry-level luxury vehicles (e.g., BMW's 3 series and Mercedes's C-class). As these brands have shifted their center of mass toward "entry luxury," so has consumer opinion shifted.

Marketer's Checklist

Few manufacturers have the resources required to implement such a sweeping overhaul of their product portfolio. Consequently, brand positions tend to change relatively little over time. Furthermore, it is far easier to erode brand equity than it is to build brand equity. Product missteps, gaps in the product pipeline, and intentional efforts to shift a brand's customer base can lead to significant deterioration in brand value.

The five findings detailed above have profound implications for most manufacturers.

- Tangible product differentiation is both critical to success and difficult to maintain on a sustained basis. A key focus of the marketing function should be to rigorously understand consumers' preferences, unmet needs, and willingness to pay, in order to maximize the "hit rate" on innovative products.
- Minimizing cost of ownership (both up-front acquisition cost and long-term ownership cost) within the segment boundary is critical. The marketing function must take an active role in balancing the drive toward lower cost of ownership with the consumer value created through innovative features and options.
- Lifestyle and emotional imagery cannot compensate for weak brands and undifferentiated products. Consumers may acknowledge a brand's "personality," but the aspects of the brand that drive consumer shopping behavior are promises that the brand represents for product excellence and cost of ownership. Image advertising and lifestyle and event marketing may help to accelerate consumers' understanding of the brand, but it cannot fundamentally change the promise. Consequently, the

number of resources applied toward lifestyle and image advertising should be scrutinized for appropriateness and effectiveness.

- For mass-market vehicles, incentives are a symptom of a weak brand—not the cause. In the absence of a strong brand, price is the only plausible way to affect near-term demand. Hence, curtailing incentives in an effort to "build brand" is not likely an economically viable option.

Many manufacturers have made brand positioning and development a key item on their marketing agenda. Yet brands are not the product of manufacturers' marketing efforts. Instead, consumers base their understanding of an automotive brand's value on their accumulated experience with that brand's products. If you want to change the brand, change the products—for the better.

Research Methodology

Our research is based on data from the Allison-Fisher Barometer of Automotive Awareness and Imagery Study (the primary source is the "Car Makes" study, which is supplemented with the "Light Vehicle" study to include Saab and Infiniti). The research and conclusions are specifically for cars. Allison-Fisher surveys car buyers on their attitudes, focusing on 24 specific attributes: excellent handling, excellent ride, excellent workmanship, good looking, good warranty program, good customer service, good safety for occupants, high trade-in value, prestigious, luxurious, really dependable, sporty, technically advanced, fun to drive, excellent acceleration, lasts a long time, name you can trust, viewed as a leader, satisfying sales experience, trend-setting vehicles, economical to operate, excellent gas mileage, good value for the money, reasonably priced.

We employed standard statistical analysis (factor analysis) to identify which of these image attributes correlate with each other and to distill the 24 attributes down to a small set of underlying, uncorrelated factors, or "meta-attributes." Attributes with a 60 percent correlation were considered part of the same factor. Two

underlying meta-attributes emerged from this distillation: product excellence and cost of ownership.

In order to further validate the dual meta-attribute model, we employed standard regression analysis techniques to demonstrate the meta-attributes' ability to predict brand opinion. The results confirmed the model and demonstrate very strong predictive power ($R^2 = 96\%$) for the model.

After identifying the two factors and determining each brand's scores on the two meta-attributes, we detected clusters of brands. These clusters not only match our intuition of how the automotive market is segmented, but are statistically valid (based on cluster analysis, another standard statistical technique).

To study how brands have changed over time, we looked at historical image attribute data, limiting ourselves to the subset of image attributes that were consistently available across the entire past decade. The original analyses (factor analysis and clustering) were repeated on this subset of image attributes and conducted on the full decade-long set of data. Brand position evolution was then studied to see which brands showed both significant (i.e., large magnitude relative to others) and consistent (i.e., same year-to-year trend) movement.

Evan Hirsh (hirsh_evan@bah.com) is a vice present of Booz Allen Hamilton based in Cleveland. He specializes in strategic marketing, business unit strategy, and performance improvement for consumer and industrial companies. Mr. Hirsh is coauthor, with Steven Wheeler, of Channel Champions: How Leading Companies Build New Strategies to Serve Customers (strategy+business/Jossey-Bass, 1999)

Steve Hedlund (shedlund@moen.com) is a vice president of strategic planning and new business development for Fortune Brands Inc. Previously, he was a principal with Booz Allen Hamilton, focusing on organizational and strategy-based transformation for automotive, aerospace, and industrial companies.

Mark Schweizer (schweizer_mark@bah.com) is a senior associate in Booz Allen Hamilton's Cleveland office. He focuses on product, sales, and marketing strategy for automotive OEMs and suppliers.

The Organization

5

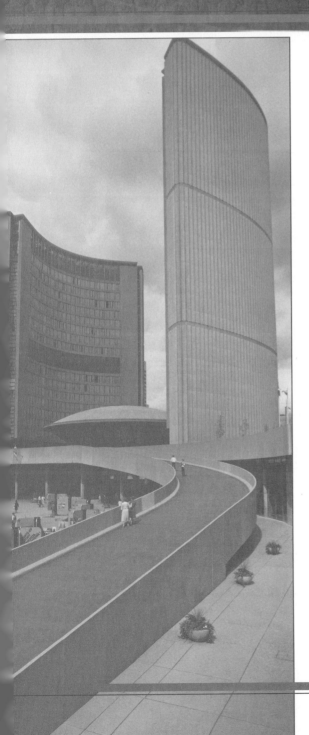

Whereas previous chapters discussed the external analysis phase of the strategic management process, this chapter begins to consider internal factors. This shift from the industry level to the organizational level reflects a change in focus from similarities, or factors that tend to affect all of an industry's organizations in a like manner, to differences, or issues specific to a particular firm in an industry. This shift also relates to theoretical perspectives discussed in Chapter 1, marking a movement from an industrial organization (IO) perspective to a resource-based view of the firm.

Crafting a strategy for an organization whose purpose and resources are not well understood by its members is a difficult task, however. This chapter discusses the role that an organization's unique mission and resources, as well as social responsibility and ethics, play in the strategic management process.

5-1 Organizational Direction: Mission, Goals, and Objectives

Mission

The reason for an organization's existence. The mission statement is a broadly defined but enduring statement of purpose that identifies the scope of an organization's operations and its offerings to the various stakeholders.

Goals

Desired general ends toward which efforts are directed.

Objectives

Specific, verifiable, and often quantified versions of a goal.

Several terms are commonly used to delineate the direction of the organization. The **mission** is the reason for the firm's existence and is the broadest of these terms. The organization's **goals** represent the desired general ends toward which efforts are directed. **Objectives** are specific and often quantified versions of goals. Unlike goals, objectives are verifiable and specific, and are developed so that management can measure performance. Without verifiability and specificity, objectives will not provide a clear direction for strategy.

For example, the mission of an Internet Service Provider (ISP) might be "to provide high-quality, reliable Internet access to the southeastern United States at a profit." Management may establish a goal "to expand the size of the firm through acquisition of small ISPs." From this goal, specific objectives may be derived, such as "to increase access numbers by 20 percent each year for the next five years." As another example, management's goal may be "to be known as the innovative leader in the industry." On the basis of this goal, one of the specific objectives may be "to have 30 percent of sales each year come from new products developed during the preceding three years."

5-1a Global Influences on Mission

An organization's mission may be closely intertwined with international operations in several ways. A firm may need inputs from abroad or sell a large percentage of its products to global customers. Consider, for example, that virtually all of Japan's industries would grind to a halt if imports of raw materials from other nations ceased, because Japan is a small island nation and its natural resources are quite limited.

Comparative Advantage

The idea that certain products may be produced more cheaply or at a higher quality in particular countries, due to advantages in labor costs or technology

Organizational mission and international involvement are also connected through the economic concept of **comparative advantage**, the idea that certain products may be produced more cheaply or at a higher quality in particular countries due to advantages in labor costs or technology. Chinese manufacturers, for example, have enjoyed some of the lowest global labor rates for unskilled or semiskilled production in recent years. As skills rise in the rapidly emerging nation, some companies have succeeded in extending this comparative advantage to technical skill areas as well. The annual salary for successful engineers in China rose to around $15,000 in 2007, a level well below their comparably skilled counterparts in other parts of the world.[1]

Global involvement may also provide advantages to the firm not directly related to costs. For political reasons, a firm often needs to establish operations in other countries, especially if a substantial proportion of sales is derived abroad. Doing so can also provide managers with a critical understanding of local markets. For example, Ford operates plants in western Europe, where manufacturing has helped Ford's engineers design windshield wipers for cars engaged in high-speed driving on the German autobahns.[2]

Source: Ablestock.com

5-1b Goals and Stakeholders

At first glance, establishing a mission, goals, and objectives for a firm appears to be fairly simple; however, because stakeholders have different perspectives on the purpose of the firm, this task can become quite complex. **Stakeholders** are individuals or groups who are affected by or can influence an organization's operations. Firm stakeholders include such groups as shareholders, members of the board of directors, managers, employees, suppliers, creditors, and customers (see Table 5-1). As owners, shareholders traditionally represent the dominant group of stakeholders. Top managers, too, should be concerned not only with the shareholders' primary objective of profits, but also with those of other stakeholders.[3] Ideally, the mission, goals, and objectives should emphasize goals of the shareholders, and balance the pressures from other stakeholders.[4]

It is not difficult to see how stakeholder goals can conflict with one another. For example, shareholders are generally interested in maximum profitability, whereas creditors are more concerned with long-term survival so that their loans will be repaid. Meanwhile, customers desire the lowest possible prices, even if offering them would result in losses for the firm. Hence, top management faces the difficult task of attempting to reconcile these differences while pursuing its own set of goals, which typically includes quality of work life and career advancement.

Stakeholders

Individuals or groups who are affected by or can influence an organization's operations.

TABLE **5-1** Suggested Goals of Stakeholders

Stakeholders	Goals
Customers	The company should provide high-quality products and services at the most reasonable prices possible.
General public	The company should provide goods and services with minimum environmental costs, increase employment opportunities, and contribute to social and charitable causes.
Suppliers	The company should establish long-term relationships with suppliers and purchase from them at prices that allow the suppliers to remain profitable.
Employees	The company should provide good working conditions, equitable compensation, and opportunities for advancement.
Creditors	The company should maintain a healthy financial posture and a policy of on-time payment of debt.
Shareholders	The company should produce a higher-than-average return on equity.
Board of directors	Current directors should be retained and shielded from a legal liability.
Managers	The company should allow managers to benefit financially from the growth and success of the company.

This balancing act is evident when one considers the clash that can occur when top management goals are pitted against those of the board of directors. Although both groups are primarily accountable to the owners of the corporation, top management is responsible for generating financial returns and the board of directors is charged with oversight of the firm's management. Some have argued, however, that this traditional *shareholder-driven* perspective is too narrow, and that financial returns are actually maximized when a *customer-driven* perspective is adopted, a view that is consistent with the marketing concept.[5] Consumer advocate and 2000 U.S. presidential candidate Ralph Nader has argued for more than thirty years that large corporations must be more responsive to customers' needs.[6]

Firms create value for various parties, including employees through wages and salaries, shareholders through profits, customers through value derived from goods and services, and even governments through taxes. Firms that seek to maximize the value delivered to any single stakeholder at the expense of those of other groups can jeopardize their long-term survival and profitability.[7] For example, a firm that emphasizes the financial interests of shareholders over the monetary needs of employees can alienate employees, threatening shareholder returns in the long run. Likewise, establishing long-term relationships with suppliers may restrict the firm's ability to remain flexible and offer innovative products to customers. Top management is charged with the task of resolving opposing stakeholder demands, recognizing that the firm must be managed to balance the demands of various stakeholder groups for the long-term benefit of the corporation as a whole.[8]

5-2 Social Responsibility

An organization's direction is governed in part by its value system. An organization's values can be seen through its stance on service to society, as well as its support for high ethical standards among its managers. These factors are discussed in this section.

Social Responsibility

The expectation that business firms should serve both society and the financial interests of shareholders.

Social responsibility refers to the expectation that business firms should serve both society and the financial interests of the shareholders. A firm's stance on social responsibility can be a critical factor in making strategic decisions. If social responsibility is not considered, decisions may be aimed only at profit or other narrow objectives without concern for balancing social objectives that the firm might embody. The degree to which social responsibility is relevant in strategic decision making is widely debated, however.

From an economic perspective, businesses have always been expected to provide employment for individuals and meet consumer needs within legal constraints. Today, however, society also expects firms to help preserve the environment, to sell safe products, to treat their employees equitably, and to be truthful with their customers.[9] In some cases, firms are even expected to provide training to unemployed workers, contribute to education and the arts, and help revitalize urban areas. Firms such as Home Depot, Coca-Cola, UPS, and Johnson & Johnson recently earned high marks for social responsibility, whereas Bridgestone and Philip Morris were at the bottom of the list.[10] Figure 5-1 illustrates the approach to social responsibility at Johnson & Johnson, a firm whose corporate reputation ranked number one in 2002 and 2003 in the Harris Interactive survey.[11]

Many economists, including such notables as Adam Smith and Milton Friedman, have argued that social responsibility should not be part of management's

FIGURE 5-1 Johnson & Johnson Credo

Our Credo

We believe our first responsibility is to the doctors, nurses, and patients,
to mothers and fathers and all others who use our products and services.
In meeting their needs everything we do must be of high quality.
We must constantly strive to reduce our costs
in order to maintain reasonable prices.
Customers' orders must be serviced promptly and accurately.
Our suppliers and distributors must have an opportunity
to make a fair profit.

We are responsible to our employees,
the men and women who work with us throughout the world.
Everyone must be considered as an individual.
We must respect their dignity and recognize their merit.
They must have a sense of security in their jobs,
Compensation must be fair and adequate,
and working conditions clean, orderly, and safe.
We must be mindful of ways to help our employees fulfill
their family responsibilities.

Employees must feel free to make suggestions and complaints.
There must be equal opportunity for employment, development,
and advancement for those qualified.
We must provide competent management,
and their actions must be just and ethical.

We are responsible to the communities in which we live and work
and to the world community as well.
We must be good citizens—support good works and charities
and bear our fair share of taxes.
We must encourage civic improvements and better health
and education.
We must maintain in good order
the property we are privileged to use,
protecting the environment and natural resources.

Our final responsibility is to our stockholders.
Business must make a sound profit.
We must experiment with new ideas.
Research must be carried on, innovative programs developed and
mistakes paid for.
New equipment must be purchased, new facilities provided
and new products launched.
Reserves must be created to provide for adverse times.
When we operate according to these principles,
the stockholders should realize a fair return.

Johnson & Johnson

Source: *Reprinted by permission of Johnson & Johnson*

decision-making process. Friedman has maintained that business functions best when it concentrates on maximizing returns by producing goods and services within society's legal restrictions. According to Friedman, corporations should be concerned only with the legal pursuit of profit, while shareholders are free to pursue other worthy goals as they individually see fit. Even if one accepts Friedman's argument, firms should act in a socially responsible manner for two primary reasons.

First, acting responsibly can reduce the likelihood of more costly government regulation. Historically, regulations over business operations often were enacted because certain firms refused to act responsibly. Had some organizations not damaged the environment, sold unsafe products, or engaged in discrimination or misleading advertising, legislation in these areas would not have been necessary. Government regulation is always possible when companies operate in a manner contrary to society's interests, even if doing so is clearly within the legal jurisdiction of the firm.

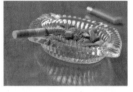

Source: Ablestock.com

Second, stakeholders affected by a firm's social responsibility stance—most notably customers—are also those who must choose whether to transact business with the firm. Prospective customers have become more interested in learning about a company's social and philanthropic activities before making purchase decisions. Those who believe a firm is not socially responsible may take their business elsewhere. The social responsibility debate aside, many executives—especially those in large firms—have concluded that their organizations must at the minimum *appear* to be socially responsible or face the wrath of angry consumers. As such, they are greatly concerned about both the actual behavior of the firm and how it is perceived. Evidence suggests that consumers want the firms that produce the products and services they buy not only to support public initiatives, but also to uphold the same values in terms of the day-to-day decisions of running the company.[12] By definition, a firm that is socially responsible is one that is able to generate both profits and societal benefits; but exactly what is good for society is not always clear.[13] For example, society's demands for high employment and the production of desired goods and services must be balanced against the pollution and industrial wastes that may be generated by manufacturing operations. The decisions made to balance these concerns, however, can be quite difficult to make (see Strategy at Work 5-1).

Source: Ablestock.com

Social responsibility is a prominent issue in some industries. Pharmaceutical manufacturers, for example, spend billions of dollars to develop drugs for treating a wide range of ailments. The costs of the drugs, however, can determine the extent to which patients will benefit from them. In the United Kingdom, government officials called on physicians to stop prescribing various drugs for Alzheimer's disease, acknowledging their benefits but arguing that they do not justify the cost.[14] The same

---

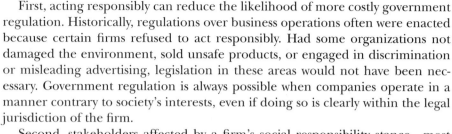

S T R A T E G Y   A T   W O R K   5 - 1

GMAbility: Social Responsibility in Action

The public emphasis that General Motors places on social responsibility is quite noteworthy. The company's "GMAbility" initiative (www.gm.com/company/gmability) highlights a number of GM activities. For example, according to its 2001 sustainability report, GM has taken action to reduce emissions and water and energy consumption, while increasing its community support and number of partnerships. GM is also active in a variety of recycling, education, hazardous waste collection, and pollution prevention programs.

GM has partnered with The Nature Conservancy, an international environmental organization. GM spends $1 million annually to assist in the preservation of land and water systems in North America, Latin America, the Caribbean, and the Asia/Pacific region.

GM also participates in a variety of philanthropic activities, such as violence reduction programs in schools, Special Olympics, and community development. For example, GM partnered with Sun Microsystems and EDS to contribute more than $211 million in computer-aided design, manufacturing, and engineering (CAD/CAM/CAE) software, hardware, and training to Virginia Tech.

Sources: R. Alsop, "Perils of Corporate Philanthropy," Wall Street Journal, 16 January 2002, B1, B4; General Motors, www.gm.com/company/gmability, accessed March 14, 2002.

realities can be true for medical procedures, especially in emerging economies. The pay-as-you-go system for medical treatment in China ultimately can deny costly life-saving treatment for the majority of its citizens who lack health insurance.[15]

In some instances, society's expectations of an organization may increase as the firm grows. For example, various constituencies have charged Wal-Mart with socially irresponsible behavior in recent years. Critics allege that the mega-retailer often competes unfairly, does not always follow fair hiring and promotion practices, and even contributes to local economic problems by abandoning strip-mall locations when larger stores are constructed. In 2004, CEO Lee Scott signaled a more assertive approach to countering such claims. As Scott put it, "When we're wrong, we change, so our detractors don't have a foothold in attacking us. Where we are right, we will fight and take each issue to the wall."[16]

A broader notion of social responsibility, **sustainable strategic management (SSM)**, has received increased attention in recent years. SSM refers to the strategies and related activities that promote superior performance from *both* market and environmental perspectives. Hence, an ideal strategy should seek market sustainability by meeting buyer demands and environmental sustainability by proactively managing finite resources. Organizations able to meet this challenge are more likely to perform well and benefit society over the long term.

> **Sustainable Strategic Management (SSM)**
>
> Strategies and related activities that promote superior performance from both market and environmental perspectives.

5-3 Managerial Ethics

Although social responsibility and managerial ethics are often grouped together in the popular business press, the terms are not synonymous. Whereas social responsibility considers the firm's ability to address issues beyond the financial concerns of the shareholders, **managerial ethics** refers to an individual's responsibility to make business decisions that are legal, honest, moral, and fair. Strategic decisions should not require managers or other employees to perform activities inconsistent with their ethical convictions concerning the role that they may be expected to play in firm activities (see Strategy at Work 5-2). The ethics test in Figure 5-2 provides an assessment of employees' ethics.

> **Managerial Ethics**
>
> An individual's responsibility to make business decisions that are legal, honest, moral, and fair.

S T R A T E G Y   A T   W O R K   5 - 2

Good Neighbor or Good Business?

After creating considerable destruction in the Caribbean, Hurricane Ivan hammered the Gulf Coast of the United States in September 2004. Because meteorologists had forecast the magnitude of the storm several days prior, many Americans soon to be affected turned to rivals Lowe's and Home Depot for plywood to board up their homes, for power generators, and for other supplies. Both retailers stepped into high gear to meet consumer needs.

Neither chain raised prices amidst the storm preparation and most stores made valiant attempts to remain open as long as possible. In one respect, Home Depot and Lowe's went the extra mile to assist customers in a crisis. In reality, however, remaining open extra hours was simply good business and helped to minimize local inventories that could be damaged if the stores were devastated by the storm.

Indeed, the two rivals were well aware of possible long-term effects that could stem from their ability to help customers prepare for the storm. As Home Depot's eastern division president, Tom Taylor, put it, "They'll remember who got them stuff. They'll remember who stayed open. The better job we can do during a hurricane, [the more] we can gain market share [after the storm]."

Could the Lowe's and Home Depot actions be described as good neighbor or good business? The answer is probably both.

Sources: D. Morse, "Competing in a Crisis," Wall Street Journal, *16 September 2004, B4, B5.*

FIGURE 5-2   Employee Ethics Test

Indicate the degree to which you agree or disagree with each statement.

Strongly Disagree	-0-	-1-	-2-	-3-	Strongly Agree

	-0-	-1-	-2-	-3-
1. Employees should not expect to inform on their peers for wrongdoings.	☐	☐	☐	☐
2. There are times when a manager must overlook contract and safety violations in order to get on with the job.	☐	☐	☐	☐
3. It is not always possible to keep accurate expense account records; therefore, it is sometimes necessary to give approximate figures.	☐	☐	☐	☐
4. There are times when it is necessary to withhold embarrassing information from one's superior.	☐	☐	☐	☐
5. We should do what our managers suggest, though we may have doubts about it being the right thing to do.	☐	☐	☐	☐
6. It is sometimes necessary to conduct personal business on company time.	☐	☐	☐	☐
7. Sometimes it is good psychology to set goals somewhat above normal if it will help to obtain a greater effort from the sales force.	☐	☐	☐	☐
8. I would quote a "hopeful" shipping date in order to get an order.	☐	☐	☐	☐
9. It is proper to use the company 800 line for personal calls as long as it's not in company use.	☐	☐	☐	☐
10. Management must be goal oriented; therefore, the end justifies the means.	☐	☐	☐	☐
11. If it takes heavy entertainment and twisting a bit of company policy to win a large contract, I would authorize it.	☐	☐	☐	☐
12. Exceptions to company policy and procedures are a way of life.	☐	☐	☐	☐
13. Inventory controls should be designed to report "underages" rather than "overages" in goods received.	☐	☐	☐	☐
14. Occasional use of the company's copier for personal or community activities is acceptable.	☐	☐	☐	☐
15. Taking home company property (pens, tape, paper, etc.) for personal use is an accepted fringe benefit.	☐	☐	☐	☐

If your score is:

0	Prepare for canonization ceremony
1–5	Bishop material
6–10	High ethical values
11–15	Good ethical values
16–25	Average ethical values
26–35	Need moral development
36–44	Slipping fast
45	Leave valuables with warden

The line between social responsibility and managerial ethics can be difficult to draw, as what may be considered by some to be socially irresponsible firm behavior may be a direct result of unethical managerial decision making. Nonetheless, while the debate over social responsibility continues, few would argue that managers should not behave ethically. When executives shun clear ethical principles, corporate scandal or even demise can follow (see Strategy at Work 5-3).

What is morally right or wrong continues to be a topic of debate, especially when firms operate across borders where ethical standards can vary considerably.

S T R A T E G Y   A T   W O R K   5 - 3

Ethical Concerns and the Corporate Scandals of 2001 and 2002

The period from mid-2001 to mid-2002 witnessed an unprecedented number of ethical allegations and corporate misdoings that jolted Americans' confidence in corporate America. In August 2002, *Forbes* published "The Corporate Scandal Sheet" in an effort to keep track of the dearth of ethical violations and allegations rampant at that time. The *Wall Street Journal* also followed in January 2003 with an extensive chronicle of events for 2002. In November 2001, Enron, once one of the world's largest electricity and natural gas traders, admitted overstating its earnings by $567 million between 1997 and 2001 and filed for Chapter 11 bankruptcy protection the following month. In another case, the astute craft and décor authority Martha Stewart sold a large number of her ImClone Systems shares one day before the company released damaging news about an experimental cancer drug, raising the specter of insider information and thus resulting in a conviction.

Although the deluge of news surrounding such scandals began to slowly subside in late 2002, public fervor concerning a perceived lack of corporate accountability and widespread corporate legerdemain has not. This fervor has been sparked further by press reports of executive prosecutions associated with these scandals several years later. U.S. governmental agencies have responded with new policies and procedures designed to foster a more complete disclosure of corporate financial doings and make it more difficult for executives to mislead investors about the performance of their firms. These actions notwithstanding, however, it is clear that a key part of the solution to this problem lies in a willingness of managers at all levels to commit to a sense of fair play and uphold ethical standards at a personal level.

Sources: R. Alsop, "Corporate Scandals Hit Home," Wall Street Journal, 19 February 2004, B1, B2; P. Patsuris, "The Corporate Scandal Sheet," Forbes, www.forbes.com/2002/07/25/account-ingtracker.html, accessed August 26, 2002; L. S. Egodigwe, J. C. Long, and N. Warfield, "A Year of Scandals and Sorrow," Wall Street Journal Interactive Edition, 2 January 2003; P. Behr, "Ailing Enron Files for Chapter 11 Bankruptcy Protection," Washington Post, 3 December 2001, A7; C. Gasparino and S. Craig, "Merrill Worker Casts Doubt on Stewart's Stop-Loss Pact," Wall Street Journal Interactive Edition, 24 June 2002.

In the United States, for example, bribes to government officials to secure favorable treatment would be considered unethical. In other countries—especially those with developing economies—small "cash tips" are an accepted means of transacting business and may even be considered an integral part of an underpaid government official's compensation.

Ethics is a key consideration, especially at top management levels. Selecting the right individual to serve as CEO can be a perilous task, especially when a leader departs abruptly. Although evaluating a person's professional qualifications is still important, personal characteristics are gaining prominence. Consider that Boeing's CEO Harry Stonecipher was dismissed in March 2005 after directors became aware of explicit e-mails to a female employee with whom he was having an affair. Events such as these have prompted directors to search for personal behavior that might disqualify them as leaders, including sexual harassment, drinking problems, or failing to file income taxes properly.[17]

Wal-Mart's Thomas Coughlin ended his twenty-seven-year stint with the firm in 2005. Originally appointed as director of loss prevention in 1978, Coughlin was promoted to director of human resources in 1983 and president of the Wal-Mart Stores division in 1999. In 2003, Coughlin was elected to Wal-Mart's board. He retired as an executive in January 2005 due to health reasons, but was forced to resign from the board two months later when a pattern of expense account abuses was uncovered. The investigation that uncovered the abuses began when

Coughlin asked a firm lieutenant to approve $2,000 in expense payments without providing any receipts.[18]

Ethical decisions are not always resolved easily and can even be observed differently at different times. In 1991, for example, the U.S. Food and Drug Administration (FDA) banned silicone breast implants in most instances, a decision that fueled the demise of many of its original marketers who lost billions of dollars in lawsuits alleging product flaws, breast cancer, and other serious health concerns. Dow Corning lost $3.2 billion in settlements and remained in bankruptcy protection from 1995 to 2004. Since that time, however, several major studies found no link between silicone implants and major diseases. In 2006, the FDA reapproved the sale of silicone implants. Hence, what was originally termed as "unethical" behavior by Dow Corning is once again being touted as an acceptable product.[19]

What constitutes ethical behavior can be viewed in a number of ways, six of which are discussed here. The **utilitarian view of ethics** suggests that anticipated outcomes and consequences should be the only considerations when evaluating an ethical dilemma. The primary shortcoming associated with this approach, however, is that a decision may have multiple consequences, some of which may be positive, others negative, and still others undetermined. For example, a decision to layoff 10 percent of an organization's workforce will harm those who lose their jobs but may help shareholders by increasing the projected returns on their investments. The long-term effect of the layoff could be positive if the organization emerges as a more competitive entity or negative if employee morale suffers and productivity declines. Hence, the utilitarian view is not always easy to apply. Research suggests that the utilitarian view is the most commonly applied perspective in organizations.[20] Note, however, that these views of ethical decision making are not always mutually exclusive. Managers often employ a combination of ethical perspectives when making decisions.

The **self-interest view of ethics** suggests that benefits of the decision maker(s) should be the primary considerations. This view assumes that society will likely benefit when its individual members make decisions that are in their own best interest. As Smith and Friedman argued, firms that attempt to maximize their returns within the legal regulations of society behave ethically. This perspective limits ethical concerns to the consideration of short-term financial benefits for the organization.

Self-interest can be viewed from either a narrow, short-run perspective or a broader, long-term perspective, however. It can be argued that one who always self-promotes short-term interests at the expense of others will suffer greater loss in the long term. For example, firms whose managers construct loopholes in their product or service warranties to promote short-term profits can ultimately alienate their customers. Hence, ethical behavior has long-term profit considerations.

The **rights view of ethics** evaluates organizational decisions to the extent to which they protect basic individual rights, such as a customer's right to privacy and an employee's right to a safe work environment. The key shortcoming of this approach, however, is that it is possible to protect individual rights at the expense of group progress or productivity.

The **justice view of ethics** suggests that all decisions will be made in accordance with preestablished rules or guidelines. Employee salaries may be administered by developing a formula that computes salary based on level of experience, amount of training, years of experience, and previous job evaluations. The key

---

Utilitarian View of Ethics

Perspective suggesting that anticipated outcomes and consequences should be the only considerations when evaluating an ethical dilemma.

Self-Interest View of Ethics

Perspective suggesting the benefits of the decision maker should be the primary consideration when weighing a decision.

Rights View of Ethics

Perspective that evaluates organizational decisions on the extent to which they protect individual rights.

Justice View of Ethics

Perspective suggesting that all decisions will be made in accordance with preestablished rules or guidelines.

shortcoming associated with the justice view is that it requires decision makers to develop rules and procedures for every possible anticipated outcome—an arduous task indeed.

The **integrative social contracts view of ethics** suggests that decisions should be based on existing norms of behavior, including cultural, community, or industry factors. Although this perspective emphasizes the situational influences on a particular decision, it deemphasizes the need for clear standards of right and wrong devoid of the situation.[21]

The **religious view of ethics** is based on personal or religious convictions. In the United States, the Judeo-Christian heritage forms a distinct notion of ethics, whereas Islam, Hinduism, and other religions comprise the majority viewpoint in distant nations. From the Christian perspective, for example, individuals should behave in ways that benefit others, treating other people as one would wish to be treated.[22] In one respect, the religious perspective counters the integrative social contracts view because it emphasizes clear principles of right or wrong with limited regard to situational variables. Needless to say, however, the religious view would result in markedly different ethical perspectives across cultures with different prominent religious traditions.

Some activities associated with strategic analysis may be questionable from an ethical standpoint. Few would argue that obtaining competitive information from one's own customers or purchasing and breaking down a competitor's products would be unethical. However, some companies have been known to extensively interview managers with key competitors for executive positions that do not exist.

Other examples illustrate the complexities of ethical issues faced by firms. In 2000, Philip Morris introduced the Merit brand of cigarettes designed to reduce the risk of fire when left unattended. The manufacturer claimed that the ultrathin paper used to wrap the tobacco burns more slowly and would cause fewer fires. Shortly after introduction, however, a company scientist reported that the cigarettes actually increase the risk of fire. Philip Morris fired the scientist in 2002 and continued to market the cigarette, although the fire-reduction claim was avoided. The U.S. Department of Justice launched a lawsuit against Philip Morris in 2004 alleging that the action was part of a broader attempt to conceal the negative effects of cigarette smoke from the public.[23]

In 2003, the Recording Industry Association of America launched several hundred lawsuits at teenagers and college students in an effort to emphasize the notion that swapping copyrighted music files via the Internet is against the law. Critics charged that "suing kids" is both bad business and unethical; industry executives argued that the law is clear and that widespread violations are taking a serious toll on its member firms.[24]

Ethics in advertising is also a key concern. Kraft, the largest food company in the United States, spends about $90 million annually advertising directly to children. In 2004 and 2005, however, the company announced plans not to direct advertisements for products such as Oreos and Lunchables to children under twelve years. When explaining the firm's decision, executives referenced the link between such products and obesity in children.[25]

Some firms and individuals indiscriminately use bulk e-mails to "spam" the public by e-mailing unwanted direct response advertisements of pornography sites, mortgage and investment services, and the like. Studies suggest that spam costs U.S. corporations billions of dollars each year due to loss

Integrative Social Contracts View of Ethics

Perspective suggesting that decisions should be based on existing norms of behavior, including cultural, community, or industry factors.

Religious View of Ethics

Perspective that evaluates organizational decisions on the basis of personal or religious convictions.

Management Focus on **Ethics**

A Memory Device for Making Ethical Decisions

Most people believe it is important that ethics take on a conscious, deliberate role in business decision making. The issue of ethics boils down to asking yourself, "What price am I willing to pay for this decision, and can I live with that price?" This process can be helped by using the word *ethics* as a mnemonic device.

E = EXPERIENCE. The values we carry with us into adulthood, and into business, are those that were modeled to us, usually by a parent, teacher, or other significant adult. How people behave and the decisions they make speak much louder and are more convincing than what they say.

T = TRAINING. Training means training yourself to keep the question of ethics fresh in your mind deliberately.

H = HINDSIGHT. Success leaves clues that we need to tap into in order to help us make that tough decision. What if the problem you face was the problem of the person you admire most in life? What would this person do?

I = INTUITION. What does your gut tell you is the right thing to do? Some call it conscience or insight. How do you know when you've gone against your gut feeling? You experience guilt, shame, remorse, or perhaps a restless night. Now the decision is what to do about it?

C = COMPANY. How will your decision affect the company, coworkers, customers, and your family? No matter the size of your decision, it affects other people in your life.

S = SELF-ESTEEM. The greatest ethical decision is one that builds self-esteem through the accomplishment of goals based on how these goals positively impact those around you.

Sources: Adapted from F. Bucaro, "Ethical Considerations in Business," Manage, *August/September 2000, 14; A. Gaudine and L. Thorne, "Emotion and Ethical Decision Making in Organizations,"* Journal of Business Ethics, *1 May 2001, 175–187.*

of worker productivity, consumption of bandwidth and other technological resources, and the use of technical support time. Although this largely illegal practice is deplored by most industry groups and Internet users, enforcement is a complicated legal endeavor.[26] Strategic managers are challenged to know where to draw the line concerning such practices.

Why do some organizations portray a pattern of unethical business practices? Anand and Ashforth identified six common rationalization tactics to explain this behavior.[27] First, individuals *deny responsibility*, rationalizing that they have no other choice but to participate in unethical behavior. One employee may contend that the practice is directly associated with another's responsibility.

Second, individuals *deny injury*, suggesting that the unethical behavior did not really hurt anyone. This perspective defines behavior only as unethical if directly injured parties can be clearly identified and then hesitates to acknowledge the injury.

Third, individuals *deny rights of the victims*, rationalizing that "they deserve what they got anyway." This perspective rationalizes unethical behavior when competitors or other related parties are alleged to be involved at least at the same level of corruption.

Fourth, individuals *engage in social weighting* by making carefully controlled comparisons. One way this is done is by character assassination of those suggesting that a particular pattern of behavior is unethical. If those condemning us are corrupt—the argument goes—then how can credence be given to their arguments? Another way this is done is by selectively comparing the unethical action to others whose actions are purported to be even more unethical. For example, falsifying an expense account for meals not eaten on a business trip is not considered a major offense when compared to someone who falsifies expenses for an entire business trip that never occurred.

Fifth, individuals can *appeal to higher values* by suggesting that justification of the unethical behavior is due to a higher order value. In this sense, one might argue that it is necessary to accept some degree of lower level unethical behavior in pursuit to ethical responsibility at a higher level. For example, a sales rep who is brought in to help resolve a dispute between a customer and another sales rep may deny the legitimate claims of the customer, rationalizing that loyalty among sales representatives is a higher order value.

Finally, individuals may *invoke the metaphor of the ledger*, arguing that they have the right to engage in certain unethical practices because of other good things they have done. For example, a manager on a business trip may justify padding a travel expense account because she has already done "more than her share" of traveling in recent months.

Improving the ethical stance of an organization is not easy, however. Treviño and Brown identify five commonly held myths concerning ethics in organizations.[28] These myths and accompanying realities are summarized in Table 5-2. In concert, they argue that ethical decision making is a complex process that extends beyond removing the bad apples from the organization and establishing formal ethics codes. It begins with proactive behavior on the part of top executives that infuses ethics into the fabric of the organization.

5-4 The Agency Problem

Ideally, top management should attempt to maximize the return to shareholders on their investment while simultaneously satisfying the interests of other stakeholders. For as long as absentee owners (i.e., the shareholders)

TABLE 5-2 Myths and Realities of Organizational Ethics

Myth	Reality
1. Ethical decision making is easy.	Ethical decision making is a complex process.
2. Unethical behavior can be traced to a limited number of bad apples in an organization.	Unethical behavior can be a systemic part of the organization's culture.
3. Ethics can be managed by developing formal ethics codes and programs.	Formal codes and programs are helpful, but ethical expectations must be part of the culture and fabric of the organization.
4. Ethical leadership is really about leader morality and honesty.	Leader morality and honesty is a good start, but the leader must also infuse ethics into the organization and hold others accountable.
5. Business leaders are less ethical today than they used to be.	Ethical concern in organizations has always been a pervasive issue.

Source: Based on L. K. Treviño and M. E. Brown, "Managing to Be Ethical: Debunking Five Business Ethics Myths," Academy of Management Executive 18(2) (2004): 69–81.

Source: Ablestock.com

Agency Problem

A situation in which a firm's top managers (i.e., the "agents" of the firm's owners) do not act in the best interests of the shareholders.

have been hiring professionals to manage their companies, however, questions have been raised concerning the degree of emphasis these managers actually place on maximizing financial returns.[29] Of course, managers emphasizing their own goals over those of the shareholders would raise serious ethical questions.

This concern has become more prominent in recent years as shares of publicly traded firms are more widely dispersed, making it harder for shareholders to exert control over a firm. For this reason, it is not uncommon to see successful, small, privately held firms seeking to stay small so the owner can remain personally in charge of the major business decisions.

The **agency problem** refers to a situation in which a firm's managers—the so-called agents of the owners—fail to act in the best interests of the shareholders. The extent to which the problem adversely affects most firms is widely debated, and factors associated with the problem can vary from country to country.[30] Indeed, some argue that management primarily serves its own interests, whereas others contend that managers share the same interests as the shareholders. These two perspectives are briefly discussed in sections 5-4a and 5-4b.

5-4a Management Serves Its Own Interests

According to one perspective, top managers tend to pursue strategies that ultimately increase their own salaries and other rewards. In particular, top executives are likely to grow their firms because increases in rewards usually accompany increases in organizational size and its greater responsibilities, even if growth is not the optimal strategy for the firm. This perspective is based on the tendency for management salaries to increase as the organization grows.[31]

Excessive CEO compensation has been widely criticized in recent years.[32] Although what is considered excessive varies among stakeholders, many CEOs have come under fire for their annual compensation. According to a number of surveys, most managers believe CEOs earn too much. During the 1980s, CEO compensation rose by 212 percent, compared to only 54 percent for factory workers, 73 percent for engineers, and 95 percent for teachers. After a brief decline in the early 1990s, CEO salaries began to climb once again.

In addition to salary, CEOs typically receive stock options and bonuses, revenues from profit-sharing plans, retirement benefits, and interest-free loans. As a result, CEOs in America's 350 largest publicly held corporations average more than $3 million annually in salary and bonuses, a figure that has declined only once in the past ten years. Recently, however, corporate boards have taken a closer look at CEO pay to ensure a tighter link between company performance and total compensation.

Hewlett-Packard's former CEO, Carly Fiorina, was one of the highest paid chief executives in the world, with a compensation package valued at nearly $90 million when she joined the company in 2000. The intriguing element of the package, however, was a grant for the equivalent of 580,000 restricted HP shares over three years, a block of stock worth $66.1 million when Fiorina's tenure began. When HP fired her in 2005, Fiorina received cash, stock, and pension benefits worth about $40 million, prompting protests from union officials and shareholders alike.[33]

Limiting CEO pay is not easy. Whole Foods Market attempted to restrict the pay of its CEO in the 1980s to eight times that of the average worker, a multiple that crept upward and was raised to nineteen times in 2006 to keep the firm from losing key leaders to competitors.[34] Hence, it is not surprising that political interest in regulating or limiting CEO pay is a hot topic. In 2007, some U.S. lawmakers supported legislation allowing shareholders to veto any CEO pay packages. A number of academics, mutual-fund trustees, institutional investors, union leaders, and politicians have taken a stand on this issue.[35] CEO pay can become a complex issue when a firm is going through a financial crisis and demanding sacrifices from the rank and file. Gerard Arpey, chairman and CEO of American Airlines (AMR), accepted stock options as part of his compensation, but turned down promotion raises in 2004.[36] In addition, many firms have discovered difficulties when attempting to reclaim pay from executives even in the case of malfeasance.[37]

CEOs in the United States earn on average far more than their counterparts in other countries; however, U.S. firms have become more likely than their global counterparts to employ non-Americans as CEOs. Interestingly, a number of studies have demonstrated that CEO salary is more closely tied to company size than to performance. Recently, however, firms have begun to tie compensation more closely to corporate performance. Most firms appear willing to continue to pay large sums to chief executives, provided the corporation performs at a comparable level. Surveys of CEO compensation practices continue to uncover special arrangements and considerable bonuses.

Pay practices in Internet businesses have also changed. Many Internet-based companies have increasingly adopted short-term incentives and bonus plans that are tied to more traditional business performance metrics, such as increased revenue or nearing profitability.

Executives may also pursue **diversification**, the process of increasing the size of their firms by acquiring other companies that may be related to the firm's core business. Diversification not only increases a firm's size but may also improve its survivability by spreading operational risks among its various business units. Diversification pursued only to spread risk, however, is generally not in the best interest of shareholders, who always have the option of reducing their financial risks by diversifying their own financial portfolios.[38] This perspective does not necessarily suggest that top management is unconcerned with the firm's profitability or market value; rather, top managers may emphasize business performance only to the extent that it discourages shareholder revolts and hostile takeovers.

Diversification
The process of acquiring companies to increase a firm's size.

The extent to which this perspective is accurate can create an advantage for relatively small, entrepreneurial organizations whose owners actively manage the firm. For this reason, such firms may be able to compete aggressively and successfully with their larger, more established competitors.

5-4b Management and Stockholders Share the Same Interests

Because managers' livelihoods are directly related to the success of the firm, one can argue that managers generally share the same interests as the stockholders. This perspective is supported at least in part by several empirical studies. One study, for example, found that firm profit—not size—is the primary determinant of top management rewards.[39] Another points to a significant relationship between common stock earnings and top executives' salaries.[40] Hence, according to these studies, management rewards rise with firm performance, a relationship that encourages managers to be most concerned with company performance.

One of the most common suggestions for aligning the goals of top management and those of shareholders is to award shares of stock or stock options to top management, transforming professional managers into shareholders. Stock option plans and high salaries may bring the interests of top management and stockholders closer together.[41] Top executives seek to protect their salaries and option plans and can do so only by delivering higher business performance. Indeed, research has suggested that as managerial stock ownership rises, the interests of managers and shareholders begin to converge to some extent.[42] This view has gained support from others, but for different reasons.[43] Many suggest that managerial jobs contain structural imperatives that force managers to attempt to enhance profits.[44] In addition, when managers are major shareholders, they may become entrenched and risk averse, adopting conservative strategies that are beneficial to themselves but not necessarily to their shareholders.

In sum, the debate over whether top managers are primarily concerned with their firms' returns or their own interests continues. Most scholars and practitioners believe both perspectives have merit, and pursue compensation models designed to bring the two sides together, such as those that emphasize stock options and profit sharing for managers instead of fixed pay levels. Many companies have adopted **employee stock ownership plans (ESOPs)** to distribute shares of the company's stock to managers and other employees over a period of time.

Employee Stock Ownership Plan (ESOP)

A formal program that transfers shares of stock to a company's employees.

5-5 Corporate Governance and Goals of Boards of Directors

Corporate Governance

The board of directors, institutional investors, and blockholders who monitor firm strategies to ensure managerial responsiveness.

Corporate governance refers to the board of directors, institutional investors (e.g., pension and retirement funds, mutual funds, banks, insurance companies, among other money managers), and large shareholders known as *blockholders* who monitor firm strategies to ensure effective management. Boards of directors and institutional investors—representatives of pension and retirement funds, mutual funds, and financial institutions—are generally the most influential in the governance systems. Boards of directors represent the shareholders and are legally authorized to monitor firm activities, as well as the selection, evaluation, and compensation of top managers. Because institutional investors own more than half of all shares of publicly traded firms, they tend to wield substantial influence. Blockholders tend to hold less than 20 percent of the shares, so their influence is proportionally less than that of institutional investors.[45]

Boards often include both inside (i.e., firm executives) and outside directors. Insiders bring company-specific knowledge to the board, whereas outsiders bring independence and an external perspective. Over the past several decades, the composition of the typical board has shifted from one controlled by insiders to one controlled by outsiders. This increase in outside influence often allows board members to oversee managerial decisions more effectively.[46] Furthermore, when additional outsiders are added to insider-dominated boards, CEO dismissal is more likely when corporate performance declines,[47] and outsiders are more likely to pressure for corporate restructuring.[48]

In the 1990s, the number of corporate board members with memberships in other boards began to increase dramatically. With outside directors of the largest 500 firms in the United States commanding an average of $151,000 in cash and equity in 2005, companies often became concerned about both potential conflicts of interest and the amount of time each individual can spend with the affairs of each company. As a result, many companies have begun to limit the number of board memberships their own board members may hold. Approximately two-thirds of corporate board members at the largest 1,500 U.S. companies do not hold seats on other boards. In addition, some firms are reconsidering board member compensation. In 2006, for example, Coke unveiled a plan that pays its board members only if the company hits earnings targets. The plan, however, does pay new members $175,000 as a signing bonus.[49]

This change has been underscored by the Sarbanes-Oxley Act of 2002, which requires that firms include more independent directors on their boards and make new disclosures on internal controls, ethics codes, and the composition of their audit committees on annual reports. Analysts have noted positive changes among boards as a result of this legislation in terms of both independence and expertise.[50] Evidence also suggests that many CEOs have become more reluctant to sit on boards of publicly held companies. Increased liability on the part of board members and recent policy changes that often restrict the number of outside boards on which a CEO may serve have also contributed to this change.[51]

Even with new disclosure regulations, it can be difficult to determine precisely what top executives earn at public companies. In 2004, for example, Regions Financial, Ryland Group, and Home Depot each reimbursed their top executives more than $3 million for personal taxes levied on executive perks. Details of such payments are not always readily available in corporate filings.[52]

Boards of directors consist of officials elected by the shareholders and are responsible for monitoring activities in the organization, evaluating top management's strategic proposals, and establishing the broad strategic direction for the firm, although few boards tend to be aggressive in this regard. As such, boards are responsible for selecting and replacing the chief executive officer, establishing the CEO's compensation package, advising top management on strategic issues, and monitoring managerial and company performance as representatives of the shareholders. Critics charge, however, that board members do not always fulfill their legal roles.[53] One reason is board members are nominated by the CEO, who expects them to support his or her strategic initiatives. The generous compensation they often receive is also a key issue.[54]

When boards are controlled by insiders, a rubber stamp mentality can develop, whereby directors do not aggressively challenge executive decisions as they should. This is particularly true when the CEO also serves as chair of the board, a phenomenon known as **CEO duality**.[55] Although research shows mixed results concerning the desirability of CEO duality,[56] insider board members may be less willing to exert control when the CEO is also the chair of the board, because present rewards and future career prospects within the firm are largely determined by the CEO. In the absence of CEO duality, however, insiders may be more likely to contribute to board control, often in subtle and indirect ways so as not to document any opposition to the decisions of the CEO. For example, the insiders may ostensibly present both sides of various issues, while carefully framing the alternatives in favor of one that may be in opposition to the wishes of the CEO.

CEO Duality
A situation in which the CEO also serves as the chair of the board.

S T R A T E G Y   A T   W O R K   5 - 4

The Growing Responsiveness of Boards

The adage on Wall Street is, "If you don't like the stock, sell it." Over the past decade, however, dismayed investors have decided to challenge the board instead. Many corporate boards have historically functioned as rubber stamps for top executives. Nonetheless, the directors of many prominent corporations have become increasingly responsible to shareholder interests, thanks in part to the increased influence of institutional shareholders. These large investment firms control substantial numbers of shares in widely held firms and have the clout necessary to pressure board members for change when needed.

Consider the case of Nell Minow. A principal at activist money-management firm Lens Inc., Minow searches for companies with strong products and underlying values that appear to be underperforming. After identifying a target, Minow purchases a substantial number of shares in the company and then advises the CEO of her ownership position. She requests a meeting with the CEO and/or the board to discuss changes that could improve the performance of the firm. Activist owners like Minow have sent a message to both top executives and boards that poor performance is not unlikely to go unchallenged.

However, a number of analysts and executives believe that further change to the system is needed. According to David Leighton, former chairman of the board at Nabisco Brands, Ltd., companies should seek out more independent and qualified board members who will consider the strategic direction of the firm more aggressively.

In some instances, boards of directors, pressured by institutional investors, have forced the turnover of top executives. In one prominent example, GM's market share declined from 44 percent to 33 percent between 1981 and 1992. In 1992, the California Public Employees Retirement System, a significant shareholder, pressured the eleven outside board members (a majority of the fifteen-member board) to reassert strategic control over the firm. As a result, the shareholder forced a complete overhaul of senior GM executives, the first since 1920. GM generated profits of $2.6 billion, $7.6 billion, and $9.7 billion in 1993, 1994, and 1995, respectively.

Sources: N. Dunne, "Adding a Little Muscle in the Boardroom," Financial Times, 10 October 2003, I; W. Royal, "Impeach the Board," Industry Week, 16 November 1998, 47–50; C. Torres, "Firms' Restructuring Often Hurt Foreign Buyers," Wall Street Journal Interactive Edition, 13 May 1996; M. L. Weidenbaum, "The Evolving Corporate Board," Society, March–April 1995, 9–16.

Pressure on directors to acknowledge shareholder concerns has increased over the past two decades. The major source of pressure in recent years has come from institutional investors, owners of large chunks of most publicly traded companies by way of retirement or mutual funds. By virtue of the size of their investments, they wield considerable power and are more willing to use it than ever before (see Strategy at Work 5-4).

Some board members have played effective stewardship roles. Many directors promote strongly the best interests of their firm's shareholders and various other stakeholder groups as well. Research indicates, for instance, that board members are often invaluable sources of environmental and competitive information.[57] By conscientiously carrying out their duties, directors can ensure that management remains focused on company performance.[58]

A number of recommendations have been made on how to promote an effective governance system. For example, it has been suggested that outside directors be the only ones to evaluate the performance of top managers against the established mission and goals, that all outside board members meet alone at least once annually, and that boards of directors establish appropriate qualifications for board membership and communicate these qualifications to shareholders. For institutional shareholders, it is recommended that institutions and other shareholders act as owners and not just investors,[59] that they not interfere with day-to-day managerial decisions, that they evaluate the performance of the board of directors regularly,[60] and that they recognize that the prosperity of the firm benefits all shareholders.

5-6 Takeovers

When shareholders conclude that the top managers of a firm with ineffective board members are mismanaging the firm, institutional investors, blockholders, and other shareholders may sell their shares, depressing the market price of the company's stock.[61] Depressed prices often lead to a **takeover**, a purchase of a controlling quantity of a firm's shares by an individual, a group of investors, or another organization. Takeovers may be attempted by outsiders or insiders, and may be friendly or unfriendly. A friendly takeover is one in which both the buyer and seller desire the transaction. In contrast, an unfriendly takeover is one in which the target firm resists the sale, whereby one or more individuals purchase enough shares in the target firm to either force a change in top management or to manage the firm themselves. Interestingly, groups that seek to initiate unfriendly takeovers often include current or former firm executives.

Takeover

The purchase of a controlling quantity of shares in a firm by an individual, a group of investors, or another organization. Takeovers may be friendly or unfriendly.

In many cases, sudden takeover attempts rely heavily on borrowed funds to finance the acquisition, a process referred to as a **leveraged buyout (LBO)**. LBOs strap the company with heavy debt and often lead to a partial divestment of some of the firm's subsidiaries of product divisions to lighten the burden.[62]

Leveraged Buyout (LBO)

A takeover in which the acquiring party borrows funds to purchase a firm.

Corporate takeovers have been both defended and criticized. On the positive side, takeovers provide a system of checks and balances often required to initiate changes in ineffective management. Proponents argue that the threat of LBOs can pressure managers to operate their firms more efficiently.[63]

Takeovers have been criticized from several perspectives. The need to pay back large loans can cause management to pursue activities that are expedient in the short run but not best for the firm in the long run. In addition, the extra debt required to finance an LBO tends to increase the likelihood of bankruptcy for a troubled firm.[64]

5-7 Summary

An organization's mission outlines the reason for its existence. A clear purpose provides managers with a sense of direction and can guide all of the organization's activities. Goals represent the desired general ends toward which organizational efforts are directed. However, managers, shareholders, and board members do not always share the same goals. Top management must attempt to reconcile and satisfy the interests of each of the stakeholder groups while pursuing its own goals. Inherent in the notion of mission and goals is the organization's position on social responsibility and the ethical standards it expects its managers to uphold.

Takeovers and leveraged buyouts have emerged as mechanisms for resolving some of the goal conflicts that occur among various stakeholder groups. The usefulness of these mechanisms continues to be widely debated, however.

Key Terms

agency problem
CEO duality
comparative advantage
corporate governance
diversification
employee stock ownership
  plan (ESOP)
goals

integrative social contracts view
  of ethics
justice view of ethics
leveraged buyout
managerial ethics
mission
objectives
religious view of ethics

rights view of ethics
self-interest view of ethics
social responsibility
stakeholders
sustainable strategic management
takeover
utilitarian view of ethics

Review Questions and Exercises

1. What is and should be the relationship between an organization's mission and its strategy?

2. What is the difference between social responsibility and managerial ethics?

3. Select a company that has published a mission statement on its Web site. Evaluate its mission statement along each of the following criteria.

   a. Is the mission statement comprehensive? Is it concise?

   b. Does the mission statement delineate, in broad terms, what products or services the firm is to offer?

   c. Is the mission statement consistent with the company's actual activities and competitive prospects?

4. Why do stakeholders in the same organization often have different goals? Would it not be best if they shared the same goals? Explain.

5. What are the key advantages and disadvantages of leveraged buyouts?

Practice Quiz

True or False

1. Goals are specific and often quantified versions of objectives.

2. If a firm is able to consistently earn above-average profits, then it is effectively balancing the goals of its stakeholders.

3. The agency problem refers to the balancing act a firm must exhibit when attempting to satisfy the myriad of governmental agencies.

4. A firm's managers may pursue diversification even if performance is likely to suffer because diversification can reduce the risk of firm failure.

5. A common suggestion for aligning the goals of top management and those of shareholders is to award shares of stock or stock options to top management.

6. Most boards of directors include both inside and outside directors.

Multiple Choice

7. The reason for the firm's existence is known as
   A. the vision.
   B. organizational goals.
   C. organizational objectives.
   D. none of the above

8. The idea that certain products may be produced more cheaply or at a higher quality in particular countries due to advantages in labor costs or technology is known as
   A. comparative advantage.
   B. competitive advantage.
   C. strategic advantage.
   D. national advantage.

9. Which of the following is not an example of a stakeholder?

   A. customers

   B. suppliers

   C. employees

   D. none of the above

10. An individual's responsibility to make business decisions that are legal, honest, moral, and fair is known as

    A. social responsibility.

    B. the social imperative.

    C. managerial ethics.

    D. all of the above

11. The board of directors is responsible for

    A. selecting the CEO.

    B. determining the CEO's compensation package.

    C. overseeing the firm's strategies.

    D. all of the above

12. Leveraged buyouts can

    A. strap the company with a large amount of debt.

    B. serve as a system of checks and balances.

    C. lead to the sale of company assets.

    D. all of the above

Notes

1. NewswireToday.com, "Software Development Engineer in India Vs China, accessed June 14, 2007, http://www.newswiretoday.com/news/4319; P. Wonacott, "China's Secret Weapon: Smart, Cheap Labor for High Tech Goods," *Wall Street Journal* (14 March 2002): A1.

2. T. Eiben, "U.S. Exporters on a Global Roll," *Fortune* (29 June 1992): 94.

3. R. Jacob, "The Search for the Organization of Tomorrow," *Fortune* (18 May 1992): 93.

4. A. L. Friedman and S. Miles, "Developing Stakeholder Theory," *Journal of Management Studies* 39 (2002): 1–22.

5. S. I. Wu and C. Wu, "A New Market Segmentation Variable for Product Design-Functional Requirements," *Journal of International Marketing and Marketing Research* 25 (2000): 35–48.

6. For an example of his early work, see R. Nader, *Unsafe at Any Speed: Design and Dangers of the American Automobile* (New York: Grossman, 1964).

7. H. A. Simon, "On the Concept of Organizational Goal," *Administrative Science Quarterly* 9 (1964): 1–22; J. Pfeffer and G. Salancik, *The External Control of Organizations* (New York: Harper & Row, 1978).

8. R. M. Cyert and J. G. March, *A Behavioral Theory of the Firm* (Englewood Cliffs, NJ: Prentice-Hall, 1963); J. G. March and H. A. Simon, *Organizations* (New York: John Wiley & Sons, 1958).

9. M. J. Verkerk, J. DeLeede, and A. H. J. Nijhof, "From Responsible Management to Responsible Organizations: The Democratic Principle for Managing Organizational Ethics," *Business and Society Review* 106 (2001): 353–378; A. E. Randel, "The Maintenance of an Organization's Socially Responsible Practice: A Cross-Level Framework," *Business and Society* 41 (2002): 61–83.

10. R. Alsop, "Survey Rates Companies' Reputations and Many Are Found Wanting," *Wall Street Journal* (7 February 2001): B1, B6.

11. R. Alsop, "Perils of Corporate Philanthropy," *Wall Street Journal* (16 January 2002): B1, B4.

12. Ibid.; A. Maitland, "No Hiding Place for the Irresponsible Business," special report in *Financial Times* (29 September 2003): 1–2.

13. R. J. Ely and D. A. Thomas, "Cultural Diversity at Work: The Effects of Diversity Perspectives on Workgroup Processes and Outcomes," *Administrative Science Quarterly* 46 (2001): 229–273.

14. J. Whalen, "Britain Stirs Outcry by Weighing Benefits of Drugs Versus Price," *Wall Street Journal* (22 November 2005): A1, A11.

15. A. Browne, "Chinese Doctors Tell Patients: Pay Upfront, or No Treatment," *Wall Street Journal* (5 December 2005): A1, A12.

16. A. Zimmerman, "Defending Wal-Mart," *Wall Street Journal Online* (6 October 2004).

17. C. Hymowitz, "The Perils of Picking CEOs," *Wall Street Journal* (15 March 2004): B1, B4.

18. J. Bandler and A. Zimmerman, "A Wal-Mart Legend's Trail of Deceit," *Wall Street Journal*, (8 April 2005): A1, A10.

19. R. L. Rundle and A. W. Mathews, "Breast Implants Made of Silicone Win FDA Backing," *Wall Street Journal* (18–19 November 2006): A1, A5.

20. D. J. Fritzsche and H. Becker, "Linking Management Behavior to Ethical Philosophy—An Empirical Investigation," *Academy of Management Journal* 27 (1984): 166-175.

21. E. Soule, "Managerial Moral Strategies—In Search of a Few Good Principles," *Academy of Management Review* 27 (2002): 114–124.

22. G. R. Weaver and B. R. Agle, "Religiosity and Ethical Behavior in Organizations: A Symbolic Interactionist Perspective," *Academy of Management Review* 27 (2002): 77–97.

23. V. O'Connell, "U.S. Suit Alleges Philip Morris Hid Cigarette-Fire Risk," *Wall Street Journal* (23 April 2004): A1, A8.

24. C. Bialik, "Will the Music Industry Sue Your Kid?" *Wall Street Journal* (10 September 2003): D1, D12.

25. S. Ellison, "Why Kraft Decided to Ban Some Food Ads to Children," *Wall Street Journal* (31 October 2005): A1, A13.

26. M. Mangalindan, "For Bulk E-Mailer, Pestering Millions Offers Path to Profit," *Wall Street Journal* (13 November 2002): A1, A17; B. Morrissey, "Spam Cost Corporate America $9B in 2002," (7 January 2003), study by Ferris Research reprinted at www.cyberatlas.com.

27. B. E. Ashforth and V. Anand, "The Normalization of Corruption in Organizations," in R. M. Kramer and B. M. Staw, eds., *Research in Organizational Behavior* 25 (2003): 1–52 (Amsterdam: Elsevier Publishing).

28. L. K. Treviño and M. E. Brown, "Managing to be Ethical: Debunking Five Business Ethics Myths," *Academy of Management Executive* 18(2) (2004): 69–81.

29. B. M. Staw and L. D. Epstein, "What Bandwagons Bring: Effects of Popular Management Techniques on Corporate Performance, Reputation, and CEO Pay," *Administrative Science Quarterly* 45 (2000): 523–556.

30. K. Ramaswamy, R.Veliyath, and L. Gomes, "A Study of the Determinants of CEO Compensation in India," *Management International Review* 40 (2000): 167–191.

31. J. E. Richard, "Global Executive Compensation: A Look at the Future," *Compensation and Benefits Review* 32(3) (2000): 35–38.

32. J. S. Dublin, "Why the Get-Rich-Quick Days May Be Over," *Wall Street Journal* (14 April 2003): R1, R3; J. S. Lublin, "Executive Pay Keeps Rising, Despite Outcry," *Wall Street Journal* (3 October 2003): B1, B4; C. Hymowitz, "Does Rank Have Too Much Privilege? *Wall Street Journal* (26 February 2002): B1; C. Dembeck, "Is Amazon.com's CEO Package Too Generous?" *E-Commerce Times Columnist* (31 August 1999); C. Dembeck, "HP's New CEO Package Is a Sweetheart Deal," *E-Commerce Times Columnist* (27 September 1999); L. Enos, "Study: Dot–Compensation Going Mainstream," *E-Commerce Times* (22 August 2000); P. Wright, M. Kroll, and J. A. Parnell, *Strategic Management:Concepts* (Upper Saddle River, NJ: Prentice Hall, 1998); C. Hymowitz, "Foreign-Born CEOs Are Increasing in U.S., Rarer Overseas," *Wall Street Journal* (25 May 2004): B1, B6.

33. R. Mark, "HP Stockholders after Fiorina Severance," *Internet News* (9 March 2006).

34. P. Dvorak, "Limits on Executive Pay: Easy to Set, Hard to Keep," *Wall Street Journal* (9 April 2007): B1, B5.

35. J. S. Lublin and P. Dvorak, "How Five New Players Aid Movement to Limit CEO Pay," *Wall Street Journal* (13 March 2007): A1, A20.

36. J. S. Lublin, "Cost-Cutting Airlines Grapple with Issue of Executive Pay," *Wall Street Journal* (25 January 2005): B1, B9.

37. P. Dvorak and S. Ng, "Companeis Discover It's Hard to Reclaim Pay from Executives," *Wall Street Journal* (20 November 2006): A1, A12.

38. D. J. Teece, "Towards an Economic Theory of the Multiproduct Firm," *Journal of Economic Behavior and Organization* 3 (1982): 39–63.

39. W. G. Lewellen and B. Huntsman, "Managerial Pay and Corporate Performance," *American Economic Review* 60 (1970): 710–720.

40. R. T. Masson, "Executive Motivations, Earnings, and Consequent Equity Performance," *Journal of Political Economy* 79 (1971): 1278–1292.

41. J. Child, *The Business Enterprise in Modern Industrial Society* (London: Collier-Macmillan, 1969).

42. S. L. Oswald and J. S. Jahera, "The Influence of Ownership on Performance: An Empirical Study," *Strategic Management Journal* 12 (1991): 321–326.

43. D. R. James and M. Soref, "Profit Constraints on Managerial Autonomy: Managerial Theory and the Unmaking of the Corporation President," *American Sociological Review* 46 (1981): 1–18.

44. C. R. Weinberg, "CEO Compensation: How Much Is Enough?" *Chief Executive* 159 (2000): 48–63.

45. S. Chen and K. W. Ho, "Blockholder Ownership and Market Liquidity," *Journal of Financial & Quantitative Analysis* 35 (2000): 621–633; J. J. McConnell and H. Servaes, "Additional Evidence on Equity Ownership and Corporate Value," *Journal of Financial Economics* 27 (1990): 595–612.

46. W. J. Salmon, "Crisis Prevention: How to Gear Up Your Board," *Harvard Business Review* 71 (1993): 68–75.

47. See B. Hermalin and M. S. Weisbach, "The Determinants of Board Composition," *Rand Journal of Economics* 19(4) (1988): 589–605; E. F. Fama and M. C. Jensen, "Separation of Ownership and Control," *Journal of Law and Economics* 26 (1983): 301–325; M. S. Weisbach, "Outside Directors and CEO Turnover," *Journal of Financial Economics* 20 (1988): 431–460.

48. P. A. Gibbs, "Determinants of Corporate Restructuring: The Relative Importance of Corporate Governance, Takeover Threat, and Free Cash Flow," *Strategic Management Journal* 14 (1993): 51–68.

49. C. Terhune and J. S. Lublin, "In Unusual Move, Coke Ties Pay for Directos to Earnings Targets," *Wall Street Journal* (6 April 2006): A1, A11; P. Plitch, "Ready and Able?" *Wall Street Journal* (24 February 2003): R3, R5; J. S. Lublin, "More Work, More Pay," *Wall Street Journal* (24 February 2003): R4, R5.

50. N. Dunne, "Adding a Little Muscle in the Boardroom," *Financial Times* (10 October 2003): I.

51. A. Raghavan, "More CEOs Say 'No Thanks' to Board Seats," *Wall Street Journal* (28 January 2005): B1, B4.

52. M. Maremont, "Latest Twist in Corporate Pay: Tax-Free Income for Executives," *Wall Street Journal* (22 December 2005): A1, A11.

53. J. H. Morgan, "The Board of Directors Is No Longer Just a 'Rubber Stamp'," *TMA Journal* 19(5) (1999): 14–18.

54. B. R. Baliga and R. C. Moyer, "CEO Duality and Firm Performance," *Strategic Management Journal* 17 (1996): 41–53; P. Stiles, "The Impact of Board on Strategy: An Empirical Examination," *Journal of Management Studies* 38 (2001): 627–650.

55. S. Finkelstein and R. D'Aveni, "CEO Duality as a Double-Edged Sword," *Academy of Management Journal* 37 (1994): 1079–1108.

56. P. Allan and A. A. Widman, "A Comparison of the Views of CEOs and Public Pension Funds on the Corporate Governance Issues of Chairman-CEO Duality and Election of Lead Directors," *American Business Review* 18(1) (2000): 49–54; W. N. Davidson III, D. L. Worrell, and C. Nemec, "CEO Duality, Succession-Planning and Agency Theory: Research Agenda," *Strategic Management Journal* 19 (1998): 905–908.

57. J. Goldstein, K. Gautum, and W. Boeker, "The Effects of Board Size and Diversity on Strategic Change," *Strategic Management Journal* 15 (1994): 241–250.

58. M. S. Mizruchi, "Who Controls Whom? An Examination of the Relation between Management and Board of Directors in Large American Corporations," *Academy of Management Review* 8 (1983): 426–435.

59. C. Wohlstetter, "Pension Fund Socialism: Can Bureaucrats Run the Blue Chips?" *Harvard Business Review* 71 (1993): 78.

60. J. A. Conger, D. Finegold, and E. E. Lawler III, "Appraising Boardroom Performance," *Harvard Business Review* 76(1) (1998): 136–148.

61. P. Wright and S. Ferris, "Agency Conflict and Corporate Strategy: The Effect of Divestment on Corporate Value," *Strategic Management Journal* 18 (1997): 77–83.

62. S. Perumpral, N. Sen, and G. Noronha, "The Impact of LBO Financing on Bank Returns," *American Business Review* 20(1) (2002): 1–5.

63. M. C. Jensen, "The Eclipse of the Public Corporation," *Harvard Business Review* 67(5): 61–74; P. H. Pan and C. W. L. Hill, "Organizational Restructuring and Economic Performance in Leveraged Buyouts," *Academy of Management Journal* 38 (1995): 704–739.

64. R. B. Reich, "Leveraged Buyouts: America Pays the Price," *New York Times Magazine* (29 January 1989): 32–40.

Insight from *strategy+business*

This chapter's strategy+business reading highlights the fact that progressive firms can meet social challenges while securing profits. South African power company Eskom anticipated the end to apartheid and has facilitated social change in the country by providing electricity to sections of the country dominated by a poor, predominantly black population.

The Company that Anticipated History

By Ann Graham

Driving along the old two-lane road from the Republic of South Africa's political capital, Pretoria, to its commercial hub, Johannesburg, a visitor sees two strikingly different nations. The first South Africa looks like an emerging economy in hypergrowth. Hundreds of acres of rolling hillsides are rapidly giving way to new four-lane highways, office parks, shopping centers, and housing developments of modest and McMansion-style homes. Parking lots in Johannesburg suburbs are jammed with BMWs, Mercedes-Benzes, and Range Rovers. A supermarket called Woolworth's resembles the American haute-healthy food emporium Whole Foods; an apparel store, Kozi Kids, looks like the Gap. Bars and restaurants cater to young, university-educated, upwardly mobile professional blacks—a category that didn't exist 15 years ago. It emerged after the 1994 national election, which brought Nelson Mandela and the African National Congress (ANC), the country's oldest black rights organization, to power.

The second South Africa consists of a predominantly black population mired in poverty. Next door to many of the new malls and mansions are sprawling shantytowns of rusting metal shacks. Men and women in tattered clothes walk from them daily through tall grasses down to the urban roads. On their heads, some balance baskets filled with fruits and vegetables or trinkets they will try to sell to travelers. Day laborers jam themselves into ramshackle minivan taxis that take them to pickup points for construction or farm work. If they're not lucky enough to land those jobs, these itinerant workers might end up in a crowded shopping center parking lot, directing cars to open spaces and hoping to receive a small tip for their service.

South Africa's president, Thabo Mbeki, calls these two South Africas the "first" and "second" economies. They are a legacy of apartheid, the system of racial segregation that governed South Africa from 1946 to 1994, effectively excluding nonwhites (who make up 79 percent of South Africa's 47 million people) from the nation's economy and politics. Even with GDP growth averaging 3 percent since 1994, and more blacks rising out of poverty to enter the first economy, whites' per capita income of 82,000 rand (US$11,000) is still more than five times that of blacks, and black unemployment remains a problem. Officially, unemployment nationwide stands at about 27 percent. Unofficially, the rate is anywhere from 40 to 75 percent among blacks.

Access to electricity is always an important first step up the economic ladder. In South Africa, Eskom Holdings Ltd. provides that first step. A government-owned corporation headquartered in the Johannesburg suburb of Sandton, Eskom generates 95 percent of the country's electricity. Many organizations debate whether their business has social responsibilities, but Eskom's core business is itself a social responsibility. Without electricity, educating children is difficult; families must heat their homes with coal or wood, a major cause of respiratory diseases; and new businesses and employment opportunities can't grow. Eskom receives 80 percent of its revenues from industrial customers, but the company also has a self-imposed mission: to deliver electricity to all individuals, especially those who, in every sense, have lived without power.

Eskom adopted this mandate not in the wake of apartheid's fall, but in the mid-1980s, when it was legally prohibited from providing electricity to black communities. The company's early embrace of "electricity for all" (as the policy is called) allowed the company to play a leadership role early on in the social transformation of South Africa. Not only did the company rethink the value of serving black customers and remake its work force to bring blacks into positions of responsibility—both in defiance of the laws then in place—but it thus positioned itself as one of the very few African companies that could make a play for international expansion. (South African Breweries, now SABMiller, is another.)

Ahead of Change

"One cannot manage change," wrote noted management author Peter Drucker. "One can only be ahead of it." That maxim could be Eskom's motto. By preparing in advance for the end of apartheid, risking its own executives' lives in the process, the company established a pivotal role for itself in the South African economy, and arguably in its culture as well. Eskom's story is the sort often recounted under the banner of corporate social responsibility, but the company's efforts were not primarily motivated by the desire for a good reputation. They had much more to do with resilience and growth as an enterprise.

Eskom's leaders take the position that because no business can perform to its full potential in a society that is failing, companies must be involved in the societal health of their country. "It's not only that society needs strong and sustainable businesses. Businesses need sustainable societies in which to operate," says Wendy Poulton, Eskom's general manager of corporate sustainability. "Our view is if you don't recognize this as a business, you're going to be out of business."

Since the inception of "electricity for all," Eskom has electrified an average of 300,000 additional homes annually. In 2006, Eskom reported delivering electricity to 3.3 million homes, compared to only 120,000 during the last years of apartheid. To be sure, this electrification rate lags behind those of other emerging economies, such as India and China, but it means that 66 percent of the South African public has electricity, which is up from 30 percent a decade ago. This rate is more than four times the percentage in the rest of sub-Saharan Africa. With wholly owned electric power operations in 20 sub-Saharan countries and partnerships in 10 others, Eskom is also trying to be an economic engine for all of Africa—intending to bring electricity to more than a billion people, many of whom still live by candles and kerosene lamps. Currently, Eskom is among the largest utilities in the world, ranking 11th in generation capacity and seventh in sales, according to its 2005 annual report. Electricity sales reached R36.6 billion (US$4.61 billion), with pretax profits of R4.6 million (US$579,710) in the 2005–06 fiscal year.

Throughout its history, Eskom has had to manage the complex relationship among South Africa's government, financial, and industrial sectors. The utility traces its origins to private entrepreneurs at the beginning of the 20th century who won the first concessions to transmit electricity to the newly discovered gold deposits of the Witwaterstrand, the mountain range in northeastern South Africa that now houses the richest gold mines on earth. In 1910, when the Union of South Africa was formed, the Transvaal provincial government, representing the heart of the mining region, declared that supplying electricity was too important a public service to leave in private hands. In 1923, when apartheid was still a relatively informal policy in the country, the Electricity Supply Commission, abbreviated to *Escom* (the spelling was later changed), was created to absorb and run South Africa's electricity assets, with no profit requirement.

Escom was one of the first parastatals—South Africa's state corporations. Together with Iscor, which produces iron and steel; Sasol, which refines liquid fuels and other products from coal; and Foskor, which mines phosphate, Escom provided the infrastructure and raw materials to grow South Africa's economy. The parastatals also provided critical support to the government's increasingly separatist regime. After 1948, when apartheid became national policy, the government and therefore Escom effectively wrote off most black townships, arguing that their inhabitants would one day return to the so-called homelands. This homeland policy, or "grand apartheid," inhibited investment in township infrastructure, schools, and other basic services. However, the demand for electricity increased among the white population—enough to drive Escom to expand its generating capacity dramatically in the 1960s and early '70s.

When the utility made plans to erect five coal-fired power stations, Dr. Ian McRae, then the head of power station operations, saw a large problem ahead: a shortage of white workers with the skills needed to staff those plants. "We realized we had all these new power stations coming on and we didn't have the people to operate them," recalls Dr. McRae.

His solution was to begin training blacks to fill these positions, even though most were illiterate and apartheid outlawed them from being anything more than unskilled laborers. At the time, the laws reserved certain jobs for whites, and white trade unions jealously guarded those rules. (Black trade unions were illegal until 1979.) Breaking the law, though, wasn't what most concerned Dr. McRae; rather, he worried whether Escom's employees would support such radical measures. So he set up meetings at each power station with trade union representatives, plant managers, and black laborers to discuss the idea of blacks' doing jobs traditionally performed by whites. Reassured that there would be minimal resistance, Dr. McRae started introducing blacks into the ranks in the new position of "operating assistant" and providing them with the training to develop their technical skills. He removed the existing educational barriers so that nonwhite operators could move into the position of shift supervisor. "I got people to agree that a good operator, with some experience, could move up," says Dr. McRae.

By the late 1970s, worldwide condemnation of apartheid had left South Africa isolated, and its economy was stagnating. Demand for power plummeted, and it soon became clear that the power stations Escom had committed to build were no longer needed. After the company jacked up prices to offset the costs of construction and operational misfires, it found itself in financial difficulty.

That's when the government stepped in. In May 1983, a commission appointed by the Minerals and Energy Ministry and led by mining executive W.J. de Villiers found fault with Escom's management of forecasting, governance, accounting, and investment. Amid the commission's inquiry, a scandal broke concerning a company accountant who had defrauded Escom of nearly $4 million; he was convicted and the finance chief was forced to resign. Escom was now a national embarrassment. The De Villiers Commission replaced its existing hierarchy with a new two-tier governance structure. An Electricity Council, appointed by and reporting to the government, represented the stakeholders, including consumers and unions, and set policy. Below that was the management board, which ran the company. For the first time, Escom would be accountable for profits and losses.

In 1984, the De Villiers Commission nominated Dr. McRae to be Escom's chief executive. For chairman of the new management board, South African President P.W. Botha chose Dr. John B. Maree. The two men, temperamentally quite different, took on financial and cultural reforms together. Dr. McRae was the consummate company man. Soft-spoken and professorial in demeanor, he had started at Escom as an artisan's apprentice in 1947. He was well-liked and respected inside the company and in the industry. Dr. Maree, a turnaround specialist, was renowned for his shrewd political instincts and his blunt management style. A former divisional chair at Barlows Ltd., one of the country's oldest and largest conglomerates, Dr. Maree came to Escom following a three-year stint as the chief executive of Armscor, South Africa's defense parastatal.

Drs. McRae and Maree began by looking inward. Using Dr. McRae's signature "walkabouts," a technique he had developed years earlier to make sure he never lost touch with his employees, they met with small groups of senior and middle managers in regional offices, power stations, and distribution and service departments. Morale was low. Consumer criticism had hurt, and Escom-bashing in the press made it worse.

At the head office, the two assembled Escom's best and brightest managers and strategic thinkers into a senior management council they called the "Top 30." A few outsiders were also invited, including Reuel J. Khoza, a management consultant recognized for his entrepreneurial acumen and commitment to social change. (In 1997, he would become Eskom's first black chairman.) Escom's leaders defined their most pressing task as fixing the fiscal mess and turning Escom into one of the world's top utilities. "John and I knew our performance had to be first class, or the government would take over," remembers Dr. McRae. "I had seen all over Africa how disastrous such political interference could be. We had to keep the government out of the engine room."

Electricity for All

Downsizing was a critical step—and a move unheard of at Escom. Over the years, Escom had developed a reputation as an undemanding workplace. People joked that Escom stood for "easy, slow, comfortable." Dr. Maree pushed through instant work-force reductions from 66,000 to 60,000. By 1995 the head count was 39,000. (Today it's just under 30,000.) A name change from *Escom* to *Eskom* symbolically cemented the shift and distanced the company from its former identity as the government's supply commission.

While Dr. Maree drove the company to higher performance, Dr. McRae started to champion the vision of "electricity for all"—a response to the change he believed was inevitable. "South Africa was facing political transition, either through armed struggle or political negotiation," he wrote in his memoir, *The Test of Leadership* (EE Publishers, 2006). "When (not if) the ANC came into power, Eskom needed to be performing to the satisfaction of everyone in our country and that included making electricity available to all, not just one third of the population."

Dr. McRae proposed that Eskom begin offering electricity directly to households in the townships.

Other executives agreed, but saw his plan as too risky, politically and financially. They weren't convinced blacks really wanted electricity; the few who could afford it complained of poor service and exorbitant bills. Furthermore, there was no commercial logic for growing a customer base of poor households, especially because at the time it was still illegal for Eskom to do so.

"To me the threat of not getting people electricity was greater," recalls Dr. McRae. "In these urban townships, there was no commercial or industrial infrastructure. What really worried me wasn't the lack of electricity; it was poverty."

Before pressing for further support within the company, he decided to see for himself if there was market demand. At great personal risk, he went to townships, where few whites had ever ventured, to ask residents directly whether they wanted electricity, and if they would pay for Eskom's service. With the help of the then-banned ANC, he met at night with people in churches and in their homes. On one visit to Soweto, Dr. McRae learned why the bills were so high: Meters were locked in cubicles on the sidewalks and were not read regularly. "When I went to those meetings, I got a clear signal that they did want electricity if the price was reasonable and they could get decent service," he says.

To buttress his argument, he pointed to the *favelas* of Rio de Janeiro. In these squatter cities, which are similar to South Africa's shantytowns, the residents were eager to buy electricity when delivery was reliable. Dr. McRae won the support of Eskom's board, and in 1989, he launched a drive to bring affordable, safe electricity to the townships.

To achieve that goal, the utility had to devise a completely new way to collect payment. There was no postal service, and most residents had no fixed address and did not hold regular jobs. Eskom came up with a revolutionary prepayment system that is still in use; an in-home metering system that changed the dynamics of the black political struggle—withholding payment was a frequent form of protest—and forever altered the business model of Eskom. The in-home system used fare cards purchased at the post office; customers inserted them into the meter to activate the electricity flow. Four lights in the meter box allowed residents to monitor how much electricity they had left. The system also helped residents and the company avoid a mishap that both hated: service disconnections for nonpayment. Township activists continued to play an advocacy role; for example, they pressed for the replacement of unreliable meters.

Meanwhile, as Dr. McRae recalls, new stories of township entrepreneurialism emerged. A man who had baked his family's bread over an open fire invested in two electric ovens, which he used to start a successful bakery business that grew to have seven employees. A skilled welder launched a business with two other men making fencing, security bars for windows, and small steel chairs. Successes like these were the clearest vindication of Eskom's prescience.

Equalizing Opportunity

As the company worked to desegregate power delivery, its leaders attacked segregation inside Eskom. Dr. Maree recalls becoming committed to the idea when the company opened its Matimba power station, near the Botswana border, in 1987. "I'll never forget one man who came up to me and said, 'Dr. Maree, electricity has no color. Eskom should not have color.' That really hit me." To be a top-performing utility, he and Dr. McRae declared, Eskom had to fast-track development of the staff from all races. They also argued that Eskom would better serve black customers if black workers at Eskom held positions of authority.

Integration was painful, especially for middle managers. "I remember sending young engineers, one black and one white, to the power stations," says Dr. Steve Lennon, who was then a middle manager and is now Eskom's managing director of resources and strategy. "They were expected to work together, but they weren't allowed to sleep in the same place. I had a fight with one station manager, and ended up transferring a black scientist to another project because of the segregation." At the same time, it was Eskom's social progressiveness and its growing reputation for technical excellence that attracted highly skilled individuals like Dr. Lennon in the first place.

And it also attracted those few black students who had beaten the odds to become engineers. When Ehud Matya graduated from engineering school in 1986, he committed to a four-year stint with Eskom. He had been the first black at his school to win an Eskom-sponsored scholarship, and Eskom had gone out on a limb to award it to him. Assigned to a team piloting a software system at Duvha Power Plant, the largest in the world, he broke the managerial color barrier. Yet lavatories and lunchrooms were still closed to him. Before the year was over, he left Eskom for a job at South African Breweries. "The race issues were more challenging than I had expected," he says.

Dr. Maree concedes that desegregating Eskom was painful for everyone, as well as time-consuming. "It took us two years to get all our regulations changed, because apartheid was still the law." To pave the way for blacks to assume executive positions, including seats on the Electricity Council, Dr. Maree worked his political connections right up to President Botha. At a meeting with the president in 1987, he says, "We agreed Eskom should take a step very few others had taken."

By the end of 1987, conditions had improved enough that Mr. Matya, for one, felt comfortable returning to Eskom. His post this time was chief of logistics at a distribution unit in Bloemfontein, a conservative Afrikaaner stronghold. "I took the job with the clear intent of being part of the transformation process," he says. Then, after the ANC assumed power in 1994, Mr. Matya became the first black manager at Duvha, where he'd once been forbidden to use the toilets. He is currently Eskom's managing director for generation and sits on the executive management committee.

Eskom's willingness to integrate its work force as far back as the 1970s paid an enormous dividend in building the company's capacity for leadership. "I joined the company in 1993, when the country's transformational initiatives were in their infancy," says Thulani S. Gcabashe, Eskom's current chief executive officer, who started as an electrification manager in Natal. "Eskom saw its chance to get an early start—make our own mistakes and learn from them. So by the time the rest of society was ready to start putting out guidelines, we were the ones being consulted. If you look at the Employment Equity Act of 1998, it is very much based on what we started doing in the 1990s." Even today, Eskom is one of the few South African corporations to consistently meet or exceed the requirements of the first post-apartheid government's 1995 Reconstruction and Development Program, which included targets for promoting affirmative action and bringing water and electricity to poor communities. In 1993, 60 percent of all Eskom employees were black, and 5 percent of the managerial, supervisory, and professional staff were black. By the time Dr. Maree retired in 1997, more than 50 percent of the managerial and technical professionals were black. The next chairman and CEO, respectively, Mr. Khoza and Mr. Gcabashe, aimed by 2000 to fill half of all supervisory personnel and top managerial positions with nonwhites. "In the end, we achieved this goal a year ahead," says Mr. Gcabashe. "We also said 1.75 million homes will have electricity by the year 2000, and we beat that goal a year ahead, too."

Eskom's nonwhite supervisory and managerial goal for 2010 is 65 percent.

Eskom's top executive team is made up almost exclusively of blacks, as is its board of directors. (Dr. Lennon is the only white member of the executive management committee.) Eskom appointed its first black chairman of the board, Mr. Khoza, in 1997. (He stepped down in 2005. His successor is Valli Moosa, a former minister of the environment.) Mr. Gcabashe is Eskom's first black CEO. (He is scheduled to retire at the end of 2007.) By contrast, as of March 2006, Sasol—South Africa's state-owned synthetic fuel and chemical company—had appointed only its second black executive director in 12 years.

As the South African government formalizes and expands its regulations on training and promoting nonwhite managers, companies scramble to formulate their compliance strategies. But Eskom has already met the government requirements, and is now concentrating on recruitment and development strategies, to fill its pipeline of managerial and technical talent in a market where such talent is in short supply.

"We start to recruit young men and women in high school and support them through university. Then we bring them into the business in a two-year training program," says Mr. Gcabashe. The Eskom Foundation, a social investment nonprofit founded by Mr. Khoza and Allen J. Morgan, a former CEO who succeeded Dr. McRae, funds health, education, and small business programs for disadvantaged South Africans. The foundation provides scholarships to promising students and helps schools develop teaching resources in math and science. Eskom is also promoting a first generation of women in management. In 1993, about 8 percent of Eskom professionals were women. Now the number is 30 percent, which includes the only female power station manager in the world, and a senior transmission manager responsible for ensuring the stability of the national grid.

Ubuntu Management

When Mr. Khoza succeeded Dr. Maree, he brought along his own visions for Eskom. As the company's first black chairman, accountable to South Africa's first black government, Mr. Khoza felt his mandate was to complete the integration of Eskom while ensuring it continued to perform at a high level.

To meet this management challenge, he applied an African humanist philosophy known as *ubuntu*. Translated from Zulu as "I am because you are, you are because we are," ubuntu is based on the idea that human beings derive their primary identity from the communities where they live and work, and that these communities must therefore demonstrate respect for people in large and small ways. Mr. Khoza says the ubuntu ethic helped him recognize that white executives held most of the skills and knowledge needed to manage the company. "I could not behave like a bull in a china shop and decree that there will be black managers tomorrow," he says. "I strove to understand the business, not just the business as it technically performs, but the people who deliver and how to motivate them to deliver."

Selling that view inside and outside Eskom was critical to Mr. Khoza's success, and he was tested almost immediately. When he arrived, Eskom's longtime head of finance, who was white, was considering a lucrative job offer. It would have been politically expedient to replace him with a black executive, but Mr. Khoza worked hard to persuade the man to stay at Eskom. "If he had left, the entire finance and treasury department would have followed him and I would have been left with a void," says Mr. Khoza. He saw an opportunity to turn the executive into a valuable ally. What won the employee over, says Mr. Khoza, "was not giving him a counteroffer in terms of money, but selling him on a philosophy."

In his book *The Power of Governance: Enhancing the Performance of State-Owned Enterprises* (coauthored with Mohamed Adam; Pan Macmillan, 2005), Mr. Khoza explains Eskom's credo since 1994: "At the heart of the transformation process was a continued commitment by Eskom and the South African government to superlative performance. This encompasses economic, financial, and operational excellence, social and environmental responsibility, and good governance." It also encompassed a new, almost obsessively detailed dedication to tracking results, in a company that had once "lost" $4 million. The 400-page 2005 annual report lists virtually everything the company achieved or did not achieve, down to the attendance records of directors at board meetings. Although some consider the report overkill, Eskom's executives and managers continually scrutinize the data to develop strategy and improve performance. For example, the company's Human Resources Sustainability Index (HRSI), described by the company as a "measure of Eskom's ongoing ability to achieve its human resources objectives," covers 26 indicators of employee health and wellness, competence, satisfaction, and race and gender equity. "One needs to institutionalize putting race, gender, and performance into a productive context," says Mpho Letlape, Eskom's managing director for human resources.

Eskom has also been a national leader in the fight against HIV/AIDS. In 1987, it launched South Africa's first workplace programs, shining a light on the then-taboo disease with education and treatment programs. It continues to add programs on AIDS awareness and prevention. "Last year, 95 of our colleagues passed away from HIV/AIDS-related diseases. That is a lot of people, but it would have been far worse if we had not started acting when we did," says Mr. Gcabashe.

Eskom sustains its social leadership without sacrificing financial performance. The company has consistently earned a profit since recovering from near-bankruptcy in 1984. It has also earned investment-grade credit ratings from Standard & Poor's, Moody's, and Fitch—a claim few state-owned utilities in developing countries can make.

Confronting the Future

Despite its many accomplishments, Eskom still faces significant challenges. Several major power outages in the Western Cape and local rolling blackouts and tension over rising electricity prices hit Eskom all at once in early 2006. Consumers grew angry, and Eskom became a campaign issue during the local government elections in March. To the country's leading business newspaper, *Business Day*, the year 2006 was Eskom's "horror year. In 12 short months, the electric utility that could do no wrong suddenly became a problem child."

Eskom has addressed the problems. The national rolling blackouts that media predicted never materialized, and the Koeberg nuclear power plant, a primary supplier for the Western Cape, is now back online. Eskom has negotiated a multiyear price agreement with the regulatory agency that keeps electricity prices in line with inflation. In July 2006, the government announced a long-range energy plan for the country, which includes a five-year, R97 billion ($12.2 billion) program—the largest in 20 years—to expand and upgrade Eskom's capacity. Two-thirds of the money will go to generation, including new coal technology, hydro, and gas options; the rest will go to distribution, transmission, new business, and renewable energy. Eskom is working with Plug Power, an American fuel cell manufacturer, and IST Holdings, a South African power industry equipment distributor and longtime Eskom supplier, on a pilot project to make fuel cells affordable. "I had a guy at one American utility tell me that unless I had 100 years of proven field experience, he didn't want to talk to me. A utility needs to be conservative, but Eskom pushes for innovation more than most," says Mark Sperry, chief marketing officer of Plug Power.

A plaque near the entrance to Eskom's headquarters marks the place where a time capsule was buried to mark the company's 75th anniversary in 1998. The capsule will be opened in 2023, Eskom's centennial year. "May the contents highlighting past achievements be a source of inspiration to those achievers of the future," the plaque says. Most of Eskom's current leaders, black and white, were there on the day that capsule was buried, and like most South Africans, they have lived through the transformation of the country and the company.

"I was born in South Africa in 1959, so I'm a product of apartheid. I was designed a racist," says Dr. Lennon. "It is one of those things that South Africans who were born in the late '50s, who went through the public education system, and who are honest with themselves, spend a lot of time thinking about and regretting. But my time at Eskom, and in South Africa, during this transition has been an incredible life experience. What is so exciting is that, as an individual, you can do a lot to create positive change."

Because the lead time for building new power stations is 20 to 25 years, Eskom will always face difficulties in anticipating power capacity needs. And politics is always a complicating factor. No matter how successful Eskom is at keeping the government out of the engine room, it still must answer to those in charge —for good and ill. Debates over pricing and privatization are never settled.

In that light, Eskom's biggest asset is arguably the resilience its leaders, white *and* black, have cultivated throughout the company since the 1980s. That resilience, in turn, has allowed it to stay in front of public-sector trends and needs, a critical capability in a government-owned power utility. "The advantage of being ahead of the game, says Mr. Gcabashe, "is not that you can dictate the terms of legislation, but you can influence the thinking around issues based on the experience you already have."

But one doesn't have to be government-owned, or African, to find inspiration in Eskom's story. These days, every company's performance is in some way tied to the social and political environment in which it operates. If Eskom is a model for companies facing such enormous changes as global warming and soaring health-care costs, then the most effective approach is not risk management as usual. Eskom thrived by anticipating the course of history and stepping out in front of change, thereby building its capacity to lead. Its example suggests that any other company can do the same.

Resources

Anton Eberhard, "The Political Economy of Power Sector Reform in South Africa," working paper no. 6, Program on Energy and Sustainable Development at the Center for Environmental Science and Politics, Stanford Institute for International Studies, April 2004, http://iisdb.stanford.edu/pubs/20183/WP6,_10_May_04.pdf: Context for Eskom's challenges as the primary electricity supplier in South Africa.

Linda A. Hill and Maria Farkas, "A Gentler Capitalism: Black Business Leadership in the New South Africa," Harvard Business School working paper no. 06-057, 2006, www.hbs.edu/research/pdf/06-057.pdf: An informative profile of another South African company's effort to recruit and develop black managers.

Charlayne Hunter-Gault, *New News out of Africa: Uncovering Africa's Renaissance* (Oxford University Press, 2006): The respected American journalist provides fresh perspective on pre- and post-apartheid South Africa, and prospects for the continent.

Reuel J. Khoza and Mohamed Adam, *The Power of Governance: Enhancing the Performance of State-Owned Enterprises* (Pan Macmillan, 2006): The former chairman of Eskom offers views on governance of state-owned enterprises and on the narrowing gap between public- and private-sector management.

Ian McRae, *The Test of Leadership: 50 Years in the Electricity Supply Industry in South Africa* (EE Publishers, 2006), www.eepublishers.co.za/ view.php?sid=943: Eskom's former chief executive tells his story.

Ann Graham (ann.graham@mac.com) is a contributing editor to *strategy+business* and its former deputy editor. Based in Bronxville, N.Y., she focuses on the role of business in society. Her latest publication, Learning for Sustainability (Society for Organizational

Corporate-Level Strategies

6

Chapter Outline

**Corporate-level
Strategy**

The strategy that top
management formulates
for the overall company
(or should be operating).

C hapter 5 laid the foundation for addressing the strategic direction within the organization. Strategies exist at three levels in any organization: the corporate or firm level, the business unit or competitive level, and the functional level. This chapter focuses on the strategy at the broadest of these three levels, the **corporate-level strategy**, or the strategy top management formulates for the overall corporation. In general, corporate-level strategy concerns precede the competitive and tactical issues related to business and functional strategies.

6-1 The Corporate Profile

The first step in formulating an organization's strategy is to assess the markets or industries in which the firm operates. The **corporate profile** identifies one or more businesses and industries in which the firm operates. A firm may choose three basic profiles: (1) to operate in a single industry, (2) to operate in multiple related industries, and (3) to operate in multiple unrelated industries.

Corporate Profile

Identification of the
industry(ies) in which a
firm operates.

Most firms start as single-business companies, and many continue to thrive while remaining active primarily in one industry. By competing in only one industry, firms such as UPS, Exxon-Mobil, and Home Depot can benefit from the specialized knowledge that it develops from concentrating its efforts on one business area. This knowledge can help the firm improve product or service quality and become more efficient in its operations. Firms operating in a single industry are more susceptible to sharp downturns in business cycles, however. For this reason, most large firms eventually pursue diversification and compete in more than one industry. Diversification allows a firm to grow, (potentially) use its resources more effectively, and make use of surplus revenues.

Firms that diversify may choose to compete in related or unrelated industries. Related diversification involves expanding into similar businesses that may complement the original or primary business. Wal-Mart—which also operates Sam's Wholesale Club—benefits from expertise derived from concentration in multiple retailing industries. McDonald's—which owns Boston Market—also operates in related industries. In contrast, General Electric (GE) operates in a vast array of unrelated businesses ranging from television sets to aircraft engines to financial services.

Although diversification can reduce the uncertainty and risk associated with operating in a single industry, participating in numerous unrelated businesses may result in uncertainties associated with losing touch with the fundamentals of each business. As a result, many scholars and executives occupy the middle ground by arguing that aggregate uncertainty is minimized when a firm diversifies its holdings, but only into related industries.[1] Relatedness, however, is ultimately in the eyes of the beholder, and may be based on clear similarities such as product lines or customers or less obvious bases such as distribution channels or raw material similarities.

Unrelated diversification is driven by the desire to capitalize on profit opportunities in a given industry and involves the corporation in businesses that typically are dissimilar. Although such an approach may reduce risk for the firm, it also carries potential disadvantages. Because their interests are spread throughout unrelated business units, strategic managers may not stay abreast of market and technological changes that affect the businesses. In addition, they may unknowingly neglect the firm's primary, or core, business in favor of one or more other units. Avoiding these pitfalls is easier when a firm's business units are related.

The key to successful related diversification is the development of synergy among the related business units. **Synergy** occurs when the combination of two organizations results in higher effectiveness and efficiency than would otherwise be generated separately. Opportunities for synergy are not always easy to identify. Synergy may occur when similarities exist in product or service lines, relationships in the distribution channels, or complementary managerial or technical expertise across business units.

Synergy between business units does not always materialize as originally planned. For example, when Sports Illustrated campaigned in 2005 to merge its Web site with the AOL Web portal to create a massive sports site, AOL balked, suggesting that Sports Illustrated had too little to offer. Several years prior, parent company Time Warner might have encouraged the partnership between its two business units under the guise of "corporate synergy," but instead the Time Warner president, Jeffrey Bewkes, told the magazine to look elsewhere for a partner. Unlike his predecessors who preached synergy among Time Warner business units, Bewkes challenged the universality of the synergy concept and began selling off less profitable businesses.[2] In another example, when CVS acquired pharmacy-benefits manager Caremark Rx in 2007, the California Public Employees Retirement System (CALPERS) voted more than 2.1 million Caremark shares and more than 3.1 million CVS shares against the deal. CALPERS officials charged that poor synergy existed between the retailer and the benefits manager.[3]

Each of the three corporate profiles includes successful firms, as no single profile proves to be the best. After selection of the corporate profile, the next consideration is the corporate strategy.

Synergy

When the combination of two organizations results in higher efficiency and effectiveness that would otherwise be achieved separately.

6-2 Strategic Alternatives at the Corporate Level

The three basic strategic alternatives at the corporate level are growth, stability, and retrenchment. The available strategies are listed in Table 6-1.

6-3 Growth Strategies

The **growth strategy** seeks to significantly increase a firm's revenues or market share. Although many top executives believe that growth is always the single best strategy for a healthy firm, this is not the case. Rather, a firm should adopt a

TABLE 6-1   Corporate-Level Strategies

1. Growth strategies
   a. Internal growth
   b. External growth
      - Horizontal related integration
      - Horizontal related diversification
      - Conglomerate unrelated diversification
      - Vertical integration
      - Strategic alliances (partnerships)
2. Stability strategy
3. Retrenchment strategies
   a. Turnaround
   b. Divestment
   c. Liquidation

Internal Growth

A corporate-level growth strategy in which a firm expands by internally increasing its size and sales rather than by acquiring other companies.

External Growth

A corporate-level growth strategy whereby a firm acquires other companies.

Merger

A corporate-level growth strategy in which a firm combines with another firm through an exchange of stock.

Acquisition

A form of a merger whereby one firm purchases another, often with a combination of cash and stock.

growth strategy only if growth is expected to result in an increase in firm value. This theme is revisited in section 6-4.

Growth may be attained primarily by two means. **Internal growth** is accomplished when a firm increases revenues, production capacity, and its workforce; it can occur by growing an existing business or creating new ones. In contrast, **external growth** is accomplished when two firms merge or one acquires the other. A **merger** occurs when two or more firms, usually of roughly similar sizes, combine into one through an exchange of stock. An **acquisition** is a form of a merger whereby one firm purchases another, often with a combination of cash and stock. Firms with large, successful businesses often acquire smaller competitors with different or complementary product or service lines. For example, Wendy's acquired the Mexican quick-casual chain Baja Fresh in 2001 and grew the chain to include almost two hundred eateries in the United States by 2003.[4] Classifying a merger as an acquisition is not always easy, however.

There are clear advantages to both internal and external growth. Internal growth enables a firm to maintain control over the enterprise by adding new products, facilities, or businesses incrementally. Internal growth enables the firm to preserve its corporate culture and image while expanding at a more controlled pace.

The attractiveness of external growth through mergers and acquisitions seems intuitively obvious: Two firms join forces and the combined organization possesses all the strengths of the individual firms. Indeed, when two firms possess complementary resources and cooperate in a friendly acquisition or merger, the results can be positive (see Strategy at Work 6-1).

External growth has its shortcomings, however. In an acquisition, the acquiring firm typically must pay a premium (i.e., an amount greater than the current share price) to obtain the firm, a process that leads to increased debt and legal fees. In addition, top managers in the acquired firm often depart the organization.

Another potential pitfall associated with mergers and acquisitions is that of blending two distinct cultures or ways of thinking, a process that can be

---

STRATEGY AT WORK 6-1

Sears and Kmart Join Forces

Kmart acquired Sears in November 2004 in an $11.5 billion deal that placed the newly combined firm—named Sears Holding Corporation—in the number three U.S. retailing position behind Wal-Mart and Home Dept. The move followed a decade of struggles by both century-old companies.

Going into the acquisition, Sears boasted more stores (2,000 versus 1,500) and employees (249,000 versus 144,000) than Kmart. From a financial perspective, Kmart was showing signs of turning around several years of dismal performance, generating $801 million in profit during the first nine months of 2004, while Sears had reported $61 million in losses. It was immediately confirmed that the total number of stores and employees would be reduced as the new firm restructures.

Those behind the deal are hoping for improved efficiencies, with each retailer adding a number of successful product lines from the other. Prior to the acquisition Sears was widely believed to be the stronger brand, bringing with it Craftsman tools, Diehard batteries, Kenmore appliances, and Lands' End apparel. Kmart's key brands included Martha Stewart, Jaclyn Smith, Joe Boxer, Route 66, and Sesame Street. Insiders expect some repositioning of the store brands, with Kmart becoming a slightly more upscale retailer and Sears moving in the opposite direction. The extent to which the two retail icons will enjoy renewed success as a team remains to be seen, however.

Source: A. Merrick and D. K. Berman, "Kmart to Buy Sears for $11.5 Billion," Wall Street Journal, 18 November 2004, A1, A8

difficult amidst the rumors or layoffs and restructuring that often accompany the deal.[5] This is especially the case across borders. For example, although carmakers Chrysler and Daimler Benz merged to form DaimlerChrysler in 1998, complete cooperation between members from the two original organizations was slow to develop. During the first few years of the merger, Mercedes executives closely guarded their technology from Chrysler for fear of eroding the Mercedes mystique. The Crossfire—a Chrysler design with Mercedes components—was introduced in 2004 and represented the first joint vehicle. The synergy never seemed to materialize, however, and most of Chrysler was sold to a private investment group, Cerberus, for $7.4 billion in 2007. After other financial considerations were taken into account, Daimler actually paid Cerberus about $500 million to take the financially strapped carmaker it had paid $36 billion for nine years earlier.[6]

External growth can take many forms, five of which are discussed in sections 6-3a through 6-3e. Although these forms are not always mutually exclusive, it is appropriate to consider each example individually.

6-3a Horizontal Related Integration

A firm that acquires other companies in the same line of business is engaging in **horizontal related integration**. Doing so allows a firm operating in a single industry to grow rapidly without moving into other industries. Hence, the primary impetus for such a strategy is a desire for increased market share. Such growth can create scale economies for the firm, increase its negotiating leverage with suppliers, and enable the firm to promote its goods and services to a large audience more efficiently and effectively.

Horizontal Related Integration
A form of acquisition in which a firm expands by acquiring other companies in its same line of business.

6-3b Horizontal Related Diversification

A firm is engaging in **horizontal related diversification** when it acquires a business outside its present scope of operation, but with similar or related **core competencies**, the firm's key capabilities and collective learning skills that are fundamental to its strategy, performance, and long-term profitability. The purpose of horizontal related diversification is to create synergy by transferring and/or sharing the capabilities among the various business units. For example, in the 1990s and early 2000s, numerous banks consolidated to gain economies of scale.

Ideally, core competencies should provide access to a wide array of markets, contribute directly to the goods and services being produced, and be difficult to imitate. When a firm lacks one or more key core competencies and acquires a business unit that possesses them, these two firms may combine complementary core competencies. For example, when a traditional retailer with a quality reputation acquires an e-tailer with a strong Internet presence and Web savvy, the idea is to combine the two capabilities so that the newly created firm can enjoy the best of both competencies.

Horizontal Related Diversification
A form of diversification in which a firm acquires a business outside its present scope of operation but with similar or related core competencies.

Core Competencies
The firm's key capabilities and collective learning skills that are fundamental to its strategy, performance, and long-term profitability.

6-3c Conglomerate (Unrelated) Diversification

When a corporation acquires a business in an unrelated industry to reduce cyclical fluctuations in cash flows or revenues, it is pursuing **conglomerate, or unrelated diversification**.[7] Whereas diversifying into related industries is pursued for strategic reasons, diversifying into unrelated industries is primarily financially driven.[8] Conglomerate diversification allows a firm to continue to grow even when its core business has matured. However, firm managers often lack the expertise required to manage a myriad of unrelated businesses.

Conglomerate (Unrelated) Diversification
A form of diversification in which a firm acquires a business to reduce cyclical fluctuations in cash flows or revenues.

6-3d Vertical Integration

Vertical integration refers to merging various stages of activities in the distribution channel. Firms in some industries tend to be more vertically integrated than those in other industries, although variations can exist among similar firms. Full integration occurs when a firm performs all activities ranging from the procurement of raw materials to the production of final outputs, whereas firms that engage in some but not all of these activities are only partially integrated. When a firm acquires its suppliers (i.e., expands "upstream"), it is engaging in **backward integration**; when a firm acquires its buyers (i.e., expands "downstream"), it is engaging in **forward integration**.

Vertically integrated firms enjoy certain advantages. Vertical integration can reduce transportation costs, provide more opportunities to differentiate products because of the increased control over inputs, and provide access to distribution channels that would not otherwise be accessible to the firm. Transactions costs between suppliers and buyers may be reduced when the same firm owns both entities. Proprietary technology can be more easily secured when information is shared among businesses owned by the same parent firm. It is often possible to reduce costs by coordinating distribution activities among the business units. It is also easier to develop and maintain high quality when a single firm controls all the businesses associated with the production of a good or service.[9]

Vertical integration also has its disadvantages. It can reduce operational flexibility because the firm is heavily invested both upstream and downstream. Vertical integration can even raise production costs and reduce efficiency because of the lack of supplier competition. Overhead costs may increase as the need and ability to coordinate activities among business units increases. Because producers within a vertically integrated firm are committed to working with suppliers owned by the same firm, it will be forced to pay higher prices for its inputs if its suppliers are not technologically competitive.[10]

6-3e Strategic Alliances (Partnerships)

Strategic alliances—often called *partnerships*—occur when two or more firms agree to share the costs, risks, and benefits associated with pursuing new business opportunities. Such arrangements include joint ventures, franchise or license agreements, joint operations, joint long-term supplier agreements, marketing agreements, and consortiums. Strategic alliances can be temporary, disbanding after the project is finished, or can involve multiple projects over an extended time. The late 1990s and early 2000s witnessed a sharp increase in strategic alliances.[11]

Broadly speaking, strategic alliances are considered to be a form of growth, but the firm does not necessarily gain revenues because there is no exchange of resources. Although many strategic alliances may be undertaken for political, economic, or technological reasons, others may be pursued as an alternative to diversification. In this context, a firm may opt to work closely with other firms to pursue various business opportunities instead of attempting to purchase the firms outright. Another key reason is the generation of greater customer value through synergy.[12] A particular project may be so large that it would strain a single company's resources or require complex technology that no single firm possesses. Hence, firms with complementary technologies may combine forces, or one firm may contribute its technological expertise while another contributes its managerial or other abilities.[13]

There are many examples of partnerships, especially where technology and global access are key considerations. IBM and Apple Computer have exchanged

Source: Comstock.com

technology in an attempt to develop more effective computer operating systems. GM, Ford, and Chrysler are jointly conducting research to enhance battery technology for electric cars. GM, Lockheed, Southern California Edison, and Pacific Gas & Electric have been working together to develop widely used electric vehicles and advanced mass transportation systems.[14]

Strategic alliances have two major advantages. First, they minimize increases in bureaucratic, developmental, and coordination costs when compared to mergers and acquisitions. Second, each company can share in the benefits of the alliance without bearing all the costs and risks itself. The major disadvantage of a strategic alliance is that one partner in the alliance may offer less value to the project than other partners but may gain a disproportionate amount of critical know-how from the cooperation with its more progressive partners.

Strategic alliances can be problematic if the partner firms do not agree explicitly on the contribution each will make to the alliance. In 2000, for example, Amazon.com and Toys "R" Us inked a ten-year deal to join forces, with Amazon agreeing to devote a portion of its Web site to Toys "R" Us products, and the toy retailer agreeing to stock certain items on the virtual shelves. Although the arrangement was touted as an example of how Internet retailers can work effectively with their traditional counterparts, the deal deteriorated several years later and ended up in court in 2006. Toys argued that Amazon broke its original commitment to use Toys as its sole provider of toys and related products, while Amazon contended that Toys did not maintain an appropriate selection of products.[15]

6-4 Stability Strategy

Although growth is intuitively appealing, it is not always the most effective strategy. The **stability strategy** *for a firm that has operations in multiple industries* maintains the current array of businesses for two reasons: First, stability enables the corporation to focus managerial efforts on enhancing existing business units, by fostering productivity and innovation. Second, the cost of adding new businesses may exceed the potential benefits. A corporation may adopt a stability strategy in leaner times and shift to a growth strategy when economic conditions improve. Stability can be an effective strategy for a high-performing firm, but it is not necessarily a risk-averse strategy.

For a single-industry firm, the stability strategy is one that maintains approximately the same operations without pursuing significant growth in revenues or in the size of the organization. Growth may occur naturally but is typically limited to the level of industry growth. Such a business may select stability instead of growth for four reasons.

First, *industry growth may be slow or nonexistent.* In this situation, one firm's growth must come at the expense of another firm. This can be particularly costly, especially when attacking an industry leader.[16]

Second, *the costs associated with growth do not always exceed the benefits.* During the cola wars of the 1980s, PepsiCo and Coca-Cola spent millions to lure consumers to their cola brands, only to realize that the costs associated with securing this market share severely dampened profits.

Third, *growth may place great constraints on quality, marketing efforts, and customer service.* Growth for small firms can create a strategic challenge as managers attempt to retain the flexibility and entrepreneurial spirit that helped found the company while making the substantial capital outlays and commitments typically associated with larger firms. Strategic managers of such firms are understandably

Stability Strategy

A corporate-level strategy intended to maintain a firm's present size and current lines of business.

hesitant to adopt growth strategies, even when financial prospects look promising, if they believe that their uniqueness may be lost in the transition. After going public in 2002, U.S. airline upstart JetBlue surpassed the $1 billion mark in revenues in 2004 and announced plans to employ as many as thirty thousand workers to operate 275 planes by 2010. With increased hiring and contract commitments, however, JetBlue risks losing its ability to respond quickly to shifts in consumer demand patterns and environmental factors, an ability that helped shape the firm's early success. As evidenced in 2007, the fast-growing airline stranded hundreds of passengers when inexperienced and overwhelmed customer and crew services did not cancel and reschedule flights appropriately during a snowstorm, an error that cost the company $30 million in payments to customers alone and eventually led to the board's removal of founder David Neeleman.[17]

Even large, established firms can experience quality challenges when they grow rapidly, as has been the case when Toyota achieved 10 percent of the global automobile market in 2004 and began to push toward a goal of 15 percent.[18] Even when Toyota surpassed its sales goal of 150,000 vehicles from its Scion division in 2006, the carmaker decided to place a sales ceiling of 150,000 Scions annually to support the brand's "underground" and hard-to-get image.[19] McDonald's turnaround between 2003 and 2007 has been widely credited to CEO Jim Skinner's decision to eschew growth for a strategy built around improving existing locations through improvements in service, food taste, ambience, value, and marketing.[20]

Finally, *large, dominant firms may not wish to risk prosecution for monopolistic practices associated with growth*. American firms, for example, may be prohibited from acquiring competitors if regulators believe their combined market shares will threaten competitiveness. Even internal growth can be problematic at times, as was the case in the late 1990s through 2001 with Microsoft's costly defense against federal charges that the company unfairly dictated terms in the software industry.

It is interesting to note, however, that declines in demand do not necessarily require a stability strategy for each firm in an industry. To the contrary, business opportunities may be presented when markets shrink. For example, F³ Fat Free Foods is a New York–based retailer of more than seven thousand food products, most of which are fat free. In the early 2000s, most analysts were proclaiming that the fat-free category was past its prime. The urban grocer was experiencing considerable success, however, due in part to the declining attention traditional grocers were paying to a hard-core segment of fat-conscious consumers.[21]

6-5 Retrenchment Strategies

Retrenchment Strategy

A corporate-level strategy designed to reduce the size of the firm.

Turnaround

A corporate-level retrenchment strategy intended to transform the firm into a leaner and more effective business by reducing costs and rethinking the firm's product lines and target markets.

Growth and stability strategies are usually adopted when firms are performing well. When performance is disappointing, however, a **retrenchment strategy** may be appropriate. Retrenchment may take one or a combination of three forms: turnaround, divestment, or liquidation.

6-5a Turnaround

A **turnaround** seeks to transform the corporation into a leaner, more effective firm, and includes such actions as eliminating unprofitable outputs, pruning assets, reducing the size of the workforce, cutting costs of distribution, and reassessing the firm's product lines and customer groups.[22] Turnarounds are often preceded by changes in the macroenvironment, industry structure, or competitive behavior. Broadly speaking, a turnaround is not as drastic a move as restructuring, although the two can work together.

Consider, as an example, what may be the most famous turnaround in U.S. history. By the late 1970s, Chrysler was on the verge of bankruptcy. Its newly hired CEO, Lee Iacocca, implemented a dramatic turnaround strategy. Many employees were laid off, while those remaining agreed to forgo part of their salaries and benefits. Twenty plants were either closed or consolidated. Collectively, these actions lowered the firm's break-even point from an annual sales level in half to about 1.2 million vehicles. It is interesting to note that Iacocca also implemented a divestment strategy (another form of retrenchment) by selling Chrysler's marine outboard motor, defense, and air-conditioning divisions, as well as all of its automobile manufacturing plants located outside the United States. By 1982, Chrysler began to show a profit after having lost $3.5 billion in the preceding four years. Over the subsequent two decades, Chrysler embarked on various forms of growth and stability strategies, merged with Daimler Benz to form DaimlerChrysler, and was eventually sold to Cerberus in 2007.

Turnarounds often focus on a change of company leadership. When Greg Brenneman replaced Brad Blum as Burger King CEO in 2004, sales had declined to the point where the fast-food chain was on the verge of losing its number two position behind McDonald's to Wendy's. Brenneman moved quickly to improve morale and relationships with franchisees, who control about 90 percent of all restaurants. He also cut costs and increased sales with an assortment of new products. As a result, customer traffic increased by 7 percent in 2005, the first annual increase in eight years.[23]

When a turnaround involves layoffs, firms must be prepared to address their effects on both departing employees and survivors. Employees may be given opportunities to voluntarily leave—generally with an incentive—to make the process as congenial as possible. When this situation occurs, however, those departing are often the top performers who are most marketable, leaving the firm with a less competitive workforce. Of course, when layoffs are simply announced, morale is likely to suffer considerably. For this reason, turnarounds involving layoffs are often more difficult to implement than anticipated.[24]

When layoffs are necessary, however, several actions can help to palliate some of the negative effects. Specifically, top management is encouraged to communicate honestly and effectively with all employees, explaining why the downsizing is necessary and how terminated employees were selected. Everyone, including the "survivors," should be made aware of how departing employees will be supported. Employees should also be encouraged to partake of services available to them, and special efforts should be made to ensure that such programs are administered in a clear and consistent manner.[25] Although these measures will not eliminate all the harsh feelings associated with layoffs, they can help keep the process under control.

Some executives are widely recognized as "turnaround specialists" and may be brought in as temporary CEOs to lead the process and orchestrate such unpopular strategic moves as layoffs, budget cuts, and reorganizations. Robert "Steve" Miller, also a major player in the Chrysler turnaround, has served as CEO of Waste Management and the automobile parts supplier Federal-Mogul, as well as a consultant on turnaround issues to such companies as Aetna. According to Miller, the CEO in a company seeking turnaround should be honest with employees from the outset and seek their input. The CEO should also spend time with customers. As Miller put it, "Listen to your customers. [They] are usually more perceptive than you are about what you need to do with your company."[26]

Step 9: What Is the Current Firm-Level Strategy?

What is the corporate profile? Is the organization attempting to grow, maintain its present size, or retrench? One need not be concerned with what the company *should be* doing at this point, but rather what *is presently being* implemented. It is important to provide sufficient detail to support the assessment of the strategy. It is also important not to assume that public references to growth in one specific division or line of business necessarily means that a firm is pursuing an *overall growth* strategy.

6-5b Divestment

Divestment

A corporate-level retrenchment strategy in which a firm sells one or more of its business units.

If it is believed that one or more of the firm's business units may function more effectively as part of another firm, then a **divestment** strategy may be pursued. Divestment may be necessary when the industry is in decline, or when a business unit drains resources from more profitable units, is not performing well, or is not synergistic with other corporate holdings. In a well-publicized spin-off, PepsiCo divested its KFC, Taco Bell, and Pizza Hut business units into a new company, Tricon Global Restaurants, Inc., in 1997. The spin-off was designed to refocus PepsiCo's efforts on its beverage and snack food divisions. Tricon's name was officially changed to Yum Brands in 2002. Yum added A&W All American Food and Long John Silver's to the portfolio shortly thereafter and has performed well.

6-5c Liquidation

Liquidation

A corporate-level retrenchment strategy in which a firm terminates one or more of its business units by the sale of their assets.

Liquidation is the strategy of last resort, and terminates the business unit by selling its assets. In effect, liquidation represents a divestment of *all* the firm's business units and should be adopted only under extreme conditions. Shareholders and creditors experience financial losses, some of the managers and employees lose their jobs, suppliers lose a customer, and the community suffers an increase in unemployment and a decrease in tax revenues. For this reason, liquidation should be pursued only when other forms of retrenchment are not viable (see Case Analysis 6-1).

6-6 BCG Growth-Share Matrix

It is often difficult to coordinate the activities of multiple business units, particularly when they are minimally related or not related at all. Corporate portfolio frameworks have been developed to provide guidelines for strategists. Although firm-specific conditions may require exceptions to the guidelines, these frameworks can provide an excellent starting point to consider strategy in firms with multiple business units. The Boston Consulting Group (BCG) original framework is one of the most widely recognized.

BCG Growth-share Matrix

A corporate portfolio framework developed by the Boston Consulting Group (BCG) that categorizes a firm's business units by the market share that the firm holds and the growth rate of the firm's respective markets.

The **BCG growth-share matrix** was developed in 1967 by the Boston Consulting Group (BCG) and is illustrated by the matrix shown in Figure 6-1. The market's rate of growth is indicated on the vertical axis, and the firm's share of the market is indicated on the horizontal axis. A firm's business units can be plotted on the matrix with a circle whose size denotes the relative size of the business unit. The horizontal position of a business indicates its market share, and its vertical position depicts the growth rate of the market in which it competes. Managers and consultants can categorize each business unit as a star, question mark, cash cow, or dog, depending on each one's relative market share and the growth rate of its market.[27]

FIGURE 6-1   The Original BCG Framework

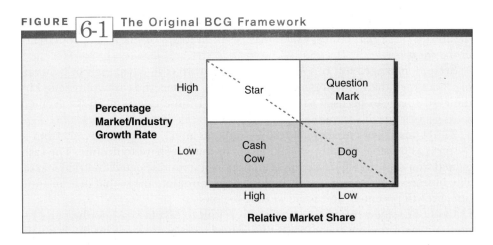

A *star* is a business unit that has a large share of a high-growth market, generally 10 percent or higher. Although stars are usually profitable, they often necessitate considerable cash to continue their growth and to fight off the numerous competitors that are attracted to fast growing markets. *Question marks* are business units with low shares of rapidly growing markets, and may be new businesses just entering the market. If they are able to grow and develop into market leaders, they evolve into stars; if not, they will likely be divested or liquidated.

A *cash cow* is a business unit that has a large share of a slow-growth market, generally less than 10 percent. Cash cows are normally highly profitable because they often dominate a market that does not attract a large number of new entrants. Because they are well established, they need not spend vast resources for advertising, product promotions, or consumer rebates. The firm may invest the excess cash generated in its stars and question marks. Lastly, *dogs* are business units that have small market shares in slow-growth (or even declining) industries. Dogs are generally marginal businesses that incur either losses or small profits, and are often liquidated.

Ideally, a well-balanced corporation should have mostly stars and cash cows, some question marks (because they can represent the future of the corporation), and few, if any, dogs. To attain this ideal, corporate-level managers have four options (see Figure 6-2). First, managers can *build* market share with stars and question marks. The key for question marks is to identify and support the promising ones

FIGURE 6-2   Alternative Strategies with Strategic Business Units

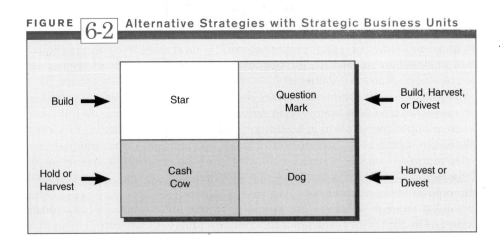

so that they can be transformed into stars. Building market share may involve significant price reductions, which may result in losses or marginal profitability in the short run.

Second, management can *hold* market share with cash cows, thereby generating more cash than building market share does. Hence, the cash contributed by the cash cows can be used to support stars and those question marks deemed most promising.

Third, management may *harvest*, or milk, as much short-term cash from a business as possible, usually while allowing its market share to decline. The cash gained from this strategy is also used to support stars and selected question marks. The businesses harvested usually include dogs, question marks that demonstrate little growth potential, and some weak cash cows.

Lastly, management may *divest* a business unit to provide cash to the corporation and stem the outflow of cash that would have been spent on the business in the future. As dogs and less promising question marks are divested, the cash provided is reallocated to stars and more promising question marks.

All things equal, healthy multibusiness unit firms should maintain a balance of business units that generate cash and those that require funds for growth. Broadly speaking, business units below the dotted line in Figure 6-1 are *revenue generators*, whereas business units above the dotted line are *revenue users*. The balance of businesses on both sides of the line can be a key factor in decisions to acquire new business units or divest old ones.

The BCG matrix heavily emphasizes the importance of market share leadership as a precursor to profitability. Some question marks are cultivated to become leaders as well, but less promising question marks and dogs are usually targeted either for harvesting or divestiture.

The BCG matrix provides managers with a systematic means of considering the relationships among business units in its portfolio. A number of limitations of this and similar frameworks have been identified, however. For example, the BCG matrix assumes that success is directly linked to high performance, a relationship that often—but not always—exists in a corporation. The model also assumes that strategic managers are free to make portfolio decisions, such as transferring capital from cash cows to question marks, without challenges from shareholders and others. Hence, although the BCG matrix serves as an excellent starting point and generates discussion on critical strategy issues, it should not be interpreted literally.

6-7 Global Corporate Strategy

Regardless of the corporate profile, a business may choose to be involved only in its domestic market, or it may compete abroad at one of three levels: international, multinational, or global. Effective operation at any of these levels often—but not always—necessitates economies of scale and a relatively high market share.[28]

Moving outside the domestic market, some companies choose to be involved on an *international* basis by operating in various countries but limiting their involvement to importing, exporting, licensing, or making strategic alliances. Exporting alone can significantly benefit even a small company. However, international joint ventures—a form of strategic alliance involving cooperative arrangements between businesses across borders—may be desirable even when resources for a direct investment are available.

Global strategic alliances are common in the automobile manufacturing industry. In 2001, GM launched a $333 million joint venture with Russian firm

OAO Avtovaz. GM provides technological support to the struggling holdover from Soviet-era industry to engineer a stripped-down version of an SUV currently offered by the Avtovaz. By engaging in the joint venture, GM gained immediate access to the market but placed its reputation on the line by putting its "Chevy" name on a vehicle produced by a technologically weak automobile producer. In 2005, the venture's annual production had reached about 50,000 sedans and SUVs—the Viva and Niva respectively—sold under the Chevrolet brand. In 2006, however, venture profits declined and GM announced plans to build its own production facilities in Russia, an indication that the joint venture may be in trouble.[29]

Automotive joint ventures are also popular in Asia. By 2005, most major Chinese automakers had secured established global partners to assist in their expansion outside of China. Shanghai Automotive Industry Corporation (SAIC) has partnered with Volkswagen and General Motors, Dongfeng Motor with Nissan and Peugeot-Citroën, and Changan with Ford and Suzuki. When Toyota outsold Ford for the first time in July 2006, Ford launched an intensive review of its brands and began to explore global alliances even more.[30]

Firms with global objectives may decide to invest directly in facilities abroad. Due to the complexities associated with establishing operations across borders, however, strategic alliances may be particularly attractive to firms seeking to expand their global involvement. Companies often possess market, regulatory, and other knowledge about their domestic markets but may need to partner with companies abroad to gain access to this knowledge as it pertains to international markets. The international strategic alliances visible among automobile producers include production facilities owned jointly by General Motors and Toyota and by Ford and Mazda.

International strategic alliances provide particular advantages to a firm. They can provide entry into a global market, access to the partner's knowledge about the foreign market, and risk sharing with the partner firm. They can work effectively when partners can learn from each other, when neither partner is large enough to function alone, and when both partners share common strategic goals but are not in direct competition. Problems that arise from international joint ventures include disputes and lack of trust over proprietary knowledge, cultural differences between firms, and disputes over ways to share the costs and revenues associated with the partnership.

Other conservative options are also available to a firm seeking an international presence. Under an **international licensing** agreement, a foreign licensee purchases the rights to produce a company's products and use its technology in the licensee's country for a negotiated fee structure. This arrangement is common among pharmaceutical firms. Drug producers in one nation typically allow producers in other nations to produce and market their products abroad.[31]

International franchising is a long-term form of licensing in which a local franchisee pays a franchiser in another country for the right to use the franchiser's brand names, promotions, materials, and procedures.[32] Whereas licensing is predominantly pursued by manufacturers, franchising is more commonly utilized in service industries, such as fast-food restaurants.

Other companies are involved at the *multinational* level, where firms direct investments in other countries, and their subsidiaries operate independently of one another. Colgate-Palmolive has attained a large worldwide market share through its decentralized operations in foreign markets.

Finally, some firms are *globally* involved, with direct investments and interdependent subdivisions abroad. For example, some of Caterpillar's subsidiaries

International Licensing

An arrangement whereby a foreign licensee purchases the rights to produce a company's products and/or use its technology in the licensee's country for a negotiated fee structure.

International Franchising

A form of licensing in which a local franchisee pays a franchiser in another country for the right to use the franchiser's brand names, promotions, materials, and procedures.

produce components in different countries, while other subsidiaries assemble these components, and still other units sell the finished products. As a result, Caterpillar has achieved a low-cost position by producing its own heavy components for its large global market. If its various subsidiaries operated independently and produced only for their individual regional markets, Caterpillar would be unable to realize these vast economies of scale.[33]

Expanding into global markets is not always easy. In 2003, for example, McDonald's announced plans to expand its cadre of 566 stores in China by approximately 100 stores annually. By that time, however, KFC had already grown to about 900 eateries in China with plans for an additional 200 units annually. McDonald's slower growth resulted from its struggle to build a network of local suppliers, many of whom are the same ones it utilizes in the United States, whereas KFC built a network of Chinese suppliers while aggressively adapting to local tastes in an effort to speed up its growth efforts. Starbuck's has about five hundred Chinese locations but has found it difficult to convert a nation of tea drinkers to specialty coffees.[34]

Some of the complexities associated with adopting a global perspective are illustrated by Kellogg's production dilemma. Some countries appreciate the vitamin fortification in Corn Flakes common in Kellogg's host country, the United States. Denmark, however, does not want vitamins added to cereal for fear that some might exceed recommended daily doses. Officials in the Netherlands do not believe vitamin D or folic acid is beneficial, but the Finns like more vitamin D to make up for sun deprivation. As a result, Kellogg plants in England and Germany have produced four different varieties of Corn Flakes since 1997 to meet the differences in demand throughout the European Union.[35]

Consider Wal-Mart. When the giant retailer first expanded outside of the United States in the early 1990s, the retailing giant made mistakes by presuming that its successful American model would succeed in disparate global markets. Golf clubs in Brazil and ice skates in Mexico were among the early casualties, and some German customers mistook the friendliness of its clerks for flirting. In the early and mid-2000s, Wal-Mart changed course, expanding by acquiring successful local retail chains, hiring locals to manage them, and learning the local tastes and culture. Wal-Mart's acquisitions of grocer Asda in the United Kingdom and retailer Cifra SA in Mexico have given the firm strong stakes in two nations without expanding its operations internally.[36] Wal-Mart has grown rapidly and enjoyed considerable success in developing markets such as Mexico where "shoppers care more about the cost of medicine and microwaves than the cultural incursions of a multinational corporation."[37]

Wal-Mart was never able to win over Germany's frugal and demanding customers from the country's strong, local discount retailers. After losing money for eight years, Wal-Mart sold its eighty-five stores to German rival Metro AG. Interestingly, the firm's largest global competitor, Carrefour, seemed to know better all along. Carrefour had operations in twenty-nine countries when Wal-Mart decided to leave Germany altogether in 2006, but the number two global retailer never had stores in Germany.[38]

Wal-Mart has faced other challenges in China where the retailer has sixty-six stores, mostly hypermarkets. Wal-Mart's global rival Carrefour has eighty stores, however, and China's top thirty domestic chain stores operate more than sixteen thousand outlets, making for a highly competitive market. Expansion outside of the most developed cities, such as Shanghai and Beijing, is a complex task indeed. China lacks a nationwide logistics network of trucks, highways, and warehouses to distribute products efficiently. Local tastes vary in a country with multiple languages and dialects and diverse climates. For example, one-half of Chinese grocery expenditures are on fresh and live produce, a necessity in a nation with few refrigerated trucks. The result is a highly fragmented market, with the top hundred retailers accounting for less than 10 percent of total retail sales. Wal-Mart is attempting to gain a national footprint by purchasing stores currently operated by Trust-Mart, a Chinese retailer known for small outlets emphasizing basic products at low prices. In 2006, Wal-Mart introduced a credit card in partnership with China's Bank of Communication, the first issued by a foreign company in a country where less than 5 percent of the population uses credit cards. As we can see, Wal-Mart will be challenged to develop its presence in China over the next decade.[39]

Firms change from domestic-oriented strategies to a global orientation for numerous reasons. Pursuing global markets can reduce per-unit production costs by increasing volume. A global strategy can extend the product life cycle of products whose domestic markets may be declining, as U.S. cigarette manufacturers did in the 1990s. Establishing facilities abroad can also help a firm benefit from cost differences associated with comparative advantage, which partially explains why athletic shoes tend to be produced most efficiently in parts of Asia where rubber is plentiful and labor is less costly. A global orientation can lessen risk because demand and competitive factors tend to vary among nations. Consider the following factors, however.

1. Are customer needs abroad similar to those in the firm's domestic market? If so, the firm may be able to develop economies of scale by producing a higher volume of the same goods or services for both markets.

2. Are differences in transportation and other costs abroad favorable and conducive to producing goods and services abroad? Are these differences favorable and conducive to exporting or importing goods from one country to another?

3. Are the firm's customers or partners already involved in global business? If so, the firm may need to become equally involved.

4. Will distributing goods and services abroad be difficult? If competitors already control distribution channels in another country, expansion into that country will be difficult.

5. Will government trade policies facilitate or hinder global expansion? For example, NAFTA facilitates trade among firms in the United States, Canada, and Mexico. Similar trading blocs, such as the European Economic Union (EEU), occur in other parts of the world.

6. Will managers in one country be able to learn from managers in other countries? If so, global expansion may improve efficiency and effectiveness, both abroad and in the host country.

Corporate growth is often pursued through expansion into emerging economies, those nations that have achieved enough development to warrant expansion but whose markets are not yet fully served. Although emerging economies such as China, South Africa, Mexico, and parts of eastern Europe are attractive in many respects, poor infrastructure (e.g., telecommunications, highways), cumbersome government regulations, and a poorly trained workforce can create great challenges for the firm considering expansion. The advantages and disadvantages of growth through global expansion should be considered carefully before pursuing expansion into an emerging market.

6-8 Summary

Two key sets of strategic decisions must be made at the corporate level. First, top executives must identify the corporate profile and determine whether the firm will operate in a single business, in more than one related business, or in more than one unrelated business. Benefits and shortcomings are associated with each profile option.

Second, strategic managers must select a corporate strategy from among three basic choices: growth, stability, or retrenchment. Additional alternatives associated with growth and retrenchment strategies must also be addressed. A firm may choose a form of corporate restructuring to support strategic attempts to revive its competitiveness and performance.

Portfolio frameworks such as the BCG matrix can assist corporate executives in managing the relationships among the firm's business units. In doing so, executives must determine the extent to which the firm will involve itself in business operations.

Global concerns represent a key consideration at the corporate strategy level. The three broad options range from conservative to aggressive, each with advantages and disadvantages, depending on the level of international involvement desired.

Key Terms

acquisition

backward integration

BCG growth-share matrix

conglomerate unrelated
  diversification

core competencies

corporate-level strategy

corporate profile

divestment

external growth

forward integration

growth strategy

horizontal related diversification

horizontal related integration

internal growth

international franchising

international licensing

liquidation

merger

retrenchment strategy

stability strategy

strategic alliances

synergy

turnaround

vertical integration

Review Questions and Exercises

1. What are the advantages and disadvantages of internal growth as opposed to growth through mergers and acquisitions?

2. Why would management adopt a stability strategy? Can stability strategies be viable over time? Why or why not?

3. When is a retrenchment strategy appropriate? What criteria can help determine what particular retrenchment strategy should be used?

4. How should the BCG matrix be applied? Are such portfolios always useful to corporate executives?

5. What are the advantages and disadvantages associated with corporations operating in centralized or decentralized fashions?

6. What factors should a firm's managers consider when determining the degree of international involvement appropriate for the organization?

Practice Quiz

True or False

1. Because firms operating in single industries are more susceptible to industry downturns, most firms eventually diversify into other industries.

2. The growth strategy is the most effective strategy for a healthy firm.

3. Synergy occurs when the combination of two organizations results in higher effectiveness and efficiency than would otherwise be generated by them separately.

4. Strategic alliances typically involve higher bureaucratic and developmental costs when compared to mergers and acquisitions.

5. Corporate restructuring involves the acquisition of business units unrelated to the firm's core business unit.

6. The BCG matrix provides managers with a systematic means of determining whether a growth, stability, or retrenchment strategy should be adopted.

Multiple Choice

7. Diversification allows a firm to

  A. concentrate its efforts on a single business.

  B. use its resources more effectively.

  C. create excess resources.

  D. all of the above

8. A firm seeking rapid growth should pursue

  A. internal growth.

  B. external growth.

  C. divestment of poor performing businesses.

  D. a restructuring strategy.

9. When a firm purchases both its suppliers and buyers, it is engaging in

  A. forward integration.

  B. backward integration.

  C. both forward and backward integration.

  D. none of the above

10. Which of the following is not a potential reason for selecting a stability strategy?

  A. The industry is not growing.

  B. Growth may place constraints on customer service.

  C. Costs associated with growth exceed its benefits.

  D. The stability inherently reduces risk.

11. Firms operating on an international basis limit their activities to

  A. importing and exporting.

  B. licensing.

  C. strategic alliances.

  D. all of the above

12. Which of the following is not an advantage of international joint ventures?

  A. Firms gain access to knowledge about a foreign market.

  B. Partners have the ability to eliminate risk associated with global expansion.

  C. Firms can learn from each other.

  D. Entry into the foreign market is secured.

Notes

1. M. Lubatkin and S. Chatterjee, "Extending Modern Portfolio Theory into the Domain of Corporate Diversification: Does It Apply?" *Academy of Management Journal* 37 (1994): 109–136.

2. M. Karnitschnig, "After Years of Pushing Synergy, Time Warner Says Enough," *Wall Street Journal Online* (2 June 2006).

3. J. Covert, "CVS Shareholders Approve Chain's Offer for Caremark," *Wall Street Journal Interactive Edition* (15 March 2007).

4. T. Bouza and G. Sama, "America Adds Salsa to Its Burgers and Fries," *Wall Street Journal* (2 January 2003): A1, A12.

5. M. A. Hitt, J. S. Harrison, and R. D. Ireland, *Mergers and Acquisitions: A Guide to Creating Value for Stakeholders* (New York: Oxford University Press, 2001).

6. N. E. Boudette, "At DaimlerChrysler, a New Push to Make Its Units Work Together," *Wall Street Journal* (12 March 2003): A1, A15; J. R. Healey, S. S. Carty, C. Woodyard, and M. Krantz, "Chrysler Sold in Unprecedented Auto Deal," *USA Today* (17 May 2007).

7. M. S. Salter and W. S. Weinhold, "Diversification via Acquisition: Creating Value," *Harvard Business Review* 56(4) (1978): 166–176.

8. L. E. Palich, L. B. Cardinal, and C. C. Miller, "Curvilinearity in the Diversification-Performance Linkage: An Examination of over Three Decades of Research," *Strategic Management Journal* 21 (2000): 155–174.

9. S. Bhuyan, "Impact of Vertical Mergers on Industry Profitability: An Empirical Evaluation," *Review of Industrial Organization* 20 (2002): 61–78.

10. R. D. Buzzell, "Is Vertical Integration Profitable?" *Harvard Business Review* 61(1): 92–102.

11. J. J. Reuer, M. Zollo, and H. Singh, "Post-Formation Dynamics in Strategic Alliances," *Strategic Management Journal* 23 (2002): 135–152.

12. B. N. Anand and T. Khanna, "Do Firms Learn to Create Value? The Case of Alliances," *Strategic Management Journal* 21 (2000): 295–315.

13. T. E. Stuart, "Interorganizational Alliances and the Performance of Firms: A Study of Growth and Innovation Rates in a High-Technology Industry," *Strategic Management Journal* 21 (2000): 791–811.

14. P. Wright, M. Kroll, and J. A. Parnell, *Strategic Management: Concepts* (Upper Saddle River, NJ: Prentice Hall, 1998).

15. M. Mangalindan, "How Amazon's Dream Alliance with Toys 'R' Us Went So Sour," *Wall Street Journal* (23 January 2006): A1, A12.

16. K. G. Smith, W. J. Ferrier, and C. M. Grimm, "King of the Hill: Dethroning the Industry Leader," *Academy of Management Executive* 15(2) (2001): 59–70.

17. S. Carey, "Amid JetBlue's Rapid Ascent, CEO Adopts Big Rivals' Traits," *Wall Street Journal* (25 August 2005): A1, A6; J. Lipton, "Storm Worries Ground JetBlue," *Forbes Online Edition* (16 March 2007); S. Carey and P. Prada, "Course Change: Why JetBlue Shuffled Top Rank," *Wall Street Journal* (11 May 2007): B1, B2.

18. N. Shirouzu and S. Moffett, "As Toyota Closes in on GM, It Develops a Big Three Problem," *Wall Street Journal* (4 August 2004): A1, A3.

19. G. Chon, "A Way Cool Strategy: Toyota's Scion Plans to Sell Fewer Cars," *Wall Street Journal* (10 November 2006): B1, B2.

20. J. Adamy, "How Jim Skinner Flipped McDonald's," *Wall Street Journal* (5 January 2007): B1, B2.

21. J. A. Tannenbaum, "Fat-Free Store Tries to Gain Weight as U.S. Gets Greasy," *Wall Street Journal Interactive Edition* (13 February 2001).

22. See M. Garry, "A&P Strikes Back," *Progressive Grocer* (February 1994): 32–38.

23. S. Gray, "Flipping Burger King," *Wall Street Journal* (26 April 2005): B1, B7.

24. M. Murray, "Waiting for the Ax to Fall," *Wall Street Journal* (13 March 2001): B1, B10.

25. *Purchasing*, "Some Specifics on How to Handle Layoffs" (16 December 1999), http://www.manufacturing.net/pur/index.asp?layout=article&articleId=CA148401&stt=001&text=some+specifics+on+how+to+handle+layoffs.

26. J. S. Lublin, "Tips from a Turnaround Specialist," *Wall Street Journal* (27 December 2000): B1.

27. B. Hedley, "Strategy and the Business Portfolio," *Long Range Planning* 10(2) (1977): 9–14.

28. J. M. Geringer, S. Tallman, and D. M. Olsen, "Product and International Diversification among Japanese Multinational Firms," *Strategic Management Journal* 21 (2000): 51–80.

29. M. Scallon, "Russia: Is Historic Auto Partnership Nearing Its End? *Radio Free Europe-Radio Liberty* (12 June 2006); G. L. White, "GM Trusts Former Soviet Auto Maker to Build Car with the Chevy Name," *Wall Street Journal Interactive Edition* (20 February 2001).

30. J. McCracken, "Ford to Review Its Ailing Brands, Explore Alliances," *Wall Street Journal* (2 August 2006): A1, A9; G. Chon, "U.S. Auto Makers' Sales Slump as Toyota Tops Ford," *Wall Street Journal* (2 August 2006): A1, A9.

31. H. Merchant and D. Schendel, "How Do International Joint Ventures Create Shareholder Value?" *Strategic Management Journal* 21 (2000): 723–737; T. L. Powers and R. C. Jones, "Strategic Combinations and Their Evolution in the Global Marketplace," *Thunderbird International Business Review* 43 (2001): 525–534.

32. P. Chan and R. Justis, "Franchise Management in East Asia," *Academy of Management Executive* 4 (1990): 75–85.

33. Wright et al., *Strategic Management*.

34. B. Dolven, "Trailing KFC, McDonald's Plans to Accelerate Expansion in China," *Wall Street Journal* (8 September 2003): A13; G. A. Fowler, "Starbucks' Road to China," *Wall Street Journal* (14 July 2003): B1, B3.

35. T. Sims, "Corn Flakes Clash Shows the Glitches in European Union," *Wall Street Journal* (1 November 2005): A1, A9.

36. G. Samor, C. Rohwedder, and A. Zimmerman, "Innocents Abroad?" *Wall Street Journal Online* (16 May 2006).

37. J. Lyons, "In Mexico, Wal-Mart Is Defying Its Critics," *Wall Street Journal* (5 March 2007): A1.

38. A. Zimmerman and E. Nelson, "With Profits Elusive, Wal-Mart to Exit Germany," *Wall Street Journal* (29 July 2006): A1.

39. M. Fong, K. Linebaugh, and G. Fairclough, "Retail's One-China Problem," *Wall Street Journal* (23 October 2006): B1, B12.

Insight from *strategy+business*

Executives are constantly searching for ways to make their firms more innovative. This chapter's strategy+business reading suggests, however, that some firms are built for innovation and market development whereas others are best equipped for industry consolidation. It is important for strategic decision makers to recognize the capabilities the organization has—and does not have—when charting a course of action. Concepts discussed in the article relate to development and execution of both corporate and business strategies.

Colonizers and Consolidators: The Two Cultures of Corporate Strategy

By Costas Markides and Paul Geroski

Take this quick test: Which innovative company created online bookselling in the 1990s? If your answer is Amazon.com, you are wrong. The idea for online bookselling—and the first online bookstore—came from Charles Stack, an Ohio-based bookseller, in 1991. Computer Literacy, a successful retail chain, also registered an Internet domain name for a bookstore in 1991. Amazon did not enter the market until 1995.

Another quiz: Which innovator came up with the idea for online brokerage services? If you answered Charles Schwab or E-Trade, again you are wrong. Two Chicago brokerage firms—Howe Barnes Investments Inc. and Security APL Inc.—launched the first Internet-based stock trading service, a joint venture called the Net Investor, in January 1995. Schwab did not launch its Web-trading service until March 1996.

Both examples highlight a simple point: The individuals or companies that create radically new markets are not necessarily the ones that scale them into mass markets. Indeed, historical evidence shows that in the majority of cases, product and service pioneers are almost *never* the ones to conquer the markets they create. For at least 20 years, the Xerox Corporation has been derided for its inability to successfully commercialize scores of new products and technologies, including, notably, the now ubiquitous personal computer OS interface, developed at its PARC research center in Northern California. In reality, Xerox's failure is more the norm than the exception.

For those brought up to believe in the enduring value of "pioneering" and "first-mover advantage," such a statement may come as a surprise. However, recent work by many scholars, including William Boulding, a professor at Duke University's Fuqua School of Business, and Markus Christen, an assistant professor at INSEAD; former Booz Allen Hamilton executives Rhonda Germany, Raman Muralidharan, Charles F. Lucier, and Janet D. Torsilieri; Steven P. Schnaars, a professor of marketing at Baruch College's Zicklin School of Business; and Gerard J. Tellis, of the University of Southern California's Marshall School of Business, and Peter N. Colder, an associate professor at New York University's Stern School of Business—as well as our own research—has shown that the widely held belief that pioneers enjoy first-mover advantages and grow to market dominance is simply wrong.

Our research, which examined the early evolution of several new markets, provided a number of clues about how markets are created, how they evolve, and what their structural features and characteristics are in their early formative years. (See "Research Methodology," following page.) In industry after industry, we saw the same pattern unfold: Upon the creation of a new market, there's a mad entry rush by scores, sometimes hundreds, of players to colonize it. At some stage in the evolution of the market, a "dominant design" emerges, which standardizes the core product or service being produced, gives it its lasting identity, and defines the identity of the market it serves. Upon the emergence of this dominant design, a shakeout and consolidation takes place in the market: The overwhelming majority of early movers that choose the wrong design go out of business; a few prescient (or lucky) ones that bet on the winning design survive, and a handful of these grow to market dominance.

For example, more than 1,000 firms populated the U.S. automotive industry at one time or another between

Source: Reprinted with permission from *strategy+business,* the award-winning management quarterly published by Booz Allen Hamilton. http://www.strategy-business.com.

its creation in 1885 and the introduction of Ford's Model T in 1908; dozens of new carmakers entered and exited the industry each year during that period. Yet by the late 1950s, only seven auto manufacturers were left in the United States. Similarly, there were more than 274 competitors in the tire market in the early 1920s. Fifty years later, no more than 23 had survived. And from a peak of 89 competitors in the television-set industry in the 1950s, only a small number of U.S.-owned manufacturers existed at the end of the 1980s—and none after 1995.

Although the survivors in the consolidation wars are those that, by definition, selected the winning design, only a handful of these lucky or insightful victors will grow to dominate the new market. The eventual market leaders are the firms that proactively and strategically invest to grow the market and attract the average customer to it. These winners are scarcely ever the early entrants. Indeed, the early entrants—we call them colonizers—are almost never the successful consolidators. Most colonizers disappear, never to be heard from again.

The fact that firms that create new product and service markets are rarely the ones that scale them into mass markets carries serious implications for the modern corporation. Our research points to a simple reason for this phenomenon: The skills, mind-sets, and competencies needed for discovery and invention not only are *different* from those needed for commercialization; they *conflict* with the needed characteristics. This means that firms good at invention are unlikely to be good at commercialization, and vice versa.

Some firms are natural colonizers, able to explore new technologies quickly and effectively and to make the creative leap from a technological novelty to a product or service that meets customer needs. What these firms are good at is creating new market niches. Other firms are natural consolidators. They are able to organize a market, turning a clever idea into something that reliably and regularly meets the promise, can attract consumers, and can be manufactured and distributed efficiently to a mass market.

Very few firms are good at both sets of activities.

Colonizers' Commitments

What skills are needed for effective pioneering? To answer this question, we need to understand how new, disruptive markets are created, and by whom. Our historical analysis of 20 markets that were created in the last 100 years shows that the creation of new markets is consistently accompanied by the same four events:

- The haphazard (and at times accidental or lucky) development of a new technology
- A flood of companies entering the uncertain (and risky) market opened by the development of this new technology
- A slow initial uptake of the products and services associated with the new technology, followed by a huge explosion of customer interest when a dominant design is established
- The death of most of the early entrants (and their products) once a design emerges as dominant

The oft-told story of the development of the Internet provides a ready example. The technologies associated with its invention and growth, including the TCP/IP protocol, the HTML programming language, and the Mosaic browser, were developed randomly. No one involved with the technology in the early days had any idea of the scope or scale of the end product. No one had a master plan that linked the development of new client-server relations to the possibility of booking a hotel room by computer from a mobile phone. This apparently unplanned, unsystematic development of the underlying technology seems to have been largely a consequence of how the work was done, and by whom—mainly scientists and engineers in research institutes and universities that were under contract, at least at the start, to the U.S. Department of Defense.

When the "finished" Internet emerged from the convergence of the three "killer" platform technologies, numerous business possibilities presented themselves. They were poorly defined, but attractive enough to draw hordes of new entrants with a variety of different types of business models. This, in turn, triggered a signal that led to massive market expansion: By introducing new applications, these colonizers made using the Internet attractive for a vast number of new types of consumers and businesses. Internet connection rates, usage, and the revenues generated by various businesses on the Net grew vertiginously.

Yet, while the World Wide Web seemed like an overnight sensation, the fact is its takeoff took decades, its existence and evolution cannot be credited to any clear customer needs. Rather, engineers "playing" with new technologies propelled the new market onto an unsuspecting population.

Our research shows that a variation on this theme introduces all radically new markets. Such markets, we find over and over, are rarely created by demand or customer needs. Demand-driven innovations can, at best, develop and extend existing markets incrementally. These innovations usually come in the form of either product extensions or process innovations; valuable as they are, they do not create disruptive new markets. Evidence shows that disruptive new markets are actually created in a haphazard manner when a new technology gets *pushed* onto a market.

This kind of innovation process is called "supply push" by economists, and it has a peculiar property: Since innovation leads demand, inventors have to aim at a very imprecise target. Indeed, most new products are *experience goods*; customers are able to form clear preferences about them only by using them. This is very important, and it carries three major implications:

- Since the new product or service does not meet an immediate, well-articulated need, it is likely that a long period of time will pass before customers adopt it. Hence, one can expect adoption rates to be slow.
- Since there are no well-articulated needs, it is impossible to be sure of the right design of a new product or service built on the new technology. Hence, the market is likely to fill rapidly with a large supply of products and product variants, as entrepreneurs make guesses about customer wants and needs.
- Since customer preferences will evolve with experience, there is likely to be as much product development postinnovation as there is before the introduction of the new product. Hence, there are likely to be plenty of opportunities for a second mover to come into the market and win a position.

All this suggests that early markets are volatile and unpredictable places, characterized by high technological and customer uncertainty. New entrants come and go, experimentation is a way of life, and high turnover is the norm. Yet these markets are also characterized by two identifiable types of fluidity: fluidity in the number of and rate by which firms enter and leave the market; and fluidity in the number of products and product/feature variants created.

To survive in such an environment—as inhospitable as it maybe exciting—colonizers must have certain traits. They must be enthusiasts. They must have deep knowledge of the basic science and technology and should be interested in pushing it as far as they can. This means that colonizers are often serial risk takers. They are willing to bet on seriously speculative projects that result in new products well beyond the frontier of current knowledge

about the relevant science and technology. Colonizers often assume that customers share their enthusiasm for science and technology, and value performance in the same way the inventors do.

Colonizers need to be flexible and adaptable so that they can respond to the developments of the new technology or of the new market. They need to be relatively open to outside influences and to have internal processes that facilitate the learning of technical information. On the other hand, they do not require marketing skills (they often need to cultivate the attentions of only a few lead risers), and they do not need production skills. Their organizations are not required to be very large or complex, so colonizers don't have to have organizational skills or the ability to build and monitor complex accounting, personnel, or service delivery systems. Typically, colonizers are quick-hit entrants; their competitive advantage arises from their ability to be flexible and agile and to hit their continually moving target accurately.

Effective Consolidators

Compare this set of skills with the competencies consolidators must have to grow niches into mass markets.

Consolidators need to win the dominant design battle and then unify the market whose potential they unleash. Typically, that means making heavy investments in exploiting scale economies, following learning curves, developing strong brands, and controlling the channels of distribution to the mass market.

Creating a dominant design and consolidating a market around it is a formidable task. To do it successfully, a firm needs to make serious investments in production, so it can consistently and efficiently produce a high-quality product. Furthermore, a consolidator needs to be able to sway consumers and create a marketplace consensus to support its proposed dominant design. That requires the consolidator to identify, reach out to, and overcome the risk aversion of the many potential customers who are unwilling to shoulder the hazards of choosing from among a developing market's multiple prototypes. Therefore, a consolidator must have the ability to build brands. Consolidators also must have the skills to create an organization that can distribute to the mass market and serve a large and continuously growing customer base.

For these and other reasons, consolidators are typically slow movers—and they ought to be. The investment in consolidating a market involves substantial sunk costs and should not be undertaken lightly. Consolidators are also risk averse. Having invested heavily in the growth of the market, they are unwilling to throw it all away by undertaking risky investments or projects that might cannibalize their installed customer base.

One can imagine the complexity of trying to set up structures, cultures, and processes that facilitate both colonization and consolidation. The incentives and investment horizons needed to do each activity well are fundamentally different and can rarely coexist. The attitudes toward risk are different. Even the mind-sets and behaviors needed for each activity are so different that coexistence is next to impossible. Perhaps this is why several researchers (e.g., Christopher Meyer and Rudy Ruggles of the now-closed Center for Business Innovation, and James Brian Quinn, emeritus professor of management at Dartmouth College's Amos Tuck School of Business) have advised established companies to "outsource" innovation.

The example of Lotus, now part of IBM, highlights how difficult it is to combine the two types of organizations. As Robert Sutton has reported in the *Harvard Business Review*, after Lotus's initial success with its "killer application" product, the spreadsheet program Lotus 1-2-3, the company brought in experienced professional managers to guide it forward. It soon discovered, however, that the structures and processes that the mature Lotus needed to function effectively were inhibiting innovation. In a now-famous experiment to demonstrate this, Lotus executives assembled the resumes of the first 40 people to join the company, changed their names, and put them into the applicant group. Not one was asked in for an interview; the professional managers who were running Lotus considered the "wacky" risk takers who had created the company too deviant from the current culture to warrant even a phone call.

Contemporary business is filled with examples that support the distinctions between colonization and consolidation skills. Apple Computer Inc. pioneered the home PC market, but was unable to scale it up. However, Apple's competencies may yet allow it to win as an online music and entertainment distribution company, expanding a niche that industry pioneer Real-Networks Inc. helped invent but has been unable to scale profitably. The Microsoft Corporation might appear to be both colonizer and consolidator; in fact, though, the company's expertise is in following and growing markets uncovered by others, whether in word-processing programs (Microsoft Word versus Word-Perfect), spreadsheets (Excel versus Lotus), operating systems (Windows versus Mac OS), or other products.

There are, of course, exceptions to this rule. 3M was successful in both discovering and commercializing the Post-it Note. But such cases are rare. If we are careful in examining how new markets are created and who the early pioneers really are, we soon see that the companies that scaled up the new markets are rarely the early entrants.

Where Dinosaurs Thrive

Consider most big, established companies in the economy. Given the skills, competencies, attitudes, and cultures they possess, it should come as no surprise to learn that their expertise is in consolidation. Established companies, by definition, have the financial resources, market power, reputation, brand-building skills, and facturing ability that consolidation of a market requires. The very firms that we have come to call bureaucracies or dinosaurs are often the ones perfectly positioned to take a niche market and scale it.

That's the good news for established firms. The bad news is that, as we have seen, such firms are not good at *creating* new markets. They often lack the curiosity and the internal incentives to apply new scientific knowledge to what seem like blue-sky projects. They also lack the entrepreneurial skills to succeed with disruptive innovations. Consolidators do not have the cultures or structures necessary to withstand the turbulent environments that characterize new markets. And they lack the attitudes and mind-sets that are required for pioneering.

The best evidence for this is the almost total vacuum during the past quarter-century of dramatic technological upheavals that began at large companies. As Richard Leifer et al. ask in the book *Radical Innovation*, "How many big companies pioneered the technologies and business models that now dominate e-commerce, personal computing, biotech, and wireless communications?" The answer, according to the authors, is none—which not only subverts the message of their own subtitle, *How Mature Companies Can Outsmart Upstarts*, but undermines the theories of many management gurus about how established firms can strategically innovate in their industries.

Prominent among these beliefs is that established companies can "learn" or "adopt" the skills and attitudes of pioneers in order to create new markets. Look, their advisors tell them: Don't you want to be like Body Shop or Cisco or Virgin? All you have to do is adopt *their* structures, cultures, and processes. Who says elephants can't dance? Just go on a diet and lose some of that excess weight, learn a few tricks, and off you go!

As we have argued in this article, this would not do the established firms much good. Attempting to incorporate the new skills into the existing organization almost always produces one of two outcomes: Either the existing culture and attitudes reject the new transplants, or the transplanted skills and attitudes take over and destroy the very things that have made the established firm a success (and that it still needs to be successful in its existing business).

This helps explain why most established firms, while they are happy to pay high lecture fees, are actually unwilling to implement the advice and ideas that academics and consultants have developed over the past few years to make industry giants more innovative. For example, Gary Hamel has proposed such ideas as making the strategy process democratic and "bringing Silicon Valley inside the organization." Similarly, Costas Markides, an author of this article, argued in 1997 and 1998 that corporations should import into their organizations those features of capitalism that promote innovation (such as decentralized allocation of resources, multiple sources of financing, and constant experimentation). This is all sensible stuff, and the ideas appear logical and creative. But how many established companies do you know that have adopted any of them? All this advice might be helpful in making a company more innovative in general, but it will not help established companies create radically new markets.

A similar point has also been made in a slightly different context by Christopher Meyer and Rudy Ruggles., too, once believed it was possible to teach established companies how to innovate with the same verve as pioneers, "codify[ing] their secrets into a replicable process that we can impose on our own organizations. But, they conceded last year in the *Harvard Business Review*, "Our attitude is shifting. We now warn companies, 'Don't try this at home.' Like many activities that involve talent and tacit learning, reconnaissance requires an inherent feel for the work and lots of practice. Not many companies can claim that inherent strength; nor can they devote much time to practicing, given that their day-to-day work is exploitation, not exploration.

This isn't to say that established firms have to give up completely on the possibility of creating new markets. Clayton M. Christensen has offered another, more viable option. Recognizing how difficult it is for colonization skills to coexist with consolidation skills, he and his colleagues, as well as Robert A. Burgelman and Leonard R. Sayles, in their 1986 book, *Inside Corporate Innovation:*

Strategy, Structure, and Managerial Skills, have advocated the creation of separate units or divisions within established organizations where new, disruptive growth businesses can be nurtured.

Resorting to a separate organizational entity is certainly possible; IBM adopted this strategy when it moved into the PC business, and so did the Royal Bank of Scotland when it created a telephone insurance service in the U.K. But such a strategy is not without problems. Our own recent research on the topic has shown that creating a separate unit to protect the pioneers from the stifling bureaucracy of the established firm is neither necessary nor sufficient for success. Costs are incurred by the failure to exploit synergies between the two businesses. The "pioneer" unit is also left exposed to attacks from established companies in the industry. Attempts to solve these problems often end up in failure because the established parent begins to apply its own mind-sets and processes to the startup's business.

A third alternative for established firms that want to create radical new markets has been proposed by Michael L. Tushman, of the Harvard Business School, and Charles A. O'Reilly III, of the Stanford Graduate School of Business. They argue that pioneering and consolidation can coexist if the company is successful in creating an "ambidextrous" organizational infrastructure. Such an organization will have successfully put in place multiple, contradictory structures, processes, and cultures. E. Leclerc, the French supermarket chain, is an excellent example of a successful ambidextrous company. (See "Focus: The Ambidextrousness of E. Leclerc.")

Although the ambidextrous organization is an admirable model, examples are unfortunately few and far between. As Professors Tushman and O'Reilly themselves admit, only a small minority of farsighted firms can claim to be ambidextrous. Most firms that try to operate this way will fail.

Finding Feeders

The final option—and the one that most companies have ignored—is for established businesses to leave the challenges of market creation to startup firms and focus their own attention and resources on consolidation.

But to become successful consolidators, they must be ready to lump into a new market just when the dominant design is about to emerge and the market is ready to take off. For such perfect timing, established firms must create, sustain, and nurture a network of feeder firms—young entrepreneurial companies that are busy colonizing new niches. Through its business development function, the established company could serve as a venture capitalist to these feeder firms. Then, when it is time to consolidate the market, it could build a new mass-market business on the platform that these feeder firms have provided.

Such a specialization of labor already exists in creative industries—movies, book publishing, and the visual and performing arts. As Richard Caves notes in his book *Creative Industries: Contracts Between Art and Commerce*, firms in creative industries are either small-scale pickers that concentrate on the selection and development of new creative talent, or large-scale promoters that undertake the packaging and widespread distribution of established creative goods.

Messrs. Meyer and Ruggles say that a small but rapidly growing industry is emerging around firms that specialize in exploration in non-entertainment industries as well, allowing mature firms to outsource their exploration needs and focus on growing the ideas into mass markets. James Brian Quinn, too, points out that strategically outsourcing innovation is now an accepted practice in a number of industries, including pharmaceuticals, financial services, computers, telecommunications, and energy systems.

Such a "network" strategy has several advantages over the "grow it inside" strategy: It allows the firm to cover more technologies and more market niches; it enables the feeder firms to compete with one another while allowing the parent company to benchmark one against the other; it is easier to manage because it bypasses the problems of trying to manage two conflicting businesses simultaneously; and it has all the traditional benefits of outsourcing.

Indeed, one can credibly argue that the outsourcing model is in fact the one that has been adopted historically by large firms, albeit in an unplanned and haphazard way. For what are colonizers if not an external source of innovation? And aren't consolidators appropriators and scalers of others' innovations? In effect, we are arguing merely for adding a consciousness to what previously has been an unconscious, random process.

Therefore, the right way forward for established, mature firms is not to build their own new business inside and then consolidate when the time is right. Rather, they should maintain and manage a feeder system of colonizer businesses—very much what pharmaceutical companies are doing with biotech and what Unilever, for example, is doing with new consumer products. Then,

when the time is right, they should move in for consolidation and scale up what their partners are doing.

We are aware that this cuts against the grain of much of the thinking of the last few years, which aimed to make established corporations more "entrepreneurial" by developing the cultures and structures of the younger startup firms. In our view, this is misplaced counsel. It's like advising a 70-year-old person how to train to win at the next Olympics—it simply won't happen!

By trying to be ambidextrous, established companies risk being "stuck in the middle." What they need to do is focus on the area where they have an advantage—and that is in consolidating good new ideas drawn from niche markets into new and valuable mass markets.

Focus: The Ambidextrousness of E. Leclerc

E. Leclerc, the French supermarket chain, gives us an example of the successes—and the challenges—of operating as an ambidextrous organization. E. Leclerc was founded in the late 1950s by Edouard Leclerc, who gave up a career as a Catholic priest to start a supermarket dedicated to offering branded products at low prices. The organization has grown to a chain of more than 500 hypermarkets. It is now expanding beyond France.

E. Leclerc is a master at balancing quite a few conflicting forces: It has achieved low cost and differentiation simultaneously; it is very decentralized in some value-chain activities and yet centralized in many others; it is broken up into many small autonomous units but still enjoys the benefits of size; it is structured as a federation of independent stores yet behaves as an integrated network; it encourages continuous experimentation with new products and concepts yet survives the inevitable losses without pain; its employees feel and act like "owners" of the organization yet own no stock; the whole organization behaves like one big family yet is a money-making machine.

How could it possibly achieve all these things simultaneously, and how does it manage such variety?

The answer has many angles. First, E. Leclerc is not a single company. The stores are owned and operated by different individuals who choose to trade under the E. Leclerc name. They are not franchisees in the conventional sense: They do not have to pay for the right to use the E. Leclerc name; in fact, they receive numerous benefits from their E. Leclerc association for which they do not have to pay anything. However, they have to abide by certain norms and regulations, including the primary rule that they will never be undersold by competitors. In addition, no individual—including members of the Leclerc family—is allowed to own more than two stores.

Each store is given total autonomy over its affairs. Each is free to decide what products to sell, what prices to charge, what promotions to run, and so on. In addition, each store can find its own suppliers and negotiate its own prices.

Such decentralization and autonomy encourage experimentation, and the structure achieves differentiation, but not at the expense of low cost. For example, each region has its own warehouse, which is owned by the member stores. On behalf of all its members, the warehouse orders and stores those products that do not need to be sold fresh. This achieves purchasing economies. In addition, a central purchasing department in Paris identifies potential suppliers and negotiates prices with them. Although individual stores do not have to use a centrally recommended supplier, this method also helps achieve purchasing economies. The use of the E. Leclerc name by all has advertising and promotional benefits and cuts costs. Finally, new E. Leclerc stores are always started by current E. Leclerc employees, who receive the financial backing and guarantees of current E. LecLerc store owners. The financial backing of a prominent local businessperson has benefits in dealing with the banks for startup capital.

Every owner is active in the management of the whole organization. All attend monthly regional meetings as well as frequent national meetings, where decisions are made and experiences exchanged.

Each store belongs to a region, and each region is "run" by a member for three years (on a voluntary basis). The regional president directs the affairs of the region and travels extensively to individual stores to offer advice, monitor plans, and transfer best practices. Furthermore, at the end of each year, each owner has to distribute 25 percent of the stores profits to its employees.

Owners also have the "duty" (not obligation) to act as a "godparent" to one of their employees. The selected employee is someone who has been identified as having high potential and who might be a future E. Leclerc owner. This individual receives continuous support and advice and, when the time comes, financial backing and moral support to start a store. If the new store fails, the "godparent" is financially responsible for liabilities.

How is so much variety managed? Information systems are used to monitor what is happening across the "federation." Frequent meetings also help owners exchange ideas and monitor progress. But the two primary mechanisms of control are (1) a common and deeply felt vision that sets the parameters within which each member store operates; and (2) a strong family culture in which everybody is treated with fairness and openness and all are equal. It is interesting that each store has its own unique culture (created primarily by the personality of the store owner), yet a common E. Leclerc culture still permeates the whole organization. This common culture sets the parameters, the norms, the shared values, and the constraints within which individuals behave. It is this shared culture that allows so much autonomy and freedom without the fear that somebody, somewhere, will do something nasty.

–C.M. and P.G.

Research Methodology

We examined the historical evolution of 20 newly created markets, from the moment they were formed until they grew to mass market. The 20 markets were television, personal computers, scientific instruments, the Internet, supercomputers, online groceries, cars, beer, Internet service provision, tires, semiconductors, baked beans, genetically modified foods, mobile phones, video recorders, satellite TV, stereo sound, typewriters, computer operating systems, and medical diagnostic imaging. We first examined what new technologies were developed that gave rise to the new products or services and how these technologies were discovered. We then studied how the new markets developed in their early years, how many companies entered and exited the market, and what kinds of product (or service) variants developed. Finally, we examined how the market developed once a dominant design emerged and what firms survived this event. Further details of this research can be found in *The Early Evolution of New Markets,* by Paul Geroski.

Resources

Rhonda Germany and Ramon Muralidharan, "The Three Phases of Value Capture: Finding Competitive Advantage in the Information Age," *s+b* First Quarter 2001; www.strategy-business.com/press/article/?art=17915

Charles E. Lucier and Jaent D. Torsilieri, "The Trillion-Dollar Race to 'E,'" *s+b* First Quarter 2000; www.strategy-business.com/press/article/?art=19162

William Boulding and Markus Christen "First-Mover Disadvantage," *Harvard Business Review,* October 2001; www.harvardbusinessonline.com

Clayton M. Christensen, Mark W. Johnson, and Darrell K. Rigby, "Foundations for Growth: How to Identify and Build Disruptive New Business," *Sloan Management Review*, Spring 2002; http://smr.mit.edu/

Gary Hamel, "Bringing Silicon Valley Inside," *Harvard Business Review*, September/October 1999; www.harvardbusinessonline.com

Gary Hamel, "Strategy as Revolution," *Harvard Business Review*, July/August 1996; www.harvardbusinessonline.com

Constantinos Markides, "Strategic Innovation," *Sloan Management Review*, Spring 1998; http://smr.mit.edu/

Constantinos Markides, "Strategic Innovation in Established Companies," *Sloan Management Review*, Spring 1998; http://smr.mit.edu/

Christopher Meyer and Rudy Ruggles, "Search Parties," *Harvard Business Review*, August 2002; www.harvardbusinessonline.com

James Brian Quinn, "Outsourcing Innovation: The New England of Growth," *Sloan Management Review*, Summer 2000; http://smr.mit.edu/

Robert Sutton, "The Weird Rules of Creativity," *Harvard Business Review*, September 2001; www.harvardbusinessonline.com

Michael L. Tushman and Charles A. O'Reilly III, "The Ambidextrous Organization: Managing Evolutionary and Revolutionary Change," *California Management Review*, Summer 1996; www.haas.berkeley.edu/News/cmr

Robert A. Burgelman and Leonard R. Sayles, *Inside Corporate Innovation: Strategy, Structure, and Managerial Skills* (Free Press, 1986)

Richard Caves, *Creative Industries: Contracts Between Art and Commerce* (Harvard University Press, 2002)

Clayton M. Christensen, *The Innovator's Dilemma: When New Technologies Cause Great Firms to Fail* (Harvard Business School Press, 1997)

Paul Geroski, *The Early Evolution of New Markets* (Oxford University Press, 2003)

Gary Hamel, *Leading the Revolution* (Harvard Business School Press, 2000)

Richard Leifer, Christopher M. McDermott, Gina Colarelli O'Connor, Lois S. Peters, Mark P. Rice, and Robert W. Veryzer, *Radical Innovation: How Mature Companies Can Outsmart Upstarts* (Harvard Business School Press, 2000)

Steven P. Schnaars, *Managing Imitation Strategies: How Later Entrants Seize Markets from Pioneers* (Free Press, 1994)

Gerard J. Tellis and Peter N. Golder, *Will and Vision: How Latecomers Grow to Dominate Markets* (McGraw-Hill, 2002)

Constantinos Markides and Constantinos Charitrou, "Competing with Dual Strategies," Working Paper, London Business School, March 2003.

Costas Markides (cmarkides@london.edu) is a professor of strategic and international management and holds the Robert P. Bauman Chair in Strategic Leadership at the London Business School. His newest book, with Paul Geroski, provisionally titled Racing to Be Second: From Creating to Conquering New Markets, will be published in 2004.

Paul Geroski (pgeroski@london.edu) is deputy chairman of the Competition Commission and a professor of economics at the London Business School. His most recent book is The Early Evolution of New Markets (Oxford University Press, 2003) Professor Geroski sits on the editorial boards of several journals and on the council of the Royal Economic Society.

Business Unit Strategies

7

Chapter Outline

A fter a firm's top managers have settled on a corporate-level strategy, their focus then shifts to how the firm's business or businesses should compete. Whereas the corporate strategy concerns the basic thrust of the firm—*where* top managers would like to lead the firm—the business or competitive strategy addresses the competitive aspect—*who* the business should serve, *what* needs should be satisfied, and *how* a business should develop core competencies and be positioned to satisfy customers' needs.

Another way of addressing the task of formulating a business strategy is to consider whether a business should concentrate its efforts on *exploiting* current opportunities, *exploring* new ones, or attempting to balance the two. Exploitation generates returns in the short term; exploration can create forms of sustainable competitive advantage for the long term. The business strategy developed for an organization seeks, among other things, to resolve this challenge.[1]

Business Unit

An organizational entity with its own unique mission, set of competitors, and industry.

A **business unit** is an organizational entity with its own mission, set of competitors, and industry. A single firm that operates within only one industry is also considered a business unit. Strategic managers craft competitive strategies for each business unit to attain and sustain competitive advantage, a state whereby its successful strategies cannot be easily duplicated by competitors.[2] In most industries, different competitive approaches can be successful, depending on the business unit's resources

Generic Strategies

Broad competitive Strategies that can be adopted by business units to guide their organizations.

Strategic Group

A select group of direct competitors who have similar strategic profiles.

Each business competes with a unique competitive strategy. In the interest of simplicity, however, it is useful to categorize different strategies into a limited number of generic strategies based on their similarities. **Generic strategies** emphasize the commonalities among different business strategies, not their differences. Businesses adopting the same generic strategy comprise what is commonly referred to as a **strategic group**.[3] In the airline industry, for example, one strategic group may comprise carriers such as Southwest Airlines and AirTran that offer low fares and no frills on a limited number of domestic routes, thereby maintaining their low-cost structures (see Figure 7-1). A second strategic group may comprise many traditional carriers such as Continental, United, and American that serve both domestic and international routes and offer extra services such as meals and movies on extended flights.

Because industry definitions and strategy assessments are not always clear, identifying strategic groups within an industry is often difficult. Even when the industry definition is clear, an industry's business units may be categorized into

FIGURE 7-1   Strategic Groups in the Airline Industry

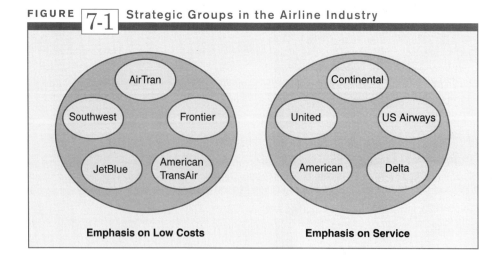

any number of strategic groups depending on the level of specificity desired. One or two competitors may also seem to be functioning between groups and thus be difficult to classify. For these reasons, the concept of strategic groups can be used as a means of understanding and illustrating competition within an industry, but the limitations of the approach should always be considered.

The challenging task of formulating and implementing a generic strategy is based on both internal and external factors. Because generic strategies by nature are overly simplistic, selecting generic approach is only the first step in formulating a business strategy.[4] It is also necessary to fine-tune the strategy and accentuate the organization's unique set of resource strengths.[5] Two generic strategy frameworks—one developed by Porter and another by Miles and Snow—can serve as good starting points for developing business strategies.

7-1 Porter's Generic Strategies

Michael Porter developed the most commonly cited generic strategy framework.[6] According to Porter's typology, a business unit must address two basic competitive concerns. First, managers must determine whether the business unit should focus its efforts on an identifiable subset of the industry in which it operates or seek to serve the entire market as a whole. For example, specialty clothing stores in shopping malls adopt the focus concept and concentrate their efforts on limited product lines primarily intended for a small market niche. In contrast, most chain grocery stores seek to serve the mass market—or at least most of it—by selecting an array of products and services that appeal to the general public as a whole. The smaller the business, the more desirable a focus strategy tends to be, although this is not always the case.

Second, managers must determine whether the business unit should compete primarily by minimizing its costs relative to those of its competitors (i.e., a low-cost strategy) or by seeking to offer unique or unusual products and services (i.e., a differentiation strategy). Porter views these two alternatives as mutually exclusive because differentiation efforts tend to erode a low-cost structure by raising production, promotional, and other expenses. In fact, Porter labeled business units attempting to emphasize both cost leadership and differentiation simultaneously as "stuck in the middle."[7] This is not necessarily the case, however, and the low-cost–differentiation strategy is a viable alternative for some businesses. Combining the two strategies is difficult, but businesses able to do so can perform exceptionally well.

Depending on the way strategic managers in a business unit address the first (i.e., focus or not) and second (low-cost, differentiation, or low-cost–differentiation) questions, six configurations are possible. A seventh approach—multiple strategies—involves the simultaneous deployment of more than one of the six configurations (see Table 7-1). The low-cost and differentiation strategies with and without focus comprise those in Porter's original framework.

7-1a Low-Cost (Cost Leadership) Strategy

Businesses that compete with a **low-cost strategy** produce basic, no-frills products and services for a mass market of price-sensitive customers. Because they attempt to satisfy most or all of the market, these businesses tend to be large and established. Low-cost businesses often succeed by building market share through low prices, although some charge prices comparable to rivals and enjoy a greater margin. Because customers generally are willing to pay only low to average prices

TABLE 7-1   Generic Strategies Based on Porter's Typology

Emphasis on Entire Market or Niche	Emphasis on Low Costs	Emphasis on Differentiation	Emphasis on Low Costs and Differentiation	Emphasis on Various Factors Depending on Market
Entire Market	Low-Cost Strategy	Differentiation Strategy	Low-Cost–Differentiation Strategy	Multiple Strategies
Niche	Focus–Low-Cost Strategy	Focus–Differentiation Strategy	Focus–Low-Cost/Differentiation Strategy	

for "basic" products or services, it is essential that businesses using this strategy keep their overall costs as low as possible. Efficiency is a key to such businesses, as has been demonstrated by mega-retailer Wal-Mart in recent years.

Low-cost businesses tend to emphasize a low initial investment and low operating costs. Such organizations tend to purchase from suppliers who offer the lowest prices within a basic quality standard. Research and development efforts are directed at improving operational efficiency, and attempts are made to enhance logistical and distribution efficiencies. Such businesses often but not always deemphasize the development of new and improved products or services that might raise costs, and advertising and promotional expenditures will be minimized (see Strategy at Work 7-1).

S T R A T E G Y   A T   W O R K   7 - 1

The Low-Cost Strategy at Kola Real

Coca-Cola and PepsiCo enjoy substantial profit margins on their soft drinks in Mexico's $15 billion market, where the two have waged intense battles for market share during the past decade. Although Coke usually came out on top, the two collectively controlled sales and distribution in almost all of the country's major markets. In 2003, Coke had more than 70 percent of Mexican sales, and Pepsi had 21 percent. Consumers in Mexico drink more Coke per capita than those in any other nation.

In the early 2000s, however, both well-known colas have been challenged by an unlikely upstart from Peru known as Kola Real (pronounced "ray-'al"). Launched in Mexico in 2001, Kola Real captured 4 percent of the Mexican market in its first two years.

Bottled by the Ananos family from Peru, Kola Real lacks all of the frills and endorsements associated with Coke and Pepsi. The strategy is simple: Eliminate all possible costs and offer large sizes at low prices. Whereas Coke and Pepsi spend nearly 20 percent of

revenues on concentrates, the Ananos family makes its own. Whereas Coke and Pepsi spend millions on promotion and manage their own fleets of attractive trucks, the Ananos family hires third parties for deliveries—even individuals with dented pickup trucks—and relies primarily on word-of-mouth advertising.

Central to Kola Real's success is the fact that the majority of Mexican cola drinkers are relatively poor and consider price to be a major factor in their purchase decisions. In Brazil, so-called B-brands (i.e., low-cost generic or store brands) now account for almost one-third of the country's cola sales. Fearing this could happen in Mexico, Coke and Pepsi have fought back with price cuts of their own, although they will not be able to challenge Kola Real's low-cost position on a large-scale basis.

Source: Adapted from D. Luhnow and C. Terhune, "A Low-Budget Cola Shakes Up Markets South of the Border," Wall Street Journal, 27 October 2003, A1, A18.

A cost leader may be more likely than other businesses to outsource a number of its production activities if costs are reduced as a result, even if modest amounts of control over quality are lost in the process. In addition, the most efficient means of distribution is sought, even if it is not the fastest or easiest to manage. It is worth noting that successful low-cost businesses do not emphasize cost minimization to the degree that quality and service decline excessively. In other words, cost leadership taken to an extreme can result in the production of "cheap" goods and services that nobody is willing to purchase.

Low-cost leaders depend on unique capabilities not available to others in the industry such as access to scarce raw materials, large market share, or a high degree of capitalization.[8] Manufacturers that employ a low-cost strategy, however, are vulnerable to intense price competition that drives down profit margins and limits their ability to improve outputs, to augment their products with superior services, or to spend more on advertising and promotion.[9] The prospect of being caught in price wars keeps many manufacturers from adopting the low-cost strategy, although it can affect other businesses as well. Other low-cost leaders have bought their suppliers to control quality and distribution. Price cutting in the airline industry led to the demise of several upstarts even before the events of 9/11, and made it even more difficult to raise fares shortly thereafter.[10]

Success with the low-cost strategy can be short lived, however. Low-cost airline AirTran, for example, boasted a 2003 profit of $101 million while Delta squabbled with its pilots throughout the year in an effort to reduce costs. Delta dominates Atlanta where AirTran also has a hub, but has had difficulty cutting costs. In 2004, however, Delta finally made headway and began cutting many of its fares, some by as much as 50 percent. By 2005, AirTran, along with other low-cost airlines, began to feel the squeeze as major airlines such as Delta became more price competitive.[11]

Imitation by competitors can also be a concern when the basis for low-cost leadership is not proprietary and can be easily duplicated. Lego discovered this fact when Canadian upstart Mega Blocks began to steal market share by making colorful blocks that not only look like Legos, but also snap into them and sell for a lower price. Lego responded by launching the Quatro line of oversized blocks aimed at the preschool market and carrying lower prices than traditional Lego playsets.[12]

Low-cost businesses are also particularly vulnerable to technological obsolescence. Manufacturers that emphasize technological stability and do not respond to new product and market opportunities may eventually find that their products have become obsolete.

7-1b Focus–Low-Cost Strategy

The **focus–low-cost strategy** emphasizes low overall costs while serving a narrow segment of the market, producing no-frills products or services for price-sensitive customers in a market niche. Ideally, the small business unit that adopts the focus–low-cost strategy competes only in distinct market niches where it enjoys a cost advantage relative to large, low-cost competitors.

The focus concept is clear in theory, but often confusing in practice. In general, a business rejects a focus approach when it attempts to serve *most* of the market. In practice, however, virtually every business focuses its efforts, at least to some extent. Because *most* is a subjective term, scholars sometimes disagree on whether a particular business should be classified as focus or not.

Focus–Low-Cost Strategy:

A generic business unit strategy in which a smaller business keeps overall costs low while producing no-frills products or services for a market niche with elastic demand.

Aldi is a clear example of a business that pursues a focus–low-cost strategy. Aldi is an international retailer that offers a limited assortment of groceries and related items at the lowest possible prices. Functional operations are tightly coordinated around a single strategic objective: low costs. Efforts are targeted to consumers with low to moderate incomes.

Aldi minimizes costs a number of ways. Most products are private label, allowing Aldi to negotiate rock-bottom prices from its suppliers. Stores are modest in size, much smaller than that of a typical chain grocer. Aldi only stocks common food and related products, maximizing inventory turnover. The retailer does not accept credit cards, eliminating the 2 to 4 percent fee typically charged by banks to process the transaction. Customers bag their own groceries and must either bring their own bags or purchase them from Aldi for a nominal charge. Aldi also takes an innovative approach to the use of its shopping carts. Customers insert a quarter to unlock a cart from the interlocked row of carts located outside the store entrance. The quarter is returned with the cart when it is locked back into the group. As a result, no employee time is required to collect stray carts unless a customer is willing to forego the quarter by not returning the cart!

Adding a focus orientation to cost leadership can enable a firm to avoid direct competition with a mass-market cost leader. In this manner, grocer Save-A-Lot has found a way to compete successfully against Wal-Mart Supercenters. Its prices are competitive with those at Wal-Mart, but Save-A-Lot pursues locations in urban areas that Wal-Mart rejected. Save-A-Lot also generates profits by opening small, inexpensive stores catering to U.S. households earning less than $35,000 a year. Save-A-Lot stocks mostly its own brand of high-turnover goods to minimize costs and eschews cost-inducing pharmacies, bakeries, and baggers.[13]

Like low-cost businesses, those adopting the focus–low-cost strategy are vulnerable to intense price competition that periodically occurs in markets with no-frills outputs. For instance, several years ago, Laker Airways successfully used the focus–low-cost strategy by providing the first no-frills, low-priced trans-Atlantic passenger service. The major airlines responded by dropping prices, eventually driving Laker out of business. The large competitors, because of their greater financial resources, were able to weather the short-term financial losses and survive the shakeout.[14] Southwest Airlines, in contrast, adopted a similar strategy and has been able to perform well despite competitive pressure from its large rivals.

To deter price competition, businesses employing the focus–low-cost strategy must continuously search for new ways to trim costs. The Irish no-frills air carrier Ryanair has surpassed Southwest in this regard. Passengers are required to pay for all food, drinks, and newspapers. Employees pay for their own training and uniforms. The airline even incorporates a strict no-refund policy, even if the airline cancels a flight. Even with an average ticket price of about $50, Ryanair faces constant pressure from its large rivals. In 2004, Ireland's state carrier Aer Lingus added routes and lowered prices in an attempt to model itself after Ryanair.[15]

Founded in 2003, Hungary's low-cost airline Wizz Air specializes in transporting Hungarians, Poles, and other Eastern Europeans to Britain and Ireland where many seek and find better paying jobs. CEO Jozsef Varadi sees buses—not other airlines—as their primary competition. Sparked by recent expansion of the European Union, Wizz Air makes economic sense for its customer base when considering fares and travel time.[16]

Like low-cost businesses that do not adopt a focus approach, focus–low-cost businesses are particularly vulnerable to technological obsolescence. Businesses that value technological stability and do not respond to new product and market opportunities may eventually find that their products have become obsolete and are no longer desired by customers.

7-1c Differentiation Strategy (No Focus)

Businesses that utilize the **differentiation strategy** produce and market to the entire industry products or services that can be readily distinguished from those of their competitors. Because they attempt to satisfy most or all of the market, these businesses tend to be large and established. Differentiated businesses often attempt to create new product and market opportunities and have access to the latest scientific breakthroughs because technology and flexibility are key factors if firms are to initiate or keep pace with new developments in their industries.

The potential for differentiation is to some extent a function of its physical characteristics. Tangibly speaking, it is easier to differentiate an automobile than bottled water. However, intangible differentiation can extend beyond the physical characteristics of a product or service to encompass everything associated with the value perceived by customers. Because such businesses' customers *perceive* significant differences in their products or services, they are willing to pay average to high prices for them.

Of the prospective bases for differentiation, the most obvious is features of the product (or the mix of products) offered, including the objective and subjective differences in product attributes. Lexus automobiles, for example, have been differentiated on product features and are well known for their attention to detail, quality, and luxury feel. United and other airlines have attempted to differentiate their businesses by offering in-flight satellite telephone and e-mail services.[17] Continental even differentiated itself by emphasizing animal cargo.[18]

Speed can also be a key differentiator. For example, according to a 2004 survey by Mintel International Group, 64 percent of Americans said that they selected a restaurant based on the amount of time they had to eat. Speed has been an essential part of the Starbucks competitive strategy, but became a key concern when service slowed after breakfast sandwiches were added to the product line in the mid-2000s. Adding these food items broadened the appeal of Starbucks, but slowed service in a segment of the market where seconds count. In contrast, competitor Caribou Coffee can make a small coffee-of-the-day in only six seconds.[19]

Timing can also be a key factor, because first movers are more able to establish themselves in the market than those who come later, as was seen for a number of years with Domino's widespread introduction of pizza delivery.[20] Factors such as partnerships with other firms, locations, and a reputation for service quality can also be important (see Strategy at Work 7-2).

When customers are relatively price insensitive, a business may select a differentiation strategy and emphasize quality throughout its functional areas. Marketing materials may be printed on high-quality paper. The purchasing department emphasizes the quality and appropriateness of supplies and raw materials over their per unit costs. The research and development department emphasizes new product development (as opposed to cost-cutting measures).

Differentiated businesses are vulnerable to low-cost competitors offering similar products at lower prices, especially when the basis for differentiation is not well defined or it is not valued by customers. For example, a grocer may emphasize fast checkout, operating on the assumption that customers are willing to pay

Differentiation Strategy

A generic business unit strategy in which a larger business produces and markets to the entire industry products or services that can be readily distinguished from those of its competitors.

The Differentiation Strategy in Residential Real Estate

Implementing a differentiation strategy can be difficult in a highly regulated industry in which competitors are forced to follow rules and even work together. Residential real estate is an example of such an industry. In most cases, a real estate agent who lists a home for a seller must work with agents from other firms who represent prospective buyers. Buyers and sellers are interested in working only with agents who can negotiate successfully with other agents to complete the transaction. When one also considers the myriad of federal, state, and local regulations concerning property disclosure, confidentiality, and the like, one can easily see why it is difficult for an agent or real estate firm to differentiate service.

Differentiation in such an industry is possible, however. Boyd Williams Real Estate Company (www.boydwilliams.com) operates in the southeastern Mississippi community of Meridian, a city of about forty thousand people. To distinguish himself from his rivals, Boyd brings his mobile office to clients' homes, offices, hotel lobbies, and even restaurants over lunch break. He is always equipped with a laptop computer, portable printer, cell phone, and digital camera. Prospective buyers can view full-color pictures of virtually every home in the market from the mobile office. This approach seeks to provide maximum efficiency and convenience to the buyer.

Interestingly, commissions available to Boyd Williams are the same as those available to other agents who do not offer the same amenities. Clearly, Williams seeks to finance his additional investment in the mobile office by allowing consumers to move through the buying process more efficiently—saving him time as well—and by increasing his volume.

Source: Adapted from Boyd Williams Real Estate Company home page, accessed March 29, 2002, www.boydwilliams.com.

a few cents more for additional cashiers and checkout lanes. If customers tend to be more concerned with product assortments and prices than with waiting times, they may shop at other stores instead.

Instituting a change in competitive strategy can be a difficult process, especially when the nature of the change involves a heightened emphasis on differentiation. For example, in 2002, Volkswagen entered the luxury market with the Phaeton, complete with doors trimmed in Italian leather, brushed chrome and chestnut, and a price tag of $70,000. Consumers found it difficult to associate Volkswagen with such refinement and the company sold only about three thousand Phaetons that year. Interestingly, upscale carmakers including such notables as BMW and Jaguar began to produce smaller, less expensive "luxury" cars, a move that received a greater welcome from consumers.[21]

7-1d Focus-Differentiation Strategy

Focus-Differentiation Strategy

A generic business unit strategy in which a smaller business produces highly differentiated products or services for the specialized needs of a market niche.

Firms utilizing the **focus-differentiation strategy** produce highly differentiated products or services for the specialized needs of a market niche. At first glance, the focus-differentiation strategy may appear to be a less attractive strategy than the no-focus differentiation strategy, because the former consciously limits the set of customers it seeks to target. However, unique market segments often require distinct approaches. For example, The Limited operates retail outlets to address multiple demographic segments simultaneously. Men are served by its Structure stores, women by its Lane Bryant stores, and children by its Limited Too stores. The Limited even targets trendy consumers with Express stores. U.S. chain Torrid features fifty-two stores and specializes in plus-size clothing for young, fashion-conscious women, a niche nonfocused retailers have not filled effectively.[22] In some cases, however, large business units are simply not interested in serving smaller, highly defined niches.

Firms can focus their efforts in several ways. Popular retailer Cabela's has even successfully targeted its efforts to men who hate to shop! The Cabela's in Michigan draws an estimated 6 million visitors to its retail store each year, mixing its outdoorsman-oriented merchandise with an aquarium, indoor waterfall stocked with trout, and realistic nature scenes. As a result, Cabela's has secured a customer base largely ignored by other retailers.[23]

In general, high prices are acceptable to certain customers who need product performance, prestige, safety, or security, especially when only one or a few businesses cater to their needs. As such, focus differentiation is most appropriate when market demand is inelastic, because high-cost products are often required to support the specialized efforts to serve a limited market niche. As a result, cost reduction efforts, while always desirable, are not emphasized.[24]

7-1e Low-Cost–Differentiation Strategy

Debate is widespread among scholars and practitioners as to the feasibility of pursuing low-cost and differentiation strategies simultaneously. Porter suggests that implementing a **low-cost–differentiation strategy** is not advisable and leaves a business stuck in the middle, because actions designed to support one strategy could actually work against the other. Simply stated, differentiating a product generally costs a considerable amount of money, which would erode a firm's cost leadership basis. In addition, a number of cost-cutting measures may be directly related to quality and other bases of differentiation. Following this logic, a business should choose *either* a low-cost *or* a differentiation strategy, but not both.[25]

Others contend that the two approaches are not necessarily mutually exclusive.[26] For example, some businesses begin with a differentiation strategy and integrate low costs as they grow, developing economies of scale along the way. Others seek forms of differentiation that also provide cost advantages, such as enhancing and enlarging the filter on a cigarette, which reduces the amount of costly tobacco required to manufacture the product.

Perhaps the best example of a business that has successfully combined the two approaches is McDonald's. The fast-food giant was originally known for consistency from store to store, friendly service, and cleanliness. These bases for differentiation catapulted McDonald's to market share leader, allowing the firm to negotiate for beef, potatoes, and other key materials at the lowest possible cost. This unique combination of resources and strategic attributes has placed McDonald's in an enviable position as undisputed industry leader, although it is facing increased competitive pressure from differentiated competitors emphasizing Mexican, "fresh and healthy," or other distinct product lines.[27]

A more recent example of the combination strategy is the relatively young airline JetBlue Airways, launched in 2000 to provide economical air service among a limited number of cities. JetBlue distinguished itself by providing new planes, satellite television on board, and leather seating. JetBlue also minimized costs by such measures as squeezing more seats into its planes, selling most of its tickets on the Internet to avoid commissions, shortening ground delays, and serving snacks instead of meals. Hence, JetBlue's differentiation efforts increased its load factor (i.e., the average percentage of filled seats), also reducing its per-passenger flight costs.[28]

Changes in the U.S. mobile home industry in the 2000s also illustrate a link between low cost and differentiation. Traditionally, mobile homes have been positioned as a low-cost, affordable housing option to low-income consumers. In 2004, about 22 million Americans, or 8 percent of the U.S. population, live in manufactured housing. Sales approached almost 400,000 units per year in the late 1990s.

Low-Cost–Differentiation Strategy

A generic business unit strategy in which a larger business unit maintains low costs while producing distinct products or services industry-wide for a large market with a relatively inelastic demand.

By 2003, however, sales had declined to about 131,000 units, a year in which about 100,000 units were repossessed from previous customers. Manufacturers such as Clayton Homes responded by targeting customers with moderate incomes, offering homes with upscale features, such as Mohn faucets, porcelain sinks, a wood-burning fireplace, and even a high-definition television set.[29]

Revenue declines within an industry may cause some of its differentiated businesses to cut costs to remain competitive. In the years following the events of 9/11, for example, British Air embarked on an aggressive cost-cutting campaign, ordering replacement jets devoid of the customary special features, trimming the total number of jets in its fleet, cutting fees to travel agents, eliminating 13,000 jobs, and even limiting menu choices for customers. Ticket prices were also reduced so that the airline could become more competitive with low-fare carriers. As a result, British Air has integrated an emphasis on low costs into its traditional differentiation emphasis.[30] Indeed, the low-cost–differentiation strategy is possible to attain and can be quite effective. Porter's point is well taken, however, because implementing the combination strategy is generally more difficult than implementing either the low-cost or the differentiation strategy alone. This strategy begins with an organizational commitment to quality products or services, thereby differentiating itself from its competitors. Because customers may be drawn to high quality, demand may rise, resulting in a larger market share and providing economies of scale that permit lower per unit costs in purchasing, manufacturing, financing, research and development, and marketing (see Strategy at Work 7-3).

A business can pursue low costs and differentiation simultaneously through six primary means: commitment to quality, differentiation on low price, process innovations, product innovations, value innovations, and structural innovations (see Table 7-2). First, commitment to quality throughout the business organization not only improves outputs but also reduces costs involved in scrap, warranty,

---

STRATEGY AT WORK 7-3

Competitive Strategy in the Fast-Food Industry

Although fast food in the United States has long been considered an economical lunch or dinner option, restaurants over the years have attempted to differentiate their products and create brand loyalty among consumers, with varying degrees of success. An advent of the 1990s was the notion of the "value menu" or "99 cents menu," whereby restaurants offered a limited number of its sandwich and other items at special prices for cost-conscious consumers. Initially, this move was seen as a necessary means of serving consumers during down economic times. The concept stuck, however, and many analysts believe it is here to stay.

While offering some sandwiches at or near the one-dollar price point, many restaurants also offer—and heavily promote—highly differentiated products in the two- to three-dollar range. Managers hope that many consumers will be lured in for the special prices, only to "move up" to the higher priced items when it is time to order. McDonald's, Burger King, and Wendy's all follow this approach to some degree on a national level. In 2002, Hardee's even introduced the "six dollar burger," a sandwich designed to compete with those offered in the six-dollar range at sitdown restaurants such as Applebee's, but for only $3.95 at Hardee's.

A new breed of fast-food restaurants is avoiding the value menu concept, however. High-end sandwich chains such as Panera Bread Company and Corner Bakery Café are sticking to a highly differentiated approach, emphasizing fresh bread and ingredients to an increasingly health-conscious market. The various strategies implemented by different, successful fast-food players demonstrate the number of viable market niches available in the industry.

Source: Adapted from S. Leung, "Fast-Food Chains Vie to Carve Out Empire in Pricey Sandwiches," Wall Street Journal, 5 February 2002, A1, A10.

TABLE $7\text{-}2$	Means of Pursuing Low Costs and Differentiation Simultaneously

1. Commitment to quality
2. Differentiation on low price
3. Process innovations
4. Product innovations
5. Value innovations
6. Structural innovations

and service after the sale. **Quality** refers to the features and characteristics of a product or service that enable it to satisfy stated or implied needs.[31] Hence, a high-quality product or service conforms to a predetermined set of specifications and satisfies the needs of its users. In this sense, quality is based on *perceptions* and is a measure of customer satisfaction with a product over its lifetime, relative to customer satisfaction with competitors' product offerings.[32]

Building quality into a product does not necessarily increase total costs, because the costs of rework, scrap, and servicing the product after the sale may be reduced; and the business benefits from increased customer satisfaction and repeat sales, which can improve economies of scale. The emphasis in the 1990s on quality improvement programs sought to improve product and service quality and increase customer satisfaction by implementing a holistic commitment to quality, as seen through the eyes of the customer. Studies suggest that when properly implemented, an emphasis on quality can improve customer satisfaction while lowering costs.[33]

Second, a lower than average price may be viewed as a basis for differentiating one's products or services. However, low prices should be distinguished from low costs. Whereas *price* refers to the transaction between the firm and its customers, *cost* refers to the expenses incurred in the production of a good or service. Firms with low production costs do not always translate these low costs into low prices. Anheuser Busch, for example, maintains one of the lowest per unit production costs in the beer industry but does not offer its beers at a low price. However, many firms that achieve low-cost positions also lower their prices because their competitors may not be able to afford to match their price level. These firms are combining low costs with a differentiation based on price.

Third, **process innovations** increase the efficiency of operations and distribution. Although these improvements are normally thought of as lowering costs, they can also enhance product or service differentiation. For example, the recent emphasis on eliminating processes that do not add value to the end product has not only cut costs for many businesses, but also increased production and delivery speed, a key form of differentiation.

Fourth, **product innovations** are typically presumed to enhance differentiation but can also lower costs. For instance, over the years, Philip Morris developed a filter cigarette and, later, cigarettes with low tar and nicotine levels. These innovations not only differentiated its products, but also allowed the company to use less tobacco per cigarette to produce a higher quality product at a dramatic reduction in per unit costs.[34]

Fifth, firms may engage in **value innovations**, modifying products, services, and activities in order to maximize the value delivered to customers.[35] Such firms seek to provide maximum value by differentiating products and services only to the extent that any associated cost hikes can be justified by increases in overall

Quality

The features and characteristics of a product or service that allow it to satisfy stated or implied needs.

Process Innovations

A business unit's activities that increase the efficiency of operations and distribution.

Product Innovations

A business unit's activities that enhance the differentiation of its products or services.

Value Innovations

Modifying products, services, and activities in order to maximize the value delivered to customers.

Structural Innovations

Modifying the structure of the organization and/or the business model to improve competitiveness.

Business Web

A system of internetworked, fluid, specialized businesses that come together to create value for customers.

Focus–Low-Cost/ Differentiation Strategy

A generic strategy in which a smaller business produces highly differentiated products or services for the specialized needs of a select group of customers while keeping its costs low.

Multiple Strategies

A strategic alternative for a larger business unit in which the organization simultaneously employs more than one of the generic business strategies.

value *and* by pursing cost reductions that result in minimal if any reductions in value. By focusing on value instead of low cost or differentiation, a firm can offer the overall combination of cost minimization and differentiation in an industry.

Finally, the importance of **structural innovations**, modifying the structure of the organization or the business model to improve competitiveness, has been highlighted in recent years. Recent approaches to structural innovation include the virtual corporation, outsourcing, and the Japanese kieretsu. The notion of **business webs,** or systems of internetworked, fluid, specialized businesses that come together to create value for customers, has gained prominence among strategic thinkers. Within the business web model, organizations do not focus solely on their own activities, but consciously develop partnerships with other businesses, each focusing on its own core competence to better achieve its mission.[36]

7-1f Focus–Low-Cost/Differentiation Strategy

Business units that adopt a **focus–low-cost/differentiation strategy** produce highly differentiated products or services for the specialized needs of a select group of customers while keeping their costs low. Businesses utilizing this strategy share all the characteristics of the previous strategies. The focus–low-cost/differentiation strategy is difficult to implement because the niche orientation limits prospects for economies of scale and opportunities for structural innovations. Many small, independent restaurants such as those specializing in ethnic or international cuisine adopt this approach, constantly seeking a balance of cost reductions and uniqueness targeted at a specific group of consumers. For example, many university towns have small eateries that emphasize a unique specialty—such as Garibaldi's barbeque pizza in Memphis, Tennessee—while also minimizing costs to remain affordable to the price-conscious college student.

7-1g Multiple Strategies

In some cases, business units utilize **multiple strategies**, or more than one of the six strategies identified in sections 7-1a through 7-1f, simultaneously. Unlike the *combination* low-cost–differentiations strategy, multiple strategies involve the *simultaneous* execution of two or more different generic strategies, each tailored to the needs of a distinct market or class of customer. For this reason, large businesses are more likely than small ones to adopt this approach. Hotels, for example, utilize multiple strategies when they offer basic rooms to most guests but reserve suites on the top floor for others.

A multiple strategy approach can be difficult to implement and confusing to customers. Many airlines utilize multiple strategies when they offer both highly differentiated (and high-priced) service via first-class seating and economical, limited-frills service in coach. To distinguish between these two classes of customers, airlines typically provide separate customer service counters, different boarding times and procedures, and better food for their first-class passengers. While this approach is not optimal in theory, it enables airlines to satisfy the needs of more than one traveling segment without flying additional aircraft.

7-2 Miles and Snow's Strategy Framework

A second commonly used framework introduced by Miles and Snow considers four strategic types: prospectors, defenders, analyzers, and reactors.[37] Miles and Snow's typology is an alternative to Porter's approach to generic strategy.

Prospectors perceive a dynamic, uncertain environment and maintain flexibility to combat environmental change. Prospectors introduce new products and services, and design the industry. Thus, prospectors tend to possess a loose structure, a low division of labor, and low formalization and centralization. While a prospector identifies and exploits new product and market opportunities, it accepts the risk associated with new ideas. For example, Amazon.com's initial launch of its Web bookstore was a major risk, one that resulted in much greater success for the company than with literally hundreds of other Internet start-ups in the late 1990s.

Prospectors typically seek **first-mover advantages** derived from being first to market. First-mover advantages can be strong, as demonstrated by products widely known by their original brand names, such as Kleenex and Chap Stick. Being first, however, can be a risky proposition, and research has shown that competitors may be able to catch up quickly and effectively.[38] As a result, prospectors must develop expertise in innovation and evaluate risk scenarios effectively.

Prospectors are typically focused on corporate entrepreneurship, or **intrapreneurship**. Whereas entrepreneurship focuses on the development of new business ventures as a means of launching an organization, intrapreneurship involves the creation of new business ventures within an existing firm. Established firms seeking to foster a culture that encourages the type of innovative activity often seen in upstarts must provide time, resources, and rewards to employees who develop new venture opportunities for the organization.

It can be argued that all businesses should be prospectors, at least to some extent. For example, Kraft revenues from traditional and "new and improved" versions of its Ritz, Kool-Aid, Maxwell House, Jell-O, and other brand products began to slip in the early 2000s. Kraft fired its CEO, Betsy Holden, in late 2003 in an effort to place a greater emphasis on new products instead of more conservative brand extensions.[39]

Defenders are almost the opposite of prospectors. They perceive the environment to be stable and certain, seeking stability and control in their operations to achieve maximum efficiency. Defenders incorporate an extensive division of labor, high formalization, and high centralization. The defender concentrates on only one segment of the market.

Analyzers stress stability and flexibility, and attempt to capitalize on the best of the prospector and defender strategy types. Tight control is exerted over existing operations with loose control for new undertakings. The strength of the analyzer is the ability to respond to prospectors (or imitate them) while maintaining efficiency in operations. An analyzer may follow a prospector's successful lead, modify the product or service offered by the prospector, and market it more effectively. In effect, an analyzer is seeking a "second-mover" advantage.[40]

Copying successful competitors can be a successful strategy when both organizations share the resources needed to effectively implement similar programs. After sales slumped in 2000 at Taco Bell, president Emil Brolick acknowledged plans to model the restaurant after Wendy's, noting Wendy's ability to gain market share without slashing prices. In 2001, Taco Bell began appealing to a more mature market with additional pricey items and fewer promotions. Although the product lines are substantially different, Brolick hopes that a similar approach for Taco Bell can produce similar results.[41]

Reactors lack consistency in strategic choice and perform poorly. The reactor organization lacks an appropriate set of response mechanisms with which to confront environmental change. The reactor strategic type also lacks strength.

In some respects, Porter's typology and Miles and Snow's typology are similar. For example, Miles and Snow's prospector business is likely to emphasize

First-Mover Advantages

Benefits derived from being the first firm to offer a new or modified product or service.

Intrapreneurship

The creation of new business ventures within an existing firm.

Case Analysis 7-1

Step 10: What Is the Current Business-Level Strategy?

One needs to examine each major business unit (if there is more than one) and identify which generic strategy best describes the strategy of each business unit. Both strategy typologies (e.g., Porter, Miles and Snow) should be applied, but additional support should also be provided. Each business has its own unique strategy based on its own combination of resources. Hence, it is also important to discuss how the organization's business-level strategy differs from others in the industry that might share the same generic strategy. What makes the organization unique? This phase of the strategy management process is critical and often neglected.

The notion of business-level strategy cannot be understood independent of industry definition because an organization's business-level strategy is expressed in terms *relative* to others in the industry. For example, the competitive strategy for retailing giant Wal-Mart might be considered that of differentiation or low-cost–differentiation strategy if the industry is defined "discount retailers," whereas it might be considered as low cost if the industry is defined more broadly as "department stores."

---

differentiation, whereas the defender business typically emphasizes low costs. These tendencies notwithstanding, fundamental differences exist between the typologies. Porter's approach is based on economic principles associated with the cost-differentiation dichotomy, whereas the Miles and Snow approach describes the philosophical approach of the business to its environment (see Case Analysis 7-1).

7-3 Business Size, Strategy, and Performance

Researchers examining the relationship between a business unit's size and its performance, relative to those of its competitors, have interesting observations. Midsize business units often perform poorly in comparison with small or large competitors, because they typically do not possess the advantages associated with being flexible like their small rivals or possessing substantial resources like their large rivals.[42] Specifically, small businesses enjoy flexibility in meeting specific market demands and a potentially quicker reaction to environmental changes. Because of their lower investments, they may be able to make strategic moves and pursue more limited revenue opportunities that would be unprofitable for midsize or large businesses. Likewise, large businesses can translate their economies of scale into lower costs per unit and may be better able to bargain with their suppliers or customers, or to win industry price wars.

Because midsize business units tend to lack the advantages of either small or large rivals, many choose to become larger or smaller to capitalize on advantages of their competitors. Specifically, they may seek to expand their operations (i.e., increase their size) to take advantage of scale economies, or they may retrench (i.e., decrease their size) to avail themselves of the advantages possessed by small companies. Either option can be difficult and may not even be feasible, depending on various competitive and industry forces.[43] It is not suggested that all midsize businesses perform poorly and should aggressively attempt to increase or decrease size. Nonetheless, strategic managers should understand the relationships between

FIGURE 7-2 **Porter's Generic Strategy Matrix**

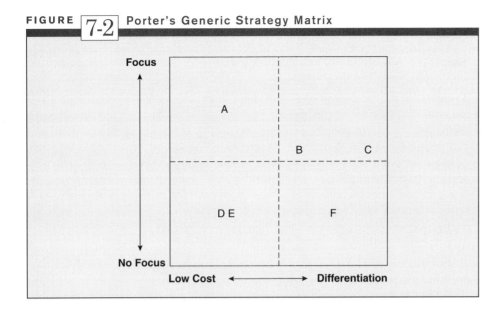

size and performance and consider them when evaluating the specific needs of their business units.

7-4 Assessing Strategies

Although the distinctions between such strategies as cost leadership and differentiation or prospectors and differentiators are readily made in theory, they are not always easy to assign in practice. Considering Porter's typology, cost leadership and differentiation may be viewed as opposite extremes on a continuum. Likewise, focus and no focus can also be seen as opposite extremes. Figure 7-2 illustrates this approach with a hypothetical industry containing six rivals. Company A is the only focus–low-cost competitor. Companies B and C—generally seen as part of the same strategic group—are slightly less focused than A; both B and C are more differentiated than A, but C is more differentiated than B. Companies D and E—clearly members of the same strategic group—employ low-cost (no-focus) strategies, whereas company E follows a differentiation (no-focus) approach. Viewing generic strategies as a matter of degree enables analysts to illustrate relatively minor distinctions between businesses employing the same generic strategy. This approach can also be applied to the Miles and Snow typology, with prospectors and defenders anchoring ends of a continuum and analyzers in the middle.[44]

Categorizing businesses in such a matrix is not easy and can be somewhat subjective. Consider Wal-Mart as an example. Traditionally, the retailer has eschewed a focus approach in favor of a one-size-fits-all approach geared at selling to most consumers. Although this approach was successful for a while, sales growth in the United States began to decline in the early 2000s. In 2006, the retailer began modifying its product mixes in many of its U.S. stores to target six groups: African Americans, the affluent, empty-nesters, Hispanics, suburbanites, and rural residents.[45] On the one hand, this move reflects an attempt by Wal-Mart to concentrate its efforts on specific markets, an approach consistent with Porter's focus strategy. On the other hand, the six groups identified together comprise the majority of the U.S. population, suggesting that Wal-Mart's competitive strategy does not qualify as a focus strategy, but as a no-focus strategy with some degree of tailoring each store to the needs of its clientele. Although it might not be appropriate to reclassify

---

Case Analysis 7-2

Step 11: What Business-Level Strategies Are Presently Being Employed by Competitors?

To analyze all the competitive options available to a business, one needs to understand the strategic approach of competitors. Because obtaining detailed information about all competitors is often difficult, a focus on the primary competitors utilizing at least one of the business strategy typologies is appropriate. The key here is to understand how different competitors in the industry utilize various strategic means to serve customers and pursue profitability. It is helpful to identify how the companies are similar and different in their strategic approaches. This insight can help strategic managers predict how competitors might respond to a change in strategy.

Wal-Mart strategy as a focus approach because of this strategic shift, a modest move toward the focus end of the continuum may be warranted.

In addition, formulating an effective competitive strategy is almost impossible without a clear understanding of the primary competitors and their strategies. Specifically, it is important to comprehend how rivals compete, what they are attempting to accomplish (i.e., their goals), what assumptions they hold concerning the industry, and what their unique strengths and weaknesses are relative to others in the industry. Developing this understanding not only helps top managers formulate strategies to position a business in the industry, but can also help them forecast any competitive responses that rivals might make if a major strategic change is implemented (see Case Analysis 7-2).

Many strategic moves are not instituted by businesses when they anticipate a competitor's activities, but in response to moves that have already been implemented. For example, by 2003, online hospitality sites Hotels.com and Expedia.com had teamed up with franchise hotels with unused capacity to fill extra rooms at discounted rates. As a result, consumers were able to secure high-quality accommodations at substantial savings. The hotel chains associated with these franchised units earn substantial profits from their reservation services and therefore began to restrict franchisees from offering rates at Web sites lower than those offered by the hotel chain's site. As one executive put it, "If we are not careful, these wholesalers will become…so big and powerful that we will have to work with them . . . And you will have to pay a premium to be on their shelves."[46]

Taking advantage of a competitor's misfortune is not always easy, however. In 2000, Bridgestone's Firestone unit was forced to recall 6.5 million tires linked to fatal accidents on Ford Explorers in a widely publicized challenge to its credibility. Goodyear, however, was unable to meet the sudden increase in demand for its tires and responded by raising prices. Although sales stabilized at Bridgestone in the early 2000s at a market share about 2 percent lower than before the recall, Goodyear's market share had declined back to its pre-recall levels by 2003. Hence, Goodyear was unable to respond effectively to Bridgestone's woes.[47]

7-5 Global Concerns

Identifying the competitive strategy of a business operating in global markets can be a complex task. Unfortunately, no simple formula exists for developing and implementing successful business strategies across national borders. A popular approach to this challenge is to think globally, but act locally. Following this logic, a business organization would emphasize the synergy created by serving multiple markets globally, but formulate a distinct competitive strategy for each specific market that is tailored to its unique situation. Others argue that consistency across global markets is critical, citing examples such as Coca-Cola, whose emphasis on quality, brand recognition, and a small world theme has been successful in a number of global markets. These two approaches represent distinct perspectives on what it takes to be successful in foreign markets. Consider several examples.

Coca-Cola's global approach to marketing the popular soft drink has been relatively consistent across borders. Some product differences exist, however, due to availability and cost factors. In Mexico, for example, Coke contains readily available cane sugar. In the United States, where customers are not believed to perceive a major difference in sweeteners, Coke changed to high-fructose corn syrup, a less expensive alternative.[48]

Compared to Coca-Cola, Yum Brands takes a more localized approach with its KFC business unit. KFC emphasizes chicken in its host country—the United States—but added fish sandwiches to menus at its Malaysian outlets in early 2006. According to KFC Holdings (Malaysia) executive director and chief operating officer To Chun Wah, "As much as our customers love our chicken products, they also want a greater variety of meat products at KFC. Our market surveys show that our customers want more than just tasty, high quality and affordable chicken but are also constantly on the lookout for new and interesting things to eat." This move reflects a clear plan to localize business strategies along the lines of taste. Outlets in Malaysia are not required to carry the fish sandwich, however. Fish sandwiches had already proven to be successful in other Asian markets, such as Beijing, Shanghai, and Taipei.[49]

Yum Brands took localization another step further in 2004 when it launched East Dawning, a bright, clean fast-food restaurant in Shanghai. East Dawning operates like Yum's KFC restaurants except that its menu and décor are Chinese. Menu offerings include Chinese favorites such as noodles, rice, soy milk, fried dough, and plum juice. Yum hopes to turn East Dawning into China's largest fast-food restaurant one day. Yum is also considering launching an Indian fast-food restaurant in India.[50]

Consider Swedish home furnishings designer Ikea. Responding to frugality in the local market, Ikea sells many of its products in China at prices well below those in other parts of the world. The Beijing store, opened in 2006, is its second largest store in the world, behind Ikea's Stockholm store, and draws an estimated three times as many visitors as its other outlets. Ikea has experienced success selling to the growing middle class in China, but at prices that would be considered bargains elsewhere in the world.[51]

There is wisdom in both global strategy perspectives—localizing and maintaining consistency across borders—although the most effective approach will depend on the mission, goals, and characteristics of the organization. In practice, businesses rarely operate at one extreme or the other. Hence, these alternative approaches can be viewed as opposite ends of a continuum. Regardless of choice, there are costs and trade-offs associated with every position along the continuum.

Tailoring a business strategy to meet the unique demands of a different market can be especially challenging because it requires that top managers understand the similarities and differences between the markets from both industry and cultural perspectives. For example, since the 1970s, Japanese automobile manufacturers have sought to blend a distinctively Japanese approach to building cars with a sensitivity to North American and European values. Honda, the first

Japanese manufacturer to operate a facility in the United States, has been most aggressive in this regard. In 2000, Mitsubishi was aggressively redesigning the Montero Sport to make it a "global vehicle" that could sell effectively in world markets. In 2001, however, the car maker dropped its one-size-fits-all approach and began to emphasize design factors unique to the critical U.S. market.[52]

Given the intense competition in most markets in the developed world, strategic managers must remain abreast of opportunities that may exist in emerging economies. India, for example, has enjoyed considerable growth in recent years. Some firms have outsourced jobs in technical areas to India where trained workers are available at considerably lower wages. Economic liberalization in the country has invited additional foreign investment into the country. India's Tata Motors helped overcome the country's reputation for poor production quality by exporting an estimated twenty thousand CityRovers to the United Kingdom in 2004.[53]

India, however, has received only a small fraction of the level of foreign investment made in China, which boasts the world's largest population and has been tabbed as a world economic leader within the next few decades. China's entrance into the World Trade Organization, declining import tariffs, and increasing consumer incomes suggest a bright future for the nation. At present, China remains a mix of the traditional lifestyle based in socialism and its own form of a neo-Western economic development. Nowhere is this friction seen best than on the roads of the capital, Beijing, where crowds of bicycles attempt to negotiate traffic with buses and a rapidly increasing number of personal automobiles. U.S.-style traffic reports have even become pervasive in a country where the world's largest automakers are fighting for a stake in what many experts believe will be a consumer automobile growth phase of mammoth proportions.[54]

When a Western firm seeks to conduct business with one of its Chinese counterparts, managers from both firms must recognize the cultural differences between the two nations. Recently, a number of consulting and management development organizations in both China and the West have been busy training managers to become aware of such differences and take action to minimize misunderstandings that can arise from them. For example, Chinese managers are more likely than Americans to smoke during meetings and less likely to answer e-mail from international partners. In the United States, it is more common to emphasize subordinate contributions to solving problems, whereas Chinese managers are more likely to respect the judgment of their superiors without subordinate involvement.[55]

Western manufacturers such as Eastman Kodak, Proctor & Gamble, Group Danone of France, and Siemens AG of Germany have already established a strong presence in China. A number of Western restaurants and retailers have also begun to expand aggressively into China, including U.S.-based McDonald's, Popeye's Chicken, and Wal-Mart. As the CEO of Yum, owner of KFC, Pizza Hut, and Taco Bell, put it, "China is an absolute gold mine for us."[56] French-based Carrefour is the largest foreign retailer in China with ninety hypermarkets in about two dozen cities. Product mixes in the Chinese stores tend to be similar to those in the domestic market, with adjustments made for local preferences. For a number of firms, the only attractive prospects for growth lie in emerging economies such as China, Brazil, and Mexico.[57]

7-6 Summary

At the business level, top managers determine how the organization is to compete effectively. According to Porter's framework, managers must decide whether to focus on a segment of the market—a strategy often appropriate for small businesses—and whether to emphasize low costs or differentiation.

Each approach has its own set of advantages and challenges. Business units may also seek to combine the low-cost and differentiation strategies, although this approach can be difficult to implement effectively.

According to Miles and Snow's framework, managers may select a prospector, an analyzer, a defender, or a reactor strategy. Each of the first three approaches can serve as an effective approach, whereas the reactor strategy is a suboptimal choice.

Top managers should also consider the roles of business size, the strategies of rivals, and opportunities in emerging markets when seeking to develop business strategies.

Key Terms

business unit

business webs

differentiation strategy

first-mover advantages

focus-differentiation strategy

focus–low-cost/differentiation strategy

focus–low-cost strategy

generic strategies

intrapreneurship

low-cost–differentiation strategy

low-cost strategy

multiple strategies

process innovations

product innovations

quality

strategic group

structural innovations

value innovations

Review Questions and Exercises

1. What is the difference between a corporate strategy and a business strategy?

2. Identify the generic business strategy configurations available to strategic managers, according to Porter's typology.

3. Is it possible for a business to differentiate its outputs and lower its costs simultaneously? Explain.

4. Identify the generic business strategy configurations available to strategic managers, according to Miles and Snow's typology.

5. How are the business strategy typologies by Porter and those by Miles and Snow similar? How are they different?

6. Why might one expect the performance level of mid-size business units to be lower than the performance level of either small or large business units?

Practice Quiz

True or False

1. The focus-differentiation strategy emphasizes low overall costs while serving a narrow segment of the market.

2. Businesses that utilize the focus strategy produce and market to the entire industry products or services that can be readily distinguished from those of their competitors.

3. The combination strategy can also be referred to as multiple strategies.

4. There is no advantage to the reactor strategic type.

5. The generic strategy typologies developed by Porter and by Miles and Snow possess both similarities and differences.

6. Midsize businesses tend to be outperformed by their smaller and larger counterparts.

Multiple Choice

7. Businesses adopting the same generic strategy are referred to as
   A. low-cost businesses.
   B. differentiated businesses.
   C. a strategic group.
   D. none of the above

8. A no-frills product targeted at the market at large is consistent with the
   A. low-cost strategy.
   B. differentiation strategy.
   C. focus strategy.
   D. none of the above

9. Which of the following is not a key advantage of the low-cost–differentiation strategy?

   A. It enables the business to compete from a cost leadership position.

   B. It is easier to implement than either the low-cost or the differentiation strategy.

   C. It allows the business to distinguish its products from the competition.

   D. It offers the prospects of high profitability.

10. Modifying the structure of the organization and/or the business model to improve competitiveness is consistent with

   A. the low-cost strategy.

   B. the focus strategy.

   C. the differentiation strategy.

   D. none of the above

11. Analyzers

   A. seek first-mover advantages.

   B. control a distinct segment of the market.

   C. display some of the characteristics of both prospectors and defenders.

   D. none of the above

12. Emerging markets are often more attractive than developed ones because

   A. competition is not as intense.

   B. consumer incomes in emerging markets are not a concern.

   C. the infrastructure in emerging markets is already developed.

   D. none of the above

Notes

1. Z. He and P. Wong, "Exploration vs. Exploitation: An Empirical Test of the Ambidexterity Hypothesis," *Organization Science* 15 (2004): 481–494.

2. I. M. Cockburn, R. M. Henderson, and S. Stern, "Untangling the Origins of Competitive Advantage," *Strategic Management Journal* 21 (2000): 1123–1145.

3. T. D. Ferguson, D. L. Deephouse, and W. L. Ferguson, "Do Strategic Groups Differ in Reputation?" *Strategic Management Journal* 21 (2000): 1195–1214.

4. R. S. Kaplan and D. P. Norton, "Having Trouble with Your Strategy? Then Map It," *Harvard Business Review* 78(5) (2000): 167–176.

5. C. Campbell-Hunt, "What Have We Learned about Generic Competitive Strategy? A Meta-Analysis," *Strategic Management Journal* 21 (2000): 127–154.

6. M. E. Porter, *Competitive Strategy* (New York: Free Press, 1980).

7. Porter, 41.

8. H. Rudnitsky, "The King of Off-Price," *Forbes* (31 January 1994): 54–55; J. A. Parnell, "New Evidence in the Generic Strategy and Business Performance Debate: A Research Note," *British Journal of Management* 8 (1997): 175–181.

9. R. D. Buzzell and B. T. Gale, *The PIMS Principles* (New York: Free Press, 1987); R. Luchs, "Successful Businesses Compete on Quality–Not Costs," *Long Range Planning* 19(1) (1986): 12–17.

10. K. Stringer, "Airlines Now Offer 'Last Minute' Fare Bargains Weeks before Flight," *Wall Street Journal* (15 March 2002): B1.

11. E. Perez and N. Harris, "Despite Early Signs of Victory, Discount Airlines Get Squeezed," *Wall Street Journal* (17 January 2005): A1, A6; E. Perez, "Fare War Menaces Air Industry," *Wall Street Journal* (6 January 2005): C1, C5; A. Johnson, "Airlines Cut Prices on Overseas Fares," *Wall Street Journal* (11 January 2005): D1, D5.

12. J. Pereira and C.J. Chipello, "Battle of the Building Blocks," *Wall Street Journal* (4 February 2004): B1, B4.

13. J. Adamy, "To Find Growth, No-Frills Grocer Goes Where Other Chains Won't," *Wall Street Journal* (30 August 2005): A1, A8.

14. "The Collapse of Laker Airways," Workers World Online, accessed April 12, 2002, www.workers.org/marcy/economy/crisis04.html.

15. K. Johnson and D. Michaels, "Big Worry for No-Frills Ryanair: Has It Gone as Low as It Can Go?" *Wall Street Journal* (1 July 2004): A1, A10.

16. D. Michaels, "Growth Market for Airlines: Cheap Travel for Immigrants," *Wall Street Journal* (7 March 2007): A1, A15.

17. S. Carey, "United to Install In-Flight E-Mail by End of Year," *Wall Street Journal* (17 June 2003): D1, D2; S. McCartney, "New In-Flight E-Mail Falls Short," *Wall Street Journal* (31 March 2004): D1, D3; D. Michaels, "New Look for Cattle Class," *Wall Street Journal* (8 December 2004): B1, B2.

18. S. McCartney, "Carrier Caters to Critters," *Wall Street Journal* (29 October 2003): B1–B2.

19. S. Gray, "Coffee on the Double," *Wall Street Journal* (12 April 2005): B1, B7.

20. M. B. Lieberman and D. B. Montgomery, "First-Mover Advantages," *Strategic Management Journal* 9 (1988): 41–58.

21. N. E. Budette, "Volkswagen Stalls on Several Fronts after Luxury Drive," *Wall Street Journal* (8 May 2003): A1, A17.

22. S. Kang, "Retailer Prospers with Sexy Clothers for the Plus-Sized," *Wall Street Journal* (27 April 2004): A1, A8.

23. K. Helliker, "Rare Retailer Scores by Targeting Men Who Hate to Shop," *Wall Street Journal* (17 December 2002): A1, A11.

24. J. Kickul and L. K. Gundry, "Prospecting for Strategic Advantage: The Proactive Entrepreneurial Personality and Small Firm Innovation," *Journal of Small Business Management* 40 (2002): 85–97.

25. Porter, *Competitive Strategy*.

26. Parnell, "New Evidence in the Generic Strategy and Business Performance Debate"; Parnell, "Reframing the Combination

Strategy Debate: Defining Different Forms of Combination," *Journal of Applied Management Studies* 9(1) (2000): 33–54; C. W. L. Hill, "Differentiation versus Low Cost or Differentiation and Low Cost: A Contingency Framework," *Academy of Management Review* 13 (1988): 401–412.

27. R. Papiernik, "McDonald's Shows It Can Market Well with Numbers, Knack for Good Timing," *Nation's Restaurant News* (1 May 2000): 15–16; J. F. Love, *McDonald's: Behind the Arches* (New York: Bantam Press, 1995).

28. S. Carey, "Costly Race in the Sky," *Wall Street Journal* (9 September 2002): B1, B3.

29. J. R. Hagerty, "Mobile-Home Industry Tries to Haul Itself out of Big Slump," *Wall Street Journal* (30 March 2004): A1, A12.

30. D. Michaels, "As Airlines Suffer, British Air Tries New Strategy," *Wall Street Journal* (22 May 2003): A1, A5.

31. ANSI/ASQC, Quality Systems Terminology, American National Standard (1987), A3-1987.

32. D. A. Garvin, *Managing Quality* (New York: Free Press, 1988).

33. United States General Accounting Office, "Management Practices: U.S. Companies Improve Performance through Quality Efforts," GAO/NSIAD-91-190, May 1991.

34. A. Farnham, "America's Most Admired Companies," *Fortune* (7 February 1994): 50–54; R. H. Miles, *Coffin Nails and Corporate Strategies* (Englewood Cliffs, NJ: Prentice Hall, 1982).

35. W. C. Kim and R. Mauborgne, "Value Innovation: The Strategic Logic of High Growth," *Harvard Business Review* 82(4) (2004): 172–180.

36. D. Tapscott, D. Ticoll, and A. Lowy, *Digital Capital* (Boston: Harvard Business School Press, 2000).

37. R. E. Miles and C. C. Snow, *Organizational Strategy, Structure, and Process* (New York: West, 1978); M. Forte, J. J. Hoffman, B. T. Lamont, and E. N. Brockmann, "Organizational Form and Environment: An Analysis of Between-Form and Within-Form Responses to Environmental Change," *Strategic Management Journal* 21 (2000): 753–773.

38. J. A. Matthews, "Competitive Advantages of the Latecomer Firm: A Resource-Based Account of Industrial Catch-Up Strategies," *Asia Pacific Journal of Management* 19 (2002): 467–488.

39. S. Ellison, "Kraft's Stale Strategy," *Wall Street Journal* (18 December 2003): B1, B6.

40. H. C. Hoppe and U. Lehmann-Grube, "Second-Mover Advantages in Dynamic Quality Competition," *Journal of Economics & Management Strategy* 10 (2001): 419–434.

41. J. Ordonez, "Taco Bell Chief Has New Tactic: Be Like Wendy's," *Wall Street Journal* (23 February 2001); B1, B4.

42. D. B. Audretsch and J. A. Elston, "Does Firm Size Matter? Evidence from the Impact of Liquidity Constraints on Firm Investment Behavior in Germany," *International Journal of Industrial Organization* 20 (2002): 1–138.

43. P. Chan and T. Sneyoski, "Environmental Change, Competitive Strategy, Structure, and Firm Performance: An Application of Data Development Analysis," *International Journal of Systems Science* 22 (1991): 1625–1636.

44. Some scholars might reject this approach, arguing that each generic strategy in a given typology represents a qualitatively distinct strategy. While this is arguably true, considering generic strategy as a matter of degree rather than kind is a useful means of illustrating strategic variations in an industry.

45. A. Zimmerman, "To Boost Sales, Wal-Mart Drops One-Size-Fits-All Approach," *Wall Street Journal* (7 September 2006): A1, A17.

46. J. Angwin and M. Rich, "Big Hotel Chains Are Striking Back against Web Sites," *Wall Street Journal* (14 March 2003): A7, A71; R. Lieber, "When Hotel Discounts Are No Bargain," *Wall Street Journal* (6 August 2003): D1, D9.

47. T. Aeppel, "How Goodyear Blew Its Change to Capitalize on a Rival's Woes," *Wall Street Journal* (19 February 2003): A1, A10.

48. C. Terhune, "U.S. Thirst for Mexican Cola Poses Sticky Problem for Coke," *Wall Street Journal* (11 January 2006): A1, A10.

49. P. Nambiar, "Grab a Fish Sandwich—at KFC," *New Strait Times* (5 January 2006): B24.

50. J. Adamy, "One U.S. Chain's Unlikely Goal: Pitching Chinese Food in China," *Wall Street Journal* (20 October 2006): A1, A8.

51. M. Fong, "Ikea Hits Home in China," *Wall Street Journal* (3 March 2006): B1, B4.

52. N. Shirouzu, "Tailoring World's Cars to U.S. Tastes," *Wall Street Journal* (15 January 2001): B1.

53. J. Slater and J. Solomon, "With a Small Car, India Takes Big Step onto Global Stage," *Wall Street Journal* (5 February 2004): A1, A9; C. Karmin, "India, Poised for Growth, Merits Closer Look," *Wall Street Journal* (19 February 2004): C1, C18; S. Thurm, "Lesson in India: Some Jobs Don't Translate Overseas," *Wall Street Journal* (3 March 2004): A1, A10.

54. K. Leggett and T. Zaun, "World Car Makers Race to Keep Up with China Boom," *Wall Street Journal* (13 December 2002): A1, A7; K. Chen, "Beyond the Traffice Report," *Wall Street Journal* (2 January 2003): A1, A12.

55. M. Fong, "Chinese Charm School," *Wall Street Journal* (13 January 2004): B1, B6.

56. L. Chang and P. Wonacott, "Cracking China's Market," *Wall Street Journal* (9 January 2003): B1.

57. L. Chang, "Western Stores Woo Chinese Wallets," *Wall Street Journal* (26 November 2002): B1, B6; B. Saporito, "Can Wal-Mart Get Any Bigger?" *Time* (13 January 2003): 38–43.

Insight from *strategy+business*

Leadership and innovation may be appealing concepts, but they are not always crucial to strategic success. This chapter's strategy+business reading refers to the alternative approach as imitation and notes that doing so reduces risk and can increase efficiency. As Carr puts it, "Innovation has its place…but it's not every place."

Mastering Imitation

For every thousand flowers that bloom, a million weeds surface. Best to cultivate from the greats.

By Nicholas G. Carr

Management thinking has for some time been dominated by two big themes: leadership and innovation. It's not hard to see why. Both are important yet amorphous subjects. As resistant to definition as they are essential to business success, they offer unbounded opportunities for exposition and exploration to researcher, philosopher, and charlatan alike.

They have something else in common, too. It's come to be assumed that leadership and innovation are universally good qualities to which all should aspire. Through high-minded training programs, reward systems, and communication efforts, companies today routinely seek to democratize innovativeness and leadership—to drive them into every nook and cranny of their organization. In one way, this phenomenon seems yet another manifestation of the peculiarly American assumption that what's good small doses must be great in large quantities. In another way, it appears to spring out of the shift from a manufacturing to a service economy, with the attendant weakening of traditional management hierarchies.

But is the phenomenon as salutary as it first appears? Is it really in the best interest of companies to try to turn all their employees into leaders, all their units into hotbeds of creativity? I'm not convinced. The cult of leadership seems especially, even insidiously, dangerous. Too often, it ends up promoting an insipid textbook form of leadership, a "five keys to success" pantomime. At worst, it breeds a particularly insufferable kind of despot—the boss who, like David Brent in the BBC series *The Office,* feels compelled to flourish his entirely imaginary "leadership qualities" in front of his beleaguered staff. The result, inevitably, is organizational cynicism.

The cult of innovation seems healthy on the face of it. In a free market, after all, innovation underpins competitive advantage, which in turn undergirds profitability. Being indistinguishable from everyone else means operating with a microthin profit margin, if not outright losses. So why not try to innovate everywhere—to let, as Chairman Mao famously put it, a thousand flowers bloom?

Here's why not: For every thousand flowers, you get a million weeds. Innovation is by its very nature wasteful. It demands experimentation, speculative investment, and failure, all of which entail high costs anti risks. Indeed, it is innovations intrinsic uncertainty that gives it its value. High risks and costs form the barriers to competition that give successful innovators their edge. If innovation were a sure thing, everyone would do it equally well, and its strategic value would be neutralized. It would become just another cost of doing business.

But the high costs and risks also make discretion and prudence paramount. The most successful companies know when to take a chance on innovation, but they also know when to take the less glamorous but far safer route of imitation. Although imitation is often viewed as innovation's homely sibling, it's every bit as central to business success. Indeed, it's what makes innovation economically feasible.

Deliberate but Dicey

So the critical first question for any would-be innovator should not be *How?* but *Where?* Deciding where to innovate—and where not to—is fundamentally a strategic exercise, requiring a clear understanding of a company's existing and potential sources of competitive advantage.

Source: Reprinted with permission from *strategy+business,* the award-winning management quarterly published by Booz Allen Hamilton. http://www.strategy-business.com.

If corporate innovation involves a deliberate but dicey attempt to create a new product or practice with commercial value, then the target should be one in which a company has an opportunity to establish a *meaningful* and *defensible* point of differentiation from its competitors. A meaningful point of differentiation is one that, to paraphrase Michael Porter, translates into either lower-cost operations or higher-value products, the two linchpins of outstanding profitability. A defensible point of differentiation is one that is resistant to rapid competitive replication. Defensible doesn't mean permanent; competition eventually erases all differences. What's important is to be able to sustain the differentiation long enough at least to offset the up-front costs and risks of innovation.

The proper focus of innovation will vary greatly from company to company, but at a high level successful businesses can be divided into two camps: process innovators and product innovators. Process innovators distinguish themselves by being more efficient in how they work; they produce fairly standardized products at a lower cost than competitors do, enabling them to earn relatively high profits at prevailing market prices (or drive competitors out of business through ruthless discounting). Process innovators tend to be the largest of all companies, dominating big, mature markets. Product innovators, on the other hand, make their mark by offering customers particularly attractive goods or services—those that offer superior functionality, more fashionable designs, or simply more enticing brand names or packaging. Their supranormal profitability, as an economist would put it, derives from the premium prices they can charge. Product innovators tend to pioneer new markets or to hold lucrative niches in older industries.

In the personal computer market, Dell stands as a classic process innovator. Its products are nothing special—they're essentially commodities that meet the prevailing needs of most buyers. But through the relentless fine-tuning of its supply, assembly, and distribution operations, Dell has gained a wide cost advantage over its rivals that has made it the fastest-growing, most profitable company in its industry—by far. Apple, on the other hand, is the model of an effective product innovator. It has carved out a profitable niche in a cutthroat business by offering distinctive and stylish products that a sizable set of buyers are willing to pay more for.

What's especially noteworthy about Dell and Apple is the discipline they bring to innovation. They innovate where creativity will buttress their core advantages, and they imitate elsewhere. You could argue, in fact, that to be a successful product innovator you need to be an adept process imitator, and to be a winning process innovator you need to be a good product imitator.

Dell, for instance, is skilled at quickly copying products and product features, which has enabled it to apply its superior process skills to a series of new markets, from servers to storage drives to switches. In some cases, it simply contracts with existing suppliers to provide it with commodity products to push through its distribution system. In challenging Hewlett-Packard in the lucrative market for printers, Dell is buying its products from Lexmark and rebranding them as its own. It thus avoids high research and development expenditures, further reinforcing its cost advantage.

As for Apple, its resurgence since the late 1990s has been as attributable to emulating processes as to churning out breakthrough products like the iMac and iBook. Soon after Steve Jobs returned as CEO in 1996, for example, he hired an operations ace, IBM and Compaq veteran Timothy Cook, to retool the company's rusty supply chain. By copying the best practices pioneered by companies like Dell, Mr. Cook dramatically reduced Apple's in-channel inventory, and the savings in working capital provided an immediate boost to profitability. On the distribution end, Apple has successfully copied efficient direct-to-customer channels such as online sales and dedicated stores.

Compare Dell's and Apple's highly disciplined innovation efforts to Gateway's shoot-anything-that-approach. Gateway started as a process innovator, becoming, with Dell, a pioneer of direct distribution, but it also tried to be a product differentiator, maintaining relatively high-cost manufacturing plants, investing more than Dell in R&D, and launching expensive brand-advertising campaigns. It innovated aggressively on the retailing end as well, pioneering the exclusive stores that Apple would later (and more successfully) copy. It even tried to be a service innovator, pursuing a highly publicized "beyond the box" strategy involving the provision of various consulting services to small businesses. By trying to innovate everywhere, Gateway failed to build a strong competitive advantage anywhere. It was unable to distinguish its products enough to escape the industry price wars, and its operating costs remained much higher than Dell's. Today, it is struggling to survive.

For purposes of illustration, I've drawn clear lines between products and processes and between innovation and imitation. In practice, those lines are usually blurred. A new industrial chemical, for example, will often arise as much through process advances in the manufacturing plant as through product breakthroughs in the research and development lab.

Even the most amazing new products will often incorporate ideas and components filched from others. In creating the iPod, its latest hit, Apple borrowed the major components from outside suppliers—the basic circuitry from PortalPlayer, the tiny hard drive from Toshiba, the battery from Sony, the digital-to-analog converter from Wolfson. It concentrated its innovation in its core strengths of engineering, design, marketing, partnering, and, most important of all, the integration of hardware and software. It's hard to think of another company that has the skill and business model required to tie together a handheld music player (iPod), an elegant PC application for playing and organizing music files (iTunes), and an online store filled with songs from all the major recording studios (iTunes Music Store).

The lesson is clear: Innovate passionately in those places where you can separate yourself from the competition. Where differentiation promises to be elusive or fleeting, be a cold-blooded imitator.

Creativity Kills Competence

Beyond the dubious economics, one of the biggest problems with unconstrained innovation is that it can end up devaluing competence. It says to employees, It's not enough to do your job extremely well: You're only truly valuable if you "think outside the box" or "push the envelope" or—pick your cliché. That can lead to distorted measurement and reward systems, misdirected activity, and ultimately the disenfranchisement of a company's best workers.

A few years ago, a firm I'm familiar with got the innovation religion, and suffered mightily as a result. After nearly a decade of strong growth, the company's sales had gone soft and its margins had narrowed. It realized, correctly, that it required an infusion of new thinking. But rather than concentrate its efforts in the two areas that might have made a real difference to its business—new product development and branding—it took an unfocused, more-is-more approach. It democratized innovation by putting it at the heart of its annual incentive-compensation program.

To earn a decent bonus, each employee had to demonstrate some form of creativity in his or her work, and each business unit had to provide examples and measures of its innovativeness.

The company's intentions were noble, but the program backfired. Dozens of piecemeal innovation initiatives were launched; even the IT help desk and the reception staff strove to reinvent their functions. The management and measurement of all these efforts required a cumbersome new bureaucracy and a small mountain of paperwork. Little thought was given to the actual business impact of the individual programs—creativity had become a good in its own right. Not surprisingly, employees and managers let their attention drift away from their day jobs, which suddenly seemed like secondary concerns, and the company's core business suffered.

The effect of the effort on individual employees was particularly distressing. The least talented workers actually embraced the program with the greatest fervor; it provided them with a respite from what they saw as the drudgery of their regular work. They became fonts of new and largely useless ideas, meticulously documenting their every passing fancy. The most competent employees, in contrast, treated the whole project as a silly game. They went through the motions, all the while complaining to one another about the emptiness of the exercise. Believing the company was rewarding smart talk over real accomplishment, they were slowly drained of their morale and motivation, and many of them ended up heading for the exit. Creativity had trumped competence, and performance took a hit.

Innovation has its place—a very, very important place but it's not everyplace. Creativity should not be allowed to shoulder competence to the verges. Acts of innovation may determine what companies do, but it's competence that determines how well they do it. Let a half-dozen flowers bloom, and keep the weeds in check.

Nicholas G. Carr (ncarr@mac.com) a contributing editor to *strategy+business* and a former executive editor of *Harvard Business Review*, is the author of *Does IT Matter? Information Technology and the Corrosion of Competitive Advantage* (Harvard Business School Press, 2004).

Functional Strategies 8

Chapter Outline

Corporate-level and business-level strategies can only be successful if they are supported by strategies at the business unit's functional levels, such as marketing, finance, production, purchasing, human resources, and information systems. Each functional area should integrate its activities with those of the other functional departments because a change in one department can affect both the manner in which other departments operate and the overall performance of the business unit. Indeed, the extent to which all of the business unit's **functional strategies** integrate can determine the effectiveness of the unit's business-level and firm-level strategies.

Although functional strategies are formulated after the corporate and business strategies have already been established, it is a good idea to consider the capabilities of functional areas while debating higher level strategies. For example, an airline considering expansion through additional international routes should consider factors such as the need for additional personnel and the organization's

Functional Strategies

The strategies pursued by each functional area of a business unit, such as marketing, finance, or production.

TABLE 8-1 Integrating Business and Functional Strategies

Strategy	Low-Cost	Differentiation	Low-Cost–Differentiation
Marketing	Emphasize low-cost distribution and low-cost advertising and promotion.	Emphasize differentiated distribution and advertising and promotion on a large scale.	Emphasize differentiated distribution and advertising and promotion on a large scale at the lowest cost possible.
Finance	Lower financial costs by borrowing when credit costs are low and issuing stock when the market is strong.	Emphasize obtaining resources and funding output improvements or innovations, even when financial costs may be high.	Emphasize obtaining resources and funding output improvements or innovations at the lowest possible cost.
Production	Emphasize operation efficiencies through learning, economies of scale, and capital-labor substitution possibilities.	Emphasize quality in operations even when the cost of doing so is high.	Emphasize quality in operations when the cost of doing so is relatively low.
Purchasing	Purchase at low costs through quantity discounts. Operate storage and warehouse facilities and control inventory efficiently.	Purchase high-quality inputs, even if they cost more. Conduct storage, warehouse, and inventory activities with extensive care, even if costs are higher.	Purchase high-quality inputs, but only if costs are low. Conduct storage, warehouse, and inventory activities with care, but only if costs are relatively low.
Research and Development (R&D)	Emphasize process R&D aimed at lowering costs of operation and distribution.	Emphasize product/service R&D aimed at enhancing the outputs of the business.	Emphasize both product/service R&D and process R&D.
Human Resource Management	Emphasize reward systems that encourage cost reductions.	Emphasize reward systems that encourage innovation.	Emphasize reward systems that encourage cost reductions and innovation.
Information Systems	Emphasize timely and pertinent information on costs of operations.	Emphasize timely and pertinent information on the ongoing processes that yield unique products/services.	Emphasize both timely and pertinent information on costs of operations and innovation processes that are meant to yield unique products/services.

Source: Adapted from P. Wright, M. Kroll, and J. A. Parnell, *Strategic Management: Concepts* (Upper Saddle River, NJ: Prentice Hall, 1998).

ability to finance additional airplanes *before* settling on the expansion plan as the preferred strategic option.

Unfortunately, managers in each functional area may not fully appreciate the interrelationships among the functions. Marketers who do not understand production may promise customers product features that the production department cannot readily or economically integrate into the product's design. Production managers who do not understand marketing may insist on production changes that result in relatively minor cost changes but fail to satisfy customer needs. For this reason, managers in all functional areas should understand how the areas integrate, and they should work together to formulate functional strategies that fit together and support the corporate- and business-level strategies.

This chapter examines functional strategies in the areas of marketing, finance, production, purchasing, human resources, and information systems. Although the relationships among functional strategies are not always clear, Table 8-1 summarizes the way functional strategies typically integrate with the business strategy using as an example the modified version of Porter's typology discussed in Chapter 7.

This chapter is organized along functions. In practice, however, many of the issues discussed herein are *cross-functional* and therefore concern more than one functional area. Production warranties, for example, are a key concern for both the production and marketing departments. These issues are discussed in the functional section where they seem to fit the best.

8-1 Marketing

The competitive strategy and the marketing functional strategy are tightly intertwined. Traditionally, marketing has been dissected into four dimensions or four Ps: price, promotion, product/service, and place (i.e., channels of distribution). The particular generic strategy adopted by the business unit influences how these various dimensions are planned and executed. The emphasis on marketing—most notably the notion of customer orientation—continues to gain prominence and places a high level of importance on marketing strategies that support the firm and business strategies.[1] From a competitive standpoint, marketing is arguably the most critical of the functional strategies and should be considered early in the development of the business strategy.

8-1a Pricing Strategies

Business units that compete with the low-cost generic strategy produce basic, relatively undifferentiated outputs and often offer low prices. Wal-Mart, for example, is known for its highly effective high-volume, low-cost strategy. Even Internet powerhouse Amazon.com has sought to follow the Wal-Mart model, cutting prices when possible in an effort to gain economies of scale (discussed in greater detail in section 8-3) through high volume.[2]

Motel 6 also incorporates such a strategy, offering clean and comfortable, low-priced rooms. Founded more than forty years ago, Motel 6 minimizes costs by offering few services, such as restaurants or conference rooms. Its simple brand name, Motel 6, even conveys the impression of economy services. Consistent with its no-frills outputs, each Motel 6 offers rooms at daily rates at or below other nearby chain motels. Promotional efforts—primarily radio spots with limited television and billboards—are relatively limited and attempt to convey to the traveling public that Motel 6 offers satisfactory economy lodging.[3]

Businesses that use the generic strategy of low-cost differentiation must market quality products and services that are distinguishable from the outputs of their competitors.[4] For example, Hampton Inn offers larger rooms with better quality furnishings than Motel 6, along with amenities such as a free breakfast buffet, swimming pool, and conference rooms. The brand name Hampton Inn is intended to convey the impression of quality and value. Average to slightly above average prices are charged for Hampton Inn rooms, depending on the competitive situation, and promotional efforts connote a differentiated quality image.

Businesses emphasizing low prices, however, often find it difficult to raise prices if it becomes necessary. Fast-food restaurants with "dollar menus" in the United States experienced declines in sales when they attempted to wean consumers from such values in the early 2000s. Automakers relied heavily on rebates to sell cars during this time—an average of over $3,000 for Chevrolets—and have experienced similar difficulties.[5]

Business units that combine the focus strategy with the differentiation or low-cost–differentiation generic strategy tend to emphasize other factors in their marketing strategies. These businesses offer unique, high-quality products and services to meet the specialized needs of a relatively small market. Most bed-and-breakfast establishments offer a limited number of rooms to discriminating travelers who seek accommodations with a local, home-oriented flavor.

Pricing strategies can involve more than simply a price point relative to the competition. Health clubs, for example, typically promote memberships by the month and offer discounts for commitments of one or two years. Research suggests that many consumers would actually save money if they chose to pay on a per-visit basis or make a higher monthly payment without a long-term commitment because they never actually use the facilities as much as they project when they join. By offering unlimited usage for a period of time, health clubs are *perceived* to be more price competitive by consumers who may or may not attain their fitness goals.[6]

8-1b Promotion Strategies

Firms operating in certain industries have been banned from advertising in the United States, although many of these regulations have been lifted. Medical professionals, attorneys, and pharmaceutical companies are now permitted to advertise their products and services, provided they meet specific requirements. Advertising can often backfire, however, if consumers perceive that expenses associated with the promotion may drive up already steep fees, as could be the case for attorney services or prescription medicines.[7]

From a marketing perspective, the Internet presently offers opportunities for integration among various media. In the early 2000s, Proctor & Gamble began sponsoring news stories on topics such as health care, parenting, and nutrition, ending each ninety-second segment with a referral to its Web site via the television station's site. For example, a story on diaper rash might conclude with a referral to the Pampers page.[8]

The Internet enables many businesses to target potential customers in an efficient manner. For this reason, Internet-based and traditional businesses have begun to use the Net as a significant part of their promotional campaigns. Following an initial boom in Internet advertising in the late 1990s, interest in Web advertising waned for several years. By the mid-2000s, however, the advent of broadband and new advertising formats, including more sophisticated animation, sparked a resurgence. Search-related advertisements—those which appear alongside search results at popular search sites—remain quite popular.[9]

8-1c Product/Service Strategies

Product decisions are a key part of the marketing mix and can be quite interesting. Consider the following examples. Honda, Nissan, and other carmakers began adding safety features in many of their 2004 models to provide SUV drivers, who place a high value on safety, with alternatives in smaller vehicles.[10] In 2003, restaurants such as McDonald's and Starbucks began installing Wi-Fi (i.e., wireless fidelity high-speed Internet access) in some of their restaurants to provide online access for customers with laptops. In some instances, one hour of access is available as an add-on to a value meal.[11] In the early 2000s, PepsiCo controlled three of the top five soft drinks in the United States. Market shares of two of the three—Pepsi and Mountain Dew—declined, however, while Diet Pepsi increased during this time. Although Diet Pepsi remained third in revenues behind its two siblings, PepsiCo announced in early 2005 that Diet Pepsi would replace Pepsi as its new flagship, a major shift in its marketing efforts.[12] Since the introduction of Coke Zero in 2005, Coca-Cola has also shifted much of its attention away from its flagship—Coca-Cola Classic—to its low-calorie alternative.[13]

Product design is also critical to all firms, regardless of the strategies they employ. Although design was traditionally associated with appearance, the concept also includes such features as designing a product for easy manufacturability so that fewer parts have to be purchased or improving the product's ability to perform its purpose.[14] Effective design now addresses aesthetics as well as other consumer concerns, including such factors as how a product works, how it feels in the hand, how easy it is to assemble and fix, and even what its prospects are for recycling. Gaining a competitive advantage through superior product design involves all functional areas. A well-designed product is attractive and easy to build, market, use, and maintain; it is also driven by simplicity.

Customer service is also a critical marketing concern. Developing and maintaining the quality of customer service can be more challenging than enhancing product quality, because the consumer perceives service value primarily at the time the service is rendered (or not rendered).[15] All functional areas must work together to provide the customer with product and service value.[16] For example, an online retailer must fulfill several customer needs. First, it must offer value to customers in their shopping. Carrying the products that customers desire at competitive prices means that the various functions must communicate with one another and cooperate closely. Next, it must make certain that its employees are able to respond to customer inquiries, either electronically or by telephone. This capability requires effective human resource management training as well as information systems management. The e-tailer must also ensure that it stocks sufficient quantities of the items that it promotes, a common problem for start-ups in the 1990s. This requires interaction among the purchasing, inventory, information systems, and marketing functions. Finally, the company must provide the clear, efficient, and secure means for

STRATEGY AT WORK 8-1

Importance of Customer Service in e-Commerce

In e-commerce, extraordinary customer service can lead to great increases in future sales through repeat visits and positive word of mouth. In addition, online shoppers expect to have prompt customer service throughout the buying experience. Research has found that as many as 40 percent of online buyers abruptly discontinue shopping at e-tailers because of unsatisfactory customer service.

Today, online shoppers are more sophisticated, with complex questions and expectations of real-time responses. Customers are beginning to expect instant service via a toll-free number, live text chat, or other such immediate response methods.

Major package carrier DHL offers customer service only by e-mail or telephone. Oliver Deschryver, chief technology officer at DHL Airways Inc., also added that text chat and collaborative browsing are definitely part of the strategy.

Nordstrom.com launched text-based chat that has the added feature of "watching," whereby online shoppers can actually view the exact colors of the fabrics while they are chatting with a customer service representative. Paul Onnen, the company's chief technology officer, hopes that this will enrich the customers' shopping experience.

Many companies are also using sophisticated software to improve online customer service. Averitt Express built a broad range of customer service applications using Domino Web Server Release 5 and Lotus Notes. Home Inc. combined customer relationship management (CRM) and e-commerce applications with Oracle Financials to integrate its online business.

As Christopher Little, vice president and general manager of GE Distribution Finance, puts it, "Our goal is complete customer fulfillment online, which means I want to keep my shop open to our customers 24 hours a day, seven days a week."

Sources: R. Spiegel, "Study: Top Customer Service Drives E-Commerce Sales," E-Commerce Times, 1 December 1999; M. Zetlin, "E-Customer Service Gets Real," Computerworld 34(44) (2000): 56–57; L. Stevens, "Companies Go beyond CRM to Pamper Online Customers," Informationweek 808 (2000): 184–188; T. Sinioukov, "Financial Services' E-Commerce Outreach," Dealerscope 42(9) (2000): 28.

customers to complete the purchase process accurately and quickly, requiring the close cooperation of information systems and human resource management (see Strategy at Work 8-1).

Product/service decisions are often difficult. Responding to market share gains by discounters such as Target, Federated Department Stores recently redesigned its stores to promote self-service, while reducing the number of sales clerks. The large retailer hopes that consumers will perceive the efficient layout as more convenient, while enabling Federated to cut costs.[17] At the same time, Saks, Macy's, and Federated have introduced upscale private label products in an attempt to lower prices while maintaining a quality image.[18]

The importance of service cannot be overemphasized. The Southwest Airlines frequent fliers appreciate that company's commitment to superior service in a friendly, professional, but sometimes comical environment.[19] Interestingly, surveys typically suggest that more than one-third of consumers choose businesses that charge high prices but provide excellent service over companies that offer low prices but mediocre service.[20]

Personal attention is an important way that some businesses provide superior service. Personal attention involves paying heed to details, addressing customers' concerns, answering technical questions, and providing service after the sale.[21] Such attention often plays an important psychological role as well because customers see how important quality is to the organization.[22]

Source: Ablestock.com

STRATEGY   AT   WORK   8 - 2

The Importance of Distribution and Production Capacity in e-Commerce Success

Despite the early failures of many dot-com start-ups, some Internet companies continue to grow. These e-tailers understand that they are facing an unprecedented challenge—how to create an infrastructure that cost effectively meets the needs and complex demands of today's sophisticated customer. To respond, many are designing and implementing multichannel distribution models to enhance distribution and improve customer service.

Customers who shop on the Internet typically check their order several times before they receive it. This means that the distribution system should be able to confirm order receipt, notify the customer of shipping details, and provide immediate notice of any problems that may occur in the process.

For example, JCPenny.com reaps success in drawing record sales with an effective distribution system. Of course, JCPenny.com does not depend solely on e-commerce for its retail sales. Other clothing merchants that have followed suit include Gap.com, EddieBauer.com, and BananaRepublic.com. BarnesandNoble.com has also successfully integrated its product inventories and distribution channels. Shipping costs have been slashed, and customers now have more options for pickups, purchase, and returns.

Innovation has not been limited to e-tailers. For example, DaimlerChrysler created its own Internet applications, one of which is known as FastCar. This Internet-based development and production system enables development and production departments to collaborate in real time.

Sources: L. Enos, "DaimlerChrysler Forms E-Business Subsidiary," E-Commerce Times, 9 October 2000; D. Christensen, "Delivering the Promise of 'E,'" World Trade 13(12) (2000): 60–61; M. Mahoney, "And the Dot-Com Survivors Are . . ." E-Commerce Times, 2 February 2001.

8-1d Place (Distribution) Strategies

Low-cost businesses typically seek distribution channels that meet the basic needs of the target market while minimizing costs. In contrast, differentiated businesses often select the most appropriate means of distribution regardless of cost and may even use the means of distribution as a way of differentiating the business (see Strategy at Work 8-2). For example, cost leader Cici's distributes its pizza through low-priced buffets and customer pickup at the restaurant, whereas Domino's has used "free" delivery—the cost of which is built into the price—as an effective means of differentiation over the years (see Case Analysis 8-1).

Source: Comstock.com

Case Analysis 8-1

Step 12: What Is the Organization's Marketing Strategy?

Given the strong link between a business's competitive strategy and its marketing functional strategy, this step can require much research and depth. What marketing efforts are underway to support the current business-level strategy? Are these efforts successful? Why or why not? Provide examples of recent promotional or public relations campaigns that support your assessment.

An effective means of assessing the marketing strategy is to analyze each of the four Ps individually. Company Web sites and trade journals are excellent sources for the type of information that should be included in this section.

8-2 Finance

The financial strategy addresses factors related to managing cash, raising capital, and making investments. Because few businesses internally generate the amount of cash necessary to grow, most resort to other means of securing financial resources. Different means of securing funds will likely be considered and prioritized depending on the corporate and business strategies selected.[23]

Low-cost businesses pursue financial strategies that are intended to minimize their financial costs. They place a great emphasis on keeping costs within the limits of the funds they are able to generate from operations. When borrowing becomes necessary, they usually try to do so when credit costs are relatively low, even if they must defer expansion plans.

In contrast, differentiated businesses are more likely to pursue financial strategies that fund initiatives such as quality improvements and product research and development (R&D) even when the cost of securing funds is relatively high. They may sell common stock, incur debt, or even seek venture capital regardless of the costs of doing so. The greatest strategic priorities are maintaining quality and enhancing differentiation, not minimizing the cost of funds.

One can assess a firm's financial strategy, as well as its performance, by examining its financial ratios and comparing them to those of key competitors or industry averages. Comparing current ratios to those in the past is also relevant. Table 8-2 lists key financial ratios that can help evaluate the financial position of the organization (see Case Analysis 8-2). However, strategic decisions should not be based on financial ratios alone. Although ratios can provide valuable insight, their usefulness is limited, because the accounting data on which they are based do not always provide a complete picture of the firm's financial position.

8-3 Production

Similar in some respects to the product dimension of the marketing strategy, the production or operations strategy outlines *how* a business generates its goods and services. Production/operations management (POM) is crucial to both manufacturing and service organizations.[24] In general, the production strategy difference between low-cost businesses and differentiated businesses is straightforward. Low-cost businesses develop production systems that minimize production costs, often by limiting customer options and product features. In contrast, differentiated businesses tend to develop systems that emphasize product and service quality and distinctiveness, even if production costs rise as a result.

Organizational size is also a key factor in production strategy decisions. Generally speaking, the range of production strategies at its disposal increases as an organization grows. Large business units can capitalize on factors that accompany their larger size. Each of these factors is associated with the **experience curve**, the reduction in per unit costs that occurs as an organization gains experience producing a product or service.[25]

Interestingly, each time a company's output doubles, production costs decline by a specific percentage, depending on the industry. The greater the percentage, the greater the role size plays in performance. For instance, with a sales volume of 1 million units, per unit costs may be $200 in a particular industry. With a doubling of volume to 2 million units, per unit costs may decline by 20 percent. Another doubling of volume to 4 million units may lower per unit costs another 20 percent. The experience curve can be observed in a wide range of manufacturing and service industries, including automobiles, personal computers, and airlines. Although the

Source: Comstock.com

Experience Curve

The reduction in per unit costs that occurs as an organization gains experience producing a product or service.

TABLE 8-2   Primer on Essential Financial Ratios

Ratio	Formula	What the Ratios Represent
Liquidity Ratios Current Ratio	$\dfrac{\text{Current Assets}}{\text{Current Liabilities}}$	Indicates how much of the current liabilities the current assets can cover; ordinarily 2:1 or better is desirable.
Quick Ratio or Acid Test or Liquidity Test	$\dfrac{\text{Current Assets – Inventory}}{\text{Current Liabilities}}$	Indicates how rapidly a business can come up with cash on short notice. Not relevant for firms where inventory is almost immediately convertible to cash (e.g., McDonald's).
Activity Ratios Asset Turnover	$\dfrac{\text{Total Revenues (i.e., Sales)}}{\text{Total Assets during Period}}$	Measures how efficiently the company's total assets are being used to generate sales.
Inventory Turnover	$\dfrac{\text{Cost of Goods Sold}}{\text{Average Inventory for Period}}$	Indicates how many times inventory of finished goods is sold per year.
Sales-to-Working Capital	$\dfrac{\text{Net Sales}}{\text{Net Working Capital}}$	Measures how efficiently net working capital (current assets – current liabilities) is used to generate sales.
Leverage Ratios Debt-to-Asset	$\dfrac{\text{Total Debt}}{\text{Total Assets}}$	Indicates the percentage that borrowed funds are utilized to finance the assets of the firm.
Debt-to-Equity	$\dfrac{\text{Total Debt}}{\text{Stockholders' Equity}}$	Indicates the percentage of funds provided by creditors as compared with owners.
Long-Term Debt-to-Equity	$\dfrac{\text{Long-Term Debt}}{\text{Stockholders' Equity}}$	Indicates the percentage of funds provided by long-term creditors as compared with owners.
Performance Ratios Gross Profit Margin	$\dfrac{\text{Gross Profit}}{\text{Total Revenue (i.e., Sales)}}$	Measures company's efficiency during the production process. Substantial variations over time could suggest financial difficulties or possibly fraud.
Return on Assets	$\dfrac{\text{Net Income before Taxes}}{\text{Total Assets}}$	Measures the return on total assets employed.
Return on Equity	$\dfrac{\text{Net Profit after Taxes}}{\text{Stockholders' Equity}}$	Measures a firm's profitability in comparison to the total amount of shareholder equity.
Return on Sales	$\dfrac{\text{Net Operating Profit before Taxes}}{\text{Net Sales}}$	Indicates ratio of return on net sales.

precise percentages are not always known, the principle of the curve can be accurately applied to most production environments.

The experience curve is based on three underlying concepts: learning, economies of scale, and capital-labor substitution possibilities.[26] **Learning** refers to the idea that employees become more efficient when they perform the same task many times. An increase in volume fuels this process, also increasing expertise. This reasoning can be applied to all jobs—line and staff, managerial and nonmanagerial—at the corporate, business unit, and functional levels. Economies of scale—the reductions in per unit costs as volume increases—can be great for businesses such as automobile manufacturers or Internet Service Providers. **Capital-labor substitution** refers to an organization's ability to substitute labor for capital, or vice versa as volume increases, depending on which combination minimizes costs and/or maximizes effectiveness. Certain U.S. manufacturers, for example, have shifted their assembly operations across the Mexican border where labor costs are much lower.

Recent developments in production technology have modified the traditional capital versus labor dichotomy. Many facilities have advanced to the point that products are manufactured while no workers are present, often during the night.

Learning

The increased efficiency that occurs when an employee performs a task repeatedly.

Capital-Labor Substitution

An organization's ability to substitute labor for capital or vice versa as production increases.

Case Analysis 8-2

Step 13: What Is the Organization's Financial Position and Financial Strategy?

What is the organization's financial strategy? Is the organization financially sound? Ratio analysis is a systematic means for analyzing the financial condition of the organization. The purpose of financial ratio analysis is to determine the financial effects on a business based on current, past, and possible future managerial business decisions. Financial ratios—expressed either as a times multiple (x) or a percentage (%)—are computed by taking numbers from a business's financial statements and converting them into meaningful relationships and indicators of the firm's financial performance. Calculating financial ratios covering the current and past fiscal years or periods of a business and then comparing them to each other and to comparable industry averages for the same time period will provide an insight into the business's financial condition and operational performance.

Calculating only the ratios of the firm being analyzed is not sufficient. Industry norms must also be considered. Because of structural and competitive factors, a ratio that may appear normal in one industry may signal cause for concern in another. Therefore, one should compare each ratio to the industry norm (when available) and provide some degree of analysis. For example, it is not sufficient to note that the days of inventory is 47.5 without also identifying the industry norm and addressing why an organization is above or below that norm. One needs to compute all of the appropriate ratios while focusing on the most critical ratios, those that differ significantly from years past or from the industry norm.

If the company competes in multiple industries, comparisons should be made to the averages for industries in which the firm operates. Alternatively, when another company or a set of companies with similar characteristics exists (e.g., PepsiCo and Coca-Cola), direct company comparisons can also be made. The key is that a company's performance is compared to the most valid and reliable set(s) of standards available, although comparing is easier with some firms than with others.

If unique characteristics of the company do not permit the calculation of all relevant ratios (e.g., inventory turnover is irrelevant for corporations that do not hold inventory), then this fact should be stated in the report. In addition, certain Web sites (e.g., www.hoovers.com) provide detailed financial analysis for many publicly traded companies.

The role of the workers in such facilities is not to produce the products but to prepare them for delivery.[27]

Low-cost businesses with large market shares tend to benefit the most from the experience curve. Differentiated businesses often attempt to gain a similar advantage by charging higher than average prices, seeking to gain market share and ultimately lower costs by offering higher quality outputs. However, differentiators do not actively capitalize on the opportunities presented by low costs, whereas managers of businesses that compete with low-cost–differentiation do.[28]

Regardless of strategy, seeking to exploit the experience curve can be risky. Increases in volume often involve substantial investments in plant and equipment and a commitment to the prevailing technology. However, as technology changes and renders the plant's production processes obsolete, outdated capital equipment may have to be discarded. Balancing current investments in plant and equipment with the risk that current technology may become dated prompts particular firms to invest in flexible manufacturing systems that can be retooled quickly to respond to market changes.

Enhancing efficiency in production is a key issue in restaurants, textile plants, and even airplane factories. In the mid-2000s, airplane producers Airbus and Boeing launched concerted efforts to simplify their production procedures and reduce assembly time. Airplane parts are now designed with a greater emphasis on how fast they can be assembled.[29]

Speed in developing, making, and distributing products and services can be the source of a significant competitive advantage.[30] In fact, an application of speed known as time-based strategy is a top priority in many organizations.[31] Companies that can deliver quality products in a timely fashion become problem solvers for their customers and are more likely to prosper. Motorola, for instance, cut the time needed to produce a cellular telephone from fourteen hours to less than two hours, while retail prices have fallen dramatically. Speed is equally important in customer service.

Source: Ablestock.com

8-3a Quality Considerations

In the late 1970s and early 1980s, strategic managers became interested in a concept borrowed from the Japanese known as quality circles, whereby managers and workers would meet to discuss and implement production changes that improved quality and efficiency. This interest evolved in the late 1980s and early 1990s into a heightening of interest in quality, broadly known as **total quality management (TQM)**.[32] Developed by W. Edwards Deming, TQM refers to the totality of features and characteristics of a product or service that bear on its ability to satisfy customer needs. Historically, quality has been viewed largely as a controlling activity that takes place at or near the end of the production process, an after-the-fact measurement of production success that occurs in the so-called quality control department. However, the notion that quality is measured *after* an output is produced has eroded, and quality is now seen as an essential ingredient of the product or service being provided and a concern of all members of the organization. Hence, from a production standpoint, producing a quality product lowers defects and minimizes rework time, thereby increasing productivity. In addition, making the operative employees responsible for quality eliminates the need for inspection.[33]

As an extension of the TQM philosophy, Six Sigma seeks to increase profits by eliminating variability in production, defects, and waste that undermine customer loyalty. Six Sigma is a systematic process that utilizes information and sophisticated statistical tools to improve production efficiency and quality. Practitioners receive training and advance to various levels of certification in Six Sigma concepts. Many companies began adopting the approach in the late 1990s and early 2000s and have reported substantial savings.[34]

Problems resulting in poor product or service quality can arise even in the best-managed businesses. Companies must guarantee an acceptable level of quality to instill confidence among buyers and avoid loss of business when such problems occur. The concept of the guarantee is both a quality and a marketing concern. Some companies even offer unlimited money-back guarantees.

In an effort to minimize short-term costs, however, many companies ignore this competitive advantage. Often, guarantees lapse after a short time or contain too many exceptional conditions to be effective competitive weapons. Managers must balance the costs associated with a superior guarantee with its benefits and tailor the package to the organization's strategy. Nonetheless, it

Total Quality Management (TQM)

A broad-based program designed to improve product and service quality and to increase customer satisfaction by incorporating a holistic commitment to quality, as seen through the eyes of the customer.

has been suggested that the following five desirable characteristics be included in service guarantees.[35]

1. The guarantee should be unconditional, with no exceptions.
2. It should be easily understood and written in simple language.
3. The guarantee should be meaningful by guaranteeing what is important to the customer and making it worth the customer's time and effort to invoke the guarantee, should the customer be dissatisfied.
4. The guarantee should be convenient to invoke and not require the customer to appeal to several layers of bureaucracy.
5. The customer should be satisfied promptly, without a lengthy waiting period.

Changes in the competitive environment can even spark quality decisions from competitors within a given industry. For example, after 9/11, many airlines engaged in vigorous cost-cutting to help stop losses that were to follow. Although some airlines eliminated meals on domestic flights, Continental actually took steps to improve cabin comfort and retain quality meals on its flights. Hence, whereas most airlines moved to address critical short-term financial concerns, Continental perceived an opportunity to emphasize quality and seek to develop long-term competitive advantage.[36]

8-3b Research and Development

Another function closely related to production is research and development (R&D). Differentiated businesses often—but not always—spend more on R&D than low-cost businesses. However, differentiated and low-cost businesses tend to pursue different types of R&D. **Product/service R&D** refers to efforts directed toward improvements or innovations in the quality or uniqueness of a company's outputs. For example, certain carmakers have been competing vigorously in the 2000s to develop high-performing and cost-competitive vehicles utilizing power sources other than gasoline.[37]

In contrast, **process R&D** seeks to reduce operational costs and make them more efficient. R&D is most important in rapidly changing industries where production modifications are most often required to remain competitive. Low-cost business units tend to emphasize process R&D to reduce their operations costs, whereas differentiators tend to place more importance on product/service R&D to produce improved and innovative outputs.

Product/service innovations can be risky. Once introduced, new products or services may not generate a level of demand sufficient to justify the R&D investment. RJR Nabisco, for example, has spent millions of dollars to develop and produce a smokeless cigarette. Although the new brands such as Premier and Eclipse were introduced with considerable fanfare, demand never materialized and the product was canceled after a short time.[38]

Interestingly, Japanese companies often abandon their new products as soon as they are introduced to force themselves to develop new replacement products immediately.[39] U.S. companies have responded by increasingly forming direct research links with their domestic competitors, asking their suppliers to participate in new-product design programs and taking ownership positions in small start-up companies that have promising technologies.[40]

8-4 Purchasing

All organizations have a purchasing function. In manufacturing firms, the purchasing department procures raw materials and parts so that the production department may process them into finished products. At the retail level, company buyers

---

Product/Service R&D

Research and development activities directed toward improvements or innovations in the quality or uniqueness of a company's outputs.

Process R&D

Research and development activities that seek to reduce the costs of operations and make them more efficient.

purchase items from manufacturers for resale to the consumer. Buyers must identify potential suppliers, evaluate them, solicit bids and price quotes, negotiate prices and terms of payment, place orders, manage the order process, inspect incoming shipments, and pay suppliers.

A business unit's purchasing strategy should be integrated with its competitive strategy. Generally speaking, low-cost businesses seek to purchase materials and supplies of basic quality at the lowest costs possible. Large organizations are able to lower costs further through their ability to demand quantity discounts. In addition, buyers that are larger than their suppliers and whose purchases represent a significant percentage of their suppliers' revenues may also possess considerable negotiating clout.

Small companies, however, can often attain low-cost purchasing through other means, such as working with other small businesses in the same industry to pool their purchasing requirements. Because of large quantities, industry networks are often able to wield as much power as a single large business in demanding quantity discounts and negotiating terms.

It is critical to note that low costs are not the only consideration in purchasing activities. Rather, low-cost businesses should seek the *best cost,* one that is as low as possible and consistent with basic quality standards of the purchased good or service. A low price is useless if the item breaks down in the production process or fails to meet customer demands. On the other hand, excessive quality unnecessarily raises costs and prices.[41]

Because their customers are willing to pay higher prices, differentiators tend to emphasize the procurement of high-quality inputs, even if they cost more than alternative offerings. In these cases, the quality of the parts or products takes precedence over cost considerations, although cost minimization is always desirable.

Purchasing is the first step in the materials management process. Indeed, purchasing also includes the operation of storage and warehouse facilities and the control of inventory.[42] Consequently, these related tasks can be efficiently and effectively conducted only if they are viewed as parts of a single operation, regardless of the business strategy employed.[43] The **just-in-time (JIT) inventory system** demonstrates the interrelationships. JIT was popularized by Japanese manufacturers to reduce materials management costs. Using this technique, the purchasing manager asks suppliers to ship parts at the precise time they are needed in production to hold inventory, storage, and warehousing costs to a minimum. As such, JIT has reduced costs for numerous large firms.

Although U.S. manufacturers have moved in the direction of JIT, this approach works particularly well in Japan where large manufacturers wield considerable bargaining power over their much smaller suppliers. Because JIT places great delivery demands on suppliers, it does not tend to work well when manufacturers do not possess great bargaining power, as is often the case in the United States. In addition, an occasional late supplier can cripple a firm's production process.[44]

A JIT system also makes a company highly vulnerable to labor strikes. For example, one of the plants that supplies parts to GM's Saturn manufacturing operations shut down for a short time due to a local labor dispute. Saturn, which uses the JIT system, suddenly found itself unable to produce any cars because it had no inventory of the more than three hundred metal parts that it purchased exclusively from the supplier whose plant was struck.[45]

Many large U.S. manufacturers seek a middle ground between traditional inventory systems and JIT. Most have reduced their number of suppliers from a

just-in-time (JIT) inventory system

An inventory system, popularized by the Japanese, in which suppliers deliver parts just at the time they are needed by the buying organization to use in its production process.

Case Analysis 8-3

Step 14: What Are the Organization's Production and Purchasing Strategies?

What approaches to production that support the current business-level strategy are in effect? Are these efforts successful? Why or why not? How does the firm's approach to production and purchasing differ from that of its competitors?

dozen or more to two or three to control delivery times and quality.[46] Companies are also strengthening their relationships with suppliers and providing them with detailed knowledge of their requirements and specifications. By working together, buyers and suppliers can improve the quality and lower the costs of the purchased items.[47]

8-5 Human Resources

The human resource management (HRM) functions include such activities as planning for future human resource (HR) needs, recruitment, placement, compensation, evaluation, and employee development. Strategic HRM seeks to build a workforce that enables the organization to achieve its goals.[48] A major detriment to effective HRM practices over the past two decades was an unprecedented wave of mergers and acquisitions. This massive restructuring of U.S. business has resulted in widespread layoffs and disillusioned, formerly loyal employees. Today, many workers no longer anticipate or even desire lifelong employment with a single firm.

Ineffective human resource policies can be detrimental to a firm, not only from a strategic perspective but also from a cost standpoint. As part of a labor agreement negotiated with the United Auto Workers, GM maintains a jobs bank where up to four hundred employees show up to work each day, do nothing, and earn wages and benefits that often exceed $100,000 annually. Collective costs of such programs to GM, Ford, and other manufacturers may be as high as $2 billion each year.[49] Such policies stifle productivity in an era when global competition demands that all of a firm's human resources work efficiently.

Strategy aside, all organizations are challenged to develop employee commitment to the company and to the job. Fostering commitment and developing a strong, competitive workforce require the creation and maintenance of attractive working conditions for employees that may include providing customized benefits, child day care, parental leave, and flexible working hours, as well as such traditional needs as training and development, job enrichment, and promotional opportunities for advancement.

In response to 9/11, numerous companies have heightened efforts to screen employees and investigate workers' history. Many argue that such efforts improve security at company facilities, whereas others cite examples of employees allegedly losing jobs over traffic violations or bounced checks. Nonetheless, today more than ever, security is a key strategy concern.[50]

An organization's strategy may be affected by the increasing diversity of the modern workforce. Women, Americans of African, Hispanic, and Asian descent, and persons with disabilities have already transformed the traditional white male image of many U.S. corporations. As a result, managers must learn to help persons from diverse backgrounds and functional areas work effectively as team members. The success of such cooperative endeavors as cross-functional teams, quality circles, and JIT inventory systems requires a unity of action that can be achieved only through the mutual respect and understanding of one's coworkers.

Although one might expect low-cost businesses to spend less on HR activities than their differentiated counterparts, this is not always the case, because attracting the best from the new workforce can support both strategies. Valuable human resources may enhance efficiency by lowering absenteeism and turnover and may promote differentiation by way of their innovative ideas and excellence in job performance.

The role played by human resources in an organization's strategic success is difficult to understate, especially in industries where turnover is historically high. Consider the fast-food industry in the United States, where it is not uncommon to experience turnover rates as high as 200 percent, compared to 10 to 15 percent at typical midsize and large organizations. Starting wages at fast-food companies generally hover around minimum wage. Some organizations have attempted to combat this problem by offering wages significantly higher than the minimum, whereas others, such as Domino's Pizza, have taken a more comprehensive approach. Domino's renamed its HR department "PeopleFirst" and started to focus more on attracting, training, and retaining exceptional store managers. The firm estimates HR costs of departing employees to be about $2,500 for hourly workers and $20,000 for managers. Domino's has experienced success with the program, reducing turnover significantly in the mid-2000s.[51]

Another key dimension of the HR strategy is that of benefits, specifically health care. Most organizations are struggling with the desire to provide health care as part of the compensation package while minimizing employment costs. To cut costs, some firms have even resorted to terminating workers who are disabled.[52] Needless to say, such decisions have strategic, legal, and ethical ramifications.

In a more narrow sense, a business unit's generic strategy can also influence specific components of its HR program. For example, a company's reward system should be tied to employee behavior that helps the business attain its goals. Hence, low-cost business units should reward employees who help reduce operating costs, differentiators should establish reward systems that encourage output improvements or innovations, and all businesses should reward excellent customer service.

8-5a Human Capital and Knowledge Management

When organizations see their employees as expenses, they tend to *minimize* the cost. However, when they see their employees as investments, they tend to *maximize* the value by managing them more strategically. Following this logic, strategic managers have recently begun to assess the value of **human capital**— the sum of the capabilities of individuals in an organization—as a source of competitive advantage.[53] According to the **knowledge management** perspective, people and their skills and abilities represent the only resource that cannot readily be reproduced by a firm's competitors if it is deemed to be a source of competitive advantage.[54] As such, high-performing firms must leverage their human capital if they are to remain successful over the long term.[55] Human capital can be developed through organizational learning.[56] Table 8-3 identifies ten factors that can promote the development of learning capabilities in an organization.

Human Capital

The sum of the capabilities of individuals in an organization.

Knowledge Management

People and their skills and abilities (i.e., knowledge capital) represent the only resource that cannot readily be reproduced by a firm's competitors. Knowledge capital must be effectively leveraged if high-performing firms are to remain as such over the long term.

TABLE 8-3 Factors that Facilitate Organizational Learning Capabilities

1. Scanning imperative	Interest in external happenings and in the nature of one's environment. Valuing the processes of awareness and data generation. Curious about what is "out there" as opposed to "in here."
2. Performance gap	Shared perception of a gap between actual and desired state of performance. Disconfirming feedback interrupts a string of successes. Performance shortfalls are seen as opportunities for learning.
3. Concern for measurement	Spend considerable effort in defining and measuring key factors when venturing into new areas; strive for specific, quantifiable measures; discourse over metrics is seen as a learning activity.
4. Experimental mindset	Support for trying new things: curiosity about how things work; ability to "play" with things. Small failures are encouraged, not punished. See changes in work processes, policies, and structures as a continuous series of graded tryouts.
5. Climate of openness	Accessibility of information, relatively open boundaries. Opportunities to observe others; problems/errors are shared, not hidden; debate and conflict are acceptable.
6. Continuous education	Ongoing commitment to education at all levels; support for growth and development of members.
7. Operational variety	Variety exists in response modes, procedures, systems; significant diversity in personnel. Pluralistic rather than monolithic definition of valued internal capabilities.
8. Multiple advocates	Top-down and bottom-up initiatives are possible; multiple advocates and gatekeepers exist.
9. Involved leadership	Leadership at significant levels articulates vision and is very actively engaged in its actualization; takes ongoing steps to implement visions; "hands-on" involvement in educational and other implementation steps.
10. Systems perspective	Strong focus on how parts of the organization are interdependent; seek optimization of organizational goals at the highest levels; see problems and solutions in terms of systemic relationships.

Source: From B. Moingeon and A. Edmondson, Organizational Learning and Competitive Advantage *(Thousand Oaks, CA: Sage, 1996), 43.* Reprinted by permission of Sage Publications Ltd.

Amazon.com makes effective use of its knowledge. As an Internet pioneer, the firm has a great deal of experience and Web savvy, enabling the firm to address new market opportunities ahead of competitors. Amazon.com also maintains a database of customer information, allowing the firm to suggest additional products that may be of interest to the consumer when shopping online. The company has even used its recommendations feature occasionally to make "faux suggestions," purchase recommendations that are not tied to a consumer's purchase history, but enable the firm to promote its new product lines to existing customers.[57]

8-5b Knowledge and Competitive Advantage

Regardless of the choice of generic strategy, the acquisition and development of knowledge can be a source of competitive advantage.[58] Five operating principles can help guide this process.[59]

1. Knowledge-based strategies begin with strategy, not knowledge. Knowledge can *support* the traditional mechanisms for serving customers and delivering value, but cannot replace them.
2. Knowledge-based strategies must be linked to traditional measures of performance. Quantifying the value of knowledge as a resource or an investment is difficult. However, performance can be evaluated only with quantifiable, objective measures.
3. Executing a knowledge-based strategy is about nurturing people with knowledge, not managing knowledge per se. Companies must develop cultures conducive to learning,

sharing, and personal growth; otherwise, its collective knowledge—housed within its people—will never be realized.

4. Organizations leverage knowledge through networks of people who collaborate, not networks of technology that interconnect. Technology cannot completely replace the need for the human interaction that transforms knowledge into market-viable innovations.

5. The engine that drives knowledge development comes from the workers' need for help in solving business problems. Company efforts to disseminate knowledge to its workers often lead to overload and frustration.

8-6 Information Systems Management

An effective information system (IS) can benefit all of a business unit's functional areas.[60] A computer-based decision support system can permit each functional area to access the information it needs and to improve coordination by communicating electronically with the other functional departments. Like HR, the link between the IS strategy and the business strategy is not always clear. An effective IS strategy can also cut internal costs while promoting differentiation and quality through a faster response to the market. Wal-Mart's system, for example, manages the reordering process on a real-time basis for the purchasing department while also providing critical data for the marketing department, such as which product combinations are most popular and the time of day certain products are likely to be purchased.

The value of quality information is not always easy to assess, but it can be great. Progressive online retailers such as Overstock.com, Delightful Deliveries, and Sierra Trading Posts collect extensive aggregate data about customer shopping habits and use it to craft personalized marketing approaches. A surfer's gender, location, or connection speed can determine whether this consumer is linked to a free shipping promotion or provided instant access to an online customer service representative. Internet searches using the words *cheap* and *discount* often pull up contextual advertisements targeted to bargain hunters. Creating a system to manage and utilize such data effectively can help retailers enhance their strategic effectiveness, regardless of business strategy.[61]

Whether an information system is conducted in-house or outsourced, it is deemed effective if it helps the business carry out its strategy. Far too many companies emphasize the hardware and software components of their functional system rather than the system's ability to satisfy customer needs.[62] Today, more than ever, the application of Internet technology to serve customers and support suppliers is typically a focal point of the IS strategy (see Case Analysis 8-4).

Case Analysis 8-4

Step 15: What Are the Current Strategies in Other Functional Areas Such as HR and Information Systems?

What HR policies that support the current business-level strategy are in effect? Are these efforts successful? Why or why not? Is the organization poised to meet HR needs (changes in the workforce, etc.) in the future? How do the firm's human resources objectively compare to those of its competitors?

What is the current state of the organization's information system? Is it supporting the implementation of the organization's business and corporate strategies? Why or why not? Does the firm have a competitive presence on the Internet? How does this presence compare to those of its competitors?

8-7 Summary

After corporate-level and business unit generic strategies are developed, top executives must align activities in the functional areas to ensure that the various departments are well coordinated and work together. Most notably, the functions of marketing, finance, production, purchasing, human resources, and information systems—including utilization of the Internet—should be considered.

In many instances, an organization's business strategy suggests appropriate characteristics of its functional strategies. Each organization should develop integrated functional strategies that support the uniqueness of its business and corporate strategies.

Key Terms

capital-labor substitution

experience curve

functional strategies

human capital

just-in-time inventory system

knowledge management

learning

process R&D

product/service R&D

total quality management

Review Questions and Exercises

1. What are the relationships among corporate-level, business unit, and functional strategies?

2. Why and how should the four Ps of marketing be aligned to support the organization's business strategy?

3. What is the difference between product and process R&D? How can each align with business strategies?

4. Relate the concept of the experience curve to the production operations of an automobile assembly plant.

5. Explain the role of business process reengineering in various functional strategies.

6. Explain the linkage that a just-in-time inventory system provides between the purchasing and production functions. What are the implications for quality?

Practice Quiz

True or False

1. Because functional strategies should be designed to support corporate and business strategies, they should not be considered until corporate and business strategies have been formulated.

2. The most appropriate means of securing funds will depend heavily on the corporate and business strategies being pursued.

3. The reduction in per unit costs that occurs as an organization gains experience producing a product or service is known as economies of scale.

4. The purchasing department in a low-cost business should always purchase raw materials at the lowest possible cost.

5. The human resources department in a low-cost business should always attempt to hire managers and workers at pay rates below those of their competitors.

6. A key characteristic of an effective information system is its ability to serve and help integrate the other functional areas of the business.

Multiple Choice

7. Functional strategies should

    A. be integrated across the business unit.

    B. support the business strategy.

    C. support the corporate strategy.

    D. all of the above

8. Which of the following is not part of the marketing strategy?

    A. pricing

    B. distribution

    C. promotion

    D. none of the above

9. The experience curve is based on which of the following?

    A. potential for capital-labor substitutions

    B. economies of scale

    C. organizational learning

    D. all of the above

10. Efforts directed toward improvements or innovations in the quality or uniqueness of a company's outputs is known as

    A. product R&D.

    B. process R&D.

    C. product innovation.

    D. structural reorganization.

11. Reducing operational costs by making the production process more efficient is known as

    A. total quality management.

    B. process R&D.

    C. product innovation.

    D. structural innovation.

12. Which of the following is not a characteristic of the just-in-time (JIT) approach to inventory?

    A. JIT is difficult on suppliers.

    B. JIT reduces inventory costs.

    C. JIT is less risky than traditional inventory approaches.

    D. JIT is popular in Japan.

Notes

1. D. Webb and C. Webster, "An Exploration of the Meaning and Outcomes of a Customer-Defined Market Orientation," *Journal of Business Research* 48 (2000): 101–112.

2. N. Wingfield, "Amazon Takes Page from Wal-Mart to Prosper on Web," *Wall Street Journal* (22 November 2002): A1, A6.

3. M. Whitford, "Motel 6 Converts Hotels to Launch Extended Stay Brand," *Hotel & Motel Management* (15 March 1999): 36.

4. M. McCarthy, "Mazda Earmarks $30 Million to Ring in Millenia," *Brandweek* (7 March 1994): 1, 6.

5. K. Lundegaard and S. Freeman, "Detroit's Challenge: Weaning Buyers from Years of Deals," *Wall Street Journal* (6 January 2004): A1, A2; J. Grant, "Carmakers 'Poised to Rebound' This Year," *Financial Times* (2 January 2004): 1, 12.

6. R. E. Silverman, "Why You Waste So Much Money," *Wall Street Journal* (16 July 2003): D1, D2.

7. T. M. Burton, "Backlash Is Brewing among Companies Who Believe Flash Ads Drive Up Costs," *Wall Street Journal* (13 March 2002): B1.

8. E. White, "P&G to Use Plugs in TV News Stories to Send Viewers to Its Web Sites," *Wall Street Journal* (7 March 2001): B1, B6.

9. M. Mangilindan, "Web Ads on the Rebound," *Wall Street Journal* (25 August 2003): B1, B6.

10. T. Zaun, "Very Defensive Driving," *Wall Street Journal* (2 June 2003): B1, B3.

11. J. Drucker and A. Latour, "New Value Meal: Big Mac, Fries, Web Access," *Wall Street Journal* (8 July 2003): D1, D5.

12. C. Terhune, "In Switch, Pepsi Makes Diet Cola Its New Flagship," *Wall Street Journal* (16 March 2005): B1, B2.

13. B. McKay, "Zero Is Coke's New Hero," *Wall Street Journal* (17 April 2007): C1, C2.

14. R. G. Schroeder, K. A. Bates, and M. A. Junttila, "A Resource-Based View of Manufacturing Strategy and the Relationship to Manufacturing Processes," *Strategic Management Journal* 23 (2002): 105–118.

15. A. G. Perkins, "Manufacturing: Maximizing Service, Minimizing Inventory," *Harvard Business Review* 72(2) (2000): 13–14.

16. J. Maas, "Customer Service: Extraordinary Results at Southwest Airlines, Charles Schwab, Lands' End, American Express, Staples, and USAA," *Sloan Management Review* 40(1) (1999): 105.

17. S. Branch, "Forget 'May I Help You?'" *Wall Street Journal* (8 July 2003): B1, B5.

18. Branch, "Going Private (Label)," *Wall Street Journal* (12 June 2003): B1, B3.

19. R. Suskind, "Humor Has Returned to Southwest Airlines After 9/11 Hiatus," *Wall Street Journal* (13 January 2003): A1, A6.

20. A. Bennett, "Many Consumers Expect Better Service and Say They Are Willing to Pay for It," *The Wall Street Journal* (12 November 1990): B1.

21. L. Dube, L. M. Renaghan, and J. M. Miller, "Measuring Customer Satisfaction for Strategic Management," *Cornell Hotel and Restaurant Administration Quarterly* (February 1994): 39–47.

22. P. Wright, "Competitive Strategies for Small Businesses," in *Readings in Strategic Management,* ed. A. A. Thompson Jr., A. J. Strickland III, and W. E. Fulmer (Plano, TX: Business Publications, 1984), 90.

23. P. R. Brown, "A Model for Effective Financial Analysis," *Journal of Financial Statement Analysis* 3(4) (1998): 60–63.

24. M. Pagell, S. Melnyk, and R. Handfield, "Do Trade-offs Exist in Operations Strategy? Insights from the Stamping Die Industry," *Business Horizons* 43(3) (2000): 69–77.

25. See Boston Consulting Group, *Perspectives on Experience* (Boston: The Boston Consulting Group, 1976); G. Hall and S. Howell, "The Experience Curve from an Economist's Perspective," *Strategic Management Journal* 6 (1985): 197–212.

26. L. E. Yelle, "The Learning Curve: Historical Review and Comprehensive Survey," *Decision Sciences* 10 (1979): 302–328.

27. T. Aeppel, "In Lights-Out Factories Machines Still Make Things Even When No One Is There," *Wall Street Journal* (19 November 2002): B1, B11.

28. R. D. Buzzell and B. T. Gale, *The PIMS Principles* (New York: Free Press, 1987), chap. 6.

29. D. Michaels and J. L. Lunsford, "Streamlined Plane Making," *Wall Street Journal* (1 April 2005): B1, B2.

30. K. Rollins, "Using Information to Speed Execution," *Harvard Business Review* 76(2) (1998): 81.

31. B. Dumaine, "How Managers Can Succeed through Speed," *Fortune* (13 February 1989): 54.

32. E. Abrahamson and G. Fairchild, "Management Fashion: Lifecycles, Triggers, and Collective Learning Processes," *Administrative Science Quarterly* 44 (1999): 708–728.

33. D. F. Kuratko, J. C. Goodale, and J. S. Hornsby, "Quality Practices for Competitive Advantage in Smaller Firms," *Journal of Small Business Management* 39 (2001): 293–311.

34. J. A. DeFeo, "Creating Strategic Change More Effectively with a New Design for Six Sigma Process," *Journal of Change Management* 3(1) (2002): 60–80.

35. C. W. L. Hart, "The Power of Unconditional Service Guarantees," *The McKinsey Quarterly* (Summer 1989): 75–76.

36. S. McCartney, "Continental Airlines Keeps Little Things, and It Pays Off Big," *Wall Street Journal* (4 February 2002): A1.

37. N. Shirouzu, "When Hybriud Cars Collide," *Wall Street Journal* (6 February 2003): B1, B5.

38. J. Levine, "Smokeless Cigarette Goes on Sale but Nothing Shows It's Safer for Smokers," *CNN Interactive*, accessed March 11, 2002, www.cnn.com/HEALTH/9606/03/cigarette.

39. P. F. Drucker, "Japan: New Strategies for a New Reality," *The Wall Street Journal* (2 October 1991): A12.

40. N. Anbarci, R. Lemke, and S. Roy, "Interfirm Complementaries in R&D: Re-examination of the Relative Importance of Joint Ventures," *International Journal of Industrial Organization* 20 (2002): 191–204.

41. E. E. Scheuing, *Purchasing Management* (Englewood Cliffs, NJ: Prentice Hall, 1989), 4.

42. T. H. Hendrick and F. G. Moore, *Production/Operations Management*, 9th ed. (Homewood, IL: Irwin, 1985), 336.

43. J. G. Miller and P. Gilmour, "Materials Managers: Who Needs Them?" *Harvard Business Review* 57(4) (1979): 145.

44. S. P. Galante, "Distributors Bow to Demands of 'Just-in-Time' Delivery," *The Wall Street Journal* (30 June 1986): B1; L. Beard and S. A. Butler, "Introducing JIT Manufacturing: It's Easier Than You Think," *Business Horizons* 43(5) (2000): 61–64.

45. J. Mitchell, "GM Saturn Ads Request Buyers to be Patient," *Wall Street Journal* (25 September 1992): B1.

46. J. Dreyfuss, "Shaping Up Your Suppliers," *Fortune* (10 April 1989): 116.

47. J. Browne, J. Harhen, and J. Shivnan, *Production Management Systems: A CIM Perspective* (Workingham, England: Addison-Wesley, 1988), 158–159.

48. A. A. Lado, "Strategic Human Resource Management," *Academy of Management Review* 25 (2000): 677–679; R. A. Shafer, L. Dyer, J. Kitty, J. Amos, and J. Erickson, "Crafting a Human Resource Strategy to Foster Organizational Agility: A Case Study," *Human Resource Management* 40 (2001): 197–212.

49. M. McCracken, "Detroit's Symbol of Dysfunction: Paying Employees Not to Work," *Wall Street Journal* (1 March 2006): A1, A12.

50. A. Davis, "Employers Dig Deep into Workers' Pasts, Citing Terrorism Fears," *Wall Street Journal* (12 March 2002): A1.

51. E. White, "To Keep Employees, Domino's Decides It's Not All about Pay," *Wall Street Journal* (27 February 2005): A1, A9.

52. J. Pereira, "To Save on Health-Care Costs, Firms Fire Disabled Workers," *Wall Street Journal* (14 July 2003): A1, A7; T. Aeppel, "Skyrocketing Health Costs Start to Pit Worker vs. Worker," *Wall Street Journal* (17 June 2003): A1, A6.

53. A. S. Huff, "Changes in Organizational Knowledge Production," *Academy of Management Review* 25 (2000): 288–293; T. H. Davenport, J. G. Harris, D. W. DeLong, and A. L. Jacobson, "Data to Knowledge to Results: Building an Analytic Capability," *California Management Review* 43(2) (2001): 117–138.

54. S. K. McElivy and B. Chakravarthy, "The Persistence of Knowledge-Based Advantage: An Empirical Test for Product Performance and Technological Knowledge," *Strategic Management Journal* 23 (2002): 285–306.

55. C. Soo, T. Devinney, D. Midgely, and A. Deering, "Knowledge Management: Philosophy, Processes, and Pitfalls," *California Management Review* 44(4) (2002): 129–150; J. Birkinshaw and T. Sheehan, "Managing the Knowledge Life Cycle," *MIT Sloan Management Review* 44(1) (2002): 85–93.

56. A. W. Sheldon, "Strategy Rules," *Fast Company* (January 2001): 164–166.

57. N. Wingfield and J. Pereira, "Amazon Issues 'Faux' Recommendation for Its Clothing," *Wall Street Journal* (4 December 2002): B1, B3.

58. J. P. Katz, "Blown to Bits: How the New Economics of Information Transforms Strategy," *Academy of Management Executive* 14 (2000): 160–162; H. Tsoukas and E. Vladimirou, "What Is Organizational Knowledge?" *Journal of Management Studies* 38 (2001): 973–994.

59. B. Manville and N. Foote, "Strategy as If Knowledge Mattered," *Fast Company* (April 1996): 66.

60. R. Sabherwal and Y. E. Chan, "Alignment between Business and IS Strategies: A Study of Prospectors, Analyzers, and Defenders," *Information Systems Research* 12 (2001): 11–33.

61. J. E. Vascallaro, "Online Retailers Are Watching You," *Wall Street Journal* (28 November 2006): D1, D3.

62. K. F. Pun and M. K. O. Lee, "A Proposed Management Model for the Development of Strategic Information Systems," *International Journal of Technology Management* 20 (2000): 304–325; P. Gottschalk, "Strategic Information Systems Planning: The IT Strategy Implementation Matrix," *European Journal of Information Systems* 8(2) (1999): 107–118.

Insight from *strategy+business*

In some respects, larger firms have an edge over smaller firms. To exercise this advantage, however, its top managers must understand when and how firm size can be an asset. This chapter's strategy+business reading makes the case that scale economies, network efforts, and economies of scope offer an advantage for larger firms, but only in certain circumstances.

The Big, the Bad, and the Beautiful

Size comes in three flavors–scale, scope, and network. Choose wisely from the menu.

By Tim Laseter, Martha Turner, and Ron Wilcox

Wal-Mart Stores Inc. dominates the retail industry. The Microsoft Corporation controls the market for PC software. General Electric Company has generated superior returns for decades. Each one ranks, on the basis of annual revenues, as the largest company of its type. Are they succeeding because they are large, or are they large because they are succeeding?

Consider three New Economy survivors: Amazon. com Inc., eBay Inc., and Cisco Systems Inc. During the Internet boom, companies pursued growth and size as key elements of their business strategy. Most failed in that pursuit. Were the few that succeeded simply lucky, or did they understand something that their competitors did not?

Size does matter, but only if you understand why and use that knowledge to create a competitive advantage. Three theories support the bigger-is-better argument: scale economies, network effects, and economies of scope. Each theory derives its logic from a different source and applies only in certain circumstances. Pursuit of size without a clear understanding of these concepts can lead to oblivion rather than dominance.

Scale Economies

The theory of increasing returns to scale, or scale economies, dates to the beginning of the 20th century and a set of British economists, including Alfred Marshall, AC. Pigou, and Nicholas Kaldor. Building upon Adam Smith's original observations, these economists reasoned that larger companies would achieve productivity advantages due to greater opportunities for division of labor.

Technically, a scale curve measures production costs as a function of facility capacity. Plotted on a logarithmic scale, the slope of the curve shows the fixed percentage reduction in cost for each doubling of capacity. Businesses with operations that offer significant economies of scale, such as wafer fabrication for integrated circuits, have steep scale curves where costs drop significantly when facility capacity increases—which is why the Intel Corporation and other chip makers regularly invest upward of a billion dollars in new higher-capacity facilities.

Other businesses, such as apparel-producing plants, exhibit very limited scale economies. Since there is little opportunity to automate the process of sewing a dress or shirt, a larger apparel plant simply contains more sewing machines. A plant with 200 sewing machines run by individual operators doesn't produce shirts and dresses much more cheaply than one with only 100 machines. There is little value in having a bigger apparel factory.

Wal-Mart now ranks as the largest company on the planet. Although retailing, in general, has relatively limited opportunities to benefit from economies of scale, Wal-Mart has prospered by leveraging scale where it matters. For example, a Wal-Mart store building does not offer dramatic scale economies. A 100,000-square-foot store costs slightly less to build per square foot than a 50,000-square-foot store, but not enough less to provide a big competitive advantage. A retail distribution network, on the other hand, exhibits significant scale economies by enabling a business to exploit a lower cost trade-off among facility costs, inventory costs, and transportation. Wal-Mart's distribution network dwarfs its smaller retail competitors' networks and produces a 1 to

Source: Reprinted with permission from *strategy+business*, the award-winning management quarterly published by Booz Allen Hamilton. http://www.strategy-business.com.

2 percent margin advantage by our estimates. Given the thin margins in retail, this advantage is significant.

Amazon.com has sought, and in some cases achieved, scale economies. Its distribution network, although a fraction of the size of Wal-Mart's, ranks among the largest networks for fulfilling direct customer orders (rather than moving full cases and pallets as a traditional retailer does). But, frankly, the scale economies in fulfillment remain relatively marginal. Amazon's key source of scale has come from its ability to amortize its massive investment in the Web shopping engine across multiple categories and also across service contracts with partner companies like Toys "R" Us Inc., the Target Corporation, and Circuit City Stores Inc. The cost of building and maintaining a user-friendly online shopping interface has proved to be beyond the means of many Amazon competitors.

Pursuing size under an assumption that you will gain scale economies in businesses with flat scale curves offers no advantage and can in fact lead to decreasing margins if the incremental size is gained through lower prices. And even where a steep slope is possible, scale advantages don't just happen. A company must seek them out and exploit them. Examples like Wal-Mart and Amazon highlight the specific sources of scale and how companies have gained competitive advantage from it.

Network Effects

Network effects came to the fore of business strategy during the height of the Internet boom to justify the phenomenal valuations of dot-com startups. Stock analysts applied the logic that the value of a network grows proportionately to the square of the number of users, a property of networks asserted by Bob Metcalfe, developer of Ethernet, a technology for connecting computers in a local area network, and the founder of the 3Com Corporation. Following what became known as Metcalfe's Law, a company's value quadrupled when the number of users doubled. Or if the number of users quadrupled, the value grew 16-fold. Given the exponential growth of the Internet population, the projected value gains were simply astronomical.

Unfortunately, even though a customer connects to a company's Web site via a computer network, the business itself does not necessarily exhibit network effects. To better understand why, we need to return to the economic arguments that predated the hype. Economists noted the existence of "network externalities" in their research covering everything from ATMs

to electricity to software. Formally, a network externality occurs when the value of participation in a network depends on how many other parties or which parties already belong to the network. Accordingly, a network effect is a demand-side argument for size versus the supply-side argument for scale economies.

Reflect on the early days of the telephone. In 1876, after participating in a demonstration call between Washington, D.C., and Philadelphia, President Rutherford B. Hayes commented: "That's an amazing invention, but who would ever want to use one?" President Hayes failed to understand the network possibilities of the nascent tool. A phone connecting a central user in one city to another offered little advantage over the existing telegraph technology. But unlike telegraphy, a telephone required no special training to use, and, accordingly, the network grew to encompass many individual users. And, as more individuals acquired telephones, the value of having a phone increased for everyone connected to the network. More recently, the Internet has produced the same effect.

Economists argue that a market leader can gain a monopolistic position from the network effect by erecting "switching barriers." A competitor with a smaller network has trouble enticing customers to join its alternative network because it offers lower network value. Microsoft's dominance of the market for personal computer operating systems and ultimately PC application software offers an excellent example. Although alternative operating systems such as Unix, Linux, and Apple OS have challenged Microsoft's DOS and Windows systems, none have displaced them—even though some proponents claimed their alternatives offered superior functionality. Why? Because PC users value the ability to exchange files with other users without risk of compatibility problems. The largest network (in this case a virtual one) offers more value to the user. Similarly, the large base of Windows users drives application developers to tailor their products to Microsoft first. This also creates greater value for the users of the dominant network.

Among Internet-based companies, eBay exhibits the most powerful network effect. As more people list items for sale on eBay, the site attracts more buyers. The more buyers who bid on an item, the greater its value to the seller. This, in turn, attracts more sellers. For comparison, consider that Amazon.com has the same number of customers as eBay, but its business model generates nominal network effects. Amazon customers benefit from the product ratings of other customers, and the acquisition of more customers improves Amazon's ability to mine its sales data to create customized purchasing recommendations, but the impact of this network effect is relatively small compared to eBay's.

As the early leader in creating an auction community, eBay built a network unmatchable by others. The site claims to have had 28 million active customers in 2002, and it offers about 16 million listings in its 27,000 categories on a typical day. UBid Inc., the second largest auction site, claims 3 million registered users bidding on its rotating stock of 12,000 branded products in 16 categories.

Even though uBid compares itself to eBay, its inherent business model offers less of a network effect. Since eBay primarily auctions used products, its customers tend to be both buyers and sellers. Competitor uBid auctions new branded products from a small base of dedicated sellers. This means the more customer-bidders there are joining the network, the higher the realized price will be on the network. This benefits the small population of sellers, but harms the disproportionately larger community of buyers.

In other words, sometimes a network, however large, produces little value. Many dot-coms focused on growth in customers as a key strategic tenet under the false assumption that size always translates into competitive advantage from scale economies and network effects. Such was the expectation of the ill-fated "last-mile delivery" companies Webvan, Kozmo, and UrbanFetch, but in reality their costs were largely variable and their customers didn't get incremental value from an increase in the customer base. (See 'The Last Mile to Nowhere: Flaws & Fallacies in Internet Home-Delivery Schemes," by Tim Laseter et al., s+b, Third Quarter 2000.) Here size added little advantage, and ill-advised pursuit of rapid growth led to their demise.

Economies of Scope

The third theory supporting the size argument, economies of scope, concerns the benefits achieved by offering more than one product or service through the same organization. Economies of scope can affect both supply and demand.

General Electric captures demand-side benefits through its ability to bundle services from its financing unit with products from manufacturing units. For example, GE has long allowed its customers to finance the multimillion-dollar purchase of its jet engines via a leasing arrangement from GE Finance. More recently, GE has pursued a service strategy of selling "power by the hour" so that an airline doesn't buy a specific engine.

Instead, a customer pays for access to a rotating stock of engines serviced and maintained by GE. On the supply side, GE Appliances combines with GE Motors and GE Aircraft Engines to purchase sheet steel in larger quantities for lower prices.

The most powerful economy of scope at General Electric, however, is probably the least tangible: Its vaunted management development system. The company can provide a breadth of experiences to its managers, who ultimately transfer best practices across disparate divisions. For example, Six Sigma, the analytical improvement process, was viewed largely as a tool for high-volume manufacturing operations until GE proved it could be applied across its wide range of businesses, including broadcast network NBC and finance arm GE Credit.

Cisco Systems offers a New Economy example of a strategy based on economies of scope. Originally a focused producer of Internet routers, Cisco launched what ultimately became a massive expansion of scope with its acquisition of Crescendo Communications in September 1993. From this initial expansion from routers to switches, Cisco made 39 additional acquisitions through 1999 and now boasts a full line of network equipment as varied as modems, wireless local area network equipment, and optical switches. Cisco thereby captured economies of scope by putting more products through the same organization. It loaded the new products into the plants of its existing contract manufacturers, and its sales organization could then offer complete solutions to its partner customers. These economies of scope helped Cisco build its dominant position as a supplier of the infrastructure of the Internet.

Such product line expansion does not necessarily lead to economies of scope. If Cisco had not consolidated the manufacturing activities of its acquisitions and enabled its sales forces to offer complete solutions, it would have captured little advantage from the broader product line.

In fact, economies of scope can be negative as well as positive. Empirical research has demonstrated the value of "focused factories," which were first described by Harvard Business School professor Steven Wheelwright in the early 1970s. Arguments for focusing on core competencies, or more colloquially "sticking to one's knitting," stem from a recognition that multi-line businesses suffer from "costs of complexity." (Sometimes described by the misnomer diseconomies of scale, the disadvantages of size are more appropriately viewed as diseconomies of scope.)

The ill-fated diversification strategy of Sears, Roebuck and Company in the 1980s offers a prime example of a failed attempt to capture economies of scope. Sears, which had owned Allstate insurance since the 1930s, set out to build a consumer-oriented financial-services business by acquiring the real estate broker Coldwell Banker & Company and the stock brokerage firm Dean Witter. The company would accrue economies of scope by locating the stockbrokers within the Sears stores and by sharing information across business units. After all, the purchaser of a new home likely needs new appliances and homeowners insurance, too.

Unfortunately, the expansion led to what marketers call perceptual incongruity. Consumers accepted that Sears was a great source for appliances and power tools, but failed to accept that it could offer equal expertise in financial services. Furthermore, the added complexity of managing the disparate businesses drained the attention of Sears management. And the core department store business began to struggle. Ultimately, Sears reversed its diversification strategy and sold off its non-retail businesses in the early 1990s.

As these examples demonstrate, neither product line expansion nor business diversification automatically generates economies of scope. Economies of scope accrue only to companies that identify and capture synergies while simultaneously managing the risk of added complexity. Thus, scope expansion provides a powerful but double-edged sword. Broader scope can provide supply-side and demand-side advantage. But increased complexity can confuse consumers and distract management from the core value proposition of a company. Although a multiline company should seek synergies across unrelated business units, beware a company that tries to justify an expansion strategy purely on the basis of economies of scope.

Defense vs. Offense

So, returning to our opening question, does size drive success or does success drive size? Although the three distinct theories described above propound solid arguments for the advantages of size, we believe that more often than not, success generates superior size rather than vice versa.

Although Wal-Mart posted $244 billion in revenues in 2002, its revenues in 1983 were a mere $4.7 billion, about one-eighth those of then-dominant retailer Sears.

Not until 1990 and 1992, respectively, did Wal-Mart pass the Kmart Corporation and Sears in total revenues. Wal-Mart grew to a dominant position because it offered a superior customer proposition. As it grows, it certainly leverages its size for further advantage—but it didn't gain its dominance simply through the pursuit of size as a strategic objective.

In fact, size may offer a more effective defense than offense. The General Motors Corporation, Wal-Mart's predecessor in defining American business, provides ample evidence of the lingering, but continually fading, value of size. GM passed Ford Motor Company as the No. 1 global producer of automobiles in 1931 and became such an icon that Charles E. Wilson, a former GM executive, proclaimed before a congressional committee in 1952, "What is good for the country is good for General Motors, and what's good for General Motors is good for the country." Today, GM remains the largest producer of automobiles in the world by revenues, but ranks eighth in profits among vehicle producers, behind Toyota, Volkswagen, Daimnler-Chrysler, BMW, Peugeot, Renault, and Honda (rankings based on an average of 2001 and 2002). Toyota has less than half the sales of GM but nearly four times the profits. Size may provide an advantage, but size without profitability is of limited value.

Size certainly offers benefits to the companies that understand and exploit it. But size alone offers a relatively weak basis for a corporate strategy. A small company that executes well offers far more potential than a large, feeble one. In the end, it's not the size that matters, but how you use it.

Tim Laseter (laseter@darden.virginia.edu) is the author of *Balanced Sourcing: Corporation and Competition in Supplier Relationships* (Jossey-Bass, 1998) and serves on the operations faculty at the Darden Graduate School of Business at the University of Virginia. Formerly a vice president with Booz Allen Hamilton, he has 20 years of experience in supply chain management and operations strategy.

Martha Turner (turner_Martha@bah.com) is a senior associate in Booz Allen Hamilton's New York office. She specializes in operations and supply chain management issues in a broad range of industries.

Ron Wilcox (wilcoxr@darden.virginia.com) is an associate professor of business with the Darden Graduate School of Business at the University of Virginia. He was formerly an economist at the Securities and Exchange Commission. His articles on business strategy have appeared in leading academic and industry journals.

Strategy Formulation

9

Chapter Outline

After a firm's external and internal environments have been analyzed, it is necessary to review its stated mission and goals to ensure that they are compatible with the firm's internal characteristics and its external environment. Reconsidering the firm's current strategic initiatives is the first step in *evaluating* its activities and thinking about what the firm *should* be doing.

After the firm's mission and ongoing strategic directions are well understood, the organization can begin to craft a strategy. The first step in this process, a **SWOT** (strengths, weaknesses, opportunities, and threats) **analysis**, enables the firm to position itself to take advantage of select opportunities in the environment while avoiding or minimizing environmental threats.[1] In doing so, the organization attempts to emphasize its strengths and moderate the potential negative consequences of its weaknesses. Sometimes referred to as TOWS, the SWOT analysis also helps uncover strengths that have not yet been fully utilized and identify weaknesses that can be corrected. Matching information about the environment with knowledge of the organization's capabilities enables management to formulate realistic strategies for attaining its goals.[2]

9-1 Strengths and Weaknesses

The first two elements of the SWOT analysis—strengths and weaknesses—represent internal firm attributes. In addition, a firm's strengths and weaknesses are considered *relative* to key competitors in its industry. In other words, customer loyalty would be viewed as a strength or weakness for an organization if it is believed to be greater in that firm than in most others in the industry. Hence, strengths can be viewed as artifacts of past success in an organization, whereas weaknesses can be seen as gaps between an organization's current position and the industry norm. As an extension of this logic, the notion of **gap analysis** seeks to identify the distance between a firm's current position and its desired position with regard to an internal weakness. When possible, a firm should take action to close the gap, especially when the gap leaves a firm vulnerable to external threats in its environment.

The **value chain** is a useful tool for analyzing a firm's strengths and weaknesses and understanding how they might translate into competitive advantage or disadvantage. The value chain describes the activities that comprise the economic performance and capabilities of the firm. Specifically, the value chain identifies primary activities (i.e., those directly related to the firm's product or service) and support activities (i.e., those that assist the primary activities) which create value for customers. As such, the value chain is a conceptual foundation for assessing firm strengths and weaknesses.

By considering all of the firm's processes from the procurement of raw materials to the delivery of a final product or service, strategic managers can identify discrete activities performed along the way that may add exceptional value to the end product or detract from it.[3] For example, in March 2002, after a gradual decline in travel agency commissions throughout the industry, Delta Airlines announced an end to most of the commissions it pays to travel agents. With Delta's ability to trim sales costs through direct selling, the airline no longer believed that domestic travel agents were adding sufficient value to justify the expense. As is often true with such moves in the airline industry, most other major airlines followed suit.[4]

Firm resources—both tangible and intangible—ultimately constitute the firm's strengths and weaknesses.[5] Merely possessing a resource, however, does not always result in any tangible benefit to the organization. Resources are translated into desired results by **strategic capabilities**, the mechanism through which individuals in an organization coordinate efforts along one or more resources to

SWOT Analysis

An analysis intended to match the firm's strengths and weaknesses (the *S* and *W* in the acronym) with the opportunities and threats (the *O* and *T*) posed by the environment.

Gap Analysis

Identifying the distance between a firm's current position and its desired position with regard to an internal weakness. All things equal, it is desirable to take action to close a gap, especially when it leaves a firm vulnerable to external threats in its environment.

Value Chain

A useful tool for analyzing a firm's strengths and weaknesses and understanding how they might translate into competitive advantage or disadvantage. The value chain describes the activities that comprise the economic performance and capabilities of the firm.

Strategic Capabilities

The mechanism through which individuals in an organization coordinate efforts along one or more resources to solve a particular problem.

solve a particular problem. Although resources and capabilities are sometimes used interchangeably, the distinction between the two is an important one.[6]

The three broad categories of firm resources are as follows:

- **Human resources:** the experience, capabilities, knowledge, skills, and judgment of all the firm's employees
- **Organizational resources:** the firm's systems and processes, including its strategies at various levels, structure, and culture
- **Physical resources:** plant and equipment, geographic locations, access to raw materials, distribution network, and technology

In an optimal setting, all three types of resources work together to provide the firm with a competitive advantage that can be sustained. According to the resource-based perspective discussed in Chapter 1, a firm must utilize resources that are long lasting and not easily acquired by rivals through imitation, transfer, or replication if it is to sustain competitive advantage. When a firm's strategic success is dependent on resources that can readily be acquired by competitors, that success is likely to be temporary. A consideration of an organization's strengths and weaknesses is a means of objectively assessing its resource base.

9-2 Human Resources

The most attractive organizational and physical resources are useless without a competent workforce of managers and employees. A firm's human resources can be examined at three levels: (1) the board of directors, (2) top management, and (3) middle management, supervisors, and employees.

9-2a Board of Directors

Because board members are becoming increasingly involved in corporate affairs, they can materially influence the firm's effectiveness. In examining their strengths and weaknesses, one should consider the following issues.

1. *Prospective contributions of corporate board members.* Strong board members possess considerable experience, knowledge, and judgment, as well as valuable outside political connections.

2. *Tenure (experience) as members of the corporate board.* Long-term stability enables board members to gain organizational knowledge, but some turnover is beneficial because new members often bring a fresh perspective to strategic issues.

3. *Connection to the firm (i.e., internal or external) and ability to represent various stakeholders.* Although it is common for several top managers to be board members, a disproportionate representation of them diminishes the identity of the board as a group apart from top management. Ideally, board members should represent diverse stakeholders, including minorities, creditors, customers, and the local community. A diverse board membership can contribute to the health of the firm.

4. *Present level of investment in the firm.* Significant stock ownership may increase the board's responsiveness to shareholders, while significant bond holdings may heighten its concern for creditworthiness and result in a risk-averse posture on strategic issues.

9-2b Top Management

Three issues should be considered relative to the strengths and weaknesses of any firm's top management.

1. *Backgrounds and capabilities of top managers.* Comprehending their strengths and weaknesses in experience, managerial style, decision-making capability, and team building is useful. Although having executives who possess an intimate knowledge of

Source: Ablestock.com

the firm and its industry can be advantageous, managers from diverse and complementary backgrounds may generate innovative strategic ideas. In addition, an organization's management needs may change as the firm grows and matures. Because firms are often started by innovative entrepreneurs who happen to be poor administrators, they often add key administrators to the top management team, which includes the group of top-level executives—headed by the CEO—all of whom play instrumental roles in the strategic management process.

2. *Tenure (experience) as members of top management.* Although lengthy tenure can mean consistent and stable strategy development and implementation, low turnover may breed conformity, complacency, and a failure to explore new opportunities. CEO turnover is even desirable when the firm is unable to meet its performance targets.

3. *Strengths and weaknesses of individual top managers.* Some executives may excel in strategy formulation, for instance, but be weak in implementation. Some may spend considerable time on internal stakeholders and operations, whereas others may concentrate on external constituents. As with the board of directors, it is helpful for board members to possess complementary skills to function well as a team. In addition, several large companies offer financial incentives to sign and retain top executives with knowledge critical to the firm.

9-2c Middle Management, Supervisors, and Employees

Even the best strategies will fail without a talented workforce to implement them. A firm's personnel and their knowledge, abilities, commitment, and performance tend to reflect the firm's HR programs. These factors can be explored by considering five key issues.

1. *Existence of a comprehensive HR planning program.* Developing such a program requires that the firm forecast its personnel needs, including types of positions and requisite qualifications, for the next several years based on its strategic plan.

2. *Strategically relevant knowledge or expertise possessed by members of the firm.* Many firms place a great emphasis on retaining high-quality individuals in critical areas such as R&D or sales. This is a vital issue when a firm is heavily involved in global competition. Interestingly, all companies claim to have the *best* workforce, but clearly this is not always the case.

3. *Emphasis on training and development.* Some firms view training and development as a strategic issue and seek long-term benefits from its training programs. In contrast, other firms view training as a short-term necessity and emphasize cost minimization in their programs.

4. *Turnover.* High turnover relative to levels among close competitors generally reflects personnel problems such as poor management–employee relations, low compensation or benefits, or low job satisfaction due to other causes.

5. *Emphasis on effective performance appraisal (PA).* Progressive firms utilize PA to provide accurate feedback to managers and employees, link rewards to actual performance, and show managers and employees how to improve performance, as well as comply with all equal employment opportunity requirements. Firms that do not adequately appraise high performers—and reward them—are more likely to lose them.

9-3 Organizational Resources

The alignment between organizational resources and business strategy is critical for long-term success. Researchers have utilized the term *dynamic capabilities* to refer to the set of specific and identifiable processes controlled by an organization, such as product development and strategic decision making.[7] In this regard, seven key issues are noteworthy.

1. *Consistency among corporate, business, and functional strategies.* To facilitate strategy integration, managers at the corporate, business unit, and functional level should be represented at each level of strategic planning. The strategy at each level should influence and be influenced by the strategy at the other levels.

2. *Consistency between organizational strategies and the firm's mission and goals.* The mission, goals, and strategies must be compatible and integrated to reflect a clear sense of identity and purpose for the organization.

3. *Consistency between the firm's strategies and its culture.* For a strategy to be effective, it must be supported by an organizational culture that emphasizes values that support it.

4. *Consistency between the firm's strategies and its structure.* It is important to note any structural changes that might be required should the organization seek to implement a major change in strategy.

5. *Position in the industry.* All things equal, firms that possess strong market positions are in a better position to implement strategic changes than those in weak positions. For firms operating globally, this assessment must be made in the various nations in which the firm operates.

6. *Product and service quality.* It is important to comprehend how quality levels of the firm's products and services compare with those of rival firms.

7. *Reputation of the firm and/or brand.* Many firms have established reputations for factors such as high quality and customer service. A 2004 *Financial Times* global survey identified strength in brands such as General Electric, Microsoft, Toyota, IBM, and Wal-Mart. In contrast, little confidence was placed on scandal-ridden firms such as Enron, Parmalat, and WorldCom.[8]

9-4 Physical Resources

Physical resources can differ considerably from one organization to another, even among close competitors. For example, Amazon.com requires different physical plants than a software consulting firm. Nonetheless, five issues concerning the strengths and weaknesses of physical resources should be considered.

1. *Currency of technology.* All things equal, competitors with superior technology and the ability to use it have a decided competitive advantage in the marketplace. This is especially true in global markets and should be assessed in each of the nations in which the firm operates.

2. *Quality and sophistication of distribution network.* Distribution networks apply to both manufacturing and service concerns. The American Airlines domination of passenger gates at Dallas–Fort Worth Airport and Delta's similar control in Atlanta give both of these service companies a competitive advantage.

3. *Production capacity.* A continual backlog of orders may indicate a growing market acceptance of a firm's product, or it may depict serious problems associated with insufficient capacity. Capacity may be expanded by increasing production shifts or obtaining additional facilities, but such measures can be costly.

4. *Reliable access to cost-effective sources of supplies.* Suppliers who are unreliable, lack effective quality control programs, or cannot control their costs well do not foster a competitive advantage for the buying firm.

5. *Favorable location(s).* Ideally, the organization should be located where skilled labor, suppliers, and customers are readily accessible.

The unique combination of a firm's human, organizational, and physical resources—as transformed into capabilities—should be emphasized in its strategy. As the firm acquires additional resources, unique synergies occur between its new and existing resources. Because each firm possesses its own distinct

Case Analysis 9-1

Step 16: What Strengths Exist for the Organization?

Step 17: What Weaknesses Exist for the Organization?

Although resources and strategic capabilities are the foundation for a firm's strengths and weaknesses, it is not necessary to discuss the transition from resources to strengths and weaknesses in this section. Rather, the organization's strengths and weaknesses should be listed, each with as much depth and justification as possible. Many possible organizational strengths and weaknesses can emanate from its resource base, including but not limited to the following:

1. Advertising	19. Labor relations
2. Brand names	20. Leadership
3. Channel management	21. Location
4. Company reputation	22. Management
5. Computer information system	23. Manufacturing and operations
6. Control systems	24. Market share
7. Costs	25. Organizational structure
8. Customer loyalty	26. Physical facilities and equipment
9. Decision making	27. Product/service differentiation
10. Distribution	28. Product/service quality
11. Economies of scale	29. Promotion
12. Environmental scanning	30. Public relations
13. Financial resources	31. Purchasing
14. Forecasting	32. Quality control
15. Government lobbying	33. Research and development
16. Human resources	34. Sales
17. Inventory management	35. Technology and patents
18. Internet presence	

To set the stage for the remainder of the analysis, it is important to state clearly how each strength has helped the organization and how each weakness has hindered it. In many instances, the strengths are the primary catalysts for the organization's successes, and its weaknesses are the main reasons why it has failed in certain endeavors.

combination of resources, the particular types of synergies that occur will differ from one firm to another. Leveraging these synergies into sustained competitive advantages is a key task of top management (see Case Analysis 9-1).

9-5 Opportunities and Threats

The last two elements of the SWOT analysis—opportunities and threats—are associated with factors outside the organization. As such, they emerge from the earlier analyses of the industry and the macroenvironment (i.e., political-legal, economic, social, and technological forces). Although an industry-level analysis may identify general factors, this stage moves to the firm level and considers how the external forces could affect the organization under consideration. For example, an analysis of the social forces affecting investment houses may identify consumer acceptance of the Internet as a social force affecting the industry. Considering online broker Ameritrade, this force may be translated into both opportunities (e.g., a growing market of potential online investors who are still utilizing traditional brokers) and threats (e.g., intense competition from the myriad of Internet sources that may erode the loyalty of current customers to Ameritrade offerings).

External opportunities and threats must not be confused with *internal* strengths and weaknesses. Factors associated with the firm such as a poor financial position, an ineffective marketing strategy, or a strong brand image are internal factors and therefore must be classified as strengths or weaknesses. In contrast, factors outside the firm such as demographic changes, competitive threats, or recent legislation are external factors and therefore must be classified as opportunities or threats. At the international level, certain external factors should be considered as prospective opportunities and threats, including the cyclical or seasonal nature of the industry in which the firm operates and the intensity of global competition.

It is also critical to distinguish between *opportunities* and *alternatives,* although the distinction can sometimes appear to be one of semantics. Opportunities represent the application of macroenvironmental forces to a specific organization. Alternatives emanate from the SW/OT matrix (discussed in section 9-6) and represent specific courses of action that the organization may choose to pursue. The two are related but must be differentiated. For example, increasing societal interest in Cajun food may present an opportunity for a restaurant. When considered relative to internal factors (via the SW/OT matrix) such as the company's existing locations in Louisiana and its strong reputation for innovative cuisine, this opportunity may lead to an alternative for the company to consider, such as introducing a new line of Cajun offerings (see Case Analysis 9-2).

Case Analysis 9-2

Step 18: What Opportunities Exist for the Organization?
Step 19: What Threats Exist for the Organization?

In the SWOT analysis, one must not only identify strengths and weaknesses, but also translate the analysis of the macroenvironment and industry into opportunities and threats. Although these issues were addressed at the industry level earlier in the analysis, they should be integrated into a discussion that highlights specifically how they present opportunities to or threaten the organization. For example, if it was previously noted that the industry rises and falls abruptly with economic conditions, then the prospects of a recession may pose a major threat for the firm. If it was noted that technological advances have not yet been incorporated into production processes in the industry, then application of this technology may become an opportunity worth considering for the organization.

There is no set target for the number of strengths, weaknesses, opportunities, or threats that should be identified. When only several of each are identified, however, it is likely that the analysis is superficial and does not address key issues. When the list becomes too long—as would be the case if all thirty-five of the items listed in Case Analysis 9-1 were associated with strengths and weaknesses—the list becomes cumbersome to manage in the remaining steps of the analysis. In this situation, it is necessary to consider pooling several items into one when feasible. For example, "expertise in advertising" and "a strong sales force" could be merged into "marketing expertise."

9-6 The SW/OT Matrix

After the SWOT analysis is completed, alternative courses of action may be analyzed by creating a **SW/OT matrix**.[9] The SW/OT matrix extends the SWOT analysis by using it as a tool for generating strategic alternatives for the firm. A matrix is created with strengths and weaknesses listed vertically on the left side and opportunities and threats listed across the top. Alternatives emerge from the combination of one or more strengths/weaknesses from the left side of the matrix with one or more opportunities/threats from the top. For example, a company that can develop and produce high-quality electronic products in a short time—a strength—could take advantage of an increased consumer interest in portable DVD players—an opportunity—by developing and marketing one, a strategic alternative. This does not mean that the company should necessarily pursue such a strategy, but merely that the alternative warrants further consideration. The SW/OT matrix is a systematic means of developing strategic alternatives available to the organization, but it requires brainstorming and creative skills as well. The SW/OT matrix helps top managers position a firm in its environment so that it leverages its strengths while minimizing the detrimental effects of its weaknesses.

In general, four categories of alternatives emerge from the SW/OT matrix, each representing the combination of one or more strengths or weaknesses with one or more opportunities or threats.

1. *Strength–Opportunity.* These "offensive" alternatives tend to be the most common and involve utilizing an organizational strength to address an opportunity.
2. *Weakness–Threat.* These "defensive" alternatives involve taking corrective action to eliminate or minimize a weakness so as to minimize the effect of a threat.
3. *Strength–Threat.* These alternatives involve utilizing a strength to eliminate or minimize the effect of a threat and may be offensive or defensive.
4. *Weakness–Opportunity.* These alternatives involve shoring up a weakness so that the organization can take advantage of an opportunity and may be offensive or defensive.

Typically, most of the individual internal-external combinations (i.e., matches between strengths/weaknesses and opportunities/threats) will not produce viable alternatives. Further, several different combinations of internal and external factors can produce the same alternative. Some of the alternatives that emerge might be eliminated from further consideration for obvious reasons (e.g., taking the action would be illegal). In addition, a given SW/OT matrix might generate a large number of alternatives in a particular category, whereas only a few may be generated in other categories. Once generated, strategic alternatives should be analyzed further.

Figure 9-1 provides a simplified example of a SW/OT matrix for McDonald's. Assume that the SWOT analysis for McDonald's identified strengths of financial stability, brand recognition, and a strong ability to produce consistent products throughout the world. Two weaknesses were identified as well: inconsistent financial performance in international markets and a heavy dependence on fried foods. The two key opportunities were economic growth in emerging economies and the increasing health consciousness of the U.S. population. Two threats were highlighted as well: the possible mandates that will raise employment costs in the United States and the increasing popularity of easy-to-prepare microwaveable foods. A thorough SWOT analysis for McDonald's would develop many more than two or three factors in each category and might even challenge the oversimplification of the factors identified in this example. Nonetheless, the number and

FIGURE 9-1   SW/OT Matrix

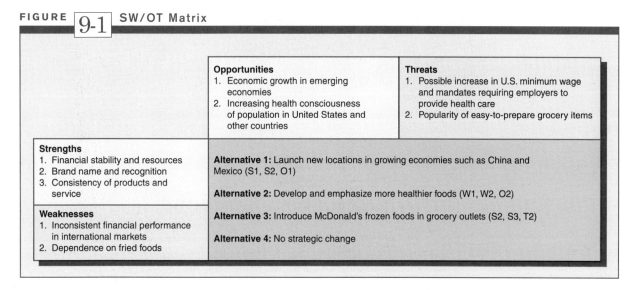

	Opportunities 1. Economic growth in emerging economies 2. Increasing health consciousness of population in United States and other countries	Threats 1. Possible increase in U.S. minimum wage and mandates requiring employers to provide health care 2. Popularity of easy-to-prepare grocery items
Strengths 1. Financial stability and resources 2. Brand name and recognition 3. Consistency of products and service	**Alternative 1:** Launch new locations in growing economies such as China and Mexico (S1, S2, O1) **Alternative 2:** Develop and emphasize more healthier foods (W1, W2, O2)	
Weaknesses 1. Inconsistent financial performance in international markets 2. Dependence on fried foods	**Alternative 3:** Introduce McDonald's frozen foods in grocery outlets (S2, S3, T2) **Alternative 4:** No strategic change	

complexity of the factors are kept to a minimum so that the process of developing alternatives can be clearly illustrated.

Following the example, three possible alternative courses of action can be identified for further consideration. First, McDonald's could emphasize its financial and brand strengths and seize an emerging market opportunity by expanding aggressively into growing economies such as China and Mexico. Second, McDonald's could address its weaknesses of declining market share and dependence on fast foods and capitalize on a greater health awareness in the United States and other parts of the world by developing and emphasizing more healthy foods. Third, McDonald's could emphasize its brand name and consistency strengths and address the threat of increased popularity of easy-to-prepare grocery items by introducing its own line of grocery products. Of course, this simple example considers only a few hypothetical items in each of the SWOT categories and does not suggest that McDonald's should *necessarily* adopt any of these alternatives.

It is worth noting that continuing to implement the current strategy in its present form—the so-called no change option—should be considered. This alternative (denoted as the final option in the previous example) should be analyzed as critically as the others. Selecting the no change alternative should *not* be considered as a low-risk option, because resisting change may be just as likely to expose a firm to great danger as embracing it (see Case Analysis 9-3).

Evaluating the pros and cons of strategic alternatives in a detailed, objective, and thorough manner is critical. Problems with implementation can often be traced to the lack of a thorough evaluation of the strategic alternatives available to a firm. For example, it is easy to assume that well-known brands will be readily accepted in new markets or that competitors will not respond effectively to major strategic changes. Even major retailers, however, can find themselves battling stiff local competition when they expand abroad.[10]

In addition, the direction of a strategic change can affect the difficulty of its implementation. In general, a business pursuing differentiation can shift to low cost more easily than a low-cost business can shift to differentiation. Because a low-cost business is likely to be associated with value rather than quality, it is difficult to convince buyers that they should pay more because its products

Case Analysis 9-3

Step 20: What Strategic Alternatives Are Available to the Organization?

Alternatives are organizational courses of action that (1) are worth considering because they offer some potentially positive benefits, and (2) are within the realm of possibilities for the organization. For starters, one alternative is to continue with the present strategy. Sometimes this alternative is the most desirable, but typically some changes are needed. Additional alternatives should be identified from the SW/OT matrix in two ways. First, one should consider more fully utilizing strengths to take advantage of existing opportunities or palliate threats if the organization is not presently doing so. For example, if an organization has excess production capacity and there exists a market not presently served, then moving into this market is worth considering. Second, one should also consider taking action to minimize the weaknesses so that the organization can pursue opportunities or minimize the effect of threats. It is critical to identify the S/W-O/T combinations that result in the identification of each alternative, but it is not worthwhile to include alternatives that are obviously implausible or unattractive (e.g., McDonald's could close its fast-food stores to concentrate on promoting frozen foods through grocery outlets) for the sake of creating a list. All of the alternatives to be considered should be viable alternatives, at least at first glance.

There is no set number of alternatives that should be generated. As with the identification of elements within the SWOT, having too few alternatives implies a superficial analysis, whereas too many alternatives can become difficult to assess.

Step 21: What Are the Pros and Cons of These Alternatives?

Some of the alternatives identified in step 20 may be mutually exclusive, whereas others may not. Inevitably, one must assess the attractiveness of each alternative. It is not appropriate to "sell" one or two that will be recommended later. Rather, pros and cons must be objectively identified for each alternative. All alternatives have costs, and some have limited prospects for success, factors which should be converted to dollars when possible. For example, quality circles may be proposed as a solution to low morale without considering the costs. Quality circles require a commitment of time (i.e., lost production) and effort if they are to be successful, and management must also be willing to implement suggestions. In the final analysis, quality circles may be desirable, but no strategy can be implemented free of cost.

Interestingly, the quality circles recommendation has another problem. Most scholars and practitioners have reported that quality circles are effective only when they are part of a larger approach to employee empowerment. As such, a quality circle alternative should consider an overall strategic change as related to the organization's human resources, not simply the implementation of a technique.

It is important to consider competitive responses in concert with this and the subsequent case analysis step. For example, a McDonald's drop in price for the Big Mac cannot be considered in isolation of a likely price cut at Burger King. In many cases, anticipated retaliation is a con of the alternative and could ultimately render the alternative as undesirable. Assuming that competitor behavior will not change over time—especially in response to a major strategic change—is shortsighted.

Step 22: Which Alternative(s) Should Be Pursued and Why?

This phase necessitates an objective and subjective analysis of the pros and cons associated with each alternative. It is critical not to select an alternative without both arguing for its selection and explaining why other alternatives were rejected. When two or more options are mutually exclusive, eliminating the options not chosen is just as important as selecting the desired choices. Although it is important to spend time analyzing the alternatives, one must resist the temptation to overanalyze and avoid making the difficult choices, a process often referred to as "analysis to paralysis."

are differentiated. Volkswagen found this out when sales plummeted after the carmaker added pricey features to the moderately positioned Golf. Many consumers simply were not willing to pay the additional charge for a vehicle whose quality and prestige was perceived to be somewhat modest.[11]

9-7 Issues in Strategy Formulation

Crafting a strategy is not an easy task, even with the assistance of tools such as the SW/OT matrix. When a strategy appears attractive, certain issues should be considered before it is implemented. Four such issues are discussed in this section.

9-7a Evaluating Strategic Change

Should an organization change course when performance declines or should it stay the course? On the one hand, its strategic managers may choose to commit to a strategic course of action for an extended time and enjoy the benefits of specialization, expertise, organizational learning, and a clear customer image. Alternatively, an organization can remain flexible so that it does not become committed to products, technology, or market approaches that may become outdated. In a perfect world, organizations commit to predictable, successful courses of action, and strategic change is only incremental. However, outcomes are not always predictable.

Source: Ablestock.com

As with many strategic issues, there are two compelling sides to this debate. When traditional firms perform poorly, their strategic managers are exhorted by business analysts to promote flexibility and strategic renewal to improve profitability. In contrast, when bold strategic changes fail, pundits assert that a company must return to its "core business." Hence, it is easy to migrate freely from one side of the debate to the other, often with convincing empirical and intuitively appealing arguments.

The needs for strategic flexibility or commitment can be debated on at least four grounds. First, a strategy tends to yield superior performance when it fits with the organization's environment. Without strategic flexibility, an organization cannot adapt to its changing external environment. Even if an organization's strategy and its environment are in concert, an environmental shift may necessitate strategic change to maintain alignment. In addition, changes in competition and technology necessitate a change in the knowledge base within the organization if it is to prosper. The state of the environment is not always fully understood by strategy formulators, and top managers may be most likely to contemplate a strategic change when perceived environmental uncertainty is high.

In contrast, however, a change in any key strategic, environmental, or organizational factor may entice strategic managers in a business to modify its strategy to incorporate these changes. However, since such variables are constantly evolving, this is a challenging process, and strategic inaction may minimize uncertainty. Indeed, a strategic change is most risky when competitors are better equipped to respond if it is deemed successful. As such, strategic change can challenge the assumptions of all organizational members and may be difficult to implement even with employee support.

Second, flexibility is necessary if an organization is to seek first-mover advantages by entering a new market or developing a new product or service prior to its competitors. Being a first mover can help secure access to scarce resources, increase the organization's knowledge base, and result in substantial long-term competitive advantage, especially when switching costs are high. Maintaining commitment to the firm's strategy can preclude movement into attractive strategic domains.[12]

However, even when strategic change results in a successful new product or service, there is no assurance that this success can be maintained. In fact, competitors may distort consumer perceptions and reap the benefits of the initial strategic change. When a consumer goods company imitates another, for example, consumers may purchase the imitation product thinking it is the original. If consumers dislike the product, this dissatisfaction can be transferred to the original. On the other hand, if the consumer likes the product, the consumer may realize that the product is an imitator and transfer the positive associations with the original product to that of the imitator. Either scenario can prove costly to the originator.

Third, even when a firm's environment is relatively stable, strategic change can be attractive when the organization's set of unique human, physical, capital, and informational resources change. Resource shifts necessitating strategic change may be more prevalent in some organizations than in others. Following this logic, strategic change can improve an organization's ability to adapt by forcing healthy changes within the business. The initial pain associated with change may be offset by the emergence of a lean, rejuvenated organization with a fresh focus on its goals and objectives.[13]

Consumer confusion may result from strategic change, however, even when the new strategy represents a better fit with the firm's resources. For example, if a business employing a low-cost strategy attempts to switch to a differentiation strategy, its price-oriented customers may become confused and leave in pursuit of another low-cost leader, while those willing to pay a premium price for differentiated products may not recognize or positively perceive the strategic change. Many will likely recall remnants of the previous strategy—perhaps advertising campaigns—and may not even consider the organization for future business.

Fourth, strategic change may be necessary if desired performance levels are not being attained by the organization. In many cases, a change in strategy may be required to improve the ability of the business to generate revenues or profits, increase market share, and/or improve return on assets or investment. In many cases, new CEOs are recruited for that purpose.

In contrast, however, the measures required to implement a change in strategy may necessitate substantial outlays of capital, thereby further denigrating the organization's financial position. Considering the Miles and Snow typology discussed in section 7-2 as an example, a shift from a prospector or analyzer strategy to a defender strategy may require investments in sophisticated production equipment to lower production costs, a characteristic more important to effective implementation of a defender strategy. Likewise, a shift from defender or analyzer to prospector may require substantial outlays to develop or enhance R&D facilities.

The decision to incorporate a substantial change in strategy can be alluring, especially when performance is poor. It is necessary, however, to recognize the costs associated with strategic change *before* committing resources.

9-7b Social Responsibility and Managerial Ethics

Strategy decisions should not be based solely on projected effects on financial performance. An organization's strategies at all levels should be compatible with its stance on social responsibility and ethics. Strategic alternatives should be considered in light of stated positions on social responsibility. Marketers of alcoholic beverages must consider whether attractive advertising campaigns may attract minors as well. A manufacturer must consider the effects of a prospective plant relocation on the community where it is currently located. Video game developers, for example, must consider how much violence is acceptable in the games they market to various age groups. Hence, every organization faces social responsibility and ethical considerations.

9-7c Effects on Organizational Resources

Executing a strategy requires resources that could be used for another purpose. The most obvious example is capital. If a firm pursues aggressive expansion into an uncharted geographical area, for example, the capital required will not be available for other purposes such as R&D or a new advertising campaign. If a firm launches a service enhancement effort by requiring sales representatives to make more frequent visits to existing customers, they will not be able to pursue new accounts as vigorously as before. These tradeoffs should be considered before a strategy is adopted.

Unfortunately, many firms do not fully consider such tradeoffs. Instead, they devise strategies whose success depends on "doing more with less." Managers and employees are stretched thin while new programs are implemented without eliminating old ones. In the end, an organization may find itself performing lots of activities, but none of them well.

9-7d Anticipated Responses from Competitors and Customers

Strategies are not implemented in a vacuum. Competitive responses should be expected when a substantial strategic change is employed. In many situations, the prospective gains associated with a strategic change will be reduced when the response is considered. For example, the development of new products may produce few new customers if competitors respond quickly by developing a similar offering.

In some cases, considering the retaliation makes an otherwise attractive strategic alternative undesirable. Consider, for example, that American Airlines could probably secure more fliers than Delta on common routes if its fares were priced below those of the rival. If American initiated a price cut, however, Delta would almost certainly match it. It is likely that the reduced fares would attract few additional fliers to either airline. Hence, both airlines would be forced to operate the same routes with virtually the same number of customers at lower routes. When competitive retaliation is considered in this example, American is probably best served not to spark a price war with Delta.

Consider another example that illustrates the fact that changes in the competitive environment do not always materialize as one might expect. When an airline hub closes, for example, one might expect flights to and from the affected city to increase in price because of the departed competitor. In the United States, however, discount airlines often fill the empty gates, actually fostering greater price competition.[14] Hence, one could argue that it may be in the best interest of traditional carriers *not* to drive less competitive rivals out of key hubs, lest they be bombarded by greater competition.

Customer responses can be difficult to predict, but responses to strategic change should be anticipated and accounted for, especially when substantial shifts in prices or product line occur. When eBay announced a hike in its fee structure in early 2005, for example, many customers took notice, closed their eBay "stores," and pursued other means of promoting and selling their wares.[15]

9-8 Summary

The SWOT analysis serves as the basis for the formulation of strategies at all levels. The SWOT summarizes the organization's internal (i.e., strengths and weaknesses) and external (i.e., opportunities and threats) characteristics. Strengths and weaknesses emanate from an analysis of human, organizational, and physical resources. Opportunities and threats are based on analyses of the macroenvironment and industry. The SW/OT matrix generates strategic alternatives by combining internal and external factors delineated in the SWOT analysis.

Before a strategy is selected, however, several other considerations should be made. These include the costs associated with strategic change, the strategy's fit with the organization's stance on social responsibility and managerial ethics, effects on organizational resources, anticipated responses from competitors, and potential difficulties in implementing the strategy.

Key Terms

gap analysis

human resources

organizational resources

physical resources

strategic capabilities

SWOT analysis

SW/OT matrix

value chain

Review Questions and Exercises

1. What is the value chain? How is it useful to strategy formulation?

2. How do a SWOT analysis and SW/OT matrix help managers in the strategic decision-making process?

3. What types of alternatives can be generated from a SW/OT matrix?

4. Should an organization change strategies when performance declines? Explain.

Practice Quiz

True of False

1. The first step in crafting a strategy is the SWOT analysis.

2. The value chain is an analytical technique for identifying organizational opportunities and threats.

3. Opportunities and threats emerge from the analysis of macroenvironmental and industry forces.

4. A factor can be both an opportunity and a strength.

5. Another name for an opportunity is an alternative.

6. Choosing the no change strategy and thereby recommending that the current strategy be continued is the least risky option.

Multiple Choice

7. The tool that enables an organization to position itself to take advantage of particular opportunities in the environment while avoiding or minimizing environmental threats is called

   A. PEST analysis.

   B. SWOT analysis.

   C. TQM analysis.

   D. none of the above

8. The description of activities that comprise the economic performance and capabilities of the firm is known as

   A. the value chain.

   B. process innovation.

   C. quality assessment.

   D. none of the above

9. To sustain competitive advantage, firms must acquire or develop resources that are

   A. difficult for competitors to imitate.

   B. long lasting.

   C. difficult for competitors to acquire on the market.

   D. all of the above

10. Physical resources include:

    A. production facilities.

    B. plant locations.

C. production capacity.

D. all of the above

11. Which of the following could not be an example of a weakness?

A. product quality

B. fierce competition

C. human resources

D. All of the above could be weaknesses.

12. Which type of alternative is always defensive in nature?

A. strength-opportunity

B. strength-threat

C. weakness-opportunity

D. weakness-threat

Notes

1. K. W. Glaister and J. R. Falshaw, "Strategic Planning: Still Going Strong?" *Long Range Planning* 32(1) (1999): 107–116.

2. P. C. Nutt, "Making Strategic Choices," *Journal of Management Studies* 39 (2002): 67–96.

3. M. Porter, *Competitive Advantage: Creating and Sustaining Superior Performance* (Boston: Free Press, 1985).

4. N. Harris and S. Carey, "Delta Ends Commissions for Most Travel Agents," *Wall Street Journal Interactive Edition* (15 March 2002).

5. J. B. Barney, "Firm Resources and Sustained Competitive Advantage," *Journal of Management* 17 (1991): 99–120; A. Lado, N. Boyd, and P. Wright, "A Competency-Based Model of Sustainable Competitive Advantage: Toward a Conceptual Integration," *Journal of Management* 18 (1992): 77–91.

6. Barney, *Gaining and Sustaining Competitive Advantage* (Upper Saddle River, NJ: Prentice Hall, 2007); D. Teece, G. Pisano, and A. Shuen, "Dynamic Capabilities and Strategic Management," *Strategic Management Journal* 18 (1997): 509–533.

7. K. M. Eisenhardt and J. A. Martin, "Dynamic Capabilities: What Are They?" *Strategic Management Journal* 21 (2000): 1105–1121.

8. M. Skapinker, "Brand Strength Proves Its Worth," *Financial Times* (20 January 2004): 1–2 (special report).

9. Based on H. Wilrich, "The TOWS Matrix—A Tool for Structural Analysis," *Long Range Planning* 15(2) (1982): 54–66.

10. S. Jung-a, "Carrefour's Korean Stores to Go Upmarket," *Financial Times* (7 October 2003): 18.

11. B. E. Boudette, "As VW Tries to Sell Pricier Cars, Everyman Image Holds It Back," *Wall Street Journal* (13 May 2004): A1, A8.

12. B. Peterson and D. E. Welch, "Creating Meaningful Switching Options in International Operations," *Long Range Planning* 33 (2000): 688–705; M. B. Lieberman and D. B. Montgomery, "First-Mover Advantages," *Strategic Management Journal* 9 (1988): 41–58.

13. Barney, "Is the Resource-Based 'View' a Useful Perspective for Strategic Management Research?" *Academy of Management Review* 26 (2001): 41–56.

14. S. McCartney, "Why Travelers Benefit When an Airline Hub Closes," *Wall Street Journal* (1 November 2005): D1, D8.

15. M. Mangalindan, "Some Sellers Leave eBay over New Fees," *Wall Street Journal* (31 January 2005): B1, B3.

Insight from *strategy+business*

Organizations are constantly changing. Sometimes change is needed simply to keep up with the environment. At other times, change must be initiated to correct key problems in strategy or performance. The problem, however, is that initiating any type of change can be difficult. This chapter's strategy+business reading offers ten suggestions for instituting change effectively.

The Ten Principles of Change Management

Tools and techniques to help companies transform quickly.

By John Jones, DeAnne Aguirre, and Matthew Calderone

Way back when (pick your date), senior executives in large companies had a simple goal for themselves and for their organizations: stability. Shareholders wanted little more than predictable earnings growth. Because so many markets were either closed or undeveloped, leaders could deliver on those expectations through annual exercises that offered only small modifications to the strategic plan. Prices stayed in check; people stayed in their jobs; life was good.

Market transparency, labor mobility, global capital flows, and instantaneous communications have blown that comfortable scenario to smithereens. In most industries—and in almost all companies, from giants on down—heightened global competition has concentrated management's collective mind on something that, in the past, it happily avoided: change. Successful companies, as Harvard Business School Professor Rosabeth Moss Kanter told *strategy+business* in 1999, develop "a culture that just keeps moving all the time."

This presents most senior executives with an unfamiliar challenge. In major transformations of large enterprises, they and their advisors conventionally focus their attention on devising the best strategic and tactical plans. But to succeed, they also must have an intimate understanding of the human side of change management—the alignment of the company's culture, values, people, and behaviors—to encourage the desired results. Plans themselves do not capture value; value is realized only through the sustained, collective actions of the thousands—perhaps tens of thousands—of employees who are responsible for designing, executing, and living with the changed environment.

Long-term structural transformation has four characteristics: scale (the change affects all or most of the organization), magnitude (it involves significant alterations of the status quo), duration (it lasts for months, if not years), and strategic importance. Yet companies will reap the rewards only when change occurs at the level of the individual employee.

Many senior executives know this and worry about it. When asked what keeps them up at night, CEOs involved in transformation often say they are concerned about how the work force will react, how they can get their team to work together, and how they will be able to lead their people. They also worry about retaining their company's unique values and sense of identity and about creating a culture of commitment and performance. Leadership teams that fail to plan for the human side of change often find themselves wondering why their best-laid plans have gone awry.

No single methodology fits every company, but there is a set of practices, tools, and techniques that can be adapted to a variety of situations. What follows is a "Top 10" list of guiding principles for change management. Using these as a systematic, comprehensive framework, executives can understand what to expect, how to manage their own personal change, and how to engage the entire organization in the process.

1. **Address the "human side" systematically.** Any significant transformation creates "people issues." New leaders will be asked to step up, jobs will be changed, new skills and capabilities must be developed, and employees will be uncertain and resistant. Dealing with these issues on a reactive, case-by-case basis puts speed, morale, and results at risk. A formal

Source: Reprinted with permission from *strategy+business*, the award-winning management quarterly published by Booz Allen Hamilton. http://www.strategy-business.com.

approach for managing change—beginning with the leadership team and then engaging key stakeholders and leaders—should be developed early, and adapted often as change moves through the organization. This demands as much data collection and analysis, planning, and implementation discipline as does a redesign of strategy, systems, or processes. The change-management approach should be fully integrated into program design and decision making, both informing and enabling strategic direction. It should be based on a realistic assessment of the organization's history, readiness, and capacity to change.

2. **Start at the top.** Because change is inherently unsettling for people at all levels of an organization, when it is on the horizon, all eyes will turn to the CEO and the leadership team for strength, support, and direction. The leaders themselves must embrace the new approaches first, both to challenge and to motivate the rest of the institution. They must speak with one voice and model the desired behaviors. The executive team also needs to understand that, although its public face may be one of unity, it, too, is composed of individuals who are going through stressful times and need to be supported.

Executive teams that work well together are best positioned for success. They are aligned and committed to the direction of change, understand the culture and behaviors the changes intend to introduce, and can model those changes themselves. At one large transportation company, the senior team rolled out an initiative to improve the efficiency and performance of its corporate and field staff before addressing change issues at the officer level. The initiative realized initial cost savings but stalled as employees began to question the leadership team's vision and commitment. Only after the leadership team went through the process of aligning and committing to the change initiative was the work force able to deliver downstream results.

3. **Involve every layer.** As transformation programs progress from defining strategy and setting targets to design and implementation, they affect different levels of the organization. Change efforts must include plans for identifying leaders throughout the company and pushing responsibility for design and implementation down, so that change "cascades" through the organization. At each layer, the leaders who are identified and trained must be aligned to the company's vision, equipped to execute their specific mission, and motivated to make change happen.

A major multiline insurer with consistently flat earnings decided to change performance and behavior in preparation for going public. The company followed this "cascading leadership" methodology, training and supporting teams at each stage. First, 10 officers set the strategy, vision, and targets. Next, more than 60 senior executives and managers designed the core of the change initiative. Then 500 leaders from the field drove implementation. The structure remained in place throughout the change program, which doubled the company's earnings far ahead of schedule. This approach is also a superb way for a company to identify its next generation of leadership.

4. **Make the format case.** Individuals are inherently rational and will question to what extent change is needed, whether the company is headed in the right direction, and whether they want to commit personally to making change happen. They will look to the leadership for answers. The articulation of a formal case for change and the creation of a written vision statement are invaluable opportunities to create or compel leadership-team alignment.

Three steps should be followed in developing the case: First, confront reality and articulate a convincing need for change. Second, demonstrate faith that the company has a viable future and the leadership to get there. Finally, provide a road map to guide behavior and decision making. Leaders must then customize this message for various internal audiences, describing the pending change in terms that matter to the individuals.

A consumer packaged-goods company experiencing years of steadily declining earnings determined that it needed to significantly restructure its operations—instituting, among other things, a 30 percent work force reduction—to remain competitive. In a series of offsite meetings, the executive team built a brutally honest business case that downsizing was the only way to keep the business viable, and drew on the company's proud heritage to craft a compelling vision to lead the company forward. By confronting reality and helping employees understand the necessity for change, leaders were able to motivate the organization to follow the new direction in the midst of the largest downsizing in the company's history. Instead of being shell-shocked and demoralized, those who stayed felt a renewed resolve to help the enterprise advance.

5. **Create ownership.** Leaders of large change programs must over-perform during the transformation and be the zealots who create a critical mass among the work force in favor of change. This requires more than mere buy-in or passive agreement that the direction of change is

acceptable. It demands ownership by leaders willing to accept responsibility for making change happen in all of the areas they influence or control. Ownership is often best created by involving people in identifying problems and crafting solutions. It is reinforced by incentives and rewards. These can be tangible (for example, financial compensation) or psychological (for example, camaraderie and a sense of shared destiny).

At a large health-care organization that was moving to a shared-services model for administrative support, the first department to create detailed designs for the new organization was human resources. Its personnel worked with advisors in cross-functional teams for more than six months. But as the designs were being finalized, top departmental executives began to resist the move to implementation. While agreeing that the work was topnotch, the executives realized they hadn't invested enough individual time in the design process to feel the ownership required to begin implementation. On the basis of their feedback, the process was modified to include a "deep dive." The departmental executives worked with the design teams to learn more, and get further exposure to changes that would occur. This was the turning point; the transition then happened quickly. It also created a forum for top executives to work as a team, creating a sense of alignment and unity that the group hadn't felt before.

6. **Communicate the message.** Too often, change leaders make the mistake of believing that others understand the issues, feel the need to change, and see the new direction as clearly as they do. The best change programs reinforce core messages through regular, timely advice that is both inspirational and practicable. Communications flow in from the bottom and out from the top, and are targeted to provide employees the right information at the right time and to solicit their input and feedback. Often this will require overcommunication through multiple, redundant channels.

In the late 1990s, the commissioner of the Internal Revenue Service, Charles O. Rossotti, had a vision: The IRS could treat tax-payers as customers and turn a feared bureaucracy into a world-class service organization. Getting more than 100,000 employees to think and act differently required more than just systems redesign and process change. IRS leadership designed and executed an ambitious communications program including daily voice mails from the commissioner and his top staff, training sessions, videotapes, newsletters, and town hall meetings that continued through the transformation. Timely, constant, practical communication was at the heart of the program, which brought the IRS's customer ratings from the lowest in various surveys to its current ranking above the likes of McDonald's and most airlines.

7. **Assess the cultural landscape.** Successful change programs pick up speed and intensity as they cascade down, making it critically important that leaders understand and account for culture and behaviors at each level of the organization. Companies often make the mistake of assessing culture either too late or nor at all. Thorough cultural diagnostics can assess organizational readiness to change, bring major problems to the surface, identify conflicts, and define factors that can recognize and influence sources of leadership and resistance. These diagnostics identify the core values, beliefs, behaviors, and perceptions that must be taken into account for successful change to occur. They serve as the common baseline for designing essential change elements, such as the new corporate vision, and building the infrastructure and programs needed to drive change.

8. **Address culture explicitly.** Once the culture is understood, it should be addressed as thoroughly as any other area in a change program. Leaders should be explicit about the culture and underlying behaviors that will best support the new way of doing business, and find opportunities to model and reward those behaviors. This requires developing a baseline, defining an explicit end-state or desired culture, and devising detailed plans to make the transition.

Company culture is an amalgam of shared history, explicit values and beliefs, and common attitudes and behaviors. Change programs can involve creating a culture (in new companies or those built through multiple acquisitions), combining cultures (in mergers or acquisitions of large companies), or reinforcing cultures (in, say, long-established consumer goods or manufacturing companies). Understanding that all companies have a cultural center—the locus of thought, activity, influence, or personal identification—is often an effective way to jump-start culture change.

A consumer goods company with a suite of premium brands determined that business realities demanded a greater focus on profitability and bottom-line accountability. In addition to redesigning metrics and incentives, it developed a plan to systematically change the company's culture, beginning with marketing, the company's historical center. It brought the marketing staff into the process early to create enthusiasts for the new philosophy who adapted marketing campaigns, spending plans, and incentive programs to be more accountable. Seeing these culture leaders grab onto the new program, the rest of the company quickly fell in line.

9. **Prepare for the unexpected.** No change program goes completely according to plan. People react in unexpected ways; areas of anticipated resistance fall away; and the external environment shifts. Effectively managing change requires continual reassessment of its impact and the organizations willingness and ability to adopt the next wave of transformation. Fed by real data from the field and supported by information and solid decision-making processes, change leaders can then make the adjustments necessary to maintain momentum and drive results.

A leading U.S. health-care company was facing competitive and financial pressures from its inability to react to changes in the marketplace. A diagnosis revealed shortcomings in its organizational structure and governance, and the company decided to implement a new operating model. In the midst of detailed design, a new CEO and leadership team took over. The new team was initially skeptical, but was ultimately convinced that a solid case for change, grounded in facts and supported by the organization at large, existed. Some adjustments were made to the speed and sequence of implementation, but the fundamentals of the new operating model remained unchanged.

10. **Speak to the individual.** Change is both an institutional journey and a very personal one. People spend many hours each week at work; many think of their colleagues as a second family. Individuals (or teams of individuals) need to know how their work will change, what is expected of them during and after the change program, how they will be measured, and what success or failure will mean for them and those around them. Team leaders should be as honest and explicit as possible. People will react to what they see and hear around them, and need to be involved in the change process. Highly visible rewards, such as promotion, recognition, and bonuses, should be provided as dramatic reinforcement for embracing change. Sanction or removal of people standing in the way of change will reinforce the institution's commitment.

Most leaders contemplating change know that people matter. It is all too tempting, however to dwell on the plans and processes, which don't talk back and don't respond emotionally, rather than face up to the more difficult and more critical human issues. But mastering the "soft" side of change management needn't be a mystery.

John Jones (jones_john@bah.com) is a vice president with Booz Allen Hamilton in New York. Mr. Jones is a specialist in organization design, process reengineering, and change management.

DeAnne Aguirre (aguirre_Deanne@bah.com) is a vice president in Booz Allen Hamilton's San Francisco office. She has 18 years of organizational and technology strategy experience serving multinational clients.

Matthew Calderone (calderone_matthew@bah.com) is a senior associate in Booz Allen Hamilton's New York office. He specializes in organization transformation, people issues, and change management.

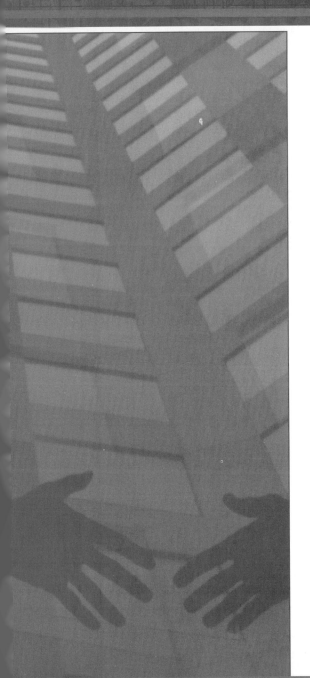

Strategy Execution: Structure 10

Chapter Outline

The best conceived strategic plans often fail from a lack of planning for their execution. Effective strategy implementation requires managers to consider many issues, including structural, cultural, and leadership concerns.[1] These considerations should be made *before* a strategic alternative is selected and then detailed *after* strategy formulation. This chapter emphasizes the relationship between strategy and structure, especially within the context of strategy execution. Leadership and cultural concerns are addressed in Chapter 11.

10-1 Organizational Structure

Organizational Structure

The formal means by which work is coordinated in an organization.

Simple Structure

An organizational form whereby each employee often performs multiple tasks, and the owner-manager is involved in all aspects of the business.

Organizational structure is the formal means by which work is coordinated in an organization. As the focus of this chapter, an organization's structure dictates reporting relationships and defines where and how the firm's work will be done. It establishes a framework for identifying levels in the organization where decisions will be made. In many respects, the structure sets the stage for strategy execution. A given structure might be appropriate for one particular strategy, but not another.

The long-standing debate among scholars is whether a firm's strategy should follow its structure or vice versa. Most practitioners, however, recognize that each is influenced by the other. In the short term, strategic managers should evaluate and consider the firm's structure when crafting the strategy, recognizing that modifying the structure is rarely easy or inexpensive. In addition, they should be willing to modify the firm's structure as required to fit with any necessary strategic change. In the long term, because a firm's strategy is a key driver of its performance, the structure should be built around the strategy to ensure its effectiveness.

Although some new businesses are launched on a large scale, many start small with an owner-manager and a few employees. Neither an organizational chart nor a formal assignment of responsibilities is necessary. Each employee often performs multiple tasks and the owner-manager is involved in all aspects of the business, a form of organization often called a **simple structure**. This structure may remain intact for only a few months in a fast growing organization or for years in a small family business such as a rural convenience or hardware store.

In organizations with a simple structure, early survival depends on an increase in demand for the company's products or services. As the organization grows to meet this demand, however, a more permanent division of labor tends to form. The owner-manager, who once was nearly involved in all functions of the enterprise, begins to play more of a leadership role and therefore assigns additional employees to more specialized functions. Growth of the firm reaches a certain point, however, where top managers must evaluate the effectiveness of the evolving system of coordinating tasks and consider modifying it if necessary, so that the structure evolves along with the strategy.

Because the simple structure is inappropriate when a firm grows beyond a certain point, other alternatives must be considered. For such organizations, the structure exists to provide control and coordination for the organization. As such, the structure designates formal reporting relationships and defines the number of levels in the hierarchy.[2] (See Figure 10-1.) There are logical reasons for organizing work along various lines. For example, work can be organized along function so employees can work only in their areas of specialty, by product

FIGURE 10-1 **Security Bank Organization Chart**

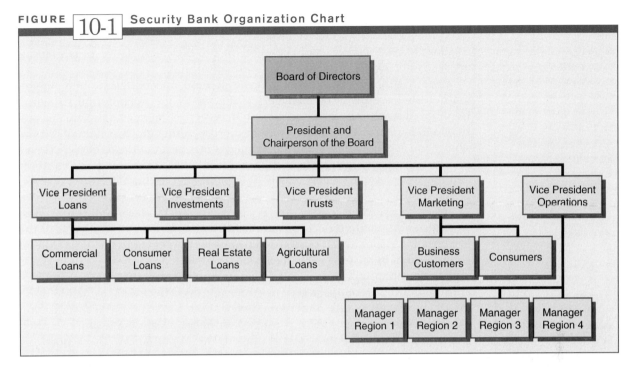

so decisions about products can be made in an integrated fashion, and along geographical lines so decisions can be tailored to unique needs of various geographical regions. It is also reasonable to assume that individuals can and should work across the structure when necessary. Nonetheless, there is no single best structure, and the one selected for any organization will have its own set of benefits and challenges. Interestingly, many large, well-known companies change structures frequently as their environments change.

The extent to which organizational activities are appropriately grouped affects how well strategy is implemented. For instance, customers may be confused when they are contacted by multiple sales representatives for the same company, each representing a different product line. In addition, it is difficult to hold a product divisional manager fully responsible for product sales if this person has little or no control over either the development or the production of the product.

In addition, firms with multiple related businesses usually require greater coordination of their business units' activities than those operating in only one business. However, as an organization becomes more complex, coordinating activities becomes more difficult, especially in organizations with related businesses.

10-1a Vertical Growth

The growth of the organization expands its structure, both vertically and horizontally. **Vertical growth** refers to an increase in the length of the organization's hierarchy (i.e., levels of management). The number of employees reporting to each manager represents that manager's **span of control**. A **tall organization** has

Vertical Growth

An increase in the length of the organization's hierarchical chain of command.

Span of Control

The number of employees reporting directly to a given manager.

Tall Organization

An organization characterized by many hierarchical levels and a narrow span of control.

Flat Organization

An organization characterized by relatively few hierarchical levels and a wide span of control.

Centralization

An organizational decision-making approach whereby most strategic and operating decisions are made by managers at the top of the organization structure (at corporate headquarters).

Decentralization

An organizational decision-making approach in which most strategic and operating decisions are made by managers at the business unit level.

many hierarchical levels and narrow spans of control; a **flat organization** has few levels in its hierarchy and a wide span of control from top to bottom. In reality, organizations fall somewhere in between the two extremes. Hence, organizations are seen as being either relatively tall or relatively flat.

When a structure is marked by **centralization**, most strategic and operating decisions are made by managers at the top of the organization structure. Centralized structures push decisions to managers at higher levels who are presumed to have greater experience and expertise. Although clear lines of responsibility and accountability exist, top managers may lack the hands-on experience that managers have at middle and lower levels. Decision making occurs slowly and the lower-level managers may be less committed to those decisions made at higher levels.

Alternatively, when a structure is characterized by **decentralization**, most strategic and operating decisions are made by managers at lower levels of the organization structure. Decentralized firms seek to overcome the difficulties of centralization by pushing each decision to the lowest level where it can be made effectively. Decentralization can take advantage of the intellectual capital that an organization develops across managerial ranks. Decisions are made more rapidly by managers with direct knowledge about a situation. Decentralization can cloud lines of accountability when poor decisions are made and can often result in poor coordination across units in the organization. These potential disadvantages notwithstanding, it is not difficult to see why many progressive organizations have moved toward greater decentralization in the last two decades.

The extent to which decision making should be decentralized depends on several factors, one of which is organizational size. In general, very large organizations tend to be more decentralized than very small ones, simply because it is difficult for the CEO of a very large company to stay abreast of all of the organization's operations. In addition, firms with large numbers of unrelated businesses tend to be relatively decentralized, whereby corporate-level management determines the overall corporation's mission, goals, and strategy, and lower-level managers make the actual operating decisions. Finally, organizations in dynamic environments must be relatively decentralized so that decisions can be made quickly, whereas organizations in relatively stable environments can be managed more systematically and centrally because change is rather slow and fairly predictable. In such cases, most decisions are routine, and procedures can often be established in advance.

John Child has studied extensively the link between firm size and number of management levels. According to Child, the average number of hierarchical levels for an organization with three thousand employees is seven levels.[3] Consequently, one might consider such an organization with fewer than seven hierarchical levels to be relatively flat, and one with more than seven to be relatively tall. Because tall organizations have a narrow span of control, managers in such organizations exercise a relatively high degree of control over their subordinates, and authority tends to be relatively centralized. Conversely, authority is more decentralized in relatively flat structures because managers have broad spans of control and must therefore grant more flexibility to their employees. Because decisions are more likely to be made at lower levels in flat organizations, it is advisable for employees to have a more generalist orientation.

From a strategic perspective, both organizational types possess certain advantages. Tall, centralized organizations foster more effective coordination and communication of the business's mission and goals to all employees. Planning and its execution are relatively easy to accomplish because all employees are centrally directed. As such, tall organizational structures may be best suited for environments that are relatively stable and predictable, although experts have begun to suggest that tall structures do not yield the same advantages today as they once did.

Flat structures also have advantages. Administrative costs tend to be less than those in taller organizations because fewer hierarchical levels require fewer managers and support personnel. Decentralized decision making also gives managers at various levels more authority, which may increase their satisfaction and motivation.[4] The greater freedom in decision making also encourages innovation. Hence, flat structures are best suited to more dynamic environments, such as those in which most Internet businesses operate. Quality tends to improve when decision making is decentralized closest to the level at which the decisions will be implemented.

Flatter organizations, with relatively few hierarchical levels and wide spans of control, tend to work more effectively in dynamic environments, whereas taller organizations may operate more effectively in stable, predictable environments. Not all of a firm's business units need to adopt the same structure. If some business units operate in relatively dynamic environments while others compete in relatively stable environments, then structural differences may be necessary.

Other factors can also influence the appropriate structure for an organization. Heavy involvement in outsourcing and offshoring is one such factor. Because outsourcing reduces internal activities, it can flatten the structure and increase decision-making speed.[5] Outsourcing can stifle the bureaucracy, enabling firms to concentrate on key strategic concerns such as shortening the cycle time for new products or new models of existing ones.

10-1b Horizontal Growth

Horizontal growth refers to an increase in the breadth of an organization's structure. The owner-manager and a few employees may perform all of the functions in a new business. With growth, however, each function expands so that no one individual can be involved in all of the company's functions, and the structure of the organization is broadened to accommodate the development of more specialized functions. Owner-managers who are unable to let go of former realms of responsibility as their new duties increase are often referred to disparagingly as micromanagers.

Increases in organizational size usually lead to additional organizational layers and bureaucracy. Although large organizations are often presumed to benefit from economies of scale and therefore be more efficient, a large firm may actually become both less efficient and less capable of meeting the needs and expectations of its customers over time. Top management often addresses the burgeoning bureaucracy by instituting a more **horizontal structure**, which has fewer hierarchies. The organizational restructuring so pervasive throughout the 1980s and 1990s has often involved forming a more horizontal structure through **downsizing**, whereby one or more hierarchical levels—typically middle managers—are eliminated. Additionally, employee layoffs often occur in order to cut costs and eliminate some of the bureaucracy that invariably accompanies multiple organizational layers. As layers are reduced, decision making becomes decentralized.

Interestingly, downsizing often fails to achieve desired results, especially in the long term. Studies suggest that approximately 50 percent of downsized

Horizontal Growth

An increase in the breadth of an organization's structure.

Horizontal Structure

An organizational structure with fewer hierarchies designed to improve efficiency by reducing layers in the bureaucracy.

Downsizing

A means of organizational restructuring that often eliminates one or more hierarchical levels from the organization and pushes decision making downward in the organization.

firms actually lower costs, and many of these firms also suffer declines in productivity. When cuts are applied equally to all departments, both efficient and inefficient ones lose employees without regard to performance level. When buyouts are offered to relatively high-paid, longtime employees, the firm can be faced with a drastic loss of critical experience. In addition, the positive changes in the formal organization created by downsizing often lead to dysfunctional consequences in the informal organization. Survivors (i.e., employees who remain after the cuts) are typically less loyal to the organization and wonder if they will be cut next. Hence, downsizing is a viable strategic alternative, but one whose long-term ramifications must be seriously considered before it is adopted.[6]

Firms occasionally seek to downsize for the specific purpose of eliminating part of the workforce so that it can be rebuilt in a different manner. Downsizing may occur after an acquisition if there are substantial cultural differences between the two firms and the acquiring firm wishes to reorient the new combined workforce.

10-2 Structural Forms

This section describes four general alternative structures that may be adopted to meet the strategic needs of the organization. Some structures tend to fit with a certain firm level of competitive strategies, although this relationship is not always clear.

10-2a Functional Structure

Functional Structure

A form of organizational structure whereby each subunit of the organization engages in firm-wide activities related to a particular function, such as marketing, human resources, finance, or production.

The initial growth of an enterprise often requires that it be organized along functional areas. In the **functional structure**, each subunit of the organization engages in firm-wide activities related to a particular function, such as marketing, human resources, finance, or production. (Figure 10-2 illustrates one example of a functional structure.) Managers are grouped according to their expertise and the resources they use in their jobs. A functional structure has certain strategic advantages. Most notably, it can improve specialization and productivity by grouping people who perform similar tasks. When functional specialists interact frequently, improvements and innovations for their functional areas evolve, which may not have otherwise occurred without a mass of specialists organized within the same unit. Working closely on a daily basis with others who share one's functional interests also tends to increase job satisfaction and lower turnover. In addition, the functional structure can foster economies of scale by centralizing functional activities.

FIGURE 10-2 A Partial Example of Functional Structure

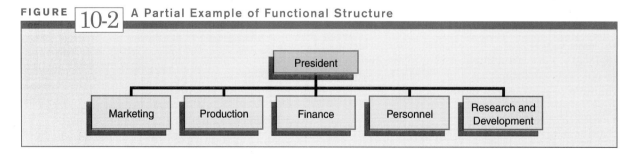

Because of its ability to group specialists and foster economies of scale, this form tends to address cost and quality concerns well. However, the functional structure also has its disadvantages. Because the business is organized around functions rather than around products or geographic regions, pinpointing the responsibility for profits or losses can be difficult. For example, a decline in sales could be directly linked to problems in any number of departments, such as marketing, production, or purchasing. Members of these departments may blame other departments when firm performance declines.

In addition, a functional structure is prone to interdepartmental conflict by fostering a narrow perspective of the organization among its members. Managers in functional organizations tend to view the firm totally from the perspective of their field of expertise. The marketing department might see a company problem as sales related, whereas the human resource department might view the same challenge as a training and development concern. In addition, communication and coordination across functional areas are often difficult because each function tends to have its own perspective and vernacular. R&D, for example, tends to focus on long-term issues, whereas the production department generally emphasizes the short run. Grouping individuals along function minimizes communication across functions and can foster these types of communication problems.

In sum, the functional structure can serve as a relatively effective and efficient means of controlling and coordinating activities. For this reason, it may be appropriate for defenders and low-cost businesses that emphasize efficiency in established markets. The current emphasis, however, is on customer service and speed, challenges that the functional structure may not be as well equipped to address. Depending on the specific issues facing an organization, a division along product or geographical lines may be more appropriate to other businesses.

10-2b Product Divisional Structure

The **product divisional structure** divides the organization's activities into self-contained entities, each responsible for producing, distributing, and selling its own products or services. This structure is often adopted when a business has several distinct product lines. For example, a software developer may organize along three product lines: business, productivity, and educational applications. Each division would have its own functional areas, such as R&D, marketing, and finance. For this reason, the product divisional structure may be most appropriate for diversified firms. This structure is used both in manufacturing and service organizations.

The product divisional structure has certain advantages. Rather than emphasizing functions, the structure emphasizes product lines, resulting in a clear focus on each product category and a greater orientation toward customer service. Pinpointing the responsibility for profits or losses is also easier because each product division becomes a **profit center**, which is a well-defined organizational unit headed by a manager who is accountable for its revenues and expenditures. The product divisional structure is also ideal for training and developing managers because each product manager is, in effect, running his or her own business. Hence, product managers develop general management skills—an end that can be accomplished in a functional structure only by rotating managers from one functional area to another.[7]

The product divisional structure also has its disadvantages. Because product divisional firms generally have multiple departments performing the same

Product Divisional Structure

A form of organizational structure whereby the organization's activities are divided into self-contained entities, each responsible for producing, distributing, and selling its own products.

Profit Center

A well-defined organizational unit headed by a manager accountable for its revenues and expenditures.

function, the total personnel expense for manufacturing is likely to be higher than if only one department were necessary. The coordination of activities at headquarters also becomes more difficult, as top management finds it harder to ensure consistency among the various departments. This problem can become substantial in large organizations with forty or more product divisions. Finally, because product managers emphasize their own product area, they tend to compete for resources instead of working together in the best interest of the company.

10-2c Geographic Divisional Structure

Geographic Divisional Structure

A form of organizational structure in which jobs and activities are grouped on the basis of geographic location .

When a firm's operations are dispersed through various locations, top executives often employ a **geographic divisional structure**, whereby activities and personnel are grouped by specific geographic locations (see Figure 10-3). This structure may be used on a local basis (i.e., a city may be divided into sales regions), on a national basis (i.e., southern region, mid-Atlantic region, Midwest region), or even on an international basis (i.e., North American region, Asian Region, Western European region). The primary impetus for the geographic divisional structure is the existence of two or more distinct markets that can be segmented easily along geographical lines. For this reason, differentiated businesses or those unable to standardize product or service lines because of geographical market differences may implement a geographic divisional structure.

There are two key advantages to organizing geographically. First, products and services may be tailored more effectively to the legal, social, technical, or climatic differences of specific regions. For example, relatively small 220-volt appliances may be appropriate for parts of Asia where living quarters tend to be limited and the American 110-volt system is not used. In addition, insurance companies are often organized along state and national boundaries because of legal differences. Second, producing or distributing products in different locations may give the organization a competitive advantage. Many firms, for example, produce components in countries that have a labor cost advantage and assemble them in countries with an adequate supply of skilled labor.

The disadvantages of a geographic divisional structure are similar to those of the product divisional structure. Often, more functional personnel are required because each region has its own functional departments. Coordination of company-wide functions is often more difficult, and area managers may emphasize their own geographic regions to the exclusion of a company-wide viewpoint.

FIGURE 10-3   A Partial Example of Geographic Divisional Structure

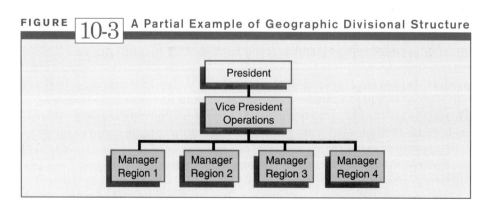

10-2d Matrix Structure

In a general sense, the functional and divisional structures—both product and geographical—can be viewed as opposite ends of a continuum. The traditional demands for quality and price may pull an organization toward the functional end, whereas demands for service and speed may pull the organization toward the divisional end. To address these demands, top managers may settle on one of the two poles or may attempt to position the organization between the extremes. One such approach that has gained considerable popularity in recent years is the matrix structure.

Unlike the other structures that are characterized by a single chain of command, the **matrix structure** is a combination of the functional and product divisional structures (see Figure 10-4). Hence, personnel within the matrix have two (or more) supervisors: a functional boss and a project boss. In one project, a project manager might pull together some members of the organization's functional departments. After the project is completed, the personnel in the project return to their functional departments. Hence, some individuals may be assigned to more that one team at the same time.

Consider that many common organizational tasks require expertise from a variety of backgrounds. Effective new product development requires contributions from such areas as R&D, marketing, and production. Enhancing a

Matrix Structure

A form of organizational structure organized around projects that combines the functional and product divisional structures.

FIGURE 10-4 **Matrix Organizational Structure**

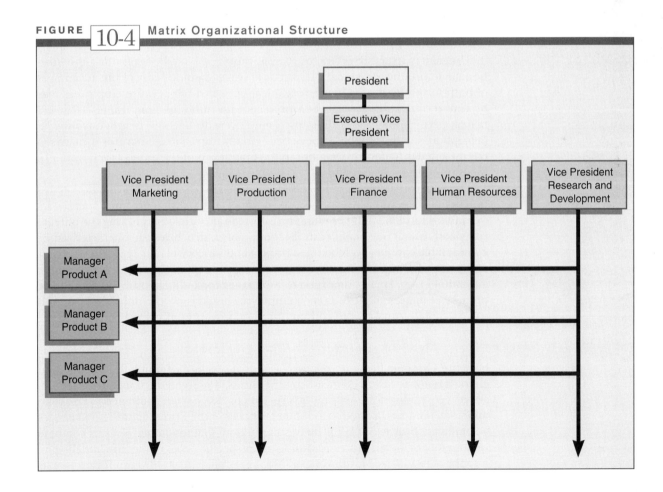

consumer product firm's e-commerce capability requires contributions from information technology, marketing, supply chain management, and merchandising. An initiative to improve customer satisfaction requires expertise in sales, inventory management, and production. The matrix structure is designed to address these multifaceted problems because it pools the necessary expertise required.

The matrix structure is most commonly used in organizations that operate in industries with a high rate of technological change, such as software development, management consulting, medical care, and telecommunications. Because of its complexity, the matrix structure is not as common as the other structures. However, recent developments in network technology have helped managers in many matrix organizations overcome some of the confusion and duplication that can accompany the structure. As such, matrix approaches are likely to continue to expand, especially in industries governed by technology.

A variation to the traditional project form of the matrix structure is reflected in the form of organization pioneered by Procter & Gamble (P&G) in 1927. At P&G, rather than a project manager being in charge of a temporary project, each of P&G's individual products has a **brand manager**. Like a project manager, the brand manager pulls various specialists, as they are needed, from their functional departments. Each brand manager reports to a category manager, who is in charge of all related products in a single category. The category manager coordinates the advertising and sales efforts so that competition among P&G products is minimized. Interestingly, P&G continues to modify its brand management approach as the environment changes, and has recently undergone a shift toward a more global orientation.[8]

The matrix structure offers four key advantages. First, by combining the functional and product divisional structures, a firm can enjoy many of the advantages of both forms. Second, a matrix organization is flexible because employees may be transferred with ease between projects with different time frames. Third, a matrix permits lower-level functional employees to become heavily involved in projects and gain valuable experience. Finally, top management in a matrix is freed from day-to-day involvement in the operations of the enterprise in order to focus on strategic leadership.

The matrix structure also has disadvantages. First, because coordination across functional areas and across projects is so important, matrix personnel spend considerable time in meetings exchanging information, ultimately growing the bureaucracy and raising personnel costs. Second, matrix structures are characterized by considerable conflict, both between project and functional managers over budgets and personnel, and among the project managers themselves over similar resource allocation issues. Finally, reporting to two managers simultaneously violates a basic premise of management (i.e., each employee should report to only one boss) and can create role conflict when different bosses provide conflicting instructions.

10-2e Assessing Organizational Structure

Structures in some firms are relatively easy to assess by examining the organization chart. It is not as easy to delineate in other firms, however. Functional, product divisional, geographic divisional, and matrix structures are often combined to create an approach uniquely tailored to the strategic needs of the firm. (Figure 10-5 illustrates a combination structure.) It is interesting to note that a number of firms combine two or more of the structures according to the specific needs of the firm and the philosophy of its top executives. Yum Brands, for example, has a division for each of its domestic restaurant holdings (e.g., KFC, Pizza Hut, Taco Bell, Long John Silvers, and

---

Brand Manager

The project manager in Proctor & Gamble's version of the matrix structure.

FIGURE 10-5   **A Partial Example of a Combination Structure**

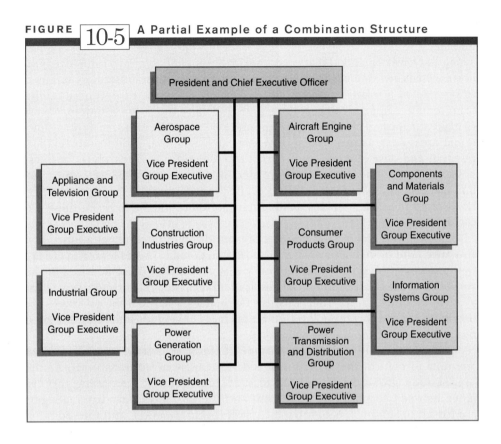

A&W Restaurants). Another division, however, is based on geography and includes units in all three of the restaurant brands located outside the United States. Hence, implementing a single, pure structure is not necessary.

Summarizing the previous sections, the appropriate structure for a given firm can depend on the following factors.

1. Level of corporate involvement in business unit operations
2. Compatibility of the existing structure with the firm- and business-level strategies
3. Number of hierarchical levels in the organization
4. Extent to which the structure permits the appropriate grouping of activities
5. Extent to which the structure promotes effective coordination
6. Extent to which the structure allows for appropriate centralization or decentralization of authority

The next section addresses a philosophical concern that can influence the structure as well.

10-3 Corporate Involvement in Business Unit Operations

Top management philosophy is a key determinant of an organization's structure, especially in large firms with multiple business units. The extent to which corporate managers are involved in business-level operations varies from one firm to another. Involvement is sometimes seen as a stabilizing force and is welcomed by top executives in business units. Some business unit managers, however, refer to "corporate" in a less than positive light and may view such involvement as interference or stifling to progress.

Studies have concluded that corporate involvement can greatly influence business profitability.[9] Some firms have diversified into unrelated businesses and tend to operate in a relatively decentralized fashion, however. In decentralization, firms tend to employ small corporate staffs and allow the business unit managers to make the most of their own strategic and operating decisions, including functional areas such as purchasing, inventory management, production, finance, research and development, and marketing. Alternatively, firms whose business units are in the same industry or in related industries usually follow a centralization pattern, whereby major decisions affecting the business units tend to be made at corporate headquarters. Many corporations operate between these two extremes.

Organizations seeking the benefits of centralization often select a functional structure. The more commonality in those functional activities across the firm's business units, the greater the tendency is to coordinate those activities at the corporate level. Centralization can result in efficiencies and consistencies across all business units. For instance, quantity discounts are larger if the purchases are negotiated at the corporate level for all business units, rather than having each business purchase them separately.

Centralization, however, can also be inefficient, especially when a firm attempts to control the activities of a diverse array of business units. As the organization grows, larger corporate staffs are required, increasing the distance between corporate management and the business units. Top managers are forced to rely increasingly on their staff for information, and they communicate downward to the business units through their staff. These processes can lead to communication and coordination problems, as well as to a proliferation of bureaucracy.

Although synergy among business units may not be minimized, decentralized corporations can often eliminate these problems because highly decentralized firms maintain only skeletal corporate staffs.[10] Many firms seeking the benefits of decentralization organize along a matrix structure. Decisions in matrix structures are typically made by content experts throughout the organization regardless of their management levels. In general, product divisional and geographic divisional structures tend to lie between the functional and matrix structures in terms of centralization and decentralization. Although there is a clear link between structure and degrees of centralization and decentralization, an organization can pursue greater centralization or decentralization within any of the structures.

10-4 Corporate Restructuring

Even after a firm matures, it is uncommon that its structure would stay the same over time. Structures are normally modified from time to time as the firm changes markets, moves into new industries, performs poorly, or hires a new chief executive.

Corporate
Restructuring

A change in the organization's structure to improve efficiency and firm performance.

A major structural change may be considered when an organization is performing well, although it most commonly occurs when performance is poor and the firm is thus pursuing a retrenchment strategy. In this situation, retrenchment is often accompanied by a reorganization process known as corporate restructuring. **Corporate restructuring** refers to a change in the organization's structure to improve efficiency and firm performance. Restructuring efforts can include such actions as realigning divisions in the firm, reducing the amount of cash under the discretion of senior executives, and acquiring or divesting business units.[11] Although corporate restructuring can refer to a simple change in structure—perhaps from a functional approach to a product divisional approach—it often accompanies more aggressive changes as well.

Source: Ablestock.com

Progressive firms restructure when it becomes clear that a change is necessary. Unfortunately, some managers resist change and ultimately may be forced to do so. Firms that *voluntarily* restructure when necessary ordinarily do not have to be concerned with hostile takeover bids or externally forced, *involuntary* restructuring. However, firms that do not manage for value may eventually be forced to restructure by outsiders, a process that is usually more costly.

Even well-known leading companies progress through product and economic cycles that require them to restructure on occasion. Fast-food giant McDonald's, for example, posted a fourth quarter 2002 loss of $344 million, its first in thirty-seven years. The firm responded with a restructuring plan that included fewer new stores, greater product and marketing emphasis on existing outlets, and store closings in 2003 in the United States and Japan, its two largest markets.[12]

When properly executed, minor or major corporate restructuring efforts can enable a firm to execute its strategies more effectively. Structural changes have a downside, however. Actions such as closing or combining offices, eliminating positions, and modifying reporting relationships may not only increase costs for a firm but can also result in other negative effects. Specifically, the concept of restructuring tends to conflict with emphasis on human resources as the key source of a firm's competitive advantage. The job cuts typically associated with restructuring can damage morale, encourage survivors to consider leaving before they are laid off, and place a greater focus on minimizing costs rather than fostering creativity and excellence. Hence, the long-term effects of corporate restructuring—especially downsizing—should be seriously considered before a plan is implemented.[13]

10-5 Summary

Successful strategy implementation requires a fit between strategy and structure. Strategic managers may choose to structure the organization around functions, products, or geography, or they may choose a matrix approach. Each structure has its own advantages and disadvantages.

There are a number of considerations when assessing an organization's structure. In the functional structure, each subunit of the organization engages in firm-wide activities related to a particular function, such as marketing, human resources, finance, or production. The product divisional structure divides the organization's activities into self-contained entities, each responsible for producing, distributing, and selling its own products. When a firm's operations are dispersed through various locations, top executives often employ a geographic divisional structure, whereby activities and personnel are grouped by specific geographic locations. The matrix structure is a combination of the functional and product divisional structures.

Corporate restructuring refers to a change in the organization's structure to improve efficiency and firm performance. Restructuring efforts can include such actions as realigning divisions in the firm, reducing the amount of cash under the discretion of senior executives, and acquiring or divesting business units.

Key Terms

brand manager

centralization

corporate restructuring

decentralization

downsizing

flat organization

functional structure

geographic divisional structure

horizontal growth

horizontal structure

matrix structure

organizational structure

product divisional structure

profit center

simple structure

span of control

tall organization

vertical growth

Review Questions and Exercises

1. What is the difference between a tall organization and a flat organization? What are the advantages and disadvantages of each?

2. What forms of organizational structure are available to strategic managers? What are the primary advantages and disadvantages of each?

3. What is the matrix structure? Why has it become so popular in recent years?

4. What is corporate restructuring?

Practice Quiz

True of False

1. Corporate restructuring is a corporate strategic approach that includes such actions as realigning divisions in the firm, reducing the amount of cash under the discretion of senior executives, and acquiring or divesting business units.

2. A flat organization has many hierarchical levels and narrow spans of control.

3. Horizontal structures have fewer managerial levels than vertical structures.

4. In general, a functional structure tends to be most appropriate for differentiated businesses.

5. Corporate restructuring refers to changes that include modifications in the organizational structure.

6. Progressive firms restructure only when firm performance declines.

Multiple Choice

7. The formal means by which work is coordinated in an organization is called the

   A. organizational structure.

   B. organizational culture.

   C. organizational dynamic.

   D. none of the above

8. An increase in the breadth of an organization's structure is known as

   A. centralization.

   B. decentralization.

   C. horizontal growth.

   D. vertical growth.

9. Which of the following structures tends to be the most centralized?

   A. functional structure

   B. product divisional structure

   C. geographic divisional structure

   D. matrix structure

10. The notion of a profit center is consistent with which form of organizational structure?

   A. functional structure

   B. product divisional structure

   C. geographic divisional structure

   D. matrix structure

11. Which form of organizational structure is actually a combination of two other forms?

   A. functional structure

   B. product divisional structure

   C. geographic divisional structure

   D. matrix structure

12. Which of the following structures tends to be the most decentralized?

   A. functional structure

   B. product divisional structure

   C. geographic divisional structure

   D. matrix structure

Notes

1. M. P. Miles, J. G. Covin, and M. B. Heeley, "The Relationship between Environmental Dynamism and Small Firm Structure, Strategy, and Performance," *Journal of Marketing Theory & Practice* 8(2) (2000): 63–78; G. Duysters and J. Hagedoorn, "Do Company Strategies and Structures Converge in Global Markets? Evidence from the Computer Industry," *Journal of International Business Studies* 32 (2001): 347–356.

2. J. Hagel, "Fallacies in Organizing Performance," *The McKinsey Quarterly* 2 (1994): 97–108; also see J. Child, *Organization: A Guide for Managers and Administrators* (New York: Harper & Row, 1977), 10.

3. Child, *Organization*.

4. L. G. Love, R. L. Priem, and G. T. Lumpkin, "Explicitly Articulated Strategy and Firm Performance under Alternative Levels of Centralization," *Journal of Management* 28 (2002): 611–627.

5. J. B. Quinn, "'Strategic Outsourcing' Leveraging Knowledge Capabilities," *Sloan Management Review* 40(4) (1999): 9–22; J. Heikkila and C. Cordon, "Outsourcing: A Core or Non-Core Strategic Management Decision," *Strategic Change* 11(3) (2002): 183–193.

6. D. Rigby, "Look Before You Lay Off," *Harvard Business Review* 80(4) (2002): 1–2; I. Suarez-Gonzalez, "Downsizing Strategy: Does It Really Improve Organizational Performance?" *International Journal of Management* 18 (2001): 301–307.

7. P. Wright, M. Kroll, and J. A. Parnell, *Strategic Management: Concepts* (Upper Saddle River, NJ: Prentice Hall, 1998).

8. J. Neff, "The New Brand Manager," *Advertising Age* 70(46) (1999): 2–3; B. Dumaine, "P&G Rewrites the Marketing Rules," *Fortune* (6 November 1989): 34–48; A. Swasy, "In a Fast-Paced World, Procter & Gamble Sets Its Store in Old Values," *The Wall Street Journal* (21 September 1989): 1; Z. Schiller, "No More Mr. Nice Guy at P&G—Not by a Long Shot," *Business Week* (3 February 1992): 54–56.

9. For example, S. Chang and H. Singh, "Corporate and Industry Effects on Business Unit Competitive Position," *Strategic Management Journal* 21 (2000): 739–752.

10. S. Hill, R. Martin, and M. Harris, "Decentralization, Integration and the Post-Bureaucratic Organization: The Case of R&D," *Journal of Management Studies* 37 (2000): 563–585; C. Hales, "Leading Horses to Water? The Impact of Decentralization on Managerial Behaviour," *Journal of Management Studies* 36 (1999): 831–851.

11. J. F. Weston, "Restructuring and Its Implications for Business Economics," *Business Economics* (January 1998): 41–46.

12. R. Gibson, "McDonald's Posts a Super-Size Loss, Lowers Growth Goals," *Dow Jones Newswires* (23 January 2003).

13. W. F. Cascio, "Strategies for Responsible Restructuring," *Academy of Management Executive*, 16(3) (2002): 80–91.

Insight from *strategy+business*

Even well-orchestrated plans can fail as a result of poor execution. In recent years, business leaders have begun to pay more attention to problems associated with strategy implementation. This chapter's strategy+business reading highlights many of these problems and provides suggestions for solving them.

The Four Bases of Organizational DNA

Trait by trait, companies can evolve their own execution cultures.

By Gary Neilson, Bruce A. Pasternack, and Decio Mendes

Every economic era has a theme. The 1960s are still recalled as the "Go-Go" years, when Wall Street was fueling mergers and conglomerations of unprecedented scale. The 1990s were the "Internet Boom" years, when a rising economic tide lifted the boat of just about any company with a plausible business model tale to tell. The agonizingly slow recovery since the Internet bubble burst has inspired the latest motif. Executives no longer believe that a strategy—consolidation, transformation, or breakaway—is enough. "We've made the right strategic decision, but my organization isn't motivated or set up right to get on with it," they are saying. "Everyone says they understand the vision, but the businesses and functions just aren't working together to get results."

Welcome to the Era of Execution

Execution has become the new mantra for this first decade of the new millennium. Larry Bossidy, who led AlliedSignal Inc.'s turnaround and its merger with Honeywell International Inc., wrote a book with Ram Charan, titled *Execution: The Discipline of Getting Things Done* (Crown Business, 2002), that's been on the business bestseller lists for more than a year. Former IBM CEO Louis V. Gerstner Jr. put forth the same message in his memoir, *Who Says Elephants Can't Dance? Inside IBM's Historic Turnaround* (HarperBusiness, 2002). In it, he says flatly that the revival of the computer giant wasn't due to vision. "Fixing IBM," he wrote, "was all about execution."

Boards of directors, increasingly impatient with CEOs who don't deliver, have climbed on the execution bandwagon too. Booz Allen Hamilton's annual study of CEO succession trends showed that forced turnover of underperforming CEOs at major corporations reached a new high in 2002,

rising a staggering 70 percent from 2001 and accounting for 39 percent of all chief executive transitions.

But is execution simply a matter of firing the CEO and bringing in a charismatic leader who can get on with "getting things done"? Not at all. Underlying the quest for an execution-driven enterprise is one central question: How does a company design its organization to execute the strategy—whatever the strategy is—and successfully adapt when circumstances change?

Execution is woven deeply into the warp and woof of organizations. It is embedded in the management processes, relationships, measurements, incentives, and beliefs that collectively define the "rules of the game" for each company. Although we often think of companies as monolithic entities, they're not. They're collections of individuals who typically act in their own self-interest. Superior and consistent corporate execution occurs only when the actions of individuals within it are aligned with one another, and with the overall strategic interests and values of the company. Performance is the sum total of the tens of thousands of actions and decisions that, at large companies, thousands of people, at every level, make every day.

Because individual behaviors determine an organization's success over time, the first step in resolving dysfunctions is to understand how the traits of an organization influence each individual's behavior and affect his or her performance. We like to use the familiar metaphor of DNA to attempt to codify the idiosyncratic characteristics of a company. Just as the double-stranded DNA molecule is held together by bonds between base pairs of four nucleotides, who sequence spells out the exact instructions required to create a unique organism, we describe the DNA of a living organization as having four bases that, combined in myriad ways, define an organization's unique traits. These bases are:

Structure. What does the organizational hierarchy look like? How are the lines and boxes in the organization chart connected? How many layers are in the hierarchy, and how many direct reports does each layer have?

Decision Rights. Who decides what? How many people are involved in a decision process? Where does one person's decision-making authority end and another's begin?

Motivators. What objectives, incentives, and career alternatives do people have? How are people rewarded, financially and nonfinancially, for what they achieve? What are they encouraged to care about, by whatever means, explicit or implicit?

Information. What metrics are used to measure performance? How are activities coordinated, and how is knowledge transferred? How are expectations and progress communicated? Who knows what? Who needs to know what? How is information transferred from the people who have it to the people who require it?

Any metaphor can he pushed too far, of course. Although the basic comparison of corporate and human DNA is often invoked in general discussions of institutional culture and conduct, we think it provides a practical framework senior executives can use to diagnose problems, discover hidden strengths, and modify company behavior. With a framework that examines all aspects of a company's architecture, resources, and relationships, it is much easier to see what is working and what isn't deep inside a highly complex organization, to understand how it got that way, and to determine how to change it. (See "Focus: Testing Quest Diagnostics' DNA.")

Structure

In principle, companies make structural choices to support a strategy (for example, the decision to organize business units around customers, products, or geography). In practice, however, a company's organizational structure and strategic intent often are mismatched. The variance can usually he exposed by, in effect, superimposing the organization chart—an efficient communicator of power and status in a firm—over a business unit's strategic plan.

A common structural problem impeding the execution of strategy is the existence of too many management tiers (deep layers), with too many individuals at each tier having too few direct reports (narrow spans). Portrayed graphically, this structure resembles an hourglass. (See Exhibit 1.) Narrower spans in the middle often result from unclear decision rights and the company's mix of motivators. Generally, a structure shaped this way indicates trouble.

There are many reasons a certain management position may legitimately call for a narrower or wider span than another position's. Managers in complex jobs that

EXHIBIT 1 The Hourglass Organization

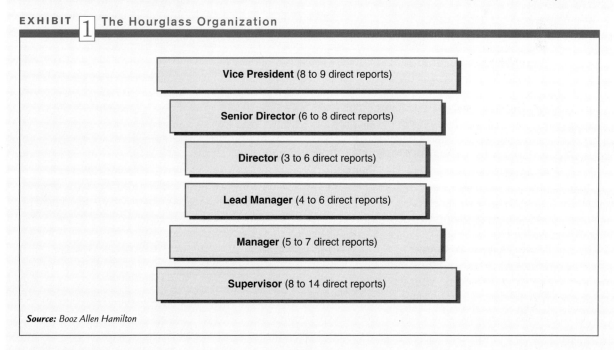

Vice President (8 to 9 direct reports)

Senior Director (6 to 8 direct reports)

Director (3 to 6 direct reports)

Lead Manager (4 to 6 direct reports)

Manager (5 to 7 direct reports)

Supervisor (8 to 14 direct reports)

Source: Booz Allen Hamilton

require them to create and maintain multiple information linkages across individual units cannot handle the same number of direct reports as managers with simpler information aggregation roles. But it's also easy for spans to become too narrow for no legitimate reason.

Consider the spans of control for three senior positions at one consumer goods company with which we have worked. As shown in Exhibit 2, the category/product line manager had five direct reports, compared with seven and 10 reports for senior managers at two best-practice companies. The vice president of sales had six direct reports, versus eight and 10 at the other companies. The manufacturing manager had only seven direct reports; in other companies, similar managers had 11 or more. We have taken this measurement at more than 100 companies, and our data indicates that this company fell well outside the range found at comparable firms.

In our experience, numbers this far off the norm provide strong evidence that a company's spans are narrower than they should be. Often this results in a structure that has too many layers as well. This became evident when we explored how senior managers at the consumer goods company spent their time. About a third of it was devoted to making plans, ensuring target corporate goals were met, and dealing with exceptions and high-impact/high-risk decisions, all appropriate roles for these managers. But they were spending far too much time (roughly 40 percent) justifying and reporting performance to senior executives above them and participating

in tactical, operational decisions with their direct reports. In other words, too much of their time was devoted to second-guessing the work of people below them and preparing reports so that superiors could second-guess their work. They should have been giving more of their time to preparing action plans to achieve the strategic and operational objectives of the company.

This structure kept the consumer goods organization from executing to its potential. Among specific dysfunctions we found:

- Because there were no clear standards that allowed basic decisions to be made at lower levels, decisions regarding such matters as authorization for PC purchases and travel were decided too high in the organization.
- Managers and supervisors tended to discourage their staffs from troubleshooting to resolve routine problems on their own.
- Managers rotated rapidly through jobs, reaching senior positions without sufficient experience. Not only did they require close supervision, but they continually struggled to figure out what they needed to know.
- The company seemed to rapidly promote its best and brightest just so it could retain them. This added unnecessary layers to the hierarchy and created more work at lower levels.
- Large cross-departmental meetings filled the workday. The rationale was to have all parties "in one room to resolve the issues."

All of this activity is costly—these are managers with salaries in the low six figures. Their compensation, plus

EXHIBIT 2 Comparing Spans of Control

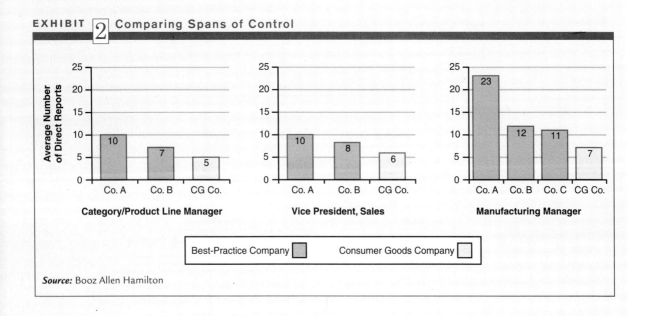

Category/Product Line Manager — Co. A: 10, Co. B: 7, CG Co.: 5

Vice President, Sales — Co. A: 10, Co. B: 8, CG Co.: 6

Manufacturing Manager — Co. A: 23, Co. B: 12, Co. C: 11, CG Co.: 7

Best-Practice Company ☐   Consumer Goods Company ☐

Source: Booz Allen Hamilton

the actual cost of their activities, pushed the company's general and administrative costs to a level that was 20 percent higher than the average of our benchmark companies. Because each of its many layers got involved in almost every decision, the company's speed to market was slowing, and it was losing share to new, more nimble competitors in several categories.

The obvious structural change was to reduce layers and increase spans—that is, to add direct reports to each manager. We recommended a new structure that resulted in a reduction of 10 percent of the positions in the management ranks across all six divisions. Ultimately, with the elimination and repositioning of managers and support staff, about 2,300 management jobs were cut, which saved the company more than $250 million.

Still, simply cutting layers and extending spans would have had little long-term effect if underlying behaviors didn't change. One way the company could do this was by setting clear standards (e.g., which PC to buy and which airline to fly) so high-level managers would not need to review every transaction and provide approvals. With a monthly report, they could easily track exceptions to the standards. Another solution: Reset promotion expectations to slow the upward movement of managers and encourage more horizontal moves—use promotions not just as a reward, but to develop a manager's breadth of experience. Long and cumbersome reporting processes designed to satisfy' the information preferences of each layer and the tremendous desire for detail also had to go. In their place would be a report on the key lagging and leading measures of critical business activity, a top-down setting of targets, and the monitoring of variances. To further dissolve the reflexive addition of layers, the company also had to do more managerial training and communicate better about the change in promotion principles. Following the restructuring and changes in management, time to market for product introductions shrank by months, enabling the company to regain the first-to-market advantage it had traditionally held.

Decision Rights

Decision rights specify who has the authority to make which decisions. Clarifying these rights puts flesh on an organization chart and makes crystal clear where responsibility lies.

Clear decision rights enable wider spans and fewer layers, which translates into lower costs and speedier execution. Unarticulated decision rights are more than a time sink; they're a central cause of substandard performance—and

even of nonperformance. An employee at a financial-services company expressed this problem quite concretely in a focus group we conducted, saying, "Responsibilities are blurred intentionally around here so everyone has an excuse for not getting involved."

At one industrial company, we found yet again that senior executives were spending too much time reviewing small projects. It turned out the company had not reassessed managers' spending-approval limits in more than 10 years. We suggested the authorization process be adjusted so that managers lower in the organization could be accountable for the final approval of more projects. The capital expenditure amount requiring CEO authorization was raised from $5 million to $15 million. The objective was to free up senior managements time to focus on the longer-term issues associated with market growth and potential acquisitions. Based on historical analysis, it was determined that raising the level at which projects required CEO authorization to $15 million would reduce the number of projects crossing the CEO's desk by 49 percent. All large projects would still come to the CEO, so the aggregate value of projects approved at the top would decline by only 13 percent.

Decision rights become blurred for many reasons, not all of them intentional. After a large industrial company completed a leveraged buyout, the management of one of its business units became the new entity's corporate management, charged with reviewing the operating decisions of all business units. That change required every level of management to take on greater decision-making responsibility—an unnatural act for executives accustomed to hands-on involvement in operating unit decisions. Rather than allow their general managers to make basic decisions about product design and resource allocation, the CEO and COO still involved themselves deeply in these activities. Meanwhile, they were neglecting other areas where their attention was expected, notably strategic planning, long-range business portfolio decisions, and the firm's financial condition.

The solution was to create a process for corporate officers to delegate decisions to the business unit's general managers. An executive committee was established to review business unit decisions, and several general managers were charged with integrating marketing, product engineering, and manufacturing. These structures and processes made effective delegation possible.

It doesn't take a leveraged buyout to distort a company's decision-rights structure. People naturally lean toward the familiar when faced with change. Executives promoted to new positions often cling to their prior responsibilities, burdening themselves with unnecessary tasks and disempowering their subordinates. The press of the urgent at the business unit level drives out the important at the corporate level. The lesser decisions seem concrete and knowable. Forward thinking and big decisions regarding long-term direction seem undefined, amorphous, and tougher to tackle.

Often the process of assigning decision rights is a response to a crisis or a shift in political power. When this happens, decisions can fall between the cracks. Or they can be made twice by different parties. Or they can be reviewed repeatedly, becoming a Sisyphean exercise in backsliding.

It is possible to assign decision rights systematically and rationally. At a global industrial company, we helped create an organizational matrix of functions, products, and geographies. The structure was under-girded by a set of specific organizational and decision-making principles, among them: responsibility does not imply exclusive Authority; different units should have joint goals and performance measures; and certain positions need to report upward to multiple managers.

Over several months, we worked with the company to apply these and several other principles to more than 300 critical decisions. Because we undertook this effort explicitly while also changing the structure, the company was able to execute its new strategy faster, and with fewer missteps. The overall change process took two years (one less than had been anticipated). The company returned to profitability, reduced its net debt by the targeted amount, and reached several other critical financial goals a year ahead of schedule.

Making decision rights explicit in companies in which they are not requires management to set rules for the most common business situations—and for each position. In effect, the company is creating a constitution that says who will decide what and under what circumstances.

The decision rights of groups must also be clear. At a consumer goods company, we saw large numbers of executives meeting frequently to resolve conflicts among functional units. It appeared that operations, finance, and marketing were each doing an excellent job of analyzing new factories, new products, and new business opportunities, but they weren't talking to one another along the way. Operations planned the perfect factory—without guidance from finance on the cost. In marathon meetings, managers from each function brought their independent analyses

together. Then they struggled to reach a joint conclusion, because each unit, by that time, was wedded to its own recommendation.

To solve this silo problem, one top executive was made responsible for managing a cross-functional team, so there would always be communication across disciplines. As a result, only a few top executives were needed to make routine decisions, and the company reduced dedicated staff support for these efforts by more than 30 percent.

Motivators

The third of the four bases in a company's DNA-like makeup involves motivation. Employees generally don't deliberately act counterproductively; they don't try to derail a company's strategy. Rather, they respond quite rationally on the basis of what they see, what they understand, and how they're rewarded. An exhortation to follow the vision and pursue the strategy is only so much air if the organization's incentives and information flows make it difficult for employees to understand and do what they're supposed to do.

An organization can send confusing signals to individuals in many ways. Think about what happens when an appraisal system inflates performance ratings. At a consumer goods company we once worked with, employees were appraised on a 1 to 10 scale. Eighty percent received a rating of 9 or above, and everyone felt good. But superior employees didn't feel they needed to do any better. Other workers thought their performance was acceptable when it wasn't. Appraisers were avoiding the unpleasant task of delivering bad performance ratings, and the organization wasn't giving them any reason to be tough. For every deficient employee who stayed at the company because the organization said he or she was competent, the company's execution suffered. Because of its unwillingness to differentiate people's contributions through performance assessments and raises, the company lost the opportunity to send important feedback to employees on what was relevant to executing the strategy—and where their performance was unsatisfactory.

Several years ago we worked with the new CEO of a technology company who had been the head of a business unit and had served for several years on the executive committee that made investment decisions. The new CEO knew from experience that the committee wasn't tough enough on new investment requests. They were a collegial group; members supported their colleagues' investment requests with the understanding their own requests would be supported in return.

The new CEO wanted a more discriminating process that would judge investment proposals on their merits. He also knew executive committee members faced little downside from approving unsound investment requests. Future bonuses might suffer if company performance wasn't good, but that money wasn't already in their pockets.

So the CEO introduced a new system to change this attitude: Each committee member was required to take out a personal loan of $1 million and invest it in company stock (the loan was guaranteed by the company, so the individuals could borrow at good rates). Unlike an outright stock grant, this scheme ensured that the executives had existing wealth at risk, and that they would lose money, and perhaps the ability to repay the debt, if they permitted poor investment decisions. With this new incentive to scrutinize investment requests, the committee became much tougher and more effective. And after a few sessions, teams began bringing better-researched and smarter investment proposals to the table because they knew if they didn't, the committee was likely to turn them down.

There are other market mechanisms that can be used to send more accurate signals to managers about the cost and value of certain activities. This approach was used successfully at a large agribusiness company that came to us for help in improving the services of its human resources department. The HR department's performance had always been judged by how well it stayed on budget. Internal customer satisfaction was rarely measured. Each customer was allocated a share of the HR budget, but these figures didn't represent the true cost of the services. Meanwhile, customers had little influence on the kind and amount of services they received. Neither HR nor its customers had an incentive to offer or ask for services tailored to the specific needs of a division.

Working with the company, we created a scorecard to measure HR performance on such things as call center response time and payroll errors. Achieving scorecard targets became a significant component of management incentives and rewards. HR's internal customers were given the right to negotiate service level agreements with HR. The true cost of services was established using outside benchmarks. Once HR's customers understood what they were paying for and could better manage their costs, they had an incentive to use HR services more wisely. Today, they often decline or reduce some services and request new ones. The market-based measurement and incentive program improved the quality of the company's HR services and reduced costs by more than 15 percent.

Organizations that are ready to implement multiple profit-and-loss statements and market-based motivational systems will find that these powerful new tools can help them operate effectively with less command-and-control oversight. But not all companies are ready for these systems; it takes strong leadership, persistence, and patience to introduce them and overcome employee resistance to using them.

Information

Underlying a company's ability to ensure clear decision rights and to measure and motivate people to apply them is one critical matter: information.

Making sure high-quality information is available and flowing where it needs to go throughout a company, all the time, is among the most challenging tasks of the modern corporation, and one of the most under-appreciated contributors to high performance and competitive advantage. A 2002 study of the management and financial performance of 113 Fortune 1000 companies over the five-year period 1996 to 2000, conducted by Booz Allen Hamilton and Ranjay Gulati of the Kellogg School of Management at Northwestern University, found that the companies with the highest shareholder returns were more focused on managing and enhancing communication with their customers, suppliers, and employees than other firms in the study.

We have seen this information-performance linkage often in practice. A few years ago, the board of an agricultural grower and processor became concerned about the company's operating efficiency. Among other problems, farm managers were using equipment without discipline—ordering a machine at will, driving it hard, and returning it with an empty gas tank, all because headquarters was responsible for maintenance and replacement costs. Our benchmark data indicated that this company's expenses were far higher than those of independent farms. We worked with corporate and farm management to develop a new business model, centered on turning each farm into an independent business. For this to happen, farm managers needed new information—specifically, individual farm P&Ls that reflected, among many other things, the cost of the equipment they used. The redesigned organization executed more efficiently, as reflected in a 48 percent jump in its imputed share price in the first year.

Better information flows did more than keep costs down; they helped allocate scarce resources far more efficiently than before. The company had a silo problem—literally and figuratively. Any field ready for harvest had a peak yield window of about 15 days. But there was only so much mill capacity during the peak window. Coordinating and timing the harvesting and milling activities fell to a hapless employee at headquarters, a central planner who relied on historical data that didn't reveal much about current conditions.

We showed in a simulation that if farm managers could bid for use of the mill on particular dates, it would strikingly improve the company's efficiency. If a manager saw that his highest-yielding acreage was ready to harvest and couldn't wait because rain was predicted, he could bid more for mill time. No longer would someone back at headquarters have to hunker down with a spreadsheet, making educated guesses based on the previous year's yield data and taking frantic phone calls from farm managers. Market-based pricing of mill time would allocate scarce resources better than a central planner could. And with this new system, decisions would reflect the real-time knowledge of the farmer in the field observing the sky, testing the ripeness of the crop, hour by hour, acre by acre.

Adaptive DNA

Although we have illustrated the four bases of organizational DNA separately to emphasize their distinct characteristics, they clearly are intertwined. Changing structure requires changing decision rights; to make effective decisions, employees need new incentives and different information. At the agricultural grower and processor, the new structure touched each of these elements—the individual farm as a business required new decision authority for farm managers, new metrics by which to measure their performance, and new rewards based on their individual success. This interdependency is evident in all of these company stories.

Considering—and changing—a company's DNA holistically means weaving intelligence, decision-making capabilities, and a collective focus on common goals widely and deeply into the fabric of the organization so that each person and unit is working smartly—and working together. It's one thing to achieve well-coordinated

intelligence among senior executives. It's another thing entirely to touch every level of an organization all the way down to the loading dock. What every employee does every day, aggregated across the company, constitutes performance.

The best organizational designs are adaptive, are self-correcting, and become more robust over time. But creating such an organization doesn't happen quickly; it can take several years to get the basics right, and there is always a need for fine-tuning. This may explain why leaders of companies that are truly ailing—and who need to reassure shareholders as fast as they can—often don't have the patience for changing decision rights, motivators, and information flows. They're more likely to cut the structure and see what happens than to take time to ensure that structural changes actually result in sustained productivity improvements and steady gains in shareholder value. But neglecting this hard work may also partly explain why some of these CEOs are no longer in charge.

No company may ever totally master the enigma of execution. But the most resilient and consistently successful ones have discovered that the devil is in the details of organization. For them, organizing to execute has truly become a competitive edge.

Focus: Testing Quest Diagnostics' DNA

DNA testing can be as valuable to corporate health as it has become to human health care. An analysis of a company's "genetic material" can isolate the underlying causes of and potential solutions to organizational dysfunctions, and even head off problems before they start.

Consider the case of the U.S.-based medical laboratory testing company Quest Diagnostics. Originally a division of Corning Incorporated, Quest Diagnostics grew in the 1990s through the acquisition of hundreds of small independent testing laboratories. Spun off from Corning in 1997, the company was losing money and battling fines for billing fraud and other abuses in a number of the laboratories it had bought. Chairman and CEO Ken Freeman, then the newly appointed leader of Quest Diagnostics, recognized that the DNA of an enterprise formed by the union of so many different entities, each born in a different time and place, with many different parents, could readily become a monster. So he was determined to focus his attention on improving organizational DNA across the entire company.

Immediately after the spin-off, Mr. Freeman and his top management team took control of key decision rights to ensure that the company's turnaround effort was coherent and driven hard. When the company acquired SmithKline Beecham Clinical Labs in August 1999, they again deliberately centralized decision rights among a small senior team. A set of integration teams headed by the leaders of both companies methodically worked through the long-term vision and short-term tactics for each area of the new company, again, to ensure consistency across the enterprise. The financial payoff was immediate: Prior to the deal, revenues had typically declined upward of 20 percent following a major acquisition. In this case, Quest Diagnostics not only didn't lose business, revenues grew at or above industry growth rates during the integration process. This was the first time such postmerger growth occurred in the industry.

As Quest Diagnostics' turnaround progressed, decision rights were decentralized gradually, first by placing supervisors into various units who led change and taught employees new behaviors, and then by empowering front-line staff. Although many parts of the Quest Diagnostics organization are now high performers and largely self-directed, it has taken seven years to get there.

Today when Quest Diagnostics acquires a company, Mr. Freeman and his team concentrate on two of the four organizational bases, *motivators* and *information*, recognizing their interdependency and combined influence on individual and organizational behavior. Among the first "gene therapies" they perform is to introduce a comprehensive and varied set of metrics that go well beyond the typical financial performance measures that most companies use. There are measures for customer retention, the time it takes to pick up a call in the call center, the time it takes to process a specimen in the labs, employee satisfaction and attrition rates, and more. The system is designed so that all employees know how they can personally influence one or more core performance measures.

The only way this information can influence the day-to-day behavior and decisions of employees throughout the organization is if decision makers have the information on hand when they need it. Quest Diagnostics posts various metrics on different timetables depending on the type of management issue: Customer retention metrics are posted at least once a month; specimen turnaround time is posted every morning.

Finally, the company ties these metrics to individuals' bonus payments so that information not only informs, but also motivates productive behavior. Since virtually everyone in the company can affect customer retention in some way, Quest Diagnostics uses the customer retention metric very broadly in its performance-based compensation programs. Ultimately, the bonuses of all 37,000 Quest Diagnostics employees depend in some way on meeting the customer retention target.

"If we have a shared goal that says we're going to reduce customer attrition, that doesn't mean it is only for people in sales. It impacts people picking up the specimens, people who draw and perform tests on the specimens, and certainly people in billing. If there are lots of complaints, the customer is going to leave. By having shared goals, you get speed and alignment," says Mr. Freeman.

To make the motivators as specific and powerful as possible, customer retention metrics are measured not just organization-wide. They are divided up by region, so that people are paid on the basis of customer retention performance in their own region, where they can have the greatest influence.

The aligning and motivating power of bringing information and incentives together is reflected in the firm's strong financial performance. Since Quest Diagnostics was spun off from Corning in 1997, the company's stock price has increased 730 percent, compared with a 41 percent increase in the S&P 500 Index during the same period. Having successfully carried out a classic turnaround and taken the lead in consolidating the industry, Quest Diagnostics is now driving growth organically and has become the clear leader in the U.S. medical laboratory testing market. Last year, the company earned $322 million on $4.1 billion in revenues.

–G.N., B.A.P., and D.M.

Resources

Jeffrey W. Bennett, Thomas E. Pernsteiner, Paul F. Kocourek, and Steven B. Hedlund, "The Organization vs. the Strategy: Solving the Alignment Paradox," *s+b* Fourth Quarter 2000; www.strategy-business.com/press/article/14114

Paul F. Kocourek, Steven Y. Chung, and Matthew G. McKenna, "Strategic Rollups: Overhauling the Multi-Merger Machine," *s+b*, Second Quarter 2000; www.strategy-business.com/press/article/16858

Chuck Lucier, Rob Schuyr, and Eric Spiegel, "CEO Succession 2002: Deliver or Depart," *s+b*, Summer 20003; www.strategy-business.com/press/article/21700

Gary Neilson, David Kletter, and John Jones, "Treating the Troubled Corporation," *s+b enews*, 03/28/03; www.strategy-business.com/press/enewsarticle/22230

Randall Rothenberg, Larry Bossidy: The Thought Leader Interview," *s+b*, Third Quarter 2002; www.strategy-business.com/press/article/20642

Michael C. Jensen, *Foundations of Organizational Strategy* (Harvard University Press, 1998)

Gary Neilson (neilson_gary@bah.com) is a senior vice president with Booz Allen Hamilton in Chicago. He works on the development of new organizational models and designs, restructuring, and the leadership of major change initiatives for Fortune 500 companies across industries.

Bruce A. Pasternack (pasternack_bruce@bah.com) is a senior vice president with Booz Allen Hamilton in San Francisco. He counsels companies in building strategic agendas, developing organizations, and transforming business models. He has published widely on leadership and organizational issues.

Decio Mendes (mendes_decio@bah.com) is a senior associate with Booz Allen Hamilton based in New York. He works with clients to improve organizational effectiveness and operations efficiency.

Strategy Execution: Strategic Change, Culture, and Leadership

11

Chapter Outline

When a new strategy is executed, an old one is discarded. The strategic change that occurs as a result is not always easy to direct. Managing strategic change can be a difficult task even when everyone agrees that it is needed and understands what will occur as a result. Even so, techniques to institutionalize the change must be developed. Barriers and resistance to change should be recognized so that strategies can be developed to overcome them.

Executing a strategy can become quite challenging, especially when a strategic change of great magnitude is involved. When the environment changes rapidly or abruptly, progressive firms take steps to capitalize on new opportunities and minimize negative effects of the changes.[1] Change can be brought about by factors such as the need to address increased competition, improve quality or service, reduce costs, or align the firm with the practices and expectation of its partners. Strategic change can be revolutionary, such as when a firm changes its product lines, markets, or channels of distribution. Strategic change can also be less radical, such as when a firm overhauls its production system to improve quality and lower its costs of operations.

Because changing strategies is often cumbersome, it may not be desirable even when changes in the macroenvironment and industry suggest problems for the current strategy. Shifting the strategic intent may confuse customers and employees, may require structural changes in the organization, and can result in major capital investments. In short, costs associated with a major strategic change are not always justified by the benefits.[2]

Evaluating the appropriateness of strategic change is a complex process. Consider several examples. In 2003, McDonald's faced its first quarterly loss as a public company. Rather than increase its efforts to market inexpensive products to children, the burger giant responded with higher priced items such as the $4.50 California Cobb salad and the $3.89 grilled chicken club sandwich, all the while retaining its dollar menu with items such as double cheeseburgers, chicken sandwiches, and side salads. As a result, revenue increased 33 percent from 2002 to 2005, while profits more than doubled. McDonald's also responded with a more aggressive approach to new product development instead of relying on its franchises to generate ideas, a slow process that led to the Big Mac in 1968, the Egg McMuffin in 1973, and the Happy Meal in 1979. The firm hired chef Dan Coudreaut as director of culinary innovation in 2004, a decision that led to the successful Asian salad and the value-priced snack wrap in 2006.[3]

Frequent strategic shifts have occurred in the airline industry since the early 2000s. Southwest Airlines has reported profits every year since its inception, fueled by a consistent reliance on low costs, no frills, and low fares. In the early 2000s, however, younger low-cost carriers such as JetBlue, Frontier, and America West experienced more rapid growth, thanks in part to a greater emphasis on factors such as entertainment, food service, and first-class seating. In late 2003, Southwest announced it would begin flying into Philadelphia—a hub for U.S. Airways—in 2004, a move signaling a possible shift from the airline's historical avoidance of busy airports ruled by major carriers.

Southwest made another similar jump when it moved into Denver International Airport in January 2006, where airport fees average around $9 per passenger as opposed to the industry average of $5. Southwest had avoided such costly airports in the past and now faces intense price competition there with Denver-based low-cost carrier Frontier Airlines, and some extent from United Airlines, which controls over half of the Denver market.[4] Some analysts believed that this strategic change marked the beginning of a departure from Southwest's strict low-cost position.[5] Others believe that Southwest's growth and success in the early 2000s, coupled with intense competition from low-price upstarts, has begun to erode Southwest's cost advantage. In an effort to remain strong, Southwest CEO Gary Kelly argues that airlines must compete daily for every customer, embrace change in the marketplace, and remember that price alone is not sufficient to generate customer loyalty.[6]

As upstarts begin to resemble their veteran counterparts, their strategies often shift as well. Budget carrier JetBlue, for example, went public in 2002 and passed the $1 billion revenue mark in 2004. In 2005, CEO David Neeleman announced plans to expand its fleet from 80 airplanes to 275 by the end of 2010.[7] As niche players like Southwest and JetBlue grow and lose their emphasis on focus, openings are created for new competitors to fill gaps they leave unserved. In 2007, upstart ExpressJet entered the scene, focusing on point-to-point service across twenty-four midsize cities where such service currently does not exist. ExpressJet maintains modest costs but offers free snacks, sandwiches, and cold pasta dishes, as well as new leather seats and satellite radio. By utilizing a fleet of fifty-seat Embraer jets, ExpressJet hopes to fill a void too small to attract major carriers with larger aircraft.[8]

Strategic change in the airline industry has not been limited to modest size carriers and upstarts. In 2006, United Airlines made a strategic shift that parted course with its large U.S. counterparts. Instead of seeking profits by cutting costs and service, United retained and even enhanced services—such as roomier seats—deciding to focus on increased revenues instead of lower expenses. United management hopes that this shift will enable the carrier to distinguish itself from the other major carriers.[9]

Strategic change of a great magnitude can be difficult to implement (see Strategy at Work 11-1). Employees resist change for a variety of reasons, including personal factors, lack of information about the change, and poor design of the support system. Simply stated, strategic change is easier said than done. For example, Home Depot launched a major effort in the early 2000s to eliminate store clutter and enhance customer service. Instead of finding sales associates eager to help them with their purchase decisions, customers were tripping over wooden pallets and dodging forklifts. Employees are now barred from stocking shelves and operating forklifts during key shopping hours. These changes resulted in improved customer service vis-à-vis rival Lowe's.[10]

The decision whether to institute a strategic change can be difficult. This chapter discusses two key areas associated with executing strategic change: organizational culture and leadership. Both dimensions must be aligned with the strategy and be managed properly if a strategy is to be implemented effectively.

11-1 Organizational Culture and Strategy

Strategic decisions rendered by top management should be consistent with the culture of the organization. **Organizational culture** refers to the shared values and patterns of belief and behavior that are accepted and practiced by the members of a particular organization.[11] It includes accepted work practices and traditions, and defines how managers and workers treat each other and can expect to be treated. It fosters peer pressure that encourages members of the organization to behave in certain ways.

Organizational Culture

The shared values and patterns of belief and behavior that are accepted and practiced by the members of a particular organization.

Decades of Strategic Change at Sears

Sears was arguably the most successful U.S. retailer until the entire retail industry began to undergo dramatic changes in the late 1970s. The Sears private-label business was eroded by the growing popularity of specialty retailers such as Circuit City, and its once low-cost structure was decimated by Wal-Mart.

The retailer's response to these changes has not always been consistent. Initially, Sears reacted by attempting to emphasize fashion with such labels as Cheryl Tiegs sportswear, but high-fashion models were not consistent with the Sears middle-America image. Sears then attempted to convert its antiquated image into a financial supermarket by purchasing Dean Witter Financial Services and Coldwell Banker Real Estate. However, in-store kiosks never caught on with customers, and the expected synergy between these two subsidiaries and the Sears Allstate Insurance and Discover Card business units failed to materialize.

Next, management modified the store's image to one that sold nationally branded merchandise along with private-label brands at "everyday low prices." The idea was to create individual superstores within each of the Sears outlets to compete more effectively with powerful niche competitors. Sears departed from its traditional practice of holding weekly sales to save on advertising expenses and inventory handling while offering new low prices, which turned out to be, in some cases, higher than old sale prices. By this time, customers were totally confused. In 1992 alone, Sears lost almost $4 billion, its worst performance ever.

In 1993, Sears terminated its big catalog operations, began spinning off some of its businesses unrelated to general merchandising, overhauled its clothing lines, eliminated more than 93,000 jobs, and closed 113 stores. In 1995, Sears reentered the catalog business. This time, instead of a big book Sears catalog, it set up joint ventures

to provide smaller catalogs. Sears provides its name and its 24 million credit card customers. Its partners select the merchandise, mail catalogs, and fill orders.

By 1996, Sears had begun to benefit from its strategic shift to moderately priced apparel and home furnishings. In 1999, Sears branched out further, developing "The Great Indoors" to attract women to the traditionally male-dominated home improvement market. This format was in response to the fragmented nature of the home remodeling business, particularly on the higher end where services such as decorating and installation are often involved. The format targeted as its primary customers women age thirty to fifty years old earning in the $50,000 range.

In late 2001, Sears announced another strategic shift designed to position the firm as a solid, even more discount-oriented retailer. The company announced the elimination of a substantial number of cashiers and other employees, the integration of centralized checkouts, and shifts in the product mix, all designed to improve efficiency in the stores.

In late 2002, Sears acquired Lands' End, a leading marketer of traditionally designed clothing and related products. By the mid-2000s, Sears had incorporated the brand into its retail outlets. Sears was acquired by Kmart in early 2005 for $11 billion, marking the beginning of a new chapter in its strategy. Financial difficulties for the newly combined firm in 2007 point to another restructuring effort in the late 2000s.

Sources: E. Scardino, "Sears Looking for the Best Fit," DSN Retailing Today, 23 February 2004; "Sears Retrenches for the Future: Retailer's Makeover Includes Layoffs and a Discount Image," National Home Center News, 19 November 2001; "Home Goods Concept Anchors Multi-Format Strategy," DSN Retailing Today, 11 December 2000, 49; K. Hutchison, "Sears to Announce Long-Term Plans, Creating Buzz among Many Analysts," DSN Retailing Today, 22 October 2001, 2–3; A. Ward, "Sears 'On Course' Despite Hard Retail Conditions, CEO Says," Wall Street Journal Interactive Edition, 9 May 1996; K. Fitzgerald, "Sears, Ward's Take Different Paths," Advertising Age, 31 July 1995, 27.

Because each organization develops its own unique culture, even organizations within the same industry and city will exhibit distinctly different ways of functioning. The organizational culture enables a firm to adapt to environmental changes and to coordinate and integrate its internal operations.[12] Ideally, the values that define a firm's culture should be clear, easy to understand by all employees, embodied at the top of the organization, and reinforced over time.

Subculture

A culture within a broader culture.

Cultures not only form at the organizational level, but also within the organizational culture. These organizational **subcultures** can develop around such factors as location, functional responsibility, or managerial level. Cultural similarities among sales representatives at an organization, for example, typically differ from those among production workers.

The first and most important influence on an organization's culture is its founder. Some founders have strong beliefs about business practice or have strict procedures for transacting affairs. Their assumptions about success—as well as those of other early top managers—form the foundation of the firm's culture.[13] For instance, the primary influence on McDonald's culture was the fast-food company's founder, Ray Kroc. Although he passed away in 1984, his philosophy of fast service, assembly-line food preparation, wholesome image, cleanliness, and devotion to quality are still central facets of the organization's culture.[14]

Whether the founder or not, a firm's CEO also plays a significant role in its culture. JCPenney CEO Mike Ullman, for example, has taken steps to loosen up the retailer's stodgy culture since joining the firm in 2004. Specifically, Ullman targeted the stringent code of conduct and in-house hiring requirements that he believed increased turnover and made recruiting more difficult. During Ullman's tenure, JCPenney replaced its art collection with employee photos and began to emphasize the use of first names and business-casual attire, including jeans on Friday.[15]

Views and assumptions concerning an organization's distinctive competence comprise one of the most important elements of culture, particularly in new organizations. For example, historically, innovative firms are likely to respond to a sales decline with new product introductions, whereas companies whose success is based on low prices may respond with attempts to lower costs even further.[16] However, it is possible to modify the culture over time as the environment changes, rendering some of the firm's culture obsolete and even dysfunctional. New elements of the culture must be added as the old elements are discarded.

Stories are also an important component of culture. Whether true or fabricated, accounts and legends of organizational members can have a great influence on present-day actions of managers and workers alike. UPS employees tell stories of drivers who go the extra mile through adverse weather to deliver packages on time. Microsoft employees retell stories of programmers who work long hours to meet demanding production schedules. These stories create expectations and can inspire workers to perform similar feats in their daily jobs.

Organizational culture can facilitate or hinder the firm's strategic actions. Studies have shown that firms with strategically appropriate cultures, such as PepsiCo, Wal-Mart, and Shell, tend to outperform other corporations whose cultures do not fit as well with their strategies. A strategy-culture fit can support strategy execution because the activities required from middle managers and others in the organization are consistent with what is already taking place. When the strategy does not fit with the culture, it is necessary to change one or both. For example, a firm caught in a changing environment may craft a new strategy that makes sense from financial, product, and marketing points of view. Yet the strategy may not be implemented because it requires significant changes in assumptions, values, and ways of working.[17] All things considered, changing a strategy is easier than changing culture, and both are often required for organizations to be successful.[18]

For many firms, achieving a strategy-culture fit means creating an **adaptive culture** whereby members of an organization are willing and eager to embrace any change that is consistent with the core values.[19] Such a culture values taking initiative and risk; exhibiting creativity, trust, and employee involvement; and desiring continuous, positive organizational change. Adaptive cultures are especially important for firms that emphasize high growth or innovation (e.g., prospectors), as well as

Adaptive Culture

A culture whereby members of an organization are willing and eager to embrace any change that is consistent with the core values.

Innovation

Developing something new.

Inert Culture

A conservative culture that encourages maintenance of existing resources.

Strong Culture

A culture characterized by deeply rooted values and ways of thinking that regulate firm behavior.

Weak Culture

A culture that lacks values and ways of thinking that are widely accepted by members of the organization.

Diversity

The extent to which individuals within an organization are different.

those operating in turbulent environments. Adaptive cultures encourage initiative and emphasize **innovation**—developing something new—whereas **inert cultures** are conservative and encourage maintenance of existing resources. For companies such as Google and eBay, an adaptive culture is an essential part of their success.

11-1a Cultural Strength and Diversity

Some cultures influence firm activities more than others. A **strong culture** is characterized by deeply rooted values and ways of thinking that regulate firm behavior. Top managers model that behavior and create peer pressure that reinforces the notion that others in the organization should behave likewise. Strong cultures develop over time, generally a decade or longer.

A strong culture that embodies appropriate values can be a valuable resource for a firm, especially when it reinforces values inherent in the organization's strategies. Effective strategy execution occurs when all facets of the organization, including the culture, mesh. Effectiveness is then likely to increase when a firm's strategy and culture reinforce each other.[20] JCPenney's strong culture grounded in its key principles on ethics and customer orientation has contributed to its success and survival as a leading U.S. retailer for over a hundred years.[21]

Conversely, when a strong culture is unhealthy and embodies destructive characteristics, it can strain firm performance. For example, such characteristics include a strong emphasis on politics to get things done, a disregard for ethical standards, territorialism among departments, and strong resistance to change. Needless to say, strong dysfunctional cultures can hinder organizational performance.[22]

Unlike a strong culture, a **weak culture** lacks values and ways of thinking that are widely accepted by members of the organization. There is no clear, widely accepted business philosophy, and managers approach their responsibilities in different ways. In general, this lack of cultural consensus does not support strategy execution.

A concept related to the notion of strong and weak cultures is **diversity**, the extent to which individuals within an organization are different. People today commonly speak of the need to pursue diversity as a means of competitive advantage. The term *diversity* can be defined in several ways, however. Some use it to reference differences over which individuals clearly have no choice, such as age, race, ethnicity, gender, and physical disability. Others extend this definition to include differences over which individuals may have control, such as marital status, religion, and sexual preference.[23] Still others use the term simply to reference differences in ways of thinking.

Research linking diversity and performance is largely inconclusive, however, in part because of competing conceptualizations of what it means for an organization's membership to be diverse.[24] Diversity's link to cultural strength is an interesting one. The latter, simpler notion of diversity—differences in ways of thinking—is strikingly similar to the concept of a weak culture. In this respect, greater diversity can hinder firm performance. Studies focusing on diverse top management teams, however, have found that diverse ways of thinking among top managers lead to more creative, comprehensive, and effective strategies.[25]

The value of diverse ways of thinking appears to be most critical during strategy formulation. A diverse top management team can pool its vast backgrounds and perspectives to create innovative strategies without blind spots. For those responsible for executing a strategy, typically middle and lower-level managers, less diversity is required. In this stage, processes for implementation may be clearly defined, and managers are simply charged with following them. Hence, a strong culture with less diversity of thought is likely preferable in this regard.

11-1b Shaping the Culture

Cultural change is a complex process. Just as cultures do not develop overnight, rarely are they changed in a short time. Culture change is possible but efforts often fail, due primarily to a lack of understanding about *how* a culture can be changed and *how long* it is likely to take.[26]

Top executives can influence and shape the organization's culture in at least five ways.[27] The first means is to systematically pay attention to areas of the business believed to be of key importance to the strategy's success. The top executive may take steps to accomplish this goal formally by measuring and controlling the activities of those areas, or less formally by making specific comments or questions at meetings. These specific areas should be ones identified as critical to the firm's long-term performance and survival, and may include such areas as customer service, new product development, or quality control.

The second means involves the leader's reactions to critical incidents and organizational crises. The way a CEO deals with a crisis, such as declining sales or technological obsolescence, can emphasize norms, values, and working procedures, or even create new ones. When Saturn's chief executive chose to destroy a group of vehicles produced with faulty coolant instead of simply draining the radiators, he sent a strong pro-quality message to his workers.

The third means is to serve as a deliberate role model, teacher, or coach. When a CEO models certain behavior, others in the organization are likely to adopt it as well. For example, chief executives who give up their reserved parking place and park among the line workers send a message about the importance of status in the organization.

The fourth means is the process through which top management allocates rewards and status. Leaders communicate their priorities by consistently linking pay raises and promotions, or the lack thereof, to particular behaviors. Simply stated, rewarded behavior tends to continue and become ingrained in the fabric of the organization. This not only applies to middle and lower-level managers, but can apply at top levels of the organization as well.

The fifth means of shaping the culture is to modify the procedures through which an organization recruits, selects, promotes, and terminates employees. An organization's culture can be perpetuated by hiring and promoting individuals whose values are similar to those of the firm and whose beliefs and behaviors more closely fit the organization's changing value system. Firms should spend the time necessary to properly screen candidates and evaluate them on their fit with the desired organizational culture. The easiest way to affect culture over the long term is to hire individuals who possess the desired cultural attributes.

11-1c Global Concerns

Global concerns can also complicate the role of organizational culture. In many respects, an organization's culture can be viewed as a subset of the national culture in which the firm operates. As such, operating outside one's own country can create special challenges in areas such as leadership and maintaining a strong organizational culture. For example, leaders of some nations resist innovation and radical new approaches to conducting business, whereas others welcome the change. Such national tendencies often become a part of the culture of the organization in those countries.

The self-reference criterion, the unconscious reference to one's own cultural values as a standard of judgment, also presents a potential problem. Managers often believe that the leadership styles and organizational culture that work in their home country should work elsewhere. However, each nation—like each organization—has its own unique culture, traditions, values, and beliefs. Hence, organizational values and norms must be tailored to fit the unique culture of each country in which the organization operates, at least to some extent. The need to customize values and norms can create special challenges, however, when firms from different countries become partners or even merge their organizations.

11-2 Strategic Leadership

Leadership

The capacity to secure the cooperation of others in accomplishing organizational goals.

Announcing a strategic change usually does little to inspire those responsible for implementing the change. The top management team has several means at its disposal to encourage managers and other employees to implement the strategy, one of which is leadership. The CEO is recognized as the organization's principal leader, one who sets the tone for its activities. A manager exhibits (managerial) **leadership** when he or she secures the cooperation of others in accomplishing a goal (see Strategy at Work 11-2).

STRATEGY AT WORK 11-2

Planning for CEO Succession

Wal-Mart's legendary CEO, Sam Walton, handed over the reigns of power to David Glass in early 1998. Only two years later, Glass transferred control to H. Lee Scott. How did Wal-Mart execute these changes in leadership, and leadership styles, without negative consequences? Five lessons for a successful CEO transition have been suggested from the Wal-Mart experience.

1. Firms should cross-train high-level executives to broaden their exposure as much as possible. Doing so prevents the learning curve for the new CEO from being too steep.

2. Firms should expose the heir apparent and other top executives to board members so they know what the board expects from top management.

3. Firms should discuss potential conflicts associated with the new roles for both the incoming and the outgoing CEOs. Plan to deal with any potential problems (like Walton, Glass stayed on in an advisory capacity after he stepped down as CEO).

4. The new CEO should conduct meetings on the other side of the executive desk.

5. Everyone involved should stay humble and not overestimate the new CEO's ability to institute rapid change.

Sources: A. Zimmerman, "Defending Wal-Mart," Wall Street Journal, 6 October 2004, B1, B10; Zimmerman, "How Wal-Mart Transfers Power," Wall Street Journal, 27 March 2001, B1, B4; B. Ortega, In Sam We Trust: The Untold Story of Sam Walton and Wal-Mart, the World's Most Powerful Retailer (New York: Times Books, 2000); P. Pitcher, S. Chreim, and V. Kisfalvi, "CEO Succession Research: Methodological Bridges over Troubled Waters," Strategic Management Journal 21(2000): 625–648.

Strategic leadership is more than managerial leadership. It involves creating the vision and mission for the firm, developing strategies, and empowering individuals throughout the organization to put those strategies into action. It includes determining the firm's strategic direction, aligning the firm's strategy with its culture, modeling and communicating high ethical standards, and initiating changes in the firm's strategy when necessary. Strategic leadership establishes the firm's direction by developing and communicating a vision of the future and inspires organization members to move in that direction.[28] Unlike strategic leadership, managerial leadership is generally concerned with the short-term, day-to-day activities.[29]

Effective strategic leadership is the link between strategy formulation and strategy execution. Without it, otherwise effective strategies will not likely be implemented as planned. Developing a firm's mission, vision, and strategies is not sufficient. Effective strategic leaders inspire managers and even nonmanagers to take the necessary steps to realize them. They build and promote an organizational culture that supports firm strategies and they set the tone for ethical behavior.

11-2a Leadership Style

Every leader has a distinctive **leadership style,** or consistent pattern of behavior exhibited in the process of governing and making decisions. Some leaders are flamboyant, whereas others are reserved and contemplative. Some seek broad-based participation when making decisions, whereas others arrive at decisions primarily on their own with little input from others. Regardless of style, participation can help build employee commitment to the firm's goals and strategies and is generally seen as a positive approach to decision making.[30]

There is little agreement on what might constitute a single best leadership style; however, two basic approaches can be identified.[31] Leaders employing a **transactional leadership** style use the authority of their office to exchange rewards such as pay and status for employees' work efforts and generally seek to enhance an organization's performance steadily, but not dramatically. By contrast, leaders employing a **transformational leadership** style inspire involvement in a mission, giving followers a vision of a higher calling, thereby seeking more dramatic changes in organizational performance. In effect, the transformational leader motivates followers to do more than they originally expected to do by stretching their abilities and increasing their self-confidence.[32] Transformational leaders also tend to promote innovation throughout the organization.

Transformational leadership is typically associated with innovation. Austrian economist Joseph Schumpeter identified five types of innovation: (1) new products, (2) new materials or resources, (3) new markets, (4) new production processes, and (5) new forms of organization.[33] It often occurs through a process Schumpeter called **creative destruction**, whereby managers consciously and constantly destroy the old by recombining its elements into new forms.

Leaders are typically categorized as transactional or transformational based on their overall pattern of behavior. Contrary to popular opinion, the transformational leader is not always a dynamic, vibrant, charismatic personality type.[34] A number of CEOs have transformed their organizations during times of turbulence without being charismatic figures. Indeed, a charismatic personality can be an asset to a transformational leader (and to a transactional

Strategic Leadership

Creating the vision and mission for the firm, developing strategies, and empowering individuals throughout the organization to put those strategies into action.

Source: Comstock.com

Leadership Style

The consistent pattern of behavior that a leader exhibits in the process of governing and making decisions.

Transactional Leadership

The capacity to motivate followers by exchanging rewards for performance.

Transformational Leadership

The capacity to motivate followers by inspiring involvement and participation in a mission.

Creative Destruction

A process whereby managers consciously and constantly destroy the old by recombining its elements into new forms.

Management Focus on **Innovation**

Johnson & Johnson Leadership Emphasizes Innovation

To say the least, Robert Wood Johnson, chairman of Johnson & Johnson, was ahead of his time when he wrote the company's credo in the 1940s. The credo took the unusual step of declaring that the organization's primary responsibility was to "the doctors, nurses, and patients . . . mothers and fathers and all others who use our products and services." This customer-driven focus had been the basis of J&J's success to that point, and it continues to pervade the company today, serving as common ground for the organization's 170 operating companies. J&J's business today is driven by three basic commitments.

1. Commitment to the credo
2. Commitment to decentralized management
3. Commitment to the long term

   Within the credo's framework—and in some ways because of it—J&J constantly emphasizes innovation, often measuring its success by the percentage of sales from products introduced in the last five years. In the 1980s, this percentage was around 30 percent. Today, it is close to 35 percent. As a result of this high level of innovation, the organization has increased its sales by more than $3 billion and added more than eight thousand new employees over the last decade.

Sources: Robert M. Fulmer, "Frameworks for Leadership," Organizational Dynamics, March 2001, 211–220; and Fulmer, Philip A. Gibbs, and Marshall Goldsmith, "Developing Leaders: How Winning Companies Keep on Winning," Sloan Management Review, Fall 2000, 49–59.

leader, to a lesser extent), but it is not a prerequisite for success (see Strategy at Work 11-3).

11-2b Leadership in Practice

Most leaders exhibit both transactional and transformational styles, to varying degrees (see Figure 11-1). Consider General Electric's Jack Welch, who retired in 2001 after two decades as CEO. Welch was known for his impatient, aggressive, and alternatively charming and overbearing image, and he pushed workers in GE plants and offices to constantly improve efficiency. However, Welch also demonstrated an uncanny charisma and strong drive as top executive. Widely known as one of America's most effective CEOs, Welch integrated components of both transactional and transformational styles.[35]

Emotional Intelligence

One's collection of psychological attributes, such as motivation, empathy, self-awareness, and social skills.

Regardless of leadership style, a leader's likelihood of success has also been tied to **emotional intelligence**, one's collection of psychological attributes, such as motivation, empathy, self-awareness, and social skills. Executives who possess a passion for their work, are socially oriented, and understand their own needs, as well as those of their subordinates, are more likely to gain the trust, confidence, and support necessary to lead their organizations.[36]

Although transformational leadership styles have gained increased popularity in recent years, transactional styles may be most appropriate in relatively predictable environments. Because predictability has become less common in recent years, however, many scholars and practitioners see a movement toward a transformation style as attractive for many organizations. Changing the predominant style in an organization, especially from transactional to transformational, can be a difficult process.

STRATEGY AT WORK 11-3

Leadership at Southwest Airlines

Herb Kelleher built Southwest Airlines into one of the most profitable and fast growing airlines in the country through an emphasis on low-cost operations. In doing so, he also managed to win the trust and respect of his employees through his leadership style.

Texas businessman Rollin King and attorney Herb Kelleher founded Air Southwest in 1967 as a regional airline linking Dallas, Houston, and San Antonio. Southwest made its first scheduled flight in 1971 and passed the billion-dollar revenue mark in 1989. Today, Southwest Airlines remains a predominantly short-haul, high-frequency, low-fare airline providing service within the United States. The Dallas-based carrier offers approximately 2,700 daily flights throughout much but not all of the country.

Southwest is a classic no-frills airline, although service is generally perceived to be excellent, and on-time performance rivals or exceeds its larger peers. Meals are not served, although passengers are encouraged to bring their own food on the plane. In addition, there are no reserved seats. The first thirty passengers to check in at the gate are allowed to board first and select their seats, followed by the next thirty, and so on. Southwest minimizes costs by operating out of smaller, less costly airports when possible.

Southwest has enjoyed twenty-nine consecutive years of profits, including 2001 when the 9/11 attacks riveted other American carriers into deep losses. High productivity, combined with the airline's lack of frills, gives Southwest a 43 percent cost advantage over its large Dallas-based rival, American Airlines. In fact, the airline has been the only major U.S. carrier to avoid layoffs and maintain a full flight schedule since that time. The company even began hiring additional employees in early 2002.

Southwest is known for its fun-loving, service-oriented culture. Flight attendants seem to be amateur comedians, a practice that subsided after the events of 9/11, but had reemerged by 2003.

Kelleher, who stepped down as CEO in 2001, helped establish a reputation for the company as one of the top employers in the United States. *Fortune* typically recognizes Southwest as one of the most admired companies in its annual surveys.

Kelleher was (and still is) genuinely respected by Southwest employees. He established excellent rapport with personnel and avoided the bitter negotiations that have characterized labor contracts at several other airlines. Through profit-sharing plans, cross-utilization of workers, and Kelleher's concern for employees, the company developed a culture of trust and loyalty. As CEO, Kelleher was highly visible. He would often take Southwest flights and frequently visited the aircraft maintenance areas. The visits were invariably upbeat and optimistic, with Kelleher dressing in a casual fashion (often in a Southwest Airlines shirt) and joking with the crew. He knew individuals' names and even sent birthday and Valentine's Day cards to each employee.

Kelleher handed over the CEO reins to VP James Parker in 2001, although Kelleher retained his position as chairman of the board.

Sources: J. Barlow, "Legendary Herb Has Done It His Way," Houston Chronicle, 22 March 2001, online edition; P. Adams, "Southwest Air Founder, Kelleher, Yielding Reins," Baltimore Sun, 20 March 2001, 1C; K. Labich, "Is Herb Kelleher America's Best CEO?" Fortune, 2 May 1994, 44–52; P. O'Brian, "Southwest Airlines Is a Rare Air Carrier: It Still Makes Money," Wall Street Journal, 26 October 1992, A1.

FIGURE 11-1 Leadership Style Continuum

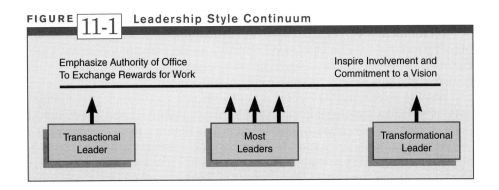

11-3 Executing Strategic Change

This chapter has outlined the benefits, costs, and considerations for implementing a strategic change. Indeed, strategic change is a complex process; and clear, detailed steps for instituting a change are difficult to develop, because organizations differ markedly in terms of industry, external environment, strategy, structure, culture, and leadership. For this reason, a simple three-step process for executing an effective strategic change is needed.[37]

This model can be applied regardless of the type of strategic change under consideration. In this context, the notion of strategic change is broadly defined and includes both changes in a strategy and changes in related factors (e.g., structure, leadership, and culture) that support the success of a strategy.

Recognize the Need for Change. First, the need for change must be recognized, and key managers in the organization must be made aware of that need. Although this step may appear simple at first, some individuals inevitably perceive the need for change before others. In addition, this task may be difficult if the organization currently seems to be doing okay. From an implementation standpoint, however, the best time to initiate change is when the organization is functionally well, not when it is in crisis. From a practical standpoint, it is difficult to execute a strategic change when only a visionary top executive sees the need to change in the first place.

Managers in poor performing firms are usually first to recognize the need for change, and often replace their CEOs with outsiders. These new leaders can sometimes make the decisions that an insider might be reluctant to make, and bring a fresh perspective to the firm and its problems. On the other hand, outsiders may have to spend months learning the business and developing a network of contacts before they can make decisions of any magnitude. However, hiring an outsider can send a message that current executives are not worthy of promotion.

An organization tends to allocate resources to the factors that led to current success, not necessarily the factors that are associated with future success. To overcome this tendency, leaders should broaden their measurement of performance to include comparisons to their competitors and to industry norms, not just last year's performance. In addition to the typical economic indicators, such as profitability, earnings per share, and market share, performance measures should also include factors such as customer satisfaction and product quality.

Create a Shared Vision. Once the need for change is established, leaders must inspire organizational members with a vision of what the organization can become if its members are willing to change. The vision might be one of excellent customer service, industry leadership, or a leaner firm following a restructuring. The change effort is not as likely to be successful when members of the firm do not share the same vision for the company's future organization.

The CEO should lead the effort and identify and model high performance standards. Transformational leaders seek to stretch their followers' abilities, and high performing organizations rarely pursue moderate goals or performance standards. Their public behavior should reflect their own excitement and energy at all levels of the organization.[38] Transformational leaders must also effectively communicate their vision to all members of the organization. A lack of vision can

Case Analysis 11-1

Step 23: How Should the Alternative(s) Be Implemented?

After alternatives have been evaluated and one or more have been selected, a plan for their execution must be developed. There are no simple outlines for effective implementation; each plan for implementation is unique to the organization and the alternatives recommended. Nonetheless, it must clearly detail precisely how the organization should implement the selected alternative(s). In doing so, potential problems may arise—many of which are an extension of some of the pros and cons aforementioned—and must be addressed. For example, if raising product quality and prices is proposed, then the problems associated with present customers who may not perceive the increase in quality or who may not be willing to pay a higher price should be considered. Hiring a consultant is not an acceptable recommendation!

Consider the following restaurant example. Suppose, based on the analysis, that it is recommended that Pizza Hut introduce a low-fat pizza. Stating that the organization should "just do it" would not be sufficient. Key questions to be considered in the plan for implementation include the following:

1. What are the characteristics of the new product (low-fat cheese, "lite" crust, etc.; actual fat and calorie levels should have been discussed in the pros and cons earlier)?
2. Should this product be implemented at all locations simultaneously? What are the pros and cons of such action?
3. How should this new product be marketed?
4. How will this new product affect sales of existing pizzas?
5. What problems have other fast-food restaurants had in delivering high-quality, low-fat products to their customers?
6. Specifically, what should Pizza Hut do to avoid the pitfalls and/or capitalize on the successes?
7. How much will this new product introduction cost?
8. How much time is necessary for training employees in the preparation of the new product?

Notice in this example that some of these issues may have been introduced in the alternative evaluation phase, and others extend beyond implementation into the control function. It is acceptable to make references to earlier statements and arguments.

One final note: The execution phase of the case analysis is required even if no major strategic changes are adopted. It is still necessary to explain in detail how the firm will execute the current strategy effectively in the coming years. It is not sufficient to suggest that the firm simply "stay the course" or "keep doing what it is already doing." Arguments such as, "If it ain't broke, don't fix it" are weak, as firms often fail because they resist change during profitable periods.

cloud organizational efforts, whereas clear communication of a vision creates a focus for the employees' efforts.

Institutionalize the Change. Finally, the firm's leadership must institutionalize the desired strategic changes. The adage "change starts at the top" is true in this regard. Without a strong commitment from the top executive and the top management team, the proposed strategic change is less likely to succeed.

The top executive must also realize that building a lasting change takes time. For example, encouraging organizational members to work and interact in different ways may require a new reward system, and changes may be necessary in systems for pay increases and promotions. Without adequate rewards, employees are unlikely to see involvement in initiating change as worthy of their efforts.[39] Minor changes in the system will likely produce minor changes in behavior.

The need for concise, accurate, and timely information is critical at all three stages of the change process.[40] Leaders should not rely exclusively on their associates for information, but should be accessible to all the members of the organization and to its customers. CEOs should also actively encourage others on their top management teams to act as devil's advocates so that group members seek agreement even in the face of conflict.

Top-down change efforts are not always successful. Top managers may attempt to institutionalize an ambitious change without pretesting, education, or employee participation, or they may follow a rigid change procedure that appeared to work elsewhere without considering unique characteristics of the organization.[41] For this reason, bottom-up approaches have been suggested whereby managers and line workers recognize the need for change and develop new strategies jointly. Regardless of approach, the importance of employee participation in the process at all levels cannot be easily understated.[42] (See Case Analysis 11-1.)

11-4 Summary

Executing a strategy can be challenging, especially when a significant strategic change is involved. Hence, the decision to institute such a change is not easy. Two key areas associated with executing strategic change—organizational culture and leadership—must be considered. Organizational culture can facilitate or hinder the firm's strategic actions. Successful strategy execution requires a strategically appropriate culture, one that is appropriate to, and supportive of, the firm's strategy. Modifying the culture is sometimes necessary, but doing so is usually difficult.

The leadership style of the top executive and the top management team is also closely linked to a firm's ability to implement a given strategy. Each leader may adopt a transactional or a transformational style, although most effective leaders utilize both styles to some extent. Effective leadership is critical when a firm seeks to implement a major strategic change.

Key Terms

adaptive culture	innovation	strong culture
creative destruction	leadership	subculture
diversity	leadership style	transactional leadership
emotional intelligence	organizational culture	transformational leadership
inert culture	strategic leadership	weak culture

Review Questions and Exercises

1. Give an example of an organization whose culture is appropriate for its strategy. Explain.

2. Strategies involving mergers and acquisitions are particularly vulnerable to cultural problems. Mergers between two organizations often are easier to accomplish on paper than in reality. Reality may reveal that the cultures of the organization fail to mesh as easily as corporate assets. Research the history of the DaimlerChrysler merger on the Internet. Learn as much as you can about cach original company's organizational culture. What cultural problems did the two companies experience? Did these problems contribute to the split in 2007?

3. Explain transformational and transactional leadership styles and give examples of each. Identify the conditions under which each is likely to be effective.

4. To what extent can leaders institute change in their organizations? Practically speaking, how is this accomplished?

Practice Quiz

True or False

1. Organizational culture can facilitate or hinder the firm's strategic actions.

2. Because each organization develops its own unique culture, even organizations within the same industry and city will exhibit distinctly different ways of functioning.

3. Transactional leaders inspire involvement in a mission, giving followers a vision of a higher calling.

4. Most effective leaders exhibit traits associated with both transformational and transactional leadership styles.

5. Because environments have become less predictable in recent years, a transformational leadership style may be most appropriate for the majority of firms.

6. The first step in initiating strategic change is to create a shared vision.

Multiple Choice

7. Deeply rooted values and ways of thinking that regulate firm behavior characterize
   A. a strong culture.
   B. a weak culture.
   C. the organizational culture.
   D. none of the above

8. A lack of values and ways of thinking in a firm characterize
   A. a strong culture.
   B. a weak culture.
   C. the organizational culture.
   D. none of the above

9. In general, an organizational culture
   A. cannot be changed.
   B. can only be changed by a charismatic leader.
   C. can be changed easily if proper procedures are followed.
   D. none of the above

10. The unconscious reference to one's own cultural values as a standard of judgment is known as
    A. emotional intelligence.
    B. the self-reference criterion.
    C. global awareness.
    D. none of the above

11. One's collection of psychological attributes such as motivation, empathy, self-awareness, and social skills is known as
    A. emotional intelligence.
    B. leadership traits.
    C. leadership style.
    D. none of the above

12. Top-down change efforts
    A. are not always successful.
    B. can be augmented through employee participation.
    C. are not necessarily more effective than bottom-up efforts.
    D. all of the above

Notes

1. R. D'Aveni, "The Empire Strikes Back: Counterrevolutionary Strategies for Industry Leaders," *Harvard Business Review* 80(11) (2002): 66–74.

2. J. A. Parnell, "Strategic Change versus Flexibility: Does Strategic Change Really Enhance Performance?" *American Business Review* 12(2) (1994): 22–30; D. D. Bergh and J. F. Fairbank, "Measuring and Testing Change in Strategic Management Research," *Strategic Management Journal* 23 (2002): 359–366.

3. S. Gray, "McDonald's Menu Upgrade Boosts Meal Prices and Results," *Wall Street Journal* (18–19 February 2006): A1, A7; J. Adamy, "For McDonald's, It's a Wrap," *Wall Street Journal* (30 January 2007): B1, B2.

4. S. Warren, "Move to Denver Signals Threat to Southwest's Low-Cost Model," *Wall Street Journal* (29 November 2005): A1, A6.

5. M. Trottman, "Southwest Air Considers Shift in Its Approach," *Wall Street Journal* (23 December 2003): B1, B5.

6. S. Warren, "Keeping Ahead of the Pack," *Wall Street Journal* (19 December 2005): B1, B3.

7. S. Carey, "Amid JetBlue's Rapid Ascent, CEO Adopts Big Rivals' Traits," *Wall Street Journal* (25 August 2005): A1, A6.

8. S. McCartney, "New Airline to Link Small, Midsize Cities," *Wall Street Journal* (30 January 2007): B11, B14.

9. S. Carey, "As Airlines Pull out of Dive, United Charts Its Own Course," *Wall Street Journal* (13 January 2006): A1, A6.

10. C. Terhune, "Home Depot's Home Improvement," *Wall Street Journal* (8 March 2001): B1, B4.

11. W. J. Duncan, "Organizational Culture: 'Getting a Fix' on an Elusive Concept," *Academy of Management Executive* 3 (1989): 229–236.

12. M. J. Rouse and U. S. Daellenbach, "Rethinking Research Methods for the Resource-Based Perspective: Isolating Sources of Sustainable Competitive Advantage," *Strategic Management Journal* 20 (1999): 487–494.

13. E. H. Schein, "The Role of the Founder in Creating Organizational Culture," *Organizational Dynamics* 12 (Summer 1983): 14.

14. J. F. Love, *McDonald's: Behind the Golden Arches* (New York: Bantam Press, 1995).

15. E. Byron, "Call Me Mike!" *Wall Street Journal* (27 March 2006): B1, B4.

16. G. A. Yukl, *Leadership in Organizations* (Upper Saddle River, NJ: Prentice Hall, 2002).

17. E. H. Schein, *Organizational Culture and Leadership* (San Francisco: Jossey-Bass, 1985), 30.

18. D. Tosti and S. Jackson, "Alignment: How It Works and Why It Matters," *Training* 31 (April 1994): 58–64; T. Brown, "The Rise and Fall of the Intelligent Organization," *Industry Week* (7 March 1994): 16–21; D. Lawrence Jr., "The New Social Contract between Employers and Employees," *Employee Benefits Journal* 19(1) (1994): 21–24.

19. M. Driver, "Learning and Leadership in Organizations: Toward Complementary Communities of Practice," *Management Learning* 33 (2002): 96–126.

20. J. W. Barnes, D. W. Jackson Jr., M. D. Hutt, and A. Kumar, "The Role of Culture Strength in Shaping Sales Force

Outcomes," *Journal of Personal Selling & Sales Management* 26: 255–270.

21. G. L. Davis, "Business Ethics: It's All Inside JCPenney Grounded in Golden Rules of Business Conduct," *Mid-American Journal of Business* 19(1): 7–10.

22. H. M. Sabri, "Socio-Cultural Values and Organizational Culture," *Journal of Transnational Management Development* 9(2,3): 123–145; D. W. Pitts, "Diversity, Representation, and Performance: Evidence about Race and Ethnicity in Public Organizations," *Journal of Public Administration Research and Theory* 15: 615–631.

23. The extent to which individuals can "control" some of these factors is widely debated, but beyond the scope of this text.

24. O. R. Richard, D. Ford, and K. Ismail, "Exploring the Performance Effects of Visible Attribute Diversity: The Moderating Role of Span of Control and Organizational Life Cycle," *International Journal of Human Resource Management* 17: 2091–2109; A. Alesina and E. LaFerrara, "Ethnic Diversity and Economic Performance," *Journal of Economic Literature* 43: 762–800; S. K. Horwitz, "The Compositional Impact of Team Diversity on Performance: Theoretical Considerations," *Human Resource Development Review* 42: 219–245.

25. S. Auh and B. Menguc, "Diversity at the Executive Suite: A Resource-Based Approach to the Customer Orientation-Organizational Performance Relationship," *Journal of Business Research* 59: 564–572.

26. A. R. Jassawalla and H. C. Sashittal, "Cultures That Support Product-Innovation Processes," *Academy of Management Executive* 16(3) (2002): 42–54.

27. Schein, *Organizational Culture and Leadership*.

28. J. R. Darling and T. M. Box, "Keys for Success in the Leadership of Multinational Corporations, 1990 Through 1997," *Sam Advanced Management Journal* 64(4) (1999): 16–20; M. Driver, "Learning and Leadership in Organizations: Toward Complementary Communities of Practice," *Management Learning* 33 (2002): 96–126.

29. W. G. Rowe, "Creating Wealth in Organizations: The Role of Strategic Leadership," *Academy of Management Executive* 15(1) (2001): 81–94.

30. G. Trumfio, "Managing from the Trenches," *Sales & Marketing Management* 146 (February 1994): 39; J. A. Parnell and E. D. Bell, "A Measure of Managerial Propensity for Participative Management," *Administration and Society* 25 (1994): 518–530.

31. D. J. Brown and R. G. Lord, "The Utility of Experimental Research in the Study of Transformational/Charismatic Leadership," *Leadership Quarterly* 10 (1999): 531–539.

32. J. M. Beyer, "Two Approaches to Studying Charismatic Leadership: Competing or Complementary?" *Leadership Quarterly* 10 (1999): 575–588.

33. J. Schumpeter, *The Theory of Economic Development* (Cambridge: Harvard University Press, 1934).

34. J. M. Crant and T. S. Bateman, "Charismatic Leadership Viewed from Above: The Impact of Proactive Personality," *Journal of Organizational Behavior* 21 (2000): 63–75.

35. M. Murray, "Why Jack Welch's Brand of Leadership Matters," *Wall Street Journal* (5 September 2001): B1, B10.

36. D. Goleman, "What Makes a Leader?" *Harvard Business Review* 76(5) (1998): 92–105.

37. N. M. Tichy and M. A. Devanna, *The Transformational Leader* (New York: Wiley, 1986).

38. A. M. Mohrman Jr., S. A. Mohrman, G. E. Ledford Jr., T. G. Cummings, E. E. Lawler III, and associates, *Large-Scale Organizational Change* (San Francisco: Jossey-Bass, 1989), 106.

39. A. J. Nurick, "The Paradox of Participation: Lessons from the Tennessee Valley Authority," *Human Resource Management* 24 (Fall 1985): 354–355.

40. W. Bennis, "The End of Leadership: Exemplary Leadership Is Impossible without Full Inclusion, Initiatives, and Cooperation of Followers," *Organizational Dynamics* 28(1) (1999): 71–80.

41. N. P. Archer, "Methodologies and Tools for E-Business Change Management," presented at the 24th Annual McMaster World Congress, Hamilton, Ontario, Canada (15–17 January 2003).

42. M. Beer, R. A. Eisenstat, and B. Spector, "Why Change Programs Don't Produce Change," *Harvard Business Review* 68(5) (1990): 158–166.

Insight from *strategy+business*

This chapter's strategy+business reading builds on last chapter's reading by delving deeper into the importance of strategy execution. Specifically, seven types of organizations are identified, four of which possess serious problems in terms of effective implementation. Understanding one's "organizational DNA" is the first step in improving a firm's ability to execute well-crafted strategies effectively.

The Seven Types of Organizational DNA

An exclusive survey shows most companies possess traits that inhibit their ability to execute.

By Gary Neilson, Bruce A. Pasternack, and Decio Mendes

"Execution" has become the new watchword in boardrooms, as CEOs and directors watch sound strategies fail at the hands of organizations that cannot or will not effectively implement them. The first step in resolving these dysfunctions is to understand how the inherent traits of an organization influence—and perhaps even determine—each individual's behavior; and how the collective behavior affects company performance.

We like to use the familiar metaphor of DNA to codify the idiosyncratic characteristics of a company. (See "The Four Bases of Organizational DNA," *s+b,* Winter 2003.) Like the DNA of living organisms, the DNA of living organizations consists of four building blocks, which combine and recombine to express distinct identities, or personalities. These organizational building blocks—structure, decision rights, motivators, and information—largely determine how a firm looks and behaves, internally and externally. (See Exhibit 1.)

EXHIBIT 1   Breaking Down an Organization's Genetic Code

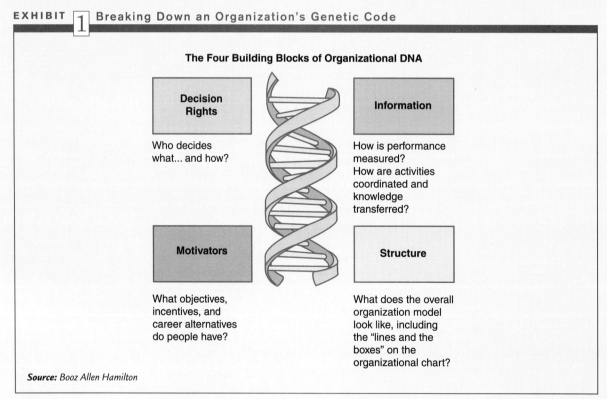

The Four Building Blocks of Organizational DNA

Decision Rights

Who decides what... and how?

Information

How is performance measured?
How are activities coordinated and knowledge transferred?

Motivators

What objectives, incentives, and career alternatives do people have?

Structure

What does the overall organization model look like, including the "lines and the boxes" on the organizational chart?

Source: Booz Allen Hamilton

Source: Reprinted with permission from *strategy+business,* the award-winning management quarterly published by Booz Allen Hamilton. http://www.strategy-business.com.

EXHIBIT 2 **Org DNA Assessments: Industry Breakdown**

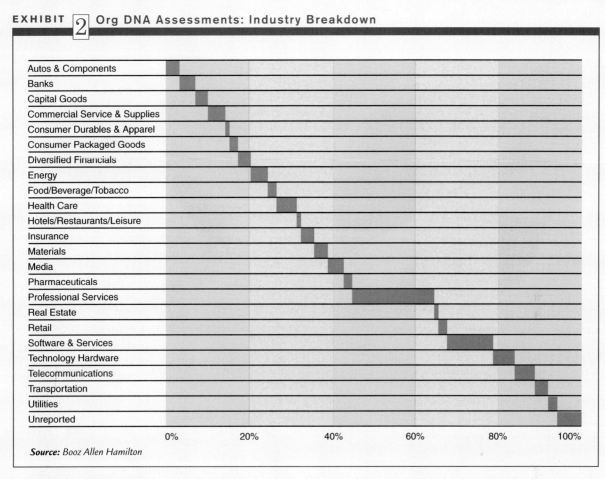

Source: Booz Allen Hamilton

Last year, we developed a short, online self-assessment tool called the Org DNA Profiler™ (www.orgdna.com) to measure an organization's relative strength in each of these four areas, on the basis of individual employees' responses to 19 questions. Survey responses are fed through proprietary software to generate one of seven prototypical organizational profiles—or, to continue the genetic metaphor, "species." (See "The Seven Organizational Species.")

We launched the Org DNA Profiler on December 9, 2003, and in the first two weeks, collected 4,007 completed assessments. (See "The Org DNA Profiler Methodology.") Respondents came from companies of all sizes in a wide variety of industries, including financial services, pharmaceuticals, telecommunications, energy, and consumer packaged goods, and represented every function and every level in the corporate hierarchy. (See Exhibits 2 and 3.)

The responses (and the thousands more we have continued to collect) prompt six observations about the prevalence of dysfunction among business organizations and the reasons for their maladies:

1. **Most organizations are unhealthy.** More than 60 percent of respondents found their organizations fit one of the four species associated with subpar performance: Passive-Aggressive, Fits-and-Starts, Outgrown, or Overmanaged.

2. **Organizational DNA changes as companies grow.** As a rule, small companies report more Resilient and Just-in-Time behaviors. As they grow, they may centralize and demonstrate more Military traits. Once their annual revenues cross the $1 billion threshold, operations necessarily decentralize, but often badly, as revealed in the higher incidence of Fits-and-Starts and Passive-Aggressive profiles. Once past the $10 billion mark, companies have obviously demonstrated some key success traits but are not necessarily free from dysfunction.

3. **Altitude determines attitude.** Survey results indicate sharp differences between senior-management responses and those of lower-level personnel, suggesting a disconnect between the organizations that senior

EXHIBIT 3 Org DNA Assessments, by Function and Position

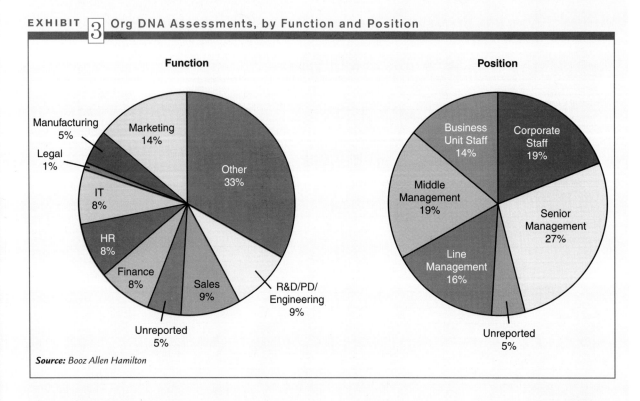

Function

Manufacturing 5%
Legal 1%
Marketing 14%
IT 8%
Other 33%
HR 8%
Finance 8%
Sales 9%
Unreported 5%
R&D/PD/ Engineering 9%

Position

Business Unit Staff 14%
Corporate Staff 19%
Middle Management 19%
Senior Management 27%
Line Management 16%
Unreported 5%

Source: Booz Allen Hamilton

executives believe they've established and the organizations they are actually running.

4. **Nonexecutives feel micromanaged.** Although senior managers appear to view their self-professed involvement in operating decisions as good, junior managers overwhelmingly reported feeling a lack of maneuvering room.

5. **Decision rights are unclear.** More than half of those completing surveys indicated they believed that the accountability for decisions and actions in their organizations was vague.

6. **Execution is the exception, not the rule.** Fewer than half of all respondents agreed that "important strategic and operational decisions are quickly translated into action" in their organizations. Poor information flows seem mostly to blame.

Unlike humans and other organisms, organizations have the ability to *change* their DNA by adjusting and adapting their building blocks. Our survey findings suggest steps companies can take both to better understand the nature of their difficulties and to improve their execution capabilities.

The Checkup

Our review of the 4,000-plus assessments showed that most organizations are unhealthy. Of the seven organizational

species, only three—Resilient, Just-in-Time, and Military—can be described as relatively free from dysfunction, or "healthy." Only 27 percent of the survey responses resulted in one of these three healthy profiles. More than 60 percent of respondents indicated that the traits and behaviors of their organizations were unhealthy in some way. Their responses describe firms unable to act decisively or effectively.

The most prevalent species was Passive-Aggressive; 31 percent of respondents reported organizational behaviors consistent with this type. Overmanaged was the second largest category, at 18 percent. The healthiest species is the Resilient firm. Yet only 15 percent of respondents indicated that their companies fit this profile. We found significant differences among industries in their degree of passive-aggressiveness, from a low of 17 percent of people in the durables and apparel sector who indicated their companies fell into this category, to a high of 40 percent among insurance-industry respondents. The surveys show that the more highly regulated the industry, the greater the level of passive-aggressive behavior. Similar variations existed among departments, with overhead and staff functions perceiving passive-aggressiveness in their companies more than manufacturing and sales personnel. (See Exhibit 4.)

EXHIBIT 4 The Prevalence of Passive Aggressiveness

Percent Passive-Aggressive by Industry [Average = 31.1%]

Industry	%
Insurance	40%
Utilities	38%
Media	37%
Health Care	36%
Banks	35%
Energy	34%
Pharmaceuticals	33%
Retail	32%
Software & Services	31%
Telecommunications	29%
Technology Hardware	28%
Food/Beverage/Tobacco	27%
Auto & Components	27%
Consumer Packaged Goods	24%
Diversified Financials	24%
Cons. Durables & Apparel	17%

Percent Passive-Aggressive by Function [Average = 31.1%]

Function	%
Legal	40%
R&D/PD/Eng	36%
Finance	33%
Marketing	33%
IT	33%
HR	30%
Sales	29%
Manufacturing	20%

Source: Booz Allen Hamilton

The surveys suggest that companies pass through different "genotypes" as they grow and that they hit a kind of Darwinian barrier when their embedded traits and behaviors hinder their ability to perform according to their aspirations. Astute managers appreciate these subtle shifts and can help their organizations transition to new models as the company expands. (See Exhibit 5.)

Specifically, in analyzing organizational behaviors by the size of the company, we see a four-step evolutionary process by which companies grow into—and occasionally out of—dysfunction:

Step 1: $0-$500 Million. Responses from small companies are more likely than those from their larger counterparts to indicate Resilient or Just-in-Time profiles—organizations that are effective at executing and adapting to change in their environment. This finding is intuitive because small companies tend to be younger, and therefore more attuned to and aligned with the vision and strategy of the founders. Moreover, their small size allows them to adapt more nimbly to market shifts.

Step 2: $500 Million-$1 Billion. As firms cross the $500 million threshold, many seem to address their growing coordination challenges by centralizing authority in a strong senior team that drives the business. Not

surprisingly, the Military profile reaches its peak in this revenue segment. In addition, we see a sharp increase in the Overmanaged profile, suggesting that many firms in this size range become bureaucratic, slow, and overly politicized as an expanding middle management starts to second-guess and interfere in lower-level decision making.

Step 3: $1-$10 Billion. Once past the $1 billion mark, organizations become too large and complex to be run effectively by a small senior team via command-and-control mechanisms. Companies are thus forced to decentralize. Given the marked increase in Fits-and-Starts profiles in this revenue range, the transition to a decentralized organizational model appears to go badly in many cases. Local managers may be given the authority to make decisions, but not the incentives or information to make them well. Passive-Aggressive profiles also increase in companies of this size, because incoherent and uncoordinated structures and processes create inertia, confusion, and ultimately a failure to execute.

Step 4: More than $10 Billion. To survive and grow to this size, companies clearly have had to figure out how to execute and adapt, and Resilient profiles do make a comeback in this segment. Even so, plenty of very large organizations still struggle to execute effectively.

EXHIBIT 5 Organizational Profiles, by Company Size

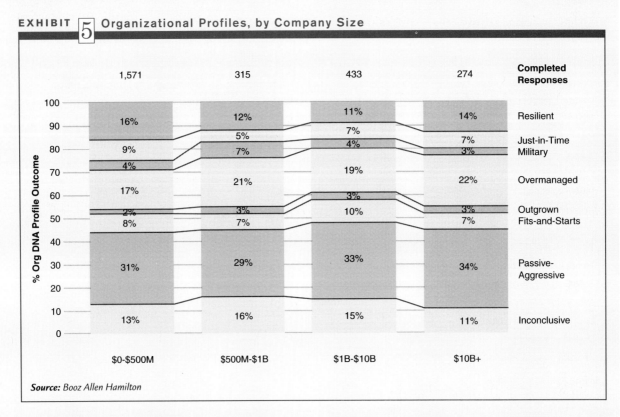

	1,571	315	433	274	**Completed Responses**
Resilient	16%	12%	11%	14%	
Just-in-Time	9%	5%	7%	7%	
Military		7%	4%	3%	
Overmanaged	4%	21%	19%	22%	
	17%				
Outgrown	2%	3%	3%	3%	
Fits-and-Starts	8%	7%	10%	7%	
Passive-Aggressive	31%	29%	33%	34%	
Inconclusive	13%	16%	15%	11%	

% Org DNA Profile Outcome

$0-$500M $500M-$1B $1B-$10B $10B+

Source: Booz Allen Hamilton

Overmanaged profiles increase and Fits-and-Starts profiles decrease in the $10 billion + segment. This finding suggests that many of the largest companies may try to "fix" a badly decentralized organization by adding layers of management and bureaucracy. Passive-Aggressive is the most prevalent profile in companies of this size, indicating that, although people may agree on the strategic plan, few are really implementing it.

But nothing is preordained. Companies are not fated to cycle through the Military, then Fits-and-Starts, and then Passive-Aggressive phases as they grow. Those firms that are aware of these patterns can anticipate and break them.

Upstairs, Downstairs

Our survey results indicate sharp differences in perception between upper management and lower-level groups, suggesting that senior executives may be out of touch with the rest of their organization. Specifically, senior managers are consistently more optimistic in their views of organizational health, a finding that echoes numerous other organizational research studies.

More than any other group in the organization, senior managers we surveyed saw their firms as "healthy."

Indeed, senior executives were twice as likely as any other group to view their companies as Resilient. Consistent with this comparative optimism, senior management answers translated into unhealthy profiles—Overmanaged, Outgrown, Fits-and-Starts, and Passive-Aggressive— almost 30 percent less often than those of other groups. (See Exhibit 6.)

Senior management's positive bias is reflected in all categories. On virtually every question that tracks to the Resilient profile, senior executives reported the "desirable" response more often than any other segment of respondents. Most strikingly, senior managers were far more willing than others in the organization to agree with the statement, "Important competitive information gets to headquarters quickly." Given the yawning gap between their perceptions of their organizations' effectiveness and that of every group that reports to them, one might question how well informed senior managers really are. As business operations grow increasingly complex and the pressure for greater accountability mounts, top management would do well to reassess data flows within the company and institutionalize access to timely, relevant, and accurate information.

EXHIBIT 6 **Organizational Profiles, by Management Positions**

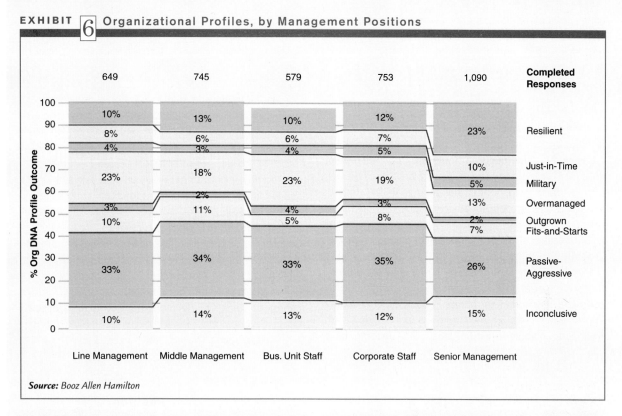

Source: Booz Allen Hamilton

These results also appear to indicate a discrepancy between senior executives' favorable perceptions of the organizational structures and processes they have established, and the actual adoption and utilization of those structures and processes. This finding is consistent with our client experience.

In contrast to their superiors, line managers and midlevel managers and business unit staff tend to be pessimistic in their assessments of organizational effectiveness. Nearly 70 percent of their surveys indicated unhealthy profiles. Line managers and business unit staff feel Overmanaged; 23 percent of them described behavior consistent with this profile. Midlevel and line managers believe their organizations struggle to pull in the same direction at the same time, as evidenced by the high incidence of Fits-and-Starts profiles.

Corporate staff personnel are slightly more optimistic. Perhaps they are far enough removed from daily operations that they are less aware of organizational problems. Most notably, they do not perceive the same Overmanaged behaviors that other nonexecutives report. One survey question that drew a consistent response across organizational levels was, "Managers above me in the hierarchy 'get their hands dirty' by getting involved in operating decisions." More than half of all respondents reported this happening "frequently," with senior managers, at 65.4 percent, citing this tendency in their companies more than any other group.

But survey results suggest this is where the consensus. Although senior managers likely view their involvement in operating decisions as good (given their overall positive bias), junior managers reported feeling in micromanaged. There is widespread agreement among business unit and corporate staffs as well as line managers, that "decisions are often second-guessed." Fewer senior managers see it that way.

There is also a disparity in beliefs regarding the role of corporate staff. Although business unit staff, line management, and middle management believe that "the primary role of corporate staff is to *support* the business units," corporate staff respondents believe their role is to *audit* those units, a view senior management overwhelmingly supports.

These differences in perception can lead to significant organizational dysfunction. Business unit personnel may feel frustrated as they spend more time reporting up the hierarchy than doing productive work. Not surprisingly, lower-level employees reported a higher incidence of "analysis paralysis" and excessively bureaucratic decision making in their organizations. Feeling distrusted, underestimated, and trapped in an overly politicized environment, those with initiative and exceptional talent may well defect.

Decisions, Decisions

If lower-level employees are feeling stifled by excessive bureaucracy and layers of micromanagement, it could be because decision rights are poorly communicated in many organizations. More than half of the Org DNA Profiler respondents indicated that they felt the accountability for decisions and actions was unclear in their organizations. This finding was consistent across all organizational levels, though senior management was slightly more sanguine.

Although decision rights are vague across the board, the lack of understanding seems particularly acute within overhead functions (e.g., human resources, finance, and information technology), where redundant "shadow staff" frequently multiply to fill the gaps left by incomplete or poorly specified responsibilities. Since so many organizations now outsource overhead functions to third-party vendors, decision rights in those organizations may be hampered by unclear service-level agreements and governance mechanisms. In line organizations (such as manufacturing and sales), decision rights—except at the lowest levels—are slightly clearer, perhaps because those organizations face more direct market pressure to resolve conflicting or poorly specified responsibilities that interfere with responsiveness to the customer.

In combination with generally unclear decision rights, lack of timely and relevant information contributes to ineffective execution. A majority of respondents at all levels reported that "field/line employees frequently lack the information they need to understand the bottom-line impact of their day-to-day choices," and a majority disagreed with the statement that "information flows freely across organizational boundaries." As always, senior managers were slightly more upbeat in their assessments, but most still took a dim view in their responses to these questions. (See Exhibit 7.)

EXHIBIT 7   **Decision Rights and Information Flows: Perceptions, by Position**

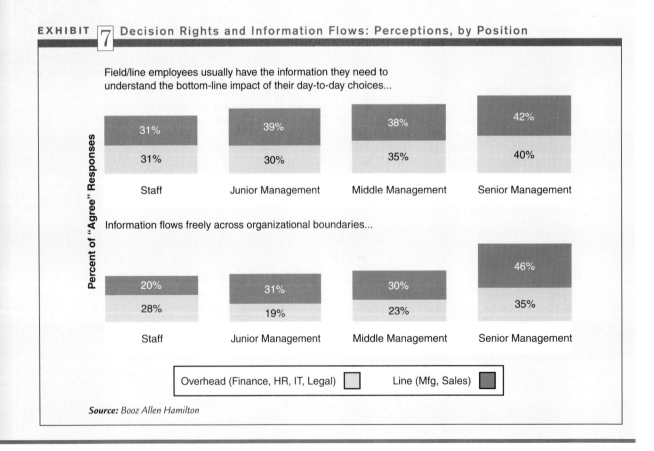

Source: Booz Allen Hamilton

Consistent with their views on decision rights, overhead employees are the most negative in their assessment of information flows. Although still sore points, information access and decision rights are less of a struggle for line organizations. Still, survey responses overwhelmingly point to the need for improved information, tools, and incentives for decision makers in all parts of the organization.

Preliminary results from the Org DNA Profiler assessment tool show that most companies today face organizational impediments to effective and rapid execution. Although 37 percent of respondents from small companies thought their organizations translated strategy into action quickly, only 29 percent of the respondents from the largest companies agreed with that statement.

Respondents at all levels in companies across industries indicated that their organizations struggle to execute decisively and effectively. Fewer than one-third of nonexecutive respondents agreed that "important strategic and operational decisions are quickly translated into action" in their organizations. Even at the most senior levels, fewer than 50 percent of respondents indicated that their companies act decisively in implementing strategy. Whether they fall into the Passive-Aggressive profile or the Outgrown, their organizational DNA is thwarting their own best efforts—and ultimate success.

As they confront their problems, companies are also contending with an increasingly complex global marketplace, where change buffets them relentlessly. According to our early results, fewer than half of the Org DNA Profiler respondents at all nonexecutive levels agreed that their companies "deal successfully with discontinuous change in the competitive environment." Even among senior managers, only half agreed with this statement.

Gene Therapy

When an organization's DNA is poorly configured, the firm exhibits unhealthy symptoms and counterproductive behaviors. The first step in fixing these problems is to identify and isolate them. That is the purpose of the Org DNA Profiler assessment tool. Using a framework that examines all aspects of a company's architecture, resources, and relationships, the tool allows management to gain insight into what is and is not working deep inside a highly complex organization.

But generating a profile is not the point; it is only an exercise designed to focus leaders on the root causes of their organizations' dysfunctions and execution problems. It is up to management to translate these findings into sustainable solutions. Using the Org DNA Profiler as a starting point for discussion, top executives, business unit heads, and staff leaders (a group that might be 10 people or more than 100) can meet to identify the impediments to effective execution in their organization and develop programs and processes to overcome them. The organizational DNA framework helps companies identify and expose hidden strengths and entrenched weaknesses so that managers can focus efforts on reinforcing what works in their organization and modifying what does not.

The Seven Organizational Species

In working with companies to diagnose and overcome organizational impediments to effective execution, we have identified seven broad types of organizations:

The Resilient Organization. This organization is flexible enough to adapt quickly to external market shifts, yet it remains steadfastly focused on and aligned with a coherent business strategy. This forward-looking organization anticipates changes routinely and addresses them proactively. It attracts motivated team players and offers them not only a stimulating work environment, but also the resources and authority necessary to solve tough problems.

The Just-in-Time Organization. Although not always proactive in preparing for impending changes, this organization has demonstrated an ability to "turn on a dime" when necessary, without losing sight of the big picture. Although it manages to hold on to good people and performs well financially, it has not made the leap from good to great. This organization tends to miss opportunities by inches rather than miles, and to celebrate successes that are marginal rather than unequivocal. Despite its frustrations, however, it can still be a stimulating and challenging place to work.

The Military Organization. Often driven by a small, hands-on senior management team, this organization succeeds through sheer force of will, the will of its top executives. It can conceive and execute brilliant strategies—sometimes repeatedly—but its middle-management bench can be shallow and short lived. This organization's biggest liability is preparing for growth beyond the tenure of its current leaders. Junior talent in this organization typically learns by seeing rather than doing, and middle management often defects as up-and-comers realize they must leave the nest to get flying experience.

The Passive-Aggressive Organization. So congenial that it seems conflict free, this is the "everyone agrees but nothing changes" organization. Building a consensus to make major changes is no problem; implementing them is what proves difficult. Entrenched, underground resistance from the field can defeat a corporate group's best efforts. Lacking the requisite authority, information, and incentives to undertake meaningful change, Line employees tend to ignore mandates from headquarters, assuming "this too shall pass." Confronted with an apathetic organization, senior management laments the futility of "pushing Jell-O."

The Fits-and-Starts Organization. Scores of smart, motivated, and talented people populate this organization, but they do not often pull in the same direction at the same time. When they do, they can execute brilliant, breakout strategic moves, but the organization typically lacks the discipline and coordination to repeat these successes on a consistent basis. It is an environment that lures intellect and initiative—smart people with an entrepreneurial bent—because the opportunities to pursue an idea and to take responsibility for executing it are abundant. The result, however, can be an organization with a disjointed self-image on the verge of spinning out of control.

The Outgrown Organization. This firm has outgrown its organizational model; it is bursting at the seams. Too large and complex to be effectively controlled anymore by a small team of top executives, it has yet to "democratize" decision-making authority. Consequently, much of the organizations potential remains untapped. By keeping power centralized, the organization tends to move slowly and often finds it cannot get out of its own way. Such firms routinely miss opportunities and consistently fail to execute effectively.

The Overmanaged Organization. Burdened with multiple layers of management, this organization tends to suffer from "analysis paralysis." When it does move, it moves slowly and reactively, often pursuing opportunities later or less vigorously than its competitors do. More consumed with the trees than the forest, managers spend their time checking one another's work rather than scanning the horizon for new opportunities or threats. These organizations, which are frequently bureaucratic and highly political, tend to frustrate self-starters and results-oriented individuals.

—G.N., B.A.P., and D.M.

The Org DNA Profiler™ Methodology

The Org DNA Profiler™ assessment tool categories organizational character based on employees responses to a five-minute survey composed of 19 questions. This assessment tool, although based on individuals' survey responses, focuses on the traits and behaviors of the organization as a whole rather than on the individuals who populate it, although certain general demographic data (e.g., position/level, division, industry, annual revenue) is collected to enhance the analysis.

Each question addresses organizational behavior with regard to one of the four building blocks of organizational DNA: decision rights, information, motivators, and structure. The responses are then fed through proprietary software that assigns the organization described to one of seven organizational species.

Resources

Jeffrey W. Bennett, Thomas E. Pernsteiner, Paul F. Kocourek, and Steven B. Hedlund, "The organization vs. the Strategy: Solving the Alignment Paradox," *s+b*, Fourth Quarter 2000; www.strategy-business.com/press/article/14114

Gary Neilson, David Kletter, and John Jones, "Treating the Troubled Corporation," *s+b enews*, 03/28/03; www.strategy-business.com/press/enewsarticle/22230

Gary Neilson, Bruce A. Pasternack, and Decio Mendes, "The Four Bases of Organizational DNA," *s+b*, Winter 2003; www.strategy-business.com/press/article/03406

Org DNA Profiler assessment tool: www.orgdna.com

Gary Neilson (neilson_gary@bah.com) is a senior vice president with Booz Allen Hamilton in Chicago. He works on the development of organizational models and designs, restructuring, and the leadership of major change initiatives for Fortune 500 companies.

Bruce A. Pasternack (pasternack_bruce@bah.com) is a senior vice president with Booz Allen Hamilton in San Francisco. He counsels companies in building strategic agendas, developing organizations, and transforming business models. He has published widely on leadership and organizational issues.

Decio Mendes (mendes_decio@bah.com) is a senior associate with Booz Allen Hamilton in New York. He works with clients to improve organizational effectiveness and operations efficiency.

Strategic Control 12

Chapter Outline

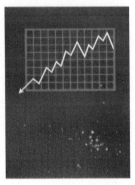

Source: Ablestock.com

Strategic Control

The process of determining the extent to which an organization's strategies are successful in meeting its goals and objectives.

The strategic management process is not complete when a strategy has been executed. It is also necessary to evaluate its success or failure, and take steps to address problems that may have arisen along the way. **Strategic control** consists of determining the extent to which the organization's strategies are successful in meeting its goals and objectives. The execution process is tracked and adjustments to the strategy are made as necessary.[1] It is during the strategic control process that gaps between the intended and realized strategies (i.e., what was planned and what really happened) are identified and addressed.

The process of strategic control can be likened to that of steering a vehicle. After the strategy accelerator is pressed, the control function ensures that everything is moving in the right direction. When a simple steering adjustment is not sufficient to modify the course of the vehicle, the driver can resort to other means, such as applying the break or shifting gears. In a similar manner, strategic managers can steer the organization by instituting minor modifications or resort to more drastic changes, such as altering the strategic direction altogether.

The need for strategic control is brought about by two key factors, the first of which is the need to know how well the firm is performing. Without strategic control, there are no clear benchmarks and ultimately no reliable measurements of how the company is doing. A second key factor supporting the need for strategic control is organizational and environmental uncertainty. Because strategic managers are not always able to accurately forecast the future, strategic control serves as a means of accounting for last-minute changes during the implementation process. In addition, competitors may respond immediately to a change in strategy, requiring that managers consider additional modifications.

The notion of strategic control has recently gained a "continuous improvement" dimension, whereby strategic managers seek to improve the efficiency and effectiveness of all factors related to the strategy. In other words, control should not be seen as an action necessary only when performance declines. Rather, managers should think critically when considering strategic control and look for opportunities to enhance performance even when things seem to be going well.

Strategic control can be exerted by the CEO, the board of directors, or individuals outside the top management team. The roles played by boards of directors, institutional investors, and shareholders who monitor firm strategies and often instigate control vary across firms. The influence of the board and others notwithstanding, ongoing strategic control is largely a function performed by the top management team. A five-step strategic control process can be utilized to facilitate this process, as depicted in Figure 12-1.

1. Top management determines the focus of control by identifying internal factors that can serve as effective measures for the success or failure of a strategy, as well as outside factors that could trigger responses from the organization.

2. Standards or benchmarks are established for internal factors with which the actual performance of the organization can be compared after the strategy is implemented.

3. Management measures or evaluates the company's actual performance, both quantitatively and qualitatively.

4. Performance evaluations are compared with the previously established standards.

5. If performance meets or exceeds the standards, corrective action is usually not necessary. If performance falls below the standard, then management must take remedial action.

FIGURE 12-1 Five-Step Strategic Control Process

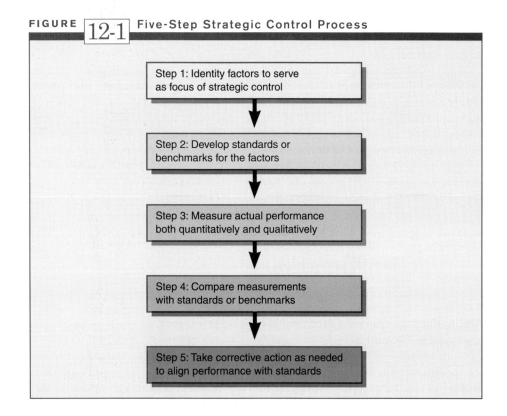

12-1 Step 1: Focus of Strategic Control

The focus of strategic control is both internal and external because it is top management's role to align the internal operations of the enterprise with its external environment. Relying on quantitative and qualitative performance measures, strategic control helps maintain proper alignment between the firm and its environment.

Although individual firms usually exert little or no influence over the external environment, macroenvironmental and industry forces must be continuously monitored because shifts can greatly influence the organization. The purpose of monitoring the external environment is to determine whether the assumptions on which the strategy is based remain valid. In this context, strategic control consists of modifying the company's operations to more effectively defend itself against external threats that may arise or become known.

Considering internal operations, top management must assess the strategy's effectiveness in accomplishing the firm's mission and goals: If the firm seeks to be the industry's low-cost producer, for example, its managers must compare its production efficiency with those of competitors and determine the extent to which the firm is attaining its goal. In the broad quantitative sense, management must assess the strategy's effectiveness in attaining the firm's objectives. For example, management can compare a firm's 3.7 percent market share with its stated objective of 4.1 percent to determine the extent to which its strategy is effective.

Firm performance may be evaluated in a number of ways. Management can compare current operating results with those from the preceding quarter or year. A qualitative judgment may be made about changes in product or service quality.

Quantitative measures may also be used, including return on investment (ROI), return on assets (ROA), return on sales (ROS), and return on equity (ROE), and growth in revenues.

A key problem with performance measurement is that one measure can be pursued to the detriment of another. The common goals of growth and profitability represent an example of this phenomenon. Many firms pursue growth by investing in R&D or new product development, or by slashing prices to gain customers. Either approach tends to reduce profits, at least in the short term. This reality was reflected in Ford's decision to cut North American production in the early 2000s and sacrifice market share to enhance profits. Ford's market share declined from about 22 percent in 2001 to below 19 percent in 2004, but profits increased steadily during this same period.[2]

12-2 Step 2: Strategic Control Standards (Benchmarks)

Profitability is the most commonly utilized performance measure and is therefore a popular means of gauging performance and exerting strategic control. Additional financial measures may also be helpful, such as many of the ratios discussed in Chapter 8.

Control standards should be established for the internal factors identified in the previous step. However, the focus should not consider past performance. Doing so can be myopic because it ignores important external variables. For example, a rise in a business's ROA from 8 percent to 10 percent may appear to be a significant improvement, but this measure must be evaluated in the context of industry trends. In a depressed industry, a 10 percent ROA may be considered outstanding, but that same return in a growth industry may be disappointing if the leading firms earn 20 percent. In addition, an increase in a company's ROA is less encouraging if performance continues to lag behind industry standards.

Competitive Benchmarking

The process of measuring a firm's performance against that of the top performers, usually in the same industry.

Often, strategic control standards are based on **competitive benchmarking**, which is the process of measuring a firm's performance against that of the top performers, usually in the same industry. After determining the appropriate benchmarks, a firm's managers set goals to meet or exceed them. **Best practices** are processes or activities that have been successful in other firms. These too may be adopted as a means of improving performance. Sources of competitive benchmarking standards are discussed in sections 12-2a through 12-2e (also see Strategy at Work 12-1).

Best Practices

Processes or activities that have been successful in other firms.

12-2a PIMS Program

PIMS (profit impact of market strategy) program

A database that contains quantitative and qualitative information on the performance of more than 5,000 business units.

The **profit impact of market strategy (PIMS) program** is a database that contains quantitative and qualitative information on the performance of thousands of firms and more than 5,000 business units. PIMS was developed in the 1960s as a result of General Electric's efforts to determine which factors drive profitability in a business unit.[3] GE's top managers and corporate staff began to assess business unit performance in a formal, systematic fashion. In 1975, other companies were invited to join the project, and the American Strategic Planning Institute (www.pimsonline.com) was founded to manage the effort. The original PIMS survey involved about 3,000 business units in 200 firms between 1970 and 1983. Data collection continued after 1983, however, with about 4,000 businesses currently included.

Each of the participating businesses provides quantitative and qualitative information to the program, such as market share, product and service quality,

Benchmarking for E-Business at UPS

The Internet currently plays a substantial role in benchmarking. According to Steve Johnson, co-director of the e-commerce program at Andersen Consulting in Chicago, "It's useful to understand where you want to go. Organizations need to find target audiences that [they're] trying to communicate with…and then, with regard to each of those target audiences, what are your specific objectives in terms of the outcomes that you're trying to achieve? And then that should lead you to a system of relevant benchmarks."

According to Mark Czarnecki, president of The Benchmarking Network Inc., an organization in Houston that runs and monitors benchmarks among companies, "Before a company can even begin to devise its benchmarks, it must first examine its core business processes. Those include developing and selling products and services to Web customers and running an organization's online operations as efficiently as possible. Once those core processes have been determined, companies need to figure out how much those processes are costing them. Then, based on that information, businesses can compare their cost structures to those of other companies and evaluate their own performance over time."

United Parcel Service (UPS) has been particularly successful at developing its e-business. UPS has been benchmarking its online tracking system every December since the site was launched in 1994. Having a benchmark to measure those requests has helped to keep UPS at the forefront of its e-commerce race with rival companies such as FedEx and DHL. According to UPS spokesman Steve Holmes, "Online tracking requests are certainly a very important benchmark that we look at, because it's probably the most widely used information that our customers access."

UPS has adopted a combination of integrated paper-based information and electronic messaging to improve efficiency in its processing of orders. UPS believes that in today's hyper-speed business environment, secure, efficient, and streamlined communications are key components. The service enables users to send and track digital files securely across the Internet. It also provides delivery confirmation, proof of receipt, and a password-protection option.

UPS has adopted this strategy in an effort to out-maneuver the U.S. Postal Service and FedEx for the steadily increasing number of Internet sales shipments. UPS continues to perform well, as it receives more than a million package-tracking requests every day through its Web site.

Sources: G. Gately, "HP and UPS Offer 'E' Alternative to Overnight Delivery," E-Commerce Times, 28 March 1999; M. Hillebrand, "UPS Offers Free Access to Online Tracking Site," E-Commerce Times, 5 October 1999.

new products and services introduced as a percentage of sales, relative prices of products and services, marketing expenses as a percentage of sales, and research and development expenses as a percentage of sales. Two profitability measures are used: net operating profit before taxes as a percentage of sales (ROS), and net income before taxes as a percentage of total investment (ROI) or of total assets (ROA). Participating firms have access to the data in aggregate form (i.e., no specific entries from other firms), whereas only limited data are available to nonparticipating organizations. Interestingly, the PIMS studies found the market-perceived quality relative to that of competitors was the single best predictor of market share and profitability.

Each of the PIMS variables has implications for strategic control. For example, top managers may discover that a business with low-quality measures may also be spending substantially less in research. R&D efforts may be enhanced to address the discrepancy. PIMS data has its limitations, however. A positive correlation between two PIMS variables, for example, does not necessarily mean that one causes the other. Hence, decision makers should exercise caution when interpreting the results.

12-2b Published Information for Strategic Control

Fortune magazine annually publishes the most- and least-admired U.S. corporations with annual sales of at least $500 million in such diverse industries as electronics, pharmaceuticals, retailing, transportation, banking, insurance, metals, food, motor vehicles, and utilities. Corporate dimensions are evaluated along factors such as quality of products and services, innovation, quality of management, market share, financial returns and stability, social responsibility, and human resource management effectiveness. Publications such as *Forbes, Industry Week, Business Week,* and *Industry Standard* also provide performance scorecards based on similar criteria. Although such lists generally include only large, publicly traded companies, they can offer high-quality strategic information at minimal cost to the strategic managers of all firms, regardless of size. Published information on three measures—quality, innovation, and market share—can be particularly useful, as discussed in sections 12-2c through 12-2e.

12-2c Product and Service Quality

Over the years, there has been a positive relationship between product and service quality—including both the conformance of a product or service to internal standards and the ultimate consumer's *perception* of quality—and the financial performance of those firms. Conforming to internal quality standards is not sufficient. Products and services must also meet the expectations of users, including both objective and subjective measures.[4]

Fortune assesses quality by asking executives, outside directors, and financial analysts to judge outputs of the largest firms in the United States.[5] Its studies consistently demonstrate a significant relationship between product and service quality and firm performance. Although the PIMS program assesses quality through judgments made by both managers and customers instead of asking executives and analysts, its findings also support a strong positive correlation between product quality and business performance.[6]

Consumer Reports is also an excellent source of product quality data, evaluating hundreds of products from cars to medications each year. Because *Consumer Reports* accepts no advertising, its evaluations are relatively bias free, rendering it an excellent source of product quality information for competing businesses. Even if the products of a particular business are not evaluated by this publication, that company can still gain insight on the quality of products and services produced by its competitors, suppliers, and buyers.

Specific published information may also exist for select industries. One of the best known is the Customer Satisfaction Index released annually by J. D. Power for the automobile industry. A survey of new-car owners each year examines such variables as satisfaction with various aspects of vehicle performance; problems reported during the first ninety days of ownership; ratings of dealer service quality; and ratings of the sales, delivery, and condition of new vehicles.[7] Numerous Internet sites (e.g., Virtualratings.com) offer quality ratings associated with industries for everything from computers to university professors.

Broadly speaking, the Internet serves as an excellent resource for strategic managers seeking quality assessments for its industry. For example, some sites (e.g., www.dealtime.com) provide consumer ratings of vendors. Although such information is not always reliable, feedback forums can provide strategic managers with valuable insight into the quality perceptions of their customers. Even Amazon.com ranks all books on sales volume and provides opportunities for readers to post comments to prospective buyers.

12-2d Innovation

Innovation is a complex process and is conceptualized, measured, and controlled through a variety of means. Some researchers use expenditures for product research and development and process R&D as a "surrogate" measure.[8] Expenditures on developing new or improved products and processes also tend to increase the level of innovation, a finding also supported by PIMS data.[9] However, it should not be assumed that all innovation-related expenditures yield the same payback.

Some firms plan and control their programs for innovation very carefully. 3M, for instance, has established a standard that 25 percent of each business unit's sales should come from products introduced to the market within the past five years. Not surprisingly, 3M invests about twice as much of its sales revenue in R&D as its competitors.[10] This approach is consistent with 3M's differentiation and prospector orientation at the business level.

12-2e Relative Market Share

Market share is a common measure of performance for a firm. As market share increases, control over the external environment, economies of scale, and profitability are likely to be enhanced. In large firms, market share often plays an important role in managerial performance evaluations at all levels in the organization. Because market share gains ultimately depend on other strategic variables, such as consumer tastes, product quality, innovation, and pricing strategies, changes in relative market share may serve as a strategic control gauge for both internal and external factors.

For successful smaller businesses, market share may serve as a strategic control barometer because some businesses may strategically plan to maintain a low market share. In this event, the strategic control of market share emphasizes variables that are not targeted at growth and includes tactics that encourage high prices and discourage price discounts. Limiting the number of product or markets in which the company competes also serves to limit small market share. A small market share combined with operations in limited product or markets may allow a company to compete in domains where its larger rivals cannot. Hence, for some companies, emphasizing increases in relative market share can trigger increases in cost or declines in quality and can actually be counterproductive.[11]

12-3 Steps 3 to 5: Exerting Strategic Control

Exerting strategic control requires that performance be measured (step 3), compared with previously established standards (step 4), and followed by corrective action (step 5), if necessary. Strategic control may be exerted in a number of different ways, such as through multilevel performance criteria, through performance itself, and through organizational variables.

12-3a Strategic Control through Competitive Benchmarking

Strategic control should occur constantly at various organizational levels and within various functions of the organization. Realistic performance targets, or benchmarks, should be established for managers throughout the organization. At the organizational level, factors such as profitability, market share, and revenue growth may be applied. The most appropriate performance benchmarks are those associated with the strategy's success, and those over which the organization has control.

Benchmarks should also be specific. For example, if market share is identified as a key indicator of the success or failure of a growth strategy, a specific market share should be identified, based on past performance and industry norms.

Without specificity, it is difficult to assess the effectiveness of a strategy after it is implemented if clear targets are not identified in advance.

Control at the functional level may include factors such as the number of defects in production or composite scores on customer satisfaction surveys. Like organization-wide benchmarks, functional targets should also be specific, such as "3 defective products per 1,000 produced" or "97 percent customer satisfaction based on an existing survey instrument."

Generally speaking, corrective action should be taken at all levels if actual performance is less than the standard that has been established unless extraordinary causes of the discrepancy can be identified, such as a halt in production when a fire shuts down a critical supplier. It is most desirable for strategic managers to consider and anticipate possible corrective measures *before* a strategy is implemented when possible.

12-3b Control through Performance

Control through performance occurs at the organizational level by comparing the company's profitability or market share growth to others in the marketplace. For example, the collective market share for cable television providers consistently declined throughout the 1990s. Many cable customers switched to less expensive satellite providers such as DirecTV and Dish Network. By the early 2000s, cable's competitive advantage of simplicity and complete local network programming had eroded in light of the satellite providers' ability to offer small, easy-to-install, and discreet satellite dishes and to include local networks as part of the service plan. As a result, cable companies began cutting rates in 2002 in an effort to regain lost market share.[12]

Because individual measures of performance can provide a limited snapshot of the firm, certain companies now use a balanced scorecard approach to measuring performance. The **balanced scorecard** measurement is not based on a single quantitative factor, but on an array of quantitative and qualitative factors, such as return on assets, market share, customer loyalty and satisfaction, speed, and innovation.[13] The balanced scorecard approach looks beyond profits by considering other factors that contribute to the overall health of the firm and position it for strong performance in the future. The key to employing a balanced scorecard is to select a combination of performance measures tailored specifically to the firm. This approach has helped a large number of firms better understand performance issues.[14]

The PIMS program provides a broad range of benchmarks against which a firm's performance can be compared. Top managers may also monitor the price of the company's stock as relative price fluctuations suggest how investors value the performance of the firm. A sudden drop in price makes the firm a more attractive takeover target, whereas sharp increases may mean that an investor or group of investors is accumulating large blocks of stock to engineer a takeover or a change in top management.

12-3c Control through Formal and Informal Organizations

Strategic control can occur directly through the formal organization or indirectly through the informal organization. The **formal organization**, the official structure of relationships and procedures used to manage organizational activity, can facilitate or impede a firm's success. When an organization's structure is no longer appropriate for its mission, strategic control can initiate a change. Top managers can exert formal control through such actions as modifying the structure or changing the reward system.

Popularity has increased for a means of exerting control through the formal organization called **business process reengineering**, which is the application

Balanced Scorecard

An approach to measuring performance based on an array of quantitative and qualitative factors, such as return on assets, market share, customer loyalty and satisfaction, speed, and innovation.

Formal Organization

The official structure of relationships and procedures used to manage organizational activity.

Business Process Reengineering

The application of technology and creativity to eliminate unnecessary operations or drastically improve those that are not performing well.

of technology and creativity to eliminate unnecessary operations or drastically improve those that are not performing well. As such, companies sought to eliminate any process that did not add value to the organization's goods and services. For example, many consumer goods manufacturers during this period began to rethink their packaging operations, and many of them eliminated large, cumbersome boxes in favor of less costly shrink-wrapping. Some analysts have noted a reemergence of this trend in the early 2000s.[15]

In the 1990s and early 2000s, some organizations shifted from functional or product divisional structures to matrix structures and experienced considerable unanticipated difficulty. Substantial structural changes cannot be easily implemented and typically require a large amount of training and development. Strategic managers at many of these firms underestimated the complications associated with transforming their organizational structures into a more complex matrix structure.

Whereas the formal organization concerns the official structure, the **informal organization** refers to the norms, behaviors, and expectations that evolve when individuals and groups come into contact with one another.[16] The informal organization is dynamic and flexible and does not require managerial decree to change. Simply stated, informal relationships can promote or impede strategy implementation and can play a greater role than the formal organization. Strategic control through the informal organization often involves attempts to modify the organization's culture.

When top executives use the formal organization effectively, the informal organization tends to reinforce the formal organization and promote the same values. However, when the organization's value system is unclear or even contradictory, the informal organization will ultimately develop its own, more consistent set of values and rewards. For example, every organization claims to reward high job performance. However, when promotions and pay increases go to individuals who have the greatest seniority (regardless of their level of performance), employees will lose motivation and develop their own set of informal rules concerning what will and will not be rewarded.

Management must recognize its limitations concerning the informal organization. Specifically, management can *influence*, but cannot control, the informal organization. The most effective means of influencing the informal organization is to develop and promote a formal organization that is consistent with the core values of the firm. The informal organization becomes dysfunctional when it develops means to address inconsistencies in the formal organization.

The relationship between the formal and informal organizations should not be underestimated. In general, any change in structure may also necessitate an appropriate modification in the organization's reward system so that the new forms of desired behavior will be properly rewarded. When management fails to align the formal organization's reward systems with new expectations, the informal organization typically changes to counterbalance the inconsistencies[17] (see Case Analysis 12-1).

12-4 Crisis Management

When a gunman killed thirty-three students and professors on the Virginia Tech campus in 2007, first responders and campus officials were thrust into a crisis of great magnitude.[18] Although university administrators should not be caught off guard, a catastrophe such as this is largely unpredictable and unavoidable. Indeed, any organization can be faced with a **crisis,** defined as any substantial disruption in operations that physically affects an organization, its basic assumptions, or

Informal Organization
Interpersonal norms, behaviors, and expectations that evolve when individuals and groups come into contact with one another.

Crisis
Any substantial disruption in operations that physically affects an organization, its basic assumptions, or its core activities.

Case Analysis 12-1

Step 24: How Should the Selected Alternative(s) Be Controlled?

How can one know in one, three, five, or ten years if an alternative has been successfully implemented? What should be done if sales or profits do not increase as planned? To facilitate answers to these questions, one needs to apply the five-step control process with as much specificity as possible.

First, identify what will be measured (i.e., how one will determine the extent to which the company is successful). Second, set the standards. For example, if ROA and "number of new profitable stores" are selected in step 1, then one might identify 15 percent ROA and twenty-two stores per year as standards or targets.

How were the standards developed? Consider the industry and past performance. If the industry mean for ROA is 15 percent, then 15 percent might be an appropriate target of performance for the company. The selected strategy can also be considered. If 110 additional retail locations are planned over the next five years, then twenty-two stores per year might be an appropriate target. It is important to clearly state how the standards were derived. Guessing, however, is not sufficient.

After performance is measured (step 3) and compared to the standards (step 4), corrective action may be taken (step 5). In the context of a case analysis, it is not possible to measure performance after the strategic recommendations are implemented. Therefore, one should suggest alternative courses of action that might be taken if the standards are not reached. Considering the preceding example, what changes (if any) should be made if only fifteen profitable stores are opened in the first two years or if ROA is only 8 percent? What changes (if any) should be made if the company reaches its target of twenty-two profitable stores, but ROA falls to 2 percent? At what point (if any) should the company consider retreating from the recommended alternative(s)? It is critical to provide considerable detail to demonstrate that all prospective future outcomes have been considered when outlining the present course of action. Of course, it is important to exert strategic control and take corrective action when necessary, not just at the end of a specified term.

Crisis Management

The process of planning for and implementing the response to a wide range of negative events that could severely affect an organization.

its core activities.[19] Such crises can include any low-probability, high-impact event that threatens the livelihood of the organization. Crises are typically characterized by ambiguity of cause, effect, and means of resolution, and a belief that the organization must respond quickly.[20] **Crisis management** refers to the process of planning for and implementing the response to a wide range of negative events that could severely affect an organization.

Some potential crisis events are more likely than others in certain types of firms. Airlines, for example, may focus crisis preparations on prospective events such as spikes in fuel prices and hijackings, whereas a small hardware store may plan for events such as the abrupt loss of a key employee or a natural disaster. Simply stated, firms can and should prepare for the crises they are most likely to face.

Crisis preparation is especially critical when a crisis can be avoided. In September 2006, for example, the Guangdong (China) Entry-Exit Inspection and Quarantine Bureau found one type of Proctor & Gamble's SK-II line of cosmetics tainted with low levels of chromium and neodymium. These metals can cause skin diseases and have been banned from cosmetics in a number of countries, including China. This situation presented a business problem—a potential crisis—for P&G. Unfortunately, the company did not address the situation effectively.

P&G initially refused to suspend sales of the SK-II line and hesitated to offer refunds to customers, doing so only after metals were discovered in more SK-II products. Angry consumers broke into a P&G office in Shanghai, resulting in widespread negative publicity in China.[21] The progression of these events caused this business problem to escalate into a crisis for the firm.

One of the most prominent examples of a crisis in recent history is the terrorist attacks on September 11, 2001, to New York City's World Trade Center and the U.S. Pentagon in Washington, D.C.[22] For some organizations, the attack resulted not only in the tragic loss of a large number of employees, but also a loss of key facilities and data.[23] Terrorism, however, represents only one form of crisis events.

Certain potential organizational crises also warrant consideration, such as fires and other natural disasters, economic crises (e.g., extortion, boycotts, bribery), and political unrest such as urban riots.[24] Even *bioterrorism*, the use of biological agents for terrorist purposes, has become a major concern. One recent survey reported that approximately two-thirds of executives are not confident that their organizations would be safe in the event of a biological or chemical attack, even though 80 percent of the organizations in question have crisis management plans in place.[25]

A more recent area of crises relates to information age activities, including computer system sabotage, copyright infringement, and counterfeiting. Criminals throughout the world can extort thousands of dollars from organizations fearful of a Web crash. So-called cyber-blackmailers may have the ability to disrupt or even halt Internet activity associated with certain sites.[26] The effects of crises on an organization can vary widely around the world and can be especially traumatic in emerging nations where recovery can be more difficult and costly.[27]

Numerous large firms faced major crises during the past few decades. Several commonly cited examples are discussed here. In 1984, gas leaked from a methyl isocyanate tank at a Union Carbide plant in Bhopal, India, killing approximately 3,800 persons and totally or partially disabling about 2,700 more. It was later learned that the leak occurred when a disgruntled employee sought to spoil a batch of the chemical by adding water to the storage tank. The incident was reported to officials at company headquarters in the United States after a twelve-hour delay, an event which sparked a widespread view that the firm was negligent and covering up details. India's Supreme Court later provided a $470 million settlement for victims and their families.[28]

In 1989, the Exxon Valdez tanker hit a reef in Prince William Sound, Alaska, spilling approximately 250,000 barrels of oil. Although there was no loss of human life, the loss of animal and bird life was extensive, and negative press was daunting. The company's untested crisis management plan said such a spill could be contained in five hours, but it was not implemented for two days. Exxon eventually spent about $2 billion to clean up the spill and another $1 billion to settle claims associated with the disaster.[29]

In 2003, The New Delhi Center for Science and Environment published a report asserting that local samples of Pepsi and Coke products contained pesticide residues at thirty times the acceptable limits in Europe. India's Parliament stopped serving the beverages and Indian nationalist activists in Allahabad smashed bottles and vandalized the property of a Coke distributor. Daily sales dropped by about one-third in less than two weeks, further curtailing efforts by the soft drink giants to spawn consumption of a product in a country where the average resident consumes less than one soft drink per month. The soft drink giants responded by questioning the methodology and credentials of the group's laboratory.[30]

In 2004, McDonald's chief executive Jim Cantalupo died suddenly from a heart attack. Less than six hours later, McDonald's board named president and chief operating officer Charlie Bell as his successor. The board had already intended for Bell to succeed Cantalupo at some point, but its quick, decisive action quelled many fears about the future of this leading fast-food chain. This response highlights the importance not only of planning for CEO succession but also of preparing for unexpected medical emergencies. Many experts suggest that boards should always be prepared for an unexpected loss of the top two executives in their firms.[31]

MSNBC and CBS Radio faced a publicity crisis in 2007 when radio talk show host Don Imus made disparaging and racially insensitive comments about members of the Rutgers University women's basketball team. CBS Radio initially suspended Imus from its radio program for two weeks, but MSNBC followed shortly thereafter by canceling its television simulcast of the program after firms began to pull their advertisements from the show and consumers threatened boycotts of other firms and the networks. CBS Radio fired Imus from the radio show several days later. The Imus incident could be seen as an extension of an ongoing broadcasting crisis for CBS, however. With Howard Stern's departure for Sirius Satellite Radio in 2005 and the growing popularity of satellite radio's talk show personalities like Andrew Wilkow, CBS is struggling to retain market share in a fiercely competitive industry.[32]

How a firm responds to a crisis can ultimately determine its survival and long-term success. Following the devastation of New Orleans from Hurricane Katrina in 2005, for example, grocer Winn Dixie contemplated closing shop in the area where it operates about 125 stores. Because Winn-Dixie was in Chapter 11 bankruptcy, the firm could exit with fewer repercussions than other grocers would face, because bankruptcy protection makes it easier to cancel costly store leases. CEO Peter Lynch saw it as an opportunity, however, choosing instead to use the millions of dollars the company would receive in insurance payments to rebuild the stores to be brighter and better stocked. Instead of departing the ravaged region, Winn-Dixie is banking on a strong rebound in New Orleans.[33]

Managing a crisis can be a complex process. Hence, it is helpful to view crisis management as a three-stage process. *Before the crisis*, organizations should develop a **crisis management team**, a cross-functional group of individuals within the organization who have been designated to develop and plan for worst-case scenarios and define standard operating procedures that should be implemented prior to any crisis event. Ideally, the team should represent all functional areas of the organization and should facilitate action necessary to prevent or minimize the effect of potential crisis events. For example, an organization anticipating labor unrest at a company facility may hire additional security guards or contract with a private agency to provide additional security.

Proactive organizations that continually assess their vulnerabilities and threats and develop crisis management plans tend to be adequately equipped when a crisis occurs. Proper preparation requires research of the literature, of the industrial sector, and of the company itself. Information is needed to properly prepare for the crisis events. When managers understand which crisis events are more likely to occur, they can plan for the event more effectively and foster a business culture that is ready to meet the challenge if and when a crisis occurs.[34]

During the crisis, an organizational spokesperson should communicate effectively with the public to minimize the effect of the crisis. For example, after being unprepared when Tylenol capsules were laced with cyanide, killing seven people in 1982, Johnson & Johnson improved its preparation, responding to a 1986 lacing incident by acknowledging the crisis with the public and instructing all consumers to return products for a refund.[35] Presentations to the public should be prompt, honest, professional, and streamlined through a single person or office.

Crisis Management Team

A cross-functional group of individuals within the organization who have been designated to develop and plan for worst-case scenarios and define standard operating procedures that should be implemented prior to any crisis event.

Source: Comstock.com

Case Analysis 12-2

Step 25: What Crisis Events Should the Firm Anticipate? What Are the Future Prospects for the Company?

Given the nature of the firm, its industry, and the recommended strategies, what crisis events are most realistic? This type of analysis varies considerably by firm and industry. Although it is impossible to anticipate and prepare for every conceivable crisis that a firm may face, attention should be placed on those that are most likely to occur, can be avoided or palliated, and are likely to result in substantial losses.

How do the strategic recommendations differ from the current strategy? Will the outlook for the company change as a result of these recommendations? Will the organization be successful in the coming decade? What strategic issues were not addressed in the recommendations that may become more important in the next few years? Why were they not addressed in the present analysis?

After the crisis, communication with the public should continue as needed, and the cause of the crisis should be uncovered. Understanding the cause can help executives minimize the likelihood that the crisis will occur again and improve preparation for the crisis if it does.[36]

Throughout these stages, three key points should be highlighted. First, organizational leaders should take crisis management seriously. Sooner or later, every organization will face a crisis, and survival may hinge on the organization's ability to manage the situation properly. Second, steps should be taken to prevent or reduce the likelihood of crisis events when such action is practicable. Finally, even when a crisis cannot be avoided, it should be handled appropriately. Managing a crisis requires an investment of time attending to specific activities before, during, and after such an event. How a crisis is managed can have a tremendous effect on the organization in both the short and long term.

Unfortunately, although few executives would reject these points, many acknowledge that their firms are not as prepared as they should be. This inconsistency occurs for three reasons. First, some executives view crisis events as largely unpredictable or unavoidable, and therefore not worthy of precious managerial time and resources. Second, many managers believe that they lack the time to adequately prepare for potential crises. Third, some leaders recognize the need for crisis planning and are willing to commit the time, but simply lack the expertise necessary to make the appropriate preparations.

Crisis management is a key component of strategic control, and arguably the entire strategic management process. Investing sufficient time, energy, and resources into preventing crises when possible and managing them when necessary can pay dividends (see Case Analysis 12-2).

12-5 Summary

The strategic control process consists of determining the extent to which the company's strategies are successful in attaining its goals. This process is accomplished through five steps. First, top management must determine what serves as a measure of a strategy's success and, therefore, needs to be controlled. Next, standards of performance should be developed for these elements. Management then measures performance along these lines both quantitatively and qualitatively and compares the actual performance to the standards. Reasons for discrepancies between actual measures and standards are analyzed, and corrective action is taken to resolve any areas where performance needs to be enhanced.

Crisis management refers to the process of planning for and implementing the response to a wide range of negative events that could severely affect an organization. Like strategic control, crisis management is an ongoing process.

Key Terms

balanced scorecard	crisis	informal organization
best practices	crisis management	PIMS program
business process reengineering	crisis management team	strategic control
competitive benchmarking	formal organization	

Review Questions and Exercises

1. What are the five steps in the strategic control process?

2. Why is it critical to identify the appropriate strategic control standards for a firm?

3. Should corrective action always be taken when performance falls below the predetermined standard? Likewise, should correction action never be taken when performance meets or exceeds the predetermined standard? Explain.

4. Explain how competitive benchmarking is used in strategic control. What are some commonly used competitive benchmarks?

5. What is crisis management and why is it important?

Practice Quiz

True or False

1. Strategic control should be ongoing and occur throughout the strategic management process.

2. The PIMS program is a government-sponsored effort to improve strategic planning effectiveness in the United States.

3. Corrective action should usually, but not always, be taken at all levels if actual performance is less than the standard that has been established.

4. Strategic control can be exerted through either the formal or informal organization.

5. Crisis management refers to efforts made to eliminate the possibility that the organization can be affected negatively by unforeseen events.

6. Crisis management involves a series of steps that can be taken before a crisis occurs, while it is occurring, and after it has passed.

Multiple Choice

7. Strategic control is important because

    A. it is difficult to know how well the firm is performing without it.

    B. the organization's environment is uncertain and always changing.

    C. lower-level managers need an effective means of providing feedback to top management.

    D. A and B only

8. The strategic control process begins by

    A. identifying appropriate performance measures.

    B. establishing standards of performance.

    C. measuring performance.

    D. taking corrective action as needed.

9. The process of measuring a firm's performance against that of the top performers, usually in the same industry, is known as

    A. competitive positioning.

    B. performance measurement.

    C. benchmarking.

    D. PIMS analysis.

10. Sources of published information for strategic control available to the public include all of the following except

    A. the *Wall Street Journal*.

    B. *Consumer Reports*.

    C. PIMS data.

    D. many trade journals.

11. Benchmarks should be
   A. broad, not specific.
   B. associated with the strategy's success.
   C. outside the firm's control.
   D. all of the above

12. Which of the following approaches bases the measurement of performance on an array of quantitative and qualitative factors instead of a single quantitative measure in the organization, such as profitability?
   A. balanced scorecard
   B. PIMS analysis
   C. competitive benchmarking
   D. none of the above

Notes

1. J. C. Picken and G. G. Dess, "Out of (Strategic) Control," *Organizational Dynamics* 26(1) (1997): 35–48.

2. J. B. White and N. Shirouzu, "At Ford Motor, High Volume Takes Backseat to Profits," *Wall Street Journal* (7 May 2004): A1, A12.

3. C. H. Springer, "Strategic Management in General Electric," *Operations Research* 21 (1973): 1177–1182.

4. L. Dube, L. M. Renaghan, and J. M. Miller, "Measuring Customer Satisfaction for Strategic Management," *Cornell Hotel and Restaurant Administration Quarterly* (February 1994): 39–47; J. M. Groocock, *The Chain of Quality* (New York: Wiley, 1986).

5. P. Wright, D. Hotard, J. Tanner, and M. Kroll, "Relationships of Select Variables with Business Performance of Diversified Corporations," *American Business Review* 6(1) (January 1988): 71–77.

6. Robert D. Buzzell and Bradley T. Gale, *The PIMS Principles: Linking Strategy to Performance* (New York: Free Press).

7. A. Taylor III, "More Power to J. D. Power," *Fortune* (18 May 1992): 103–106.

8. Buzzell et al., *The PIMS Principles*; P. Wright, M. Kroll, C. Pringle, and J. Johnson, "Organization Types, Conduct, Profitability, and Risk in the Semiconductor Industry," *Journal of Management Systems* 2(2) (1990): 33–48.

9. P. Fuhrman, "No Need for Valium," *Forbes* (31 January 1994): 84–85.

10. K. Kelly, "3M Run Scared? Forget about It," *Business Week* (16 September 1991): 59.

11. W. E. Fruhan Jr., "Pyrrhic Victories in Fights for Market Share," and R. G. Hamermesh, M. J. Anderson, and J. E. Harris, "Strategies for Low Market-Share Businesses," in *Strategic Management*, ed. R. G. Hamermesh (New York: Wiley, 1983), 112–125, 126–138.

12. P. Grant, "The Cable Guy Cuts His Rates," *Wall Street Journal* (25 September 2002): D1, D2.

13. R. Kaplan and D. Norton, *The Balanced Scorecard: Translating Strategy into Action* (Boston: Harvard Business School Press, 1996); Kaplan and Norton, *The Strategy Focused Organization* (Boston: Harvard Business School Press, 2001).

14. M. L. Frigo, "Strategy and the Balanced Scorecard," *Strategic Finance* 84(5) (2002): 6–8; E. M. Olson and S. F. Slater, "The Balanced Scorecard, Competitive Strategy, and Performance," *Business Horizons* 45(3) (2002): 11–16.

15. N. P. Archer, "Methodologies and Tools for E-Business Change Management," presented at the 24th Annual McMaster World Congress, Hamilton, Ontario, Canada (15–17 January 2003); E. Abrahamson and G. Fairchild, "Management Fashion: Lifecycles, Triggers, and Collective Learning Processes," *Administrative Science Quarterly* 44 (1999): 708–728.

16. D. Krackhardt and J. R. Hanson, "Informal Networks: The Company behind the Chart," *Harvard Business Review* 71(4) (July–August 1993): 104–111.

17. G. A. Miller, "Culture and Organizational Structure in the Middle East: A Comparative Analysis of Iran, Jordan and the USA," *International Review of Sociology* 11 (2001): 309–324; H. Kahalas, "How Competitiveness Affects Individuals and Groups within Organizations," *Journal of Organizational Behavior* 22(1) (2001): 83–85.

18. C. Dade and G. Fields, "Gunman Kills 32 People on Virginia Tech Campus," *Wall Street Journal Online Edition* (16 April 2007).

19. J. Burnett, *Managing Business Crises: From Anticipation to Implementation* (Westport, CT: Quorum, 2002).

20. C. Pearson and J. Clair, "Reframing Crisis Management," *Academy of Management Review* 23, 59–76.

21. M. Fong and L. Chao, "P&G Stumbles in China," *Wall Street Journal Interactive Edition* (25 September 2006).

22. D. N. Greenberg, J. A. Clair, and T. L. Maclean, "Teaching through Traumatic Events: Uncovering the Choices of Management Educators as They Respond to September 11th," *Academy of Management Learning & Education Journal* 1(1) (2002): 38–54.

23. J. W. Greenberg, "September 11, 2001: A CEO's Story," *Harvard Business Review* 80(10) (2002): 58–64; P. 't Hart, L. Heyse, and A. Boin, "New Trends in Crisis Management Practice and Crisis Management Research: Setting the Agenda," *Journal of Contingencies & Crisis Management* 9(4) (2001): 181–188.

24. A. H. Miller, "The Los Angeles Riots: A Study in Crisis Paralysis," *Journal of Contingencies and Crisis Management* 9(4) (2001): 189–199; C. Pearson and I. Mitroff, "From Crisis Prone to Crisis Prepared: A Framework for Crisis Management," *Academy of Management Executive* 7(1) (1993): 48–59.

25. "BioTerrorism Response Plans Doubted; Organizations Feel Vulnerable Despite Contingency Planning, According to Survey at International Biosecurity Summit," *Business Wire* (26 November 2002); J. A. Parnell, W. R. Crandall, and M. L. Menefee, "Management Perceptions of Organizational Crises: A Cross-Cultural Study of Egyptian Managers," *Journal of the Academy of Strategic and Organizational Leadership* 1(1) (1997): 8–19.

26. C. Bryan-Low, "Tech-Savvy Blackmailers Hone a New Form of Extortion," *Wall Street Journal* (5 May 2005): B1, B3.

27. A. Miller, "The Los Angeles Riots: A Study in Crisis Paralysis," *Journal of Contingencies and Crisis Management* 9(4): 189–199; Parnell et al., "Management Perceptions of Organizational Crises"; Pearson et al., "From Crisis Prone to Crisis Prepared."

28. Bhopal.com Information Center, accessed November 26, 2002, www.bhopal.com.

29. A. Tanneson and L. Weisth, "FT Report: Mastering Leadership," *Financial Times* (22 November 2002).

30. J. Slater, "Coke, Pepsi Fight Product-Contamination Charges in India," *Wall Street Journal* (15 August 2003): B1, B4.

31. C. Hymowitz and J. S. Lublin, "McDonald's CEP Tragedy Holds Lessons," *Wall Street Journal* (20 April 2004): B1, B8; R. Gibson and S. Gray, "Death of Chief Leaves McDonald's Facing Challenges," *Wall Street Journal* (20 April 2004): A1, A16.

32. B. Steinberg, B. Barnes, and E. Steel, "Facing Ad Defection, NBC Takes Don Imus Show Off TV," *Wall Street Journal* (12 April 2007): B1.

33. J. Adamy, "The Aisles of Optimism," *Wall Street Journal* (3 October 2005): B1, B6.

34. L. Barton, *Crisis in Organizations II* (Cincinnati: South-Western Publishing Co., 2001); R. R. Ulmer, "Effective Crisis Management through Established Stakeholder Relationships," *Management Communication Quarterly* 14 (2001): 590–615.

35. P. Shrivastava, I. I. Mitroff, D. Miller, and A. Miglani, "Understanding Industrial Crises," *Journal of Management Studies* 25 (1988): 205–303.

36. Special thanks to John E. Spillan, Ph.D., The Pennsylvania State University, DuBois Campus, for his insight and suggestions concerning the role of crisis management in the strategic management of organizations.

READING 12-1

Insight from *strategy+business*

In the past, many industries contained firms that approached their business activities in similar ways. Today, as this chapter's strategy+business reading explains, new entrants are taking markedly different approaches to organizing their business activities. Many are providing their customers with superior value and are challenging their traditional counterparts for industry leadership.

Format Invasions: Surviving Business's Least Understood Competitive Upheavals

By Bertrand Shelton, Thomas Hansson, and Nicholas Hodson

Two of the most intense competitive wars in modern business history are being waged simultaneously today—both centered in the United States, but already spreading to Europe and beyond. General Motors and Ford, once global leaders in automobile manufacturing but now unprofitable and losing market share, seem helpless to defend their home markets against intruders like Toyota and Nissan. Among airlines, household names like United and US Airways have been driven into bankruptcy by intruders once viewed as niche carriers, such as Southwest Airlines. In both cases, struggling incumbents offer the same explanations: weakened industry demand, excessive labor costs, legacy pension obligations, and rising oil prices.

But these standard explanations are misleading. In the 1990s, incumbents like GM, Ford, United, and US Air (now US Airways) were already losing market share and money whenever they faced the intruders directly. Only rising markets elsewhere kept them profitable. Today, even if their employment costs were equalized, their pension obligations were lifted, and crude oil prices returned to $28 per barrel, they would still have higher costs and lower quality than their new competitors.

The real explanation is format invasion. Every business has a format—its own distinctive way of organizing the many activities involved in delivering its product or service. Incumbents suffer (as GM, Ford, United, and US Airways have suffered) when intruders enter their markets wielding new types of business formats. These new ways of assembling commonplace assets deliver familiar goods and services at massively lower cost, often 20 to 40 percent lower, while maintaining or improving quality. The traditional market leaders fail to recognize the power and potential of their competitors' new formats. They cling instead to their old familiar formats, and gradually but inevitably lose ground to the new ones.

Some business observers credit technological innovation as being the most critical factor in transforming an industry. But successful new formats do not rely on new or proprietary technology. Indeed, incumbents often have broader and deeper technological capabilities than intruders. Instead, new formats achieve their massive cost advantage by changing several of the business's main functions at once, often reaching backward to include suppliers or forward to include distributors. These changes are tightly interlinked: The new format "works" only when it's adopted as a whole, which makes the transition to a new format daunting for incumbents.

Other observers equate market development and growth with a "killer app"—a new feature or hit product, like the Chrysler minivan, the Apple iPod, or Pfizer's Viagra. Hence the frenetic chase for the new feature or hit product that will open the wallets of an existing market segment or galvanize a new one. But a new business format has little to do with innovative features or technological novelty. Rather, *massively lower cost* is the killer app in many markets —as companies as diverse as Dell, Inditex (Zara) apparel, Countrywide Financial, Nucor, Wal-Mart, and Charles Schwab, as well as Toyota and Southwest Airlines, have shown. Toyota's lean manufacturing methods, which ruthlessly eliminated the waste in its production systems, led to costs far below those of the Big Three Detroit automakers. Southwest's point-to-point format for air travel vastly reduced the ground and flight costs inherent in the "hub-and-spoke" format of the airline industry's established leaders. In recent decades, intruders wielding new business formats have trounced traditional incumbents across a wide range of industries: personal-computer manufacturing, car care, mortgage lending, stockbrokerage, steel, and many varieties of retailing, from groceries to books to gasoline.

An effective format invasion throws open for question the prevailing operating assumptions of an industry.

Consider, for example, two recent format invasions in the European gasoline retail sector. The predominant format for the past several decades was the large, self-service gas station combined with a convenience store, which had supplanted the older format of small, full-service gas stations with repair bays. Jet, now a subsidiary of ConocoPhillips, has entered the Scandinavian market with a wholly new format: a completely unattended gas station. Effectively, it is a giant vending machine. By eliminating the station manager, cashiers, and other support costs, the new stations require only half as much margin per liter of gas to earn an attractive return. They can offer an almost unbeatable combination of low prices and convenient locations.

Meanwhile, in the United Kingdom and France, grocery chains have initiated a different kind of format invasion in the same sector, moving aggressively into gasoline, leveraging their existing stores and infrastructure to sell gasoline at much lower costs and prices. Gasoline is just one more product for a grocery chain, whose entire motor fuel department need be only a handful of people, compared with the hundreds employed by the old-format oil companies to support similar market share levels.

Both new formats are coming to the United States. Grocers, general merchandisers, and warehouse clubs have all begun offering gasoline, many of them using unattended operations like Jet's. They now serve about 10 percent of the U.S. national gasoline market, and much more in some markets, notably Texas. It remains unclear which variant of these new formats will win, with the answer likely varying by local market. But one thing seems clear: The traditional format is losing, and will continue to lose.

It may seem remarkable that this pattern recurs so often. Yet that's the reality of format invasions. Highly sophisticated incumbent companies, with years of experience and strong market positions, ignore and resist a new format's opportunities to reduce cost, while upstart new entrants embrace and exploit them. Intruders wielding new business formats in just this way have shattered traditional competitors across a wide swath of industries, in countries ranging from the United States to France to Japan. As a result, companies championing new business formats are among the largest creators of shareholder value. Conversely, incumbent companies' failure to respond effectively accounts for a great deal of shareholder value destruction. (See Exhibit 1.)

The pattern continues. New format invasions seem to be occurring now in industries as diverse as fashion apparel, commercial aircraft, and wireless communications. And (investors, take note) we see many established companies responding to format invasions with the same tactics that have failed other incumbents before. But there is good news for executives of established companies. Format invasions are not overnight successes; there is time to respond. And incumbents need not be losers. Established companies in large industries—armed as they are with substantial assets, intellectual capital, and customer relationships—can defeat the invasions and emerge as winners, if they recognize:

- Where new formats come from
- How new formats take over a market
- Why incumbent companies so often fail to respond to new formats
- How to take advantage of a new format.

Birth: Reconceiving Costs

Over time, an industry's prevailing format becomes a victim of its own accomplishments. The quest within one company to earn a premium or bring down costs in targeted activities succeeds—and is then copied across the industry. Competitors may become less distinct, in both features and performance, and the category commoditizes. Growth may slow, but the industry can carry on in a state of equilibrium for quite a long time.

Then an innovative new format appears. One day, somebody reexamines the activities common across the industry and discovers or develops a completely new way of performing them. Quite often, this new pattern involves a focus on activities that the industry's leading companies had not noticed, much less singled out for attention. But by focusing on these overlooked factors, the innovator finds ways to configure or reconfigure the company's assets, people, and processes to greatly reduce the activities' costs.

Southwest Airlines provides a famous contemporary example. Once in the air, Southwest is no more efficient than its traditional competitors. But Southwest was the first airline to focus its institutional attention on the least interesting part of aviation: the time an airplane sits at the gate. By dramatically reducing that turnaround time and ruthlessly applying the same logic to all its operations, Southwest developed a 40 percent or greater cost advantage that its old-format competitors seem helpless to meet. (See "Airline Invasions: 'Barbarians' at the Gates," page 9.)

For a not-so-famous example, take Inditex, the European apparel maker best known for its major brand, Zara. In the mid-1990s, European fashion apparel was dominated by specialty brands that put out new lines of clothing each season, hoping to catch the eye of trend-conscious consumers. These firms were on a

EXHIBIT 1   Shareholder Return for New-Format Intruders vs. Old-Format Incumbents*

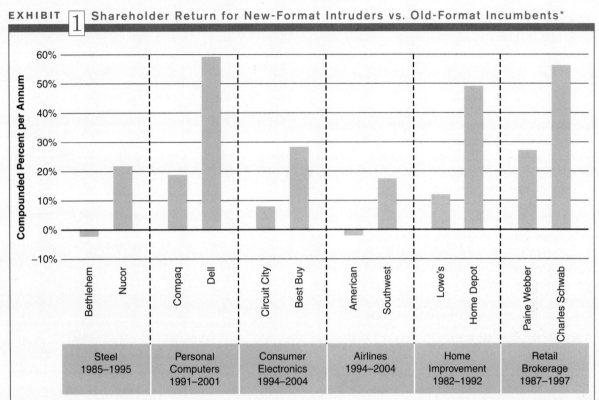

Steel 1985–1995	Personal Computers 1991–2001	Consumer Electronics 1994–2004	Airlines 1994–2004	Home Improvement 1982–1992	Retail Brokerage 1987–1997

*The shareholder impact of format invasion. Each pair of format battle contenders contrasts an incumbent on the left bar with an intruder on the right, during the peak decade of conflict in that industry.

Source: Booz Allen Hamilton; CompuStat

relentless treadmill, designing, sourcing, and distributing product for each season on an eight- to 12-month cycle. Although this was highly profitable if a firm's seasonal offering "hit the market"—selling a good proportion of product at full retail price—such good seasons were invariably interspersed with weaker ones, when much of the product sold only at heavy markdowns. Since all players had essentially identical business formats, they competed to reduce manufacturing costs by sourcing from China, India, and other low-cost locales.

Zara took a wholly different approach. Management realized that the biggest cost in fashion apparel is not in production and distribution (fabric, cutting, stitching, shipping, etc.) but in the margin forgone in marked-down sales of unpopular product. As a result, Zara created a business format capable of delivering a design from sketch to shelf in six weeks or less, allowing its designers and merchants to observe trends and respond rapidly, rather than making educated guesses about what customers might want eight months in the future. This approach

has its costs: Zara's manufacturing facilities are located in relatively high-cost Spain. However, Zara sells around 80 percent of its product at full price, twice the percentage most competitors achieve. Confident that its product portfolio is mostly "hits," Zara can price its product profitably at about 25 percent less than competing brands. The resulting extraordinary sales volumes have generated very attractive returns, fueling rapid expansion.

New formats often migrate; they jump across categories, customer segments, and geographies. Sam Walton borrowed Wal-Mart's supercenter concept—general merchandise plus food—from France's hypermarkets. Toys "R" Us transported the self-serve supermarket from groceries to toys. Southwest Airlines started in 1971 as an intrastate airline in Texas. Only in the last 10 to 15 years did Southwest break out from being a short-haul regional player to become a national force—and only within the past five to 10 years have airlines such as Ryanair and JetBlue successfully carried the Southwest format into markets without a similar point-to-point competitor.

Takeover: Capturing Demand

Time and time again, intruders in a wide variety of industries around the world have used the same tactics successfully to invade and take over existing markets. Invasions typically occur in four stages:

Stage I—Equilibrium. At the outset, incumbent-format firms serve their entire market. These firms play by variations on the same business rules, using largely the same approaches to product design, production, and marketing. Of course, each has its own slight distinctions in features, amenities, and pricing, and one or another company may tweak those to gain a temporary advantage. But these aren't decisive, since each player quickly imitates the others' worthwhile improvements.

This period can last for decades. U.S. supermarkets replaced neighborhood stores as the main purveyors of groceries in the 1950s. They lived in quiet equilibrium until Wal-Mart and the warehouse clubs finally invaded their markets with new formats in the 1990s.

Stage II—Intrusion. Most markets have a considerable amount of price-sensitive demand hanging around—both customers willing to change suppliers for a discount ("penny switchers") and noncustomers willing to start buying if prices fall low enough. For a new-format intruder, these customers represent a very attractive startup market. They don't value "frills"; they prefer a bare-bones offering at a lower price, and they don't have much loyalty to incumbent brands. So the intruder tailors its initial offering to their preferences, stripping out amenities that the new format could otherwise provide, to reduce costs still further.

Capturing these customers requires a careful pricing strategy. They don't look just for a good price, but for the absolute best price, gravitating elsewhere if the price goes even modestly higher. A successful intruder exploits this pattern, translating its cost advantage into prices at the very bottom of the market. These prices attract customers in extraordinary volume that more than compensates for the margin lost in the discount. Thus, a relatively low price, near the market bottom, is not as profitable as the lowest price at the market bottom. In the early stages of invasion, this phenomenon works to the advantage of the lowest-cost intruders.

At the same time, even price-sensitive customers know the difference between "bare bones" and "shoddy." They're naturally suspicious that a below-market price reflects inferior product quality or poor service. So a typical successful intruder works hard to build and maintain a reputation for candor, no-frills quality, reliability, and excellent customer service. It secures its relationship with customers through the openness of its menu and the clarity of its choices. The tendency of a new format to improve its product's quality and consistency helps establish that reputation.

Stage III—Expansion. The extraordinary profits that flow from the new format's huge cost advantage nurture rapid expansion: double-digit growth at margins hitherto unheard of in the industry. Format innovations aren't usually patentable technologies, so additional entrants soon emerge, imitating the new format. They would naturally prefer to compete against the old-format players than to compete against one another, so these imitators target market segments—customers, products, or geographies—into which the new format hasn't yet penetrated. A free-for-all ensues, as the new-format intruders race to occupy as much market "space" as they can.

Old-format incumbents may try to meet the intruders' low prices. But that seldom lasts long, since the incumbents labor under two disadvantages: the significantly higher costs inherent in the old format, and the broader amenity set they have customarily offered. So they typically redefine their target market upward, forsaking the price-driven customers now flocking to the intruders. There is a tempting but ultimately short-sighted rationale for abandoning these customers: Many of them are new to the category, "so we never actually *lost* them."

Retreating up-market relieves the incumbents' immediate pressures, but only postpones the problem. As the new format proliferates, it further erodes the old-format players' business, draining away their volume and depressing their prices. Their financial returns deteriorate, and investment in the old format gradually ceases.

The recent flurry of activity among European airlines nicely illustrates this expansion phase. Ryanair, easyJet, and a plethora of other new-format competitors have piled into the European air-travel market. They expanded far more rapidly than their acknowledged model, Southwest, did in the U.S., precisely because the U.S. example demonstrated how much potential the new format has.

The intensifying financial pressures on old-format European carriers already have eliminated some (Swissair, Sabena) and encouraged others to merge (KLM with Air France). Yet some of these incumbents remain convinced that the new-format upstarts are "for backpackers, not for businesspeople" and "cannot extend into long-haul markets"—as one executive at a traditional European airline told us quite recently.

Stage IV—Consolidation. The new-format players continue to expand, broadening their target market beyond price-sensitive customers. Adding amenities without giving up the new format's cost advantages becomes their next challenge; if they surmount it, they become very attractive to mainstream customers.

As the mainstream fills up with new-format players, competition among them pushes prices down toward the new format's long-run level, reducing their margins to more "normal" levels. At that point, the remaining traditional-format players must crumble, or retreat into minor niches. Meanwhile, the toughening environment gradually forces the new-format players to switch their attention from expansion to grinding competition among themselves—through incremental efficiencies, differentiated amenities, or intensified sales campaigns—with better performers acquiring weaker ones. Eventually, equilibrium is reestablished and the new business format dominates the market.

Incumbents: Misperceiving the Threat

We have found no cases in which an incumbent responded to a new business format successfully without essentially adopting it. It's true that many incumbents survive for quite some time in the face of a format invasion; they prune product lines, retrench operations, and scale back investment (if only because the business is generating less cash than it previously did). But none prosper over the long run unless they adopt the new format. No economically sound alternative seems to exist. Why do incumbents so consistently fail to recognize this, and let the intruders take away their markets?

Two classic misperceptions lie behind this common development. First, incumbents often mistakenly ascribe the new format's cost advantage to better factor prices, such as lower wages and benefits for employees or lower prices paid to suppliers. That explanation, despite being attractively straightforward, misses the central point—that the new format uses fewer resources, rather than merely paying less for those it uses.

This misperception sets incumbents on a path of fruitless confrontation with unions and suppliers. They reason that if their competitors got better factor prices, it was because they themselves hadn't been "tough" enough. Automakers, supermarkets (under pressure from Wal-Mart), and traditional airlines provide ready examples of old-format players distracted by these confrontations.

Second, incumbents often confuse the intruders with "value" or "budget" companies. In their view, the "value" company is making a niche play, appealing to the most price-conscious customers in its market. A "value" make of automobile is smaller, with a less-powerful engine and fewer extra features than a mainstream car, and thus carries a lower price tag. Similarly, a "value" department store offers no-frills products and fewer services and amenities than a mainstream store in the same market, at a lower price point. But these "value" companies rely on the same traditional business format as their mainstream competitors: They all face the same menu of trade-offs between amenities and price. The "value" companies just make different choices from that menu—choices attuned to the price conscious customers they've targeted. These traditional-format "value" competitors don't threaten the market's mainstream traditional companies.

In contrast, new-format companies create a different and better menu for themselves by operating in strikingly new ways that slice out slabs of cost. (See Exhibit 2.) The new format can deliver either a high or low level of features and amenities less expensively than the old format. Format invaders thus represent a long-term threat to the mainstream traditional companies in the sector, unlike other companies that merely pitch their offerings at the "value" end of the market.

This misperception fatally weakens the incumbents' efforts to counter the new-format intruders at each stage in the cycle. Early on, seeing the intruders as simple "value" companies, the incumbents may try competing head-to-head against them with a "value" offering of their own, providing lower features and amenities at a lower price, but still based on the old format. Examples include General Motors' Vega, an early (1970s) response to low-end import cars, and the lower-priced "value" subsidiaries of mainstream airlines.

Of course, the incumbents' "value" offerings can't truly meet the intruders' pricing head-to-head: Their cost disadvantage forces them to seek some premium above the intruders' price. But that misses the central point of the intruders' entry tactics—that price-sensitive customers respond to prices *at* the market bottom, not *near* it. Near-bottom pricing causes the incumbents to give up margin without commanding much volume. So the incumbents' "value" offerings quickly fail.

EXHIBIT 2 | Strategic Options for Old and New Formats*

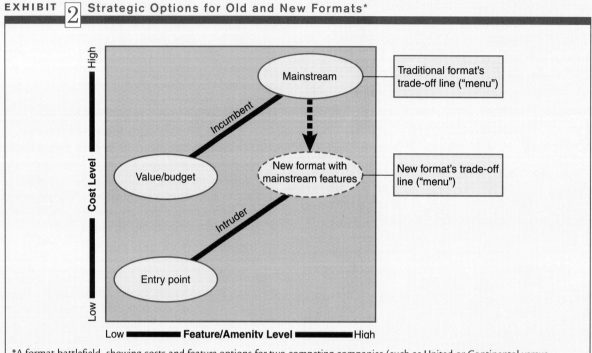

*A format battlefield, showing costs and feature options for two competing companies (such as United or Continental versus Southwest or JetBlue). The old-format incumbent is typically found in the high-cost/amenity quadrant, at upper right, and may provide a less expensive "value/budget" offering (Shuttle-by-United or CalLite). But the new-format intruder will always have lower costs. Incumbents can adopt their own version of the new format (the dotted oval), with mainstream features that the intruder may not have introduced.

Source: Booz Allen Hamilton

Later, the same misperception leads incumbents to believe they can retreat up-market safely, since they believe the new-format intruders can't follow. But in fact, the intruders have no such limitation—their new format can combine high features or amenities with low costs. Toyota's lean business format produces the top-of-the-line Lexus as well as the entry-level Corolla. Similarly, Target and Wal-Mart use the same extraordinarily efficient business format; Target has merely chosen to focus it on customers and merchandise that are farther upscale than Wal-Mart's.

Conversely, incumbents often reject the notion of adopting the new format on the grounds that doing so would require abandoning their up-market feature and amenity offering, and thus cause an unthinkable revenue loss. They fail to see a major opportunity: that *the company can combine high features and amenities with the new format's low costs.* There is a realistic opportunity, for instance, for a traditional airline to continue

providing high levels of service while adopting Southwest's more efficient production model. (In Exhibit 2, the traditional airline could move down the dotted line to the new format with mainstream features.)

This confusion also seems to underlie Harvard Business School Professor Clayton Christensen's well-known views on format competition. Professor Christensen argues that innovative products and business formats (or "value networks," as he calls them) begin life underperforming the requirements of a market's core customers. Later, as the intruder's performance improves, it gains the ability to enter the incumbents' core markets. Whatever the merits of this view with respect to technological innovations such as improved disk drives, it does not apply to new business formats. The choice of business format and the choice of amenity level are largely independent of each other. Most format innovations indeed appear at the low end of the market, but this is only because that represents the simplest and most expedient route for the intruder to monetize its innovation.

When a new-format intruder offers more features and amenities than its traditional competitors do, they will not necessarily be the same mix. The new format makes some amenities easier and some harder to provide, so the intruders do what any seller would do: accentuate their advantages. Airline passengers, for example, may wait a bit longer for connecting flights on Southwest, but they get nonstop flights more frequently. Retail customers may drive a bit farther to shop at a "big box" store, but they can choose from a broader variety of goods. In any case, these differences tend to be modest; the new format's lower costs and prices swamp any differences in its amenity mix.

Late in the cycle, as new-format intruders take ever more market share, the increasingly strapped incumbents often start to merge. From one perspective, these mergers appear inevitable and beneficial: Old-format companies face a contracting market, which simply cannot support as many of them as it before (even if the overall market remains robust). However, the traditional companies often expect more from this kind of industry consolidation than it can provide. Too often, they view consolidation as a real fix, rather than seeing it correctly as another step in their decline. This is because they view their collective overcapacity as the problem, rather than recognizing it as a symptom of the format invasion.

The Incumbent's Opportunity

Some incumbents have responded successfully to a format invasion. When they do, the results are extraordinarily profitable. We've looked at several companies that took on a format invasion successfully, and at several others that more or less tried but failed. Nothing we've seen indicates that the companies that made a successful transition to a new format had any greater depth of technical, financial, or operational resources than the peers they left behind. Nor did we find that they had "less to lose" by giving up the old format. But the winners adhered to a few basic principles, while avoiding some clear pitfalls.

The experience of Best Buy and Circuit City over the past decade comes close to being controlled experiment on this point. At the outset, nothing about Best Buy's market position or format distinguished it from Circuit City. If anything, Circuit City had more resources with which to innovate. But Best Buy identified and acted upon an opportunity where Circuit City did not.

In 1980, Circuit City was a rapidly growing electronics retailer, with a better format than traditional TV dealers. Customers viewed floor samples, made their selection—usually with help from a commissioned salesperson—and paid for the merchandise. They then took their receipt to a separate pick-up window, near the store exit, to collect their purchases. Many other retailers copied this format, including a small but successful electronics chain named Sound of Music, based near Minneapolis.

Then, in 1981, a Sound of Music store in Roseville, Minn., was hit by a tornado, forcing managers to hold a clearance sale with the inventory stacked on the sales floor. It was an unexpectedly wild success. Through this random event, company founder Richard Schulze discovered that a discount, no-frills, self-serve value proposition could be both very attractive to customers and very profitable for the company. After a couple of years of experimentation, Mr. Schulze opened his first warehouse-style, truly self-serve superstore in 1983, changing the company's name to Best Buy at the same time. The following year Mr. Schulze, sensing his new format's cost advantage over the incumbent leader, Circuit City (still thriving at that time), committed his company to a "won't be undersold" pricing policy. Mr. Schulze continued to adjust the new format during the next few years; in 1989, he launched a "grab and go" store, with salaried rather than commissioned salespeople.

Between 1994 and 2004, Best Buy gradually eclipsed Circuit City—earning a compound total shareholder return of 28 percent per year while Circuit City managed just 8 percent (despite a rapidly expanding market for consumer electronics). Circuit City lost market leadership in the sector beginning in 1997, but continues to follow its old format strategy. By now, it's a troubled company.

Companies that successfully survive a format invasion seem to have four common attributes:

1. *Successful incumbents start with a clear and accurate vision of how the new format works for their competitors—how it serves customers adequately at much lower cost.* Undeniably, that's hard work. A new format focuses on unfamiliar aspects of the business; an accurate vision must grasp what that new focus is. But the new format differs from the traditional format in so many ways—spread across so many parts of the business yet knitted so closely together—that it's hard to see. The successful companies don't just assemble a factual, detailed view of the new format; they fit those details into a realistic overall picture.

2. *Successful incumbents undertake the new format as an integrated whole, recognizing its tightly interlinked nature.* Too often, incumbents experiment halfheartedly with imitating a new format, layering bits and pieces of it onto their existing business. They modify just one element of their traditional business at a time, or they make a modification but don't pursue its implications through the rest of the business. Few companies have an appetite for making a flying leap to a whole new operating model—which is another way of explaining why so few incumbents make the transition to a new format. But the alternative—piecemeal adoption—just won't produce results.

3. *Successful incumbents adapt the new format in ways that don't compromise its cost advantages.* They provide a basic-level offer that meets the intruders' bottom-level prices profitably at the *basic* amenity level. This reclaims the bottom-of-market volume that they would otherwise forfeit to the new-format competitor. To this, they may add products or services with more features or amenities than the intruder has yet offered. They resist the temptation to blend the new format with the traditional format—an approach usually justified as "we're doing it, but our way." That approach rarely succeeds. After all, the new format moved away from the old to achieve some specific objectives; it's hard to move back without compromising them. These blends often fritter away much of the new format's cost advantage without any decisive offsetting gain in customer appeal.

4. *Successful incumbents make the new format their core business, not a side offering.* Assuming that a competitor's new format has already proved itself in the marketplace, execution is needed. Launching a side experiment signals that management sees the new format as a niche offering, with no bridge to changing the core business. It's easy for an organization to get excited at the outset about an experiment and invest a lot of energy in it ("Finally, we are actually doing something about the new format threat"), but it's ultimately ineffectual.

The story of the Home Depot format invasion of the 1980s, and the response by Lowe's Companies Inc. in the 1990s, shows how an incumbent company can come successfully to terms with a new format. Traditionally, Lowe's sold construction materials, mainly to professional homebuilders, through an extensive chain of small full-service outlets. In 1982, Home Depot introduced "big box" retailing in a "home improvement center" format: a much larger store (90,000 square feet versus 15,000 for a Lowe's outlet) with dramatically lower unit operating costs, due mainly to the labor savings from scale and self-service. The new format spread rapidly and profitably,

displacing traditional-format competitors—largely hardware and building supply stores.

Throughout the 1980s, Lowe's struggled to respond, trying to blend its traditional format with the new home improvement center. The company built larger stores (25,000 square feet) and modified its offerings and layout to accommodate both professionals and consumers. It didn't work. By 1988, Lowe's had fallen behind Home Depot in size, profitability, and shareholder returns. (See Exhibit 1.)

At that point, almost a full decade after the birth of Home Depot's format, Lowe's finally recognized the new format's power. In 1989, the company built an experimental home improvement center. In 1992, management committed to the format and started converting to new stores rapidly. (See Exhibit 3.) Since then, the profitability, growth, and shareholder returns of Lowe's have exceeded those of Home Depot.

Strategy for Survival

Format invasions seem almost certain to continue, probably with increasing frequency, as ideas for new formats flow ever more easily across industry and regional boundaries. The lessons for established companies in those markets seem clear.

- **Scan your markets regularly for format invaders.** Whenever a competitor—especially a new entrant—starts gaining market share by offering familiar products at below-market prices, suspect the possibility of a format invasion. If the new format continues growing, what will you do? Look askance at assumptions that the new format will apply only to some "value" niche. In particular, question any plans or actions that would forfeit down-market segments.

- **Understand the competitor's new format thoroughly,** including the full potential of its cost and quality advantages. Recognize that its "logic" will likely be unfamiliar, so aim to see it on its own terms. In particular, resist the temptation to assume that the intruder's success depends simply on lower factor prices, selling below costs, or other measures you could never emulate (even if these elements are truly in the picture somewhere). Then, translate that understanding into a forecast of the new format's likely success over the next five to 10 years. Caution: Incumbents often unconsciously water down these forecasts on grounds of "realism." With a new format, forecasting extraordinary growth *is* realism.

- **Approach the new format as an opportunity.** At this point, you're likely well ahead of most incumbents

EXHIBIT 3 The Evolution of Lowe's Retail Format

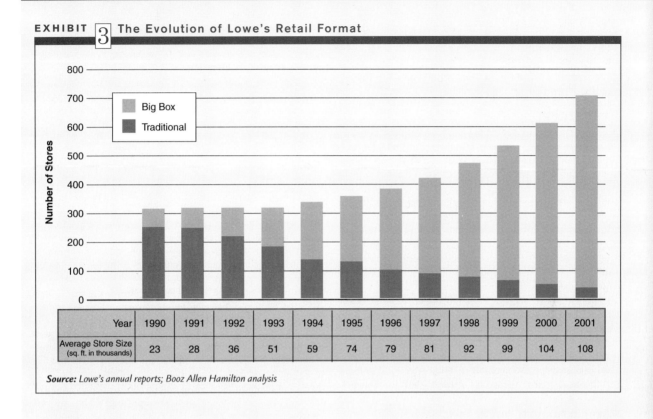

Year	1990	1991	1992	1993	1994	1995	1996	1997	1998	1999	2000	2001
Average Store Size (sq. ft. in thousands)	23	28	36	51	59	74	79	81	92	99	104	108

Source: Lowe's annual reports; Booz Allen Hamilton analysis

facing a successful new-format competitor. So you now have a significant opportunity to grow and profit at your traditional competitors' expense. In a mature market, the new format may well be the best opportunity available to your company. Make an assessment of its potential; then (if warranted) focus the company on seizing it.

- **Design your moves from the market back.** A practical plan for exploiting the new format does *not* start from your company's current position. Rather, it starts by asking, How could we imitate our most successful new-format competitor, with parity offerings, parity costs, and parity prices leading to growth and profits equaling theirs? (You won't necessarily implement this parity plan, but it forces your company's thinking away from its traditional format and toward the new one.)
- **Be cautious in adding features and amenities.** They may well be justified to build market share by appealing to mainstream customers, but that will happen only if they reinforce the new format's core advantages. (That's one reason why understanding the new format thoroughly is important.) A test: Does your new plan include a bare-bones offering that profitably matches your new-format competitors head-to-head on price and features? (If it doesn't, then your design has probably slipped away toward a less profitable "blended" format.)

- **Make the new format your mainstream business.** It's natural to field-test a new business format before committing to it wholeheartedly. But experimentation and niche marketing can become ends in themselves. Any plan for a test should define a successful outcome and the rollout plan that will follow, carrying the new format into the heart of your business.
- **Don't get distracted by merger possibilities.** Against the backdrop of a format invasion, combinations among traditional competitors present the illusion of progress. Unfortunately, because the combined incumbent remains fundamentally disadvantaged, the merged company's greater scale seldom provides enough benefits to offset the burdens of an old format. (However, a company that has adopted the new format successfully may find it worthwhile to acquire other old-format companies and bring them through the same transition.)

As for the two biggest format invasions going on right now, we don't know whether the incumbent automakers or airlines will survive or succumb. Some may well retain industry leadership, growing their businesses and delivering attractive shareholder returns over the long term. If so, they will do it by finally adopting and adapting the superior new formats that have overtaken them—the formats that enabled the Southwest Airlines and Toyotas of the world to succeed and prosper in the same economic and market conditions in which the old formats proved to be uncompetitive.

Resources

Clayton M. Christensen, Scott D. Anthony, and Erik A. Roth, *Seeing What's Next: Using the Theories of Innovation to Predict Industry Change* (Harvard Business School Press, 2004): A theory of disruptive success that partly, but not completely, meshes with the format invasion concept.

Jeff Ferry, "Flextronics: Staying Real in a Virtual World," *s+b,* Winter 2004, www.strategy-business.com/press/article/04408: A Singaporean contract manufacturer emulates Toyota's innovations.

Victoria Griffith, "Welcome to Tesco, Your Glocal Superstore," *s+b,* First Quarter 2002, www.strategy-business.com/press/article/11670: Of the *s+b* retail case studies, the most relevant format-renewal example.

Tom Hansson, Jürgen Ringbeck, and Markus Franke, "Flight for Survival: A New Business Model for the Airline Industry," *s+b,* Summer 2003, www.strategy-business.com/press/article/21966: More detailed view of the airline format invasion and its cost consequences.

Art Kleiner, "The Next Wave of Format," *Deeper News,* 2001, www.well.com/user/art/formats.pdf: Manifesto about Internet and media formats as socially created, not technological, innovations.

William Leach, *Land of Desire: Merchants, Power, and the Rise of a New American Culture* (Vintage, 1993): Early 20th-century format invasions among department stores, fashion merchandisers, and investment banks.

Chuck Lucier, "Herb Kelleher: The Thought Leader Interview," *s+b,* Summer 2004, www.strategy-business.com/press/article/04212: The cofounder of Southwest Airlines explains the strategy underlying his airline's cost advantage.

Costas Markides and Paul Geroski, "Colonizers and Consolidators: The Two Cultures of Corporate Strategy," *s+b,* Fall 2003, www.strategybusiness.com/press/article/03306: Cultural change for enabling resilience among incumbents.

James Womack and Daniel T. Jones, *Lean Solutions: How Producers and Customers Achieve Mutual Value and Create Wealth* (Simon & Schuster, 2005): Wholesale Toyota-inspired manufacturing and service redesign.

Bertrand Shelton (shelton_bert@bah.com) is a vice president in Booz Allen Hamilton's San Francisco office. He has advised leading petroleum, financial-services, aerospace, and consumer goods companies in North America, Europe, and Japan. He focuses on helping companies facing market discontinuities, such as format invasions, technology shifts, and deregulation.

Thomas Hansson (hansson_tom@bah.com) is a vice president in Booz Allen Hamilton's Los Angeles office. He focuses on new business development, growth, mergers and acquisitions, and pricing issues for a variety of corporate sectors, and has written extensively on new operating models and business formats in the global airline industry.

Nicholas Hodson (hodson_nicholas@bah.com) is a vice president with Booz Allen Hamilton in San Francisco. He has advised companies in Europe and the United States in the retailing, fashion apparel, petroleum, wireless, and aerospace industries on issues including organization design, strategy-based transformation, and new format development.

Case Analysis

Case studies provide opportunities to apply the principles discussed in the concepts portion of the text. These concepts are easier to understand when they are seen at work in ongoing enterprises. The twenty-five-question model presented in the text provides a clear and comprehensive approach to completing a case project. Several additional considerations are discussed in the following sections.

There are two different types of case studies in the text. Thirty *real-time cases* provide company snapshots and resources for researching firm activities in real time. Twelve *traditional cases* provide detailed information about a particular situation facing an organization at a point in time. Traditional cases can either be analyzed in the time frame in which they are presented—typically several years ago—or brought to the present by supplementing the case with additional research.

Preparing for the Case Project

Case studies are often assigned as team projects. The following suggestions should be considered, especially when approaching the case project as a team.

- **Start early.** Develop a basic understanding of the strategic management process and the twenty-five-question case analysis model before you begin your research; however, feel free to begin your research while you are still reading and studying the text material. Get acquainted with your company and its situation early. The Web sites provided for each case is a good place to start.

- **Do not overisolate the steps in the research process.** If you are working as part of a team analyzing a case, then exchange information frequently with your team members. For example, if you are investigating the effect of various social forces that influence an industry, you will probably uncover information along the way that may be useful to team members working in different areas. It is also helpful to keep a copy of the twenty-five questions with you as you read and take notes as necessary. If you are reading the annual report and come across some material of new technology affecting the industry, then make a quick note of this under "technological forces" for future reference. In addition, dividing up the sections among team members and proceeding to complete the work independently is discouraged, because earlier sections must flow logically into later sections. Perform the steps in order!

- **Keep clear records of all potentially useful information you find.** Print or save electronic copies of all articles that might be useful in your analysis and make sure that these files contain complete bibliographical information for use in citing your sources later. Doing so will keep you from attempting to locate an article you saw previously, a daunting task when you cannot remember the source.

- **Plan to spend a considerable amount of time reading and collecting information before writing the report.** As you read more about a firm, its competitors, and its industry, the most prominent ideas will begin to gel in your thinking. This process often takes time. Schedule frequent sessions of casual reading (remembering to print or save copies of articles as appropriate) before you reach conclusions or start to write the report.

- **Investigate multiple sources of information early.** Depending on the firm and industry you investigate, you will probably find several particular Internet sources of information to be most useful, whereas others may be of limited value. Test many different Internet sources of information for your case to determine which ones are most promising before investing considerable time collecting information from one or two sources.

- **Establish a timetable for completing the analysis and agree to it in writing.** Establish your own completion target for the project at least a few days before it is due and set benchmarks for completing various parts of the analysis. As a general rule, you might expect to spend the first third of your time reading everything you can about the firm and its industry. The second third may be spent compiling this research and writing the sections that describe the industry, its macroenvironment, and the firm. The final third may be spent analyzing the research you have done, including the SWOT analysis through implementation and control. Case projects typically suffer when 80 percent of the work is done in the last 20 percent of the time allotted. In addition, written agreements with timetables can be invaluable if team members are unwilling or unable to meet their own responsibilities.

- **Communicate.** Stay in touch with your team members and your professor as needed. If you have questions along the way, do not hesitate to ask for assistance.

Researching the Case Project

Each of the real-time cases provides a brief overview of an interesting company, identifies key case analysis tips and current issues, and provides links to several Internet sources of information on the organization. Each of the traditional cases provides detailed information about an organization, its industry, and challenges faced by the company. For traditional cases, your instructor may ask you to analyze the case in the time frame it was written or conduct additional research on the firm.

In general, the most current information available on a large organization can be found online. Requesting an investor's package from a firm or visiting one of its locations can also be helpful, but may take too much time.

The first Internet site of interest is the company Web site. Most major publicly traded firms provide extensive Web pages that discuss the firm's business units, key products, financial position, and current issues it faces. The company Web site is an excellent place to start to learn about a company, and the links to press releases and/or investor information can be especially helpful. In addition, competitor Web sites can be useful sources of information, although a firm's Web site is designed to promote the organization, not provide objective information.

Additional Web sites may include key competitors, industry associations, and trade journals. Most industries are represented by one or more industry or trade associations. These organizations provide useful information about trends and other issues to its member firms and may also publish a trade journal. An example of a trade association is the American Booksellers Association (www.bookweb.org), which provides a wealth of information and trends about the industry. Because trade associations represent the interests of an industry, their published views may not always be objective. Most trade associations do not require a subscription for current articles, although some require either a subscription or registration, which is often free, to access the entire site.

The Internet is replete with a wide variety of unusual information sources. A dissatisfied customer may launch a Web site devoted to the dissemination of negative information about a company (see www.allstateinsurancesucks.com for an example). Individuals or organizations may post the results of their research studies on an organization or industry. These sources can be quite helpful in the research process, but their reliability must be considered. Links to such sites are provided in some cases.

In addition to case-specific sources of information, the "Strategic Management Research Links" section below provides links to key Internet resources that can be helpful for conducting a strategic analysis on any company. Research sites and URLs are always changing, so some of the links included in the list may not be current. An updated version of this page maintained by the author is available when you register for your online edition of the text at www.atomicdog.com. You are encouraged to utilize this Web page as a starting point for your research.

Citing your sources is critical when preparing a case analysis. *Whenever any information obtained from an external source is presented, the reference must be included at the appropriate point in the report, and complete bibliographical information must be provided. Whenever information is repeated verbatim, quotation marks must be used as well.* Familiarize yourself with your institution's policies concerning citations and plagiarism.

The popular business press will report on activities within most large firms. The best sources are usually available online, although most charge for full access. The *Wall Street Journal* (http:wsj.com), the *Economist* (www.economist.com), and *Financial Times* (www.ft.com) require subscriptions to access articles online, although brief free trial periods are often available. University libraries often have subscriptions to extensive databases such as ABI/Inform and Lexis-Nexis, providing a wide range of search access to articles in many publications that would otherwise charge for that access. Other sources such as www.magportal.com and www.findarticles. com provide free search access to articles in a variety of business and trade publications.

Strategic Management Research Links

Recommended Research Links

Web site	URL
Annual Reports provides links to numerous annual reports.	www.annualreportservice.com
Annual Report Gallery provides links to numerous annual reports.	www.reportgallery.com
Bizjournals.com offers links to articles in a number of business periodicals. Search by company name, keyword, or industry. Most articles come from local business periodicals in the United States, so information gleaned from this source may not be readily available elsewhere.	www.bizjournals.com
CEO Express represents an elaborate array of links to business research sites. Some information requires a subscription.	www.ceoexpress.com
Company News on Call contains news releases from more than 1,500 companies provided by PR Newswire during the past three years. This is a great way to access press releases.	www.prnewswire.com/cnoc/cnoc.html
CNN Interactive News Search contains a free search of CNN news items.	www.cnn.com/SEARCH
e-Commerce Times is an excellent news source specifically for e-commerce. This can be very useful for firms heavily involved in e-commerce.	www.ecommercetimes.com
DSN Retailing Today is an excellent research source for retailers. This is an excellent publication for retailers. Free registration is required.	www.dsnretailingtoday.com
FindArticles is an exhaustive search engine for articles from numerous periodicals.	www.findarticles.com
Forrester Market Research is an excellent source for learning about business trends, although many reports can be costly.	www.forrester.com
Google is a popular Internet search engine. Enter the names of companies or industries for a search.	www.google.com
Hoover's is an excellent source of company information and financial reports. This is one of the most comprehensive sites for case research, but complete access requires a subscription. Many college and university libraries have a license, but one must access the site through the library's Web site.	www.hoovers.com
IndustryLink is an extensive directory of links to industry Web sites. Many of the links may not be useful, but the lists are quite thorough.	www.industrylink.com
Industry Week offers an eclectic array of articles of various companies, especially those in manufacturing.	www.industryweek.com
Magportal is an exhaustive search engine for articles from numerous periodicals, many of them with free access.	www.magportal.com
Newstrawler allows a search of multiple news sources simultaneously, many of them located outside of the United States.	www.newstrawler.com
Morningstar is an excellent source of financial information, including financial ratios.	www.morningstar.com
Reuters is an excellent source for business and other news (free subscription may be required).	www.reuters.com
The Standard is an excellent news source specifically for e-commerce.	www.thestandard.com
Wall Street Journal is a premier source of business information. A subscription is required for most research, but a free trial may be available. Articles over one month old are not available free of charge at the Web site.	http://wsj.com
Yahoo Finance provides firm overviews, financial information, and more.	http://finance.yahoo.com
Yahoo News Search is one of the oldest and most popular news searches on the Internet.	http://dailynews.yahoo.com/headlines/ts

Other Research Links

These sites may be more limited in scope but may be useful to a given research project.

Web site	URL
ASAE allows you to find professional and trade associations for some industries; searching is not always easy on this site.	www.asaenet.org
Bigcharts.com allows for easy financial comparisons of two companies.	www.bigcharts.com
Bpubs.com offers links to articles in a number of business periodicals.	www.bpubs.com
Business.com is a good source of business news, although many of the sites and links may not be useful.	www.business.com
Business Week is a popular business periodical. Free registration may be required.	www.businessweek.com
CNN Money provides a wealth of financial information.	http://money.cnn.com/services/search
Economist is a premier information source for business research from a European perspective. A subscription is required for most information, but a free trial may be available.	www.economist.com
Edgar Database is the U.S. government site for company reports. This is not always easy to navigate, but the information is extensive. See http://www.10kwizard.com for printable Edgar reports.	www.sec.gov/edgarhp/htm
Europages contains information for researching firms in Europe.	www.europages.com
Fast Company is an excellent source for strategic management articles, although most are on personalities or issues, not companies or industries.	www.fastcompany.com
Financial Times is a premier information source for business research from a European perspective. A subscription is required for most information, but a free trial may be available.	www.ft.com
Fortune 500 is a listing of America's largest firms. An article search is also available.	www.fortune.com/fortune/fortune500
Globalist provides interesting information on the international business environment.	www.theglobalist.com
Impact Articles provides an interesting array of articles, although search results are limited.	www.impactarticles.com
Internet Public Library is the starting point for an exhaustive series of links to find information about anything on the Web.	www.ipl.org
Marketing Power is a marketing-oriented site sponsored by the American Marketing Association.	www.marketingpower.com
Motley Fool provides information on many organizations.	www.motleyfool.com
NAICS is the current North American industry classification scheme.	www.census.gov/epcd/www/naics.html
Newswise is an interesting source of business news, often from unusual sources. Free registration may be required.	www.newswise.com
SIC is the old (but still cited) U.S. government industry classification scheme.	www.osha.gov/oshastats/sicser.html
Washington Times Business contains current business news.	www.washingtontimes.com/business

Finalizing Your Report

Professors use different grading schemes for evaluating the quality of a case analysis. However, the extent to which the twenty-five questions identified in the text are addressed accurately and in detail will likely be a major factor in the assignment of a grade. These questions are summarized as follows:

1. Introduce the organization. Is the case well organized and cited?
2. What is the specific industry and its competitors?
3. Who has succeeded and failed in the industry, and why?

4. What is the potential profitability of the industry?

5. What political-legal forces affect the industry?

6. What economic forces affect the industry?

7. What social forces affect the industry?

8. What technological forces affect the industry?

9. What is the current firm-level strategy?

10. What is the current business-level strategy?

11. What are the business strategies of the major competitors?

12. What is the current marketing (functional) strategy?

13. What is the financial position and (functional) strategy of the organization?

14. What are the current production and purchasing (functional) strategies?

15. What are the current strategies in other functional areas, such as HR and information systems?

16. What strengths exist for the organization?

17. What weaknesses exist for the organization?

18. What opportunities exist for the organization?

19. What threats exist for the organization?

20. What strategic alternatives are available to the organization?

21. What are the pros and cons of these alternatives?

22. Which alternative should be pursued and why?

23. How should this alternative be implemented?

24. How should this alternative be controlled?

25. What crisis events should the firm anticipate? What are the future prospects for the company?

After a draft of the case analysis has been prepared, it is useful to *reconsider each of these questions* concerning the extent to which the analysis does the following:

• Provides a clear and accurate answer to the question

• Provides as much detail as possible to understand the issues

• Provides citations in proper format for all sources used

• Follows the guidelines presented in the text and specifically in the case analysis box for that question

In addition, consulting with your professor concerning grading policies, formats for oral and/or written reports, and other issues unique to each situation is strongly suggested.

Case Studies

The following *real-time case studies* are presented in this text.

1. Allstate

2. Amazon.com

3. American Express

4. Anheuser-Busch, Inc.

5. AutoZone

6. Avon

7. Bank of America

8. Bed Bath & Beyond

9. Black & Decker

10. Circuit City

11. Costco

12. Dell

13. Delta Airlines

14. Dollar Tree Stores

15. Fedex

16. Ford

17. Home Depot

18. International Paper

19. Jack in the Box

20. Kroger

21. Lands' End

22. Mattel

23. Nike

24. Papa John's

25. Pfizer

26. Southwest Airlines

27. Starbucks

28. Walgreens

29. Wal-Mart

30. Yum Brands

The following *traditional case studies* are presented in this text.

1. Aries Catering and Aries Tours

2. Kraft Foods

3. Michael Petrov

4. Shipyard Brewery

5. EasyCar.com

6. WestJet

7. IPC Media

8. Kodak at a Crossroads

9. Fleet Sheet

10. Phoenix Organic

11. Chipco

12. Dixie Chicks

Real-Time Cases

Real-Time Case 1: Allstate

Allstate was founded in 1930 as a subsidiary of retailing giant Sears. As the retailer embarked on its great expansion, Allstate sold auto insurance through all of the new stores. Following World War II, the popularity of the automobile in the United States sparked continued growth for Allstate. In the late 1950s, Allstate added life insurance and continued to grow for the next several decades.

In the 1980s, Sears became interested in expanding its financial services operations. The retailer sought to become a diversified financial services company, launching the Discover Card through Allstate's Greenwood Trust Company. Hard times followed for the retailer, however, especially on the traditional retail side of the business. Sears changed course and began to divest its holdings in financial businesses. Sears sold 20 percent of Allstate in 1993 and the remainder in 1995.

In 2000, Allstate added online and telephone distributions and acquired Provident National Assurance Company. To reduce distribution expenses, Allstate eliminated 4,000 jobs that year, turned its agent-employees into independent contractors, and launched an integrated distribution system that allowed customers to transact business via the Internet, telephone, or traditional agent.

Allstate entered the car repair business in 2001 with its purchase of Sterling Collision Centers. An intense effort aimed at adding new Sterling outlets throughout the United States followed, although some critics have suggested that an auto insurer owning a body shop constitutes a conflict of interest.

The 2005 hurricane season resulted in substantial catastrophic losses in the insurance industry, including $5.67 billion for Allstate. Thomas Wilson succeeded Edward Liddy as CEO in 2006.

Today, Allstate is the second-largest personal lines insurer in the United States behind State Farm. Although the firm maintains a global presence, Allstate's current focus is on the United States and Canada. Allstate's subsidiaries include Allstate Life and Allstate Protection. Allstate Financial provides life insurance and investment products aimed at affluent and middle-income consumers. Allstate also operates the nationwide Allstate Bank.

Perspectives

- "Multinational marketing campaigns change the way Allstate does business," *Life Insurance International*, 14 September 2004. Insurance companies have begun to target various ethnic groups. Allstate launched "The Urban Initiative" in 1994 to increase sales in America's ethnic inner cities. Advertisements feature African American and Hispanic families. Allstate continues this effort today.

- "In hurricane's wake, insurers focus on customer service," *CRM Buyer*, 7 September 2004. Hurricanes and other natural disasters offer insurance companies an opportunity to differentiate themselves by providing excellent customer service.

- Saunders, J., "Lawmakers grapple with insurer's woes," *Daytona Beach News*, 6 February 2005. States often establish and oversee insurers who provide various forms of insurance to individuals and businesses not able to secure insurance from the industry. Citizen's Property Insurance Corporation is Florida's such provider.

- Kuykendall, L., "Allstate hit with $2.8 million verdict in Hurricane Katrina claims case," *Wall Street Journal*, 16 April 2007. A jury awarded $2.8 million to the owners of a Slidell, Louisiana, home who contended that their home was destroyed by wind, not by flood as Allstate argued. Typical homeowner policies cover damage from wind, but not floods.

Case Challenges

- How has Allstate been affected by recent developments in the Internet? Do these changes create opportunities or threats?

- How can Allstate rebound from the negative publicity it has received in recent years concerning allegations of less than fair claims?

- What strategic changes, if any, should be taken in response to the steep catastrophic losses of 2005 and the litigation in the aftermath?

Internet Sites of Interest

- Corporate Web site: www.allstate.com
- Web sites of key competitors: www.statefarm.com, www.geico.com, www.farmers.com
- American Insurance Association: www.aiadc.org
- Alliance of American Insurers: www.allianceai.org
- Insurance Information Institute: www.iii.org
- A site of interest: www.allstateinsurancesucks.com

Real-Time Case 2: Amazon.com

In 1994, recent Princeton graduate and Wall Street executive Jeff Bezos became interested in particular Web-based retail ventures. He examined a variety of different products and identified what he believed was an exceptional opportunity for "e-tailing" books. He left his job, began working out of the garage of his rented home, and raised several million dollars of start-up capital.

In 1995, Bezos opened a 400-square-foot office in Bellevue, Washington, and launched Amazon.com, billed as "the world's largest bookstore." In 1996, Amazon.com had become one of the most successful Web-based retailers, with revenues of almost $16 million. In 1997, Bezos took Amazon.com public and annual sales rose to $147 million. In that same year, Amazon.com became the sole book retailer on AOL's public Web site and Netscape's commercial channel. In 1998, Amazon.com launched its online music and video stores. It also began to sell toys and electronics and expanded its European reach with the acquisition of online booksellers in the United Kingdom and Germany

In 2000, Amazon.com launched a ten-year partnership with Toysrus.com to co-brand a toy and video game store. In the following year, Amazon.com cut 15 percent of its workforce as part of a restructuring plan that also forced a $150 million charge. Amazon.com also partnered with Borders in 2001 to manage the rival's Web operation. AOL invested $100 million in Amazon.com in 2001, and in the fourth quarter of 2001, Amazon.com showed its first profit, albeit a small one.

Amazon.com is active in acquisitions, including the firm's 2004 acquisition of Joyo.com, China's largest online e-tailer of books, music, and related items. Amazon.com also has numerous partners, including Gap, Lands' End, and Tivo. Its online partnership with Border's ended in 2007, however.

Today, Amazon.com offers a wide variety of products in addition to books, including free electronic greeting cards, online auctions, CDs, videos, DVDs, toys and games, electronics, kitchenware, and computers. The company competes with publishers, distributors, manufacturers, and physical-world retailers. International sales account for approximately 15 percent of revenues, with domestic books, music, and DVD sales accounting for 60 percent of the total.

Perspectives

- Foster, L., "Amazon's growth strategy pays off," *Internet Retailing*, 23 April 2004. Amazon marked it first profitable year in 2003 and made progress toward a second one in 2004 by pursuing growth through low prices.

- Freehill, L., "Arizona companies rely on eBay, Amazon.com for online selling," *Arizona Daily Star*, 6 July 2004. Building site traffic is a difficult challenge for small e-businesses, which is why many partner with high-traffic firms such as Amazon.com and eBay.

- Lam, J., "Microsoft, Amazon unite to battle e-mail scammers," *Wall Street Journal Online*, 29 September 2004. Microsoft and Amazon filed suit against a Canadian firm for allegedly sending millions of unsolicited e-mails using Microsoft's hotmail e-mail service and forging the name of Amazon. This was not the first time the two large firms joined forces to combat scammers and it will probably not be the last.

- Trachtenburg, J. A., "Border's business plan gets a rewrite," *Wall Street Journal*, 22 March 2007, B1. Border's announced that it would end its online partnership with Amazon.com and reopen its own branded e-commerce Web site in early 2008.

Case Challenges

- Who is Amazon's competition? Is it even possible to identify the industry in which Amazon.com operates?

- There has been a general trend toward "bricks and clicks"—the combination of Internet and traditional retailing outlets. How has Amazon.com succeeded as an e-tailer without brick-and-mortar operations?

- Given its Internet base, can Amazon.com's success be easily duplicated by copying its Web materials? Is this an inherent disadvantage of Internet businesses that adopt prospecting strategies?

- With the myriad of Web sites that offer price comparisons that exist for book and other e-tailers (e.g., www.bestbookbuys.com), is it possible for Amazon.com to maintain a strong customer base without an extreme emphasis on low prices?

Internet Sites of Interest

- Corporate Web site: www.amazon.com
- Profiles on prospective competitors: www.business.com
- Web site of a key book competitor, Barnes & Noble: www.barnesandnoble.com
- Web site of a key music competitor, CDNow: www.cdnow.com
- Web site of a key online auction competitor, eBay: www.ebay.com
- *The Industry Standard*: www.thestandard.com
- *E-Commerce Times*: www.ecommercetimes.com
- American Booksellers Association: www.bookweb.org
- National Retail Federation: www.nrf.com
- DSN Retailing Today: www.dsnretailingtoday.com

Real-Time Case 3: American Express

American Express was formed in 1850 as a delivery services company, but soon emerged as a leader in travel-related services. In 1868, the firm developed a money order to compete with the government's postal money order. In 1891, American Express introduced the notion of a traveler's check.

During World War I, the U.S. government nationalized and consolidated all express delivery services. After the war, American Express incorporated as a provider of overseas freight and financial services and exchange provider. The famous American Express charge card was introduced in 1958. The firm acquired Fireman's Fund American Insurance (which it later sold) and Equitable Securities in 1968.

Under the leadership of James Robinson, CEO from 1977 to 1993, American Express bought brokerage Shearson Loeb Rhoades in 1981 and investment banker Lehman Brothers in 1984, establishing a Shearson-Lehman business unit. Its 1987 launch of Optima, a revolving credit card (as opposed to its traditional charge card), did not succeed. Following mounting losses, Harvey Golub was appointed CEO in 1993 and charged with turning around the firm.

In 1994, American Express divested its brokerage operations (as Shearson) and its investment banking (as Lehman Brothers). In 1997, Kenneth Chenault was appointed president and chief operating officer. He replaced Golub as chairman and CEO in 2001, a year in which the firm suffered from bad investments in below-investment grade bonds, resulting in a $1 billion loss. In addition, the firm's employees at its New York City headquarters located across from the World Trade Center were displaced by the 2001 terrorist attacks. Its headquarters did not reopen until May 2002.

American Express remains active in acquisitions, divestments, and partnership. In 2004, the firm partnered with Industrial and Commercial Bank of China to issue its branded credit cards in that country. In 2005, American Express sold its American Financial business (formerly American Express Financial Advisors), the firm's insurance and investments arm.

Today, American Express is a leader in global travel, traveler's checks, and credit cards. The firm has more than 2,200 locations in more than 200 countries and is the world's largest issuer of traveler's checks. Approximately 80 percent of its revenue is derived from the United States.

Perspectives

- Sidel, R., and Lieber, R. "AmEx tries to have it both ways with banks," *Wall Street Journal Online*, 30 September 2004. American Express plans its first alliance with a U.S. bank, MBNA. Bank partnering has proven to be highly effective for leaders Visa and MasterCard. Previously, the two leaders—associations owned by thousands of banks—prohibited U.S. banks from simultaneously issuing cards on rival networks run by American Express and Discover. In 2001, however, a federal district court ordered Visa and MasterCard to eliminate the rules and the decision became final in 2004 when the Supreme Court affirmed the decision by rejecting an appeal to hear the case. Currently Visa leads the industry with 443.4 million cards, followed by MasterCard with 317.5 million, Discover with 53.3 million, American Express with 37.5 million, and Diners Club with 1.5 million.

- "American Express sets out its stall," *Retail Banker International*, 5 August 2004. American Express Chairman and CEO Kenneth Chenault discussed strategic objectives, including an emphasis on average card member spending, card attrition, and average assets per financial client.

- Sidel, R., and Davis, A., "Discover seeks a rediscovery," *Wall Street Journal*, 26 November 2004. In 2003, Visa led consumer credit card spending with 53.3 percent, followed by MasterCard, American Express, and Discover at 30.4 percent, 11.0 percent, and 5.2 percent, respectively. Discover has embarked on an aggressive growth strategy to gain ground on American Express.

- "American Express trimming rewards," *Deseret News*, 3 August 2006. American Express announced plans to scale back some of the rewards offered to its cardholders in an effort to control costs. The firm had recently reported $62 million in pretax expenses for reward payouts.

Case Challenges

- The American Express card is not as widely accepted as those of its rivals Visa and Mastercard. How can American Express differentiate its credit card from these two competitors, as well as a host of retailer-affiliated cards?

- Was the American Express sale of its Financial Advisors business a wise move? Why or why not?
- How has American Express created synergy through the acquisition and development of highly related business units?
- Could the large size of American Express be considered as both an advantage and a disadvantage?

Internet Sites of Interest

- Corporate Web site: www.americanexpress.com
- Web sites of key competitors: www.citigroup.com, www.visa.com, www.jpmorgan.com
- Travel Industry of America: www.tia.org
- American Society of Travel Agents: www.astanet.com

Real-Time Case 4: Anheuser-Busch, Inc.

George Schneider founded Anheuser-Busch in St. Louis in 1852. In 1860, the brewery was sold to Eberhard Anheuser and several other investors, although Anheuser later bought out the others. Adolphus Busch married into the family in 1861, hence the Anheuser-Busch connection. Budweiser was first introduced in 1876. By 1907, production peaked at approximately 1.6 million barrels per year. Between 1919 and 1933, the company survived prohibition by producing such products as malt syrup, ice cream, and even a chocolate beverage. Following the end to prohibition, sales climbed again, reaching 2 million barrels per year by 1938 and 3 million barrels by 1941.

Anheuser-Busch acquired the St. Louis Cardinals baseball team in 1953. In 1957, Anheuser-Busch passed Schlitz as beer industry revenue leader. In 1959, the Busch Entertainment theme park division was established. Throughout the 1950s, 1960s, and early 1970s, new breweries were periodically added, with production reaching 30 million barrels by 1974.

Anheuser-Busch launched its Eagle Snacks unit in 1982 and introduced Budweiser in the United Kingdom and Japan in 1984 through licensing agreements. In 1996, the company sold the Cardinals baseball team and stadium for $150 million and closed its Eagle Snacks unit, completing its departure from the food business.

Internationally, Anheuser-Busch acquired interests in brewers in Mexico in 1993, in China in 1995, and in Brazil and Argentina in 1996. Although Anheuser-Busch sold its interest in its Brazilian brewer in 1999, the company subsequently purchased nearly 20 percent of top Chilean brewer Compania Cervecerias Unidas to enhance its Latin American presence. Nonetheless, Anheuser-Busch's international market share remains quite small.

Anheuser-Busch leads the U.S. beer market with a whopping 48 percent share via thirty different varieties, led by Budweiser, the nation's top-ranked beer. The company also produces Bud Light, Michelob, and Busch, as well as an array of specialty brews, and has theme park holdings, including Busch Gardens and SeaWorld. In 2004, Anheuser-Busch acquired Harbin Brewery, China's fourth-largest brewer. As of 2006, the firm owned about 35 percent of Mexico's largest brewer, Grupo Modelo.

Anheuser-Busch produced 157 million barrels of beer in 2006, produces its own labels and cans, and is the largest aluminum recycler in the United States. The company also tests and markets several low-alcohol and nonalcoholic beverages, such as 180 blue, an energy drink introduced in 2006. August Busch IV currently serves as chairman and president.

Perspectives

- Cancelada, G., "Anheuser-Busch set to take over brewery, expand presence in China," *St. Louis Post-Dispatch*, 10 July 2004. After outbidding SABMiller PLC, Anheuser-Busch completed its takeover of Harbin Brewery, China's fourth-largest brewer. Anheuser-Busch already has a brewery in Wuhan and holds a minority stake in China's largest brewery Tsingtao.

- Cancelada, G., "Anheuser-Busch has always had success with ad campaigns in radio," *St. Louis Post-Dispatch*, 28 July 2004. Anheuser-Busch's success can be attributed in part to the firm's marketing prowess, including its success in developing winning radio campaigns.

- "Anheuser-Busch boosts stake in Tsingtao," *Modern Brewery Age*, 18 April 2005. Frustrated by stagnant growth prospects in the United States, AB tripled its holdings in the Chinese brewery.

- "Anheuser wants world to know beer is healthy," *Wall Street Journal*, 9 December 2005, B1, B4. Anheuser-Busch has teamed up with notable Harvard epidemiologist Meir Stampfer in an effort to publicize the health benefits of beer consumption. Specifically, Stampfer is noting a number of published studies suggesting that moderating alcohol consumption can result in lower rates of heart attack, diabetes, and other ailments. Wine producers have already made similar claims.

- "Statement by Joseph A. Califano, Jr. Chairman and President of The National Center on Addiction and Substance Abuse at Columbia University and Former U.S. Secretary of Health, Education and Welfare on Anheuser-Busch's 'Spykes,'" *Marketwire*, April 2007. Califano challenges Anheuser-Busch to stop selling "Spykes," a prepackaged beer additive with caffeine and 12 percent alcohol. Califano argues that the product lures underage drinkers.

Case Challenges

- It is easy to become enamored with a company when it has enjoyed so much success over the years. What are Anheuser-Busch's weaknesses?

- Anheuser-Busch controls almost one-half of the U.S. beer market. Is it possible that the company may become a target of government prosecution for anticompetitive activity if it continues to grow rapidly?

- To what extent can Anheuser-Busch control or influence public sentiment concerning such social issues as drinking and driving, underage drinking, and alcohol abuse? How does publicity surrounding products such as Spykes affect Anheuser-Busch's reputation in this regard?

Internet Sites of Interest

- Corporate Web site: www.anheuser-busch.com
- Brewery tour online: www.budweisertours.com
- Web site of a key competitor: www.millerbrewing.com
- Beer Net industry information: www.beernet.com
- Beer Institute: www.beerinstitute.org
- Distilled spirits: www.discus.health.org
- Home Wine and Beer Trade Association: www.hwbta.org
- National Beer Wholesaler Association: www.nbwa.org
- National Soft Drink Association: www.nsda.org

Real-Time Case 5: AutoZone

Joseph "Pitt" Hyde opened the first Auto Shack auto parts store in 1979 in Forrest City, Arkansas. Having served on the board of directors at Wal-Mart for seven years, Hyde adopted the giant retailer's model and concentrated on smaller markets in the South and Southeast, emphasizing service and everyday low prices. The auto parts retailer enjoyed early success and grew to almost 200 stores by 1984. Shortly thereafter, the Duralast private label was launched and the company changed its name to AutoZone. By 1991, the retailer had amassed nearly 600 stores and went public. Sales topped $1 billion in 1992.

John Adams replaced Hyde as CEO and chairman in 1997. In 1998, AutoZone acquired Chief Auto Parts, converting its 560 stores, mostly in California, into AutoZones the following year. The company also acquired Adap's 112 Auto Palace stores in the Northeast. In the early 2000s, emphasis shifted from acquisition to internal growth. In 2003, AutoZone amassed 12 percent of the $36 billion do-it-yourself (DIY) automotive aftermarket. By 2004, AutoZone had grown into the leading automotive aftermarket retailer with over $5 billion in annual revenues.

AutoZone stores sell parts under a variety of brand names and private labels and offer diagnostic testing services, but they do not sell tires or perform repairs. A typical store stocks over 20,000 parts. Most AutoZone stores are freestanding, with the remainder located in strip malls.

AutoZone targets the DIY consumer with cars more than seven years old (i.e., what the company calls OKVs—"our kind of vehicles"). Today, the company also continues to grow its do-it-for-me business by selling to professional repair shops through its AZ Commercial program, although not all stores participate in this endeavor. Future prospects for both segments bode well for AutoZone, however, as the DIY segment is expected to grow at a rate of about 5 percent over the next decade, whereas the do-it-for-me segment is expected to grow at a rate of 6 percent.

William Rhodes became CEO in 2005 and began revitalizing its stores. He mandated one of two standard layouts in all stores at a cost of about $5 million (about $2,000 per store). Storefronts were dedicated to luring in potential customers rather than a haphazard array of products selected by each individual manager. Rhodes's program has shown some initial signs of success.

Today, AutoZone operates more than 3,800 retail auto parts stores in the United States and about 100 in Mexico. Advance Auto Parts is number two in the industry with over $3 billion in sales and about 3,000 stores. Other key competitors include Pep Boys, CSK, and O'Reilly, as well as discount retailers such as Wal-Mart and Target. AutoZone emphasizes internal growth, opening about 150 to 200 additional stores per year.

Perspectives

- "Pep Boys hit speed bump on auto service," *Mercury News*, 2 September 2004. Unlike AutoZone, rival Pep Boys both sells auto parts and offers service for customers who do not wish to complete the work themselves. Pep Boys, however, has reported declines in the service side of its business.

- Howell, D., "Rallying the troops to get back into the profit zone," *DSN Retailing Today*, 6 September 2004. Much of AutoZone's success may be linked to its unique merchandising approach, including unusual mixes of products through the stores.

- Condon, B. "Cheapskates," *Forbes*, 19 June 2006. AutoZone's store revitalization—spearheaded by CEO William Rhodes—is showing signs of improving performance, in terms of both sales and (primarily) profits.

Case Challenges

- Is automotive aftermarket retail an attractive industry? Why or why not?

- How can AutoZone differentiate itself from rivals O'Reilly Automotive and Advance Auto Parts?

- Is international expansion an attractive alternative for AutoZone? Why or why not?

Internet Sites of Interest

- Corporate Web site: www.autozone.com

- Web sites of key competitors: www.advanceautoparts.com, www.pepboys.com, www.napaonline.com

- Automotive Aftermarket Industry Association: www.aftermarket.org

- Automotive Parts Rebuilders Association: www.apra.org

Real-Time Case 6: Avon

Avon Products, Inc. is a global manufacturer and marketer of beauty and related products, including cosmetics, toiletries, fragrances, jewelry, gifts, home furnishings, and health and wellness offerings. Unlike most of its rivals, Avon's business consists primarily of Internet and direct selling by 4 million independent contractors worldwide who serve as company representatives. Headquartered in the United States, Avon operates in over 100 countries, including Canada and Mexico, as well as in other parts of Latin America, Europe, and Asia. In 2002, Avon operated seventeen manufacturing facilities worldwide.

Avon was launched in 1916 and later began to emerge as one of the most successful beauty and cosmetic marketers in the world, primarily supported by housewives who sold the products as a means of generating extra income. By 1970, Avon had grown into the undisputed world leader in cosmetics. In the mid-1970s, however, the company suffered as a global recession made its products less affordable and women in the West began to leave home in search of full-time employment. Following this period, Avon began to market more intently to younger women and teenagers and even launched the slogan, "It's not your mother's makeup."

In the late 1980s and early 1990s, Avon expanded its product line considerably, introducing Avon Color cosmetics in 1988, preschool toys and sleepwear in 1989, and apparel in 1994. "Avon calling" has been central to the New York City–based firm's advertising campaigns in recent years.

Slow growth in the United States, however, led to another "makeover" for Avon, as the company began to drop several product lines in favor of brands with greater global promise. In 2001, the company revised its Web site, allowing Avon reps to sell products through their own personal Web sites with assistance from the youravon.com site. In 2002, Avon announced a $100 million investment in research and development aimed at fostering a greater global presence. In 2003, Avon launched a new cosmetics line called "mark," targeted to the sixteen to twenty-four age category. In 2004, Avon signed actress Salma Hayek to an exclusive global advertising and promotional agreement. Avon also launched its first men's catalog, *M—The Men's Catalog*, in late 2004.

Avon has over 5 million independent representatives worldwide and launched a four-year restructuring plan in 2005 that includes layoffs, outsourcing, closing plants, and opening new distribution centers. Avon has also been successful promoting its firm as "the company for women" by providing business opportunities for women worldwide and supporting women's charities. Part of the firm's mission is to develop its Avon Foundation into the largest women's foundation in the world. The group actively supports projects associated with economic empowerment and health issues.

Perspectives

- "Avon predicts market up by 50 percent," *China Daily*, 25 June 2004. Avon's expansion into China continues as the direct selling giant predicts a 50 percent growth in sales there in 2004. Avon expects sales in China to reach $400 million by 2007. (China banned direct sales in 1998 but had allowed ten foreign companies to continue to do so—including Avon—as long as their sales representatives were tied to retail stores.)

- "Avon targets men in new magazine," *Chicago Sun-Times*, 25 October 2004. Avon's launch of *M—The Men's Catalog* is geared toward the family man, the career man, and the athlete.

- "A bit less blush at Avon," *Business Week Online*, 5 February 2004. Avon has big plans for growth outside of the United States.

- Fong, M., "Avon's calling, but China opens door only a crack," *Wall Street Journal*, 26 February 2007. China lifted a nationwide ban on direct selling in 2005, but replaced it with a complicated set of regulations. For example, Avon is prohibited from using health professionals in their advertisements, and commissions are capped at 30 percent. It can take weeks for prospective sales representatives to receive a government-issued license.

Case Challenges

- How do recent changes in the macroenvironment affect Avon?
- Is Avon's direct selling approach outdated? Why or why not?
- Is Avon's recent global thrust appropriate for the company? Why or why not?

Internet Sites of Interest

- Corporate Web site: www.avon.com
- Web sites of key competitors: www.revlon.com, www.thebodyshop.com
- Cosmetic, Toiletry, and Fragrance Association: www.ctfa.org
- Cosmetic News: www.cosmeticnews.com
- Fashionlines: www.fashionlines.com

Real-Time Case 7: Bank of America

Bank of America is the third-largest bank by assets in the United States behind Citigroup and J.P. Morgan Chase. Following its 2004 acquisition of Fleet Boston, the bank boasted the most extensive branch network in the industry, encompassing over 5,700 locations in twenty-one states and the District of Columbia. The firm's coverage is especially strong in California, Texas, and Florida. Bank of America also owns about one-fourth of one of Mexico's largest banks, Santander Central Hispano.

Bank of America is a diversified firm, operating in four principal business segments. The most substantial segment is consumer and commercial banking and includes traditional banking services such as deposits, loans, and credit cards. Bank of America offers brokerage and related services to institutional clients within the global corporate and investment banking segment, featuring its subsidiary, Bank of America Securities. Its asset management segment primarily serves institutional investors and individual investors with substantial portfolios. The firm also purchases stakes in various businesses through its equity investment segment.

Bank of America was established in 1874 as Commercial National Bank, later to become American Trust Company, American Commercial Bank, and finally North Carolina National Bank (NCNB) in 1960. Following its expansion outside of North Carolina, NCNB renamed itself NationsBank in 1991. Acquisitions continued throughout the 1990s. The firm acquired Chicago Research & Trading in 1993, Boatmen's Bancshares in 1997, and Barnett Banks in 1998. Following a merger with BankAmerica in 1998, the new company was renamed Bank of America.

In the early 2000s, however, emphasis shifted from external to internal growth. Today, Bank of America is aggressively expanding its number of branches, locating in retail establishments such as Wal-Mart and Starbucks. The firm's advertising campaigns highlight full service, convenience, and accessibility. Bank of America is expanding its branch network and is aggressively targeting consumer deposits, supported by about $150 million in advertising.

In September 2003, a New York attorney general's investigation into illegal after-hours trading named Bank of America's Nations Funds. In 2004, the company spent tens of millions of dollars in fines and repayments to settle with investors who may have lost money because of the improprieties.

In the mid-2000s, however, Bank of America shifted its attention once again to external growth, acquiring broker-dealer Fleet Securities for $48 billion in 2004 and MBNA, the largest affinity credit card issuer in the United States, for $35 billion in 2005. In 2006, it purchased a 9 percent stake in China Construction Bank and a 5 percent stake in General Motors. While its global footprint continues to expand, Bank of America operates about 5,700 locations in the United States.

Perspectives

- Freer, J., "Expanding locally, Bank of America thinks 'retail,'" *South Florida Business Journal*, 15 August 2003. Bank of America has experienced considerable growth by opening branches in retailers such as Wal-Mart and Starbucks.

- Thomke, S., "How Bank of America turned branches into service-development laboratories," *HBS Working Knowledge*, 5 May 2003. Bank of America's systematic research and development efforts through its Innovation & Development Team takes an interesting approach aimed as developing new services for its customers.

- Stempel, J., "Bank of America downplays big growth targets," *Reuter's*, 26 January 2005. Rumors abound concerning Bank of America's future acquisition plans, but the strategic direction of the firm remains unclear.

- Jordan, M., and Bauerlein, M. "Bank of America casts wider net for Hispanics," 13 February 2007. In an effort to tap the growing Hispanic market, Bank of America has begun to offer credit cards to consumers without social security numbers, namely illegal immigrants. Although the bank defended the move, critics charged that the bank crossed the line when it began to knowingly offer services to individuals who are violating federal law.

Case Challenges

- Should Bank of America pursue acquisitions instead of internal expansion to further its growth objective?

- Is the Internet an opportunity or a threat for Bank of America? Why?

- Although Bank of America's size offers a number of scale economies, is the firm vulnerable to smaller banks that offer a high degree of personal service?
- Was Bank of America's decision to offer credit cards to individuals without social security cards—mostly illegal immigrants—a wise strategic move? Why or why not?

Internet Sites of Interest

- Corporate Web site: www.bankofamerica.com
- Web sites of key competitors: www.citigroup.com, www.jpmorganchase.com, www.wachovia.com
- American Bankers Association: www.aba.com
- America's Community Bankers: www.acbankers.org
- Independent Community Bankers of American: www.icba.org
- *American Banker*: www.americanbanker.com
- *ABA Banking Online*: www.ababj.com

Real-Time Case 8: Bed Bath & Beyond

Warren Eisenberg and Leonard Feinstein launched what is today known as Bed Bath & Beyond in 1971 with one small linens store in New York and another in New Jersey. BBB had expanded into only two states—California and Connecticut—by 1985, at which time the firm launched its first successful superstore, a format that became a prototype for all future outlets. The company went public in 1992, and total retail square footage quadrupled between 1992 and 1996.

The retailer opened twenty-eight new stores in fiscal 1997, thirty-three stores in fiscal 1998, and forty-five stores in fiscal 1999, when it reached the $1 billion mark in sales. The company opened seventy stores in 2000 and another eighty stores in 2001. In March 2002, BBB acquired Harmon Stores Inc., a health and beauty aid retailer with twenty-seven stores.

Today, BBB is a nationwide chain of superstores selling domestics merchandise and home furnishings, including large selections of department-store-quality brand name and private-label products. The company's domestics merchandise line includes items such as bed linens, bath accessories, and kitchen items. The company's home furnishings line includes cookware, general housewares, cutlery, glassware, and general home furnishings. The company operates about 740 stores, each averaging about 42,000 square feet, with some stores exceeding twice the average. BBB emphasizes service, selection, and everyday low prices—a formula that has helped the firm stay ahead of its closest competitor, Linens-n-Things. The company is engaged in a continued growth initiative.

Management attributes its success in part to the freedom it gives its store managers with regard to inventories, new products, and layouts. The firm's decentralized structure allows store managers to have more control than their peers at other retailers. The company ships merchandise directly to retail outlets, eliminating the expense of a central distribution center and reducing warehousing costs.

BBB acquired the small East Coast chain buybuy Baby in 2007. Founders Warren Eisenberg and Leonard Feinstein remain in control of the firm, but have slowly reduced their holdings in BBB to about 2 percent each.

Perspectives

- Byrnes, N., "What's next for Bed Bath & Beyond?" *Business Week Online*, 19 January 2004. Bed Bath & Beyond became a large chain by catering to local tastes. The firm's current rapid growth strategy could undermine this formula for success, however.

- Thau, B., "Bed Bath looks beyond: Company eyes more growth," *HFN*, 28 June 2004. Operating in the 600-store range in 2004, Bed Bath & Beyond is targeting 1,000 stores in the near future.

- Duff, M., "Harmon builds presence with stand-alone stores: Bed, Bath & Beyond fosters synergies between businesses," *DSN Retailing Today*, 7 February 2005. After purchasing the twenty-seven-unit Harmon health and beauty aids chain in 2002, BBB has increased promotion, added stores, and built synergy between Harmon and BBB stores.

- Duff, M., "Bed Bath & Beyond's Feinstein calls 2004 'best year ever,'" *DSN Retailing Today*, 11 July 2005. BBB enjoyed considerable success in 2004 and plans to continue its growth strategy.

Case Challenges

- Is the industry for Bed Bath & Beyond limited to other specialty retailers? To what extent are discount retailers such as Wal-Mart and Target prime competitors of Bed Bath & Beyond?

- Is Bed Bath & Beyond likely to remain a successful retailer without a substantial emphasis on Internet business?

- Is Bed Bath & Beyond pursuing a low-cost, a differentiation, or a combination business strategy?

Internet Sites of Interest

- Corporate Web site: www.bedbathandbeyond.com
- Web site of a key competitor, Linens-n-Things: www.lnt.com
- Web site of a key competitor, The Container Store: www.containerstore.com
- National Retail Federation: www.nrf.com
- International Housewares Association: www.housewares.org

Real-Time Case 9: Black & Decker

Black & Decker is the leading producer of power tools and accessories in the United States. The firm markets its products worldwide, emphasizing the United States, United Kingdom, and Latin America with more recent ventures into Europe and Asia. Best known for its Black & Decker and Dewalt brand names, the firm also produces Price Pfister plumbing products, Kwikset security hardware, SnakeLight flashlights, Dustbuster vacuum cleaners, and a variety of electric lawn and garden tools, including hedgers and trimmers.

Black & Decker was formed in 1910 by business partners Duncan Black and Alonzo Decker, although the first power tool was not introduced until 1916. The company's first manufacturing facility was built in Towson, Maryland, in 1917, and sales grew to $1 million annually two years later. The firm was active internationally at that time, expanding into Japan, Australia, and Russia. A second manufacturing facility in the United Kingdom was opened in 1939.

In 1984, Black & Decker acquired General Electric's housewares operations, much of which was sold in 1998. In 1986, the firm launched a major restructuring effort resulting in the closing of five production facilities. Black & Decker has aggressively pursued cost reductions during the past decade, moving many of its manufacturing plants from the United States and the United Kingdom to Mexico, China, and Central Europe. In 1995, DeWalt power tools were introduced to Europe and the firm launched joint ventures in India and China.

Most of Black & Decker's products are sold through retailers, with home improvement giants Lowe's and Home Depot accounting for approximately 10 percent of the company's revenues. A limited number of its products are distributed through Wal-Mart. The company maintains a small number of reconditioning centers and factory outlets where new and refurbished products are sold directly to the public.

In 2003, Black & Decker purchased Baldwin Hardware, a manufacturer of architectural and decorative home products, and Weiser Lock, a manufacturer of custom-designed locking devices, from Masco Corporation. In 2004, the firm acquired Pentair's Tool Group, adding brands such as Delta and Porter-Cable. Black & Decker acquired portable power products manufacturer Vector Products in 2006.

Perspectives

- Mirabella, L., "Black & Decker buys Minnesota-based tool business for $775 million," *Baltimore Sun*, 20 July 2004. Black & Decker's 2004 acquisition of Pentair's Tools Group for $775 million was the firm's largest acquisition in more than a decade. The acquisition adds brands Porter-Cable and Delta to the Black & Decker line, which already contains its own brand name and the DeWalt professional line. The acquisition is designed to shore up market share in areas where Black & Decker has struggled, such as woodworking equipment, compressors, and pressure washers.

- "Black & Decker laying off 350 people at Jackson plant," *Associated Press*, 19 January 2005. Black & Decker announced plans to eliminate 350 jobs in a Tennessee Porter-Cable plant to transfer the work to plants in Reynosa, Mexico, and McAllen, Texas.

- Kridler, K., "Towson-based Black & Decker buys toolmaker Vector Products for $160M," *Baltimore Daily Record*, 2 March 2006. Black & Decker acquired Vector Products in an effort to expand into the portable power products market. Vector products include power inverters, vehicle battery chargers, and rechargeable spotlights.

Case Challenges

- To what degree is Black & Decker's success contingent on its distribution through home improvement giants Home Depot and Lowe's, as well as discount retailers such as Wal-Mart and Target?

- Is international growth an attractive option for Black & Decker? Why or why not?

- Could Black & Decker experience a backlash from U.S. consumers if it continues to move manufacturing operations abroad?

Internet Sites of Interest

- Corporate Web site: www.blackanddecker.com
- Web sites of key competitors: www.americanstandard.com, www.danaher.com, www.makita.com
- National Retail Hardware Association: www.nrha.org

Real-Time Case 10: Circuit City

Sam Wuertzel launched Circuit City as a television retailer in Richmond, Virginia, under the Ward's name in 1949. During the 1950s and 1960s, Ward's expanded its product lines and began to acquire appliance retailers. In 1975, the firm opened an electronics superstore in Richmond, the first of its kind in the United States. The store was an immediate success.

In 1981, Ward's acquired New York City–based Lafayette Radio Electronics, but was unable to compete successfully there. The firm refocused its efforts on the electronics superstore concept and changed its name to Circuit City in 1984. Richard Sharp was named CEO in 1986 and emphasized distribution efficiency and the development of information systems. Following sales declines associated with the recession of the early 1990s, Circuit City began to open mall stores—initially under the Impulse name and later changed to Circuit City Express—and promote its credit card.

In 1993, Circuit City ventured out of its electronics base, opening its first used-car dealership CarMax. Competitive pressure in the electronics industry intensified, however, and BestBuy surpassed Circuit City in sales in 1996.

Circuit City began to develop its online interest in the late 1990s. In 1999, the firm partnered with ISP CompuServe to offer $400 rebates for PC purchasers who signed up for a year's service with the ISP. In 2000, Alan McCollough was named CEO and Circuit City immediately launched an aggressive remodeling program that included the elimination of major appliances in favor of more profitable consumer electronics. McCollough also became chairman of the board in 2002. During that year, Circuit City spun off its CarMax business unit to place greater emphasis on its electronics business. Circuit City sold its credit card operations to Banc One in 2004.

Circuit City currently has over 640 locations throughout the United States, with over 800 in Canada operated by subsidiary InterTAN. Stores range anywhere from about 10,000 to over 40,000 square feet, with an emphasis on such products as consumer electronics, satellite television systems, computers, and entertainment software. To improve customer service, the company eliminated its practice of paying sales commissions in 2003.

Circuit City and BestBuy remain two close and similar rivals. In the early 2000s, Circuit City had more stores than its main rival, but BestBuy amassed greater sales. By the mid-2000s, however, BestBuy proved the stronger of the two, prompting a series of cost-cutting measures at Circuit City in 2006 and 2007. Circuit City appointed former BestBuy executive Philip Schoonover as CEO in 2006.

Perspectives

- Gilligan, G. J., "Circuit City makes progress on plan to move stores into bustling trade areas," *Richmond Times-Dispatch*, 2 July 2004. In the 1990s, the firm often cut costs by selecting less than optimal locations, but paid the price when rival BestBuy rapidly expanded into these markets with more attractive locations. Today, Circuit City has changed course and continues to relocate stores to sites in more robust trade areas.

- "Best Buy gets better," *HFN*, 12 April 2004. Circuit City rival BestBuy is becoming more "customer centric" by offering promotions, services, and store sets tailored to specific stores and customer groups. The firm has tested the concept in several stores and is expected to expand it to the entire chain within a few years.

- Lloyd, M. E., "Circuit City to cut costs, consider alternatives," *Wall Street Journal*, 29 March 2007, B4. Following a drop in revenue and intense price competition for big-screen TVs, Circuit City announced a cost-cutting plan that includes layoffs, store closings, outsourcing, and possibly a sale of its international business, InterTAN. Growth in the coming years is still expected, but not at the rates previously projected.

Case Challenges

- How can Circuit City differentiate itself from rival BestBuy? Is such differentiation necessary?
- Was it necessary for Circuit City to eliminate its sales commissions in 2003? Why or why not?
- How can Circuit City stave off threats from price-cutting online competitors?

Internet Sites of Interest

- Corporate Web site: www.circuitcity.com
- Web sites of key competitors: www.bestbuy.com, www.compusa.com, www.radioshack.com
- National Retail Federation: www.nrf.com
- *DSN Retailing Today:* www.dsnretailingtoday.com

Real-Time Case 11: Costco

The first Price Club Warehouse was opened in San Diego in 1975 by Sol Price, Robert Price (Sol's son), Rick Libenson, and Giles Bateman. The firm originally sought to sell merchandise in volume at deep discounts only to small businesses, but later expanded the concept to include government, utility, and hospital employees. By 1980, the company had four stores in Arizona and California and went public.

During the 1980s, the company expanded to the eastern United States and Canada. In 1988, Price Club acquired grocery distributor A. M. Lewis and launched Price Club Furnishings. In the early 1990s, however, competition intensified from Sam's Club and Pace. In 1992 and 1993, Price Club's joint venture with retailer Controladora Comercial Mexicana led to the opening of two Price Clubs in Mexico City.

Later in 1993, Price Club merged with Costco Wholesale. During the 1990s, the firm expanded its international interest, launching outlets in Great Britain, Japan, and South Korea. Price Club changed its corporate name to Costco Companies in 1997 and again to Costco Wholesale in 1999.

Costco became the largest wholesale club operator in the United States, operating about 500 membership warehouses—each amassing about $115 million in sales—and serving about 40 million members. Most of its outlets are located in the United States and Canada, but additional stores can be found in Mexico, Japan, South Korea, Taiwan, Puerto Rico, and the United Kingdom. Membership costs around fifty dollars per year and is available to businesses and individuals.

Costco's business model emphasizes rock-bottom prices on a limited selection of mostly name brand products in a wide range of merchandise categories. A typical outlet carries about 4,000 products ranging from alcoholic beverages and appliances to fresh food, pharmaceuticals, and tires. Costco also offers its members insurance, financial, and travel services. Its subsidiary, Costco Wholesale Industries, operates a manufacturing business in food packaging, meat processing, and jewelry to support retail efforts.

Much of Costco's success can be attributed to its ability to minimize costs by negotiating fiercely with suppliers. The company never requires its members to pay more than 14 percent above the firm's cost for goods.

Perspectives

- Lieber, R., "American Express, Costco offer new rebate card," *Wall Street Journal Online*, 1 September 2004. American Express announced a new rebate credit card available only to Costco members.

- Dunn, J., and Vuong, A., "Growth of big-box retailers leads to increase in discrimination lawsuits," *Tribune Business News*, 21 September 2004. During the last decade, Costco, Home Depot, and Wal-Mart expanded vigorously and hired tens of thousands of hourly employees, many of whom later became managers. All three firms, however, have been the targets of class action lawsuits alleging race and sex discrimination.

- Craig, D., "Envy of its peers: Costco: Retailer of the year," *DSN Retailing Today*, 19 December 2005. Costco has enjoyed substantial success in the past decade, as evidenced by rapid growth, rising profits, and sound business practices.

- Bary, A., "'Costco' more gains coming," *Wall Street Journal*, 18 February 2007. Although Costco's recent success has been factored into its stock price, analysts suggest that continued growth and strong performance may be on the horizon. Costco aims to double its stores to about 1,000 by 2017.

Case Challenges

- What are the strategic limitations faced by membership clubs?

- Does Costco compete with nonmembership retailers such as Wal-Mart and Target? Why or why not?

- How does Costco's business model differ from that of traditional discount retailers? Is this model likely to be more successful in the coming years?

- Can Costco compete successfully on a large scale outside of the United States and Canada? Why or why not?

Internet Sites of Interest

- Corporate Web site: www.costco.com
- Web sites of key competitors: www.samsclub.com, www.bjswholesale.com
- National Retail Federation: www.nrf.com
- *DSN Retailing Today:* www.dsnretailingtoday.com

Real-Time Case 12: Dell

By the time Michael Dell enrolled at the University of Texas in 1983, he was already a successful entrepreneur. Although his initial academic interest was not business, he launched a venture selling random-access memory (RAM) chips and disk drives for IBM PCs out of his dorm room. When his business grossed $80,000 a month the following year, Dell decided to drop out of college and focus on his new enterprise full time.

Dell began making and selling IBM clones directly to consumers rather than through retail outlets. His direct marketing strategy resulted in price reductions of about 40 percent off retail. International sales offices were added in 1987 and Dell went public the next year.

When profits declined in 1990, Dell responded with cuts in inventories and an assortment of new products. In 1991, Dell began to allow select retailers to sell its PCs at direct mail prices, a strategy it would abandon several years later. In the following years, the firm opened markets in Latin America, Japan, and Australia. Dell also began manufacturing servers.

In 1996, Dell began selling PCs through its Web site. Growth continued, and in 1998, the company increased manufacturing in the Americas and Europe and added a production and customer facility in China. In 1999, Dell launched a $999 PC; however, declines in the PC market took its toll on the company. In 2001, the firm eliminated about 5,000 jobs to cut costs. Dell acquired Microsoft software support specialist Plural in 2002.

Today, Dell has operations primarily in the United States, Canada, Latin America, Europe, the Pacific Rim, Japan, Australia, and New Zealand. Dell offers PCs, servers, storage devices, and a wide variety of hardware components, as well as integration, training, and support. Although Dell has sought to develop many new products, desktop PCs account for approximately 50 percent of revenues, with notebook computers accounting for approximately 25 percent. Dell has grown aggressively in parts of Asia, including India, China, and Malaysia.

In 2004, founder and chairman Michael Dell stepped down as CEO and was succeeded by company president Kevin Rollins. Michael Dell remained as chairman, however, but retook control of the company from Rollins in 2007.

Perspectives

- Morrison, S., "It's gloves off in the computer business," *Financial Times*, 8 June 2004, 29. Average prices for PCs continue to drop, sparked by a price war between Hewlett-Packard and Dell as the two large rivals vie for market share.

- Dickie, M., and Morrison, S., "Dell cools on low-cost PC sales in China," *Financial Times*, 17 August 2004, 25. Dell is backing off its attempts to promote low-priced PCs in China due to fierce price competition there. Dell plans to continue targeting corporate sales there, but will emphasize higher end products to Chinese consumers.

- Lawton, C., "Consumer demand and growth in laptops leave Dell behind," *Wall Street Journal*, 30 August 2006, A1, A19. Historically, Dell's success has been built on its direct sales model, with an emphasis on bulk sales of desktop PCs to corporations. Recently, however, corporate and government business has slowed. Although significant growth has occurred in the consumer market, consumers prefer laptops to desktop PCs and seem to have a preference for preconfigured units at retailers such as BestBuy and Circuit City.

- Foley, S. "Dell founder in control as CEO is ousted," *The Independent (London)*, 1 February 2007. Founder Michael Dell retook control of the firm after the board ousted CEO Kevin Rollins amid a decline in performance and an SEC investigation into the firm's accounting practices.

Case Challenges

- How did and does Dell's marketing strategy differ from that of its major competitors such as Compaq and Hewlett Packard?

- Sales of personal computers grew rapidly in the 1980s and early 1990s, but have leveled off in the 2000s. Is it possible for Dell to continue to grow in such a heavily saturated market?

- Will Dell face significant problems of CEO succession when Michael Dell eventually leaves the firm?

Internet Sites of Interest

- Corporate Web site: www.dell.com
- Web sites of key competitors: www.gateway.com, www.hp.com, www.ibm.com
- Computer and Communications Industry Association: www.ccianet.org
- *PC World*: www.pcworld.com

Real-Time Case 13: Delta Airlines

Atlanta-based Delta Airlines provides scheduled air transportation for passengers and cargo throughout the United States and around the world. Delta serves over 300 cities in more than fifty countries. Founded as the world's first crop-dusting service in 1924, Delta has grown to become the third-largest airline in the world behind United and American.

The firm launched no-frills Delta Express in 1996 to compete with low-cost producers such as Southwest and JetBlue. Although a success at first, costs began to rise rapidly in subsequent years. In 2003, Delta revised its concept of a budget carrier and launched Song, a brand that subsumed Delta Express shortly thereafter. Most Song routes connect major Northeast cities with Florida leisure travel destinations.

Like other global airlines, Delta was affected substantially by 9/11. As a result, Delta quickly eliminated a number of flights and reduced its workforce by 15 percent. Additional reductions have followed.

Delta held takeover talks with Continental in 1998, but Continental later joined with Northwest instead. In 2002, Delta entered into a marketing alliance with Continental and Northwest Airlines that included *codesharing*, whereby two or more airlines list the same flight as their own to streamline passenger bookings. The alliance also allows for reciprocal frequent flyer and airport lounge access arrangements.

Delta currently operates a fleet of over 800 aircraft with U.S. hubs located in Atlanta, Cincinnati, New York City, and Salt Lake City. Passenger revenues account for over 90 percent of Delta's total revenues, with cargo and other revenues accounting for the remainder. Delta's "SkyTeam" global marketing alliance includes Air France, AeroMéxico, South African Airways, and Korean Air Lines, among others.

Following continued financial difficulties, Delta announced a restructuring plan in late 2004 that included the sale of Atlantic Southeast Airlines, the elimination of Delta's Dallas–Fort Worth hub, and about 10 percent of its workforce. Its effort to stave off bankruptcy was unsuccessful, however. A subsequent restructuring effort included an expansion of international routes in 2005 and 2006. The U.S. Airways $10 billion hostile takeover bid in early 2007 was unsuccessful. Delta remained under Chapter 11 protection until mid-2007.

Delta owns about 40 percent of computer reservation system Worldspan, a limited partnership that operates a computer reservation system (CRS) for the travel industry. Northwest and American Airlines own the remainder of the partnership. Delta also owns about 18 percent of online travel agency Orbitz.

Perspectives

- Perez, E., "Delta unveils its turnaround plan," *Wall Street Journal Online*, 9 September 2004. After weeks of speculation, Delta announced the details of its campaign to keep the airline out of bankruptcy. The strategy includes a major realignment of its routes aimed at reducing costs, an emphasis on long-haul and international flights, closing the airline's hub at Dallas–Fort Worth, cutting 7,000 jobs, and expanding flights at hubs in Atlanta, Cincinnati, and Salt Lake City.

- Kirsner, S., "Song's startup flight plan," *Fast Company Online*, June 2003. Song represents Delta's attempt to recapture some of the market lost by traditional airlines to low-cost competitors such as Southwest.

- Dade, C., and Carey, S., "Delta Air creditors reject hostile bid by U.S. Airways," *Wall Street Journal*, 1 February 2007. The U.S. Airways attempt to acquire Delta in early 2007 was not successful.

- Adams, M., "Delta expects to soar after exiting Chapter 11," *USA Today*, 24 April 2007, B1–B2. Delta's turnaround, including nineteen months in Chapter 11 protection, is chronicled. Much of Delta's success is attributed to its movement away from the East Coast and Florida—where low-cost rivals such as JetBlue, AirTran, and Southwest Airlines have driven down fares—to more profitable international routes where discount airlines are not active.

Case Challenges

- Is Delta positioned well if another terrorist attack involving aircraft occurs in the United States? Explain.

- As a full-service carrier, should Delta really be concerned with low-fare carriers?

- Is Delta's future success inextricably tied to that of its rivals? If so, how can Delta differentiate itself from other full-service carriers?

Internet Sites of Interest

- Corporate Web site: www.delta.com
- Web site of one of the top three airlines ranked by revenues, United: www.ual.com
- Web site of one of the top three airlines ranked by revenues, American Airlines: www.aa.com
- Air Transport Association (the primary trade association; an excellent source of current industry information): www.airlines.org
- Air Transport Action Group: www.atag.org
- International Air Transport Association: www.iata.org
- Industry news from Airwise: http://news.airwise.com

Real-Time Case 14: Dollar Tree Stores

In 1986, Douglas Perry, Macon Brock, and Ray Compton founded Dollar Tree Stores as an offshoot of retail chain K&K Toys. In 1991, the founder sold K&K Toys to the parent company of KayBee Toys, to place full emphasis on developing the dollar store concept—offering all products at a fixed price of one dollar. At that time, strategic issues included shifting the company away from closeouts, growth, and locating stores in more economical strip centers rather than malls.

Dollar Tree went public in 1995, and in 1996 acquired Chicago-based retail chain Dollar Bills, some of whose stores still bear the former company's name. Dollar Tree acquired California retail chain 98 Cent Clearance Centers in 1998, New York State retail chain Only $One in 1999, and Pennsylvania-based, single-price retail chain Dollar Express in 2000. The acquisition effort continued when Dollar Tree bought Greenbacks, adding its 96 stores in 2003, and Deal$-Nothing Over a Dollar, adding another 138 stores in 2006. Dollar Tree continues to expand internally as well, opening fully automated distribution centers in an effort to improve its operating efficiency and support its ongoing expansion.

Merchandise in a typical store includes candy and food, housewares, seasonal goods, health and beauty care, toys, stationery, and gift items. About one-half of Dollar Tree's merchandise is imported, most notably from China. The company continues to operate about 3,100 discount stores in forty-eight states with the following names: Dollar Tree, Dollar Express, Dollar Bills, Only One Dollar, and Only $One. Stores are located primarily in high-traffic strip centers anchored by mass merchandisers and supermarkets. New stores also tend to be larger than older ones, approaching 15,000 square feet.

Dollar Tree customers tend to be price conscious with respect to the products they are purchasing, and in many respects come to Dollar Tree because they perceive the prices at other discount retailers such as Target and Wal-Mart to be excessive. Dollar Tree offers low prices and exceptional convenience, due to small store layouts and simplicity of checkout (i.e., all products are the same price).

Perspectives

- Howell, D., "Five and dime stores may be dead, but Dollar Tree keeps on growing," *DSN Retailing Today*, 16 December 2002. Dollar Tree's formula for success is outlined.

- Howell, D., "Dollar Tree to acquire Greenbacks: Similar size, product mix cited as impetus for purchase," *DSN Retailing Today*, 9 June 2003. Dollar Tree's acquisition of the ninety-six-unit, privately held chain Greenbacks gave the company a foothold in six western states in which the retailer lacked a presence.

- "'Thrill of hunt' at Dollar Tree," *MMR*, 3 May 2004. Dollar Tree completed its acquisition of Salt Lake City–based Greenbacks, integrating its 100 stores in 2003. With 300 new Dollar Trees opened during the same year, Dollar Tree passed the 2,500 store mark by year's end and increased square footage by about 30 percent.

- Hudson, K., "Can the Dollar Stores Rebound?" *Wall Street Journal*, 21 September 2005. After years of double-digit gains in revenues, sales at dollar stores appear to have leveled off, suggesting that competitors such as Dollar Tree will be hard pressed to increase earnings through sales growth.

- Hudson, K., "Dollar General lags behind rival," *Wall Street Journal*, 26 March 2007, B5. Dollar Tree faces intense competition from stores that price everything at one dollar as well as large general merchandise chains such as Dollar General and Family Dollar, which operate over 8,000 and 6,000 stores, respectively.

Case Challenges

- Dollar Tree grew in the late 1990s almost exclusively through acquisition. Is this means of external growth favorable to an internal growth strategy? Is it likely to be a viable option in the coming decade?

- Why is Dollar Tree able to offer its products at prices below those of discount chains such as Wal-Mart and Target, firms with greater economies of scale?

- With annual inflation, it will become more difficult for Dollar Tree to continue offering all of its products at the one dollar price level. How might such a company ease into offering its products at higher prices? Would doing so undermine the company's image?

Internet Sites of Interest

- Corporate Web site: www.dollartree.com
- Web sites of key competitors: www.dollargeneral.com, www.familydollar.com
- National Retail Federation: www.nrf.com
- RetailNet: www.retailnet.com
- *DSN Retailing Today:* www.dsnretailingtoday.com

Real-Time Case 15: FedEx

Between 1969 and 1971, Fred Smith secured $90 million in financing to launch Federal Express, a service that originally provided overnight and second-day delivery to twenty-two major cities in the United States. FedEx began delivery in 1973, and the company enjoyed immediate success. FedEx was the first major air transport firm to implement a "hub and spoke" system, whereby all packages were flown to a central location (Memphis) each night and redistributed by air to their destinations in the predawn hours. The airline shift from parcels to passengers and the strike at UPS in 1974 all contributed to the firm's early market share gains. FedEx went public in 1978.

By the late 1980s, FedEx had begun to move internationally, purchasing Tiger International (also known as Flying Tigers) and carriers in Japan and Italy. In 1989, FedEx doubled its international volume. In 1995, FedEx created Latin American and Caribbean divisions and became the first U.S. express carrier to offer direct flights to China.

In 1996, FedEx introduced the first Internet-based shipping management system, known as interNetShip. Another UPS strike in 1997 sent 850,000 packages a day to FedEx, creating more opportunities for the firm. In 1998, FedEx averted a pilot strike of its own, prompting the company to outsource more of its flights.

In 2000, Federal Express adopted its nickname FedEx as its official company name. Today, FedEx provides transportation, e-commerce, and supply chain management services, including worldwide express delivery, ground small-parcel delivery, small quantity freight delivery, and supply chain management services.

FedEx remains the world's leading express delivery company, with more than 60,000 drop-off locations, 670 aircraft, and about 40,000 vehicles, delivering over 3 million packages to about 220 countries and territories every business day. FedEx has even partnered with the U.S. Postal Service to provide air transportation for postal express shipments, an arrangement that allows FedEx to utilize post offices' critical package drop-off locations. FedEx acquired Kinkos in early 2004 in an effort to serve a broader array of shipping and office-related needs, particularly those of small business owners. In 2007, FedEx acquired its Chinese partner, DTW Group, and launched the first one-day guaranteed service in the country later in the year.

FedEx has organized its operations into multiple businesses: FedEx Ground, FedEx Express (which accounts for almost 70 percent of revenues), FedEx Freight, FedEx Custom Critical, and FedEx Kinkos.

Founder Fred Smith remains the CEO and owns approximately 6 percent of FedEx shares. Smith is known as a popular and cagey leader, both inside and outside of the company.

Perspectives

- Keane, A. G., "Searching for shippers," *Traffic World*, 12 January 2004. In an effort to increase its shipping business, UPS acquired Mail Boxes Etc. in 2001, renaming them UPS stores in 2003. FedEx kept pace in 2004, acquiring Kinkos for $2.4 billion.

- Creamer, M., "DHL bets on flexibility as it moves on FedEx, UPS in U.S.," *Advertising Age*, 6 September 2004. DHL is embarking on a challenge to the express delivery market in the United States controlled by UPS and FedEx by emphasizing superior customer service.

- Dade, C., "FedEx says profit gains may be sluggish," *Wall Street Journal*, 22 March 2007, A11. The close link between FedEx performance and overall economic conditions is discussed.

- Stanley, B., "FedEx raises stakes in China market," *Wall Street Journal*, 21 March 2007, A12. FedEx launched the first one-day guaranteed delivery service in China in mid-2007, offering time-definite service between nineteen major cities and day-definite service between more than a couple hundred others.

Case Challenges

- The Internet has alleviated the need for overnight delivery of many documents. How has FedEx survived and even prospered in the midst of this key technological change?

- Should FedEx be partnering with a key competitor and protected government entity, the U.S. Postal Service?

- Do FedEx and UPS offer the same delivery services, or has each chosen to focus on different forms of delivery and customer needs? Explain.
- Was FedEx wise by moving aggressively into China? Can the Chinese market support FedEx's one-day delivery services? Explain.

Internet Sites of Interest

- Corporate Web site: www.fedex.com
- Web sites of key competitors: www.ups.com, www.airborne.com, www.dhl.com
- *Transport News*: www.transportnews.com

Real-Time Case 16: Ford

Henry Ford founded Ford Motor Company in 1903 in Dearborn, Michigan. In 1908, Ford assembly lines produced the company's first car, the Model T. Henry Ford is often quoted as saying that a customer could have a Model T in any color, as long as it was black. By the late 1910s, more than one-half of all vehicles on the road were Fords. In 1919, the firm bought back all of its outstanding shares and did not go public again until 1956.

Ford bought Lincoln in 1922, and the Model T was replaced with the Model A in 1932. Market share fell behind GM and Chrysler in the late 1930s, and Ford did not return to second place again until 1950. Ford introduced the infamous Edsel in 1958 and the popular Mustang in 1964.

Ford, like other domestic automakers, was hurt by the oil crisis of the 1970s. The company responded by cutting its workforce and closing plants during the 1980s. Ford purchased 75 percent of Aston Martin in 1987 (and the remaining shares in 1994). In 1988, the company introduced the Ford Taurus and Mercury Sable, and its domestic market share increased to 21.7 percent.

Ford diversified in the 1980s and 1990s, acquiring car rental agencies Hertz in 1994 and Budget in 1996 (which it sold the following year). Ford also established a one-third ownership state in Mazda in 1997. In that same year, Ford sold its heavy-duty truck unit to Daimler-Benz and spun off 19 percent of Hertz in an IPO. During this time, international expansion was also evident. In 1997, Ford began building a minibus line in China. Ford purchased Volvo's auto manufacturing operations in 1999, as well as several other related businesses.

In 2001, Ford announced a 50-50 truck-building joint venture with Navistar to produce a common medium-duty chassis customized for Ford and Navistar vehicles. In early 2002, Ford embarked on far-reaching cost-cutting measures, including the elimination of 35,000 jobs worldwide, the closure of three North American assembly plants, and the discontinuation of the Ford Escort, Mercury Cougar, Mercury Villager, and Lincoln Continental. In 2004, Ford announced plans to establish a second manufacturing plant in China.

Ford also operates Ford Motor Credit, a financial services division consisting primarily of vehicle-related financing, leasing and insurance, and renting and leasing of cars and trucks. Over 80 percent of firm revenues are still derived from its automotive division, which presently includes Ford, Mercury, Lincoln, Aston Martin, Jaguar, and Volvo. Ford Motor Credit and Hertz generate most of the remaining revenues. Henry Ford's great-grandson, William Clay Ford Jr., became chairman in 1998 and was also named CEO in 2001.

After five years at the helm and a failed restructuring effort, Ford remained as chairman of the board, but was replaced as CEO by Boeing executive Alan Mulally in 2006. Ford's "Way Forward" restructuring program seeks to cut costs in the company's North American operations—including health care expenses—trim production capacity, cut its workforce, and build more customer-focused vehicles. Leaders hope Ford will return to profitability by 2009 or 2010.

The Ford family still owns about 40 percent of the company's voting stock.

Perspectives

- Kerwin, K., "How would you like your Ford?" *Business Week Online*, 9 August 2004. Ford is shifting away from the one-size-fits-all model pioneered by Henry Ford in the early 1900s. In 2004, Ford completed a $400 million refurbishment of an 80-year-old manufacturing plant in Chicago that is capable of making eight different models. This move is part of Ford's continuing effort to better satisfy consumer taste in a fragmented car market.

- Power, S., "Ford takes hard line at Jaguar," *Wall Street Journal Online*, 20 September 2004. Following a stream of losses, Ford announced cuts of 1,150 jobs at its Jaguar plant in Coventry, England, marking an effort to restructure operations at its British luxury brand.

- Langley, M., "Ford Motor names Mulally of Boeing as Chief Executive," *Wall Street Journal Online*, 5 September 2006. After difficulties implementing a restructuring plan, Ford selected Alan Mulally to replace William Clay Ford, Jr. as CEO.

- Ball, G., "Car makers mobilize over CO2 curbs," *Wall Street Journal*, 9 April 2006, A6. Ford, GM, and DaimlerChrysler's AG Chrysler group have joined forces to support an economy-wide carbon reduction policy rather than one aimed only at the auto industry. Ford and others worry that a policy targeting the auto industry through substantial changes in fuel economy could be devastating to U.S. carmakers.

Case Challenges

- Is it necessary for Ford to produce and/or sell a large proportion of its vehicles abroad in order to maintain its strong domestic market position in the coming decade?

- A number of analysts have suggested that world carmakers will likely consolidate into only two or three within the next twenty years. Should Ford actively pursue any specific mergers and acquisitions at this point? Why or why not?

- How can and should Ford address environmental concerns? Explain.

Internet Sites of Interest

- Corporate Web site: www.ford.com

- Ford's Volvo group: www.volvo.com

- Web site of a key competitor, General Motors: www.gm.com

- Web site of a key competitor, DaimlerChrysler: www.daimlerchrysler.com

- Web site for Japanese automaker Mazda (Ford currently owns part of the company): www.mazda.com

- *Automotive News*: www.autonews.com

- American Industry Action Group: www.aiag.org

- American Automobile Manufacturers Association: www.aama.org

- American Automobile Association: www.aaa.com

Real-Time Case 17: Home Depot

After losing their jobs in the home improvement industry, Bernard Marcus and Arthur Blank founded Home Depot in 1978. Home Depot was conceptualized as a retailer focused on the needs of the do-it-yourself (DIY) market, specializing in building materials and lawn and garden equipment. Three stores were launched in the Atlanta area in 1979, and four stores in South Florida were added in 1981. The firm posted sales of $50 million that year and went public. By 1983, Home Depot had opened stores in Louisiana and Arizona with total sales exceeding $250 million.

Home Depot expanded into California in 1985 and the firm amassed a total of sixty stores and sales of $1 billion by 1986. Home Depot continued to grow and entered the northeastern United States and Canada in subsequent years. By 1997, Home Depot had reached 500 stores. In that same year, Marcus stepped down as CEO (but remained chairman) and was succeeded by Blank. Home Depot added a direct-mail interest by acquiring mail-order firm National Blind & Wallpaper Factory and direct marketer Maintenance Warehouse.

Home Depot launched Villager's Hardware stores in New Jersey in 1999, a 40,000-square-foot outlet designed to compete with traditional hardware stores. The firm also began to add large appliances to many of its stores. In 2000, Marcus and Blank became co-chairmen and former General Electric executive Robert Nardelli was named president and CEO.

Aggressive expansion continued in 2001 when Home Depot added another 200 stores and acquired Total Home, a small home improvement chain in Mexico. Marcus and Blank stepped down as co-chairmen and Nardelli assumed the role in addition to his CEO responsibilities. Having abandoned its Villager's Hardware concept in the previous year, Home Depot opened its first small store—about 60,000 square feet—in New York City in 2002. The firm continued its expansion into Mexico, acquiring Del Norte, a small chain in Juarez. Home Depot operates over 100 stores in Canada and has opened a business-development office in China.

Today, Home Depot is the world's largest home improvement chain and second-largest retailer after Wal-Mart, operating approximately 2,150 stores throughout the Americas. Home Depot continues to focus on the DIY customer, with more than 40,000 products stocked in a 130,000-square-foot facility. Contractor sales have risen to about one-third of the total, however, and have received greater attention. Home Depot acquired roofing installer IPUSA and windows installer RMA Home Services in an effort to expand its service offerings. Recent competitive pressure by Lowe's has caused Home Depot to aggressively upgrade its old stores while continuing its growth efforts, and contributed to CEO Robert Nardelli's ouster in 2007, who was replaced by Frank Blake.

Perspectives

- Vereen, B., "Dissecting Home Dept's new strategy," *Retail Merchandiser*, 1 May 2004. Home Depot's growth efforts have turned from large markets to small ones. In response to similar moves by rival Lowe's, Home Depot has broadened its product line and redesigned its stores to improve its prospects in smaller markets.

- DeGross, R., "Online overhaul a winner for Home Depot," *Atlanta Journal and Constitution*, 20 July 2004. Home Depot's Web site overhaul in late 2003 appears to have paid off. Consumers not only can shop online, but can also obtain more detailed product information and advice on performing repairs. Visits to the site have increased by over one-third in one year, surpassing visits to the site of rival Lowe's.

- Dunn, J., and Vuong, A., "Growth of big-box retailers leads to increase in discrimination lawsuits," *Tribune Business News*, 21 September 2004. During the last decade, Costco, Home Depot, and Wal-Mart expanded vigorously and hired tens of thousands of hourly employees, many of whom later became managers. All three firms, however, have been the targets of class action lawsuits alleging race and sex discrimination.

- Terhune, C., "Home Depot, seeking growth, knocks on contractor's doors," *Wall Street Journal*, 7 August 2006. Since Chairman and CEO Bob Nardelli arrived at Home Depot in 2000, sales growth has slowed to about 12 percent a year, compared to 19 percent in previous years. The company stock price, as well as per-store sales, also declined from 2000 to 2005. Home Depot has increased its emphasis on the lucrative contractor market in an effort to rejuvenate growth.

- Cox, R., and Silva, L., "A Home Depot blueprint," *Wall Street Journal*, 13 February 2007, C16. Home Depot is considering closing its supply operations and focusing more on its more profitable retail operations.

Case Challenges

- Is it necessary for Home Depot to emphasize both the DIY and contractor markets to build and maintain economies of scale?
- Is competitive pressure from Lowe's causing Home Depot to modify its competitive strategy?
- Do international opportunities exist for Home Depot beyond North and South America?

Internet Sites of Interest

- Corporate Web site: www.homedepot.com
- Web sites of key competitors: www.truserv.com, www.lowes.com
- National Retail Federation: www.nrf.com
- *DSN Retailing Today:* www.dsnretailingtoday.com

Real-Time Case 18: International Paper

International paper was launched in 1898 when eighteen northeastern pulp and paper firms consolidated to reduce costs. Growth was not rapid in much of the 1900s, although the firm acquired a number of small, related businesses. Following some diversification in the 1960s and 1970s, International Paper began to refocus its efforts on paper and pulp. In the 1980s and 1990s, International Paper embarked on a series of key acquisitions, including office paper provider Hammermill Paper, paper manufacturer Arvey, composite wood products firm Masonite, and paper-products firm Federal Paper.

International Paper engaged in a restructuring effort after a loss in 1997. The firm sold $1 billion in assets and trimmed its workforce by about 10 percent. The following year, IP acquired Weston Paper & Manufacturing and Mead's distribution business. In 1999, IP acquired rival Union Camp for $7.9 billion.

The acquisitions continued in 2000 when IP bought Shorewood Packaging for $850 million and Champion International for $9.6 billion. Interestingly, the firm restructured again in 2001, trimming another 10 percent of its workforce. In 2003, IP began an effort to sell about 17 percent of its timberland—about 1.5 million acres—to improve its financial position.

At first glance, IP's myriad of acquisitions and divestments over the past decade may be difficult to comprehend. Divestitures alone between 2000 and 2002 totaled about $3 billion. However, a closer look reveals that IP has been aggressively acquiring businesses that support its core paper, packaging, and forest products focus, while divesting of businesses that may only have been tangentially related.

Today, International Paper is the world's largest forest products company. IP is involved in a full array of production of printing and writing papers, pulp, tissue, paperboard, packaging, plywood, and other wood products. IP also processes forest products including pine lumber, engineered wood, laminates, and particleboard. Approximately three quarters of revenues are distributed somewhat evenly among paper packaging, paper distribution, and printing papers.

IP has a number of international holdings including Papeteries de France, Scaldia in the Netherlands, and Impap in Poland. In addition, the firm controls about 9 million acres of forest in the United States and 900,000 acres in Brazil and Russia. In 2006, IP announced a job venture with Ilim Pulp, Russia's leading forestry products supplier.

Perspectives

- "International Paper profit jumps but costs rise," *Reuter's*, 3 February 2005. IP's profit environment improved in 2004, but costs continue to increase.

- "International Paper cutting 209 jobs," *Pittsburgh Business Times*, 4 February 2005. IP is aggressively shifting production among facilities.

- "IP completes Box USA acquisition," *Box Biz*, 6 July 2004. As part of its external growth efforts, IP acquired industrial packaging provider Box USA in 2004.

- Sherwood, J., "Why Europe's paper firms struggle," *Wall Street Journal Online*, 22 January 2007. World paper prices have declined about 20 percent during the past six years because of increased exports from China. Paper companies hope prices will rise again as Chinese domestic demand rises in the coming years.

Case Challenges

- During the last several years, IP has engaged in both rapid acquisition of highly related businesses and divestment of less related businesses. Is this an effective strategy?

- Are economies of scale essential for firms in the forestry products industry?

- Could IP face any potential political or publicity problems associated with environmental concerns in the United States and elsewhere?

Internet Sites of Interest

- Corporate Web site: www.internationalpaper.com
- Web site of a key competitor, Georgia Pacific: www.gp.com
- Web site of a key competitor: www.weyerhaeuser.com
- Web site of a key competitor, Boise Cascade: www.bc.com
- Alliance for Environmental Technology: www.aet.org
- American Forest & Paper Association: www.afandpa.org
- National Paper Trade Association: www.paperfiber.com
- Packaging Online: www.packaging-online.com

Real-Time Case 19: Jack in the Box

In 1951, Robert Peterson launched a chain of drive-thru restaurants located primarily in California, Texas, and Arizona. From the beginning, Jack in the Box restaurants featured a clown named Jack who greeted motorists ordering through a two-way speaker device encased inside Jack's head. Business operations have been conducted under various names and public, private, and subsidiary affiliations, including Foodmaker, Ralston Purina, and currently (public) Jack in the Box, Inc.

In response to a key company food poisoning incident, Jack in the Box implemented the industry's first comprehensive Hazard Analysis & Critical Control Points (HACCP) system for managing food safety and quality in 1994. Jack in the Box continues to support tougher legislation to mandate food-safety systems throughout the fast-food industry, and actively partners with national consumer organizations to educate the public about the best techniques families can use to protect themselves against home-based food poisoning.

Jack in the Box is known as a fast-food innovator, introducing the first breakfast sandwich and prepackaged portable salad. Whereas other fast-food restaurants are often hesitant to make major product line changes, Jack in the Box continuously modifies its offering to provide customers with an ever-changing array of food items.

In the mid-2000s, Jack in the Box began to emphasize pricier, more upscale items on its menu. The firm hopes to succeed with such higher margin products as deli sandwiches while retaining its traditional customer base.

Jack in the Box currently operates more than 2,000 restaurants in the western and southern United States, most of which are company owned, as well as 300 Qdoba Mexican Grill fast-casual restaurants. The restaurant targets the adult market with a broad and changing selection of distinctive, innovative products, including hamburgers, specialty sandwiches, tacos and other ethnic products, finger foods, breakfast foods, unique side items, and dessert items. The restaurant chain is adding about forty-five Jack in the Box locations and ninety Qdoba locations in 2007. Restaurant sales accounted for over 90 percent of the firm's revenues.

Perspectives

- Linecker, A. C., "Restaurant chain serves up a new strategy," *Investor's Business Daily*, 4 June 2004, A5. Jack in the Box is in the midst of a transition from volume-oriented, lower priced sandwich offerings to more of an upscale look. The challenge is to secure new customers with the changes in product line and aesthetics without driving away too many of the traditional ones.

- Green, F., "Jack in the Box benefits from diversified menu," *San Diego Union-Tribune*, 13 May 2004. Jack in the Box's launch of new gourmet Pannido sandwiches and other upscale products have resulted in increased profits.

- "Jack in the Box debuts bacon breakfast Jack," *Nation's Restaurant News*, 22 January 2007. Jack in the Box continues to develop a number of new food products, ranging from economical offerings such as the $1.29 bacon breakfast Jack to upscale sandwiches like the $4.59 Sirloin Steak 'n' Cheddar ciabatta sandwich.

Case Challenges

- Jack in the Box is a well-known fast-food restaurant chain in many parts of the Southwest and California. However, the chain has not penetrated markets in much of the remaining sections of the country. Should Jack in the Box continue to concentrate its efforts on a limited geographical area?

- In an industry where all competitors appear to market similar products via a ninety-nine cent menu, how has Jack in the Box succeeded in differentiating itself from its rivals? What more can and/or should be done in this regard?

- Jack in the Box has only recently begun to combine its restaurants with its proprietary convenience store, Quick Stuff. Should Jack in the Box pursue the combination store concept more aggressively?

Internet Sites of Interest

- Corporate Web site: www.jackinthebox.com
- Web sites of key competitors: www.mcdonalds.com, www.burgerking.com, www.whataburger.com
- *Nation's Restaurant News*: www.nrn.com
- National Restaurant Association: www.restaurant.org

Real-Time Case 20: Kroger

Bernard Kroger was only twenty-two when he launched the Great Western Tea Company in 1883. Growing to 40 stores in the Cincinnati area, the company became known as Kroger Grocery and Baking Company in 1902. Kroger continued to grow rapidly in the 1900s and 1910s, acquiring a number of smaller grocery stores. The company acquired Piggly Wiggly stores in six states in the late 1920s, as well as most of the rival's corporate stock (which it did not sell until the early 1940s). Kroger reached 5,575 stores before the stock market crash in 1929. Interestingly, Bernard Kroger sold his shares and retired just one year prior to the crash.

After a brief decline in the number of stores during the depression, Kroger began to grow again in the following three decades. In the 1970s, Kroger changed growth strategies and began to pursue growth by enlarging its existing stores. During this decade, Kroger added only a small number of new stores, but its total floor space nearly doubled.

In the 1980s and 1990s, Kroger returned to its external growth prowess, acquiring several regional grocery chains. In 1999, Kroger acquired Fred Meyer, operator of about 800 stores mainly in the western United States. In 2000, the company bought twenty Hannaford stores in Virginia, as well as twenty additional stores in Nebraska. In 2001, Kroger acquired additional stores in New Mexico, but also announced a restructuring plan to cut expenses, resulting in the layoff of about 1,500 employees.

Today, Kroger is the leading supermarket chain in the United States (if Wal-Mart is not considered in this category), operating more than 2,500 supermarkets, 800 convenience stores, 125 supermarket fuel centers, and 430 jewelry stores. The company also manufactures and processes food for private-label sales in its own supermarkets. Kroger stores are primarily located in the Midwest, South, and West, although it continues to acquire smaller supermarkets throughout the country, as well as poor performing outlets of its major competitors,

from time to time. Retail operations account for about 98 percent of company revenues.

In 2007, analysts speculated that a leveraged buyout was in the works for Kroger, a rumor rejected by CEO David B. Dillon.

Perspectives

- "Kroger to launch Smith's Marketplace in Utah," *Drug Store News*, 1 March 2004. Kroger continues to develop its grocery/general merchandise combination superstore concept via Smith's Marketplace.

- Hale, J., "Kroger predicts labor trouble," *Danville Register & Bee*, 5 February 2005. Negotiations with the United Food and Commercial Workers Union represent a constant challenge for Kroger.

- Marcial, G. G., "Shopping at Kroger—for toys and furniture," *Business Week Online*, 7 February 2005. Kroger is taking a lesson from Wal-Mart as it begins to offer more high margin, nonfood items in many of its stores.

- Berman, D. K., "Kroger moves into sights of private-equity firms," *Wall Street Journal*, 6 April 2007, C3. Although rumors about Kroger will explore a leveraged buyout, there is no confirmation from Kroger executives.

Case Challenges

- What forms of differentiation are available to supermarket chains? What forms is Kroger using effectively?

- Should Kroger continue it acquisition strategy in the future? Why or why not?

- Does the Internet pose specific opportunities or threats to Kroger? How should Kroger prepare to meet these challenges?

Internet Sites of Interest

- Corporate Web site: www.kroger.com
- Web site of a key competitor, Albertson's: www.albertsons.com
- Web site of a key competitor, Safeway: www.safeway.com
- *Supermarket News*: www.supermarketnews.com
- National Retail Federation: www.nrf.com

Real-Time Case 21: Lands' End

Copywriter Gary Comer launched Lands' End (the misplaced apostrophe resulted from an early typographical error in a company catalog and has remained ever since) in 1963, a Chicago-based mail-order supplier of sailboat hardware and equipment. In the mid-1970s, Comer began to emphasize clothing and soft luggage, and subsequently eliminated sailboat hardware from the product line. In 1979, Lands' End moved its warehouse and fulfillment operations to rural Dodgeville, Wisconsin.

In 1981, Lands' End launched a national advertising campaign to promote the company's brand name. The company grew following the campaign, emphasizing folksy catalog copy to sell traditional clothing in basic colors. Lands' End went public in 1986.

In 1990, Comer stepped down as CEO and was replaced by Richard Anderson. During this same year, the firm experienced a significant inventory and fulfillment crisis. As sales declined in the early part of the year, Lands' End cut inventories and released a myriad of new products. Christmas orders surged, however, and Lands' End was unable to fulfill customer demand on its promised same-day basis. As a result, the company lost sales and incurred substantial shipping costs by fulfilling back orders at its own expense. The situation improved in the following year.

In 1991, Lands' End introduced its first catalog in the United Kingdom and opened a distribution center there shortly thereafter. Former L. L. Bean executive William End was named CEO in 1993, but was replaced by Michael Smith in 1994. In the same year, the company was shipping small mailings of catalogs in France, Germany, and the Netherlands from its UK distribution center. Lands' End opened an outlet store in the United Kingdom and started selling products online in 1995. Product line debates and sales declines led to another round of management changes in 1998, when David Dyer replaced Smith as CEO. Restructuring followed, as more than 10 percent of the salaried workforce was eliminated.

Lands' End has been active on the Web in recent years, including new sites in 1999 in Germany, Japan, and the United Kingdom. In the United States, products are marketed on the Internet, as well as through traditional catalogs. Lands' End is the leading online clothing retailer in the United States and arguably one of the most successful since the Web's development.

Present emphasis is placed on traditionally styled apparel, bed and bath items, casual clothing for adults and children, accessories, shoes, and soft luggage. Lands' End is organized into four segments, including (1) adult apparel, (2) specialty goods, (3) international operations, and (4) shipping, handling, and gift wrap operations. The company seeks to provide the highest levels of quality and service in the industry, along with an unequivocal ironclad guarantee. Sears bought Lands' End in 2002 for nearly $2 billion but has struggled to build the anticipated synergy. Sears and Kmart merged in 2004. In 2006, Sears opened about seventy-five separate store-in-store Lands' End shops inside Sears retail stores.

Perspectives

- Hajewski, D., "Sears-Kmart merger may mean new beginning for Lands' End," *Seattle Times*, 5 January 2005. Plans for Lands' End may change with the Sears-Kmart merger.

- Scardino, E., "Sears looking for best fit: Can Lands' End be the Kenmore of clothing?" *DSN Retailing Today*, 23 February 2004. The prospects for integrating Lands' End into Sears shortly after the acquisition are discussed.

- Anderson, G., "The Lands' End brand plan: Insanity or genius?" *RetailWire*, 11 December 2006. Lands' End president David McCreight explains that the retailer is trying to develop a one-stop shopping experience for its customers. Proponents of the move argue that doing so may expand the strength of the Lands' End brand to other Sears product lines, a necessary move to branch out beyond its core business. Opponents call the move "brand suicide."

Case Challenges

- How and why did Lands' End succeed as an online retailer during the late 1990s and early 2000s when other Internet businesses failed?

- How important is further international expansion to the success at Lands' End?

- Should Lands' End shift to an Internet-only business model to reduce mailing and other costs, or should the company maintain its traditional catalog approach as well?

Internet Sites of Interest

- Corporate Web site: www.landsend.com
- Web sites of key competitors: www.llbean.com, www.gap.com, www.spiegel.com
- *The Industry Standard*: www.thestandard.com
- *E-Commerce Times*: www.ecommercetimes.com
- National Retail Federation: www.nrf.com
- American Apparel and Footware Association: www.apparelandfootwear.org

Real-Time Case 22: Mattel

Founded in 1948 by Elliot and Ruth Handler, Mattel, Inc. designs, manufactures, and markets a variety of toy products for infants, boys, and girls worldwide. Mattel distributes most of its toys through retailers, with a small percentage sold directly to the public. The company employs more than 25,000 people in 36 countries and sells products in more than 150 countries.

Major brands of the number-one toymaker in the world include the famous Barbie dolls, Hot Wheels and Matchbox cars, Magna Doodle, and Fisher-Price, as well as products based on characters from Disney, Sesame Street, Barney, Blues Clues, Winnie the Pooh, and even Harry Potter. About one-third of the company's revenues are derived from Barbie-related products. Major rivals include Hasbro, Jakks Pacific, and Leap Frog.

Mattel developed a number of core toy lines in the 1950s and 1960s. Barbie was introduced in 1959, joined by companion Ken in 1961. Mattel entered the preschool market with the See 'N Say talking toy in 1965 and launched Hot Wheels in 1968.

In the 1970s, however, the company moved into several nontoy areas, acquiring Western Publishing and the Ringling Brothers–Barnum & Bailey Combined Shows circus. The Mattel Children's Foundation was established in 1978 and has since been funded exclusively by cash donations from Mattel.

Mattel underwent a major restructuring in the mid-1980s when the company divested itself of all assets not related to toys and cut toy production capacity by about 40 percent. In the 1990s, the company acquired some related businesses, including Aviva Sports, International Games, Fisher Price, Tyco, Kransco, and American Girl (then the Pleasant Company) in 1998. The company even made an unsuccessful bid for rival Hasbro in 1996. Mattel acquired The Learning Company in 1999 and sold it after mounting losses only a year later. During 2003, the Mattel Children's Foundation distributed cash grants of almost $6 million, including a grant of $5 million to the Mattel Children's Hospital at UCLA.

Mattel announced the breakup of Barbie and Ken in 2004 after over forty years together, and Barbie sales declined in the months shortly thereafter and has suffered as a result of intense competition from MBA's Bratz dolls. Mattel announced a reorganization of its core toy business in 2005 and acquired Hong Kong–based electronic toy company Radica Games in 2006 in an effort to expand its appeal to older children and young adults. Mattel unveiled its new generation of Barbie dolls in 2007.

Today, Wal-Mart, Target, and Toys "R" Us account for about half of Mattel's sales. About one-third of the company's revenues come from outside of the United States.

Perspectives

- Marsh, P., "Bandai sets sights on number one spot," *Financial Times*, 10 March 2003, 19. Japanese firm Bandai, the world's number-three toymaker, is known for such toys as Hello Kitty and Strawberry Shortcake. Bandai, roughly half the size of industry leader Mattel (Hasbro is number two), plans to embark on a number of acquisitions and alliances in the coming years to challenge Mattel.

- Palmeri, C., "March of the toys—out of the toy section," *Business Week Online*, 29 November 2004. Toys are no longer confined to toy stores and the toy sections within department stores. Many are winding up in checkout lines and music sections, and even in arts and crafts stores.

- "Mattel, Nickelodeon team up," *Los Angeles Business*, 10 May 2004. Mattel is partnering with Nickelodeon to market its toys in Latin America.

- Pruitt, A., "Mattel's net drops; Fisher Price, Hot Wheels brands boost sales," *Wall Street Journal*, 16 April 2007. Fisher Price and Hot Wheels brands are selling well, but MGA's Bratz line is taking a toll on Barbie.

Case Challenges

- Is Mattel too dependent on retail giants such as Wal-Mart, Toys-R-Us, and Target?

- How important is it for Mattel to develop the "winning toy" each year? How important is the Barbie franchise in this effort?

- Having secured the number-one position in the United States, should Mattel focus its efforts on global markets?

Internet Sites of Interest

- Corporate Web site: www.mattel.com
- Web site of the firm's main rival: www.hasbro.com
- Web sites of key competitors: www.leapfrog.com, www.jakkspacific.com
- Toy Industry Association: www.toy-tia.org
- International Council of Toy Industries: www.toy-icti.org
- Game Manufacturers Association: www.gama.org
- American Specialty Toy Retailing Association: www.astratoy.org

Real-Time Case 23: Nike

Phil Knight and Bill Bowerman met at the University of Oregon in 1957. In 1962, they formed Blue Ribbon Sports to manufacture high-quality running shoes. In the following year, they began selling Tiger shoes—manufactured by Onitsuka Tiger in Japan—out of cars at track meets in the United States. The company became Nike in 1972, named for the Greek goddess of victory.

By 1979, the company had secured 50 percent of the U.S. running shoe market. Nike went public in 1980. The shoemaker expanded into other sports with Michael Jordan's "Air Jordan" in 1985 and the cross trainer in 1987. Nike signed Tiger Woods to a $40 million endorsement contract in 1995 and continued its prowess into most major sports. The company acquired competitor Converse in 2003 and currently competes with such shoemakers as Adidas and Reebok. Much of Nike's success may be attributed to its ability to sign major sports stars to endorse its products, most recently LeBron James for an estimated $90 million.

Today, Nike is the number-one shoemaker in the world and controls over 20 percent of the athletic shoe market in the United States. The company designs and markets shoes for basketball, baseball, golf, cheerleading, volleyball, and other sports—in addition to Cole Haan dress and casual shoes and a line of athletic apparel—in about 200 countries. Approximately half of the company's revenues come from outside of the United States. Chairman, CEO, and cofounder Phil Knight still owns controlling shares in the company.

In addition to distribution through an estimated 27,000 retail shoe and sporting goods stores in the United States and 30,000 abroad, Nike operates about 175 of its own Niketown stores, NikeGoddess shops for women, and factory outlet stores. The company also operates twenty-four distribution centers worldwide, although it dropped Sears as a retail outlet in 2005.

Nike has continued to expand its product offerings to a variety of sports-related categories, including apparel, clothing bags, two-way radios, and even heart monitors. Nike's late 1980s advertising slogan, "Just Do It," is still widely renowned as highly effective and memorable. Although Nike has been highly successful throughout Europe, the firm closed all of its Paris operations in 2004 because of difficulties with its French franchise operator.

Adidas acquired Reebok in 2006 and presents a formidable challenge to Nike's industry leadership position. Nike veteran Mark Parker succeeded Bill Perez as CEO in 2006.

Because most of its shoes are manufactured by contractors in low-wage companies, Nike has been a constant target of human rights activists citing poor wages and alleging child labor violations and substandard working conditions. Nike has taken steps to improve conditions, but critics continue to charge that more should be done.

Perspectives

- Gapper, J., "The big bucks that keep Nike in the big league," *Financial Times*, 4 November 2003, 19. The cost of big league endorsements notwithstanding, it is argued that Nike's success is attributable at least in part to its ability to secure such athletes as Michael Jordan and LeBron James.

- Holmes, S., and Bernstein, A., "The new Nike," *Business Week Online*, 20 September 2004. Nike has transitioned from a "fly by the seat of your pants" shoemaker in its early days to a more professionally managed firm.

- Kang, S., "Nike gets back to basics," *Wall Street Journal*, 2 April 2007, B1. In the past, Nike has flooded retailers with multiple variations of its "swoosh" products, complicating manufacturing efforts and confusing customers. It has moved to simplify its product lines and refocus efforts on the most popular products.

Case Challenges

- How critical are Nike's expensive endorsements to the company's success? Are the endorsements worth the money? Explain.

- To what extent, if any, is Nike liable for the actions of its manufacturing contractors with regard to employment issues and human rights violations?

- Could private-label athletic shoes pose a serious threat to Nike in the future?

- How might the Adidas acquisition of Reebok create strategic problems for Nike?

Internet Sites of Interest

- Corporate Web site: www.nike.com
- Web sites of key competitors: www.reebok.com, www.addidas.com
- Sporting Goods Manufacturers Association: www.sgma.com
- American Apparel & Footwear Association: www.americanapparel.org

Real-Time Case 24: Papa John's

Papa John's is the third-largest pizza chain in the United States behind Pizza Hut and Domino's. The company operates about 3,000 pizzerias in the United States and about thirty other countries. Papa John's typically offers delivery and carry-out options, but no restaurant seating. CEO John Schnatter founded Papa John's in 1985 at age twenty-three and owns 30 percent of the company.

Papa John's has always distinguished itself from the pizza crowd by using only fresh ingredients, concentrating on quality, and limiting the number of nonpizza items on the menu. The company frequently comes out on top in national taste tests and customer service surveys. Papa John's has received the top customer satisfaction rating among all national fast-food restaurant chains every year from 1999 to 2004, as measured by the American Customer Satisfaction Index.

Customer satisfaction successes notwithstanding, Papa John's has secured only about 7 percent of the quick-service pizza segment, behind Pizza Hut with 20 percent and Domino's with 12 percent. Other competitors include Pizza Inn, Little Caesar's, and Cici's, a rapidly growing pizza restaurant featuring a low-priced buffet offered around the clock. In addition, each location usually features independent pizzerias that have only one or a few locations.

In 2002, Papa John's initiated a move to close underperforming stores and open new ones only when prospects are very strong. For example, the company opened 103 franchised restaurants and 10 company-owned stores in 2002, while closing 76 franchised restaurants and 19 company-owned stores. As a result, revenues became stagnant in 2002 and 2003.

The Papa John's menu includes pizza with limited side items such as breadsticks and chicken strips. Bottled soft drinks are also available. Papa John's traditional pizza crust is made fresh, topped with 100 percent mozzarella cheese, meats with no fillers, and fresh vegetables. Locations abroad also emphasize pizza quality, but menus are adapted to local tastes.

During 2003 and 2004, Papa John's has closed unprofitable stores, while selling a number of units to franchisees. The firm has also emphasized global expansion as of late. Papa John's opened its first store in Russia in late 2003 and expanded its number of stores in Canada and the Bahamas in 2004. Papa John's appointed Blockbuster executive Nigel Travis as CEO in 2005.

Papa John's operates quality control (QC) centers that offer economies of scale and deliver fresh ingredients to stores twice weekly. Domestic franchises are required to purchase dough and spice mix from the QC centers or approved suppliers to ensure consistent quality. The firm consistently scores well in independent evaluations of quality, including consecutive top rankings in the *Restaurants & Institutions* survey of national take-out and delivery pizza chains in 2004 to 2006.

Perspectives

- White, J., "Come to papa," *Pizza Today*, 2004 September. Papa John's has experienced storybook growth since its inception in 1985. Today, the restaurant's emphasis on "better ingredients, better pizza" seems to keep it focused and successful.

- "Papa John's opens first Chinese pizza outlet in Shanghai," *Business Daily Update*, 27 October 2003. Papa John's opened its first pizza outlet in China, the beginning of an aggressive growth effort for the firm there.

- "Papa John's earns top rating among national take-out and delivery pizza chains in *Restaurants & Institutions'* survey," *Business Wire*, 4 December 2006. About 3,100 consumers rated 120 national and regional restaurant chains on eight customer satisfaction attributes. Papa John's earned the highest score in 2006 and its best score ever.

Case Challenges

- Why does Papa John's seem to be pursuing a stability strategy in a market where some of its key competitors are expanding rapidly?

- To what extent do low-cost pizza providers such as Little Caesar's and Cici's pose a threat to Papa John's?

- Should Papa John's develop eat-in restaurants like Pizza Hut or stick to delivery and carry-out?

Internet Sites of Interest

- Corporate Web site: www.papajohns.com
- Web sites of key competitors: www.dominos.com, www.pizzahut.com, www.cicispizza.com
- Pizza Marketplace: www.pizzamarketplace.com
- *Pizza Today*: www.pizzatoday.com
- *Restaurants & Institutions*: www.rimag.com
- *Nation's Restaurant News*: www.nrn.com
- National Restaurant Association: www.restaurant.org
- Restaurant News Resource: www.restaurantnewsresource.com

Real-Time Case 25: Pfizer

Pfizer was founded in 1849 in Brooklyn, New York, by Charles Pfizer and Charles Erhart and was incorporated in 1942. The company experienced considerable growth during the half century following its incorporation. After its merger with Warner-Lambert in 2000 and the company's acquisition of rival Pharmacia in 2003, Pfizer became the world's largest research-based pharmaceuticals firm.

During this same period, however, the company shed some of its nonpharmaceutical businesses, including the Schick-Wilkinson Sword shaving products division, the Tetra fish-care division, and the Adams confectionary business. Currently, Pfizer's subsidiaries include Warner-Lambert, Goedecke, and Parke-Davis.

Pfizer currently markets eight of the world's top twenty-five drugs. The firm's best-known products include pain management drug Celebrex, erectile dysfunction therapy Viagra, antidepressant Zoloft, and cholesterol control aid Lipitor. In addition, Pfizer provides some over-the-counter (OTC) drugs, including Ben Gay rubs, Neosporin antibiotic ointment, Unisom sleep aid, cold remedies Benadryl and Sudafed, and a variety of skin and eye care products. Pfizer also has a veterinary products division.

In 2003, Pfizer amassed $45 billion in sales worldwide, well ahead of its closest rival GlaxoSmithKline. The company depends heavily on a limited number of highly successful drugs, however. In 2003, ten different drugs accounted for over 80 percent of the firm's sales.

Pfizer's growth and success may be attributable to a number of factors, including the firm's recent acquisitions and its ability to work effectively within various government regulations. The company has enjoyed substantial success marketing its prescription drugs directly to consumers. Pfizer has also been able to leverage its research and development efforts by developing several highly successful and lucrative prescription drugs. In an industry recognized for its R&D capabilities, Pfizer is known as a leader.

One of Pfizer's most visible drugs is the "little blue pill" Viagra, which received FDA approval in 1998. Pfizer enjoyed market dominance at first with this product, but intense competition from rivals, including Bayer's Levitra and Lilly's Cialis, ensued shortly thereafter. Nonetheless, the product name remains a household word in the United States and many parts of the world. Three of Pfizer's drugs—its current flagship, cholesterol-lowering Lipitor, Norvasc, and Zoloft—accounted for $2 billion in sales in 2006.

Pfizer replaced CEO Hank McKinnell in that year and appointed Jeffrey Kindler as his replacement. In 2007, Kindler announced an amendment to McKinnell's 2006 restructuring plan that included the elimination of 10,000 jobs and the closure of three research facilities and three manufacturing plants.

Perspectives

- Bowe, C., and Dyer, G., "Pfizer to make up for patent losses with biotech purchases," *Financial Times*, 3 May 2004, 3. Pharmaceutical firms are under constant pressure to develop new products, especially as the patents for existing drugs expire. Faced with the upcoming loss of several key patents and a lack of replacements on the horizon, Pfizer is positioning itself to purchase biotechnology companies. This change marks a shift from a strategy emphasizing licensing in marketing rights to one emphasizing promising experimental drugs.

- Herper, M., "Pfizer accused of burying Celebrex study," *Forbes*, 31 January 2005. The consumer group Public Citizen accused Pfizer of "burying" the results of a study suggesting a heightened risk of heart attack for patients who take Pfizer arthritis drug Celebrex.

- Johnson, A., "Pfizer overhaul faces timing dilemma," *Wall Street Journal*, 23 January 2007, A2. CEO Jeffrey Kindler announced a restructuring plan in 2007 that includes eliminating 10,000 jobs—about 10 percent of its U.S. workforce—and closing three research facilities and three manufacturing plants. These measures are designed to stave off potential financial losses when the patent on Pfizer flagship Lipitor expires in 2010.

Case Challenges

- Evaluate the effectiveness of Pfizer's recent acquisitions and divestments.

- How can Pfizer maintain its leadership position in the world pharmaceutical industry?

- Considering this industry, how important have factors not associated with R&D become in recent years?

Internet Sites of Interest

- Corporate Web site: www.pfizer.com
- Web sites of key competitors: www.bayer.com, www. merck.com, www.novartis.com
- American Association of Pharmaceutical Scientists: www.aaps.org
- American Pharmaceutical Association: www.aphanet.org
- World Health Organization: www.who.int/en
- Pharmaceutical Research and Manufacturers of America: www.phrma.org
- Association of the British Pharmaceutical Industry: www. abpi.org.uk
- Pharmacist.com: www.pharmacist.com

Real-Time Case 26: Southwest Airlines

Texas businessman Rollin King and attorney Herb Kelleher founded Air Southwest in 1967 as a regional airline linking Dallas, Houston, and San Antonio. Southwest made its first scheduled flight in 1971 and passed the billion-dollar revenue mark in 1989. Today, Southwest Airlines remains a predominantly short-haul, high-frequency, low-fare airline providing service within the United States. The Dallas-based carrier offers approximately 2,700 daily flights throughout much, but not all, of the country.

Southwest is a classic no-frills airline, although service is generally perceived to be excellent and on-time performance rivals or exceeds its larger peers. Meals are not served, although passengers are encouraged to bring their own food on the plane. In addition, there are no reserved seats. Each passenger is allowed to board and select a seat based on arrival time at the gate. Southwest operates out of smaller airports when possible.

Southwest was the first carrier to establish an Internet home page. The company offers a ticketless travel system to reduce its commissions for travel agents, operates its own reservation system, and sells a substantial portion of its tickets through its own Web site. Interestingly, Southwest spends about one dollar to book a ticket online, compared to six to eight dollars per ticket when booking through agents. The airline's frequent flier program, known as Rapid Rewards, is among the most generous in the industry.

Southwest has enjoyed twenty-nine consecutive years of profits, including when 9/11 riveted other American carriers into deep losses. In fact, the airline has been the only major U.S. carrier to avoid layoffs and maintain a full flight schedule since that time. The company even began hiring additional employees in early 2002.

Southwest is known for its fun-loving, service-oriented culture. Every flight attendant seems to be an amateur comedian, an approach that subsided after 9/11 but had reappeared again by 2003. Chairman Herb Kelleher, who stepped down as CEO in 2001, helped establish a reputation for the company as one of the top employers in the United States. *Fortune* typically recognizes Southwest as one of the most admired companies in its annual surveys. Southwest is nearly 85 percent unionized, but has experienced only one strike.

In 2001, Southwest's average one-way airfare was about $83, with an average passenger length of 690 miles. As a major U.S. carrier, Southwest provided about 90 percent of all discount domestic air travel. Passenger revenue accounted for approximately 97 percent of firm revenues. Employees own approximately 13 percent of the company.

In the early 2000s, growth among other low-cost carriers such as Frontier, JetBlue, and America West exceeded that at Southwest. Unlike the Texas-based carrier, competitors were offering such frills as first-class service, in-flight entertainment, and meal service, prompting Southwest to rethink its strict application of low-cost, no-frills service.

Gary Kelly was appointed CEO in 2004. Southwest has since added service to Denver, Philadelphia, and San Diego. Prior to this time, Southwest focused primarily on less costly and less busy airports where no single airline controlled a high percentage of the traffic. Analysts believe that Southwest may be embarking on a gradual strategic shift that reflects its rapid growth.

Perspectives

- Warren, S., and Trottman, M., "Southwest's Dallas duel," *Wall Street Journal*, 10 May 2005, B1, B4. Southwest has prospered despite the 1979 Wright amendment which prohibited the airline from scheduling direct flights from Dallas Love Field to airports that are not located in Texas or a contiguous state. In May 2005, the airline launched www.setlovefree.com in an attempt to overturn the law (which occurred in 2006).

- Nazareno, A., "Dallas-based Southwest Airlines faces turbulence ahead as costs creep skyward," *San Antonio Express-News*, 18 September 2004. Prior to this time Southwest has been able to weather the storm of increasing fuel prices amidst growing price competitiveness in the market for airline tickets. With costs rising further, continuing to do so will be difficult.

- Michaels, D., and Trottman, M., "Fuel may propel airline shakeout," *Wall Street Journal*, 7 September 2005. The mid-2005 spike in fuel prices seems to have hurt traditional airlines such as Delta the most, whereas budget carriers such as Southwest and Ryanair could actually benefit from the process. Fuel prices represent a smaller percentage of total costs in short-haul flights, such as those championed by Southwest

- Warren, S., "Keeping ahead of the pack," *Wall Street Journal*, 19 December 2005. With Southwest's continued growth, its early-2006 expansion into costly Denver International Airport, and increasing competition from several low-price upstarts, some analysts believe that Southwest Airline's low-cost advantage is eroding. An interview with Southwest CEO Gary Kelly reveals his perspective on the issues, as well as his tips for managing competition.

- Reed, D., "At 35, Southwest's strategy gets more complicated," *USA Today*, 11 July 2006. Southwest is considering a change to its no-assigned seat policy and could implement a change as early as 2008. Such a change could further signal Southwest's strategic shift away from that of a small, low-cost airline to one that looks more like that of its traditional rivals.

Case Challenges

- Because Southwest competes primarily in short-haul routes at low fares, should traditional carriers such as American and Delta be considered as primary competitors? What about other transportation providers such as Amtrak and Greyhound?

- Why was Southwest the only major U.S.-based airline to turn a profit in 2001?

- Can Southwest engage in strategies that look more like those of traditional airlines without losing its personal, fun-loving image?

Internet Sites of Interest

- Corporate Web site: www.southwest.com
- Web site of one of the top three airlines ranked by revenues, American (AMR): www.amrcorp.com
- Web site of one of the top three airlines ranked by revenues, United: www.ual.com
- Web site of one of the top three airlines ranked by revenues, Delta: www.delta.com
- Web site of low-cost competitor, JetBlue: www.jetblue.com
- Web site of low-cost competitor, AirTran: www.airtran.com
- Web site of Ireland's up and coming budget carrier, Ryanair: www.ryanair.com
- Air Transport Association (the primary trade association; an excellent source of current industry information): www.airlines.org
- Industry news from Airwise: http://news.airwise.com

Real-Time Case 27: Starbucks

Starbucks was founded in 1971 in Seattle by Gordon Bowker, Jerry Baldwin, and Ziv Siegl. By 1982, Starbucks had five retail stores and was selling high-quality whole bean and ground coffee products to restaurants and espresso stands in the Seattle area. In that same year, Howard Schultz joined Starbucks to manage retail sales and marketing. After convincing the firm to open a downtown Seattle coffee bar in 1984, which was successful, Schultz left Starbucks to open his own coffee bar, Il Giornale, which served Starbucks coffee. Schultz acquired Starbucks in 1987, and locations were opened in Chicago and Vancouver. The company published its first mail-order catalog in 1988. In 1991, Starbucks became the first U.S.-based privately held company to offer stock options to all employees. The company went public in 1992.

Today, the Starbucks coffee shops and kiosks can be found in a variety of shopping centers, office buildings, bookstores, and other outlets. The Starbucks product line includes food and beverage items such as coffee, coffee beans, and pastries, as well as accessories such as mugs and grinders. The Starbucks beans are also marketed to restaurants, airlines, hotels, and directly to the public through mail-order and online catalogs. Interestingly, Starbucks is capitalizing on taste changes that pre-date the company's founding. In the early 1960s, American adults consumed an average of three cups of coffee each day. Today, consumption has declined to less than two cups, with only half of American adults as coffee drinkers. During this time, decaffeinated coffee sales soared. In addition, a new category of intensely loyal coffee drinkers was born. This group of adults consumes specialty or premium coffees, including regular and decaffeinated versions with a variety of origins and flavors. Sales of specialty coffee has climbed from about $45 million annually to well over $2 billion today, accounting for about 20 percent of all coffee sales.

Because Starbucks markets both whole beans and coffee beverages, its competition comes from two distinct groups of firms. A number of regional coffee manufacturers distribute premium coffees in local markets, while several large national coffee manufacturers, such as Nestle, Proctor & Gamble, and Kraft General Foods, market and distribute specialty coffees in supermarkets. Coffee beverages are distributed by restaurants, grocery stores, and coffee retailers. Seattle's Best Coffee is a fierce competitor.

Chairman Howard Schultz projects that Starbucks will grow from its present 6,000 stores to over 20,000 stores, 75 percent of which are in the United States. Today, there are more than 13,000 Starbucks in thirty-five countries. Over 7,500 of these coffee houses—mostly in the United States—are company owned. Starbucks also owns and franchises Seattle's Best Coffee and has moved into China. Retail stores account for over 80 percent of revenues, with specialty operations accounting for the remainder.

Perspectives

- Sowa, T., "Starbucks offers glimpse of global strategy at Spokane, Washington luncheon," *Spokesman Review*, 12 June 2004. About 2,000 of Starbucks 8,000 stores are located outside of the United States, with the strongest holdings in Japan, England, and China. Starbucks plans to continue to grow aggressively and open stores in a number of global markets.

- Gray, S., and Merrick, A., "Latte letdown: Starbucks set to raise prices," *Wall Street Journal Online*, 2 September 2004. Citing higher costs for milk and commodities, Starbucks announced an across-the-board price hike. Analysts disagree as to whether projected increases of about 5 percent to most menu items will significantly affect demand.

- Gray, S., and Smith, E., "At Starbucks, a blend of coffee and music creates a potent mix," *Wall Street Journal*, 19 July 2005, A1, A11. Starbucks has become a major player in the music business. Some of the CDs and bands promoted by the chain of coffee shops are Starbucks exclusives.

- Adamy, J., "Starbucks stirred to refocus on coffee," *Wall Street Journal*, 26 February 2007, A12. Starbucks has branched out from its coffee roots in recent years but plans to refocus its strategy on the core business.

Case Challenges

- What are some of the challenges associated with the Starbucks aggressive growth strategy?

- Could an unanticipated change in coffee consumption patterns disrupt Starbucks in the same way that it paved the way for the company's growth in the 1980s?
- What problems might arise from Starbucks's efforts to expand rapidly into nations such as China and Mexico?

Internet Sites of Interest

- Corporate Web site: www.starbucks.com
- National Retail Federation: www.nrf.com
- Hawaii Coffee Association: www.hawaiicoffeeassoc.org
- National Coffee Association USA: www.ncausa.org

Real-Time Case 28: Walgreens

Walgreens is the leading drugstore chain in the United States, operating 5,600 stores in forty-eight of the U.S. states and in Puerto Rico. The firm also operates three mail service facilities and thirteen distribution centers throughout the country.

Walgreens was founded in 1901 and incorporated in 1909 in Chicago. Like other drug stores in the early twentieth century, Walgreens emphasized a soda fountain and a lunch counter. By 1929, the firm had amassed 394 stores and $47 million in revenues. By the 1950s, Walgreens had begun a shift to self-service stores, but rapid growth did not occur until the late 1970s and early 1980s. Walgreens passed the 1,000-store milestone in 1984 and continued to grow steadily.

Prescriptions account for about 65 percent of company sales, with the rest coming from over-the-counter (OTC) medications, cosmetics, toiletries, photo processing, and grocery items. Approximately 90 percent of prescriptions are paid by third parties, generally insurance companies. About 70 percent of stores offer drive-thru pharmacies and almost all offer one-hour in-store photo processing. Walgreens's closest rival is CVS, although competition from pharmacies in grocery stores and discount retailers such as Wal-Mart has intensified.

With more consumers using health insurance to pay for prescription drugs, retailers receive the same payment from insurers for a given drug and consumers pay the same co-pay regardless of pharmacy. Hence, convenience has replaced price as the most important factor in the pharmacy side of the business. In this regard, "convenience" includes such factors as the acceptance of a given insurance plan, store hours, waiting periods, options for telephone and Internet refills, and the availability of grocery or other items that a consumer might wish to purchase while picking up a prescription.

Walgreens has responded to this emphasis on convenience by developing highly visible and accessible freestanding stores in high-traffic locations. Many of the stores are open twenty-four hours a day. As such, Walgreens continues to emphasize building new stores rather than acquiring them from smaller rivals. In recent years, Walgreen has opened more than 1,000 new stores and remodeled countless others. The company projects to have more than 7,000 stores in the United States by 2010.

Walgreens has benefited from constant increases in U.S. expenditures on prescription drugs, a trend which is projected to continue well into the future.

Perspectives

- "Among drug chains, Walgreen's dominates," *MMR*, 28 June 2004. Walgreen's success in the drug market in St. Louis is highlighted.
- Sivy, M., "Walgreen is evergreen," *CNN Money*, 14 January 2005. Thanks to its continued growth, Walgreens continues to enjoy success among a number of competitors that are not performing as well.
- Kaiser, R., "Walgreen's confident in strategy for battle," *Chicago Tribune*, 13 January 2005. Like other traditional pharmacies, Walgreens is feeling the heat from mail-order competitors. Walgreens believes it will prevail, however.
- Merrick, A., "Walgreen pretties up," *Wall Street Journal*, 8 February 2007, B2. Major drug store chains have been catering to consumer preferences for exclusive brands. Walgreen introduced expensive European lines of cosmetics in about 1,000 of their stores in 2006.

Case Challenges

- Is low price an important factor in the drug store industry? Explain.
- Is the Walgreens rapid growth strategy realistic? Why or why not?
- Should Walgreens consider expansion outside of the United States? Why or why not?

Internet Sites of Interest

- Corporate Web site: www.walgreen.com
- Web sites of key competitors: www.cvs.com, www.eckerd.com, www.riteaid.com
- National Association of Chain Drug Stores: www.nacds.org
- American Pharmaceutical Association: www.aphanet.org
- National Pharmaceutical Association (UK): www.npa.co.uk
- National Retail Federation: www.nrf.com

Real-Time Case 29: Wal-Mart

Sam Walton began his career in retailing as a J.C. Penney management trainee. He later leased a five-and-dime store in the rural community of Newport, Arkansas, in 1945. Five years later, he launched Walton 5 & 10, and by 1962, Walton owned fifteen Ben Franklin stores under the Walton name. Walton envisioned a rapid expansion of chain discount stores in small towns, a concept rejected by Ben Franklin. As a result, Sam and his brother James "Bud" Walton opened the first Wal-Mart Discount City in 1962. Wal-Mart Stores reached eighteen stores with sales of $44 million in 1970, and the company went public.

The company continued to avoid the competition by opening stores in small and midsized towns. The company amassed 276 of its own stores with annual sales in excess of $1 billion by 1980. Three years later, the first Sam's Wholesale Club was opened, touting a cash-and-carry, membership-only warehouse format. Rapid growth continued through the 1980s and 1990s.

Today, the Bentonville, Arkansas-based firm operates almost 7,000 stores—about 60 percent in the United States—including traditional discount stores, supercenters that also sell groceries, and Sam's Wholesale Clubs, as well as some Internet sales. Wal-Mart has stores in all fifty states and is the leading retailer in Canada and Mexico (through its Wal-Mart de México division). Wal-Mart also operates stores in Germany, Korea, Japan, and China, as well as other nations in Asia, Europe, and South America. The heirs of the late Sam Walton (Wal-Mart's founder) own about 38 percent of the company.

It is almost impossible to separate Wal-Mart from its founder. The flamboyant leader was known for his charismatic style, emphasis on customer service, and high esteem for Wal-Mart employees. In fact, Walton is responsible for the first widespread use of "associates," a term which connotes more respect for those who work for the large retailer. This commitment is seen in Wal-Mart's contribution of about 6 percent of each associate's salary to the company's profit sharing plan. Associates can take their share in cash or stock when they leave the company. It is not unusual for 20-year employees to accumulate $500,000 or more in company stock.

More than anything, however, Walton instilled a bias for action in managers and associates alike. Store change is constant, as opportunities for improvement were constantly being sought. Within each store, department managers act as entrepreneurs and are encouraged to innovate. CEO David Glass continued Walton's commitment to cost control, innovation, greater emphasis on the upscale market, and a customer-centered culture until the top job was handed to Lee Scott in 2000. Following an incessant stream of criticism alleging such practices as unfair price competition and employment discrimination, Scott launched a concerted effort in late 2004 to defend Wal-Mart's record, both as a successful retailer and a good corporate citizen. Wal-Mart is under constant pressure from environmental groups and organized labor, and defends itself against the most lawsuits of any firm in the United States.

Wal-Mart made an interesting move in 2006, lowering the prices of 300 generic prescription drugs to four dollars for a thirty-day supply. Continued growth efforts—especially in international markets—are anticipated. A smaller, neighborhood store format that carries both grocery and household items and sales of major appliances such as LCD televisions is also in the strategic mix.

Perspectives

- Zimmerlin, A., "Defending Wal-Mart," *Wall Street Journal*, 6 October 2004, B1, B10. CEO Lee Scott vigorously defends Wal-Mart against its critics and offers insight into the company's philosophy of business.

- Buckley, N., "Wal-Mart in offensive to boost image," *Financial Times*, 9 September 2004, 30. Wal-Mart has been the brunt of criticism alleging unfair business and labor practices. CEO Lee Scott announced that the company will embark on a concerted effort to put its story across.

- Stringer, K., "Wal-Mart's growth surge leaves dead stores behind," *Wall Street Journal Online*, 15 September 2004. Wal-Mart's success in many cities has resulted in moves to larger stores, often leaving "dead" ones that used to anchor strip malls unoccupied. This has created a growing problem for local economic developers.

- Sandoval, R., "Mexican retailers fight for survival against Wal-Mart," *Dallas Morning News*, 13 March

2004. Three large Mexican grocery chains—Gigante, Comercial Mexicana, and Soriana—attempted to fuse their purchasing units to challenge Wal-Mart's clout, but Mexico's competition commission rejected their plan. The stores are appealing the decision.

- Culp, E., "Juggernaut Wal-Mart goes slow in Germany," *Sunday Business (London)*, 26 September 2004. Germany is the only company in the world where Wal-Mart is not profitable. Strategists are speaking more of adapting Wal-Mart's offerings to German consumers in an effort to revive the company's ninety-two stores there.

- Dunn, J., and Vuong, A., "Growth of big-box retailers leads to increase in discrimination lawsuits," *Tribune Business News*, 21 September 2004. During the last decade, Costco, Home Depot, and Wal-Mart expanded vigorously and hired tens of thousands of hourly employees, many of whom later became managers. All three firms, however, have been the targets of class action lawsuits alleging race and sex discrimination.

- Lyons, J., "In Mexico, Wal-Mart is defying its critics," *Wall Street Journal*, 5 March 2007. Wal-Mart is performing well in Mexico. Like many of their rural American counterparts, Mexican shoppers are "more concerned about the cost of medicine and microwaves than the cultural incursions of a multinational corporation."

Case Challenges

- It is easy to become enamored with a company when it has enjoyed so much success over the years. What are Wal-Mart's weaknesses?

- Does Wal-Mart's new neighborhood store format run counter to the cost-cutting emphasis that is at least partially responsible for the success of its traditional stores? Explain.

- What challenges can Wal-Mart expect with its international expansion efforts?

Internet Sites of Interest

- Corporate Web site: www.walmart.com
- Web site of a key competitor: www.target.com
- National Retail Federation: www.nrf.com
- *DSN Retailing Today:* www.dsnretailingtoday.com

Real-Time Case 30: Yum! Brands

In 1997, PepsiCo spun off three of its restaurant holdings—Pizza Hut, Taco Bell, and Kentucky Fried Chicken (KFC)—to focus more on its core beverage business. The resulting company, Yum Brands, Inc. (formerly Tricon Global Restaurants) now posts sales in the global fast-food industry second only to McDonald's. Yum boasts over 34,000 locations in more than 100 countries, the largest number in the industry, although the firm trails McDonald's in terms of revenue. KFC has about 14,000 outlets, more than one-half of which are located in one of more than eighty countries outside of the United States. KFC also accounts for almost half of the quick-service chicken business in the United States. Pizza Huts has about 12,600 outlets throughout the world and leads the U.S. pizza market with a 15 percent market share. Almost all of its Taco Bells are located in the United States, where the brand controls about 60 percent of the Mexican fast-food segment.

Prior to the spin-off, PepsiCo had sought to create synergy among its beverage, fast-food, and snack food businesses, but only with limited success. For example, because the beverage business was owned by the same parent company (PepsiCo) that also owned several prominent fast-food businesses, Pepsi was always guaranteed a substantial piece of the lucrative fast-food market for soft drinks. In the late 1980s, however, Coca-Cola began to market its soft drink line aggressively to non-PepsiCo fast-food vendors such as McDonald's and Burger King. Coke was quick to remind these restaurants that contracts with Pepsi provided direct financial support to KFC, Taco Bell, and Pizza Hut. As a result, Coke was successful in securing contracts with a number of fast-food companies, a factor that many analysts believe led to PepsiCo's decision to spin off the three restaurants.

In March 2002, Yum acquired Long John Silvers and A&W Restaurants to its portfolio of businesses for $320 million, and changed its name to Yum! Brands.

About 80 percent of Yum's restaurants are franchised. About 3,600 multibranded units have been opened in recent years. Yum controls about 2,600 units in China, where the restaurant earns about 15 percent of its global revenues.

Yum experienced a public relations crisis in early 2007 when a video camera filmed rats roaming a New York City Taco Bell-KFC combination unit. Yum quickly closed the store until its sanitation could be verified.

Perspectives

- "Yum! Chewing hard to digest Chinese fast food," *China Daily*, 19 August 2004. Yum Brands, which already operates a number of KFC and Pizza Hut restaurants in China, has launched its first Chinese-style restaurant brand there, East Dawning.

- Garber, A., "Thinking outside the box: Fast feeders not only are redesigning menus but also remodeling stores in an attempt to win back customers from casual competitors," *Nation's Restaurant News*, 20 October 2003. The more contemporary fast-casual restaurants have taken a bite out of the fast-food industry. Competitors such as Yum and McDonald's are fighting back with menu changes and store redesigns.

- Slaughter, M., "Yum heard 'round the world," *The Motley Fool*, 2 February 2005. Yum's recent growth is primarily due to its growth outside of the United States, particularly in China.

- "Yum shuts Taco Bell-KFC unit over rat video flap," *Nation's Restaurant News*, 5 March 2007. Yum closed the New York Taco Bell-KFC combination store in New York where video cameras recorded rats roaming unabated in the store.

Case Challenges

- Do all of Yum's business units compete in the same fast-food industry, or does each compete in a different industry based on product type?

- What kind of synergy can Yum create among its restaurants? What challenges does the firm face?

- McDonald's is known globally for a strong brand image and unrivaled consistency. What lessons can Yum learn from McDonald's?

- In early 2001, Yum appointed David Novak as CEO, replacing Andy Pearson. How has Novak's appointment changed Yum's strategic direction?

- In March 2002, Yum announced the acquisition of the Long John Silver's and A&W Restaurants chains. How can Yum effectively integrate these two chains into its portfolio?

Internet Sites of Interest

- Corporate Web site: www.yum.com
- Link to the Taco Bell business unit: www.tacobell.com
- Link to the Pizza Hut business unit: www.pizzahut.com
- Link to the KFC business unit: www.kfc.com
- Link to Long John Silver's business unit: www. ljsilvers.com
- Link to A&W Restaurants business unit: www.awrestaurants.com
- Website of a key competitor, McDonald's: www.mcdonalds.com
- *Restaurants & Institutions*: www.rimag.com
- *Nation's Restaurant news*: www.nrn.com
- National Restaurant Association: www.restaurant.org
- Restaurant News: www.restaurantnews.com

Traditional Case 1: Aries Catering and Aries Tours of Armenia

As Avetik Ghukasyan walked out of his new office on the ground floor of a small building at 43 Giulbenkyan on a quiet tree-lined street in Yerevan, Armenia, he mulled over the perplexing problems he faced as a businessman in this recently-created free market economy. It was now 2003 and seven years had passed since he had launched his catering business; however, there were still serious issues to deal with on a regular basis. To begin with, he and other Armenian entrepreneurs had to deal with labor problems fostered by the 50 years of Communist domination. The older people had no sense of the importance of a work ethic, and the younger people were discouraged over the lack of opportunities in their native country. There was also a lack of role models to encourage hard work as a way of improving oneself. He wondered how he could run a successful business with such serious labor constraints. How, he mused, does one motivate employees to be productive when the culture has never supported a strong work ethic.

In addition, there was growing competition from other catering businesses and the local hotels that made it more and more difficult to make a living. In the state-owned businesses of the past, there was no competition; so this was a totally new environment in which to operate a company. And, if this were not enough, another problem was the fact that the legislature had not yet passed laws to assist with the launching and operation of private business. Avetik wondered how he could deal with these specific problems that plagued his and other Armenian companies and also the larger problems caused by the government which had moved very slowly in enacting laws to encourage small business. The latter problem seemed to be beyond his control.

Background on Avetik Ghukasyan

Avetik had grown up in Yerevan, the capital of Armenia. He had spent most of his life living under the Communist regime that had encompassed much of Eastern Europe and the Trans-Caucasus region in which Armenia was located. In 1983, Avetik received a degree in mechanical engineering from Yerevan State University. Then from 1983 until 1991 he had worked at a number of different state-owned factories.

After the collapse of the Soviet Union, he was hired as the assistant to the Minister of Education and Science. For the first time in his life, Avetik became a bureaucrat. At the end of 1991 and just before the collapse of the Soviet Union when Gorbachev was taken into custody, his boss had resigned. This prompted Avetik to go abroad to study business administration. He had saved up a little money, so he decided to go to Melbourne, Australia, and after a year received a graduate certificate in Business Administration.

When Avetik returned to Armenia, he found his country in crisis. They were at war with Azerbaijan, there was no electricity, no radio, no jobs, no telephones and no money.

He found Armenia to be essentially a "dead country" in 1992 and 1993. They had a tough winter in 1992, and this made matters worse. Avetik was offered a job with USAID[1] which had a small office in Yerevan. He was given a position handling tasks related to energy, humanitarian projects, the micro economy, banking and finance. He worked in this office for 2 years and found it to be a worthwhile experience. This position had given him an opportunity to meet many new friends and to have a good exposure to business people.

At one of the parties hosted by USAID, Avetik met his future wife, Hasmik ("Jasmine") Barkhudaryan. After their marriage, he and Hasmik had a son and then 4 years later a girl. In 2003, the children were 7 and 3 years old, and he looked forward to being able to provide a good life for both of them.

Development of Aries Catering and Aries Tours

After leaving his job with USAID in 1995, Avetik followed the desire that had been growing in him to be an entrepreneur. He knew he wanted to begin

This case has been reprinted with permission of Dr. Marlene M. Reed, School of Business, Samford University, and Dr. Rochelle R. Brunson, Chair, Department of Management, Alvin Community College.

a small business, and the only type of business he could think of that he believed he knew enough about was catering. In early 1996, he launched Aries Catering with a partner named Marguerita. At this time, this was the first and only professional catering business in Armenia.

Perhaps because of their monopolistic position in the industry and the growing need for this type of service, the business broke even during the first year of operation. Another reason for success was their ability to operate the company as a home-based business with no expenditures or fixed assets initially. In the second year of operation, Demand grew faster than they were able to handle; so Avetik and Marguerite decided to split up and each have a catering business. They knew they would have to absorb the Growth in the volume of orders; otherwise, competitors would enter the industry. For two years, they had the only two businesses in the industry, and then competition finally appeared.

In the third year, Avetik's wife joined him in the business. After he saw how well she was doing with the catering business, Avetik gave the entire business to her. She soon became the exclusive caterer for the Head of the Catholic Church in Armenia for parties at Christmas and Easter. Around 200 people normally attended each of these parties. Aries Catering also catered for the Pope when he came to Armenia.

Avetik searched for a new business to start, and he immediately thought of opening a tour business because he had been serving as a free-lance interpreter. Due to his ability to speak fluently in Armenian, Russian and English, he often found himself working with visiting dignitaries and business people. His fluency with languages had a natural fit with his wife's catering business. He interpreted at conferences, and his wife provided the food service for the attendees.

With the launching of Aries Tours, Avetik began providing the following services:

- Airport pickup
- Hotel reservations
- Badges and folders for the conferees
- Catering (by his wife's company)
- Interpreting

Then in 2001, Avetik became involved with a Bed and Breakfast network in Armenia. He found this new venture so intriguing that he invested in a B & B himself in Southern Armenia in a town named Sisicen. Because of the perceived need for development in the operations of such establishments, Avetik hosted a training course for other B & B owners at his own B & B. As a result of the training course, he signed contracts with 12 B & B owners to serve as their reservation agent. Avetik reasoned that as the economy grew, there would be greater interest in visiting some of the country's natural attractions—especially for those Armenians who were part of the Diaspora (the dispersion). Because of conflicts with Turkey and Azerbaijan in the past and difficulties with the economy in the present, many native Armenians had moved to Russia, Europe and America—especially California.

When people had asked Avetik why he had not moved to Russia or the United States because of his fluency in Russian and English, he stated that he could never think of doing so because his heritage was in Armenia. Certainly he could make more money abroad, but he loved his country and wanted to live there.

Background on the Armenian Economy

With the demise of the Soviet Union, the Armenian economy suffered greatly. Immediately after the Russians left, the unemployment rate in the country grew to 80 percent, an earthquake killed 28,000 people and an embargo by Turkey and Azerbaijan stopped the flow of all oil and gas supplies.[2] The Azerbaijani problem was exacerbated by ethnic cleansing against Christian Armenians cut off in a small island of Armenia in Muslim Ajerbaijan. Armenia had been the first Christian nation in 301 A.D., and it was now completely surrounded by Muslim countries. The rapid increase in the unemployment rate was the result of several factors. One was the fact that Moscow stopped paying for public works. Secondly, Armenia was no longer a favorite vacation destination for the CIS (Commonwealth of Independent States–the successor of the Soviet Union).

Thirdly, Moscow no longer bought Armenian-manufactured bits. It had been the practice of the Soviet Union before its demise to farm out the manufacturing of selected parts of products throughout the countries of the Union. After the fall of

Communism in the Soviet Union, these countries no longer had a market for the specific parts that they had been manufacturing. For example, the parts for one automobile might be produced in several different countries and assembled in yet another country. Now there was no longer a unifying central planning commission to bring these parts together in a finished product.

Because Russia was no longer paying for public works, the entire infrastructure of Armenia began to deteriorate. Citizens of countries located in the former Soviet Union had been taught for decades to believe that the government would always subsidize the things that the citizenry needed. However, under the new free-market economy, the people were learning that the individual states were no longer in a financial position to do this. The streets were rapidly deteriorating, the "government" water that flowed into houses for a few hours each morning caused problems for households that forgot to open up their pipes for this inflow of water, and the water and sewer pipes which were above ground and often angled up over roadways also needed some reworking.

As late as 2003, all of the members of the CIS except Russia were still posting deficits in trade within the Commonwealth. Whereas Russia posted a surplus in trade with other CIS nations of 3.48 billion dollars (exports of 9.143 billion dollars and imports of 5.66 billion dollars), Armenia had a deficit of 109.4 million dollars (exports of 58.5 million dollars and imports of 143 million dollars).[3]

As far as GDP growth was concerned, Armenia's real GDP growth was expected to slow from 9.6 percent in 2001 to an annual average of 6.2 percent in 2003.[4] Although a 9 percent growth rate sounded aggressive by world standards, the base itself had been very low. The government was attempting to finalize a poverty reduction strategy and a national anti-corruption strategy in 2003–2004. These strategies were important because they were cited by the IMF (International Monetary Fund) and the World Bank as conditions for continued assistance in the development of Armenia.

A problem facing all businesses in Armenia was the lack of a strong work ethic in the country. Under the Communists, workers were assured of lifetime employment by nationalized companies, and there was almost no way for a worker to be fired. A common saying in Eastern Europe was that under the Soviets, "The people pretended to work, and the government pretended to pay them." The abrupt change to a free market economy was difficult for people who could not lose their jobs earlier, and there was little incentive or desire to work any harder than was necessary to keep their jobs.

Bribery of government officials to bring goods into the country or operate within the country was often considered by many people as simply another cost of doing business. In addition, the legislature had been slow in developing laws to support the development and growth of new businesses.

Another serious constraint on business formation and growth in Armenia was the very inefficient telecommunications system. Under the Soviets, it took years for a family to get a telephone in their home. In the first part of the twenty-first century, one might buy a mobile phone, yet there were serious problems with operating the phone. The nationalized telephone company ArmenTel still held a monopoly in telephone service in the country. Since ArmenTel had been sold in 1998 to Greece's Hellenic Telecommunications Organization (OTE), the company had enjoyed a continued monopoly of telephone services. However, a spokesperson for the World Bank stressed that the opening of the Armenian telecom sector to competition was critical for economic development.[5]

Another serious problem that plagued owners of companies in the former Soviet Union was a lack of understanding of the basic principles of marketing. Under the Soviets, national companies were expected to produce a certain quota of goods each year; however, they were never included in decisions regarding the distribution of those goods. Marketing was, in fact, supplanted by mere distribution of products and goods. A common saying in the countries of the CIS was that under Communism customers were treated like slaves. One would never think of asking the customer what he/she thought about a specific product. This was an unnecessary task since only one product or service would be offered in a particular product class, and that was what the customer was forced to purchase.

Another serious problem for the country was the flight of bright young workers to Russia and the

West to seek jobs. These young adults would secure a job in another country and send money home to their families in Armenia. Many observers warned that the brightest minds were leaving the country. A saying in Armenia was "planes come in empty and go out full."

Avetik's Dilemma

As he got into his van parked on the street, Avetik reviewed in his mind the dilemma he was facing with his business. Both the catering and tour businesses had grown appreciably, but now he was having problems finding workers who wanted to give a day's work for a day's pay.

In addition, he had to think of ways to make his business different enough to compete successfully with the hotels that had invaded his business for the conference trade and restricted his profitability. Under Communism, there had been only one producer of a good, and the rewards went to national companies that produced a large supply of goods—whether there was a market for them or not. Now, a successful businessperson had to operate in a competitive environment and discover ways to market a unique product or service.

There were also problems with the lack of laws to promote the launching and operation of businesses in the country. He wondered if there was anything that he could do about this or if this should be written off as an "uncontrollable" factor.

Notes

1. USAID was created in 1961 by President John F. Kennedy with the signing of the Foreign Assistance Act. It is an independent federal government agency that receives overall foreign policy guidance from the Secretary of State and extends assistance to countries recovering from disaster, trying to escape poverty and engaging in democratic reforms.
2. Benedetto, Joe (April 2002). "Where will the jobs be?" Design Engineering, Vol. 48, Issue 3, page 14.
3. "All members but Russia post deficit in trade within CIS in first half of 2003" (September 3, 2003). Moscow: Interfax News Agency, page 1.
4. "Business outlook: Armenia" (September 9, 2002). Country Monitor. New York: Vol. 10, Issue 35, page 9.
5. "World Bank praises government move against telecommunications monopoly" (September 22, 2003). Info-Prod Research, page 1.

Traditional Case 2: Kraft Foods in the Era of the Category Killer

Bryon K. Langenfeld and Rebecca J. Morris (faculty supervisor)
University of Nebraska at Omaha

Kraft Foods—And so it Begins

Kraft Foods was the second-largest food and beverage manufacturer in the world.[1] Around the globe, consumers were familiar with many of their brands, such as Kraft, Nabisco, Toblerone, Crystal Light, Maxwell House, Post, and Oscar Mayer. They were present in 145 countries around the world and employed a workforce of over 100,000 internationally.[2] Kraft had deep roots in the consumer package goods industry that dated back to the 1780s. Throughout their long history, Kraft added to its portfolio through acquisitions and mergers. The most recent acquisition was Nabisco Brands in 2000. However, Kraft was faced with a new challenge.

The company posted a fifth consecutive quarterly profit decline in October 2004, reportedly due to rising costs and increased competition.[3] In response to declining profits, Chief Executive Roger Deromedi launched a restructuring program expected to trim 6,000 jobs and close twenty plants over three years. The costs of the program outweighed the savings; in 2004, the program cost $508 million but saved $84 million.[4] Meanwhile, Kraft's last significant new brand launch was DiGiorno pizza in 1995. Once admired for its new product prowess, the cupboards at Kraft were bare. Deromedi believed that "building new brands is not the true measure of success within consumer products. Driving incremental volume is."[5]

Kraft was faced with a fork in the road. As the company built their large brand portfolio through acquisitions and mergers, they accumulated many B and C category brands and products. Large customers, such as Wal-Mart, gave preferential treatment to manufacturers of the top seller in a given category, or category killer.[6] In an industry where only number one would do, Kraft was reevaluating their noncategory killers as an answer to their declining profit trend.

The Recipe for a Food Manufacturing Giant

The wealth of brands and products owned by Kraft Foods of the early twenty-first century was largely built under the stewardship of Phillip Morris Companies Inc., later known as Altria. The diversified tobacco giant's entrance into the food industry came in 1985 when it acquired General Foods Corporation. It next acquired Kraft, Inc. in December 1988, and then in March 1989, Philip Morris combined the two food companies under a new subsidiary called Kraft General Foods, Inc. General Foods and Kraft operated separately until early 1995, when the two units were merged as Kraft Foods.[7] Then in December 2000, Philip Morris purchased Nabisco Holdings Corp., merging it into Kraft Foods. In June 2001, Philip Morris sold 16.1 percent of Kraft Foods to the public, retaining the remaining shares.[8] Prior to its acquisition by Philip Morris, General Foods earned a reputation as a pioneer in the acquisition and integration of smaller food companies and built a huge multinational, multiproduct corporation.

Ingredient One: The Rise of General Foods

The groundwork for General Foods was laid by Charles W. Post, a health enthusiast. He tried to create a noncaffeine alternative for coffee drinkers with a cereal beverage he called Postum. With a paid-in-capital of $100,000, Post incorporated the Postum Cereal Company, Ltd., in 1896. Post continued to bring new products to the table, such as Post Toasties and Krinkle. Within five years of its incorporation, Postum Cereal Company's capital had risen to $5 million. The Postum employed 2,500 people and its factories covered more than twenty acres.[9]

Upon Charles's death in 1914, Marjorie Post, his daughter, took over the company and helped launch the expansion that created the company known as General Foods. The transition began in 1925 with the acquisition of the Jell-O Company; it was the premier desert brand at that time. In 1926, the company absorbed Swans Down cake flour, and just one year later Minute tapioca, Baker's coconut and chocolate, and Log Cabin syrup were acquired.[10] In 1928, the Postum Company acquired Maxwell House Coffee. In 1929, the company made another significant acquisition when it paid $22 million for a controlling interest of the General Foods Company, owned by Clarence Birdseye. Birdseye perfected new techniques for freezing vegetables and meat.

In 1932, General Foods purchased the Sanka Coffee Corporation. General Foods's earnings, which had reached $19.4 million in 1929, dropped to $10.3 million in 1932. In 1933, however, they began to rise again as consumer purchasing power strengthened. Gaines Dog Food Company was added in 1943, and the next year General Foods acquired Yuban premium coffee to its already strong coffee line.[11]

In 1953, General Foods acquired the Perkins Products Company which held the powerhouse of powdered beverage mixes—Kool-Aid. Years later, General Foods added a number of other products to its beverage division, including Tang, Country Time, and sugar-free Crystal Light.[12] In 1954, the company entered the salad dressing market with its purchase of 4 Seasons, Inc., and Open Pit in 1960. General Foods was an established giant in the food industry by the mid-1960s. The company's outstanding success was based on new product development, sweeping market research, and enormous advertising budgets.

In 1981, General Foods made its largest acquisition to date when it bought Oscar Mayer & Co., the leading American hot dog maker, for $470 million.[13] General Foods was trying to reduce its dependence on the coffee trade, but Wall Street critics charged that with the purchase of Oscar Mayer, the company was opening itself up to the wildly cyclical, low-margin packaged-meat business. Regardless, the merger gave General Foods access to an extensive refrigerated supply network. In addition, the acquisition afforded General Foods a high profile in the refrigerated meat section at the supermarket—Oscar Mayer was the largest national brand of lunch meats, and its Louis Rich turkey products unit was top in that growing segment of the market.[14]

In November 1985, Philip Morris Companies Inc. purchased General Foods for $5.6 billion.[15]

Philip Morris had long been known as an aggressive marketer. Its chairman, Hamish Maxwell, aimed to decrease Philip Morris's reliance on the declining tobacco market. Philip Smith became CEO of General Foods in January 1987 and began a massive reorganization of the company by splitting its business into three core product lines—coffees, meats, and assorted groceries. The following year, the General Foods Oscar Mayer division introduced Lunchables, a line of convenient meals that featured meat, cheese, and crackers. Meantime, Philip Morris acquired Kraft, Inc. in 1986, which led to the 1989 combining of General Foods and Kraft under Kraft General Foods, Inc.

Ingredient Two: The Rise of Kraft Foods Company

One of Kraft, Inc.'s primary predecessor companies was established by James L. Kraft, the son of a Canadian farmer. In 1903, Kraft started a wholesale cheese distribution business in Chicago. By delivering cheese to their door, Kraft hoped to relieve grocers of the need to travel daily to the cheese market. Business was dismal at first, and it was later reported that Kraft lost $3,000 and his horse the first year.[16] The business eventually took hold and James was joined by his four brothers. In 1909, the business was incorporated as J. L. Kraft & Bros. Company. The company's growth was fueled by new product development and innovative advertising. As early as 1911, Kraft mailed circulars to retail grocers and advertised on elevated trains and billboards. Later, he was among the first to use color advertisements in national magazines. By 1914, the company sold thirty-one varieties of cheese throughout the country, and that year it opened its own cheese factory in Illinois.[17]

In 1928, Kraft merged with Phenix Cheese Corporation, the maker of Philadelphia Brand cream cheese. The newly formed Kraft-Phenix Cheese Corporation had captured 40 percent of the nation's cheese market by 1930 and boasted operations in Canada, Australia, Britain, and Germany. In 1929, National Dairy, another growing dairy company, set out to acquire Kraft-Phenix; the merger was complete in 1930.[18] After the merger, Kraft settled down to introduce many of the brands that later formed the heart of its consumer product line; Velveeta pasteurized process cheese spread was introduced in 1928; Miracle Whip salad dressing and Kraft caramels came in 1933; the famous Macaroni and Cheese dinner in 1937; and Parkay margarine in 1940.[19] Through innovative advertising on the radio, the public quickly adopted the new products. In 1945, the Kraft Cheese Company became Kraft Foods Company.

New product introductions continued with sliced process cheese in 1950 and Cheez Whiz pasteurized process cheese spread in 1952. During the late 1950s and the 1960s, Kraft continued to expand its product line, adding new products such as jellies and preserves in 1956, "jet-puffed" marshmallows in 1959, barbecue sauce in 1960, and individually wrapped cheese slices in 1965.[20] Kraft held a conservative business strategy during the 1970s. Unlike other major food companies, Kraft did not seek acquisitions to shore up sagging profits; new product introductions also slowed during this time.[21]

In 1980, the merger of Dart and Kraft was launched. Dart Industries was an aggressive, innovative, and rapidly growing diversified company with subsidiaries in chemicals, plastics, glass, cosmetics, electric appliances, and land development. Its most successful and recognized business line was Tupperware. Industry analysts doubted that such a diverse company, Dart & Kraft, Inc., would succeed. Several subsidiaries experienced managerial problems or proved vulnerable to the recession of the early 1980s. In 1986, the company decided to dissolve the six-year-old merger. Kraft, Inc. retained all of the product lines it had brought to the 1980 merger.[22]

A Food Manufacturing Giant Is Made

In December 1988, Philip Morris purchased Kraft for $12.9 billion. In March 1989, Philip Morris merged the Kraft and General Foods units into one giant entity called Kraft General Foods. As a result of the merger, the company became the largest food marketer in the United States. Profits at Kraft General Foods grew at an average rate of more than 20 percent in its first two years. The company's size proved to be a competitive advantage; it saved $400 million through initial consolidations and its purchasing power multiplied. It also had bargaining

and influence power on its customers largely driven by the immense brand portfolio.

Size had its drawbacks, however. The company was slow to respond to demand in some markets. For example, Kraft waited until 1990 to introduce Touch of Butter, well after other food producers responded to the public's growing concern about excess cholesterol. In addition, tensions were mounting between the Kraft and General Foods forces within the company. The company's sales in the North American market grew only 1 percent in 1991. Several of the company's most important product categories lost market share that year, including cheese, processed meats, and frozen dinners. In 1992, Kraft General Foods Marketing Services was formed. The purpose of this unit was to assist in coordinating marketing strategies and bridge gaps between the different opportunities. Late 1992, the operating units of Kraft General Foods were realigned. In November 1993 came the launch of yet another restructuring, this one designed to eliminate 14,000 jobs and close forty plants worldwide. In January 1993, the firm completed the $450 million purchase of RJR Nabisco Holding Corp.'s cold cereal business, gaining the Shredded Wheat products.[23]

With the financial results of Kraft General Foods continuing to disappoint analysts and being under criticism for moving too slowly to integrate the operations of Kraft and General Foods, the management was shaken up in late 1994. A major restructuring, the fourth since 1989, was launched to merge into a single organization called Kraft Foods, Inc. Continuing the drive to improve margins, Kraft Foods made some selective divestitures and acquisitions leading to the 2000 acquisition of Nabisco Holding Corp.

To complete its third major food company acquisition, Philip Morris had to pay $14.9 billion in cash plus assume $4 billion in debt.[24] Philip Morris completed its acquisition of Nabisco in December 2000 and immediately began integrating the Nabisco operations into those of Kraft Foods. In March 2001, Philip Morris created a new holding company for the combined operations of Kraft Foods and Kraft Foods International, known as Kraft Foods Inc. (lacking the comma of the previous Kraft Foods, Inc.). The previous Kraft Foods was renamed Kraft Foods North America, giving the new Kraft Foods two main units: Kraft Foods North America and

Kraft Foods International. The two CEOs of these units, Betsy D. Holden and Roger K. Deromedi, respectively, were named co-CEOs of Kraft Foods Inc. In June 2001, Philip Morris sold a 16.1 percent stake in Kraft Foods to the public, retaining the remaining shares.[25] The second largest IPO in U.S. history, the offering raised $8.68 billion, which Philip Morris used to reduce debt it had incurred in acquiring Nabisco.[26]

The U.S. Food Manufacturing Industry—Competition

Total retail sales of food and beverage products rose 6.2 percent in 2003, to $911 billion, from $857.5 billion in 2002. In 2003, the top ten publicly traded U.S. food and beverage producers generated approximately $180.5 billion in total food and beverage sales. Although the biggest firms, such as Kraft, had a great deal of power, the food markets remained fairly fragmented. According to the U.S. Census Bureau, approximately 29,365 establishments manufactured food in 2002 (see Exhibit 1).[27]

The U.S packaged food industry remained highly fragmented overall, despite the presence of several large companies. The typical food company was small and produced a limited number of products for regional or specialized markets. Regional firms also served as contract manufacturers of private-label goods for grocery store chains. In contrast to smaller players, the top national firms enjoyed significant brand name recognition. To manage their operations and create economies of scale, they focused on multimillion-dollar products that were sold nationally.[28]

EXHIBIT 1 Top Twenty Publicly Held U.S. Food and Beverage Companies, 2003 (Ranked by sales, in millions of dollars)

Rank	Company	2002	2003	Change
1	Kraft Foods Inc.	29,273	31,010	4.3%
2	PepsiCo Inc.	25,005	26,971	7.9%
3	Tyson Foods Inc.	23,367	24,549	5.1%
4	The Coca-Cola Co.	19,564	21,044	7.6%
5	ConAgra Foods	24,056	19,839	−17.5%
6	Coca-Cola Enterprises	16,889	17,330	2.6%
7	General Mills	7,949	10,506	32.2%
8	Pepsi Bottling Group Inc.	9,216	10,265	11.4%
9	Sara Lee Corp.	9,219	9,778	6.1%
10	Dean Foods Co.	8,991	9,185	2.2%
11	Kellogg Co.	8,304	8,812	6.1%
12	H. J. Heinz Co.	9,431	8,237	−12.7%
13	Smithfield Foods Inc.	7,356	7,905	7.5%
14	Campbell Soup Co.	6,133	6,678	8.9%
15	Hormel Foods Corp.	3,910	4,200	7.4%
16	Hershey Foods Co.	4,120	4,173	1.3%
17	Interstate Bakeries	3,532	3,526	−20.0%
18	Proctor & Gamble Co.	3,801	3,238	−14.8%
19	PepsiAmericas	3,240	3,237	−10.0%
20	Wrigley	2,746	3,069	11.8%

Source: Company Reports.

The Global Food Industry

The largest food manufacturer in the world was Nestle Foods, S.A. Nestle Foods not only competed in U.S. food markets with Kraft Foods but also in international markets. As the largest food producer in the world, Nestle was recognized and respected as the leader of the pack. Kraft's North America division faced off with Nestle related to U.S. markets while Kraft's Global division took the food war overseas to fight internationally.

The Food Manufacturing Industry—Barrier to Entry

Domestic food companies generally fell into two groups: those engaged in the early or middle stages of making a processed food product, and those involved in the later stages. Early to middle stage firms, referred to as "agribusinesses," engaged in activities such as harvesting, milling, or processing of raw agricultural commodities. Companies such as Archer-Daniels-Midland, Cargill, and Corn Products International Inc. were examples. Companies engaged in the late stages of consumer food production were generally referred to as food manufacturers or food packagers. These companies, which included Kellogg, Heinz, Hershey, Kraft, and ConAgra Foods, sold their finished goods to the food retailers, which in turn sold the products to consumers.

Barriers to enter the food industry were relatively low on a local level; the technological skills and financial resources were not substantial. Marketing and distribution were the most significant costs for a small-scale food manufacturer, but they could be reduced when neighboring food establishments were located close to the manufacturer. The barriers to entry on a larger scale were very high. The capital requirements needed for manufacturing facilities alone could be prohibitive. The high costs of marketing and distribution made large-scale entry into the industry unreasonable.[29]

The Food Manufacturing Industry—Regulation

Almost all food products in the United States were subject to regulations administered by the Food and Drug Administration (FDA) or, for products containing meat and poultry, the USDA. These agencies enforced statutory prohibitions against misbranded and adulterated foods, established ingredients and/or manufacturing procedures for certain standard foods, set standards of identity for food, determined the safety of food substances, and established labeling requirements for food products. Additionally, individual states had their own regulatory process. Some states required a license and inspected food. A third regulatory influence in the food manufacturing industry was the governmental agricultural programs that affected the commodities used as inputs to the manufacturers. These programs had substantial effects on prices and supplies and were subject to congressional review.[30]

The Food Manufacturing Industry—Current State and Trends

Food manufacturers were facing higher commodity and input costs. Following several years of mostly benign increases, key commodity prices rose and remained at elevated levels for several quarters.[31] Meanwhile, high competition limited manufacturers' ability to raise prices. At the same time, demand fell for high-carbohydrate product categories such as breads and pasta, because of the low-carbohydrate diet craze. Many companies committed a substantial amount of money to develop new low-carb products. In addition, they increased market spending for various other product offerings. All of these pressures increased the cost of doing business in the U.S. packaged food industry.[32]

Consumers' use of price and perceived value continued to increase as the basis for purchasing decisions. This trend strengthened the growth of private-label (or store) brands; this came at the expense of their branded counterparts. It also contributed to the sluggish trend in sales growth, because private-label products carried lower prices than branded goods. For retailers, however, their profit margins on private-label products were generally wider than those on branded products, and many were actively pursuing strategies to further increase sales of store brands. Sales volume was further stifled as food manufacturers enlisted selective price increases in certain categories to offset rising commodity costs; retailers pushed the increase on to their customers.[33]

The most significant trends affecting food companies were consumers' growing concern with health and nutrition, ethnic diversity of the U.S. population, and spreading influence of Wal-Mart Stores, Inc. During the last decade, Americans became increasing concerned with their health, spending billions of dollars each year on gym memberships, spa treatments, and organic, natural, and packaged "better-for-you" foods. It was estimated that roughly 54 million Americans were dieting at any given time, and that an additional 32 million altered their consumption behavior in some way because of one dieting philosophy or another. Media attention increased Americans' awareness of the health risks associated with obesity, and this concern reflected in their food and consumption.

Demand for "better-for-you" foods increased significantly in the late 1990s and early 2000. Consumer buying patterns supported this trend: Sales of low-sugar, low-cholesterol, low-fat products continued to rise, while high-carbohydrate categories such as fresh bread and pastas showed declines.[34] In the early 1990s, less than 1 percent of a food company's portfolio was dedicated to health and wellness products, according to industry sources. In the early twenty-first century, that portion was likely to be about 5 percent, moving steadily toward 10 percent. ConAgra Foods was one of the first to take initiative in this area with the introduction of Healthy Choice. PepsiCo, which owned Frito-Lay, Quaker Oats, and several other brands, countered with olestra-based Wow! chips. Kraft Foods was criticized for being behind the curve in terms of healthy food innovation. The trend toward healthier eating was likely to continue, fueled largely by the aging U.S. population. The aging of the baby boom generation was the primary long-term demographic trend affecting the nation's food companies. This generation, then between the ages of forty and fifty-eight, was more focused on nutrition and weight maintenance.[35]

The preference for low-carbohydrate, high-protein foods was a dietary trend that had significant impact on food manufacturers. The Atkins and South Beach diets were the most popular regimens in North America in the early 2000s. It was estimated that some 20 million Americans followed some form of low-carb, high-protein diet. The trend became so mainstream that it had a strong influence on nondieters as well, further boosting the number of "carb watchers" in the United States. Results of a July 2004 Gallup poll showed that 27 percent of consumers actively avoided carbs, compared to just 20 percent the year before.[36] Indications in late 2004 indicated the low-carbohydrate mania may be slowing.

Convenience and taste remained the driving forces behind consumers' food and beverage spending. Modern lifestyles dictated that meals be easy to prepare and serve. One factor behind the demand for convenience was the increasing number of women in the workforce. As of September 2004, women accounted for 46.4 percent of the U.S. civilian labor force, up from 34 percent in 1964.[37] In addition, the number of American families headed by two wage earners or by a single working parent steadily increased. Dual-income and single-parent families tended to buy more prepared meals, both fresh and frozen, than did traditional families with a breadwinner and a stay-at-home parent. Ready meals constituted one of the fastest growing products areas in the food market. Ready meals were generally sold at higher prices and generated more profit for food companies than packaged foods.

The ethnicity of America was constantly changing; from 2000 through 2005, the minority segments of the U.S. population grew at much faster rates than the non-Hispanic white populations. The U.S. Hispanic population saw the biggest growth; it became the country's largest minority group in 2002.[38] In that year, the U.S. Census Bureau counted 37 million Hispanics, up nearly 70 percent since the 1990s and an estimated 18 percent of the total U.S. population. By 2010, immigration and relatively high birth rates were expected to raise that number to 44 million.[39] Asian American populations were growing at the second fastest rate. The U.S. Census Bureau estimated that by 2010, numbers for this group would increase 23 percent over 2002, to 14.6 million.[40] Analysts believed the purchasing power of Hispanics would grow at twice the rate of the overall population by 2015. For example, privately owned Goya Foods Inc. emerged as the best-known Hispanic food company in the United States. The company went from $8.5 million in sales in 1976 to $750 million in 2003, according to the *Wall Street Journal*.[41]

Retail sales at traditional grocery stores grew at a slow average annual growth rate of 3 percent from 1995 through 2004, according to the U.S. Census Bureau retail trade data.[42] Meanwhile, growth in nontraditional retail segments caused a dramatic shift in the food industry. Mass merchandisers and convenience stores became the fastest growing distribution channels for food, led by super-retailer Wal-Mart Stores Inc. With an estimated $103.2 billion in grocery sales in 2003, according to *Supermarket News*, Wal-Mart was the largest food retailer in the United States with over 13 percent total market share. The chain's food sales saw a compound annual growth rate of 16 percent from 1990 through 2000. In comparison, retail sales at the largest U.S. supermarket chain, Kroger Co., had a compound annual growth rate of about 9 percent over the same period, reaching $53.8 million. Wal-Mart was expected to continue to gain market share from other food and beverage distribution channels. Some of the largest names in food manufacturing—Kraft, General Mills, Kellogg, and Hershey—realized over 10 percent of total sales at Wal-Mart, and the figure was growing rapidly.[43]

Because the U.S. food industry was mature, pricing flexibility was limited. Brand awareness was the best way to develop customer loyalty, leading to a method to enhance pricing power. Brand loyalty was the Holy Grail for all U.S. consumer product companies, including those in the packaged food and beverage industries. Not surprisingly,

food companies were among the nation's leading advertisers. Private-label goods, lower priced products sold under a store's own name, remained a constant threat to other branded goods. This was heightened during times of economic weakness. Private-label sales in supermarkets, in dollar terms and in physical volume, increased steadily from 1995 to 2003.[44] According to the Private Label Manufacturers Association (PLMA), a trade group, sales of store brands in supermarkets totaled $42.9 billion in 2003, up 2.2 percent from the prior year, while private-label sales in drug chains increased 7.7 percent to $3.8 billion. In 2003, private-label goods accounted for approximately 20.7 percent of all units sold in supermarkets and 12.6 percent of units sold in drug chains. In dollar terms, private-label goods represented 16.3 percent of supermarket sales and 11.2 percent of drugstore sales.[45]

The Plague of Declining Profits

Kraft Foods posted its sixth consecutive quarterly profit decline in the fourth quarter of 2004. Kraft's CEO Roger Deromedi claimed rising costs and price pressures from private labels put the squeeze on earnings.[46] Kraft's earnings were down 23 percent from the previous year (see Exhibit 2).

Over the summer of 2004, Kraft announced price increases on certain products to offset ballooning costs for ingredients such as milk, meat, and coffee. But those price increases, which Kraft said helped boost its revenue 4.7 percent during the quarter, were not strong enough to compensate for increases in

EXHIBIT 2 Comparative Net Earnings of Top Five Food and Beverage Companies (Millions of Dollars)

	2004	Change	2003	Change	2002	Change	2001	Change	2000
Kraft Foods	2,665	23.33%	3,476	2.42%	3,394	80.34%	1,882	−5.95%	2,001
PepsiCo	4,187	17.45%	3,565	7.74%	3,309	24.54%	2,657	21.71%	2,183
Tyson Foods	403	19.58%	337	12.01%	383	335.23%	88	41.72%	151
Coca-Cola Co.	4,847	11.50%	4,347	42.52%	3,050	−23.15%	3,969	82.32%	2,177
ConAgra Foods	880	13.55%	775	−0.19%	776	21.56%	639	67.04%	382

Source: Company Reports.

EXHIBIT 3 Comparative Revenues of Top Five Food and Beverage Companies (Millions of Dollars)

	2004	Change	2003	Change	2002	Change	2001	Change	2000
Kraft Foods	32,175	3.76%	31,010	4.33%	29,723	−12.26%	33,875	27.68%	26,532
PepsiCo	29,261	8.49%	26,971	7.40%	25,112	−6.77%	26,935	31.79%	20,438
Tyson Foods	26,441	7.71%	24,549	5.06%	23,367	117.35%	10,751	50.20%	7,158
Coca-Cola Co.	21,962	4.36%	21,044	7.56%	19,564	−2.63%	20,092	−1.79%	20,458
ConAgra Foods	14,522	26.80%	19,839	28.20%	27,630	1.60%	27,194	6.50%	25,535

Source: Company Reports.

commodity and oil costs. Kraft said net earnings fell to $2.67 billion from $3.48 billion in 2003. Revenue rose to $32.18 billion, up from $31.01 billion in 2003 (see Exhibit 3).[47]

The company was in the midst of a restructuring program set in motion by Deromedi to boost flagging sales and profit. The program, which began in January 2004, was designed to trim 6,000 jobs and close twenty plants over three years. The costs of the program so far outweighed the savings; the program cost $508 million but saved $84 million.[48] As part of that program, Deromedi considered the sale of certain Kraft's brands.

Kraft Slims Down

With private labels eating into Kraft shares, the CEO wanted its brands either number one or gone. Kraft bulked up in the early 2000s, gobbling up ten rivals. The feast included Nabisco Holdings Corp. for $19 billion in late 2000, resulting in the biggest packaged-food maker in the United States with products in almost every aisle of the grocery store. CEO Deromedi decided it was time for Kraft to slim down. He began with the November 2004 sale of Kraft's Life Savers and Altoids candies to Wm. Wrigley Jr. Co. for $1.5 billion in cash.[49] "And more will follow," Deromedi said, as Kraft divested itself of other laggard and peripheral product lines to concentrate on the blockbuster brands that topped their categories worldwide. Deromedi indicated, "We want the products that consumers and retailers are more excited about."

Clearly, the pressure was on the fifty-one-year-old Deromedi, who became Kraft's sole CEO in 2003,

when co-CEO Betsy Holden was demoted to global marketing president. Like other consumer goods companies, Kraft scrambled to give Wal-Mart Stores Inc. and other retailing giants what they wanted. Bulking up to gain leverage with the retail behemoths fueled much of Kraft's expansion in the first place, but that strategy failed. With Wal-Mart and others increasingly interested only in the briskest-selling products, it turned out that suppliers were better off with a clutch of category killers than a cartful of so-so sellers. But dealing with Wal-Mart was not Kraft's only problem. Many were of its own making, from turmoil within its executive suite to oversaturated store shelves with too many variations of the same old product. How many different kinds of Oreos did consumers really want? At the same time, other consumer products companies, notably Procter & Gamble, were far more skillful in navigating the retailing shelves with nifty new products. In addition, management at Kraft's parent, Altria Group, was putting the squeeze on Kraft to shape up in advance of a possible spin-off of its controlling stake by 2006.[50]

Kraft's Diet on New Product Introductions

Management at Kraft Foods pointed to fear of fat, more competition from private labels, and skyrocketing costs to explain missed earnings. The one thing the management did not recognize, however, was Kraft, the icon of Oreo and Mac & Cheese innovation, had not launched a significant new brand since DiGiorno pizza in 1995. Kraft's machinery for developing new brands seemed to have broken down. Kraft had been admired for its new product prowess ever since James Kraft started selling cheese to Chicago grocers out of a horse-drawn wagon. Miracle Whip, created by a then-revolutionary "emulsifying machine," made a splash at the 1933 World's Fair. Launched just after World War II, Minute Rice dramatically slashed the time needed to cook rice. Then came processed cheese slices, Cheez Whiz, and Shake 'N Bake. Even Lunchables created an entirely new category.[51]

Kraft's new-product cupboard was bare. It enjoyed decent harvests for most of the 1990s, but the famine seemed to have set in after the departure of two key executives. As parent Altria Group, then Phillip Morris, prepared to take 16 percent of Kraft public, it lost CEO Bob Eckert (now Mattel's CEO) and his predecessor, Jim Kilts, who ran Gillette. Both men were champions of new-product development and left big holes when they bolted. After the IPO in June 2001, Kraft attempted to operate with dual CEOs: marketing whiz Betsy Holden, a seventeen-year Kraft veteran, running North America and the more analytical Roger Deromedi handling international duties; but profit growth soon collapsed because of pricing and marketing mishaps. As the head of Kraft's pizza business, Holden launched DiGiorno, but as CEO she botched the two major new-product launches of her tenure: Both microwaveable Chips Ahoy and FreshPrep dinner kits were disasters. With the company still digesting its Nabisco acquisition and adjusting to Wall Street's demands, Kraft seemed less and less willing to take big risks, instead focusing on much safer line extensions such as chocolate crème Oreos.

A former Kraft R&D executive observed that Eckert and Kilts "used a whole lot more intuition and gut feel rather than relying on numbers." The people who took over, he said, just seemed to want to milk aging brands, or as he put it, "rearrange deck chairs on the Titanic."[52] In December 2003, amid a huge shortfall in Kraft's cookie business, the board demoted Holden and handed the reins to Deromedi. Holden then headed global marketing, with responsibility for new-product development. She oversaw a relatively large R&D group, with an operating budget of $380 million and 2,100 employees over five locations. As at any packaged goods company, products were hatched in the lab by food scientists working with marketing and manufacturing specialists—and some ideas also came from brand managers. Analysts indicated, however, that Kraft's bureaucratic culture often killed good ideas in the cradle. Besides, the R&D chief, Holden, was widely viewed as powerless by the organization.

Holden insisted innovation will "define our success," but Deromedi did not seem destined to return Kraft to its history of modern culinary marvels. Instead, he threw even more marketing money at Kraft's big brands. Furthermore, Deromedi argued that "building new brands is not the true measure of success within consumer products. Driving incremental volume is."[53] R&D expenditures for Kraft Foods steadily increased since their last marked decline in the first quarter of 2003. Contrary to their lack of new products, Kraft continued to increase R&D funding (see Exhibit 4).

EXHIBIT 4 Kraft Foods R&D Expenditures (Millions of Dollars)

	2004	Change	2003	Change	2002	Change	2001
1st Quarter	1,646	8.29%	1,520	−2.44%	1,558	−43.71%	2,768
2nd Quarter	1,657	9.37%	1,515	0.60%	1,506	−56.51%	3,463
3rd Quarter	1,596	4.59%	1,526	8.23%	1,410	−41.66%	2,417
4th Quarter	3,993	46.59%	2,724	17.67%	2,315	25.14%	1,850
Annual	6,658	7.39%	6,200	8.60%	5,709	−45.62%	10,498

Source: Company Reports.

Kraft Enters the Low-Carb Craze Late

Just as the low-carb craze began to fizzle, Kraft geared up heavily by launching a full lineup of twenty-six convenience foods based on the carb-restricting South Beach Diet. Although South Beach Diet creator Dr. Arthur Agatston stated that his approach was not low carb, most retailers and analysts agreed that South Beach was still linked in consumers' minds with the fad diet that hit its high around 2004.[54] That made Kraft's ambitious introduction of a range of South Beach Diet products—from frozen dinners to cereal bars—look more than slightly late to the party. The push in April 2004 was pegged to the paperback rollout of *The South Beach Diet*, which was on the New York Times bestseller list and sold more than 8 million copies since Rodale launched the hardback in April 2003.[55]

Kraft's partnership with Dr. Agatston began modestly in October 2004 with the addition of a "South Beach Diet–recommended" burst on more than 200 products across thirty-eight of its brands, including Sugar-Free Jell-O, Planters nuts, and Boca Burgers. The new initiative created a stand-alone brand for cereals, meal-replacement bars, refrigerated sandwich kits, and frozen entrees. Prudential securities analyst John McMillin said the South Beach Diet line, seemingly "a year or two late," is likely a defensive rather than an offensive move, intended to protect its own product lines from the likes of Atkins. But, he said, "It's not necessarily going to help Kraft grow."[56]

Kraft's Next Move

CEO Deromedi was evaluating which brands to auction off next. As with the sale of Altoids and Life Savers to Wrigley, he began to look at secondary brands or those where Kraft lacked the clout with retailers to turn things around. Analysts and consultants figured Oscar Mayer was most likely. Despite being the leader in bacon, hot dogs, and luncheon meats in the United States, with $2.1 billion in annual sales, it had been losing out to cheaper store brands and had little brand recognition overseas. Kraft's $1.2 billion-a-year Post cereals division, a distant number three that also was ceding market share, was on the block as well.[57]

Long term, of course, Deromedi could not make Kraft grow by slimming down. In fact, he said he might take some proceeds from divestitures and make acquisitions,[58] acquisitions that rounded out and complimented the categories that Kraft was a leader.

What Was a CEO to Do?

With profits posted at another consecutive loss, what strategy was Deromedi to enlist to turn the trend around? Several variables fed into Kraft's profitable shortcoming, yet the CEO was focused only on trimming the pantry; the same pantry that had been dry for years of new products and line extensions. Was a simple strategy of divestures and acquisitions the best course of business to regain their strategic advantage?

See Exhibits 5 and 6 for Kraft's annual balance sheet and income statement for 2000 to 2004.

Notes

1. *Standard and Poor's Industry Survey* 172(49, sec. 1) (New York: McGraw-Hill, 2004), 1–33.
2. http:\\www.kraft.com
3. Kraft Foods Annual Reports.
4. D. Carpenter, "Food Industry Nudged toward Changes," *Associated Press Online* (14 January 2005): 1.
5. B. Daly, "Wrigley Gets Altoids, Life Savers," *Daily Deal* (16 November 2004): 1.
6. S. Ellison, "Retailers' Appetite for Top Sellers Has Food Firms Slimming Down," *Wall Street Journal* (28 October 2004): A1.
7. G. Burns, "Will So Many Ingredients Work Together?: Philip Morris Puts Its Food Operations into One Kraft Empire," *Business Week* (27 March 1995): 188.
8. J. Bowman, "Kraft Offers Public Its Riches," *Chicago Sun-Times* (28 June 2001).
9. C. Dudley, *Post City, Texas* (Austin: State Historical Association, 1952).
10. J. Ferguson, *General Foods Corporation: A Chronicle of Consumer Satisfaction* (New York: Newcomen Society of the United States, 1985).
11. Kraft, Inc., *Through the Years* (Glenview, IL: Kraft Inc., 1988).
12. Ferguson, *General Foods Corporation*.
13. O. Mayer, *Oscar Mayer & Co.: From Corner Store to National Processor* (New York: Newcomen Society in North America, 1970).
14. Ferguson, *General Foods Corporation*.
15. Kraft, *Through the Years*.
16. Ibid.
17. Ibid.
18. Ibid.
19. http:\\www.kraft.com
20. Kraft, *Through the Years*.
21. J. Boland, "Putting It All Together: For Dart & Kraft the Future Still Looks Super," *Baron's* (21 June 1982): 13.

5 Kraft Foods Inc, Annual Balance Sheet ($ Millions)

	Dec 2004	Dec 2003	Dec 2002	Dec 2001	Dec 2000
Assets					
Cash and Equivalents	282	514	215	162	191
Net Receivables	3,541	3,369	3,116	3,131	3,231
Inventories	3,447	3,343	3,382	3,026	3,041
Other Current Assets	2,452	898	743	687	689
	------------	------------	------------	------------	------------
Total Current Assets	9,722	8,124	7,456	7,006	7,152
Gross Plant, Property and Equipment	16,483	15,805	14,450	13,272	13,042
Accumulated Depreciation	6,498	5,650	4,891	4,163	3,637
	------------	------------	------------	------------	------------
Net Plant, Property and Equipment	9,985	10,155	9,559	9,109	9,405
Investments at Equity	0	0	0	0	0
Other Investments	0	0	0	0	276
Intangibles	35,811	36,879	36,420	35,957	31,584
Deferred Charges	3,569	3,243	2,814	2,675	2,623
Other Assets	841	884	851	1,051	1,031
	------------	------------	------------	------------	------------
Total Assets	59,928	59,285	57,100	55,798	52,071
Liabilities					
Long-term Debt Due in One Year	750	775	352	540	713
Notes Payable	2,045	1,096	1,115	681	146
Accounts Payable	2,207	2,005	1,939	1,897	1,971
Taxes Payable	170	451	363	228	258
Accrued Expenses	3,906	3,534	3,400	3,877	3,637
Other Current Liabilities	0	0	0	1,652	865
	------------	------------	------------	------------	------------
Total Current Liabilities	9,078	7,861	7,169	8,875	7,590
Long-term Debt	9,723	11,591	12,976	13,134	24,102
Deferred Taxes	5,850	5,856	5,428	5,031	1,446
Other Liabilities	5,366	5,447	5,695	5,280	4,885
Equity					
Capital Surplus	23,762	23,704	23,655	23,655	15,230
Retained Earnings	7,099	5,228	2,347	(177)	(1,182)
Less: Treasury Stock	950	402	170	0	0
	------------	------------	------------	------------	------------
Common Equity	29,911	28,530	25,832	23,478	14,048
	------------	------------	------------	------------	------------
Total Equity	29,911	28,530	25,832	23,478	14,048
	------------	------------	------------	------------	------------
Total Liabilities and Equity	59,928	59,285	57,100	55,798	52,071
Common Shares Outstanding	1,705	1,722	1,731	1,735	1,455

Source: Company Reports.

	Dec 2004	Dec 2003	Dec 2002	Dec 2001	Dec 2000
Sales	32,175	31,010	29,723	33,875	26,532
Cost of Goods Sold	19,383	18,024	17,011	16,851	13,418
Gross Profit	12,792	12,986	12,712	17,024	13,114
Selling, General, and Administrative Expense	6,598	6,200	5,709	10,416	8,240
Operating Income before Depreciation	6,194	6,786	7,003	6,608	4,874
Depreciation, Depletion, and Amortization	879	813	716	1,642	1,034
Operating Profit	5,315	5,973	6,287	4,966	3,840
Interest Expense	679	678	854	1,452	615
Nonoperating Income/Expense	13	13	7	15	18
Special Items	(703)	38	(173)	(82)	172
Pretax Income	3,946	5,346	5,267	3,447	3,415
Total Income Taxes	1,274	1,866	1,869	1,565	1,414
Minority Interest	3	4	4	0	0
Income before Extraordinary Items and Discontinued Operations	2,669	3,476	3,394	1,882	2,001
Preferred Dividends	0	0	0	0	0
Available for Common	2,669	3,476	3,394	1,882	2,001
Savings Due to Common Stock Equivalents	0	0	0	0	0
Adjusted Available for Common	2,669	3,476	3,394	1,882	2,001
Extraordinary Items	0	0	0	0	0
Discontinued Operations	(4)	0	0	0	0
Adjusted Net Income	2,665	3,476	3,394	1,882	2,001
EPS Basic from Operations	2	2	2	1	1
Dividends Per Share	1	1	1	0	NA
Com Shares for Basic EPS	1,709	1,727	1,734	1,610	1,455

Source: Company Reports.

22. "Dart & Kraft Turns Back to Its Basic Business—Food," *Business Week* (11 June 1984): 100.

23. V. Anderson, "Another Bid to Put Pep Back in Kraft's Step," *Crain's Chicago Business* (9 January 1995): 3.

24. N. Deogun, "Philip Morris Aggress to Acquire Nabisco," *Wall Street Journal* (26 June 2000): A3.

25. J. Bowman, "Kraft Offers Public Its Riches," *Chicago Sun-Times* (28 June 2001).

26. http:\\www.kraft.com

27. *Standard and Poor's Industry Survey.*

28. Ibid.

29. Ibid.

30. Ibid.

31. S. Ellison, "Kraft's Earnings Decline Again, as Commodity Prices Take Toll," *Wall Street Journal* (19 October 2004): B6.

32. S. Thompson, "Kraft Shows Late for the Beach Party," *Advertising Age* 76(2): 1.

33. Ellison, "Kraft's Earnings Decline Again."

34. D. Carpenter, "Kraft Net Drops 28 Percent on Higher Costs," *Associated Press* (26 January 2005): 1.

35. Carpenter, "Food Industry Nudged Toward Changes."

36. "South Beach Diet Recommended," *Business Wire* (3 January 2005): 1.

37. *Standard and Poor's Industry Survey.*

38. http://www.census.gov

39. *Standard and Poor's Industry Survey.*

40. http://www.census.gov

41. Ellison, "Retailers' Appetite for Top Sellers Has Food Firms Slimming Down."

42. *Standard and Poor's Industry Survey.*

43. Ellison, "Retailers' Appetite for Top Sellers Has Food Firms Slimming Down."

44. *Standard and Poor's Industry Survey.*

45. M. Boyle, "Kraft's Arrested Development," *Fortune* 150(10): 44.

46. http:\\www.kraft.com

47. Ellison, "Kraft's Earnings Decline Again."

48. S. Ellison, "Kraft Revises Its Reporting Structure," *Wall Street Journal* (11 January 2005): A16.

49. Daly, "Wrigley Gets Altoids, Life Savers."

50. Ellison, "Retailers' Appetite for Top Sellers Has Food Firms Slimming Down."

51. M. Arndt, "Why Kraft Is on a Crash Diet," *Business Week* 3910: 46.

52. V. Vishwanath, "Inside Kraft's Leadership Corridor," *Leader to Leader* 2004(34): 27.

53. Boyle, "Kraft's Arrested Development."

54. Thompson, "Kraft Shows Late for the Beach Party."

55. "South Beach Diet Recommended."

56. Thompson, "Kraft Shows Late for the Beach Party."

57. "Kraft Realigns Its Reporting Structure," *Associated Press Online* (10 January 2005): 1.

58. S. Thompson, "Food Giant Spawns Generation of Orphans," *Advertising Age* 75(40): 4.

Traditional Case 3: Michael Petrov

Stuart Rosenberg, Dowling College

Natasha Petrov could see the look of concern in the eyes of her husband, Michael, as the two of them prepared to leave their Levittown, New York, home on a Saturday morning in May 2006, to take the thirty-minute drive to New Age Laundromat, in College Point, New York. One of them would take this drive daily, ostensibly to pick up cash that had been collected by the attendants at the laundromat in the prior twenty-four hours, but also to have some face time with the attendant as well as the customers. Since this was a Saturday, however, and both of them were on their day off from their regular jobs, Michael as a safety inspector for the Metropolitan Transit Authority and Natasha as a freelance consultant in the computer industry, they took advantage of the opportunity to drive in together. From College Point, they would swing past Clean-Rite Laundromat, in Glen Cove, New York, to also pick up cash and to check in on business.

As Michael started the engine of his recently purchased white Lincoln Continental, a car that he had always equated with success, Natasha turned toward him and gently placed her left hand on his shoulder. "Misha," she asked affectionately, "Why do you always worry about the business so much?"

Michael, a small, restless man with an irrepressible laugh, shook his head emphatically. "Natasha, I am happy with New Age's growth. I am happy with the location. The laundromat has fit in well with the local community." He sighed deeply. "I am concerned about Clean-Rite."

Michael purchased Clean-Rite in August 2001. He and Natasha had decided a few years earlier that even though they both worked long hours in their full-time jobs, they would make an investment in a business as means to generate a cash flow and an additional source of income for their family. After researching different types of business investments, they decided to refinance the mortgage on their house to enable them to purchase the laundromat in Glen Cove, on the north shore of Long Island, about twenty minutes from Levittown.

Clean-Rite did well from the start, with sales climbing each week, as a result of strategies they developed that had not been offered by the prior owner, and given the growth of the business in Glen Cove, Michael and Natasha decided to expand, and they sought a second location for a laundromat, which they ultimately found in College Point, in the borough of Queens, in New York City. Unlike the business in Glen Cove, which was previously a laundromat, the store in College Point had been vacant. After Michael refinanced his house a second time, as well as using the equity from Clean-Rite, to obtain the capital necessary to make the investment in the new business, New Age Laundromat opened its doors in April 2005.

"Misha," said Natasha, several minutes later, at about the time that the relative tranquility of Long Island had transformed to the hustle and flow of College Point, Queens, "We have worked hard to build up two businesses. They are different, but they are both good."

Michael smiled at his wife nervously. "That's true, Natasha. What troubles me, though, is that I don't know how much more we can get out of Clean-Rite. The business grew well the first year, like New Age has, but since then the growth has slowed. Maybe the life of these businesses is only five years. You take what you can, and you move on to a new location."

"I don't agree with you," Natasha chided. "Both laundromats bring in income. If one is down a little, the other can pick it up. We are an important part of both communities. We have loyal customers. We have done well. We have talked about making this more than a part-time thing. We are now considering a third location—East Rockaway—and we know it's not easy driving back and forth every day. (See Figure 1 for a map of the locations of the laundromats.) But if we continue to expand, we do have options. We can take on a partner."

"It is a family business," Michael said emphatically, still shaking his head.

Since they both had full-time jobs, their responsibilities as it applied to the business were divided evenly between them. Accordingly, it was decided that Natasha was responsible for human resource matters and Michael was responsible for technical resource matters.

FIGURE 1 Queens and Long Island, New York

Source: http://www.triboroughhomecare.com

As the car pulled into a space on College Point Boulevard a half a block from New Age Laundromat, Natasha put her hand on her husband's shoulder and smiled at him warmly. "Misha, we have worked very hard and I am very proud of what we have accomplished. Never forget that it wasn't so long ago that we came to this country with nothing."

Family History

Michael Petrov, age forty-seven, had immigrated to the United States fifteen years earlier from the Ukraine. His home was the industrial city, Zaporozhye, not far from Kiev and Chernobyl. His sole purpose for coming to America was for the opportunity to build a career.

Michael left the Ukraine during Perestroika, the period that began in June 1987 when Mikhail Gorbachev, the leader of the Soviet Union, introduced the economic restructuring of the Soviet economy. Although reforms were established, the economy worsened and the quality of life deteriorated, leading to the eventual destruction of the Soviet Union in December 1991. On the day that Michael was to fly to the United States from Moscow, the city was in chaos. The army had positioned tanks in the streets and Michael was

relieved that the military allowed his flight to leave. Following the dissolution of the Soviet Union, the Ukraine became one of fifteen independent republics faced with the challenge of rebuilding its economy. Michael has never returned.

Having received his formal training as a teacher in the Ukraine, Michael realized that he would need to start over in the United States. He only had a tourist visa, so he applied to the government for political asylum. He was denied, as he was told that the Ukraine needed to hold on to people with his level of education. One week prior to his deportation, however, he won a green card in the Department of State's annual lottery. He would become a U.S. citizen within four years.

When he arrived in New York, Michael came with $200 in his pocket. He lived in basements of houses and he worked seven days a week. He washed dishes in restaurants, pumped gas, worked in auto body shops, and saved his money. He learned English and he studied engineering and business.

In 1992, Michael met Natasha, who had recently emigrated from southern Russia, near Chechnya. Natasha had received formal training as a pediatrician, but with her strong background in chemistry and mathematics, she decided to become a computer analyst in the United States. After a brief courtship, they married. In 1995, they took out a $90,000 mortgage and, together with their savings, they bought their house in Levittown at a price of $138,000.[1] Shortly thereafter, Michael sent for his parents, who were happy to move to the United States to live with their son and daughter-in-law.

Michael was very driven. He had wanted to evolve into something better than what his parents had achieved in the Ukraine. He was pleased to have his U.S. citizenship and he was clearly bothered when people would dismiss all immigrants as second class and undeserving of the opportunities of living in the United States.

I do not like that the illegal immigrants who have been coming here from Mexico and some other countries are permitted to stay without recourse. While I understand that they satisfy a need for cheap labor in the U.S., there are too many problems with social welfare. These people are living off of other people who pay taxes. We certainly can't deport them. These

367

people are largely good people, but they need to learn English, they need to become legal citizens, and they need to pay their fair of taxes. Otherwise, things are not equal. I too am an immigrant. I too have worked hard. But I am paying taxes that help to send these people's children to school and to provide them with medical care. These other immigrants need to assimilate into American culture, just as I did. The U.S. government is doing a disservice to these people in the long run. The country will suffer from segregation not only based on income differences, but also based on cultural differences. The government needs to formulate a plan to deal with the problems of immigration. And these people need to be motivated, and not to be content with what they have. Look at me...I am an American capitalist!

Michael was reaping the benefits of the American dream. From a personal and a financial perspective, he was living relatively comfortably.

He often remarked to Natasha, "I resent it when people fail to recognize the personal struggles and sacrifices that we've made in our lives. It has not been easy."

They had always envisioned their family business to merely be a secondary source of income, but it was unmistakably a labor of love and it consumed a significant amount of their time.

Clean-Rite Laundromat, Inc.

Michael and Natasha researched different types of service businesses to invest in before deciding that a laundromat would be the safest venture. They reasoned that they would need to minimize their risk since they had never run a business before. They determined that a laundromat would generate a slow but sure return on investment. Michael believed that if they didn't make too many mistakes, their investment would work for them.

They had narrowed the choice down between a laundromat and a restaurant. Michael ultimately concluded that when people are pinched financially they would cut back on eating away from home. Conversely, he believed that people needed to do their laundry regularly. A laundromat, he reasoned, would not be subject to economic fluctuations.

Once they zeroed in on the type of service business, they needed to find a laundromat that was affordable. During the second half of 2000 and the first half of 2001, they took several road trips with David, a professional broker in the sale and resale of laundromats, who had been introduced to Michael by one of his MTA coworkers named Luis. In each of the neighborhoods that they visited, the three areas of focus were (1) the percentage of renters, (2) the level of competition, and (3) the incidence of crime. An unfavorable finding for any of these three factors were deemed to be deal-breakers, but perhaps most important was that the demographics of the neighborhood needed to show a high percentage of renters. They found this to be the case in Glen Cove, a community that with its strong Hispanic population seemed to indicate to Michael that the renters would consist largely of families with a lot of children.

The preexisting laundromat in Glen Cove that Michael purchased and renamed Clean-Rite had 600 square feet of space. It had sixteen washers and fourteen dryers. At the time of purchase, the laundromat had been operational for nine years. (See Figure 2 for a photo of Clean-Rite Laundromat.)

The laundromat, which was on the border with the next town, Locust Valley, had virtually no threat of new competitors. The reason for this was that Locust Valley, a community that was affordable to mostly households on the upper end of the economic scale, prohibited sewer systems. Without

FIGURE 2 Clean-Rite Laundromat, Inc.

access to a sewer, any new laundromat in this area would need to invest $500,000 in a water treatment system.

Given the low level of competition and the location's close proximity to his home, Michael was eager to make use of his equity, and he used his house as collateral so that he could purchase the business for $125,000.[2] He and Natasha both possessed a powerful motivation to learn how to run a business, and this was their opportunity.

After introducing the drop-off service in Glen Cove, the business really took off. Clean-Rite was embraced by the community, as word spread among local residents about this useful service, and sales revenue grew by more than 20 percent in the first year. Michael and Natasha were excited about their business venture, and after a couple of years, they decided to seek out a second location.

New Age Laundromat, Inc.

For the second location, they wanted the opportunity to build the business from scratch. This would involve a different process altogether, where they wouldn't see a return on their investment for a longer period of time. They could take the chance of spending money without getting anything back in the near term, however, because there was now a steady flow of income from the first business. They borrowed $400,000 to start up the second business, once again placing their investments (i.e., the equity in their home and first business) at risk in the event that the new business would fail.

Following a lengthy search of much of the New York metropolitan area,[3] the location that Michael ultimately identified for the new laundromat was on the main commercial thoroughfare in College Point, Queens. Michael selected a middle-class neighborhood, populated mainly by renters who did not have access to washing machines and dryers in their homes. "The location must be in a solid working class community," was his mantra.

The different neighborhoods throughout New York City had varying levels of crime, and although the previous tenant, a furniture store, had at least six different owners and some encounters with the police, Michael concluded that the neighborhood was relatively safe and free of gangs. He would say to Natasha, "I want to help improve the quality of

life for the residents of this community, and I want to provide a clean and safe service that would be a source for jobs in the neighborhood."

To further protect his customers, Michael purchased a video surveillance system for $2,000. With this system, Michael was able to monitor the store not only from a computer in the office that he set up downstairs at the laundromat, but also from his home computer. He reasoned that from a psychological standpoint, his attendant would feel safer knowing that the boss was watching. Michael put up signs in the laundromat that indicated there was a surveillance system in effect. This made the customers feel safer, too, he felt. New York State law prevented him from installing a microphone as part of the surveillance system, for privacy reasons. He justified the investment to Natasha, "Besides location, I want to emphasize safety, and having the camera differentiates my laundromat from others."

Michael established the same hours of operation at New Age as he had at Clean-Rite. The laundromat would be open from 7:00 A.M. until 11 P.M., Monday through Friday, and from 6 A.M. until 11 P.M. on Saturday and Sunday.

New Age had 1,500 square feet of space. The construction of the laundromat, which included all the plumbing and electrical requirements, represented a cost of $150,000. The period of time that elapsed prior to the start of the actual construction seemed rather long to Michael, as he learned that he needed to wait for the necessary permits from the New York City Department of Buildings and from the utility, Consolidated Edison. This waiting period in connection with the construction was six months. The physical construction of the laundromat, on the other hand, took only two months.

"In retrospect," Michael acknowledged, "the construction process might have moved more swiftly had we hired an attorney." However, in the interest of cutting his expenses, he went through this process only with his general contractor. Together, they took advantage of a service that had recently been instituted by Mayor Bloomberg known as 311, whereby individuals dial in and are given access to information and guided through the red tape of dealing with various city agencies. "By dealing with the city without an attorney, I figure that we saved

FIGURE 3 New Age Laundromat, Inc.

approximately $25,000 in legal expenses." (See Figure 3 for a photo of New Age Laundromat.)

Michael decided to have fifty-five machines installed in the new laundromat, twenty-seven washers and twenty-eight dryers. The cost of this equipment, all of which was manufactured by Dexter, was $250,000. Michael financed the construction along with the cost of this equipment with the $500,000 loan from his bank.[4]

Additional equipment other than washers and dryers was installed in the new laundromat as well. These machines, however, were installed primarily as a customer service, and they included a soda machine, gaming machines, an automatic teller machine, two television sets, and two vending machines.

"The soda machine was installed free of charge by PepsiCo," he explained, "on the condition that I stock the machine exclusively with Pepsi products." His only other expense related to the soda machine would be for electricity. Any profits derived from it were his to keep. The cost of the gaming machines that were installed in the back of the laundromat was picked up by the vendor, Sunstar Vending Corporation. Michael was allowed to keep a percentage of the profits. Similarly, the ATM was the property of a third party, but Michael kept a small percentage of the profits.

Michael purchased the two televisions and had them mounted on the walls of the laundromat, again with the intention of differentiating his business from rival laundromats in the neighborhood that did not provide this additional service for their customers.

The vending machines provided a significant source of income for the business. One of these machines contained detergent and laundry products. The other contained snacks. Michael bought the products for these machines at Costco and BJ's, the warehouse stores, and also at Jetro, a vendor of food and cleaning supplies. Michael used three sources for vending sales to take advantage of price differences. Profits from vending were 200 percent over their cost.

Unlike Clean-Rite, which had no real competition, competitors did exist in College Point for New Age. When Michael was considering the location, he walked in to the closest laundromat, which was two blocks away. He could tell from his cursory inspection that the laundromat had not seen capital improvements for several years. The owners were Chinese. To Michael, they came across as unfriendly to their customers because they did not speak English. It was a family business, and they did not hire workers from outside their family. Michael checked their pricing, and when he opened New Age a short while later, he made sure his services were twenty-five cents cheaper across the board.

Six blocks away was another laundromat, also run by a Chinese family. They owned the building, and it had a parking lot. Michael recognized that a parking lot could be a definite asset, but given the cost, it was not realistic. He was confident that most of his customers were within walking distance of their apartments, and he intended to provide customer service in other ways. "I know who my customers are, and I feel that I know what they want," he would proudly say.

In its first week of operation, New Age's sales revenue was $600. For the week of April 8, 2006, exactly one year later, the sales revenue was $6,000. Sales were not consistent, however, as Michael found sales during the winter and at month-end, when families had to pay bills, to drop. Sales were averaging $5,500 per week, and clearly, Michael and Natasha were pleased. Based on location, demography, and potential competition, they projected weekly sales to rise to $7,000 after another year, and

370

EXHIBIT 1 Income Statements

	2005	2004	2003	2002	2001
CLEAN-RITE LAUNDROMAT, INC.					
Sales	220,800	213,600	204,000	185,400	150,000
Operating Expenses	187,680	175,172	157,080	133,488	99,000
Earnings before Interest and Taxes	33,120	39,448	46,920	51,912	51,000
Interest Expenses	0	0	0	0	0
Earnings before Taxes	33,120	39,448	46,920	51,912	51,000
Taxes Paid	6,624	7,690	9,384	10,382	10,200
Net Income	26,496	30,758	37,536	41,530	40,800
NEW AGE LAUNDROMAT, INC.					
Sales	285,960				
Operating Expenses	214,470				
Earnings before Interest and Taxes	71,490				
Interest Expenses	35,714				
Earnings before Taxes	35,776				
Taxes Paid	7,155				
Net Income	28,621				

to $10,000 after five years. (See Exhibit 1 for the income statements on Clean-Rite and New Age.)

Laundry Services

The two types of customers at both laundromats are walk-in customers and drop-off customers. At both locations, walk-in customers represented 60 percent of the business and drop-off customers represented 40 percent.

The four different types of washers, depending on the size of the load, range from $1.50 to $5 per load. From smallest to largest, the washers handled twenty, twenty-five, forty, and fifty-five pound loads.[5] The dryers were all twenty-five cents for every eight minutes.

For the drop-off customers, the charge for folding service was seventy-five cents per pound. One of the differences between the two locations, driven by a difference in demographics between the Glen Cove location and the College Point location, was that Clean-Rite provided free delivery for drop-off customers. Roughly one quarter of the drop-offs at Clean-Rite utilized this, the motivation for

which was again differentiated service and a loyal customer base. Michael's father did the deliveries. The amount of driving required was not excessive, but Michael sometimes felt guilty for obligating his seventy-seven-year-old father, and he wondered perhaps if he'd sell the Glen Cove location, then his father would not have to work so hard.

Staffing

Michael employed three female attendants at each location. All of them were Hispanic, which was critical, in that these employees were from the community that the laundromats served. Moreover, the attendants needed to speak Spanish, because some of the laundromats' customers only spoke Spanish.

The customers at Clean-Rite were 70 percent Hispanic. The customer base was relatively homogenous, given seasonal employment on Long Island that tended to bring in a large supply of workers from Mexico and other Spanish-speaking countries. The neighborhood in College Point was more diverse, and the customers at New Age included immigrants from Europe and Asia, as well as from Hispanic countries.

Unemployment was higher in College Point, so Michael found it easier to find good employees at the new location. The key for him was that his attendants could build a relationship with the customers, regardless of location. They needed to be clean and personable. In addition, Michael liked to employ female attendants who were attractive, as he believed that they would help to draw male customers to the laundromat.

The attendants were started at the minimum wage. They were all full time, so in 2005, Michael paid approximately $38,000 in salary expenses at each location. The attendants were paid by check, with the appropriate deductions taken for social security. Michael also provided disability insurance, which he noted was three times more expensive for women than for men.

Many of Michael's operating costs were fixed (e.g., rent, depreciation). His utility costs were variable, as were his maintenance costs, based on the usage of his laundromats.

Technological Innovation

Michael dreamed about an additional aspect that would further enhance his laundromats' business practices. The washers and dryers in his laundromats only took cash. Some laundromats, though, have machines that work off a smart card system. Michael knew that such a system, where the store would be less cash dependent, could have a competitive advantage, but at 600 and 1,500 square feet, respectively, neither Clean-Rite nor New Age seemed to be ideal candidates for such an investment. He knew that larger laundromats, generally 4,000 to 5,000 square feet, invested in these systems, since otherwise there would be too much cash on the premises at any one time. He was not aware of any laundromats near his locations that utilized smart cards, however. The ones that he was familiar with were in Manhattan, the Bronx, and Brooklyn, and in the towns on Long Island with large Hispanic populations, such as Hempstead and Brentwood. At $20,000 to install the system, and at $300 per machine, Michael saw this now as cost prohibitive. Nonetheless, if he were to add a larger laundromat to his business portfolio, he could envision the many benefits that such a system could deliver for his customers. For the walk-ins, he could utilize variable pricing. For the drop-offs, a smart system could track everything except tips, including customer history and trends. Similar to the point of sale systems at most dry cleaners, such an innovation would certainly look professional to the customer, and given the right situation, Michael would make the necessary investment for this.

Far Rockaway

By early 2006, Michael and Natasha were back on the road, seeking out another laundromat. Through their contact, David, they discovered that a 4,000-square-foot laundromat was up for sale in Far Rockaway, in Queens, sixteen miles from College Point. Once known as "The Playground of New York," the popularity of this area as a resort declined in the second half of the twentieth century, the result of the accessibility of newer vacation spots as well as increased urbanization. Several public housing projects were built in the area through the years, the make-up of the community had changed, and consequently, the incidence of crime had increased. In 2006, Far Rockaway was struggling as a community economically, something that was quite apparent to Michael and Natasha as they surveyed the area.[6]

Yet the idea of branching out challenged their earlier criteria in seeking out potential facilities.

The asking price for the laundromat was $500,000, the same price that Michael paid to build New Age. The attraction clearly was that with the size of this facility, Michael could justify the installation of a smart card system. He figured that an investment in such a system could knock out any competition within a one-mile radius, as he firmly believed that technology would make a difference in this business.

Having a third business appealed greatly to Michael and Natasha. To make it happen, however, certain questions would have to be resolved: Would Michael be able to obtain the necessary financing to purchase a third business? Alternatively, should he sell Clean-Rite, where growth has plateaued, in order to be able to buy the new location? More fundamentally, though, were Michael and Natasha capable, both physically and emotionally, of further expansion of their family business?

The Decision

Michael was greeted fondly by his patrons as he entered New Age Laundromat and Natasha ushered him behind the front counter. "You see," she said softly, "We are successful."

Michael nodded, opening the cash register. "Do you think we can take on more?"

"Yes, I do. This is our life, Misha." She paused briefly, then continued, "It is good to expand. We can create a third corporation, to provide a shelter if the situation doesn't pick up at Clean-Rite. And you have always said that we can continue to take on long-term debt. The secret is to avoid short-term debts, right?"

"Natasha," he explained, "Our rent and utility bills are choking off our profits. Our rent is $3,100 a month for New Age and utilities here are $6,000 a month. In addition, we are paying $600 a month in property taxes, which is ridiculous, since the building that we are in was built in 1924. These costs are out of line at Clean-Rite, too, and because our growth there has slowed down, our operating costs are eating into our margins. And we can't increase prices to deal with our higher costs, since our customers have low incomes. We simply can't use New Age to hold up Clean-Rite."

"Well, maybe we can increase our volume of sales with the new location…"

Michael snapped. "Did you see the neighborhood? Do you think our little laundromat can turn it around?" He noticed one of the customers at a dryer looking toward him, and he lowered his voice. "Clean-Rite is a small store. The equipment is still good, but because of its physical limitations, I don't think it pays to replace the equipment when it begins to break down."

"I'm not sure," Natasha replied. "Whatever we get out of Clean-Rite is gravy, as far as I'm concerned. After all, we have no debt at all there."

Michael shrugged. "All right, give me a little more time to think about it. These are important questions. Our little business venture has certainly taken on a life of its own. And like you, I am passionate about it. I want to keep making improvements. Let's take another ride out to Far Rockaway. Let's see if we should move forward there. And let's look at our numbers. I want to do what's best."

Michael stepped in front of the counter. A little girl was crying and he lifted her out of her stroller to kiss her gently on her cheek.

Notes

1. It was perhaps fitting that Michael and Natasha find their home in Levittown, the brainchild of William Levitt, who capitalized on the housing crunch in the years following World War II, offering affordable housing to returning GIs and their families, in the form of small, detached, single-family houses that became the archetype community for the New York City suburbs and the American dream. Note that after ten years, their home had more than tripled in value, to $450,000.
2. The purchase price included the cost of all the existing equipment in the laundromat.
3. Perhaps the primary constraint in this search involved how reasonable the distance would be for Michael or Natasha to routinely drive to the new location from their Levittown home.
4. The property for New Age Laundromat was leased.
5. The cost of these machines ranged from $1,500 to $6,000. Clearly, when New Age Laundromat was being constructed, Michael needed to consider this, coupled with the need to optimize his space with the right mix of machines.
6. Reported crimes as a percentage of the population in the 101st precinct, which included Far Rockaway, was 1 percent according to the NYPD (for the calendar year 2003). Michael did not realize, however, that this was the identical rate for the 109th precinct, which covered College Point. His perception was that crime was worse in Far Rockaway.

Traditional Case 4: Shipyard Brewing Company: Offloaded in a Zero Growth Industry

In April, 1999 Fred Forsley and Alan Pugsley, the founders of the Shipyard Brewing Company (SBC), received an email from a senior executive of Phillip Morris Inc. Phillip Morris was the owner of the Miller Brewing Company that was SBC's co-owner. The message announced that executives from another Phillip Morris business unit, Kraft, had replaced Miller's CEO, VP of Marketing and the Director of Sales. Fred and Alan were immediately concerned because the three former Miller executives were the people that they had negotiated their partnership with in November 1995. The partnership resulted in Miller performing the marketing function of SBC with Fred and Alan operating all of the brewing activities. They were fearful that the change in senior management at Miller might result in other changes that could adversely affect SBC's relationship with Miller.

In June 1999 Fred and Alan received a visit from Miller's general manager for SBC, its financial manager and a lawyer. The Miller executives were cordial but very businesslike as they explained that due to strategic changes at Miller and Phillip Morris, the joint ventures and/or acquisitions within the craft brewing industry into which Miller had entered in 1995 were all to be terminated. This meant that SBC and Celis of Miller's former American Craft Specialty Brewing Company (ACSBC) were to be sold or liquidated. ACSBC was the Miller organizational unit where SBC was located. Fred and Alan were reminded that the original ACSBC had been rolled into Miller corporate in 1996 at the time of Miller's shift from "portfolio" to "priority" sales strategy. The Miller executives further reminded Fred and Alan of the declining sales growth of the craft brewing industry that had fallen to 0 percent in 1998. The trend was inconsistent with Miller's goals of concentrating marketing resources on its priority brands, Miller High Life, Miller Lite, and the other Miller brands.

Fred and Alan were told that they would be able to bid competitively for Miller's 50 percent share of SBC. They were also told that the price range would be typical of a 40,000-barrel annual capacity brewery, rather than the actual 96,000-barrel capacity that SBC had grown to become. The Miller executives realized that it would take time for SBC to arrange the necessary details for a buy-back

After the Miller people had left, Fred and Alan returned to the conference room. They talked about the meeting that had just concluded. They also reminisced about the origins of their company, its rapid growth and their excitement when they teamed up with Miller for what they believed would be significant marketing support for SBC. They were grateful for the very fair price range that Miller would accept. Fred and Alan had a good relationship their bank, Peoples Heritage Bank of Portland, Maine. They felt confident that they would be able to raise the necessary funds. Where they were worried was that they knew that SBC had lost sales momentum in the past couple of years. The fact that Miller wanted out of the craft-brewing segment of the beer industry was a clear signal that Miller didn't expect the craft beer industry to be profitable for them in the future. Fred and Alan knew that they had to increase sales volume immediately and continuously over the next several years to achieve efficient brewing at SBC in an industry that was not growing and might have become over-crowded.

Craft Brewing Industry

The craft brewing industry[1] had experienced spectacular growth in sales and in the number of brewers from 1985 to 1995. The craft brewers produced primarily ales which were distinctive alternatives to the lighter brews distributed by the large national companies. From 1996 the growth slowed and ultimately diminished to 0 percent by 1998 (see Exhibit 1).

During the previous six years, 1992–1998, the number of new microbreweries and brewpubs that opened was dramatic. During the industry's growth there were large numbers of brand names. Most brewers distributed only in their local areas, but the number of regional specialty brewers had increased steadily. By 1996 many microbreweries and brewpubs began closing as the industry retrenched (see Exhibit 2).

EXHIBIT 1 Craft Beer Industry Annual Production (000) Barrels 1985 - 1991

Year	Barrels	% Growth
1985	75	
1986	127	69 %
1987	220	73 %
1988	316	43 %
1989	491	55 %
1990	635	29 %
1991	854	34 %

Source: Brewers Association, 736 Pearl St., Boulder, CO. 80306
Info@brewersassociation.org; www.beertown.org

Craft Beer Industry: U.S. Regional Specialty Breweries, Microbreweries & Brewpubs Operating

Year	Sales Growth	Brewpubs	Microbreweries	Regional Specialty	Total
1992	39%	183	106	6	295
1993	40%	237	136	9	382
1994	50%	329	196	16	541
1995	47%	497	281	27	805
1996	26%	694	375	33	1,102
1997	4%	857	428	35	1,320
1998	0%	921	438	38	1,397

Source: Vol. 40. May/June, 2003. The New Brewer, The Journal of the Brewers Association. Info@brewersassociation.org; www.beertown.org

EXHIBIT 2 Craft Beer Industry Brewpubs and Microbrewery Openings and Closing

Year	Micros		Brewpubs	
	Openings	Closings	Openings	Closings
1992	20	7	39	7
1993	32	3	69	14
1994	65	2	102	6
1995	92	3	195	24
1996	116	16	217	20
1997	92	39	215	53
1998	55	45	150	79

Source: Vol. 40. May/June, 2003. The New Brewer, The Journal of the Brewers Association. Info@brewersassociation.org; www.beertown.org

The sales volume at SBC declined during this period, as well (see Exhibit 3).

Shipyard Background

SBC began as extension of Federal Jack's brewpub in Kennebunkport, Maine. In 1992 Federal Jack's was founded as a result of Fred's recommendation to open a brewpub in order to revive an under performing retail complex in town. In the early spring of that year Fred had been hired as a real estate consultant for the complex. He researched the idea of setting up a brewpub in the retail complex using the same brewing recipe and beer brands as a successful Portland brewpub, Gritty McDuff's. Using the Gritty brands failed to materialize, but during the negotiations Fred met Alan Pugsley, a brew-master trained at

EXHIBIT 3 Shipyard Brewing Company Annual Sales (barrels)

Month	1994	1995	1996	1997	1998
January	0	1300	3211	1827	1310
February	0	1356	2779	2005	1552
March	0	2728	3339	2182	1784
April	0	2328	3560	2802	2126
May	624	2985	3173	3333	2337
June	1316	2869	4374	3595	2633
July	1258	2887	4001	4448	2533
August	1466	3181	3798	3703	2862
September	1071	2299	2997	2534	1930
October	1201	3253	2761	2470	1857
November	1404	2795	2515	1869	1780
December	1490	2474	2562	1869	1780
Year Total	9,829	30,456	39,070	32,895	25,297

the Ringwood Brewery in Hampshire, England under the tutelage of Peter Austin. Austin was already considered the father of the craft brewing industry when he founded Ringwood in the 1970s. Separately, Peter Austin and Alan Pugsley had set up numerous breweries in many countries and both had notable reputations.

Fred and Alan both liked the idea of a brewpub and partnered, establishing Federal Jack's brewpub in June 1992. Fred saw the brewpub initially as a way to bolster traffic at the retail complex and as an entrepreneurial venture. Alan viewed the partnership as an opportunity to brew authentic English style ales and have the satisfaction of owning part of the pub. The brewpub was located on a site with historic significance, "The Shipyard," where in the 19th century three shipbuilding companies built schooners. Federal Jack was the name of one of the schooners chosen to be depicted on the label of SBC's first brew, Shipyard Export Ale. The brewpub had a seven-barrel batch system with an annual capacity of 1,800-barrel annual capacity and brewed two ales initially, Shipyard Export and Goat Island Light (named for an island off the southern Maine coast). Alan described Shipyard Export as blond or golden ale with a light coppery hue, full bodied yet lighter in flavor. Goat Island Light was a very light, low calorie brew with its own very distinctive flavor with notable body and the character missing in many light ales.

Ale sales at Federal Jack's were good from the pub's opening and continued throughout the summer season, but declined as the tourist trade diminished. In order to brew efficiently, sales had to be increased. As a result, Fred and Alan created the Kennebunkport Brewing Company (KBC) for selling the brews off the premises. In the fall 1992 Fred had gained 20 pub and restaurant accounts and received good feedback and solid sales growth allowing KBC to operate its 1,800-barrel annual capacity efficiently. The pub and restaurant channel of distribution effectively reached the target market of 21 to 50 year olds, which were the greatest consumers of beer. They realized from their experience at Federal Jack's that pubs and restaurants were effective channels for new ale trials and awareness building of the KBC brews.

Sales continued to grow steadily from the fall of 1992 through the summer of 1993. In September of 1993, Fred commenced the City of Portland's approval process for acquiring a vacant foundry for the purpose of renovating the building for a new brewery. The foundry's property happened to be the site of Henry Wadsworth Longfellow's birthplace and was located just off the waterfront, adjacent to Portland's Old Port. This part of Portland had many pubs and restaurants and drew Maine people from out of town and tourists. In November Fred and Alan closed on the property. In April 1994, the Portland brewery opened and with it the company named was changed to the Shipyard Brewing Company (SBC). Through the spring of 1995, SBC continued to open additional accounts at restaurants, pubs and

FIGURE 1

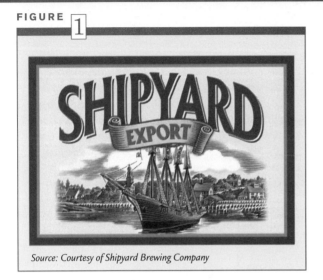

Source: Courtesy of Shipyard Brewing Company

in retail stores and further penetrated Maine. It had also begun expansion into the southern New Hampshire, sections of Massachusetts and selected areas within Vermont and Connecticut. Throughout SBC's relatively short existence, it had introduced additional brews that contributed to the growth in sales volume. Along with new brew introductions and sales volume increases were brewing capacity investments that enabled SBC to meet the demand. All of these brews had labels that were similar to the original label designs of Shipyard Export Ale and Goat Island Light (see Figure 1). Product sheets were given to all of the Shipyard dealers and distributors to remind them of SBC's full line of ales (see Figure 2a and 2b).

FIGURE 2a

The Shipyard Brewing Company

86 Newbury Street
Portland, ME 04101
(207) 761-0807
1-800-BREW-ALE
www.shipyard.com

	SHIPYARD EXPORT	IPA	Light	SHIPYARD STOUT	SHIPYARD BROWN ALE	PALE ALE CHAMBERLAIN	OLD THUMPER
MALT	2-Row British Pale Ale, Crystal	2-Row British Pale Ale, Crystal & Malted Wheat	2-Row British Pale Ale, Malted Wheat	2-Row British Pale Ale, Crystal, Chocolate, Black & Roasted Barley	2-Row British Pale Ale, Crystal, Chocolate & Roasted Barley	2-Row British Pale Ale, Crystal & Chocolate	2-Row British Pale Ale, Crystal & Chocolate
HOPS	Cascade, Willamette & Tettnang	Fuggles	Hallertau & Mount Hood	Warrior, Cascade, Tettnang & Goldings	Willamette, Cascade, & Tettnang	Cascade, Tettnang & Fuggles	Challenger, Progress & Goldings
YEAST STRAIN	Top-Fermenting English	Top-Fermenting English	Top-Fermenting English	Top-Fermenting English	Top-Fermenting English	Top-Fermenting English	Top-Fermenting English
AVAILABILITY	Year Round	Year Round	Year Round	Year Round	Year Round	Year Round	Year Round
FLAVOR CHARACTERISTICS	Malty with a hint of sweetness up front & a dry hoppy finish	Smooth, dry & crisp flavor with floral aromas & apple plum palate	An easy drinking, crisp & dry beer with only 97 calories and 7.4 carbohydrates per 12 oz serving	Initial malt & caramel flavor with a dry roasted finish	Smooth texture and mellowness, sweet finish, hint of chocolate & maple	Dry & crisp up front with an aromatic hoppy finish	Hint of sweetness with fruit aromas, smooth texture, dry hoppy finish
FOOD PAIRINGS	Pork & chicken	Roasted chicken & grilled seafood	Shellfish, salads, & other light fare	Wonderful with desserts, especially anything chocolate	Pairs well with hamburgers and other traditional pub fare	Great with pork or pizza	Hearty casseroles and stews
COLOR	Golden Copper	Light Copper	Light Golden	Jet Black	Brown	Copper	Light Copper
AVAILABLE FORMATS	12 oz Bottle, 22 oz Bottle, Keg	12 oz Bottle, Keg, Cask Conditioned	12 oz Bottle, Keg	12 oz Bottle, 22 oz Bottle, Keg	Captain's Collection, Keg	Captain's Collection, 22 oz Bottle, Keg	12 oz Bottle, 22 oz Bottle, Keg, Cask Conditioned
FIRST BREWED	June 1992	April 1997	April 2004	August 1993	April 1993	April 1995	October 1994
OG	1052	1055	1032	1052	1045	1055	1060
ALC.%VOL./VOL.	5.1%	5.8%	3.2%	4.7%	4.0%	4.9%	5.8%

Source: Courtesy of Shipyard Brewing Company

Shipyard Seasonals

86 Newbury Street Portland, ME 04101 (207) 761-0807 1-800-BREW-ALE www.shipyard.com	Summer Ale		Winter Ale	Longfellow		Brewer's Choice	THE SHIPYARD It's The Taste!
	Seasonal	Seasonal	Seasonal	Seasonal	Seasonal	Seasonal	Notes:
MALT	2-Row British Pale Ale, Munich & Malted Wheat	2-Row British Pale Ale, Malted Wheat & Light Munich	2-Row British Pale Ale, Munich, Malted Wheat, Caramalt & Crystal	2-Row British Pale Ale, Crystal, Chocolate & Roasted Barley	2-Row British Pale Ale, Crystal, Chocolate & Torrified Wheat	2-Row British Pale Ale, Crystal, Roasted Barley, Chocolate, & Torrified Wheat	
HOPS	Hallertau	Hallertau & Willamette	Fuggles, Goldings, Tettnang, Mt. Hood, & Progress	Northern Brewer, Cascade, Tettnang, Goldings	Cascade, Tettnang, Fuggles & Goldings	English Challenger, Styrian Goldings & East Kent Goldings	
YEAST STRAIN	Top-Fermenting English	Top-Fermenting English	Top-Fermenting English	Top-Fermenting English	Top-Fermenting English	Top-Fermenting English	
AVAILABILITY	April - August	September - October	November - February	November - December	November - January	February - March	
FLAVOR CHARACTERISTICS	Mellow malted wheat flavor with less hoppy characteristics	Hints of pumpkin, cinnamon & nutmeg aromas and flavors; a crisp refreshing beer	Complex malt/hop character, malty sweet up front with a dry hop bite at the finish	Full-bodied, strong ale with a distinct roasted barley character	Rich nutty ale with a hoppy finish	Smooth, full-bodied ale with a nice smoky taste up front and a crisp hop bite at the back	
FOOD PAIRINGS	Great with seafood	Lamb, turkey, BLTs & pumpkin pie	Beef, pork & hearty dishes like stew	Hearty casseroles, stews & steak	Perfect with desserts or as a dessert itself	Great with hamburgers and other traditional pub fare	
COLOR	Golden	Golden	Coppery-Orange	Dark Brown	Deep Amber	Dark Brown	
AVAILABLE FORMATS	12 oz Bottle, Keg	12 oz Bottle, Keg	12 oz Bottle, Keg	Captain's Collection, 22 oz Bottle, Keg	12 oz Bottle, 22 oz Bottle, Keg	12 oz Bottle, Keg	
FIRST BREWED	June 1995	August 2002	September 2000	October 1995	December 1993	February 2005	
OG	1050	1048	1058	1062	1070	1059	
ALC.%VOL./VOL.	4.8%	4.8%	5.2%	5.8%	6.7%	5.4%	

Source: Courtesy of Shipyard Brewing Company

Positioning

The SBC ales were authentic English style ales with flavors varying from full bodied to lighter ales. Alan believed that their ales were distinctive from the lighter beers distributed by the national American companies, because of their flavors, body and colors. The different flavors made SBC ales good choices with a variety of foods. They chose the names Shipyard Export Ale and Goat Island Light because they related to SBC's Maine Coast location. Further, they believed the names would convey a traditional image for their brews, since the schooner-shipbuilding era was long since past. Oil paintings by Maine artists of 19th century schooners were used for SBC's logo and labels, when it eventually bottled the brews. As SBC's product line expanded, the same theme and label style were used.

The Management Team

Fred, SBC and KBC's president, was previously a real estate consultant in Portland. He was a charismatic person and tried to maintain a friendly and open culture around the brewery. Both Fred and Alan believed that if they exhibited a carrying attitude toward their employees, the employees would respond positively in terms of their contributions to the company and take pride in the SBC product line. He held open forum meetings on an ad hoc basis for all employees. Fred and Alan both believed that that type of business culture was most productive for a small and growing company. This same attitude was carried toward their suppliers and members of the channel of distribution. Fred viewed them as "partners" and believed that good relationships with them were critical in producing and selling quality brews. Fred liked to say that he wanted to "kill'em with kindness" and that it would be an approach they strove to take. This meant that Fred always tried to build mutually beneficial relations and to be as supportive of SBC's business constituents as possible.

Alan was the brew-master. He carefully selected which suppliers to use for hops, malts, yeast and other supplies and equipment. Alan knew exactly the types of ingredients that would yield the desired flavor and body of the brews he crafted. Once suppliers were in place, Alan tried to maintain long term relationships with them and viewed them as partners in SBC's brewing processes. Alan also did the brewery's hiring. He selected people based on their genuine desire to become a brewer and make quality ales that they would be proud of, as well as their ability to be a loyal team player. He also felt that employees that believed in crafting superior brews would give informal testimony about the quality of the brews to their friends.

In the spring 1993, Bruce Forsley, Fred's cousin, joined KBC to assist in building the sales distribution network. Bruce was experienced in the restaurant and tavern industry and was the co-owner of two restaurant-taverns, the Silver Street Tavern in Waterville, Maine and the Silver Street Grille in Portland.

Promotion

By issuing press releases and networking with the media, SBC received publicity from numerous newspapers stories that cited its awards, new brew introductions and plant expansions. SBC was selected Portland's best micro brew in 1994 and was awarded the World Beer Tasting Gold medal for its Blue Fin Stout. In the summer of 1994 a huge mural of the Federal Jack schooner, much like the label of Shipyard Export Ale, was painted on the most prominent wall of the brewery.

Fred believed that in order to expand sales he must communicate SBC's core values to all constituents and at all opportunities. He did this through conducting numerous tours of the brewery, issuing press releases and making personal contacts to key people in Portland and SBC's channel members. Fred believed that SBC values were: quality authentic English style ale, locally brewed, viewing all channel of distribution members as "partners" and a genuine commitment to the community in general. Tours were also given for the general public and tourists. In the summer months, a van was used to pick up tourists from the Old Port and shuttle them to the brewery. Also, SBC opened a store at the brewery and sold a variety of quality products bearing the SBC logo, including: tee shirts, baseball hats, sweatshirts, mugs, book on brewing and jackets.

Fred and Alan believed it was important for SBC to be active in the community. The company sponsored numerous non-profit organization events, for example: outdoor events like "Let's Go Boating", an area boat show; "Beach to Beacon" the internationally known, 10k road race from Cape Elizabeth to Portland Head Light; the M.S. Regatta, a yacht race off Portland's Eastern Promenade; skiing and tennis events. At these events Shipyard banners were displayed at appropriate locations. Also, for community events where volunteer appreciation parties were held, SBC often donated Shipyard Export Ale. Other community events sometimes received a direct contribution of funds. SBC had also contributed funds to the York County Education Fund that benefited York County high school seniors. It also contributed funds to York County Technical College's culinary arts program.

In addition, SBC was a regular exhibitor at regional and national tradeshows and brew exhibitions. These events were important for meeting key people and contributed to word of mouth advertising.

Distribution and Packaging

Fred and Bruce continued to expand sales by securing additional pubs and restaurants. The company displayed and sold its brews at the Portland International Jetport. When making sales calls, Fred and Bruce, as well as the two reps that were hired, emphasized that SBC brewed authentic

English style ales and noted Alan's reputation as a brew-master. Fred believed that taking a personal approach to the sales calls was important for establishing a relationship with these accounts. The reps made servicing and new account calls on all of the outlets: pub, restaurant, convenience, liquor and grocery chain stores. All deliveries were handled by independent distributors, as was required by law. In all cases, the SBC reps made special effort to maintain the "kill'em with kindness" approach that Fred and Bruce successfully used. For restaurant and pub accounts they offered educational support for the wait-staff that included product sampling, food pairings and insights into the brewing process. They explained how to have beer dinners, serving the appropriate brew with each course. Shipyard pint glasses, napkins, and table tents were offered as promotional support, along with tee shirts for interested wait-staff. Sales incentives such as gift certificates were also used to build follow through with the wait-staff personnel. In addition, the pubs and restaurants in Maine received cooperative radio advertising support. SBC offered to have its Shipyard jingle, "your ship has come in . . . Shipyard Ale" used at the end of radio ads for happy hour events when SBC brews were featured. He viewed this kind of promotion as synergetic with the other promotional efforts and valuable support for the pub owner. They always gave SBC Product Sheets that showed all of the brands with their brewing details and food pairings (see Figure 2a and 2b).

Grocery, convenience and liquor stores were targeted as well. The bottled brews that were sold to these stores were packaged in 12 ounce, six and twelve packs and limited offerings of 22 ounce bottles. Later, when more brews had been added, SBC offered the Captains Collection, which was a twelve pack that contained a variety of the SBC brews. The retail prices were between $6.49 and $7.99 for six packs and between $9.99 and $12.99 for the twelve packs. These prices were very competitive with other craft brewers and super-premium beers. Shipyard Export Ale six packs retailed at $5.99. It was priced lower than the others because it was SBC's core brand and had higher production volume. SBC offered its distributors' sales reps incentives for opening a certain number of new retail accounts, such as: LL Bean's gift certificates, weekend travel

opportunities to Florida and sometimes cash. These outlets valued the addition of SBC brands to their offerings as another way of giving distinctive product choices to their customers. Fred and Bruce supported these accounts with merchandising aids that included banners, static pictures for coolers, shelf cards and border display wrap for around the bottom of cases that were displayed. For more important accounts neon signs, mirrors with the Shipyard logo and framed acrylic prints of the Shipyard label were offered. The SBC Product Sheet was always given as a summary of all of the brews and their varying characteristics. The amount of point of sales support was regulated by state statutes and limited to $300 per year and a maximum of $1,000.

Miller Time

In early 1995, the Miller Brewing Company was looking for fast growing craft breweries to add to its American Specialty Craft Beer Company (ASCBC). ASCBC was already marketing brews of the Celis Brewing Company from Austin, Texas and Jacob Leinenkugel Brewing Company of Wisconsin. One of Miller's key distributors had talked to a SBC distributor, which lead to a Miller meeting with SBC. At this time Fred and Alan were searching for an additional partner or other sources of capital to enable the company to grow faster. Fred and Alan ultimately negotiated a deal with Miller executives in November 1995. The partnership resulted in Miller conducting the marketing side of the business with Fred and Alan retaining the brewing operations.

In 1995 Miller had implemented its "portfolio" selling strategy. This meant that all of Miller brands were grouped together so that its sales force could sell their whole portfolio of beer. This included the ACSBC brands and Miller's national brands that included Miller High Life, Miller Lite, Miller Beer and Miller Draft. About the same time that SBC partnered with Miller, Molson of Canada, Fosters of Australia and Presidente from the Dominican Republic had been acquired. The portfolio strategy allowed the Miller's sales force to draw upon a variety of resources to sell their entire portfolio of beers. Miller used exclusively large distributors, rather than specialty distributors, since that was needed to accommodate the volume that Miller generated with all of its brands. According to Bruce, Miller also tended to "pay up front" for its market share. What this meant was that Miller would spend for media advertising for its brands and then attempted to influence its distributors to follow its lead and expend effort on Miller brands. It was a forceful approach, according to Bruce.

In early 1996, Miller installed a Krones bottling line at the SBC valued at approximately $5.5 million. That capital investment and other equipment increased its capacity to 96,000 barrels annually. The Krones bottling process enabled SBC to increase its products' quality because less air got into the bottles during bottling and improved seals for its caps. Higher quality glass bottles were also used. As a result, shelf life was extended from 3 to 12 months. The labor needed for bottling was cut in half and improved the brewing safety systems. Further, Alan had access to Miller's labs and expanded his brewing knowledge.

In July 1996 Miller decided to shift its sales approach because its major brands were facing keen competition from other national brewers. Miller changed its strategy from "portfolio" to "priority" selling. This meant that instead of Miller providing marketing resources to all of its brands, including the ASCBC, it concentrated the resources on its priority brands, Miller High Life, Miller Beer, Miller Draft and Miller Lite. Each brand now reported directly to the Miller marketing management. The change was a major shift in Miller's marketing strategy and hurt the specialty brews and lower market share brands, as they did not receive the marketing support they had enjoyed under the "portfolio" strategy.

Miller's management approach with the SBC was one of careful annual marketing planning and budgeting. This manner of marketing management was more bureaucratic than the more free-wheeling, entrepreneurial approach that Fred used before partnering with Miller. During 1996-97 Miller's marketing management directed Fred to focus upon out of state sales expansion. Maine and Hew Hampshire markets were doing okay and Miller management believed that those markets were about saturated. Fred followed Miller's direction and worked on gaining distributors in outlying areas where Miller was strong and the SBC brand had relevance. Miller believed that other coastal communities would relate to the SBC brand. These markets included: Long Island and Buffalo, New York, the New Jersey shore, Annapolis, Atlanta and Chicago. Fred worked hard in attempting to establish personal relationships with new distributors, but his travel and entertainment expenses were high. When a new distributor had agreed to handle the SBC brands, the regular Miller sales force took over from Fred. The shift to Miller's the sales force brought the culture of a big corporation to the channel member relationships, which was different from the more personal approach used by Fred. As a large corporation, Miller had a lot of sway with the distributors who sometimes resisted since many distributors were independent businesses and were primarily concerned with the products that made the best profit for them.

Other difficulties with the distributors surfaced. For example, in July 1996 MDI, an independent distributor in Illinois, joined the Miller distribution network. Eight months later, MDI bought the rights to market Sam Adams, which enjoyed higher margins and greater sales volume. It lost interest in supporting Miller brands, including SBC's. In New Jersey a change from a successful independent distributor previously used by SBC to six Miller distributors resulted in serious loss of sales. Since 1996, when Miller shifted to "priority" sales strategy, SBC received less and less marketing support.

In 1996 SBC received a contract from Magic Hat Brewery to brew 8,000 barrels, which turned out to be 20% of that year's production. Wharf Rat, a Baltimore microbrewer contracted brewing with SBC for a lesser quantity. In 1997 the Miller management required SBC to end the contract brewing stating that it was a distraction.

In April 1997, SBC successfully opened a brewpub at the Orlando International Airport. This was the first ever brewpub in an airport in the U.S. The high traffic of the airport and the southern location were viewed with excitement by Fred because he felt that it would gain solid awareness for the SBC brands in the South. Also in 1997, SBC won two awards for its Old Thumper. It received a silver medal in the Real Ale Festival and was voted "one of the best beers in America" by *Men's Health Magazine*.

In 1997–98 the craft beer industry suffered what Alan referred to as a "wobble." The craft beer industry that had enjoyed expansive growth but now it had slowed to zero. According to Fred, retailers were confused with the numerous craft brands that had been introduced during the craft beer industry growth years. SBC sales declined. Fred and Alan were concerned and knew that they needed to receive reasonable sales per brand to justify keeping them on the shelf. Miller management noting the trend in the craft beer industry and the difficulties SBC was having with its distributors in its more distant markets, directed Fred to drop out of New York, Illinois, New Jersey, Maryland and Georgia. In the fall of 1998 in an effort to boost volume, Fred convinced Miller to allow SBC to contract brew 3,500 barrels for a small Maine brewery, Sea Dog.

The Future

As Fred and Alan mulled over the meeting that they had just concluded with the Miller managers, the idea of being "offloaded" had given them mixed feelings. All in all, the relationship with Miller was a positive joint venture. They were excited about the chance to buy-back their company. They felt confident that the bank would support them, since SBC had grown steadily and made their loan payments on time. In addition, Miller had been very fair in setting a price in the range of a 40,000-barrel brewery and not the 96,000-barrel facility that SBC

had become. Cooling their enthusiasm was their belief that the craft brewing industry might be overcrowded. Further, SBC had lost its sales momentum in the past two years, since Miller had directed SBC to pull out of numerous markets.

Fred and Alan estimated that they needed to boost sales 5 percent per year for the next several years to achieve brewing efficiency. They wonder about what marketing strategy they should follow. Were there product, packaging or brand changes that should be made? What geographic markets should they concentrate upon? How should they promote the SBC brews now that Miller was not involved?

Note

1. As of October 27, 2003 and posted on the Association of Brewers, Boulder, CO website, www.beertown.org, defined several categories of brewers: microbreweries produce less than 15,000 barrels per year; brewpubs are restaurant-breweries that sells the majority of their beer on site and less than 15,000 barrels per year; contract breweries hire another company to produce their beer; regional brewery has a capacity of between 15,000 and 2,000,000 barrels annually; regional specialty brewery is a regional brewery whose flagship brew is an all malt or specialty beer; craft brewer is any of the above whose majority of sales are considered craft beers.

Traditional Case 5: easyCar.com

This case was prepared by Thomas C. Leach, University of New England, and is intended to be used as a basis for class discussion.

> At easyCar we aim to offer you outstanding value for money. To us value for money means a reliable service at a low price. We achieve this by simplifying the product we offer, and passing on the benefits to you in the form of lower prices.[1]

This was the stated mission of car rental company easy-Car.com. EasyCar was a member of the EasyGroup family of companies, founded by the flamboyant Greek entrepreneur Stelios Haji-Ioannou, who was known simply as Stelios to most. Stelios founded low-cost air carrier easyJet.com in 1995 after convincing his father, a Greek shipping billionaire, to loan him the $5 million (Note: In January 2003, $1 = ε1.52 = U.S. $1.61) needed to start the business.[2] EasyJet was one of the early low-cost, no frills air carriers in the European market. It was built upon a foundation of simple point to point flights, booked over the Internet, and the aggressive use of yield management policies to maximize the revenues it derived from its assets. The company proved highly successful, and as a result Stelios had expanded this business model to industries with similar characteristics as the airline industry. EasyCar, founded in 2000 on a $10 million investment on the part of Stelios, was one of these efforts.

EasyCar's approach, built on the easyJet model, was quite different than the approaches used by the traditional rental car companies. EasyCar rented only a single vehicle type at each location it operated, while most of its competitors rented a wide variety of vehicle types. EasyCar did not work with agents—over 95 percent of its bookings were made through the company's website, with the remainder of bookings being made directly through the company's phone reservation system (at a cost to the customer of ε0.95/minute for the call). Most rental car companies worked with a variety of intermediaries, with their own websites accounting for less than 10 percent of their total booking.[3] And like easyJet, easyCar managed prices in an attempt to have its fleet rented out 100 percent of the time and to generate the maximum revenue from its rentals. EasyCar's information system constantly evaluated projected demand and expected utilization at each site and adjusted price accordingly. Because of its aggressive pricing, easyCar was able to achieve a fleet utilization rate in excess of 90 percent[4]—much higher than other major rental car companies. Industry leader Avis Europe, for example, had a fleet utilization rate of 68 percent.[5]

It was January 2003. EasyCar had broken even in the fiscal year ending September 2002[6] on revenues of 27 million.[7] This represented a significant improvement over 2001, when easyCar had lost 7.5 million on revenues of 18.5 million.[8] While pleased that the company had broken even in only its 3rd year in operation, Stelios had set aggressive financial goals for easyCar for the next two years. Plans called for a quadrupling of revenues in the next two years in preparation for a planned initial public offering in the second half of 2004. EasyCar's goal was to reach $100 million in revenue and 10 million in profit for the year 2004. The 100 million revenue goal and $10 million profit goal were felt necessary to obtain the desired return from an IPO. It was thought that, with this level of performance, the company might be worth about $250 million.[9] In order to achieve these financial goals, the company was pushing to open an average of 2 new sites a week through 2003 and 2004 to reach a total of 180 sites by the end of 2004.[10]

The Rental Car Industry in Western Europe

The Western European rental car industry consisted of many different national markets that were only semi-integrated. While there were many companies that competed within this European rental car industry, a handful of companies held dominant positions, either across a number of national markets or within one or a few national markets. Industry experts saw the sector as ripe for consolidation.[11] Several international companies—notably Avis, Europcar, and Hertz—had strong positions across most major European markets. Within most countries, there was also a primarily national or regional company that had a strong position in its home market and perhaps moderate market share in neighboring markets. Sixt was the market leader in Germany, for example, while Atesa (in partnership with National) was the market leader in Spain. Generally these major players accounted for more than half of the market. In Germany, for example, Sixt, Europcar, Avis, and Hertz had a combined 60 percent of the ε2.5 billion German rental car market.[12] In Spain, the top five firms accounted for 60 percent of the ε920 million Spanish rental car market. Generally, these top firms targeted both business and vacation travelers and offered a wide range of vehicles for rent. Exhibit 1 provides basic information on these market-leading companies.

In addition to these major companies in each market, there were many smaller rental companies operating in each market. In Germany, for example, there were over 700 smaller companies,[13] while in Spain there were more than 1600 smaller companies. Many of these smaller companies operated at only one or a few locations and were particularly prevalent in tourist locations. There were also a number of brokers operating in the sector, such as Holiday Autos. Brokerage companies did not own their own fleet of cars but basically managed the excess inventory of other companies and matching customers with rental companies with excess fleet capacity.

Overall, the rental car market could be thought of as composed of two broad segments, a business segment and a tourist/leisure segment. Depending on the market, the leisure segment represented somewhere between 45 percent and 65 percent of the overall market, and a large part of this segment was very price conscious. The business segment made up the remaining 35 percent to 55 percent of the market. It was less price-sensitive than the tourist segmentand more concerned about service quality, convenience, and flexibility.

The Growth of EasyCar

EasyCar opened its first location in London, on 20 April 2000, under the name easyRentacar. In the same week, easyCar opened locations in Glasgow and Barcelona. All three locations were popular easyJet destinations. Vehicles initially could be rented for as low as ε15/day plus a one-time car preparation fee of ε8. Each of these locations had a fleet consisting entirely of Mercedes A-class vehicles. It was the only vehicle that easyCar rented at the time.

EXHIBIT 1 Information on easyCar's Major European Competitors

	easyCar	Avis Europe	Europcar	Hertz	Sixt
Number of Rental Outlets	46	3,100	2,650	7,000	1,250
2002 Fleet Size	7,000	120,000	220,000	700,000	46,700
Number of Countries	5	107	118	150	50
Largest Market	UK	France	France	U.S.	Germany
Who Owns Company	EasyGroup/ Stelios Haji-Ioannou	D'Ieteren (Belgium) is majority shareholder.	Volkswagen AG	Ford Motor Company	Publicly Traded
European Revenues	ε41 million	ε1.25 billion	ε1.12 billion	ε910 million	ε600 million
Company Website Company Website	www. easycar.com	www. avis-europe.com	www. europcar.com	www. hertz.com	ag. sixt.com

Source: Information in this table came from each company's website and on-line annual reports. European revenues are for vehicle rental in Europe and are estimated based on market share estimates for 2001 from Avis Europe's website.

EasyCar had signed a deal with Mercedes, amidst much fanfare, at the Geneva Motor Show earlier in the year to purchase a total of 5000 A-class vehicles. The vehicles, which came with guaranteed buy-back terms, cost easyCar's parent company a little over e6 million.[14] Many in the car rental industry were surprised by the choice, expecting easyCar to rely on less expensive models.[15] In describing the acquisition of the 5000 Mercedes vehicles, Stelios had said:

> *The choice of Mercedes reflects the easy-Group brand. EasyRentacar will use brand new Mercedes cars in the same way that easyJet uses brand new Boeing aircraft. We do not compromise on the hardware, we just use innovation to substantially reduces costs. The car hire industry is where the airline industry was five years ago, a cartel feeding off the corporate client. EasyRentacar will provide a choice for consumers who pay out of their own pockets and who will not be ripped off for traveling mid-week.*[16]

EasyCar quickly expanded to other locations, focusing first on those locations that were popular with easyJet customers, including Amsterdam, Geneva, Nice, and Malagra. By July of 2001, a little over a year after its initial launch, easyCar had fleets of Mercedes A-class vehicles in 14 locations in the UK, Spain, France, and the Netherlands. At this point, easyCar secured $27 million from a consortium of Bank of Scotland Corporate Banking and NBGI Private Equity to further expand its operations. The package consisted of a combination of equity and loan stock.

While easyCar added a few sites in the second half of 2001 and early 2002, volatile demand in the wake of the September 11 attacks forced easyCar to roll out new rental locations somewhat more slowly than originally expected.[17] Growth accelerated, however, in the spring of 2002. Between May 2002 and January 2003, easyCar opened 30 new locations, to go from 18 sites to a total of 48 sites. This acceleration in growth also coincided with a change in easyCar's policy regarding the makeup of its fleet. By May of 2002, easyCar's fleet consisted of 6000 Mercedes A-class vehicles across 18 sites. Beginning in May, however, easyCar began to stock its fleet with other types of vehicles. It still maintained its policy of only offering a single vehicle at each location, but now the vehicle the customer received depended on the location. The first new vehicle easyCar introduced was the Vauxhall Corsa. According to Stelios,

Vauxhall Corsas cost easyCar $2 a day less than Mercedes A-Class so we can pass this saving on to customers. Customers themselves will decide if they want to pay a premium for a Mercedes. EasyGroup companies benefit from economies of scale where relevant but we also want to create contestable markets among our suppliers so that we can keep the cost to our customers as low as possible.[18]

By January 2003, easyCar was also using Ford Focuses (4 locations), Renault Clios (3 locations), Toyota Yarises (3 locations), and Mercedes Smart cars (2 locations) in addition to the Vauxhall Corsas (7 locations) and the Mercedes A-Class vehicles (28 locations). Plans called for a further expansion of the fleet, from the 7000 vehicles that easyCar had in January to 24,000 vehicles across 180 rental sites by the end of 2004.[19]

In addition to making vehicles available at more locations, easyCar had also changed its policies for 2003 to allow rentals for as little as one hour, and with as little as one hour's notice of rental. By making this change, Stelios felt that easyCar could be a serious competitor to local taxis, buses, and trains and even car ownership. EasyCar expected that, if it made car rental simple enough and cheap enough, some people living in traffic-congested European cities who only use their car occasionally would give up the costs and hassles of car ownership and simply hire an easyCar when they needed a vehicle. Tapping into this broader transportation market would help the company reach its ambitious future sales goals.

Facilities

EasyCar had facilities in a total of 17 cities in 5 European countries, as shown in Exhibit 2. It primarily located its facilities near bus and train stations in the major European cities, seeking out sites that offered lower lease costs. It generally avoided prime airport locations, as the cost for space at, and in some cases, near airports, was significantly higher than most other locations. When easyCar did locate near an airport, it generally chose sites off the airport, in order to reduce the

EXHIBIT 2 easyCar Locations in January 2003

Country	City	Number	Number Near an Airport
France	Nice	1	1
France	Paris	8	0
Netherlands	Amsterdam	3	1
Spain	Barcelona	2	0
Spain	Madrid	2	0
Spain	Majorca	1	1
Spain	Malagra	1	1
Switzerland	Geneva	1	1
UK	Birmingham	2	0
UK	Bromley	1	0
UK	Croydon	1	1
UK	Glasgow	2	1
UK	Kingston-Upon-Thames	1	0
UK	Liverpool	2	1
UK	London	15	0
UK	Manchester	2	1
UK	Waterford	1	0
Total	5 Countries, 17 Cities	46	9

Source: easyCar.com website, January, 2003.

cost of the lease. Airport locations also tended to require longer hours to satisfy customers arriving on late flights or departing on very early flights. EasyCar kept its airport locations open 24 hours a day, whereas its other locations were generally only open 07:00–23:00.

The physical facilities at all locations were kept to a minimum. In many locations, easyCar leased space in an existing parking garage. Employees worked out of a small, self-contained cubicle within the garage. The cubicle, depending on the location, might be no more than 15 m² and include little more than a small counter and a couple of computers at which staff processed customers as they came to pick up or return their vehicles. EasyCar also leased a number of spaces within the garage for its fleet of cars. However, because easyCar's vehicles were rented 90 percent of the time, the number of spaces required for at an average site, which had

a fleet of about 150 cars, was only 15–20 spaces.[20] To speed up the opening of new sites, easyCar had equipped a number of vans with all the needed computer and telephone equipment to run a site.[21] From an operational perspective, it could open a new location by simply leasing 20 or so spaces in a parking garage, hiring a small staff, driving a van to the location, and adding the location to the company's website. Depending on the fleet size at a location, easyCar typically had only one or two people working at a site at a time.

Vehicle Pick-Upup and Return Process

Customers arrived to a site to pick up a vehicle within a prearranged one-hour time period. Each customer selected this time slot when he or she booked the vehicles. EasyCar adjusted the first day's rental price based on the pick-up time. Customers who picked their cars up earlier in the day or at popular times were charged more compared to customers picking up their cars later in the day or at less busy times. Customers were required to bring a printed copy of their contract, along with the credit card they used to make the booking and identification. Given the low staffing levels, customers occasionally had to wait 30 minutes or more to be processed and receive their vehicles, particularly at peak times of the day. Processing a customer began with the employee accessing the customer's contract online. If the customer was a new easyCar customer to the site, the basic policies and possible additional charges were briefly explained. The employee then made copies of the customer's identification and credit card and took a digital photo of the customer. The customer was charged an ε 80 refundable deposit, signed the contract, and was on his or her way.

All vehicles were rented with more or less empty fuel tanks with the exact level dependent on how much gasoline was left in the vehicle when the previous renter returned it. Customers were provided with a small map of the immediate area around the rental site, showing the location and hours of nearby gas stations. Customers could return vehicles with any amount of gas in them as long as the "low fuel" indicator light in the vehicle was not on. Customers who returned vehicles with the "low fuel" indicator light on were charged a fueling fee of ε 16.

Customers were also expected to return the vehicle within a prearranged one-hour time period, which they also selected at the time of booking. While customers did not have to worry about refueling the car before returning it, they were expected to thoroughly clean the car. This clean car policy had been implemented in May of 2002 as a way to further reduce the price customers could pay for their vehicle. Prior to this change, all customers paid a fixed preparation fee of ε 11 each time they rented a vehicle (up from the ε 8 preparation fee when the company started operations in 2000). The new policy reduced this up-front preparation fee to ε 4 but required customers to either return the vehicle clean or pay an additional cleaning fee of ε 16. In order to avoid any misunderstanding about what it meant by a clean car, easyCar provided customers with an explicit description of what constituted a clean car, both for the interior and the exterior of the car. This included that it had to be apparent that the exterior of the car had been washed prior to returning the vehicle. The map that customers were provided when they picked up their cars that showed nearby gas stations also showed nearby car washes where they could clean the car before returning it. While easyCar had received some bad press in relation to the policy,[22] 85 percent of customers returned their vehicles clean as a result of the policy.

When a customer returned the vehicle, an easyCar employee checked to make sure that the vehicle was clean and undamaged and that the low fuel indicator light was not on. The employee also checked the kilometers driven. The customer was then notified of any additional charges. These charges were subtracted from the ε 80 deposit and the difference refunded to the customer's credit card (or, if additional charges exceeded the ε 80 deposit, the customer's credit card was charged the difference).

Pricing

EasyCar clearly differentiated itself from its competitors with its low price. In addition, pricing also played a key role in easyCar's efforts to achieve high utilization of its fleet of cars. EasyCar advertised prices as low as ε 5/day plus a per rental preparation fee of ε 4. Prices, however, varied by the location and dates of the rental, by when the booking was made, and by what time the car was to be picked up and returned. EasyCar's systems constantly evaluated projected demand and expected utilization at each site and adjusted price accordingly. Achieving the ε 5/day rate usually required customers to book well in advance, and these rates were typically only available on weekdays. Weekend rates, when booked well in advance, typically started a few euros higher than the weekday rates. As a given rental date approached, however, the price typically went up significantly as easyCar approached 100 percent fleet utilization for that day. Rates could literally triple overnight if there was sufficient booking activity. Generally, however, easyCar's price was less than half that of its major competitors. EasyCar, unlike most other rental car companies, required customers to pay in full at the time of booking and, once a booking was made, it was non-refundable.

EasyCar's base price covered only the core rental of the vehicle—the total price customers paid was in many cases much higher and depended on how the customer reserved, paid for, used, and returned the vehicle. EasyCar's price was based on customers booking through the company's website and paying for their rental with their easyMoney credit card. EasyMoney was the easyGroup's credit and financial services company. Customers who chose to book through the company's phone reservation system were charged an additional ε 0.95/minute for the call and those who used other credit cards were charged ε 5 extra. All vehicles had to be paid for by a credit or debit card—cash was not accepted. The base rental price allowed customers to drive vehicles 100 kilometers per day—additional kilometers were charged at a rate of ε 0.12/km. In addition, customers were expected to return their cars clean and on-time. Customers who returned cars that did not meet easyCar's standards for clean were charged an ε 16 cleaning fee. Those who returned their cars late were immediately charged e120 and subsequently charged an additional ε 120 for each subsequent 24-hour period in which the car was not returned. EasyCar explained the high late fee as representing the cost that they would likely incur in providing another vehicle to the next customer. Customers wishing to make any changes to their bookings were also charged a change fee of ε 16. Changes could be made either before the rental started or during the rental period but were limited to changing the dates, times, and location of the rental and were subject to the prices and vehicle availability at the time the change was being made. If the change resulted in an overall lower price for the rental, however, no refund was provided for the difference.

Beginning in 2003, all customers were also required to purchase loss/damage insurance for an additional charge of ε 4/day that eliminated the customer's liability for loss or damage to the vehicle (excluding damage to the tires or windshield of the vehicle). Through 2002, customers were able to choose whether or not to purchase additional insurance from easyCar to eliminate any financial liability in the event that the rental vehicle was damaged. The cost of this insurance had been ε 6/day, and approximately 60 percent of easyCar's customers purchased this optional insurance. Those not purchasing this insurance had either assumed the liability for the first ε 800 in damages personally or had their own insurance through some other means (e.g., some credit card companies provide this insurance to their cardholders at no additional charge for short-term rentals paid for with the credit card).

EasyCar's website attempted to make all of these additional charges clear to customers at the time of their booking. EasyCar had received a fair amount of bad press when it first opened for business after many renters complained about having to pay undisclosed charges when they returned their cars.[23] In response, easyCar had revamped its website in an effort to make these charges more transparent to customers and to explain the logic behind many of these charges.

Promotion

EasyCar's promotional efforts had through 2002 focused primarily on posters and press advertising. Posters were particularly prevalent in metro systems and bus and train stations in cities were easyCar had operations. All of this advertising focused on easyCar's low price. According to founder Stelios:

You will never see an advert for an easy company offering an experience—it's about price. If you create expectations you can't live up to then you will ultimately suffer as a result.[24]

In 2002, easyCar spent $1.43 million on such advertising.[25]

EasyCar also promoted itself by displaying its name, phone number, and website address prominently on the doors and rear windows of its entire fleet of vehicles and took advantage of free publicity when the opportunity presented itself. An example of seeking out such publicity occurred when Hertz complained that easyCar's comparative advertising campaign in the Netherlands that featured the line "The best reason to use easyCar.com can be found at hertz.nl" violated Dutch law that required comparative advertising to be exact, not general. In response, Stelios and a group of easyCar employees, dressed in orange boiler suits and with a fleet of easyCar vehicles, protested outside the Hertz Amsterdam office with signs asking "What is Hertz frightened of?"[26]

In an effort to help reach its goal of quadrupling sales in the next two years, easyCar recently hired Jennifer Mowat into the new position of commercial director to take over responsibility for easyCar's

European marketing. Ms. Mowat had previously been eBay's UK country manager and had recently completed an MBA in Switzerland. Previously, Stelios and easyCar's managing director, Andrew Fitzmaurice, had handled the marketing function themselves.[27] As part of this stepped-up marketing effort, easyCar also planned to double its advertising budget for 2003, to ε 3 million, and to begin to advertise on television. The television advertising campaign was to feature easyCar's founder, Stelios.[28]

Legal Challenges

easyCar faced several challenges to its approaches. The most significant dealt with a November 2002 ruling made by the Office of Fair Trading (OFT) that easyCar had to grant customers seven days from the time they made a booking to cancel their booking and receive a full refund. The OFT was a UK governmental agency that was responsible for protecting UK consumers from unfair and/or anti-competitive business practices. The ruling against easyCar was based on The 2000 Consumer Protection Distance Selling Regulations. These regulations stipulated that companies that sell at a distance (e.g., by Internet, phone) must provide customers with a seven-day cooling-off period, during which time customers can cancel their contracts with the company and receive a full refund. The law exempted accommodation, transportation, catering, and leisure service companies from this requirement. The OFT's ruling concluded that easyCar did not qualify as a transportation service company because consumers had to drive themselves, and so they were not receiving a transport service, just a car.[29]

EasyCar had appealed the OFT's decision to the UK High Court on the grounds that it was indeed a transportation service company and was entitled to an exemption from this requirement. EasyCar was hopeful that it would eventually win this legal challenge. EasyCar had argued that this ruling would destroy the company's book-early-pay-less philosophy and could lead to a tripling of prices.[30] Chairman Stelios was quoted as saying:

> It is very serious. My fear is that as soon as we put in the seven-day cooling off periods our utilization rate will fall from 90% to 65%. That's the difference between a profitable company and an unprofitable one.[31]

EasyCar was also concerned that prolonged legal action on this point could interfere with its plans for a 2004 IPO.

OFT, for its part, had also applied to the UK High Court for an injunction to make the company comply with the ruling. Other rental car companies were generally unconcerned about the ruling, as few offered big discounts for early bookings or non-refundable bookings.[32]

EasyCar's new policy of posting the pictures of customers whose cars were 15 days or more overdue was also drawing legal criticism. EasyCar had recently received public warnings from lawyers that this new policy might violate data protection, libel, privacy, confidentiality, and human rights laws.[33] Of particular concern to some lawyers was the possibility that easyCar might post the wrong person's picture, given the large number of customers the company dealt with.[34] Such a mistake could open the company to costly libel suits. The policy of posting the pictures of overdue customers on the easyCar website, initiated in November of 2002, was designed to reduce the losses associated with customers renting a vehicle and never returning it. The costs were significant, according to Stelios:

> These cars are expensive, ε 15,000 each, and we have 6,000 of them. At any given time, we are looking for as many as several tens which are overdue. If we don't get one back, it's a write-off. We are writing off an entire car, and its uninsurable.[35]

Stelios was also convinced of the legality of the new policy. In a letter to the editor responding to the legal concerns raised in the press, Stelios said:

> From a legal perspective, we have been entirely factual and objective and are merely reporting the details of the overdue car and the person who collected it. In addition, our policy is made very clear in our terms and conditions and the photo is taken both overtly and with the consent of the customer. . . . I estimate the total cost of overdue cars to be 5 percent of total easyCar costs, or 50p on every car rental day for all customers. In 2004, when I intend to float easyCar, this cost will amount to ε 5 million unless we can reduce our quantity of overdue cars.[36]

In the past, easyCar had simply provided pictures to police when a rental was 15 or more days overdue. It was hoped that posting the picture would both discourage drivers from not returning vehicles and shame those drivers who currently had overdue cars into returning them. In fact, the first person easyCar posted to its website did indeed return his car 2 days later. The vehicle was 29 days late.[37]

The Future

At the end of 2002, Stelios had stepped down as the CEO of easyJet so that he could devote more of his time to the other easyGroup companies, including easyCar. He had three priorities for the new year. One was to turn around the money-losing easyInternetCafe business, which Stelios had described as "the worst mistake of my career."[38] The 22-store chain had lost ε 80 million in the last two years. A second was to oversee the planned launch of another new easyGroup business, easyCinema, in the spring of 2003. And the third was to oversee the rapid expansion of the easyCar chain so that it would be ready for an initial public offering in the second half of 2004.

Notes

1. EasyCar.com website.
2. "The big picture—an interview with Stelios" *The Sunday Herald* (UK), 16 March 2003.
3. "Click to Fly," *The Economist*, 13 May 2004.
4. Simpkins, E. "Stelios isn't taking it easy," *The Sunday Telegraph* (UK), 15 December 2002.
5. Avis Europe plc 2002 annual report, p. 10 accessed online at http://ir.avis-europe.com/avis/reports on 16 August 2004.
6. Simpkins, E. "Stelios isn't taking it easy," *The Sunday Telegraph* (UK), 15 December 2002.
7. "Marketing: Former eBay UK chief lands top easyCar position," *Financial Times Information Limited*, 09 January 2003.
8. Burt, T. "EasyCar agrees deal with Vauxhall," *Financial Times*, 30 April 2002, p. 24.
9. Hodgson, N. "Stelios plans easyCar float," *Liverpool Echo*, 24 September 2002.
10. Simpkins, E. "Stelios isn't taking it easy," *The Sunday Telegraph* (UK), 15 December 2002.
11. "Marketing Week: Don't write off the car rental industry," *Financial Times Information Limited*, 26 September 2002.
12. "EasyCar set to shake up German car rental market," *European Intelligence Wire*, 22 February 2002.
13. "EasyCar set to shake up German car rental market," *European Intelligence Wire*, 22 February 2002.
14. Hodgson, N. "Stelios plans easyCar float," *Liverpool Echo*, 24 September 2002.
15. Felsted, A. "EasyCar courts Clio for rental fleet," *Financial Times*, 11 February 2002, p. 26.
16. EasyCar.com website news release, 1 March 2000.
17. Burt, T. "EasyCar agrees deal with Vauxhall," *Financial Times*, 30 April, 2002, p. 24.
18. EasyCar.com website news release, 2 May 2002.
19. "Marketing Week: EasyCar appoints head of European marketing," *Financial Times Information Limited*, 09 January 2003.
20. Simpkins, E. "Stelios isn't taking it easy," *The Sunday Telegraph* (UK), 15 December 2002.
21. Simpkins, E. Stelios isn't taking it easy," *The Sunday Telegraph* (UK), 15 December 2002.
22. Hyde, J. "Travel View: Clearing up on the extras," *The Observer* (UK), 7 July 2002.
23. Stanton, J. "The empire that's easy money," *Edinburgh Evening News*, 26 November 2002.
24. "The big picture—an interview with Stelios" *The Sunday Herald* (UK), 16 March 2003,
25. "Marketing Week: EasyCar appoints head of European marketing," *Financial Times Information Limited*, 09 January 2003.
26. EasyCar.com website news release, 22 April 2002.
27. "Marketing Week: EasyCar appoints head of European marketing," *Financial Times Information Limited*, 09 January 2003.
28. "Campaigning: EasyGroup appoints Publicis for easyCar TV advertising brief," *Financial Times Information Limited* 31, January 2003.
29. Macintosh, J. "EasyCar sues OFT amid threat to planned flotation," *Financial Times*, 22 November 2002, p. 4.
30. "Marketing Week: EasyCar appoints head of European marketing," *Financial Times Information Limited*, 09 January 2003.
31. Mackintosh, J. "EasyCar sues OFT amid threat to planned flotation." *Financial Times*, 22 November, 2002, p. 4.
32. Mackintosh, J. "EasyCar sues OFT amid threat to planned flotation." *Financial Times*, 22 November, 2002, p. 4.
33. Sherwood, B., & Wendlandt, A. "EasyCar may be in difficulty over naming ploy," *Financial Times*, 14 November, 2002, p. 2.
34. Sherwood, B., & Wendlandt, A. "EasyCar may be in difficulty over naming ploy," *Financial Times*, 14 November, 2002, p. 2.
35. "e-business: Internet fraudsters fail to steal Potter movie's magic & other news," *Financial Times Information Limited*, 19 November 2002.
36. Haji-Ioannou, S. "Letters to the Editor: Costly effect of late car return," *Financial Times*, 16 November 2002, p. 10.
37. Hookham, M. "How Stelios nets return of his cars," *Daily Post* (Liverpool, UK), 14 November 2002.
38. Bentley, S. "The worst mistake of my career, by Stelios" *Financial Times*, 24 December, 2002.

Traditional Case 6: WestJet

This case has been prepared by Eldon Gardner, Faculty of Management, The University of Lethbridge, from publicly available information and with the assistance of WestJet's Marketing Department. Permission to disseminate this case for publication was requested from and granted by WestJet in May 2004 even though such permission was not required since the case is based on public information. The accuracy of the information in the case has been verified by WestJet. Copyright © 2003 held by Eldon Gardner, The University of Lethbridge.

WestJet: Setting the Stage

As Clive Beddoe and the rest of the WestJet (WJA) management team surveyed the competitive landscape in January 2003, they had reason for considerable pride in what they had accomplished over the years since the founding of the airline in 1996. The organisation had been profitable consistently over the last several years (24 consecutive quarters and soon to be 25), and it had expanded its presence to become a recognised competitor for the dominant airline in Canada—Air Canada. Now the stage was set for the next phase of expansion for WJA as it began to acquire new aircraft and expand its routes across Canada with the possibility of service to US destinations in the future.

There were many questions to be answered as these expansion plans took shape over the next ten years or so:

1. Where should WJA expand and when?

2. How should it finance aircraft purchases since 15 aircraft had just been ordered for delivery by the end of 2003, costing about $750 million (Canadian), and 15 more aircraft were to be purchased over the next four years?

3. Is there any reason to change from the acquisition of Boeing 737-700 series aircraft?

4. What would competitors do, especially Air Canada, as WJA continued expanding?

5. Should alliances be formed and with whom to enhance future growth opportunities?

6. But above all else, how could WJA maintain its record of profitability and growth amidst all of these other requirements for the future?

These were the challenges facing management as the year 2003 unfolded. Clive Beddoe and his colleagues wanted to continue to see WJA grow and prosper so that they, and the rest of WJA's shareholders (including many employees), would prosper, too. The financial community in Canada had a very high opinion of WJA at this time and its record of success; Beddoe and the rest of his management team wanted to keep that reputation, going on to even bigger, and better, things.

Recent Events

The airline business had been hit hard since the terrible events of September 2001, and WJA, along with everybody else, had been forced to adjust to the new realities of the business. Increased air security taxes in Canada, fewer passengers, greater security precautions, and a general fear of what could happen in the future had all combined to create an uncertain environment for the industry and passengers alike. Not only that, but the largest airlines in the world, including American Airlines and United Airlines, were in serious financial trouble, with United Airlines entering Chapter 11 bankruptcy protection in December 2002 and American Airlines almost forced to do the same in April 2003 but for last minute employee wage concessions. While the picture was not totally bleak, the turmoil in the industry was far from over.

If these problems were not enough, the threat of war in the Middle East was causing uncertainty about increased fuel prices for all airlines, and fuel surcharges were being added to Canadian airline tickets. Many travellers were also finding that the extra costs of all of these taxes and surcharges (ATSC [security tax], Nav-Canada, Insurance, and Airport Improvement Fees) were making short-haul travel in the air cost prohibitive, causing cut-backs in flights by all of the major airlines.

The financial implications of all of these varied problems were of considerable concern to airline executives all over the world, including those at WJA. How could the organisation maintain its record of profit growth and share price increases in the face of such uncertain times? The US economy was almost at a standstill, and that put risks in the way of the Canadian economy because of its dependence on the US. It also meant that interest rates could rise in Canada if there was a need. The Governor of the Bank of Canada had indicated that inflation was a serious concern, and that he would not hesitate to raise interest rates if he thought it necessary to curb the inflation threat. Rising interest rates would certainly affect WJA's plans for airplane acquisitions and the costs of financing them.

History

WJA came into being as a result of the actions of four Calgary entrepreneurs: Clive Beddoe, Mark Hill, Tim Morgan, and Donald Bell. They saw the potential for a low-cost air carrier in Western Canada with a low-cost structure along the lines of Southwest Airlines in the United States. With this idea in mind, capital was raised to purchase three Boeing 737-200 aircraft, and then additional capital was raised to commence operations in February 1996. Initial routes included Vancouver, Kelowna, Calgary, Edmonton, and Winnipeg. Later in 1996, WJA added Victoria, Regina and Saskatoon. Expansion continued in 1997 and later in 1999 to add additional cities as far north as Grand Prairie, Alberta and Prince George, B.C. and as far east as Thunder Bay, Ontario.

The head office of the company was in Calgary, Alberta, (where the company intended to stay) with primary service facilities at the Calgary Airport. With these facilities, and additional financing in 1999, WJA expanded its network further to include Hamilton and Ottawa, Ontario, and Moncton, New Brunswick. Later, in 2001, WJA added Fort McMurray, Alberta, Comox, B.C., and Sault Ste. Marie and Sudbury, Ontario. In 2002, WJA added service to London and Toronto, Ontario, and plans were in the works to add Halifax, Nova Scotia, Windsor, Ontario, Montréal, Québec and St. John's and Gander, Newfoundland in 2003.

Financing Activities

To facilitate the financing of expansion and the acquisition of headquarters and service hangars in Calgary, WJA launched an Initial Public Offering of shares in July of 1999. The sale of 2.5 million common shares at $10 each raised sufficient funds to allow purchase of additional aircraft in addition to facilities needs. This $25 million was an extremely important part of WJA's expansion plans and activities.

In December 2000, a further issue of 2.2 million shares was sold in Canada at $22.50 (raising $49.5 million), and that was followed with an issue of 2.5 million shares in February 2002 at a price of $27.50 (raising $68.75 million). The total financing for WJA from 1999 to 2002 was $143.25 million raised in three equity issues, providing 7.2 million shares to the financial markets.

In early 2003, there were about 75 million shares outstanding to management, the employees and the public, along with nearly 6 million share options to employees and management. Long-term (non-equity) obligations were in excess of $80 million in early 2002, and they would rise as new equipment was acquired through new financing arrangements. WJA acquired 10 Boeing 737-700 aircraft in 2001-2002 through a lease financing arrangement with GE Capital Corporation. WJA had just announced (late in 2002) financing arrangements with ING Group (the Netherlands) and the Export-Import Bank as loan guarantor (Ex-Im bank in the US guarantees loans for foreign buyers of US products.) for US $477.8 million (about $750 million Canadian) for the purchase of 15 Boeing 737-700 aircraft up to the end of 2003. The loan for each airplane would be for 12 years, with each one taking effect as the airplane was acquired. The Ex-Im Bank had agreed in principle to a loan guarantee, similar to the one on these 15 planes, for an additional 15 planes to be acquired by February 2006. These 30 Boeing 737-700 aircraft would be used to expand operations and gradually phase out the Boeing 737-200 series airplanes that are currently in service. Four of these financed planes were acquired in 2002 and deposits on future aircraft deliveries were paid, adding about $50 million per plane (Canadian) to the debt. The rest of the debt would be added by the end of 2003, massively increasing the debt position of WJA. The total equity value of WJA at the end of January 2003 was over $1 billion Canadian at the current share price, so the increase in debt did not appear to be excessive.

Business Plan

WJA had established itself in Western Canada with a strong presence using its base in Calgary. The Calgary International Airport was its primary hub in the area. In moving eastward in Canada, WJA decided to make its hub the Hamilton airport in Hamilton, Ontario rather than Toronto's Pearson Airport because of the cost and niche market advantages. However, WJA has added six landing slots in Toronto to its operations, and has announced plans to expand further east with its entrance into Windsor, Montréal, Halifax, Gander and St. John's.

The original fleet of aircraft was Boeing 737-200 series planes, configured for 125-passenger capacity. WJA did not offer first class or business class seating. The range of the aircraft was just over 4,000 km, but these planes were not used for transoceanic travel; WJA only flew over the North American continent.

A new series of aircraft, the Boeing Next Generation 737-700 series, was added to the fleet beginning in May 2001 and continuing for the foreseeable future. These planes had a passenger capacity of 140, and a range of just over 6,000 km. They, too, would be used for North American travel only. WJA had no aspirations to develop intercontinental routes at this time. There were plans, however, to expand into US air space with new routes to the south in the future.

WJA planned to use both types of aircraft—the Boeing 737-200 and the Boeing 737-700—for the next eight years or so until the Boeing 737-200 series planes were ready for retirement. They would be phased out as the new series of planes was phased in. Since WJA had options to purchase more Boeing 737-700 series aircraft each year up to 2008, the old aircraft would be kept only as long as they were appropriate for use. Also, the Boeing 737 was the most widely used airplane in the world; thus, WJA was safe in assuming that it would be able to maintain all of its fleet as long as it needed to do so. It was also clear that WJA obtained significant operating efficiencies by maintaining the use of only one type of aircraft, and it was committed to this continued operating efficiency until a significantly better alternative came along.

The choices of destinations depended on the possible demand and the ability to obtain landing slots at the proposed airports. Since these landing slots each had a cost, along with rental of space at the airports involved, expansion was not to be undertaken too quickly. WJA had been careful not to expand too quickly in the past, and there was no intention of making such a mistake in the future. Some of the Canadian routes that WJA served were not served by Air Canada, but many of them were being served by one of Air Canada's so-called discount subsidiaries, namely Jazz, Zip or Tango. In fact, these subsidiaries were being used by Air Canada to compete directly with WJA in the discount market. The battle for market share in many of WJA's markets was far from over, as it appeared that Air Canada had no intention of giving up easily. So far, however, WJA had been able to compete effectively and profitably in the markets it served, as its low-cost structure allowed it to profitably sell seats, while Air Canada's high-cost structure would mean financial losses if it charged the same prices. The significant difference between the seat-mile cost of WJA and other low-cost carriers and that of Air Canada and other high-cost carriers could be clearly seen when cost structures were examined. Studies in the US demonstrated that the difference can be 30 percent or more from the high to the low.

WJA was not a full service airline in the sense of what people had seen in the past from the major airlines. It offered snack and beverage service as opposed to meal service on its flights, even four or five hour ones; however, guests could purchase cheap "Grab 'n Go" meals at most airports before boarding their flights. The primary benefit for its customers was that it was possible to get inexpensive flights from one point to another on relatively short notice with minimal hassle. WJA also minimised the paper work with ticketing so that the cost of this operation was low. WJA was a part of the Air Miles® reward program for collectors, as it made available flights and bookings for members.

Strategic alliances had not yet been formed with any other airlines, but that possibility could not completely be discounted. At some point, perhaps such an alliance or alliances could be an appropriate action for WJA to take. However, that time, in the opinion of Clive Beddoe and his team, had not yet arrived. Such alliances would only be undertaken when it was apparent that they would be beneficial to all parties concerned—but not yet!

People

The entrepreneurs that had started WJA were still an active part of it in early 2003. They included Clive Beddoe, Donald Bell, Thomas (Tim) Morgan, and Mark Hill. In addition, WJA had added Alexander (Sandy) Campbell, William (Bill) Lamberton, and Fred Ring to the executive team.

Members of the Board of Directors included Clive Beddoe and Tim Morgan from executive team, along with Brian Gibson (Toronto), Ronald Greene (Calgary), Murph Hannon, (Calgary), Wilmot Mathews (Toronto), Donald MacDonald (Calgary), Larry Pollock (Edmonton) and Allen Byl (Calgary).

Clive Beddoe, the Executive Chairman, President and CEO of WJA, was a successful entrepreneur with a strong background in financial planning and strategic management. He was a private pilot with a keen interest in aircraft, and he had been a part of the team from the beginning.

Donald Bell was the former owner of a computer company in Calgary, and he used these skills in his position as Senior Vice-President, Customer Service and Co-Chief Operating Officer. He was, in addition to customer service, responsible for reservations and information technology, along with flight attendants and airports. He was a licensed Boeing 737 pilot (captain).

Tim Morgan was an aviation industry member for more than 20 years, with a wide range of experience in operations and in dealing with Transport Canada and other government agencies. He was Senior Vice-President, Operations and Co-Chief Operating Officer, responsible for flight operations and maintenance.

Mark Hill was the Vice-President, Strategic Planning, with responsibility for growth, route development and industry analysis. He was the author of the WJA business plan that was used to obtain its original financing.

Sandy Campbell was Senior Vice-President, Finance and Chief Financial Officer (CFO). He joined WJA in May 1996, shortly after its founding and became CFO in 1997. He was previously with Time Air and Canadian Regional Airlines, working in financial areas. He was responsible for most financial areas of WJA.

Bill Lamberton was Vice-President, Marketing and Sales, having joined WJA in 1995 just prior to its start-up. He had 15 years of experience with Canadian Airlines International in marketing prior to joining WJA. He was responsible for schedule design and distribution, advertising, product development, revenue management, corporate communications and travel agency relationships.

Fred Ring was Vice-President, People with responsibility for recruiting, compensation and benefits, performance management, leadership development, occupational health and safety, customer service agent and sales super agent training, and corporate security. He joined WJA in 2001 after 32 years in education.

The other members of the Board of Directors (other than executives) included the following people:

1. Brian Gibson, Senior Vice-President of Equities, Ontario Teachers' Pension Plan Board;

2. Ronald Greene, Chairman of the Board of Denbury Resources, Inc. (and a significant shareholder of WJA);

3. Murph Hannon, President of Murcon Development Ltd., a private investment company;

4. Wilmot Mathews, retired Vice-Chairman and Director of Nesbitt Burns Inc., currently President of Marjad Inc., a personal investment company;

5. Donald MacDonald, President of Sanjel Corporation, an oilfield pumping services company;

6. Larry Pollock, President and Chief Executive Officer of Canadian Western Bank and Canadian Western Trust;

7. Allen Byl, Chairman of WestJet Pilot's Association, and the company's PACT (Pro-Active Communications Team) representative on the Board of Directors.

Current Financial Position

In appendices 1, 2 and 3 can be found the balance sheets, consolidated income statements and statements of cash flows respectively for the fiscal years 1998, 1999, 2000, 2001 and 2002. These financial statements provide a fairly complete picture of the financial position of WJA over the five year period from 1998-2002. The growth and expansion of the organisation is obvious as is the continuing pattern of earnings growth. Appendix 4 provides stock price charts for WJA for 2002–2003 (daily) and 1999-2003 (weekly).

In the financial statements, it is wise to keep in mind that WJA has considerable equipment under lease as well as equipment purchased. While the fifteen, new aircraft were to be purchased with financing from ING, there was no requirement that future aircraft acquisitions (the 15 additional Boeing aircraft up to 2006) need be purchased. They could also be acquired with long-term leases. The impact on the financial statements would not be much different, but with leases there could be cancellation clauses that provided more flexibility than with purchases. Thus, WJA was not locked in to purchasing 30 aircraft over the next three to four years—only 15 of them, and the timing was still flexible on all purchases.

It should also be noted on the income statements, for example, the changing importance of various categories of expenses. Fuel, for example, had become a much more significant component of cost than it once was. This had given rise to the fuel surcharges that were being levied by airlines, including WJA. The price of oil, worldwide, was very important to airlines, and it was virtually impossible to arrange futures contracts for long periods into the future. Even if futures contracts for oil were purchased, they could not eliminate all of the risk.

The other significant factor to note was the employee profit sharing plan that was part of expenses for WJA. A portion of employee compensation could be provided by this profit sharing plan, and a portion of executive compensation had been through stock purchases or stock options. Employees and the managers had a portion of their income from WJA dependent on its profits; and the approximately 85 percent of people that contribute on average 13 percent of their salaries to the Employee Share Purchase Plan (which is matched dollar for dollar by the corporation) can benefit from a growing share price.

Next Steps

While many of the future aspects of WJA were known with some certainty—for example, its aircraft purchases had been planned for several years into the future—there were other aspects of the business that were much less certain. As noted earlier, the directions for the airplane expansion program were fairly widely known, but the directions for expansion of routes were not publicly disclosed for obvious strategic reasons. WJA would hardly be adding capacity at the rate it was planning if it did not have specific plans for use of the aircraft capacity that was being added. Where WJA would go next to maintain its highly successful expansion program was not being announced until the executive team was ready to do so. While a few new routes in Canada were publicly disclosed in 2003, WJA had been careful not to expand too rapidly in too many directions at once. Clive Beddoe had publicly stated that one day WJA would be in every city in Canada, and this provided ample opportunities for expansion. With Air Canada in the picture, WJA was careful about a price war on a large scale, but its low-cost structure always allowed it to price its service below that of Air Canada while leaving itself room for profitability on each individual route. A large scale price war for many destinations at once would be disastrous for all concerned—there was no upside to a price war of that sort. Thus, expansion was generally undertaken a few destinations at a time, picking the niches one by one in a carefully planned way so that large scale competition did not happen all at once.

This was where the complexities of the financial planning came into play. Where could the revenues be generated that would pay for the nearly $750 million in new aircraft that would come on stream in the next few months? The debt position of WJA was becoming significantly different from what it had been. At the end of 2002, WJA had a debt to equity ratio of 1.82 to 1, but company financial planners felt that it could tolerate a ratio of up to 3 to 1. What routes would generate additional revenue and which routes were best suited to the new aircraft so that this debt could be easily repaid with no financial repercussions? The new airplanes could fly from coast to coast in the US or Canada or from the extreme north to the extreme south of North America's populated areas. WJA's airplanes would open up the continent to service virtually anywhere. The obvious key was to target the routes where the revenue possibilities were the greatest and the competition could be handled successfully.

The second part of the financial plan would, therefore, have to address competitive reactions to WJA's expansion. Air Canada had already indicated its willingness to compete by having its subsidiary, Zip, offer trips at a loss to try to take business away from WJA. Such an action does, however, violate Canadian competition law and could lead to fines or penalties for Air Canada and/or its subsidiary. If WJA decided to compete with US-based airlines, there was no doubt that it would have to expect serious competitive reactions from them. However, competition laws in the US are equally restrictive, and a low-cost carrier can generally expect to be treated fairly under the law. Great care had to be taken in figuring out what to do next, but opportunities abounded. WJA was not anxious to repeat the mistakes of the larger US airlines that were teetering on the brink of or already in bankruptcy. Even Air Canada had had its share of financial problems over the last several years and was now under court protection from its creditors. WJA was not willing to join other airlines in financial distress. If its strategy was carefully

planned and wisely executed, there was no reason that it would.

The final piece of the puzzle was the price of jet fuel in the immediate and long-term future. There were many questions about what could or would happen to prices in 2003-2004. WJA would have to deal with whatever happened, just like everyone else. The strike in Venezuela had disrupted North American supplies, and with a possible war in the Middle East there was no telling what might happen there. Jet fuel prices would likely remain volatile for a number of months to come, and they continued to climb during the spring of 2003 to levels not seen in more than 10 years, since the Gulf War of 1991. How customers would react to fuel surcharges was another matter. They could simply stay home and refuse to travel at all or limit their travel significantly, thus reducing revenues for WJA.

The next few months were going to be interesting and challenging for all airlines, and WJA wanted to be one of the airlines that did well throughout these times. For Clive Beddoe and his team, there were many challenges ahead (as noted from the beginning of the case). They just wanted to be as successful in facing them in the future as they had in the past.

WestJet Airlines Ltd. Balance Sheets as at December 31 (in thousands of Canadian dollars)

	2002	2001	2000	1999	1998
Assets					
Current assets:					
Cash and short-term investments	$100,410	$58,942	$79,025	$50,740	$13,500
Accounts receivable	20,532	12,211	6,477	5,168	5,240
Income taxes recoverable	---	779	---	---	---
Prepaid expenses and deposits	19,759	11,643	6,099	4,123	3,479
Inventory	2,314	2,155	604	462	500
	143,015	85,730	92,175	60,493	22,719
Capital assets (net)	605,124	300,685	239,320	121,974	88,523
Other long-term assets (net)	36,066	7,488	5,677	4,131	---
Total Assets	$784,205	$393,903	$337,172	$186,598	$108,242
Liabilities and Shareholders' Equity					
Current liabilities:					
Accounts payable and accrued liabilities	$67,008	$42,019	$43,616	$21,059	$14,663
Income taxes payable	7,982	---	10,471	7,410	---
Advance ticket sales	44,195	28,609	18,764	10,907	7,218
Non-refundable passenger credits	15,915	12,599	6,996	3,863	2,940
Current portion of long-term debt	32,674	8,470	9,336	6,550	4,051
Current portion of obligations under capital lease	7,290	3,398	1,597	137	78
	175,064	95,095	90,780	49,926	28,950
Long-term debt	198,996	41,305	40,953	29,341	21,861
Obligations under capital lease	16,352	14,400	8,519	335	322
Future income tax	38,037	20,933	15,828	12,509	7,748
	428,449	171,733	156,080	92,111	58,881
Shareholders' equity:					
Share capital	211,549	129,268	125,390	69,039	39,536
Obligation to issue share capital	---	---	---	---	209
Retained earnings	144,192	92,902	55,702	25,448	9,616
	355,756	222,170	181,092	94,487	49,361
Total Liabilities and Shareholders' Equity	$784,205	$393,903	$337,172	$186,598	$108,242

WestJet Airlines Ltd. Consolidated Income Statement for the periods ending December 31 (in thousands of Canadian dollars)

	2002	2001	2000	1999	1998
Revenues:					
Passenger revenues	$643,174	$452,910	$315,931	$193,715	$118,612
Charter and other	36,822	25,483	16,588	9,859	6,825
	679,996	478,393	332,519	203,574	125,437
Expenses:					
Passenger services (Airport operations—2002)	88,586	95,613	64,090	43,955	31,386
Maintenance	81,973	72,317	49,512	31,854	22,129
Aircraft fuel	111,737	84,629	55,875	30,480	20,490
Sales and marketing	44,707	30,862	21,763	13,907	9,452
Reservations	20,106	17,777	12,497	9,550	4,917
General and administration	39,791	20,893	12,147	9,410	6,545
Flight operations (And navigational charges in 2002)	75,759	20,916	13,923	8,826	5,709
In flight	27,284	16,104	10,972	7,531	3,465
Employee profit share provision	15,233	10,311	13,549	6,633	1,702
Aircraft leasing	35,822	15,284	6,770	2,687	1,448
Depreciation and amortisation	52,637	34,332	17,959	8,272	5,087
	593,635	419,038	279,057	173,105	112,330
Earnings from operations	86,361	59,355	30,469	30,469	13,107
Non-operating income (–expense):					
Interest income	3,078	2,837	2,463	1,657	453
Interest expense	–7,038	–5,086	–2,937	–2,871	–1,137
Gain on disposal of assets	97	187	-282	93	8
Gain on foreign exchange	346	986	---	---	---
	–3,517	–1,076	–756	–1,121	–676
Earnings before income taxes	82,844	58,279	52,706	29,348	12,431
Income taxes:					
Current	12,526	15,974	18,102	7,696	335
Future	18,438	5,105	4,350	5,820	5,579
	31,064	21,079	22,452	13,516	5,914
Net earnings	51,780	37,200	30,254	15,832	6,517
Retained earnings, beginning of period	92,412	55,702	25,448	9,616	3,099
Retained earnings, end of period	$144,192	$92,902	$55,702	$25,448	$9,616
Earnings per share:					
Basic	$0.70	$0.81	$0.72	$0.63	$0.28
Full diluted	$0.69	$0.79	$0.69	$0.58	$0.28

WestJet Airlines Ltd. Statement of Cash Flow for the periods ending December 31 (in thousands of Canadian dollars)

	2002	2001	2000	1999	1998
Cash provided by (–used in):					
Operations:					
Net earnings	$51,780	$37,200	$30,254	$15,382	$6,517
Items not involved in cash:					
Depreciation and amortisation	52,637	34,332	17,959	8,272	5,087
Gain (–loss) on disposal of capital assets	–97	–187	–633	–93	–8
Unrealized loss on foreign exchange	---	50	---	---	---
Future income tax	18,438	5,105	4,350	5,820	5,579
Cash flow from operations	122,758	76,500	51,930	29,831	17,175
Decrease (–increase) in non-cash working capital	38,866	–9,139	35,483	17,948	6,759
	161,624	67,361	87,413	47,779	23,934
Financing:					
Increase in long-term debt	190,366	8,947	22,417	15,314	20,759
Repayment of long-term debt	–8,471	–9,461	–8,019	–5,335	–2,422
Issuance of common shares	84,634	3,878	57,699	30,591	2,144
Share issuance costs	–3,672	---	–2,369	–2,356	–87
Issuance of performance shares	---	---	---	---	12
Increase (–decrease) in other long-term assets	–32,257	–2,230	–3,818	–4,195	---
Decrease in obligations under capital lease	–6,088	–2,483	–137	–96	–75
	224,512	–1,349	65,763	33,923	20,331
Investments:					
Aircraft additions	–320,871	–60,518	–97,269	–39,318	–42,717
Aircraft disposals	---	---	12,239	---	---
Other capital asset additions	–24,031	–26,271	–40,043	–5,350	–4,933
Other capital asset disposals	234	694	182	206	99
	344,668	–86,095	–124,891	–44,462	–47,551
Net change in cash	41,468	–20,083	28,285	37,240	–3,286
Cash, beginning of period	58,942	79,025	50,740	13,500	16,786
Cash, end of period	$100,410	$58,942	$79,025	$50,740	$13,500

WestJet Share Price Charts. Daily 2002–2003

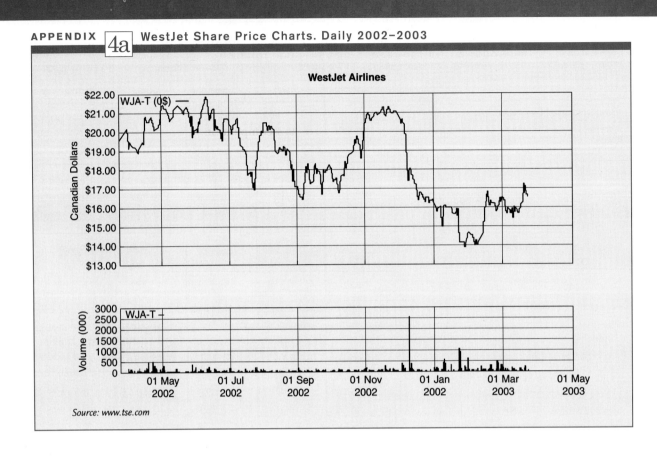

Source: www.tse.com

WestJet Share Price Charts. Weekly 1999–2003

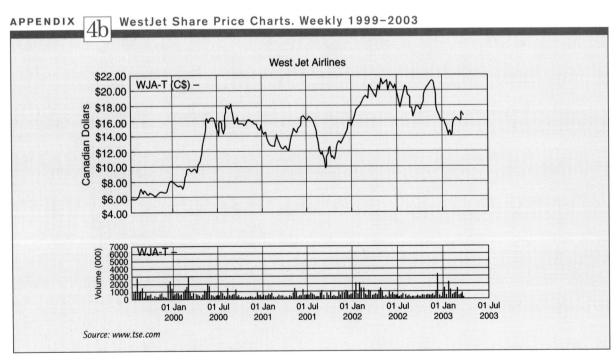

Source: www.tse.com

Traditional Case 7: IPC Media: Challenges of a British Magazine Publisher

This case was written by Professor Marlene M. Reed, Baylor University, and Professor Rochelle R. Brunson, Alvin Community College, as the basis for class discussion rather than to illustrate either effective or ineffective handling of an administrative situation.

In April 2007, IPC Media, the United Kingdom's leading consumer magazine publisher, packed up its headquarters at the King's Reach Tower just south of the Thames River in London and moved a few blocks away to a building next to the Tate Museum of Modern Art. This was not the only major upheaval in the past several years. The company had been bought out by Time, Inc. in 2001, and now they were facing some serious challenges to magazine publishing in the early years of the twenty-first century.

Strategic decisions facing the company were such considerations as whether to focus its resources on expanding current publications or investing in launching new titles; developing new products internally or through acquisitions; increasing profits by cutting costs or increasing total circulation or both; finding a way to deal with the price deflation that had recently occurred in the market for consumer magazine; and identifying appropriate strategies for a company operating in a mature industry.

History of IPC Magazines and Reed Elsevier plc

In 1963, a merger occurred between the Oldhams Press, Fleetway Publications, and George Newnes—the three leading magazine publishers in the United Kingdom. This newly merged organization was blended with the Mirror Group to form International Publishing Corporation (IPC). The company had a long history since Oldhams, Fleetway, and Newnes were originally formed in 1890, 1880, and 1881, respectively.

Eight titles launched in the late 1800s which became the property of IPC were still being published in 2007. They were *Country Life, Horse & Hound, Shooting Times, Yachting World, Amateur Gardening, Cycling Weekly, Amateur Photographer,* and *The Railway Magazine.* In the early years of IPC, various competitions were created to promote the company's magazines. One of the most interesting competitions was offered by the fledgling magazine *Answers* in 1889. This magazine awarded the then unheard of fortune of one pound sterling a week for life to any reader who could guess the amount of gold and silver in the Bank of England on a given date.

The company continued to grow through the early and middle twentieth century. In the 1940s, IPC women's weeklies played a key wartime role by keeping up the morale of Britain's women and supplying important information on behalf of the government. With the arrival of commercial television in Britain in 1955, *TVTimes* magazine was first published by the ITV (commercial) stations themselves, but IPC acquired the company in 1989.

IPC was acquired in 1970 by Reed International plc, a leading world publisher and information provider with principal operations in the United States and Europe. Reed International originally had viewed its purchase of IPC Magazines as a chance to enter the print media industry in the United Kingdom. In 1993, Reed merged with Elsevier, a Dutch publisher specializing in scientific and professional publication

Reed Elsevier in 1994 began to narrow its strategic focus to an emphasis on the high value-added areas of information, emphasizing science, business, and other professions. In late 1994, Reed Elsevier purchased LexisNexis,[1] making a major strategic commitment to computer delivered information. In mid-July 1995, Reed Elsevier issued a press release indicating a decision to divest itself of the portion of its portfolio dedicated to the consumer markets. The press release stated:

The Board of Directors of Reed Elsevier plc announced today its intention to dispose of the Company's newspaper businesses in the UK and the Netherlands, the consumer book business and its consumer magazine titles in the United States and the Netherlands.

However, the press release continued:

IPC Magazines, the UK's largest publisher of consumer Magazines, will be Reed Elsevier plc's only consumer publishing activity. IPC has long been the market leader and is expected to remain in a secure position within this large and growing consumer magazine market.

The businesses for which Reed Elsevier sought buyers were the following:

1. **Reed Regional newspapers:** a leading UK regional newspaper publisher
2. **Dagbladunie:** the publisher of two of the Netherland's leading national newspapers and a number of regional titles
3. **Reed Consumer Books:** a leading trade, children's and illustrative book publisher operating in the United Kingdom and Australia.
4. **Consumer Magazines:** consisting of fourteen Cahners Publishing titles serving the bridal, child care, and boating sectors in the United States and six titles by Bonaventura in the Netherlands.

At the end of 1994, the businesses which were targeted for divestiture had produced an operating profit for the year of 76 million pounds sterling.[2] This accounted for 11 percent of the operating profit of Reed Elsevier. The book value of these businesses at the end of 1994 was reported to be in the vicinity of 700 million pounds sterling.

In 1994, Reed Elsevier's combined businesses had generated an operating cash flow of 670 million pounds sterling. The combination of strong internal cash flow and the proceeds from the intended sale of the consumer businesses were expected to provide substantial resources to enhance the company's position as a leading provider of information to professionals and businesses.

By August 1997, the London newspapers were reporting rumors that Reed Elsevier had decided to sell IPC after all. When asked about the rumors, Reed Elsevier declined to comment. At about this time, Reed Elsevier sold its Tigerprint greeting card business and major children's book titles, including *Thomas the Tank Engine* and *Winnie the Pooh.* Concurrently, it acquired a string of trade magazines from Walt Disney, undertook a venture with Microsoft, and bought MDL Information Services, a company which specialized in managing research and development information.

While these transactions were occurring, Reed Elsevier was considering a merger with Wolters Kluwer, its Dutch rival of ten years, to form a group valued at 19.4 billion pounds sterling. Wolters Kluwer was a Dutch publishing company that focused on the delivery of professional information, concentrating on medical, scientific, tax, and accounting publishing. In 1995, Wolters Kluwer had outbid Reed Elsevier for the 1.5 billion purchase of U.S. tax specialist CCH which derived 30 percent of its revenues from electronic delivery. The proposed Reed Elsevier-Wolters Kluwer merger, scheduled to go before the shareholders in 1998, would create one of the world's largest publishers of business magazines and online information (see Figure 1).

On October 27, 1997, Reed Elsevier formally announced its intention to sell IPC

Magazines. This was seen by industry analysts as an attempt to focus more of the company's efforts on the information superhighway. The only IPC title that Reed proposed to keep was the *New Scientist,* because its content was consistent with the company's emphasis on professional information as opposed to purely consumer information. A problem for Reed Elsevier, according to one analyst was that "... consumer magazines cannot be lucratively converted into electronic format, on CD-Roms, on-line databases or the Internet, to satisfy a demand for high margin must-have information for business and the scientific, legal and other professions where Reed Elsevier has increasingly set its store." By moving to electronic delivery of must-have information, Reed believed it would become less and less advertising dependent. In addition, the combined Reed Elsevier and Wolters Kluwer produced a relatively small 11 percent consumer titles.

Companies Competing to Buy IPC in 1997

Because of IPC's dominant market share in the United Kingdom as a publisher of consumer magazines, Reed Elsevier had no problem finding prospective buyers for the magazine unit. The company received offers from potential purchasers from all over the globe.

Three companies quickly emerged as the most likely buyers. These companies were the U.S.-based Hearst Corporation, the British publisher Emap

FIGURE 1 New Giant in Specialist Publishing

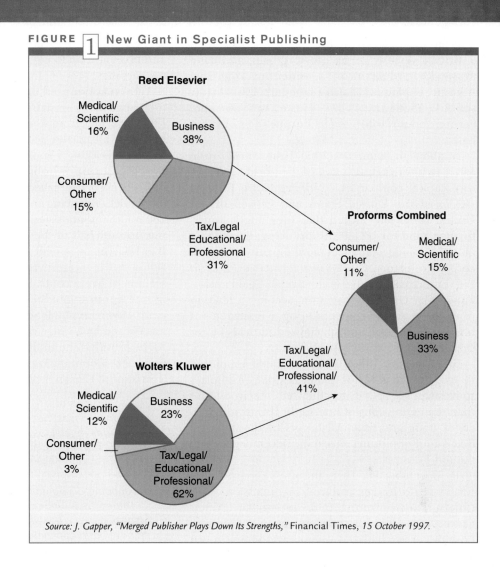

Reed Elsevier

Medical/
Scientific
16%

Business
38%

Consumer/
Other
15%

Tax/Legal
Educational/
Professional
31%

Proforms Combined

Consumer/
Other
11%

Medical/
Scientific
15%

Tax/Legal/
Educational/
Professional/
41%

Business
33%

Wolters Kluwer

Medical/
Scientific
12%

Business
23%

Consumer/
Other
3%

Tax/Legal/
Educational/
Professional/
62%

Source: J. Gapper, "Merged Publisher Plays Down Its Strengths," Financial Times, 15 October 1997.

plc, and the German media giant Bertelsmann AG. Estimates of the possible prices of the sale ranged from 700 million pounds sterling up to 1 billion pounds sterling. Emap was mentioned more frequently in the business journals and newspapers than the other two companies, because IPC had been their main rival in the UK market for consumer magazines. The synergy which could be produced by two companies appealing to the same market segment and the cost-cutting possibilities were obvious advantages for Emap. With a market value of about 1.8 billion pounds sterling and little debt, Emap could afford to buy IPC.

One possible roadblock to a merger between IPC and Emap would be regulatory concerns since the two companies held the majority market shares in the UK consumer magazine industry. Whereas IPC had a total circulation of 10 million for its titles, Emap had a circulation of 6.6 million. Analysts anticipated that if governmental authorities did not block the merger on competition grounds, they would certainly demand that any new company divest itself of some titles.

In November 1997, Time Warner, the giant American magazine and television group, announced a bid for IPC. Time Warner suggested

403

if its bid were successful, it would probably launch a British version of its glossy gossip magazine *People*. Richard Atkinson, president of Time Inc. Atlantic, explained that his company was "deadly serious" about IPC. Time Warner was also concerned about reinforcing its European publishing base.

At about the same time that Time Warner indicated an interest in IPC, two of the world's top venture capital companies, Kohlberg Kravis Roberts (KKR) of the United States and Cinven of the United Kingdom, hinted that they might jointly finance a bid for IPC. If this occurred, it would be one of the biggest management buyouts in British corporate history. Cinven was formed in 1977 as the venture capital arm of the British Coal Pension Fund. The company had now become a leading provider of private equity funding to management buyouts in Europe and specialized in deals larger than 10 million pounds sterling.

SBC Warburg Dillon Read had been appointed to handle the sale for Reed Elsevier. Warburg's spokesman suggested that they had received more than ten expressions of interest in IPC from a variety of trade and financial buyers by the time the first round of bidding closed on December 18 (see Exhibit 1).

By December 28, 1998, the press reported that KKR was no longer involved in discussions with Cinven. The frontrunner in the race to buy IPC was Cinven with a bid for the company of 860 million pounds sterling. This bid was put together by Cinven and an IPC Magazine management team headed by CEO Mike Matthews. Though this bid was at the midpoint in the earlier range of market valuations, it was the highest bid. The bid represented eleven times IPC's 1997 earnings before interest, depreciation and taxes and up to eighteen times estimated after-tax earnings.

Cinven announced on January 5, 1998, that contracts had been exchanged for the acquisition of IPC Magazines from Reed Elsevier. The transaction had kept all parties at Cinven and IPC who were involved working almost twenty-four hours a day over the Christmas holidays.

The Cinven deal called for 580 million pounds sterling in debt financing and the rest of the payment of 280 million pounds sterling in equity. Cinven would put up over half of the equity, and it was reported that IPC's management team led by Mike Matthews would buy a "meaningful" equity stake with a consortium of banks controlling the rest. The headlines in one business journal about this part of the deal read "Media Empire Is Sold to Bosses." While Cinven was backed by a range of equity partners, Goldman Sachs provided the underwriting for all of the debt financing. Commenting on the deal, Brian Linden, a director of Cinven, said:

> *The acquisition of IPC Magazines represents an exceptional investment opportunity for us. The Group has a culture of excellence and rarely does such a high quality and profitable portfolio of titles become available within the publishing industry, especially when also supported by an outstanding distribution business.*
>
> *Under our independent ownership, IPC Magazines can now concentrate on enhancing its position in consumer markets by exploiting its brand strengths, continuing to launch new titles, and through acquisitions. We will provide the resources necessary to develop the group to its full and exciting potential.*

EXHIBIT 1 Summary of Bidding War for IPC in 1997

Company Bidding	Date	Type of Company
Hearst Corporation	October 1997	U.S.-based publisher
Emap PLC	October 1997	British publisher of consumer magazines
Bertelsman AG	October 1997	German media giant
Time Warner	November 1997	U.S.-based magazine and television giant
Kohlberg Kravis Roberts	November 1997	U.S. venture capital firm
Cinven	November 1997	British venture capital firm

The Buyout by Time, Inc.

Although Time Warner was unsuccessful in its earlier bid, in October 2001, Time, Inc. (the publishing division of Time Warner) was able to buy IPC Media for 1.15 billion pounds sterling from Cinven. This was the biggest magazine deal in the United Kingdom and the biggest transatlantic media deal ever. IPC had become the United Kingdom's leading consumer magazine publisher with approximately 100 brands, selling 350 million magazines each year. The focus of the media company was on five areas: women, television, home and garden, leisure, and men's lifestyle and entertainment. Its titles included Britain's biggest-selling magazines *What's on TV* plus *TVTimes, Woman, Woman's Own, Marie Claire, NME, Country Life,* and *Horse & Hound.* In 1998, IPC had purchased Link House Media which added thirty brands to its portfolio, and they continued to launch additional new titles of their own.

In order for the deal between Time, Inc. and Cinven to be completed, European Union regulatory clearances had to be secured and the customary conditions had to be met. All of the formal steps were followed, and the deal was finally executed toward the end of 2001. Don Logan, chairman and CEO of Time, Inc., said of the acquisition:

> This is the perfect acquisition for AOL Time Warner because it accomplishes key strategic goals for the company. With some of the best known consumer publishing brands in Europe, IPC provides Time Inc. with an important presence within the European consumer publishing sector. This acquisition also furthers AOL Time Warner's goal of expanding our operations Outside of the U.S.

The Future of IPC Media and Consumer Magazines

The first decade of the twenty-first century was a challenging time for the print media in the United Kingdom. The industry simultaneously was experiencing increasing paper prices, a slowdown in advertising revenues, and flattening circulation revenues. The industry also was receiving pressure on profit growth because of the strong pound sterling in the international currency markets. By 2004, the threat of consumer magazine price deflation was apparent. Between 2002 and 2003, the average cover price of weekly and monthly magazines fell in real terms. This was attributed to heavily discounted launches of new magazines in major markets. Since the fastest route to growth appeared to be taking market share through launch, the major British publishers were following this strategy which ultimately increased pressure to reduce prices and maintain market share.

In 2004, IPC Media named Andy Cowles, former art director at Rolling Stones, as group creative director. Cowles's primary mandate was to work on revitalizing its offerings in the men's market with the launch of *Nuts*, a men's weekly. By 2007, *Nuts* was the world's leading lifestyle magazine for men. However, launching a new magazine was a costly venture. When IPC launched the new weekly women's magazine *Pick Me Up* in 2005, it gave away more than 3.5 million free copies of the magazine's first edition. While it was possible in past years to launch a successful mainstream magazine from one's kitchen table, that was no longer true. It had become increasingly difficult and expensive to launch a national consumer magazine and much of that was due to changes in the way magazines were sold in Britain. The number of news agents was falling with many of them converting to a convenience store format where magazines are a much smaller part of the product mix.

Meanwhile, supermarkets had emerged as the key channel of distribution for magazine sales. Supermarkets' share of total magazine sales had more than doubled from 11 percent in 1995 to 29 percent in 2002.

By 2007, the big British publishers had refocused on their core businesses. Both IPC and EMAP had been distracted earlier by the dot-com industry, and IPC had changed its name in 2000 to IPC Media to reflect that concern (see Web site at www.ipcmedia.com). While IPC Media was still in the hands of Cinven, the management group that had put together the buyout was looking for an exit strategy to sell off the company. That exit strategy finally came with the appearance of Time Inc.

Also during this decade, the area of "must have" information for scientific and business purposes had become a high-margin operation and was attracting the interest of many industry participants. However, they were encountering

EXHIBIT 2 IPC's Competition—Consumer Magazines: Top Five off the Shelf

IPC Media

Market Share: 22%

Owner: Cinven then Time Inc.

Top Titles: *Loaded, Country Life, Woman's Own, Marie Claire, NME, Nuts, Now*

EMAP Metro, EMAP Elan

Market Share: 13%

Owner: EMAP Group

Top Titles: *FHM, Elle, New Woman, Smash Hits*

BBC Magazines

Market Share: 6.5%

Owner: BBC

Top Titles: *Radio Times, Top of the Pops, Gardener's World, Good Food*

H. Bauer

Market Share: 6%

Owner: Bauer

Top Titles: *Bella, Take a Break, TV Quick*

National Magazines

Market Share: 3%

Owner: Hearst Corporation

Top Titles: *Good Housekeeping, Esquire, Cosmopolitan, Country Living*

difficulties converting consumer magazines into electronic formats. In fact, this latter challenge was the deciding factor in Reed Elsevier's decision to divest IPC.

Because of pressure on profits by increasing paper costs and flat circulation revenues, a favorable strategy in the print media industry appeared to be an emphasis on cost cutting. At the same time, much of IPC's success as the leader in British magazine publishing (see Exhibit 2) had come from a high level of launch activity in new titles. At the conclusion of the deal with Cinven, Mike Matthews (IPC's CEO at the time) commented that IPC had been restrained from buying titles by Reed Elsevier's lack of enthusiasm for consumer magazines.

Even British book publishers were facing challenges in 2007. Bloomsbury Publishing plc, the publisher of the Harry Potter books, reported a huge slump in 2006 annual profits. However, it forecast improved earnings in July 2007 when the final installment of the boy wizard books would be released. The company reported it was under great pressure to find new sources of revenue as their popular Harry Potter series came to an end.

IPC's research indicated that over 80 percent of the population in the United Kingdom were readers of consumer magazines. Analysts had suggested that IPC's stable of titles contained many successful titles but also some dogs. They also suggested that many of IPC's consumer titles had performed less well than rivals owned by companies such as Emap. Another possible strategy for IPC Media was to enter the markets of developing countries of the world that would be underrepresented by consumer magazine titles.

Although IPC originally had launched titles in the fishing area, Emap had come to dominate this market with total circulation almost four times IPC's. Certainly, IPC would have to make a decision about the future of titles that they owned such as

Angler's Mail and *Case & Aviary Birds.* There were other sectors in which IPC had titles, but a weak presence. One of those sectors was golf. IPC had already left the motoring market by selling *Classic Cars* to Emap. Analysts wondered if they would do the same thing with golf. Another title that stood by itself was *Aeroplane.* This market sector was dominated by Key Publishing whom some felt might be considered for a bid target by IPC.

By 2007, IPC Media had watched its recently launched magazine *Now* surge to the top of the celebrity magazines. This had been a very competitive market, and Richard Desmond of Northern and Shell (NAS) was a small player who had attempted to reduce the risks of launching in this segment by lowering cover prices to try to price competition out of the market. Almost a quarter of retail sales in the first decade of the millennium came from magazines launched in the past six years. Interest in the home also was seen to be a growing interest, and BBC magazines, H. Bauer Publishing, and National Magazine Company were planning new launches in this area.

On the question of advertising revenues, the availability of advertising was primarily a function of economic activity and the prevailing phase of the business cycle. Even if advertising revenues were to continue to grow, so would the number of uses of those revenues among a crowded number of mass media businesses such as digital TV channels. In commenting on the earlier bidding war for IPC, one observer suggested that two of the shrewdest venture capital houses were willing to pay a high price for what appeared to be a mature company in a mature business at the top of the industry life cycle. Then later, Time, Inc. paid an even higher price for this publishing giant.

By 2007, IPC Media was a 120-year-old market leader in a mature industry. Some of the important decisions facing the company appeared to be in the area of strategy development related to the possible launching of titles in new areas such as business and recreation or the acquisition of such titles from other companies; maintaining its profitability in the face of price deflation in some segments of the market and rising costs for raw materials; and expanding its publications into the growing markets of the European Union and developing nations.

Notes

1. LEXIS-NEXIS is a U.S. legal and business information database service. Along with International Thomson's WestLaw, it dominates the U.S. market for online legal information.
2. At the time, 1 pound sterling was equal to approximately $1.65.

Traditional Case 8a: Kodak at a Crossroads: The Transition from Film-Based to Digital Photography

Boris Morozov, University of Nebraska at Omaha

Rebecca J. Morris (Faculty Supervisor), University of Nebraska at Omaha

"It's not clear with Kodak if they can successfully compete in the digital world. Are they a buggy whip manufacturer?"[1]

> David Winters, Chief Investment Officer
> Franklin Mutual Advisers, Inc.

"It's a challenging strategy, there's no question about it. This is about our belief in where the company can go, and in our ability to bring growth back to the company in the next three or four years."[2]

> Daniel Carp, CEO
> Eastman Kodak Company

On September 25, 2003, Eastman Kodak Company (Kodak) CEO, Daniel Carp, announced to investors that the company would stop making major investments in its consumer film business after a three year decline in sales. Kodak would devote its cash resources to transform itself into a "digital-oriented growth company." By the end of trading on the day of the announcement, Kodak's stock fell to an 18-year low. Institutional investors criticized Kodak's announced strategy, expressing annoyance at the company's intention to invest in inkjet printing, a business dominated by Hewlett Packard.[3] People at the company's meeting said that Mr. Carp did not provide enough detail on how the strategy would affect earnings before 2006.[4] Investment analyst, Shannon Cross, expressed the concerns of many investors saying, "There are so many questions with regard to Kodak's future strategy…the track record we've seen out of management in terms of being able to hit targets and implement a strategy has been pretty spotty."[5]

Since January 1, 2000, when Mr. Carp took over as chief executive of Kodak, the company's revenues and net income had declined, its shares had dropped by 66 percent, and Standard & Poor's (S&P) had cut Kodak's credit rating by five grades.[6] Kodak had reduced its workforce by 49 percent since 1989, cutting 7,300 employees in 2002.[7] Plans were announced to eliminate up to 6,000 jobs in 2003 to stem future losses, cutting Kodak's traditional photography divisions in Rochester, New York to fewer workers than the firm had employed during the Great Depression.[8] Kodak's income statements for 1993–2003 are presented in Exhibit 1. It's balance sheets for the eleven year period ending 2003 pare presented in Exhibit 2.

Despite investing over $4 billion into digital research and related technologies since the early 1990's, Kodak was characterized as a firm struggling to find its footing in the world of digital photography. Analysts gave Kodak only two to three years to find its way or find itself fading into history. "The question is, can Kodak come up with the new products, the new insights that make sense out of digital?' asked a marketing professor from the Rochester Institute of Technology. "They have to be able to execute fast. They've got to differentiate themselves because they're going very heavily into a commodity market."[9]

The switch by consumers to digital photography was coming much faster than expected and Kodak's traditional film, papers and photofinishing businesses were declining. By the end of 2003, analysts expected that digital cameras would begin to outsell film cameras for the first time in the United States. The digital photography industry was fast-paced and more crowded, offering razor thin profit margins. Kodak was clearly at a crossroads. Would the strategy announced on September 25, 2003 position the company for growth, or would the company continue to decline?

Kodak's Challenges in 2003

With the slogan "you press the button, we do the rest," George Eastman put the first simple camera into the hands of consumers in 1888. In so doing, he changed an awkward and intricate process into something easy to use and accessible to nearly everyone. Since that time, the Eastman Kodak Company had led the way with an abundance of new products and processes to make photography simpler, more useful and more enjoyable. However, in 2003, Kodak's CEO Daniel Carp faced

EXHIBIT 1   Eastman Kodak: Annual Income Statement 1993–2003 ($ in millions except per share)

	2003	2002	2001	2000	1999	1998	1997	1996	1995	1994	1993
Sales	13,317.00	12835	13234	13994	14089	13406	14538	15,968.00	14,980.00	13,557.00	16,364.00
Cost of Goods Sold	8,130.00	7,391.00	7,749.00	7,105.00	6,731.00	6,372.00	6,986.00	7,423.00	7,046.00	6,442.00	6,952.00
Gross Profit	5187	5444	5485	6889	7358	7034.00	7,552.00	8545	7934	7,115.00	9412
SG&A Expense	3,339.00	3,260.00	3,333.00	3,747.00	3,986.00	4,119.00	4,956.00	5,438.00	5,039.00	4,570.00	6,290.00
Operating Income Before Deprec.	1,848.00	2,184.00	2,152.00	3,142.00	3,372.00	2,915.00	2,596.00	3,107.00	2,895.00	2,545.00	3,122.00
Depreciation and Amortization	830	818	919	889	918	853	828	903	916	883	1111
Operating Profit	1,018.00	1366	1233	2253	2454	2062	1768	2204	1979	1662	2011
Interest Expense	148	173.00	219.00	178.00	142.00	110.00	131.00	112.00	108.00	177.00	635.00
Non-Operating Income/Expense	-23.00	-66.00	-29.00	96.00	141.00	210.00	57.00	209.00	109.00	-143.00	18.00
Special Items	-651	-164	-888	-39	-344	-56	-1641	-745	-54	-340	-538
Pretax Income	196.00	963.00	97.00	2,132.00	2,109.00	2,106.00	53.00	1,556.00	1,926.00	1,002.00	856.00
Total Income Taxes	-66.00	153.00	32.00	725.00	717.00	716.00	48.00	545.00	674.00	448.00	381.00
Minority Interest	24	17	-11								
Income Before Extraordinary Items	238.00	793.00	76.00	1,407.00	1,392.00	1,390.00	5.00	1,011.00	1,252.00	554.00	475.00
Preferred Dividends	0.00	0.00	0.00	0.00	0.00	0.00	0.00	0.00	0.00	0.00	0.00
Available for Common	238	793	76	1407	1392	1390	5	1011	1252	554	475
Savings Due to Common Stock Equivalents	0.00	0	0	0	0	0	0	0	0	0	0
Adjusted Available for Common	238.00	793.00	76.00	1,407.00	1,392.00	1,390.00	5.00	1,011.00	1,252.00	554.00	475.00
Extraordinary Items	0	0	0	0	0	0	0	0	0	-266	-2182
Discontinued Operations	27.00	-23	0	0	0	0	0	277.00	0.00	269.00	192.00
Adjusted Net Income	**265.00**	**770.00**	**76.00**	**1,407.00**	**1,392.00**	**1,390.00**	**5.00**	**1,288.00**	**1,252.00**	**557.00**	**-1,515.00**
EPS Excl. Extra Items & Disc Op	0.83	2.72	0.26	4.62	4.38	4.30	0.01	3.00	3.67	1.65	1.44
EPS Incl. Extra Items & Disc Op	0.92	2.64	0.26	4.62	4.38	4.30	0.01	3.82	3.67	1.66	-4.62
EPS Diluted Excl. Extra Items & Disc Op	0.83	2.72	0.26	4.59	4.33	4.24	0.01	3	3.58	1.63	1.44
EPS Diluted Incl. Extra Items & Disc Op	0.92	2.64	0.26	4.59	4.33	4.24	0.01	3.82	3.58	1.63	-4.62
EPS Basic from Operations	2.37	2.77	2.37	4.73	5.09	4.42	3.52	4.50	3.77	2.40	2.60
EPS Diluted from Ops	2.37	2.77	2.37	4.70	5.03	4.37	3.46	4.50	3.77		
Dividends Per Share	1.15	1.8	1.77	1.76	1.76	1.76	1.76	1.6	1.6	1.6	1.6
Com Shares for Basic EPS	286.50	291.5	290.6	304.9	318	323.3	327.4	337.40	341.50	335.70	328.30
Com Shares for Diluted EPS	286.60	291.70	291.00	306.60	321.50	327.80	331.90			340.20	331.20

EXHIBIT 2 Eastman Kodak: Annual Balance Sheet 1993-2003 ($ millions)

	2003	2002	2001	2000	1999	1998	1997	1996	1995	1994	1993
ASSETS											
Cash & Equivalents	1,261.00	578	451	251	393	500	752	1,796.00	1,811.00	2,068.00	1,966.00
Net Receivables	2,389.00	2,234.00	2,337.00	2,653.00	2,537.00	2,527.00	2,271.00	2,738.00	3,145.00	3,064.00	3,463.00
Inventories	1,075.00	1,062.00	1,137.00	1,718.00	1,519.00	1,424.00	1,252.00	1,575.00	1,660.00	1,480.00	1,913.00
Other Current Assets	730	660	758	869	995	1,148.00	1,200.00	856	693	1,071.00	679
Total Current Assets	5,455.00	4,534.00	4,683.00	5,491.00	5,444.00	5,599.00	5,475.00	6,965.00	7,309.00	7,683.00	8,021.00
Gross Property & Equip	13,277.00	13,288.00	12,982.00	12,963.00	13,289.00	13,482.00	12,824.00	12,585.00	12,652.00	12,299.00	13,311.00
Accumulated Depreciation	8,183.00	7,868.00	7,323.00	7,044.00	7,342.00	7,568.00	7,315.00	7,163.00	7,275.00	7,007.00	6,945.00
Net Property & Equipment	5,094.00	5,420.00	5,659.00	5,919.00	5,947.00	5,914.00	5,509.00	5,422.00	5,377.00	5,292.00	6,366.00
Investments at Equity	426	382	360	0	2	3	25	31	74	@CF	@CF
Other Investments	310	53	85							338	187
Intangibles	1,678.00	981	948	947	982	1,232.00	548	581	536	616	4,312.00
Deferred Charges	1,147.00	972	482	0	0	0	0	0	0	0	0
Other Assets	708	1,027.00	1,145.00	1,855.00	1,995.00	1,985.00	1,588.00	1,439.00	1,181.00	1,039.00	1,439.00
TOTAL ASSETS	14,818.00	13,369.00	13,362.00	14,212.00	14,370.00	14,733.00	13,145.00	14,438.00	14,477.00	14,968.00	20,325.00
LIABILITIES											
Long Term Debt Due in One Year	457.00	387	156	150	2	78	3	245.00	0.00	0.00	350.00
Notes Payable	489.00	1,055.00	1,378.00	2,056.00	1,161.00	1,440.00	608.00	296.00	586.00	371.00	305.00
Accounts Payable	834.00	720.00	674.00	817.00	940.00	947.00	943.00	966.00	799.00	703.00	737.00
Taxes Payable	654	584	544	572	612	593.00	567.00	603	567	1,701.00	420
Accrued Expenses	1,696.00	1,739.00	1,635.00	1,358.00	1,460.00	1,289.00	1,080.00	1,160.00	731.00	616.00	609.00
Other Current Liabilities	1,177.00	892.00	967.00	1,262.00	1,594.00	1,831.00	1,976.00	2,147.00	1,960.00	2,344.00	2,489.00
Total Current Liabilities	5,307.00	5,377.00	5,354.00	6,215.00	5,769.00	6,178.00	5,177.00	5,417.00	4,643.00	5,735.00	4,910.00
Long Term Debt	2302	1164	1666	1166	936	504	585	559	665	660	6853
Deferred Taxes	81	52	81	61	59	69	64	102	97	95	79
Minority Interest	45.00	70	84	93	98	128	24				
Other Liabilities	3819	3,929.00	3,283.00	3,249.00	3,596.00	3,866.00	4,134.00	3,626.00	3,951.00	4,461.00	5,127.00
TOTAL LIABILITIES	11554	10592	10468	10784	10458	10745	9984	9704	9356	10951	16969
EASTMAN KODAK EQUITY	38,324.00	38323	38322	36861	36495	36130	35765	35,400.00	35,034.00	34,669.00	34,304.00
Total Preferred Stock	0.00	0.00	0.00	0.00	0.00	0.00	0.00	0.00	0.00	0.00	0.00
Common Stock	978.00	978.00	978.00	978.00	978.00	978.00	978.00	978.00	974.00	966.00	948.00
Capital Surplus	842.00	849.00	849.00	871.00	889.00	902.00	914.00	910.00	803.00	515.00	213.00
Retained Earnings	7296	6840	6834	7387	6850	6052	5141	6006	5277	4493	4234
Less: Treasury Stock	5852	5890	5767	5808	4805	3944	3872	3160	1933	1957	2039
Common Equity	3,264.00	2777	2894	3428	3912	3988	3161	4734	5121	4017	3356
TOTAL EQUITY	3,264.00	2,777.00	2,894.00	3,428.00	3,912.00	3,988.00	3,161.00	4,734.00	5,121.00	4,017.00	3,356.00
TOTAL LIABILITIES & EQUITY	14818	13369	13362	14212	14370	14733	13145	14438	14477	14968	20325
COMMON SHARES OUTSTAN.	286.58	285.933	290.93	290.485	310.421	322.798	323.067	331.84	345.89	339.76	330.57

challenges similar to those George Eastman faced over a century ago: How to make the process of printing the picture even easier in an era of digital technologies.

The economy was in a recession in 2003, major market indexes were still at a low level and investors were cautious. As a result of an unfavorable economic situation, shareholder wealth had been cut to a portion of what it was during the phenomenal technology-based run-up of the market in the late 1990's. The bursting of the technology bubble proved that the absence of a strong profit-generating business model could not be replaced with information technology solutions.

Kodak's moves paralleled those at many companies whose comfortable business models were threatened by rapid changes in information technology. When asked whether Kodak had moved into digital photography soon enough Carp replied, "I saw my first digital camera inside Kodak in 1982. Today, we're arguably one of the top three providers of digital cameras in the U.S. So we did the right thing. At the same time, we shouldn't have walked away from the historical film businesses before they turned down, because it would have destroyed value."[10]

Under slumping economic and competitive market conditions, Kodak faced tough pressure from its existing competitors as well as from new rivals in the area of digital photography (called by Kodak—"Infoimaging"). Infoimaging was the use of technology to combine images and information—creating the potential to profoundly change how people and businesses communicated.[11] Also, it was a $385 billion industry composed of devices (digital cameras and personal data assistants (PDAs)), infrastructure (online networks and delivery systems for images), services and media (software, film and paper) enabling people to access, analyze and print images.

Although Kodak had invested $4 billion[12] into digital research and related technologies and spent many years perfecting its digital cameras, Kodak's status as an iconic brand was threatened by the technological shift away from its cash-cow business of traditional film and film processing. In July 2003, Kodak reported flat sales and a 60 percent drop in second-quarter profits.

When announcing the latest rounds of workforce reductions in July, 2003, Carp expressed his perspective on Kodak's challenges saying, "I think we're at the point where we have to get on with reality. The consumer traditional business is going to begin a slow decline, though it's not going to fall of a cliff." Was Kodak closer to the edge of the cliff than Carp thought? Could Kodak survive and thrive in the digital shift? Or would Kodak fade from history like a piece of film exposed to the light?

Growth in Digital Photography

Three years into the 21st century and the digital camera market was expanding at a fast pace. This was a major transfer from the previous decade of consumer photography as a largely mature market. Color film photography (also known as "traditional photography") was a technology rich in history and closely tied to the art world. Eastman Kodak popularized color photography after the introduction of Kodachrome slide film in 1935.[13] Color print photography using 35mm film grew rapidly in 1961 after the introduction of Kodacolor II print film.[14]

Demand for Digital Cameras

Digital photography was catching on fast in mainstream America as digital camera prices fell and image quality increased. The number of U.S. households owning a digital camera passed 1 million in 1997. By 2002, more than 23 million households owned digital cameras. This represented a 57 percent increase over 2001. Demand for digital cameras was expected to continue to increase with more than 33 million households expected to own a digital camera in 2003. The growth in digital cameras is shown in the figure below. Figure 1 also shows the decline in the number of households owning traditional film cameras. The 2.6 percent decline in traditional film cameras in 2002 was attributed in part to the growing demand for digital cameras and the rising popularity of one-time use cameras. Market research projected continued further declines in traditional camera ownership.[15] Declines were also projected for sales of traditional film (down by 4 percent) and film processing (down by 3 percent) in 2003.

Although digital photography was making significant inroads with the mass market, technically sophisticated users were adopting digital technology

FIGURE 1 Number of Households Owning Cameras Film vs. Digital Modes (Number of U.S. households in March 2003 = 108.7 million)

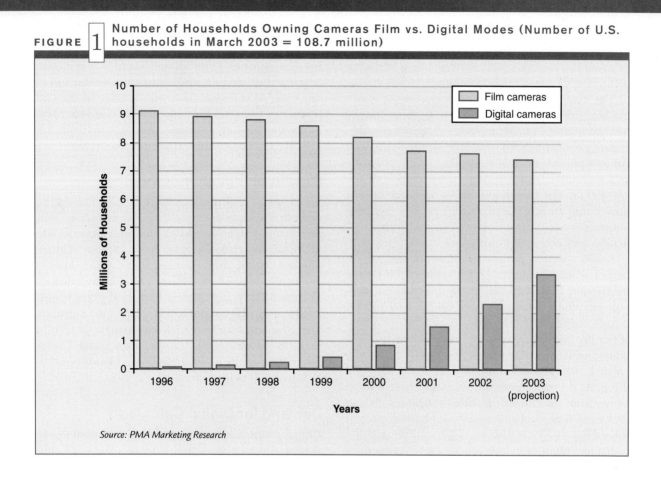

Source: PMA Marketing Research

at a higher rate. Among Internet-connected U.S. households, the estimate was that 60 percent had converted to digital cameras by the end of 2002.

Digital cameras generated a significant portion of industry revenues, accounting for $2.96 billion in revenues for 2002. This figure represented an increase of 22 percent over 2001 revenues. Revenues for traditional film, film processing, and traditional cameras had declined during this same period as shown in Figure 2.

Industry experts predicted that the consumer shift to digital photography would be nearly complete by 2008 with sales of digital cameras nearly replacing sales of traditional film cameras (such as 35 mm film cameras).[16] One-time use cameras would continue to be popular, thus providing continued, although reduced, demand for film processing services.

What made digital cameras so attractive for consumers? Digital cameras gave users capabilities that were not possible with traditional cameras. Experts attributed the growth in digital photography to four factors—instant preview, sleek design, features and price.[17] The technology of digital cameras allowed users to instantly view the shots they had taken and reshoot until they were satisfied with the results. The sleek design of many digital cameras made carrying one a fashion statement or a must-have item for teenagers and young professionals. Camera features also allowed digital users to capture short movies and to manipulate the images using photo-editing software that often came bundled with the camera. Price declines had made digital cameras much more affordable.

Michelle Slaughter, Director of Digital Photography Trends at InfoTrends Research Group

412

FIGURE 2 Consumer Photographic Market Revenue (in billions of $)

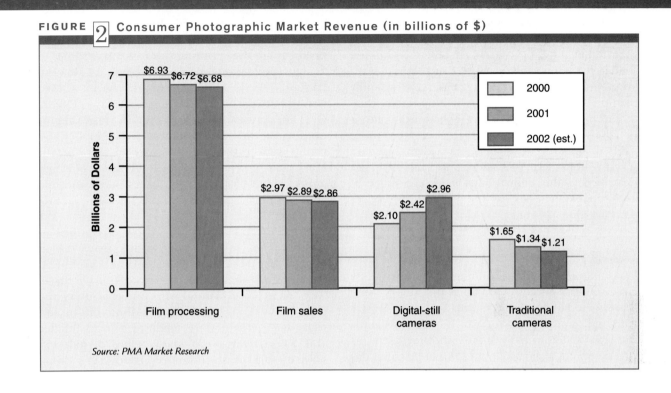

Source: PMA Market Research

described digital cameras as an "essential communications device" for consumers.[18] "Consumers are becoming accustomed to the immediacy of digital photography and are integrating digital photos into their daily communications with friends and family and for work. As a result, digital cameras have a higher intrinsic value to consumers than film cameras. This, in turn, paves the way for digital camera sales to exceed film camera sales," predicted Slaughter.

Although the price of digital cameras had declined sharply, the average price of a digital camera was still significantly more expensive than for 35 mm cameras. In 2002, the average price for a digital camera was $328.[19] When compared with an average price of $137 for a 35 mm camera, it was no surprise that more than half of digital camera buyers were in households where the annual income was $75,000 or more. Half of the digital camera buyers in 2002 were between the ages of 35 and 54. Buyers in this age group and income bracket were in the prime segment for capturing family photos and often traveled more frequently. Age and income statistics for digital camera buyers in 2002 are shown in the table below.

Percentage of Consumers Who Bought Digital Cameras in 2002

By Age	
Age Group	Percent
18–24	9%
25–34	25%
35–54	50%
55 or older	17%
By Income	
Household Income	Percent
Less than $25,000	6%
$25,000–$49,999	19%
$50,000–$74,999	23%
$75,000 or more	52%

Source: Yin, S. (July 1, 2003). Picture This, American Demographics, pg. 6.

Although market research showed that men tended to purchase digital cameras more frequently than females (58 percent vs. 42 percent), women tended to be the primary users of the equipment.[20] Women were described as the preservers of family memories and were increasingly using digital cameras to capture birthday parties, holiday celebrations or family vacations. Women were becoming more likely to spur the decision to buy a digital camera for the household.[21] Women with children were described as the "most photo active consumers"[22] and were expected to lead the demand for services such as digital printing.

Digital Printing Trends

Early adopters of digital photography consistently cited sending photos by e-mail as the number one reason for taking pictures with digital cameras.[23] Although mothers might email friends and family the latest batch of baby photos, showing them off to a crowd gathered around a computer screen did not provide the same gratification and ease of use as looking at photos in an album. Consumers saw the ability to preview digital photos and to print only those they wanted as one of the strengths of the medium.

Few digital images ever actually printed on paper. In 2000, only 12 percent of all digital images taken were printed. By 2002, this had increased to 20 percent of images taken.[24] Trends in the destination for digital images are shown in the table below.

Destination of Digital Pictures After Capture

Picture Destination	Year		
	2000	2001	2002
Save, store or keep	63%	68%	71%
Email	16%	13%	13%
Print	12%	14%	20%

Source: Photo Marketing Assocation International, (April, 2003). The Path From Pixels to Print: The Challenge of Bringing Digital Imaging to the Mass Market.. Retrieved November 22, 2004 from http://www.pmai.org/pdf/0403_pixels_to_prints.pdf.

The low ratio of printed photos to digital images was a big problem for the companies wanting to profit from the printing process. According to analysts estimations, companies such as Hewlett-Packard (NYSE: HPQ), Lexmark (NYSE: LXM), Canon (NYSE: CAJ), Seiko Epson, Olympus (NYSE: CAJ) and Eastman Kodak (NYSE: EK) made almost nothing on the printers they sold. The money and profits were in the materials used to make prints. For instance, in summer 2003, HP saw profit margins of about 65 percent on inkjet paper and ink, and roughly 30 percent margins on laser printing supplies.[25]

Consumers had a wide variety of options to choose from in obtaining prints from digital images. Digital photographers printed 2.1 billion images from digital cameras in 2003. Of these, 77 percent were printed with home printers, 6.4 percent were ordered from online photo services, 8.7 percent were made at a local retailer and 3.6 percent were made using digital self-service kiosks. Consumers reported using "some other means" to produce 4.2 percent of all digital prints in 2003.[26]

Most consumers used their personal computers and home printers for printing their digital pictures, however, these were often perceived as lower quality, more time consuming and more expensive than traditional film prints. More than half of digital camera users indicated they would print more digital images if they could make high-quality prints on their home printers.[27] Almost as many also indicated the printing of digital images at home would need to be easier and less time-consuming. Consumers often got confused while transferring pictures from their digital cameras to their computers. "There are so many ways for people to get into trouble when they try to print photos at home," said Kristy Holch, principal at Infotrends Research Group.

Online photo services provided another option. Services such as Snapfish, Shutterfly and Ofoto allowed consumers to upload their photos, preview, crop and manipulate them and obtain high quality snapshots by mail. Pictures could further be shared online with friends and relatives via online albums. Custom calendars, cards, books and mouse pads could be ordered with the customer's photos. Prints were priced significantly less than those printed at home at 19-29 cents per print versus the 62 cent cost of a print made on a Kodak Easyshare printer.[28] Disadvantages to online photo services included slow photo uploads (especially for consumers with dial-up Internet connections) and the four to six days it took to receive the prints by mail.

In September 2003, 18.4 million people visited online photography sites that could be used for sharing and printing, according to Nielsen//Net Ratings. Yahoo! Photos had 4.7 million unique visitors, followed by the Time Warner AOL unit, You've Got Pictures, with 2.7 million. Ofoto and Snapfish each had 1.67 million users and Kodak's online site drew 1.5 million.

Local retailers such as Costco, Wal-Mart and Walgreens provided another option for obtaining prints of digital images, however, these services failed to catch on with consumers. Many consumers did not realize that they could drop off their digital camera's memory card at the photo counter for printing. Others were reluctant to entrust the expensive memory cards to film processors. Retailers attempted to resolve these problems by adding self-service photo printing kiosks in their stores. Consumers could use the kiosks to edit photos and make their own prints from digital memory cards. Retailers launched advertising emphasizing ease of use and the immediacy of prints from the kiosks to overcome consumer's lack of awareness of this option. Expectations for growth in print volume at self-service kiosks were strong. "As digital camera users begin to use photo kiosks, print volumes on photo kiosks will increase dramatically," reported Kerry Flatley, a research analyst.[29] "Digital camera customers…will use photo kiosks as a high-volume source for their original photo prints," Flatley stated.

Impact on Demand for Traditional Film

The widespread adoption of digital photography had had a toll on demand for traditional film and film processing. The volume of prints made from traditional films in 2002 declined by 700,000 over 2001 volumes. During the same time frame, digital prints grew by 1.3 million units. Digital images accounted for 6.1 percent of the total volume of prints made in 2002, up from only 2.4 percent in 2001.[30] Film sales were expected to decline by 4 percent in 2003 as shown in Figure 3.

One-time-use cameras were popular with consumers due to their convenience and low price, although the growth had slowed from 25 percent in 1999 to 8 percent in 2003. Film processing which included both film rolls and one-time-use cameras had declined significantly over the period from 1999 to 2003 due to the decrease in the use of traditional film among digital camera owners and the economic slow down.

Other Digital Imaging Options

Another interesting market situation was developing—photo-capable cell phones. According to a survey done by experts in September 2003, more cell phones with integrated digital cameras were sold in the first half of the year than digital cameras.[31] Research group Strategy Analytics stated 25 million camera phones were purchased by consumers worldwide in the first half of year 2003, compared with only 20 million digital still cameras.

"This is a milestone event, but it is just the first step towards the industry goal of getting a camera phone in every pocket," said Neil Mawston, senior analyst at Strategy Analytics' Global Wireless Practice. Mobile operators wanted to get customers to send picture messages regularly over their recently enhanced networks, in hopes of replicating the surprise success of text messaging. As the market for voice calls was getting more competitive, non-voice data revenues could prove vital for operators' profitability.

However, security and privacy concerns among companies represented one potential problem for the camera phone market. Besides, Strategy Analytics said camera phones represented no major threat to the digital still camera market because the difference in picture quality between the two technologies was too great. A Canon marketing director expressed the view of most camera manufacturers, calling even the two-megapixel camera phone just a "distraction." "It's good to have mobile phone cameras," the marketing

FIGURE 3

Annual Change in Unit Sales of Film Rolls, One-Time-Use Cameras, and Film Processing

Trends: 1993 through 2003

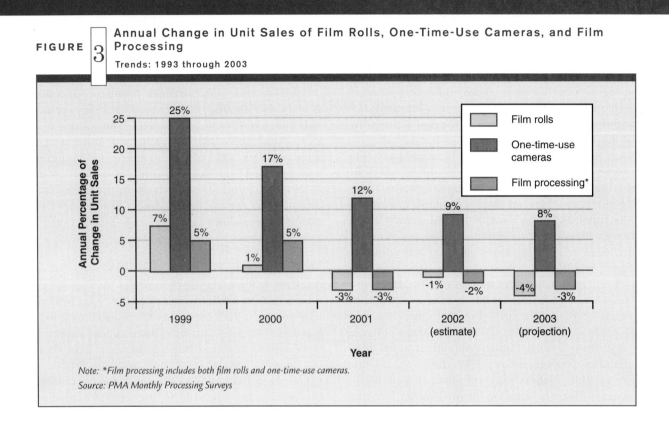

Note: *Film processing includes both film rolls and one-time-use cameras.

Source: PMA Monthly Processing Surveys

director said, "but their functionalities are limited in terms of storage, picture quality, zooming functionality, and power supply. Consumers will still go for the 'real camera' even though they have camera phones. Cameras on phones are just add-ons to give phones more functionalities."[32]

The Economist reported that camera-phones might create a "nightmare scenario" for the traditional photography industry by hastening the decline of printed photos.[33] As camera phones improved, consumers might view images on-screen on phones, PCs, televisions, or even by beaming photos to a wireless-enabled picture frame. If this came to pass, "printing could become a niche, like film is expected to," said Chris Chute of IDC.[34] Increased popularity of on-screen photo viewing would prove damaging for the photography industry, which depended on revenues from film processing and printing. Digital photography was threatening the first source of revenue. If camera-phones caught on, cell phone operators could capture the second

source, earning revenues by charging users for transmitting images.

Global Trends in Photography

Income distribution among countries influenced the sales of the cameras around the world. While sales of digital cameras were booming in developed countries like the U.S. and Japan, consumers from emerging economies such as China bought for traditional cameras.

China was developing into a center of photography—and was doing so more rapidly than anyone would have expected only a few years ago. More than five million cameras were sold in China in 2002, and 400,000 of these were digital models (see Figure 4). This figure was set to increase, and Chinese consumers were expected to buy more than three million digital cameras by 2005. However, there were also other reasons why China was so important for the photographic and imaging sector, since every market segment was still

416

FIGURE 4 Camera Sales in China

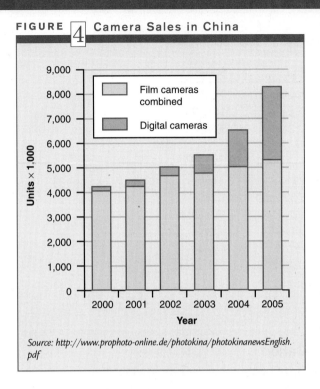

Source: http://www.prophoto-online.de/photokina/photokinanewsEnglish.pdf

FIGURE 5 Market Shares in Digital Imaging

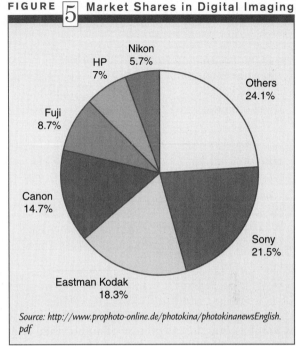

Source: http://www.prophoto-online.de/photokina/photokinanewsEnglish.pdf

growing in this country, not just the one for digital devices.

There were still a lot of additional sales potential left unexploited. Per capita consumption of films in China in 2003 was a mere 0.1 a year compared to an average of 3.1 films in Europe and 3.6 films per year in the U.S. China was still a long way from reaching market saturation even though film sales were rapidly increasing. Revenues from digital camcorders, photographic paper, data projectors, scanners and printers were growing rapidly as well.

Competitive Standings and Digital Strategies

In the segment of traditional photography, Kodak's main brand competitors were Canon USA, Sony Electronics Inc, and Fuji film. According to analysts' estimations, Kodak's competitors in the digital photography industry (or, as it was called by Kodak - *Info Imaging*) were Sony, HP, and Fuji Film (Kodak's biggest competitor in the area of traditional photography).

Eastman Kodak captured 18.3 percent of the market, compared with the 15.3 percent share it had in the first six months of 2003. Sony (nyse: SNE) led the market with a 21.5 percent share, with Canon (nyse: CAJ), Fuji (nasdaq: FUJIY), Hewlett-Packard (nyse: HPQ) and Nikon following Kodak with 14.7 percent, 8.7 percent, 7 percent and 5.7 percent, respectively.[35] The market shares are shown in Figure 5.

Although Kodak was a major player in the photography market (both digital and traditional), it was far from being the biggest (see table below). Eastman Kodak's earnings before taxes, depreciation, and amortization (EBITDA) of $1.2 billion were just a fraction of its closest competitor Fuji film's of $3.11 billion. Other competitors Sony and Canon had EBIDTA of $7.06 and $6.05 billion respectively.

Sony

Sony was on the digital wave since the mid-1990's,[36] when it introduced its first Play Station. Nobuyuki Idei, Chairman and CEO, played a key role in moving Sony into the digital network era

417

Competitor Comparison For 2003

	Kodak	Canon	Fuji	Sony
Market Capitalization	8.32B	43.19B	15.80B	36.56B
Employees	70,000	98,873	72,569	161,100
Revenue Growth	-3.00%	11.80%		9.10%
Gross Margin	32.17%	50.31%	41.64%	25.28%
EBITDA	1.20B	6.05B	3.11B	7.06B
Operating. Margins	2.79%	14.21%	6.20%	1.25%
Net Income	238.00M	2.62B	532.00M	169.89M
Earnings Per Share	0.83	2.948	1.036	0.09
Price Earnings Ratio	34.96	16.69	29.71	440.44

by emphasizing the integration of audio visual and information technology products. He was responsible for Sony's image campaign, "Do you dream in Sony?" and helped coin the term "digital dream kids."[37]

Sony was a Japanese consumer electronics and multimedia giant. The firm produced music, movies and television shows as well as the devices to bring them to the consumer. The electronics division produced video game consoles, PDAs, DVD and MP3 players, digital camcorders, digital cameras, computers and car audio products.

A team of developers gathered at a Sony laboratory in 1995 to "develop a digital still camera filled with enjoyment."[38] Sony's Cyber-Shot cameras were developed as the first "self-shooting" digital still cameras. Unburdened by a legacy in traditional film, Sony developers relied on their experience as a leading consumer technology company to develop a full line of digital cameras targeted to men and women between the ages of 25-55. Sony positioned their cameras at a premium or fair price based on cutting-edge technology and design. "You'll never see Sony offer a $99 camera," predicted one senior digital imaging analyst.[39] Sony's digital cameras ranged from about $180 for a point-and-shoot model to just under $1,000 for an advanced-featured "Pro" model.

Canon

Japan's Canon Inc. had come a long way since its days as a producer of cheap cameras. Much of Canon's success against its archrival had come on the watch of the company's president, Fujio Mitarai. A nephew of a Canon founder, Mitarai spent 23 years working in New York before returning to Japan in 1995 to head the company. Canon operated in the document reproduction markets producing copiers, fax machines and scanners. Canon's optical segment produced diverse products such as television broadcast lenses and semiconductor manufacturing equipment. The camera division produced camcorders, binoculars, lenses, and digital cameras. Canon was relatively late to the market with its digital products, but the products it had introduced were hits.[40]

Canon U.S.A. Inc., a subsidiary of Canon Inc. (NYSE:CAJ), on 11/21/2001 launched a marketing campaign featuring its PowerShot digital cameras and Bubble Jet printers working in concert to showcase Canon's leadership in digital photo solutions for the 2001 holiday season.[41] "The camera and printer are the stars of this 'production' number from beginning to end. Canon has a 60-year history in optics/lens technology for cameras, as well as creating its own printing technology—a combination our competitors cannot claim. By showcasing the 'digital duet' of our digital cameras and printers, we show the viewer that Canon products create picture perfect results that are unmatched by our competition," said Rick Booth, assistant director of advertising for the Canon Photographic Products Group.

Canon offered digital cameras for a wide variety of users at different price points. A simple point-and-shoot model was priced at slightly less than $200, while a professional-level digital single lens reflex (SLR) camera sold for almost $8,000.

Fuji

Fuji, a long time rival of Kodak, offered a complete portfolio of imaging, information, and document products, services, and e-solutions to retailers, consumers, professionals, and business customers. They went digital since 1998, when they introduced the first digital camera. "Fuji's solution was to start a suite of online options to share, order, pay for and collect digital photos," Dane Anderson, of International Data Corp (IDC), pointed out. By the summer of 2003, Image Intelligence™ was Fuji's program for digital photography. This system was an integrated system of digital image-processing software technologies that came from the culmination of nearly 70 years of imaging expertise.

Fuji's products such as traditional film, photo paper, developing chemicals and nondigital printers accounted for 42 percent of the firm's 2003 sales. Experts expected the percentage of sales due to traditional photography to shrink to 31 percent by 2006.[42]

Fuji introduced digital minilabs in the market. A minilab was a service similar to traditional picture printing where consumers could print their digital printers by dropping off their digital memory cards and returning later to pick up finished prints. Fuji Films with more than 5,000 labs in the market place had about 60 percent of the U.S. digital minilab market, including deals to put machines in 2,500 Wal-Mart and about 800 Walgreen outlets. Those two chains handled about 40 percent of the U.S. photo-processing market.

Hewlett Packard (HP)

HP provided consumer and enterprise customers with a full-range of technology-based products, including personal computers, servers, storage devices, networking equipment and software. The company also included an IT service organization that was among the world's largest. Known primarily by consumers for its dominance in computer printers, HP expanded into the digital imaging segment as a way to continue to fuel demand for HP printers and ink cartridges.

HP's breadth also provided an important advantage to consumers according to HP Vice President, Chris Morgan. "We think consumers are going to want their products to be interoperable. Digital photography is a natural extension given our strength in computing and image processing," said Morgan. Consumers will "want to move content from camera to computer to email or DVD, from camcorder to computer to TV, or just skip the computer and go directly from device to playback system. That plays to our advantage. No only are we the No. 1 consumer computer company in the world, we think that our understanding of big-business ecosystems will be a powerful advantage in helping us develop these solutions," he continued.[43]

HP's digital cameras ranged from about $100-$400. As part of the firm's strategy to provide solutions that were "interoperable" or that allowed consumers to connect various devices, HP offered several different camera and photo printer bundles and camera and docking station bundles.[44]

HP had a PC dubbed PhotoSmart, which had a built-in docking slot for uploading photos only from HP's latest digital cameras and unified photo software that handled downloading, storing, exchanging and printing photos.

HP was also trying to get more people to share digital pictures electronically because that got more people making prints. HP's Instant Share software allowed consumers to preprogram e-mail addresses and photo-sharing Web sites into their cameras. After making pictures, users specified where they wanted them sent and the pictures were mailed the next time the camera was connected to the PC.

Nikon

Nikon was well known for its traditional photography products—35 mm cameras, lenses and other consumer optical products. Nikon also produced equipment used in the manufacturing of semiconductors and a broad range of other optical products such as binoculars, microscopes, eyewear and surveying equipment. Imaging products such as camera equipment comprised 57.6 percent of Nikon's net sales in 2003.[45]

Nikon targeted amateur photographers with its line of "Coolpix" cameras. These cameras ranged in price from about $140-$850. The "Coolpix" line offered a full range of stylish and simple to use cameras designed to appeal to the first-time user and the more advanced photography hobbyist. Nikon also offered a line of digital single lens reflex (SLR) cameras that targeted advanced and professional photographers that wanted high-featured, easy-to-use digital cameras. Digital SLR cameras permitted the use of interchangeable lens and were designed to provide sharper, clearer images at faster shutter speeds than other digital cameras. Nikon digital SLR cameras ranged in price from $900 (camera body only) to well over $1,200. Nikon used the trademarked phrase, "Nikon . . . If the picture matters, the camera matters" in the marketing of its cameras.[46]

Kodak's Photography Unit

Eastman Kodak was primarily engaged in developing, manufacturing and marketing traditional and digital imaging products, services and solutions for consumers, professionals, healthcare providers, and other commercial customers. The company operated in four segments: Components Group, Health Imaging (18 percent of company's total revenue), Commercial Imaging (11 percent of total sales), and Photography (70 percent of revenue).

The Photography segment included traditional and digital product offerings for consumers, professional photographers and the entertainment industry. This segment combined traditional and digital photography and photographic services in all its forms—consumer, advanced amateur, and professional. Kodak manufactured and marketed various components of these systems, including films (consumer, professional and motion picture), photographic papers, processing services, photofinishing equipment, photographic chemicals and cameras (including one-time-use and digital).

Product and service offerings included kiosks and scanning systems to digitize and enhance images, digital media for storing images and a network for transmitting images. In addition, other digitization options were available to stimulate more pictures in use, adding to the consumption of film and paper. These products served different groups of customers like amateur photographers, as well as professional, motion picture and television customers. Technically, Eastman Kodak provided the services of picture creation to every one who requested it, adjusting these services for specific groups of consumers.

Since Kodak's "bread-and-butter" unit was its photography unit, the stock's price performance heavily depended on this unit's performance. The firm's stock price declined from mid-$80 to $20 per share (see Figure 6) as revenues from traditional photography declined. In June 2003, Standard & Poor's (S&P) Rating Service placed Kodak on a CreditWatch with negative implications, expressing concerns that economic, competitive and leisure travel pressures would continue to impair Kodak's sales and earnings.[47] S&P analysts expressed concern that Kodak's transition to digital imaging would hurt future profitability for the firm by reducing high-margin film sales. Kodak's migration to digital technologies might also require additional restructuring as the firm adapted to evolving market conditions. Kodak's financial statements are provided in Exhibit 1 and Exhibit 2.

Kodak's restructuring actions prior to 2003 were primarily of a tactical nature. Three modifications between 1999 and 2003 indicated that company's traditional film and photography businesses, while still hugely important as a source of cash, were becoming less of a central focus in a world where images were increasingly captured as bytes and bits. These modifications signaled management's attempt to keep up with market, meaning that Eastman Kodak was losing the role of market maker.

Tough Choices for a Traditional Photography Company

Although it did not announce a change to a digital strategy until 2003, Eastman Kodak was moving towards this objective through acquisitions of the smaller companies, successful in the digital area. "Digital imaging is going to be like the cellular telephone business," Fisher [former Kodak's CEO] predicted in 1997. "Highly competitive, very high

FIGURE 6 Eastman Kodak Co.

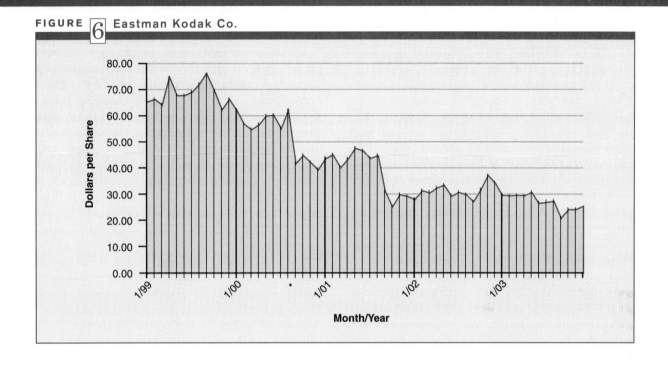

growth, good profits for the leader, but not for the followers."[48]

In general, Kodak's performance in the new market conditions was varied. In some areas it was successful, in others it was not. Kodak President and Chief Operating Officer Antonio Perez had conceded that the company was behind the curve in printers, an area it regarded as key to its future digital profits. This was not for lack of effort. A joint attempt in year 2000 to introduce a desktop photo ink-jet printer with Lexmark flopped, partly because the product's direct-to-camera interface never caught on. Most consumers made their digital prints via PC-to-printer links. Kodak said its newly introduced system for docking a thermal printer with a PC, designed for greater ease of use, was faring much better, and would generate a respectable $100 million in sales in its first year [2003].

Kodak entered the market segment of digital minilabs. However, due to technical problems, it suffered some losses. Kodak purchased machines made by a manufacturing partner that broke down frequently, printed pictures of poor quality and frustrated customers. Fuji Photo Film Co.'s rival Frontier machines, meanwhile, were gaining

market share. Kodak changed its minilab partner to Noritsu Koki Co. of Japan. As result of this change, Kodak mentioned that the machines had been "well received."

Phogenix, a joint venture between Hewlett-Packard and Kodak to develop smaller digital photo printers for retail outlets, crumbled in May 2003 because the technology already had become obsolete by the time the machines were brought to market. In a joint statement, Matthias Freund, Chairman of the Phogenix Board of Directors and Chief Operating Officer of Kodak's Consumer Imaging Products and Services business, and Mary Peery, Member of the Phogenix Board of Directors and Senior Vice President of HP's Digital Imaging & Publishing business, said, "Both HP and Kodak believe the technology being developed by Phogenix continues to offer a viable solution for on-site digital photo processing. However, based on the anticipated return on invested capital for the parent companies, each company has separately decided to focus its own investments on other opportunities."[49]

The Phogenix labs, small enough to fit in stores typically unequipped to house typical automated film-developing machines, would have cost retailers

421

about $40,000, but could produce only about 250 prints an hour, compared with more than 1,000 for the Noritsu mini-lab [Fuji's minilab]. Fuji's system cost $139,000 to $245,000, analysts estimated.

Kodak had had some notable digital successes. Kodak's popular EasyShare cameras were the second-best-selling digital cameras in the U.S. in the first half of 2003, behind only those of Sony. After successfully focusing on the lower-end of the camera market, Kodak was planning to begin selling more-expensive digital cameras aimed at tech-savvy shutterbugs. The company was diversifying its products line's depth and width, aiming at new segments of the market.

Finally, Kodak believed it had a strong management team. CEO Daniel Carp was considered to have good leadership skills. He was helped by other specialists, known for their extensive experience in the digital photography industry. Executive by executive, he replaced a top management cadre steeped in the ways of traditional photography with a team that had almost a pure digital pedigree. Except for Mr. Carp, almost every senior executive was from outside the company. Mr. Carp's management team was composed from new hires from Lexmark International Inc., Hewlett-Packard, General Electric Co. and Olympus Optical Co.

Shift from Traditional Photography to Digital Photography

On September 25, 2003, Kodak unveiled its digitally oriented strategy. "We are acting with the knowledge that demand for traditional products is declining, especially in developed markets," Carp said. "Given this reality, we are moving fast—as digital markets demand—to transform our business portfolio, with an emphasis on digital commercial markets. The digital world is full of opportunity for Kodak, and we intend to lead it, as we have led innovation in the imaging industry for more than a century."[50]

Kodak was among the last photographic giants to announce its digital plans. The truly global scale of Kodak's operations represented an additional complexity for Kodak. While some parts of the world were outgrowing "the shoes" of traditional photography (e.g. developed countries like the U.S., Western Europe and Japan), other parts of the world still exhibited growth opportunities for old film production.

Kodak recognized that on one hand, there were growth opportunities in areas that provided 30 percent profit margins (traditional film). These opportunities were in unstable emerging economies of countries like China, India, and the Russian Federation. On the other hand, opportunities in new digital photography looked better than those in traditional photography. The expected growth rate of the digital photography industry was about 26 percent until 2012. However, pursuing these opportunities would require substantial capital investment of up to $3 billion (according to stock analysts).

Daniel Carp's PowerPoint presentation for the September announcement showed that Kodak's new strategy would be based on three pillars—commercial imaging, health imaging and consumer imaging.[51] Additional "pillars" under construction were inkjet printers, commercial workflow management and flat-panel displays.

The digital and film imaging strategy focused on four components: "(1) Manage the traditional film business for cash and manufacturing share leadership; (2) Lead in distributed output; (3) Grow the digital capture business, and (4) Expand digital imaging services."[52]

Under the first of these components, Kodak planned to reduce costs in its traditional film businesses and cut back on marketing expenditures for film (shifting instead to processing). The firm would continue to offer high margin, premium products such as "Perfect Touch" processing and High Definition film in developing markets, while establishing leadership in emerging markets such as China and Russia.

Leading in distributed output referred to Kodak's plan to capture more of the demand for digital prints, whether produced in retail locations or at home. Kodak's plan called for the development of improved minilabs and kiosks that could print images faster and by increasing the number of kiosks by 50,000 by 2004. Kodak's home output strategy centered on the printer dock that allowed Kodak EasyShare users to transfer images directly from their cameras to a printer through a docking station. Users could then select and print images without a PC. Increasing use of Kodak's online photo service, Ofoto, was also a part of this strategy.

The digital capture business component referred to the further development of Kodak's digital cameras. Kodak intended to obtain a top three worldwide market position for digital cameras by 2006. This goal would be reached by becoming the industry standard for ease of use and by moving to more sophisticated cameras.

Kodak planned to expand its digital imaging services by expanding the products and services offered through Ofoto to include items such as picture frames, calendars and photo albums. Kodak also planned to develop kiosks that could print images from mobile phones. Roll out of this product had already begun in Asia and Europe and was expected to be ready for the U.S. market by the end of the fourth quarter of 2003.

On October 22, 2003, about 60 institutional shareholders met in New York City to examine other strategy alternatives, objecting to Carp's "risky" strategy of investing $3 billion into emerging digital markets.[53] Investors attending the meeting controlled about 25 percent of Kodak's stock. They felt that Kodak had been struggling with the transition to digital photography for almost ten years and that while it had enjoyed some success, the progress had not been enough especially given the billions of dollars that had already been spent. Investors pushed for radical cost cuts to quickly boost earnings, but had not yet come to an agreement about any long term strategies for Kodak.

Carp argued that the cost-cutting plans touted by the investors "really aren't viable, practical options" and that Kodak had few alternatives other than slashing its dividend and pouring its resources into digital technologies.[54] Herbert A. Denton, President of Providence Capital, the hosts for the meeting, said, "We want them (Kodak) to let us under the tent and really show us why this strategy is best."[55] Was Carp's strategy best? Would Kodak's transition to a digital strategy be enough to help them reach their goal of becoming a $20 billion company by 2010?[56]

Traditional Case 8b: Kodak at a Crossroads: The Years 2003–2007

Rebecca J. Morris, University of Nebraska at Omaha

"We are showing the momentum we need to achieve our goals."[57]

Antonio M. Perez, Chief Executive Officer
Eastman Kodak Company

"The odds are 50-50 that Kodak will be a profitable company by 2008, and these are not odds I like to bet on."[58]

Naveed Yahya, Chief Investment Officer
Fischer Investment Group

In September 2003, Kodak had announced its transition from a traditional film-based photography company to a "digital-oriented growth company." The announced digital and film imaging strategy focused on four components: "(1) Manage the traditional film business for cash and manufacturing share leadership; (2) Lead in distributed output; (3) Grow the digital capture business, and (4) Expand digital imaging services."[59]

Although shareholders and numerous investment analysts openly criticized the strategy, Kodak began implementing the new digital vision for the company. Since 2003, Kodak had pared costs through layoffs and plant closings in the traditional film division, sold off underperforming business units, and increased its research and development investment in ink-jet printers. In 2007, the question still remained—would Kodak's transition to a digital strategy beginning in 2003 be enough to help it reach its goal of becoming a $20 billion company by 2010?[60]

Trends in Digital Photography

Improved Technologies and a Shorter Product Life Cycle

Like most technologies, the market for digital photography continued to change rapidly in the years since 2003. Technological innovations improved the resolution of digital cameras (increased the mega pixels captured and thus improved the quality of the photos when enlarged). Improvements in optical and electronic technologies and subsequent reductions in production costs resulted in the introduction of higher margin, digital single-lens reflex (SLR) cameras into the market. These cameras featured interchangeable lenses and appealed to consumers buying their second digital camera and to photography enthusiasts who could utilize the traditional camera lenses they already owned on the new SLR digital camera bodies. Many digital SLR models offered significantly better image quality than point-and-shoot digital cameras due to their use of larger imaging chips. Industry insiders expected strong growth in the digital SLR segment of the market as consumers looked for more capabilities and flexibility in their digital cameras. Canon, Nikon, Sony, and Panasonic dominated the market for low-cost digital SLRs in 2007.

Camera makers found the product life cycle of the digital era to be markedly different than the rather stable product life cycle of traditional photography. For example, the Nikon top-of-the-line F-series of film cameras had been redesigned only six times over almost 50 years of production.[61] By 2006, new features-laden digital camera models had been introduced every few months rather than years apart. Makoto Kimura, president of Nikon Imaging, summed up the change, saying, "In the past, as a camera maker we were able to take it easy, watch what was happening. Now, we've had to revitalize ourself."[62]

Industry analysts believed that the faster product life cycle and the demands for technological innovations favored consumer electronics companies rather than traditional camera makers—in manufacturing and in distribution. Electronics companies such as Sony possessed the ability to design and manufacture many of the components integral to digital cameras, whereas traditional photography companies, such as Kodak, lacked these capabilities and had to purchase components from other electronics companies.[63] Distribution of cameras also shifted with the digital age in a way that favored consumer electronics companies. Consumers were increasingly purchasing even relatively expensive digital cameras at electronics chains, such as Best Buy, Staples, and Circuit City, rather than at smaller specialty photography shops. Consumer electronics companies already understood the inventory and logistics demands of the national chains while traditional photography companies struggled to gain valuable shelf space. As one researcher put it, "A new wave of technology has given the newcomers the upper hand. For the consumer electronics companies, digital photography has been all upside, while the photo industry was stuck in a slow evolution stage."[64]

Gains in Cell Phone Camera Quality and Usage

Technological improvements in the resolution of photos captured on cell phones increased significantly since 2003. In 2006, Nokia offered a cell phone model with Wi-Fi capabilities and an integrated 3–mega pixel camera.[65] Other cell phone manufacturers offered phones with an integrated 2–mega pixel camera. Consumers increasingly expected that their cell phones would contain an integrated camera. Approximately 30 million U.S. cell phone owners used their phones to capture images in 2005, an increase of 180 percent over the previous year.[66] By 2009, nearly 70 percent of cell phones were expected to contain cameras with multi–mega pixel resolutions.[67] Analysts further

expected that the improved resolution of the integrated cameras in most cell phones would decrease the demand for disposable traditional film cameras and could have a negative impact on low-end stand-alone digital cameras.[68] Because consumers carried their cell phones with them constantly, the integrated cameras provided a convenient way to capture images during their daily activities as well as special events, such as concerts and parties. Improvements in cell phone connections to wireless networks also made it easy for users to upload and share images with friends and family. Figure 1 depicts the increase in digital image captured using cell phones.

Maturing U.S. Demand

There were signs that the digital camera market was maturing in 2006. After growing by almost 670 percent from 2000–2005, unit sales of digital cameras were slowing with an increase of only 26 percent forecasted for 2009.[69] Prices of digital cameras were also declining, making profitability more difficult for makers of low-end cameras. For example, digital cameras with less than 4 mega pixels of resolution dropped in price by 40 percent in 2006.[70] In contrast, higher-end digital SLRs tended to maintain the same price points, adding value for consumers

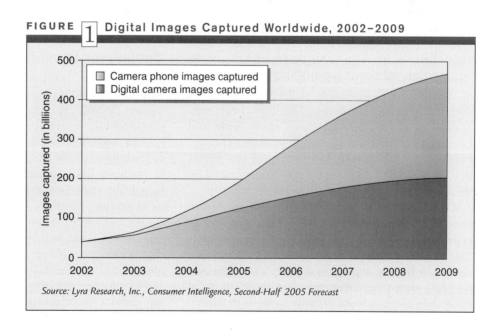

FIGURE 1 Digital Images Captured Worldwide, 2002–2009

Source: Lyra Research, Inc., Consumer Intelligence, Second-Half 2005 Forecast

by packing each successive model with even more features.

There was a glimmer of hope for some growth in the digital photography industry as some analysts believed that U.S. consumers were upgrading their digital cameras more frequently than had been previously expected. The replacement rate was estimated at every two to three years rather than every four years, as initially predicted.[71] However, demand was expected to decline in 2007 and beyond as many consumers had completed their upgrade cycle and fewer new consumers were entering the market.

An expected slow down in the U.S. economy further contributed to a slowdown in demand for digital cameras. Higher interest rates were beginning to depress consumer spending in 2005 as the percentage of disposable income that U.S. households paid for their mortgages and consumer debt was increasing.[72]

Growth Possibilities Abroad

Digital camera sales were expected to slow down in North America in 2007 but remained strong in Europe and Japan. Emerging markets were also expected to provide growing demand as camera prices fell.[73] In 2007, digital cameras were in strong demand in Central and Eastern Europe. Unit sales of digital cameras showed substantial increases in Russia (up 30 percent), Ukraine (up 70 percent), Poland (up 15 percent), Hungary (up 18 percent), and the Czech Republic (up 7.7 percent) over 2005 sales.[74] Although more cameras were purchased, sales revenues actually declined as a result of declining prices due to technology advances and competitive pressures. The top three vendors in the region in 2006 were Canon, Sony, and Olympus (in order of share).[75] Analysts expected continued sales growth in the region but noted that demand for digital cameras had matured in the Czech Republic.[76]

China was seen as a market with enormous potential for digital camera sales due to improving economic conditions and China's more open posture to the rest of the world as the 2008 Olympic Games in Beijing approached. Sales were expected to grow from approximately 3 million units in 2004 to between 6.5 and 10 million units in 2008.[77] Growth in Chinese disposable income in the major industrialized cities, such as Beijing, Shanghai, and Guangzhou, had created a market of 400 million potential customers for products such as digital cameras.[78] Interest in photography was keen among Chinese consumers as more Chinese began traveling abroad and wished to take home photos from their trips. The World Tourism Organization predicted that approximately 100 million Chinese would travel abroad in the year 2020 (an increase of 500 percent over 2003 figures).[79]

Digital camera sales to consumers outside urban areas in China were expected to be slower. Lower disposable income and need for higher-priority items, such as household appliances, caused rural Chinese consumers to delay their purchase of digital cameras.[80] Furthermore, distribution channels in rural areas were not well developed. No major electronics chain equivalent to Best Buy or Circuit City existed outside the major cities.[81]

Contrary to earlier industry predictions, Chinese consumers did not buy traditional film cameras as their purchasing power increased but preferred to leapfrog the older technologies to buy the latest digital camera models.[82] Sales of traditional film cameras and film canisters declined much more rapidly in China than had been anticipated, leaving companies that had depended on selling these products at risk of being jumped over by the newer technologies, such as digital cameras and camera-phones.[83] By 2006, more Chinese consumers owned camera-phones than digital cameras.[84]

Battling for Market Share

The disruptive technology of digital photography had proved challenging for many traditional camera makers. In 2006, Konica Minolta announced that it would withdraw completely from the photography industry—despite being the third-largest producer of traditional photo film.[85] Nikon announced plans to gradually halt production of five models of traditional film cameras, leaving only two film cameras in its product portfolio.[86] Other traditional camera companies, such as Canon, thrived in the new digital world. Canon had become the world leader in digital cameras with an almost 19 percent share in 2006.[87]

Consumers were offered more choices in the digital camera marketplace as companies in the consumer electronics industry began offering digital cameras. Notable examples included Samsung, a consumer electronics company with a strong position in the camera-phone segment, and Hewlett-Packard, with strongholds in printers and personal computers. Consumer electronics companies were formidable entrants into the digital photography industry due to their strong brand awareness with consumers, established distribution channels, and experience with many of the technologies involved in creating digital cameras.

The competitive position of the companies in the digital camera industry rose and fell as consumers demanded more features, improved technologies, and lower prices. The U.S. market shares of the top ten digital camera makers are shown as Exhibit 1. Analysts believed that the strong gains shown by Canon and Nikon from 2005–2006 were due to their introduction of low-cost digital single-lens reflex cameras (SLRs).[88]

Worldwide, Canon led in digital camera sales with an 18.7 percent share in 2006.[89] Sony followed with a 15.8 percent share, while Kodak was third at 10 percent.[90] Both Canon and Sony benefited from consumer interest in single-lens reflex models as well as growing demand in emerging markets. Sony's share of the global market increased as a result of its purchase of the digital single-lens reflex division of Konica Minolta in 2006.[91] In the digital SLR segment of the industry, Canon held 46.7 percent share in 2006, followed by Nikon with 33 percent share and Sony with 6.2 percent share.[92]

In segmented market share, significant differences were evident in the purchasing preferences of male versus female consumers. Men preferred Canon, while women preferred Kodak.[93] Analysts attributed the gender difference to women's preference for simplicity and desire for high-quality prints that could be shared with family and friends. Kodak met these needs for women with itspoint-and-shoot camera models and the EasyShare docking station. Men preferred the SLR models offered by Canon, while Kodak was their fourth most popular choice behind Sony and Olympus.[94]

Gender differences were also observed in what users did with their digital photos. More women than men (63 percent versus 53 percent) believed digital prints to be more important.[95] Women printed approximately 35 percent of the digital photos they took, while men printed only 25 percent.[96] Men "took the picture and put it in the computer. But then it was like a roach motel for pictures. They never got out," one industry insider reported.[97]

EXHIBIT 1 Top Ten U.S. Digital Camera Makers

	2006			2005			2004	
	Shipments	Market Share	Change from Previous Year	Shipments	Market Share	Change from Previous Year	Shipments	Market Share
Canon	6,068,500	20%	21%	5,000,000	18%	39%	3,587,600	16.1%
Sony	4,940,800	17%	3%	4,780,000	17%	10%	4,330,000	19.4%
Kodak	4,867,000	16%	−31%	7,050,000	25%	44%	4,880,000	21.9%
Nikon	3,045,700	10%	31%	2,326,400	8%	68%	1,381,600	6.2%
HP	2,185,100	7%	3%	2,130,600	8%	18%	1,804,900	8.1%
Olympus	1,856,500	6%	−5%	1,964,800	7%	−15%	2,317,400	10.4%
Samsung	1,496,400	5%	120%	680,500	2%			
Fujifilm	1,444,700	5%	−19%	1,780,600	6%	0%	1,782,600	8.0%
Panasonic	1,046,300	3%	199%	350,000	1%			
Casio	955,000	3%	136%	405,000	1%			

Source: Williams, M. (February 5, 2007). Kodak Loses Out in US Camera Market, Macworld, www.macworld.com/news/2007/02/05/cameras/index. php, Accessed on June 19, 2007.

	Number of Digital Camera Models	Highest Price & Resolution	Lowest Price & Resolution	Traditional Film Cameras?	Number of Photo Printers	Online Photo Printing Service
Canon http:// www.usa.canon.com	7 Digital SLRs 24 Point & Shoot	$3,799.95 12.8 MP	$249.99 7.1 MP	Yes	10 Inkjet 7 Compact Photo Printers	None
Sony http:// www.sony.com	3 Digital SLRs 2 Full-Featured 11 Point & Shoot	$1,099.95 10.2 MP	$129.99 7.2 MP	No	1 Inkjet 2 Compact Photo Printers	Image Station
Kodak http:// www.kodak.com	No Digital SLRs 10 Full-Featured 24 Point & Shoot	$449.95 7.1 MP	$94.95 5MP	Only Single Use Models	3 All-In-One 8 Compact Photo Printers	Kodak Gallery
Nikon http:// www.nikonusa.com	5 Digital SLRs 17 Point & Shoot	$1299.99 10.2 MP	$115.99 5MP	No	None	None
HP http:// www.shopping.hp.com	No Digital SLRs 7 Point & Shoot	$269.99 10MP	$109.99 5MP	No	9 Inkjet 3 Wide Print Inkjets 8 Compact Photo Printers	Snapfish

Definitions:

Digital SLRs: Digital single-lens reflex cameras that typically offered interchangeable lenses and more advanced features.

Full-Featured: Advanced camera models typically offering higher-quality lenses with superior zoom capabilities.

Point & Shoot: Simple to use cameras with fewer user-controlled options.

MP: Mega pixels—the greater the number of mega pixels the larger the images could be enlarged without quality problems.

Inkjet: Printers with photo capabilities as well as regular printing capabilities.

Compact Photo Printers: Dedicated photo printers that did not typically produce prints larger than 5x7 inches.

All-in-One Printers: Printer, scanner, fax combinations offering photo printing capabilities.

Source: All prices and number of models obtained from company Web sites accessed on June 18, 2007. Prices for Canon and Nikon obtained from http://www.BestBuy.com.

Although digital camera makers recognized gender differences in purchasing and usage behaviors, care was taken to address the needs and preferences of both men and women when designing and marketing photography products. For example, Canon utilized Russian tennis star Maria Sharapova in television advertising because she appealed to both men and women.

Representative data on the number of camera models and suggested retail prices offered by the top five digital camera companies are provided as Exhibit 2.

Kodak Since 2003

In 2003, Kodak announced an aggressive four-year plan to transform the company into a digital photography firm, replacing declining revenues and profits in the traditional film segment with growing digital revenues and profits. Job cuts and plant closures were prominent aspects of the firm's restructuring plans. From the company's peak in 1988, Kodak had cut 115,000 employees through divestitures, plant closings, and layoffs. Kodak expected to end 2007 with only 30,000 employees.[98] Although job cuts would eventually represent cost reductions and improvements to the firm's bottom line, restructuring costs since 2003 were estimated to total $3.8 billion.[99] Investment analysts believed that the high costs of Kodak's shift to a digital strategy would be worth the price if the company was successful at growing profits from itsdigital products.[100] Other analysts were unconvinced, saying, "We are increasingly skeptical that EK (Kodak) can efficiently generate digital revenue growth and we think additional plant closings, job cuts and development costs will continue depressing results."[101] Some analysts worried that the continual charges against earnings and mounting debt might leave Kodak strapped for important funds for research and development.[102] Competitive pressures in digital photography made innovation important but raised concerns for some analysts. Kodak "lost their magic touch. There are way too many people producing similar technology better," one analyst said.[103]

Important events in Kodak's history since 2003 are shown as Exhibit 3. Annual balance sheets and income statements for Kodak for the years 2004–2006 are shown as Exhibit 4 and 6.

Leadership of Kodak also was in transition during this period. In May 2005, Antonio M. Perez replaced Daniel Carp as chief executive officer of Kodak. Perez had come to Kodak in 2003 after working 25 years for Kodak's competitor, Hewlett-Packard.[104] Perez brought his extensive expertise in digital imaging technologies to Kodak and quickly became the leader of Kodak's digital transformation. Perez had been instrumental in formulating Kodak's restructuring strategy as he was Kodak's president and chief operating officer in 2003.[105] Despite the ongoing criticism of investment analysts, Perez remained optimistic about Kodak's prospects, saying,

"We said in 2003 that it would take us four years to transform this company. The first two years were loaded with restructuring costs, and the

analysts are reacting to that. My response is: Well, hello, we are following our plan. We said we'd grow digital revenue and profits, and generate a healthy amount of cash, and we are doing all that."[106]

One of the important changes championed by Perez was Kodak's new business model in inkjet printers. Kodak was upending the traditional business model in inkjet printers. Instead of pricing the printer devices low and making profits on high-priced ink cartridges, Kodak planned to sell higher-priced printers that used significantly less expensive printer cartridges. For example, Kodak's new line of all-in-one printers was priced at $149–$299, at least $50 more than comparable models.[107] The cost of the Kodak printer cartridges was significantly less, however, running $10 for black ink and $15 for the color cartridge.[108] The Kodak printers were expected to save consumers 50 percent over the lifetime of the printer due to the cheaper printer cartridges.[109]

Although some analysts reacted positively to the new pricing model, others were doubtful, saying,

"They (Kodak) are not fools, they are going after the sweet spot of the market, the people who print a huge number of photos at home, but they are up against big companies that can give a haircut to their own prices if they want."[110]

There was also some skepticism that consumers would pay more initially in order to save money over the lifetime of the product. A market research analyst described the consumers' perspective, saying, "When it comes to printers, consumers look for the features they want, then find the least expensive device that offers them. It is only later that they get sticker shock, when they're spending $50 for ink."[111] For its part, HP had adopted a "wait-and-see" posture regarding Kodak's new printer pricing model. If Kodak's printers gained share, HP was prepared to respond. Kodak "is going into a gunfight with a knife," responded Nils Madsen, marketing director for HP inkjets.[112]

Kodak predicted that it would take at least three years for the new printers to be profitable.[113] Despite reporting a narrower first-quarter net loss in 2007, Kodak's financial results were continuing to show signs of stress. Sales of Kodak's digital camera group (including digital cameras, printers,

EXHIBIT 3 Key Events for Kodak 2003-2007

Date	Event
January 26, 2005[a]	Kodak's digital revenue rose 40% in the fourth quarter of 2004, more than offsetting a 16% decline in revenue for traditional film products.
February 2, 2005[b]	Kodak announced that, for the first time, Kodak held the leading market share for digital cameras in the United States with 21.9% share.
March 2005[c]	Kodak changed the name of Ofoto, the online photo-sharing and printing site it had acquired, to Kodak EasyShare Gallery.
May 11, 2005[d]	Antonio M. Perez was announced as the next CEO of Kodak. Perez took over on June 1, 2005. Former Kodak CEO, Daniel Carp, retired at age fifty-seven.
January 5, 2006[e]	Kodak announced a ten-year partnership with Motorola to develop mobile camera-phones with Kodak sensors.
January 12, 2006[f]	Nikon stopped making most of its traditional film cameras.
January 30, 2006[g]	Kodak's digital revenues for 2005 exceeded revenues from traditional film for the first time. Digital revenues were 54% of total sales.
March 2006[h]	Konica Minolta announced that it was exiting the photography industry. Some of the firm's photography assets were sold to Sony.
August 1, 2006[i]	Kodak announced that it would outsource the production of all digital cameras to Flextronics, a leading electronics manufacturing services provider headquartered in Singapore.
January 10, 2007[j]	Kodak announced the sale of the health care imaging division to ONEX for $2.35 billion. Half of the proceeds were to be used for debt reduction. The sale of the division resulted in a decrease of 8,100 employees for Kodak.
February 1, 2007	Kodak announced the first quarterly profit in eight quarters. Revenues for digital photography products had declined by 13%.
April 26, 2007[k]	Kodak announced a partnership with BestBuy to create the BestBuy Photo Center. The center provided Kodak's EasyShare Gallery to BestBuy online consumers. The partnership would also provide for display of Kodak Gallery's photo gifts (mugs, purses, etc.) in BestBuy stores. BestBuy would also offer pre-paid cards for prints and gifts.
May 2007[l]	Kodak's digital consumer group sales (cameras, printers, and retail printing) fell 14% due to Kodak's decision to stop offering low-end digital cameras and an industry-wide decline in printing snapshots.
May 14, 2007[m]	Kodak announced a partnership with Target to produce a co-branded site that permitted consumers to order photo prints online and pick them up in Target stores. The partnership also provided for display of Kodak Gallery's photo gifts in Target stores and for pre-paid photo cards.

Notes

a. Kodak Press Release (January 26, 2005). Kodak Has Preliminary 4th-Quarter Reported Net Loss of 4 Cents Per Share. http://www.kodak.com. Accessed on June 18, 2007.

b. Kodak Press Release (February 2, 2005). KODAK Consumer Digital Photography Products Soar. http://www.kodak.com. Accessed on June 18, 2007.

c. Ibid.

d. Kodak Press Release (May 11, 2005). Kodak Board Elects Current President Antonio M. Perez as Chief Executive Officer. http://www.kodak.com. Accessed on June 18, 2007.

e. Kodak Press Release (January 5, 2006). Motorola and Kodak Announce Global Mobile-Imaging Partnership. http://www.kodak.com. Accessed on June 18, 2007.

f. M. Fackler. (January 12, 2006). Nikon Plans to Stop Making Most Cameras That Use Film. New York Times, Pg. 11.

g. Kodak Press Release (January 30, 2006). Kodak's 4th-Quarter Sales Rise 12% to $4.197 Billion. http://www.kodak.com. Accessed on June 18, 2007.

h. Down with the shutters (March 25, 2006). The Economist, Pg. 76.

i. Kodak Press Release. (August 1, 2007). Kodak Announces Agreement with Flextronics for Design, Production and Distribution of Its Consumer Digital Cameras. http://www.kodak.com. Accessed on June 18, 2007.

j. Kodak Press Release. (January 10, 2007). Kodak to Sell Health Group to Onex for Up to $2.55 Billion. http://www.kodak.com. Accessed on June 18, 2007.

k. PR Newswire. (April 26, 2007). Kodak Gallery and BestBuy Team Up to Offer Retail Customers New and Easy Ways to Enjoy Their Digital Pictures. http://www.mergentonline.com. Accessed on June 18, 2007.

l. Kodak Press Release. (May 1, 2007). Kodak Reports 1st Quarter Sales of $2.119 Billion. http://www.kodak.com. Accessed on June 18, 2007.

m. PR Newswire. (May 14, 2007). Target and Kodak Gallery Partnership Creates Complete Digital Photo Solution. http://mergentonline.com. Accessed on June 18, 2007.

EXHIBIT 4 **Kodak's Annual Balance Sheet 2004–2006 (in Millions of Dollars)**

	December 2006	December 2005	December 2004
Assets			
Current Assets			
Cash	1,469.0	1,665.0	1,255.0
Net Receivables	2,777.0	2,860.0	3,100.0
Inventories	1,202.0	1,140.0	1,158.0
Other Current Assets	109.0	116.0	135.0
Total Current Assets	5,557.0	5,781.0	5,648.0
Net Fixed Assets	2,842.0	3,778.0	4,512.0
Other Noncurrent Assets	5,921.0	5,362.0	4,577.0
Total Assets	14,320.0	14,921.0	14,737.0
Liabilities and Shareholders' Equity			
Current Liabilities			
Accounts Payable	3,502.0	3,421.0	4,521.0
Short-Term Debt	64.0	819.0	469.0
Other Current Liabilities	1,405.0	1,249.0	—
Total Current Liabilities	4,971.0	5,489.0	4,990.0
Long-Term Debt	2,714.0	2,764.0	1,852.0
Other Noncurrent Liabilities	5,247.0	4,701.0	4,084.0
Total Liabilities	12,932.0	12,954.0	10,926.0
Shareholders' Equity			
Preferred Stock Equity	—	—	—
Common Stock Equity	1,388.0	1,967.0	3,811.0
Total Equity	1,388.0	1,967.0	3,811.0
Shares Outstanding (mil.)	287.5	287.2	286.7

Source: http://www.hoovers.com/eastman-kodak. Accessed on June 18, 2007.

	December 2006	December 2005	December 2004
Total Revenue	13,274.0	14,268.0	13,517.0
Cost of Goods Sold	9,906.0	10,617.0	9,548.0
Gross Profit	3,368.0	3,651.0	3,969.0
Gross Profit Margin	25.4%	25.6%	29.4%
Operating Expenses:			
SG&A Expense	2,239.0	2,848.0	3,026.0
Depreciation & Amortization	1,331.0	1,402.0	1,030.0
Operating Income or Loss	(202.0)	(599.0)	(87.0)
Operating Margin	—	—	—
Nonoperating Income	118.0	44.0	161.0
Nonoperating Expenses	262.0	211.0	168.0
Income Before Taxes	(346.0)	(766.0)	(94.0)
Income Taxes	254.0	689.0	(175.0)
Net Income After Taxes	(600.0)	(1,455.0)	81.0
Continuing Operations	(600.0)	(1,455.0)	81.0
Discontinued Operations	(1.0)	150.0	475.0
Total Operations	(601.0)	(1,305.0)	556.0
Total Net Income	(601.0)	(1,362.0)	556.0
Net Profit Margin	—	—	4.1%
Diluted EPS from Total Net Income ($)	(2.09)	(4.73)	1.94
Dividends per Share	0.50	0.50	0.50

Source: http://www.hoovers.com/eastman-kodak. Accessed on June 18, 2007.

and retail printing) fell 14 percent during the first quarter of 2007.[114] Traditional film revenues declined 13 percent over the previous year.[115] Kodak was losing less money; however, investors were expecting more. "Kodak needs not only to restructure, but to change its business. That's a bigger project. They don't have an overnight fix," said one investment fund manager.[116] Sacrificing current earnings to focus on long-term success was a gutsy decision and members of the investment community wondered whether Kodak's executives had the fortitude to continue to pursue it and whether the path Perez had outlined for the company was indeed the right path. One investment manager summarized his perspective, saying,

> "That company (Kodak) used to be my favorite example of an old-tech company behind the eight ball. Kodak has crossed the Rubicon and gotten past denial. It may be struggling to figure out which road to take, but finally the company understands that the one it was on was getting it nowhere. You know what happens if you sit back and let history happen to you, so you've got to take a shot, and that's what they're doing."[117]

Had Kodak taken the right shot? Was it on the road to profitability? Would Kodak become a $20 billion company by 2010 as it had planned, or was Kodak soon to become extinct?

Notes

1. Wolf, C. (September 26, 2003). Kodak Stock Plummets as Dividend Cut: Slashed by 72%, *Bloomberg News*, pg. FP03.
2. Ibid.
3. Deutsch, C.H. (October 23, 2003). Some Positive News Aside, Kodak's Quarterly Profit Falls 63%, *The New York Times*, Section C, Column 1, pg. 9.
4. Wolf, C. (September 26, 2003). Kodak Stock Plummets as Dividend Cut: Slashed by 72%, *Bloomberg News*, pg. FP03.
5. Dobbin, B. (October 23, 2003). Kodak Works Through Profit Drop, *The Times Union*, Pg. E4.
6. Wolf, C. (September 26, 2003). Kodak Stock Plummets as Dividend Cut: Slashed by 72%, *Bloomberg News*, pg. FP03.
7. Ibid.
8. Ibid.
9. Dobbin, B. (October 23, 2003). Kodak Works Through Profit Drop, *The Times Union*, Pg. E4.
10. Online Extra: What It 'Boils Down To' for Kodak. (November 23, 2003). *Business Week*
11. http://www.kodak.com
12. *Associate Press,* (July 28, 2003). Kodak Struggles to Find Its Focus, *The Leader-Post,* pg. B5.
13. *Milestones—The Chronology.* (n.d.) Retrieved December 6, 2004, from http://kodak.com/US/en/corp/kodakHistory/1930_1959.shtml
14. Mutz, A. (March 26, 2993). Digital Photography Fundamentals and Trends, Retrieved December 6, 2004, from http://www.codesta.com/knowledge/technical/digital_photography/printable_version.aspx.
15. Photo Marketing Association International, (April, 2003). The Path from Pixels to Print: The Challenge of Bringing Digital Imaging to the Mass Market. Retrieved November 22, 2004 from http://www.pmai.org/pdf/0403_pixels_to_prints.pdf.
16. Press Release, (June 25, 2003), Digital Cameras Will Nearly Replace Film Cameras by 2008, According to New Report by InfoTrends Research Group, Retrieved November 29, 2004, from, http://www.infotrends-rgi.com/home/Press/itPress/2003/6.25.03.html.
17. Ismail, I. (June 7, 2004). Digital Photography Is Hot. *New Straits Times Press* (Malaysia), Pg. 9.
18. Press Release, (November 19, 2003). Worldwide Consumer Digital Camera Sales to Reach Nearly 53 Million in 2004, Retrieved November 29, 2004, from, http://www.infotrends-rgi.com/home/press/itPress/2003/11.19.03.html.
19. Yin, S. (July 1, 2003). *Picture This, American Demographics,* pg. 6.
20. Photo Marketing Association International, (April, 2003). The Path from Pixels to Print: The Challenge of Bringing Digital Imaging to the Mass Market. Retrieved November 22, 2004 from http://www.pmai.org/pdf/0403_pixels_to_prints.pdf.
21. Business Wire, (October 12, 2004). Digital Camera Ownership Moving Deeper into Mainstream Market, According to New InfoTrends/CAP Ventures Study, obtained from LexisNexis.
22. Photo Marketing Association International, (April, 2003). The Path from Pixels to Print: The Challenge of Bringing Digital Imaging to the Mass Market. Retrieved November 22, 2004 from http://www.pmai.org/pdf/0403_pixels_to_prints.pdf.
23. Ibid.
24. Ibid.
25. Ferrari, A. (October 30, 2003). *The Push For More Digital Photo Prints,* Retrieved December 6, 2004, from, http://www.forbes.com/2003/10/30/cx_af_1030printing.html.
26. Dalton, Jr., R. A. (September 26, 2004). In a Tech World, It's a Snap, *Newsday,* pg. E06.
27. Photo Marketing Association International, (April, 2003). The Path from Pixels to Print: The Challenge of Bringing Digital Imaging to the Mass Market. Retrieved November 22, 2004, from http://www.pmai.org/pdf/0403_pixels_to_prints.pdf.
28. Dalton, Jr., R.A. (September 26, 2004). In a Tech World, It's a Snap, *Newsday,* pg. E06.
29. Press Release, May 20, 2002. New Wave of Photo Kiosk and Digital Print Solutions Driven By Digital Photography, Retrieved November 30, 2004, from,

http://www.infotrends-rgi.com/home/Press/itPress/2002/5.20.02.html.

30. Photo Marketing Association International, (April, 2003). The Path from Pixels to Print: The Challenge of Bringing Digital Imaging to the Mass Market. Retrieved November 22, 2004 from http://www.pmai.org/pdf/0403_pixels_to_prints.pdf.

31. Camera phones outselling digital cameras—report (September 26, 2003). Retrieved December 6, 2004, from, http://www.forbes.com/newswire/2003/09/26/rtr1092489.html.

32. Ismail, I. (June 7, 2004). Digital Photography Is Hot, *New Straits Times* (Malaysia), Pg. 9.

33. Mobile Snaps, *The Economist*, July 3, 2003.

34. Ibid.

35. Ferrari, A. (August 9, 2004). Digital Imaging's Winners and Losers. Retrieved December 3, 2004, from, http://www.forbes.com/infoimaging/2004/08/09/cx_af_0809imagingupdate_ii.html.

36. Sony History. Retrieved December 6, 2004, from, http://www.sony.ca/sonyca/view/english/corporate/corporate_sonyhistory1.shtml.

37. Executive Biographies. Retrieved December 6, 2004, from, http://www.sony.com/SCA/bios/idei.shtml.

38. Cybershot: The Roots. Retrieved December 6, 2004, from, http://www.sony.net/Products/cybershot/the_roots_01.html.

39. Bulik, B. S. (May 31, 2004). Sony, Kodak Lead U.S. Battle for Share in Digital Cameras, *Advertising Age*, 75(22).

40. Klebinkov, P. and Fulford, B. (July 23, 2001). Canon on the Loose. Retrieved December 6, 2004, from http://www.forbes.com/global/2001/0723/036_3.html.

41. Business Wire, (November 21, 2001). New Canon Marketing Campaign Highlights "Digital Duet" of Digital Cameras and Printers. Retrieved November 30, 2004, from Lexis/Nexis.

42. *Business Week*, (February 23, 2004). Fuji's Digital Picture Is Developing Fast. Retrieved November 29, 2004, from, http://www.businessweek.com/print/magazine/content/04_08/b3871064.html.

43. *Business Week* (December 9, 2003). HP's Strategy: Connect "Device Islands." Retrieved November 29, 2004, from, http://www.businessweek.com/technology/content/dec2003/tc2003129_2679_tc137.htm.

44. Digital Cameras. Retrieved November 29, 2004, from, http://www.shopping.hp.com.

45. Nikon Portfolio. Retrieved November 29, 2004, from, http://www.nikon.co.jp/main/eng/portfolio/index.htm.

46. Nikon USA Homepage. Retrieved November 29, 2004, from, http://www.nikonusa.com/home.php.

47. *Business Week*, (June 19, 2003). Kodak Debt Placed on CreditWatch Negative. Retrieved November 29, 2004, from, http://www.businessweek.com/print/investor/content/jun2003/pi20030619_9134_pi036.htm?chan=pi&

48. Chakravarty, S. N. (January 13, 1997). How an Outsider's Vision Saved Kodak. Retrieved December 6, 2004, from, http://www.forbes.com/forbes/1997/0113/5901045a_3.html.

49. HP, Kodak to Dissolve Phogenix Venture (May 23, 2003). Retrieved December 6, 2004, from, http://www.printondemand.com/MT/archives/000142.html.

50. Kodak Press Release, (September 25, 2003). Retrieved November 29, 2004, from, http://www.kodak.com/eknec/PageQuerier.jhtml?pq-path=2709&pq-locale=en_US&gpcid=0900688a8022df48.

51. Kodak Strategy Review, (September 25, 2003). Retrieved December 6, 2004, from, http://media.corporate-ir.net/media_files/IROL/11/115911/Reports/Carp_Sept25.pdf.

52. Kodak Strategy Review: Digital and Film Imaging (September 25, 2003). Retrieved December 6, 2004, from, http://media.corporate-ir.net/media_files/IROL/11/115911/Reports/Masson_sept25.pdf.

53. Symonds, W. (November 24, 2003). Not Exactly a Kodak Moment, *Business Week*, pg. 44.

54. Ibid.

55. Deutsch, C. H. (October 23, 2003). Some Positive News Aside, Kodak's Quarterly Profit Falls 63%, *The New York Times*, Section C, Column 1, pg. 9.

56. Kodak Press Release, (September 25, 2003). Retrieved November 29, 2004, from, http://www.kodak.com/eknec/PageQuerier.jhtml?pq-path=2709&pq-locale=en_US&gpcid=0900688a8022df48.

57. Deutsch, C. H. (November 1, 2006). Kodak Posts Another Loss On Its Way to Going Digital, *New York Times*, Pg. 1.

58. Ibid.

59. Kodak Strategy Review: Digital and Film Imaging, (September 25, 2003). Retrieved December 6, 2004, from, http://media.corporate-ir.net/media_files/IROL/11/115911/Reports/Masson_sept25.pdf.

60. Kodak Press Release, (September 25, 2003). Retrieved November 29, 2004, from, http://www.kodak.com/eknec/PageQuerier.jhtml?pq-path=2709&pq-locale=en_US&gpcid=0900688a8022df48.

61. Austen, I. (February 20, 2006). They're Out of Film: Digital Moves to Top-Tier Cameras, *The New York Times*, Pg. 1.

62. Ibid.

63. Ibid.

64. Ibid.

65. Sarmad, A. (January 11, 2006). Camera-Phones Improve, *The Wall Street Journal*, Pg. D4.

66. Ibid.

67. Datamonitor, (June 2006). Eastman Kodak Company Profile, Reference Code 550.

68. Ibid.

69. Down with the shutters, (March 25, 2006). *The Economist*, Pg. 76.

70. Benderoff, E. (January 8, 2007). Gadget Forecast: Pixels Up, Prices Down, Sales Hot, *Chicago Tribune*, Pg. 3.

71. Choe, S. (January 3, 2007). U.S. Digital Camera Sales Soar on Urge to Upgrade, But How Long Will It Last, *Associate Press Financial Wire*.

72. Datamonitor, (June 2006). Eastman Kodak Company Profile, Reference Code 550.
73. Ibid.
74. IDC Press Release. (April 4, 2007). Digital Camera Shipments Flying High as Market Value Dips in Central and Eastern Europe, Says IDC, http://www.idc.com/getdoc.jsp?containerId=pr2007>04>03)124814, accessed June 15, 2007.
75. Ibid.
76. Ibid.
77. (October 2004). Product focus-Chinese Digital Camera Sales to Soar. *Market: Asia-Pacific*, Pg. 2.
78. Ibid.
79. Meredith, R. (November 15, 2004). Middle Kingdom, Middle Class, *Forbes*, Pg. 188.
80. (October 2004). Product focus-Chinese Digital Camera Sales to Soar. *Market: Asia-Pacific*, Pg. 2.
81. Ibid.
82. Yee, A. (January 9, 2006). Chinese Hunger for Digital Gives Perez a Lesson, *Financial Times*, Pg. 25.
83. (September 21, 2006). Technology Leapfrogs: Behind the Bleeding Edge, *The Economist*, Pg. 16.
84. Ibid.
85. Down with the shutters, (March 25, 2006). *The Economist*, Pg. 76.
86. Fackler, M. (January 12, 2006). Nikon Plans to Stop Making Most Cameras That Use Film, *The New York Times*, Pg. 11.
87. Williams, M. (February 5, 2007). Kodak Loses Out in US Camera Market, *Macworld*, www.macworld.com/news/2007/02/05/cameras/index.php, Accessed on June 19, 2007.
88. Ibid.
89. Tomkins, M.R. (April 4, 2007). IDC Reports on 2006 Digicam Market, http://www.imaging-resource.com/NEWS/1175724860.html, Accessed on June 19, 2007.
90. Ibid.
91. Ibid.
92. Ibid.
93. Bulkeley, W. M. (July 6, 2005). Softer View: Kodak Sharpens Digital Focus on its Best Customers, *The Wall Street Journal*, Pg. A1.
94. Ibid.
95. Ibid.
96. Ibid.
97. Ibid.
98. Deutsch, C.H. (February 9, 2007). Kodak Cuts Another 3,000 Jobs. *The New York Times*, Pg. 1.
99. Ibid.
100. Ibid.
101. Business Week Online. (May 7, 2007). Kodak Prints More Red Ink. Pg. 23–23. http://www.businessweekonline.com. Accessed June 11, 2007.
102. De Aenlle, C. (February 17, 2007). Market Values: History Offers Hope and Fear for Kodak. *The New York Times*. Pg. 6.
103. Ibid.
104. Executive Biography. http:www.kodak.com. Accessed on June 18, 2007.
105. Ibid.
106. Deutsch, C.H. (February 9, 2007). Kodak Cuts Another 3,000 Jobs. *The New York Times*, Pg. 1.
107. Ibid.
108. Hamm, S. Lee, L. & Ante, S.E. (February 19, 2007). Kodak's Moment of Truth, *Business Week*, Pg. 42–49.
109. Castelluccio, M. (March 2007). Kodak's Comeback, *Strategic Finance*, Pg. 57.
110. Deutsch, C.H. (February 9, 2007). Kodak Cuts Another 3,000 Jobs. *The New York Times*, Pg. 1.
111. Ibid.
112. Hamm, S. Lee, L. & Ante, S.E. (February 19, 2007). Kodak's Moment of Truth, *Business Week*, Pg. 42-49.
113. Deutsch, C.H. (February 9, 2007). Kodak Cuts Another 3,000 Jobs. *The New York Times*, Pg. 1.
114. Bulkeley, W.M. (May 5, 2007). Kodak's Loss Narrows as Spending, Costs Drop, *The Wall Street Journal*, Pg. A.5.
115. Transcript of Sales & Earnings Conference Call. (May 4, 2007). http://www.kodak.com. Accessed on June 18, 2007.
116. De Aenlle, C. (February 17, 2007). Market Values: History Offers Hope and Fear for Kodak. *The New York Times*. Pg. 6.
117. Ibid.

Exhibit 3

a. Kodak Press Release (January 26, 2005). Kodak Has Preliminary 4th-Quarter Reported Net Loss of 4 Cents Per Share. http://www.kodak.com. Accessed on June 18, 2007.
b. Kodak Press Release (February 2, 2005). KODAK Consumer Digital Photography Products Soar. http://www.kodak.com. Accessed on June 18, 2007.
c. Ibid.
d. Kodak Press Release (May 11, 2005). Kodak Board Elects Current President Antonio M. Perez as Chief Executive Officer. http://www.kodak.com. Accessed on June 18, 2007.
e. Kodak Press Release (January 5, 2006). Motorola and Kodak Announce Global Mobile-Imaging Partnership. http://www.kodak.com. Accessed on June 18, 2007.
f. Fackler, M. (January 12, 2006). Nikon Plans to Stop Making Most Cameras That Use Film. *The New York Times*, Pg. 11.
g. Kodak Press Release (January 30, 2006). Kodak's 4th-Quarter Sales Rise 12% to $4.197 Billion. http://www.kodak.com. Accessed on June 18, 2007.
h. Down with the shutters, (March 25, 2006). *The Economist*, Pg. 76.
i. Kodak Press Release. (August 1, 2007). Kodak Announces Agreement With Flextronics for Design, Production and Distribution of its Consumer Digital Cameras. http://www.kodak.com. Accessed on June 18, 2007.
j. Kodak Press Release. (January 10, 2007). Kodak to Sell Health Group to Onex for Up to $2.55 Billion. http://www.kodak.com. Accessed on June 18, 2007.

k. PR Newswire. (April 26, 2007). Kodak Gallery and BestBuy Team Up to Offer Retail Customers New and Easy Ways to Enjoy their Digital Pictures. http://www.mergentonline.com. Accessed on June 18, 2007.

l. Kodak Press Release. (May 1, 2007). Kodak Reports 1st Quarter Sales of $2.119 billion. http://www.kodak.com. Accessed on June 18, 2007.

m. PR Newswire. (May 14, 2007). Target and Kodak Gallery Partnership Creates Complete Digital Photo Solution. http://mergentonline.com. Accessed on June 18, 2007.

Traditional Case 9: The Fleet Sheet

This case was written by Professor Marlene M. Reed, Baylor University, and Professor Rochelle R. Brunson, Alvin Community College, as the basis for class discussion rather than to illustrate either effective or ineffective handling of an administrative situation.

At precisely 8:00 A.M. on Friday, February 16, 2007, faxes began printing out simultaneously in the offices of English-speaking companies all over the Czech Republic. Among the news of the Czech Republic translated into English that day was an interesting political insight gleaned from two newspapers.

> *After serving as adviser at the Czechoslovak Central Bank, Josef Tosovsky spent a year in London as deputy head of Zivnostenska Banka's branch. The bank allegedly financed Eastern European and KGB spy operations. After the Velvet Revolution, Tosovsky was called home to run the Central Bank. The Communists were reportedly behind his appointment.*

It was this kind of honest, straightforward evaluation of the Czech economy and government that had made the Fleet Sheet so popular to foreign companies and their managers. For Erik Best, founder of the Fleet Sheet, there were many decisions to be made concerning the future of the company as well as his own future.

He had begun the business on February 22, 1992, because of a perceived short-term need by Western companies rushing into Czechoslovakia after the Velvet Revolution for economic and political information that they could understand. He had envisioned that in a few years these companies would train Czech nationals to take over their operations in the country, and the English-speaking Westerners would withdraw. That had not happened, and he now wondered if he had a "going concern" that lacked a sound organizational and legal structure to survive into the future. He also wondered how long an operation such as his would continue to be a viable venture because of rapidly changing technology and greater access to news through the Internet. It was now the summer of 2007, and Erik knew he needed to make some decisions for the future.

Erik's Education and Early Work Experience

Erik was born in North Carolina; and when he was eleven years old, his family moved to Montana. He went to high school there and wrote for the high school newspaper. He also became a part-time staff sports writer for the *Missoulian*—the local newspaper. Near the end of his senior year in high school, Erik was offered a journalism scholarship to Vanderbilt University; however, he turned it down because at that time he was not sure he wanted to be a journalist. In the back of his mind, he had thought for some time that he wanted to be involved in business or politics or perhaps both. He decided to attend Georgetown University, and he received a degree in Foreign Service from Georgetown in 1985.

In the summers while working on his undergraduate degree at Georgetown, he also studied the Russian language at Middlebury College in Vermont, a school well known for its concentration on international affairs. He subsequently received a master's degree in Russian from Middlebury in the summer of 1985. Perhaps the educational experience that had the greatest impact upon Erik's life was a required four months' stint in Moscow. When he had completed his degree at Middlebury, he entered the master's program at the University of North Carolina at Chapel Hill and received his M.B.A. degree in 1987.

The Move to Prague

Erik Best, a fluent speaker of the Russian language and one conversant in other Slavic languages, became enamoured with the historic changes taking place in Eastern Europe. Never in the twentieth century had the opportunity existed to be a part of such a great transformation. Never before in history had countries formerly living under a Socialist government with centrally planned economies tried to make the transition to a free market economy where Adam Smith's "Invisible Hand" would be responsible for moving resources into their most advantageous usage.

Therefore, when the offer was made to Erik by the M.B.A. Enterprise Corps to join them in their work in Czechoslovakia, he quickly accepted. In February 1991, Erik packed his bags and moved to Prague. He immediately fell in love with the country and found the Czech language very similar to Russian. In explaining his love of Prague to others, Erik would state, "I have always loved music, and there is no city in the world so rich with music as Prague. There are classical concerts daily in concert halls, churches, town squares, on the breathtaking Charles Bridge, private chambers, large public halls and under street arches. There are violinists and accordionists playing on street corners and in Metro stations. I have heard that there are more musicians per capita in the Czech Republic than anywhere else in the world. After all, it was in Prague that Mozart wrote the opera 'Don Giovanni' and found greater acclaim than in his own Austria. It was also the home of composers Dvorak and Smetana. This is one of the reasons I feel at home in this city."

The Situation in Eastern Europe

In the early 1990s, the breakup of centralized Socialist economies was occurring all over Eastern Europe. Simultaneously, there was a rapid growth of the private sector in Russia and the surrounding countries of Poland, Czechoslovakia, and Hungary. One of the challenges in the burgeoning market economies was creating small businesses out of large enterprises and also launching entirely new ventures where none had been before. In fact, the development of the small business sector had been the most successful manifestation of the movement to a market economy. Small businesses had also been the greatest success story in the privatization process. Auctions of small businesses and the restitution of property in these countries had led to the restoration of some family businesses.

However, numerous problems beset these newly created companies. In some cases, the venture was merely additional work added to one or two other jobs to keep the entrepreneur afloat with increasingly higher inflation rates and increasingly stagnant wage rates. Many small businesses were forced into operating illegitimately to deal with unfair and cumbersome legal procedures in the regulatory environment, or to avoid the attention of the Mafia or corrupt officials. It became very difficult to work out a secure contract for lease of property, and the banking system was not equipped to deal with the needs of small business.[1]

Another serious problem was the lack of experience in running private businesses that existed in Eastern Europe. Most hopeful entrepreneurs had lived all of their lives in a Socialist economy and had no training or knowledge related to the way in which one becomes an entrepreneur. It was into this environment that many organizations from the West sent consultants to assist with the revitalization of the economy as a free market. The M.B.A. Enterprise Corps was one such operation.

Origination of Idea for the Fleet Sheet

After working in Prague for a year, it became clear to Erik that international companies that had established offices and operations in the Czech Republic had difficulty in obtaining accurate and timely information on political and economic trends in the country upon which to make business decisions. From his work as a management consultant, he knew that decision makers in companies are very busy, and those operating in the Czech Republic would need information that was very concise and written in English. At the time, no such product was available in the country. It occurred to him that a one-page faxed bulletin would be the best format for such a paper. The fax was also an inexpensive medium to use. He knew that in the beginning there would not be much news to report, and a one-page sheet of paper would probably hold all he needed to print.

By early 1992, he had worked out all of the details to begin the business; and on February 22 he published the first issue. Erik believed that if he had four or five subscribers in the first month, the product would be successful. In fact, approximately twenty subscribers signed up in the first month of operations. By early spring of 2007, there were about a thousand subscribers receiving the Fleet Sheet on a regular basis.

Believing that the life cycle of his product would be relatively short, Erik took little thought to establishing a permanent structure for his business. He set it up as a sole proprietorship, and did not bother with a business plan since the operations of the company were uncomplicated and easy to establish.

By 2007, he had eight staff members in the company. Some of the staff came in the very early morning to review newspapers and begin translating the news from Czech to English. Other members of the staff came in around 7:30 A.M. and were involved in distribution and client support.

Erik assumed the major responsibility for picking out the most important news to be translated and distributed in the Fleet Sheet. He believed a key competitive advantage of the Fleet Sheet was its emphasis on a quality product that reported useful Czech economic and political news. Occasionally, the Sheet would make a person unhappy by interpreting something incorrectly. However, if Erik agreed with the person's argument, he would admit it and print a retraction. He had found it important to listen to customer complaints and recognize the needs of the customer. He attempted to treat his readers as equal partners. The name for his paper came from the fact that it was issued in a timely manner, and also in reference to Fleet Street in London where all of the major newspapers once resided before moving to the Docklands.

The Pricing Strategy

Erik realized immediately that the major publication constraint would be the number of people he could physically fax copies of the Fleet Sheet to in a short time. This was primarily due to the fact that he knew there would be a limitation on the number of telephone lines that he could get. He also knew that another constraint was the budget of the companies and when they needed to have the news. The larger multinational companies, he speculated, would be willing to pay a higher price to get the information very early in the morning. On the other hand, smaller companies beset with fewer complicated decisions would probably be willing to pay a lower price to have the information later in the day. Some businesses might need the information only once a week.

On the basis of this assessment, Erik constructed a pricing structure that averaged three to four dollars per day for the customer who wanted the

Fleet Sheet faxed early in the morning, and for the smaller companies who needed the Fleet Sheet faxed to them only once a week, the price would drop to fifty to seventy-five cents per issue. There would be intermediate pricing between the two end points. Therefore, the large companies and lawyers for whom "time is money," could have access to all of the Czech political and economic news early in the morning so that they could make astute and timely decisions based upon realistic information. The companies that did not need information in a timely manner could enjoy the benefit of a discounted price for the information. The graduated pricing strategy would also make the distribution of the paper manageable. It seemed to be an effective pricing strategy: Pricing based upon when the subscriber receives the news. The attractiveness of the pricing strategy was that anyone could afford the Fleet Sheet.

In order to insure the timeliness of the paper, Erik initially guaranteed the larger companies that if they did not receive their fax of the Fleet Sheet before 9:00 A.M. each day, it would be free. However, the fax was never late, and Erik simply dropped this guarantee since no one worried about getting a fax late.

Marketing of the Fleet Sheet

The marketing of the Fleet Sheet was multi-pronged. The first thing that Erik did was to advertise in English-language publications such as the *Prague Post, Business Central Europe* (published by *The Economist*), *The American Chamber of Commerce Newsletter*, and in the Czech press in very select publications read by the elite. He was surprised that his subscribers had been not only people from English-speaking countries, but also the Dutch, French, German, and even some Czech companies that realized having the news abbreviated for them saved valuable time.

The company also engaged in direct marketing. They found out about new companies moving to town from the American Chamber of Commerce, people Erik met, personal contacts, and by word of mouth. With all new contacts, the company immediately apprised them of the product they were offering. Erik found that his satisfied subscribers let other people know about the service, and many new customers came from referrals. One reason his subscribers had been well satisfied was because Erik made an effort to dig into the important issues facing businesses in the Czech Republic. He also attempted to give people analysis rather than a simple reporting of the news. He found that clients read the Fleet Sheet because of the selection of articles that were covered.

The following testimonials by satisfied customers were published on the company's Web site:

> "Nearly the entire finance community in Prague is reading the Fleet Sheet, so I must too. I find I rely on it more than I probably should."
>
> Jiri Kunert, Chairman and CEO, Zivnostenska Banka

> "Most anybody can translate the headlines. The Fleet Sheet is successful because it understands the Czech market and gets to the real issues. It tells me what I need to know."
>
> William D. Harter, General Manager, Seagram

> "I read the Fleet Sheet before anything else in the morning. My Czech colleagues also find it useful."
>
> Ian Ferguson, Managing Director, Tabak

> "I read the Fleet Sheet because it's the first source of news for the foreign community in the Czech Republic, and I find it extremely important to know just what it is that everyone else knows."
>
> Jiri Pehe, Political Analyst

A more recent addition to his marketing activities had been using e-mail to whet the appetite of potential subscribers. (See Figure 1.) When anyone e-mailed him, Erik immediately added the name to a list of people who receive a summary of the day's Fleet Sheet articles twice a week. The purpose of this was to acquaint them with the value of subscribing to the Fleet Sheet for daily faxes. Understanding the animosity some people have to receiving "junk e-mails," Erik added a notice at the bottom of the e-mail that explained:

> If you do not wish to receive such messages in the future, please simply let us know and we will remove your name from our list.

Few people ever asked to have their names removed, and many signed up as regular subscribers. This was

FIGURE 1   Fleet Sheet's Final Word

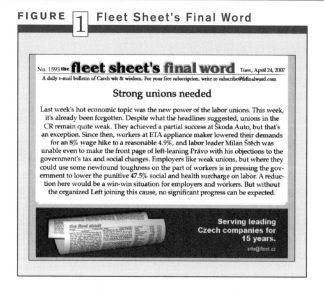

probably because the e-mail was only sent to individuals whom Erik believed would have an interest in Czech news.

In the late 1990s, Erik developed a Web site for his company. The Web address was http://www.fleet.cz. He believed that the Web site had enormous market potential for his company. It would now be possible for the company to place a page on the Web site that was a sampling of the Fleet Sheet for interested individuals and companies. Erik believed this had the potential to generate an even greater number of subscribers than did the e-mail synopses.

In the past, Erik had offered the entire archives on disk. A company would pay about $500 a year to subscribe to the service. However, he decided to put all of his archives from the past eight years on the Web site. The service was free, but one had to register to have access to it. This registry began to generate a good source of names for the e-mail synopses which were intended to develop enough interest from the reader to cause him or her to subscribe to the fax service.

Erik hoped that his Web site would be of sufficiently high quality for people to continue to read it. He was gambling on the belief that a company could make more money in the long run by using its archives as a marketing tool to generate more subscriptions than by selling the archives as some companies such as the *Wall Street Journal* had done.

People occasionally asked Erik why he didn't go to e-mail entirely as the medium for publishing and distributing the Fleet Sheet. His response was, "There is the problem of protecting intellectual property. Unless you can encrypt it, you may have a copyright infringement of your material. In fact, Stephen King's most recent story which was published originally on the Internet was encrypted, but someone broke the code. Another problem with encryption is that the message can only be sent to a specific person—not a company. Therefore, there are some real problems with encrypting the information on the Internet."

Hurdles for the Business

Unlike most start-up businesses, the Fleet Sheet was profitable from the very beginning. Erik made an early decision to rent office space and computers initially. Whenever it became clear that the Fleet Sheet was a viable business, he did invest in some assets for the company such as necessary equipment.

Concerning the success of the company, Erik mused, "The revenues of the company have grown every year because the Czech Republic was seen early as the darling of the West, and they also received a great deal of media attention. Under more realistic conditions, many of the companies would not have come here." However, in the last couple of years of the 1990s, there had been a decline in subscribers. Erik often contemplated how recent world economic events might be affecting the circulation of the Fleet Sheet.

As to the last hurdle, Erik commented, "We have had to fend off six or seven competitors who began to offer the same service that we were offering—a faxed bulletin with important political and economic news. It was a blatant rip-off of our product. The success of the Fleet Sheet drew other companies into the market."

Erik speculated:

The drastic price reduction the competition offered in the beginning served to lower the overall revenue size of the market. I have often wondered if there is a big enough market to support ONE such publication over the long run, much less numerous competitors in a smaller revenue pool.

However, he also observed:

The reason we survived was due to the overall quality of the paper. Business people know quality when they see it, and they immediately know that the Fleet Sheet is professionally done.

Government regulations which had been devastating to many businesses in the Czech Republic had been minimal for the Fleet Sheet. The company did not require a large number of licenses or drug approvals as did the large pharmaceutical companies operating in the country. However, they had been faced with government bureaucracy—especially in the distribution of their product. The government informed them that they had to send the Fleet Sheet to hundreds of libraries at the company's own expense. This, of course, would have made the company nonprofitable; and no one would have read the paper anyway. They decided to take a risk and send the paper to only selected libraries where they believed there was a greater chance of someone reading the Fleet Sheet. Fortunately, the regulation was changed in the early part of 2000 so that the company would no longer be required to distribute the paper in this manner.

In the late 1990s, Erik decided to add an advertisement to the Fleet Sheet. The ad was priced at $400 a day and was rotated among four or five different companies' ads. (See Figure 2.) If he should decide to add another advertisement, Erik would probably have to add another page to the fax. Faxing charges are minimal, the primary cost would be additional staff to prepare another page. However, he wondered if the primary focus of the paper—relevant information in a concise format—would be maintained. People don't mind taking the time to read one page of the most concise political and economic news of the day, but would they read two pages?

In the spring of 2007, approximately one thousand subscribers to the Fleet Sheet paid an average of $2.50 each per day to receive the publication. In addition, each additional subscriber brought in 90 percent in profits and only 10 percent in variable costs. Erik speculated about whether a new format with two pages would reduce rather than increase subscribers.

Erik had always used Adobe Acrobat to format the paper, and the faxed paper was very easy to read. If he went to an e-mail publication of the paper altogether, there could be a text format that would not be limited to one or two pages, but he wondered if that would affect the integrity of the product. They had done so well in the past with the concise format of a one-page fax. Would people sit at their computers and read through a lengthy e-mail the way they read through a newspaper or fax that they can hold in their hands? Erik speculated,

FIGURE 2 Fleet Sheet with Ad

the fleet sheet

No. 3363 — *Today's news, today* — Prague, Fri., June 3, 2005

Business

(MFD/1) Finance Minister Bohuslav Sobotka threatened yesterday to propose greater regulation of banks if they do not voluntarily agree to make it easier for customers to compare services and to switch institutions. CEO Pavel Kavánek of ČSOB said there was no reason to go on the war path before negotiations had been held. CEO Jack Stack of Česká spořitelna said that a task force should be created. (MFD/6) He said that banks, the appropriate ministries and consumer groups should take 90 days to put together a voluntary code of conduct for banks. What the industry needs are such things as a customer bill of rights, a quick and easy system for handling disputes, comprehensible contracts, fewer bureaucratic requirements from the state and a standard way of defining "interest," he said. If there is a legal fight, he said, no one will gain from it. (LN/3) He also hinted that the attack on banks might have been coordinated by the SOS consumer group, antitrust office and ministry. (P/17) Deputy Minister Tomáš Prouza said that bank rate cards are more like complex detective stories than clear guidelines for a price analysis. He also called on the public to express its views (at www.mfcr.cz), because "without pressure from bank customers, it is not possible to create a truly competitive atmosphere."

(HN/17) Antitrust Chair Josef Bednář said there is currently no instrument for protecting against competition violations by Český Telecom. He wants to regain the regulatory power he lost to the ČTÚ Telecoms Office. Operators prefer the status quo and warn that the sharing of regulatory power would lead to legal uncertainty. The Senate must now decide on the issue.

(P/1) Analyst Jan Vejmělek of KB said that the recent drop in the euro's value is only partially the result of the French and Dutch No votes. Also playing a role, he said, is the improved position of the U.S. economy. He played down speculation of the possible demise of the common currency.

(P/1) Deputy Premier Martin Jahn submitted a "strategy for economic growth" to the Tripartite Council yesterday that, among other things, calls for immediate deregulation of state-controlled residential rent. He said that he knows immediate deregulation is not politically viable and that for this reason he, as a cabinet minister, will support Development Minister Radko Martínek's deregulation proposal (which spreads deregulation over six years). Paroubek said that Jahn's proposal is a "semi-finished product" and that the elements of an "anti-social character" it contains must be eliminated. The plan also calls for introducing school tuition and charging for visiting a doctor. Paroubek also said he will probably recommend a change in the makeup of Jahn's team of (economically liberal) experts, because it is too one-dimensional. Senate Vice President Petr Smutný (ČSSD) said that Jahn was nominated to the cabinet by ČSSD and that he should respect this. ODS Vice Chair Petr Nečas said Jahn is making fun of everyone and should immediately resign as deputy premier after having submitted such a document (that goes against ČSSD's ideas). (P/16) Economic experts praised Jahn's strategic growth document but said that it has little chance of surviving politically. David Marek of Patria said that the proposal is missing a diplomatic element. Kamil Janáček of KB said that it was a good intellectual exercise but unfortunately one that will not be put into practice.

Eurotel

(P/4) A key meeting takes place today between Paroubek, Health Minister Milada Emmerová, doctors, unions, hospitals and health insurers. Two other meetings were inconclusive, and Paroubek asked all sides to be more modest about their ideas for solving the financial problems of healthcare. Also, Emmerová will confront the public on TV Nova's "Kotel" show tonight. (P/19) MD Ivo Žídek of Sanofi Aventis said that an expert committee should be formed for healthcare reform, as was the case for pension reform. He suggested that measures should be implemented for making sure that life-saving drugs are reimbursed but for reducing amounts spent on others.

(HN/3) The police recommended that CEO Marek Dospiva of Penta be charged regarding financial operations five years ago at Lázně Jáchymov spa company. If convicted, he could face two years in prison.

(MFD/4) František Příplata, a businessman from Uherské Hradiště, was given an eight-year sentence in Romania yesterday for being an accomplice to the murder of a local trade-union boss. He was involved in a privatization deal that was opposed by the union leader. He denies any involvement in the murder, but Foreign Minister Cyril Svoboda said recently that he trusts the Romanian justice system in this case.

(P/13) JCDecaux said it is considering suing BDO CS for a study claiming that the company's outdoor-advertising contract with Prague is one-sided. JCDecaux said the study did not take into account the Kč 1bn it invested into ad structures. It added that it does not expect any profit from the 25-year contract until the last 5-6 years.

(MFD/B1) Škoda Auto indicated yesterday that it will begin making the Yeti compact SUV in three years.... Futaba of Japan opened a car-parts plant in Havlíčkův Brod yesterday. (HN/8) PKN Orlen announced that it has a requirement to make buyback offers for Unipetrol, Spolana and Paramo. (HN/20) Amway's sales rose 6.4% last year, to Kč 217.5m. (P/1) Three accidents blocked the Prague-Brno highway for most of yesterday. (P/5) The number of Czechs vacationing in Bulgaria rose by 30% last year, to 102,045. (HN/16) Daniel Křetínský

Euro (fixing)	30.345	-0.055
Dollar	24.744	-0.113
Pound	44.929	-0.073
Slovak crown 100	77.920	+0.420
3-month Pribor	1.76	0.00
Dow Jones	10553.5	0.0%
DAX	4532.2	+0.1%
Nikkei	11277.0	0.0%
Český Telecom	460.50	+0.1%
ČEZ	427.40	+1.7%
Erste Bank	1229.00	+1.1%
Komerční banka	3054.00	-0.3%
Philip Morris ČR	17466.0	+3.7%
Unipetrol	139.95	-2.3%
Zentiva	836.50	+0.5%
PX 50	1166.4	+0.68%

of Sparta said the image of Czech soccer is much worse than the reality. (MFD/2) The CR will take over command of a 1,600-strong KFOR unit in Kosovo.

Politics

(P/3) Klaus said yesterday during a trip to Finland that approval in the CR of the EU constitutional treaty would be unconstitutional. The head of his legislative department, Jan Bárta, argued that unless several changes were made to Czech constitutional law, ratification of the EU document would be unconstitutional. MEP Jan Zahradil of ODS said that those who favor continuing with the ratification process are proposing something that would be in violation of valid EU treaties. (MFD/2) Bárta said that if the CR continues in the ratification process, he will logically advise the president not to sign the treaty. The head of the Senate's constitutional committee, Jiří Stodůlka of KDU-ČSL, said that it would create a serious constitutional crisis if Klaus went against the will of Parliament or the people by failing to sign the treaty.

(P/8) Pavel Verner of Právo says that KDU Chair Miroslav Kalousek is driving ČSSD toward ODS and might be ruining his party's chances of being in the next Czech government. On two recent occasions, Kalousek has used the media to contradict ČSSD. Verner suggests that not being in the next government could have significant consequences for KDU as a political party.

(P/1) Officials from the CR, Poland, U.S. and other countries met in Ostrava this week for exercises that are part of the Proliferation Security Initiative. The objective of the two-year-old initiative is to halt the spread of weapons of mass destruction.

(HN/2) Klaus caught his Finnish counterpart, Tarja Halonen, off guard in Helsinki yesterday when he said during a press conference that she has a personal reason for wanting the ratification of the EU treaty to continue. He hinted that Finland would like it if the treaty were signed when it holds the rotating presidency of the EU next year. Before Halonen had time to respond, Klaus said he was only joking.

Published by 9 a.m. Mon-Fri except holidays by E.S. Best s.r.o., P.O. Box 67, 130 11 Prague 3, Tel. 420 221 004 315 Fax 420 224 221 580 info@fleet.cz Unauthorized use or copy prohibited. © 2005

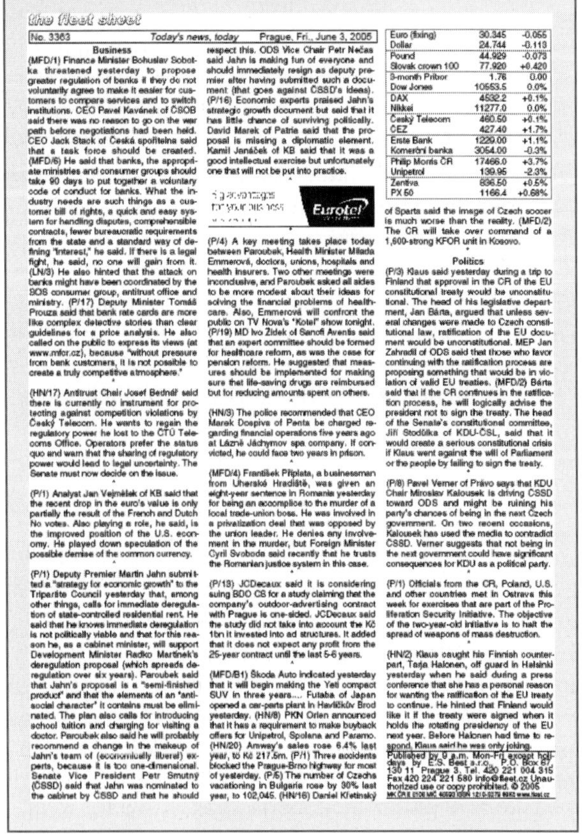

"If you could produce the same experience of reading a newspaper on the Internet, it would be good. However, our present computer monitors prevent this from occurring." Erik also wondered how a company could build a brand name and attract a loyal readership over the Internet. On the Internet, one must click through so many pages to get to the desired material, that the opportunity cost of one's time becomes very expensive.

When Erik began his venture in 1992, he firmly believed it would be a short-term operation bridging the gap until a new economy was established and other sources of information became available. With that in mind, he had spent little time pondering an appropriate legal structure for the business. He had initially set the business up as a sole proprietorship, but now he wondered if he should have established it as an LLC. He would also have developed a long-term strategy for the company. He wondered if it was too late to develop a business plan for the Fleet Sheet and alter its legal structure. He knew he would have to fill out some forms and notify the U.S. government of his actions, but perhaps he should do that. Erik wondered if a change in the legal structure of the organization would have capital gains tax implications if he decided to sell the business. He never assumed the business would last this long or he might have spent more time in planning rather than launching the business in two weeks.

Erik's Dilemma

Erik wondered if this business could survive indefinitely into the future. He also wondered what factors would have an impact on its remaining as a "going concern." Some foreign companies had already begun to close their offices in the Czech Republic because of the difficulties of doing business there, and the German banks were beginning to focus on Germany and not other countries. Even if the multinationals decided to stay in the country and there continued to be a market for the Fleet Sheet, he wondered what format it might take in the future. And then there was the question of the Internet. Would people have such quick access to data on the Internet that a service such as his would become obsolete?

Erik also thought about future competition. Would other companies try to offer the service he was offering at a lower price? Would subscribers be enticed by lower prices even though the quality of the product might be inferior?

When Erik had first begun his business, he was not making what he considered an adequate salary; and he often speculated that it would be very easy to close the business and go to work somewhere else. However, by the spring of 2007, the business was doing so well and he was making a very good salary that might be difficult to duplicate somewhere else. Erik thought it humorous to contemplate all of the problems that one encounters when a business becomes successful.

Note

1. S. Lyapura, and A. A. Gibb, "Creating Small Businesses out of Large Enterprises," *Small Business in Transition Economies* (London: Intermediate Technology Publications, Ltd., 1996), 34–50.

Traditional Case 10: Phoenix Organic: Valuing Sustainability While Desiring Growth

This case was prepared by Eva Collins and Stephen Bowden, University of Waikato, New Zealand and Kate Kearins, Auckland University of Technology, New Zealand and is intended to be used as a basis for class discussion. The views represented here are those of the authors and do not necessarily reflect the views of the Society for Case Research. The authors' views are based on their own professional judgment. No part of this work may be reproduced or used in any form or by any means without a written permission of the Society for Case Research. The assistance of Phoenix Organic is gratefully acknowledged.

"I believe that there are some significant issues related to sustainability for businesses that get beyond a certain point." Chris Morrison, Managing Director

For business school students wanting to do business differently, Phoenix Organic should be an inspiration. Start by collecting empty beer bottles after a night at the pub(s), wash off the labels and cigarette butts, and refill them with potent home brew. Sell them at a profit to a cult market and 18 years later in 2004, lean back and enjoy the fruits of a $NZ6.5 million[1] business.

All of the above is correct but it wasn't that simple. The reality was that the founders of Auckland-based Phoenix Organic made a series of strategic decisions that, coupled with some good luck and more hard work, allowed them to claim a niche in New Zealand's beverage industry. And they did it while maintaining their vision to create a business that was good for the planet and good for the health of its people. The founders were united in their enthusiasm for growth. The question was how—through new products, such as the Chai, that Phoenix had launched, through channels such as supermarkets or service stations, through developing overseas markets such as Australia or Malaysia, or through some combination?

How It All Started

In the late 1980s, "it was all very subsistence. We literally were just hanging in there and I worked nights doing dishes in a restaurant, and we were definitely hand-to-mouth," remembered Roger Harris, Director of Sales and Marketing and also one of Phoenix's founders. Phoenix relied on government business development money and personal scrimping to get the company going in those early days.

Harris met Managing Director, Chris Morrison, and partner Deborah Cairns in 1986—all part of a circle of people involved in organic urban gardening. Morrison and Cairns had started a small business making naturally fermented Ginger Fizz[2] in their Auckland flat. "We used to go around the pubs and pick up the old Steinlager bottles and take them home and soak them in our bath to get the cigarette butts out and all that filthy stuff," Morrison remembered. A friendly restaurant owner let them sterilize the bottles, which they then took back and refilled with Ginger Fizz using a jug and funnel. "All very primitive," Morrison admitted, but a product whose natural properties they all felt attuned to.

Morrison and Cairns made Ginger Fizz for about a year. The business started to grow, taking over more of the couple's time. Cairns dropped out of the course she was taking and the couple had the first of four children. All was well, if hectic and slightly chaotic, when Morrison met Harris. "He had a similar vision to us—to make a healthy alternative to the drinks out there, one with a premium edge," Morrison said. Harris tells it slightly differently. "I think they saw me as the big mouth that wouldn't shut up . . . that could be quite useful out there in the trade, selling," he said.

Harris had his work cut out for him. The product, sold under the brand, Ginger Fizz, was developing a strong following, but was a challenge to market and sell to café s. "I was out there growing distribution, but the product was not ideal. One of the problems was that it really needed to be treated as a very volatile, fresh product, but the perception was that it was just another soft drink." He had to explain to puzzled café owners that the ginger fizz had to be handled gently and refrigerated—or it would blow up! The ginger fizz had a kick that could be downright dangerous. In hot weather it

443

could explode and ricochet around the old van that Harris used for deliveries. Once a crate took off like a rocket and smashed against the roof of the van. Harris decided the business needed to upgrade. "I thought, there's got to be a better way, we can't keep doing this, it's going to kill me."

From a Flat to a Firm

Phoenix Organic[3] began in 1986 as a part-time partnership—almost a hobby for the three founders. "We had lived it quite fluid and loose and I think that was a good idea because you just don't know what is going to happen," Harris said. But moving the business to a different level required the trio to make some very strategic decisions about what they wanted to achieve.

Harris believed there was one key decision that saw Phoenix grow from a little known bathtub brew to an internationally recognized brand: pasteurization. "That was a significant quantum leap for us, the day we learnt finally how to pasteurize," he said. With that technological leap, a whole range of new opportunities opened up, including the chance to modify its only product, its flagship ginger fizz. The three realized that there were a number of negatives with the brand—not the least of which was its tendency to explode.

"I could see at that point that we needed to re-brand and we needed to exit from Ginger Fizz for a number of reasons. It was a real enthusiast product and it had a lot of cult around it, but it needed to change, it needed to reflect what we now knew about the market and where we wanted to head. So we made that change," Harris said.

Morrison agreed that the technological advance of pasteurization changed the company dramatically. "It expanded our range," he said, which meant moving into new premises and hiring more staff. In 1987, the Phoenix label was designed as the business moved from the flat to the back of a health shop in West Auckland. Phoenix moved to leased premises in 1987 and in 2001 moved to their current location, a two-acre property with custom-built premises and plenty of room for expansion. Phoenix customized the current West Auckland premises to adapt to their business of manufacturing and distributing beverages. They built a food grade kitchen (plant) for bottling beverages with bottling lines and pasteurizer.

Making a Range of Drinks

The process for making drinks was pretty simple. First, ingredients were inspected and tested to ensure they were of the required standard before being blended each evening for the following day's production. Usually two drinks in the same bottle format were prepared—two organic juices, or two sparkling waters, for example. More quality assurance tests were carried out prior to bottling. Phoenix had two bottling lines—one for juice products and one for carbonated products, each operating at around 100 bottles per minute. Once filled, bottles were sealed with aluminum caps and passed through a spray tunnel pasteurizer to ensure the drinks were free of micro-organisms. Bottles were then labeled and boxed before being sent to the onsite warehouse awaiting delivery to point of sale. With a shelf-life of twelve months, drinks were produced to order and distributed within three weeks. Waste and recalls were minimal.

The product range had expanded from the early Ginger Fizz, which became Phoenix Ginger Beer. In 1990, Phoenix Lemonade and Phoenix Cola were added, both with honey as the sweetener. Then came a range of Phoenix sparkling fruit flavored waters, including the unusual Phoenix Feijoa - seldom found outside New Zealand.[4] Later came Phoenix sparkling mineral water, vegetable juice and Chai tea (see Exhibit 1 for a complete list of Phoenix products). In 2004, the company was considering adding a liquid chocolate that café s could use to make hot chocolate. Phoenix produced five to six million bottles of drinks each year. Ginger beer (without the explosive fizz) was still one of its leading products, at around 7 percent of sales. Very close behind were Phoenix orange mango, apple and feijoa juice. Phoenix organic juices were increasing in popularity, 30-50 percent annually. Phoenix sparkling feijoa water was also popular.

Filling the Niche

The company's founders wanted Phoenix to be something new, something different. "We knew at the beginning that we wanted to break the monotony, the sameness and the oligopoly of the brand[s] in those days. Eighteen years ago [in New Zealand] it was Coke and Frucor and if you wanted

444

EXHIBIT 1 Phoenix Organic Products in 2004

Range	Products	Container	Ingredients (varies per product)	Claims*
Honey Sweetened Drinks	Lemonade Natural cola Ginger beer	330ml resealable green glass bottle	Carbonated water, honey, juice, concentrate natural flavor, yeast, root ginger	GE···FREE
Sparkling Fruit Flavored Waters	Lime Blackcurrant Melon Feijoa	330ml resealable clear glass bottle	Carbonated water, honey, juice or juice concentrate, natural fruit flavor, vitamin C (ascorbic acid)	GE···FREE
Sparkling Mineral Water	Sparkling mineral water	330 ml resealable clear glass bottle	Carbonated mineral water	Sourced from a deep aquifer naturally filtered through 220 meters of solid rock for over 50 years. Bottled straight from New Zealand source
Vegetable Juices	Vegetable juice	250ml & 1l resealable clear glass bottles	Organic vegetable juices, tomato 62%, carrot 27%, celery 9.9%, spinach 0.9%, beetroot 0.5%, sea salt	Can cleanse and repair the body IFOAM ACCREDITED 484 GE···FREE
Organic Juices	Orange mango & apple juice Pear & apple juice Apple juice Feijoa & apple juice Guava & apple juice Boysenberry & apple juice	275ml resealable clear glass bottles Also available in 1l resealable clear glass bottles	Organic juice/juice concentrate, organic puree, natural fruit flavor, natural fruit aroma, vitamin C (ascorbic acid)	IFOAM ACCREDITED 484 GE···FREE
Organic Drinks	Organic lemonade Organic cola Organic ginger beer	330ml resealable green glass bottles Also cluster packs of 4	Carbonated water, organic sugar, organic fruit concentrate, natural flavoring, yeast, root ginger	IFOAM ACCREDITED 484 GE···FREE
Natural Herbal Drinks	Wildberry herbal, Orange Mango herbal, Guava Apple herbal	250ml clear glass bottles	Filtered water, fruit juice concentrate, fruit puree, natural flavor, vitamin C, herbal extracts	Revitalize, energize, relax
Chai	Phoenix chai (Chai latte)	Concentrate	Filtered water, spices, tea, organic sugar, natural flavors, emulsifier (lecithin), sea salt, citric acid. Contains caffeine	GE···FREE

* The GE-Free/monarch butterfly symbol implies an association with the non-profit organisation GE-Free New Zealand in food and environment (Rage Inc.) that promotes making the New Zealand environment and food free of genetically engineered organisms http://www.gefree.org.nz/about.htm. IFOAM – International Federation of Organic Agricultural Movements—See Appendix 1 for more details on these symbols.

anything else, you were looking at the wrong country," Harris said.

Phoenix intentionally targeted the developing café culture. Coca-Cola had dominated for years. But Harris argued that while Coca-Cola made plenty of money, it also left a gap in the market. "There was a whole trade that was emerging called the café trade and it needed products that were packaged, that had the point of difference, that reflected the premium, that could command those margins, that could carry the retail value," he said. Phoenix tried to tap into that new market by developing what café s needed and wanted.

Early on, Phoenix spotted that café s needed to distinguish themselves in ways that would justify charging $NZ3–$NZ4 for a drink. Harris said that Coca-Cola's approach had been to go in and offer café owners the standard "big red box" (the fridge that distributors supply with their products) and the usual beverage suspects. But the Coca-Cola brand, which was so powerful in many ways, was a handicap here. "Coke was going to, just by the presence of their branding alone, say something to the audience about what the product was. It says, 'lunchbar, lunchbar, lunchbar'. And that turns off big chunks of their audience."

According to Harris, café owners knew that they did not have many realistic choices. Phoenix, small and smart enough to be flexible and innovative, attempted to fill that niche. In 2004, its success was demonstrated by its presence in some 2,000 cafés in New Zealand, a market penetration of close to 70 percent.

From the beginning, in 1986, Harris would go to cafés and say, "I know you have needs over and above what I can meet. So what I'll get you is a fridge where we'll design the product layout, and we'll put Coke in there. We'll put water in there; we'll put fresh orange juice in there. All we want is an agreement with you that gives us enough of the fridge to get the volume we need to pay for the fridge and make this a profitable business." In return, Phoenix got to occupy prime fridge real estate. "We own eye level, we own down to your navel, and they can have the rest," Harris commented. Customer service was maintained by Phoenix delivery people who did more than just re-stock Phoenix product for cafés, but were responsible for the customer relations with café owners.

The Ties that Bind

Ask Chris Morrison why he thinks Phoenix has been so successful and he will cite the relationships Phoenix had built up with suppliers and customers. "We've built up respect and trust with our market and those things don't happen over night. We're not a flash in the pan, we've done the hard yards, and we've built it up with no money. I think that's why we've been successful and why we're in quite a strong position now - because we've paid our dues, and really been fairly modest about it. And made sure that we have good relationships with people, not only customers, but our suppliers, and the whole spectrum of people we deal with in the company."

Even though it had grown into a multi-million dollar company in 2004, Phoenix still had a strong 'family business' flavor to it. Morrison preferred to deal with small companies that could buy into "the Phoenix way of doing things." And in return, he said, "We really cement the relationship, people feel like they are being looked after by us, it's very much a personal approach."

The emphasis on strong relationships extended to the company's 25 staff (see Figure 1 for Phoenix's organization chart). Due to the small number of staff, Phoenix management took a very hands-on approach to staff management and had a strong relationship with all staff which allowed them to communicate freely and show a personal interest in both their working day and their personal life. Phoenix encouraged open communication with weekly departmental meetings and bi-monthly company wide meetings.

The company prided itself on upskilling staff, listening to their needs and being responsive. For example, staff were encouraged and supported to pursue diplomas or degrees with the company reimbursing fees upon successful completion of each course. Having staff that were relatively happy at their work meant that productivity went up and turnover went down. "That's a huge benefit to the company, and so I think it's very important to put a lot of energy in that area", Morrison said. "We are very fortunate to have great staff at Phoenix and we try very hard to look after everyone."

Morrison also realized that some jobs were repetitive and of limited scope by their very nature. "It's damn hard for people to come to work every day and work on a production line and load bottles

446

FIGURE 1 Phoenix Organic Management and Board Structure in 2004

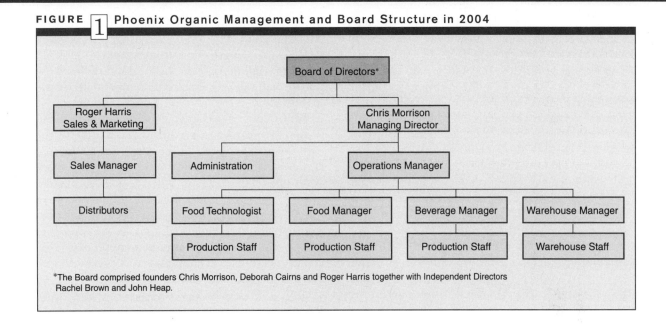

*The Board comprised founders Chris Morrison, Deborah Cairns and Roger Harris together with Independent Directors Rachel Brown and John Heap.

eight hours a day...that can be pretty tough," he said. So, social activities outside work were seen as important too. At the end of each summer (the company's busy period), staff went away for an all-expenses-paid long weekend within New Zealand. In 2003, they went to Great Barrier Island. Since 2002, in the winter, most of Phoenix staff went skiing in Queenstown for four days, with the company paying 50 percent of the costs. Families were also invited to both trips, however Phoenix did not pay for those costs. Morrison said these events had been a great success.

Riding the Organic Wave

Harris saw Phoenix benefiting from a growing global public awareness of food safety issues such as mad cow disease.[5] "The owners of the supermarkets in New Zealand suddenly lit up one day and said, 'hey, what are organics?'" Harris said. Suddenly, supermarket buyers were being told to start taking organics seriously. "It was just unprecedented," Harris recalled.

Phoenix decided to take advantage of the significant market shift represented by the rising interest in organics (see Appendix 1 for more background information on organics). The company had been tracking world media for a long time and believed that organics was a global trend that would eventually hit New Zealand. When Morrison and Harris started to get early intelligence that suggested the wave was coming soon, they moved. "We had a strategy session about three years ago [in 2001] that decided we wanted to create an umbrella organic brand," Harris said. "Chris and I thought, 'We've been in organics forever, we're not going to be left on the sideline. This is our opportunity.'"

The plan was designed to work with the café trade, but also be the vehicle to help Phoenix make it big in supermarkets. The plan was to develop an organic food brand, starting with jams and salsas, complementary to its beverage products, ultimately making Phoenix a household name for all organics. It seemed like a great idea at the time. It wasn't.

Harris was up-front about what he thinks went wrong. "It's a mistake for organizations which are fast growing and relatively light in terms of size to try and pick off too many different diverse areas. It becomes a distraction. It's incredibly tempting. You're really growth-addicted."

Phoenix encountered a number of difficulties with the organic food concept. The big supermarkets did take more organic products, but they often segregated them into small organic sections instead of mainstreaming them with similar products. In Harris's words, they were 'ghetto-ized.' For Phoenix, it was the kiss of death. "I could see this problem of having too diverse an offer and not having the resources to really do the thing properly," Harris said. "We were going to run the risk of basically stretching ourselves too thin, exhausting our resources trying to keep too many different balls up in the air."

Phoenix did not abandon the supermarket channel for its beverages, however. Harris found specialists to help Phoenix tailor beverage products to that trade. In 2004, Phoenix's beverages were in all the national supermarket outlets and accounted for about 20 percent of its business. But selling to supermarkets demanded new strategic thinking. "As we start to develop product for supermarkets, we're looking at what the need is there and we're starting to see that the single serve beverage isn't actually the main answer. We need cluster packs, we need one liter bottles, we need bulk," Harris said. However, Phoenix could approach both the two main supermarket chains in New Zealand and others as "the largest organic beverage company in the country."

Getting Enough

Phoenix was totally committed to organics and in the future hoped to have all of its beverages fully certified as organic by BioGro, New Zealand's leading internationally accredited organic certification body. BioGro certification was an additional cost for Phoenix because BioGro audits required a paperwork trail for all organic ingredients right through to the finished product. For Morrison it was worth it. "I think it's really important for organic businesses to make sure that they're squeaky clean and that consumers can see that they can trust those businesses when they see the word organic and especially certified organic products."

Some products were 'natural' rather than 'organic." Phoenix Operations Manager, John Evans, explained that natural "is a term that gets bandied around. For us there are no preservatives, no chemicals. In our natural cola, we are using natural honey versus a traditional sugar source. We don't have caffeine in it where every other cola does" (see Appendix I for additional background information on natural products). Going organic raised some

significant issues for the company. "Our ingredients are often up to 100% more expensive, plus we often have to carry ingredients from season to season," Morrison said. And organics aside, Evans pointed out that the natural flavors used by Phoenix could cost two to three times more than did artificial substitutes.

For organic ingredients, demand far outstripped supply. "We can't just go out in the middle of the down season and say I'd like some more strawberries, because there aren't that many organic strawberry growers," Morrison noted. About 60 percent of the company's production was organic. Some of Phoenix's natural products were being converted to organic, but it remained a challenge merely to source enough certified organic ingredients.

Producers of certified organic products also faced challenges with scale of economies.

- Production costs for organic foods are typically higher because of greater labor inputs per unit of output and because greater diversity of enterprises means economies of scale cannot be achieved
- Post-harvest handling of relatively small quantities of organic foods results in higher costs because of the mandatory segregation of organic and conventional produce, especially for processing and transportation
- Marketing and the distribution chain for organic products is relatively inefficient and costs are higher because of relatively small volumes (www.ifoam.org).

With the market overall, and supermarkets in particular, wanting to give only a 20 percent premium for organic products there was little margin for certified organic producers. "This has meant we have had to work more efficiently and smarter than our competitors. Sourcing a range and quantity of ingredients is also difficult and requires good long term planning and strong relationships with suppliers," Morrison said. "Strategically it's tough. But we're market leaders in this area, and it gives us an edge. And it also keeps our competitors at bay. They'll have a look at it and think the margins aren't there, it's too hard, it's too difficult. There's only a certain amount of suppliers and Phoenix already has good relationships with them."

Saving the World and Making Money

Phoenix was a privately held company. Morrison estimated total sales at about $NZ6.5 million in 2004, up from $NZ4 million in 2002 and $NZ5 million in 2003. Phoenix had been growing at 25–30 percent per annum with similar predictions for the immediate future. Morrison acknowledged that it was not easy for a business to grow at that rate without outside capital. "Cash flow is extremely tight," he said, although inventory turnover was relatively efficient at under three weeks. The land Phoenix bought in 2001, and its new buildings and planned extensions for 2004, were mainly financed through borrowing. Profits were continually ploughed back into the business. Morrison was reluctant to accept the compromises and loss of control that would likely come with outside capital. "We built this company. We don't necessarily want somebody else telling us to do it a different way. We're quite happy with the results we've achieved; we think we're doing it quite well."

Exports made up 10 percent of sales and were, Morrison predicted, the most likely source of future growth. Sales in Australia had increased from less than $NZ10,000 a month to $NZ60–70,000 a month with the deployment of personnel into Sydney on a one-week-a-month basis. When considering further expansion into Australia, Morrison suggested that the next step might be to use a contract manufacturer. He felt that investing in plant and equipment in Australia would be too expensive given current debt levels.

According to its Mission Statement, "Phoenix Organics aimed to be NZs premier organic beverage company, to be strong in both the domestic and export markets and to be an example of a successful sustainable business." Social and environmental sustainability was one aspect of the business that Morrison, was unwilling to compromise on. Even in the bathtub days, the three founders always tried to make their products in an ethical manner, providing a healthy, natural premium product with the least impact on the environment. They believed that the market had caught up to their early thinking. "In the last 10 years we've seen more interest from the market in things that are important to us—safety, accountability, values, integrity and sustainability," Morrison said.

Gradually, Phoenix had evolved from an instinctive, ad hoc approach to sustainability to adopting internationally recognized sustainability frameworks. In 1996, the local council's Cleaner Production Program got Phoenix management thinking more about its water, waste and energy reduction systems. Three years later the founders were introduced to The Natural Step, a Swedish framework for sustainability that they implemented at Phoenix (see Appendix 2). The company even had a Sustainability Director, employed part-time, Rachel Brown. "My role is to ensure that everything the company does operates in a way that is environmentally and socially responsible," Brown said. From her earlier cleaner production role involving Phoenix, Brown had gone on to the Auckland Environmental Business Network, which Morrison eventually chaired through its nationwide transformation to the Sustainable Business Network in 2002.

Creating (and Implementing) a Strategic Sustainability Plan

Brown, Morrison and others spent time coming up with a long-term sustainability plan that covered five key areas (see Exhibit 2 for Phoenix's Sustainability Plan). The plan considered staffing issues, reduction of fossil fuel use, avoiding persistent chemicals, protecting the environment and using resources efficiently. Sticking to this plan meant some hard choices. To offset the environmental impacts of the fossil fuels used in transportation, Phoenix ran a GreenFleet[6] program and encouraged Auckland distributors to use low sulphur diesel.

The choice between glass and plastic illustrated the dilemmas associated with having a sustainability philosophy that goes beyond the "win-win"[7] version of sustainability, where business will do what is good for the environment and society to the extent that it is good for business in financial terms. The "win-win" approach means that business does the easy things that have pay-off, like conducting energy and waste audits, and bringing in more efficient equipment. But beyond these initiatives, sustainability is likely to impose costs on business where payback is either lacking or quite indirect. It would have been a lot cheaper for the company to stop using glass bottles and put everything into plastic. Plus, plastic was lighter than glass was and required less fuel per shipment. But plastic was a non-renewable resource and Brown believed (although she did not cite any scientific studies) that plastic contamination of the beverages could potentially cause long-term health effects for people. Glass also fitted better with the company's up-market image. "What are the social implications? What are the economic implications?

Mission Statement

Phoenix Organics aim to be New Zealand's premier organic beverage company, to be strong in both the domestic and export markets and to be an example of a successful sustainable business.

Create a quality product and a brand of integrity and longevity that is the consumer brand of choice.

Phoenix Organics has built products behind a brand that consumers can trust. We will produce products that are in line with our sustainable principles and values. Phoenix have consistently produced drinks that fully satisfy our customers needs. We recognise that our customers need transparency and therefore have open lines of communications. We are working on improving this with our new updated website. We do not produce short term fad products but concentrate on products of high integrity with longevity.

Create a positive and supportive work environment where people have pride in working for Phoenix Organics.

Phoenix creates a positive working environment by

- We are currently running an apprenticeship programme which all production workers are invited and encouraged to participate in. This allows staff to upskill on the job. Participants who complete each stage receive a certificate which results in a sense of achievement and can lead to more interesting work and better financial rewards.

    These benefits can of course be taken to other employment.

- We encourage and support staff who are looking at or are doing more formal diplomas or degrees. We will reimburse fees partially or fully upon successful completion of each paper.

- Phoenix supports a healthy work team. We will financially support sports teams and sporting activities staff participate in. We have provided bikes to employees to ride to work on if they choose this form of transport.

- We have supported a staff member towards their 3 week trip to Outward Bound.

- We encourage a strong social club. Each year we have a summer long weekend away for the entire company. Also supported by the company is a ski trip. We have a yearly Christmas party for the staff and also a children's Christmas party as well.

- We encourage open communication with weekly departmental meetings. 6 bi-monthly company wide meetings. We have also run sustainability workshops and a values meeting (to determine how our staff view the company, products and owners)

- Induction process—all new staff are thoroughly briefed before beginning work at Phoenix on Occupational Safety and Health Standards, the history and background of the company, the culture of this company and our sustainability practices.

Develop educational processes for organics, sustainability and a GE free environment, and communicate Phoenix Organics values.

Phoenix regards organics and sustainability as the very core of the company. We are committed to the concept of NZ moving towards becoming an eco-nation. Every new drink at Phoenix will be certified organic. We will also over time convert all our natural products to certified organic.

We are actively involved with and support sustainable business initiatives. We show-case our business and its journey towards sustainability.

We are working with the local council Waitakere City, to get organic garden programmes up and running with local schools.

We support active environment causes such as the anti-GE Movement.

Integrate Phoenix Organics within the community.

Phoenix enjoys being part of our local community in Waitakere City. We participate in many community events and initiatives—such as

- setting up the Waitakere/Rodney "Organic Cluster" of businesses.
- participating in the local branch of Habitat for Humanity.
- worked with Unitec on educational programmes regarding sustainability.
- our organic garden in schools programme is an exciting new venture for our business.
- we are a founding member of the Sustainable Business Network

Develop and implement an Environmental Management Plan based upon the Natural Step methodologies.

The Natural Step (TNS) has been running in our company for over 3 years and continues to provide us with a framework on which we are continually building a comprehensive and progressive environmental management programme.

Reduce Dependence on Fossil Fuels and Metals (System Condition One)

Phoenix is dependent on fossil fuels for transportation. Raw materials are imported from around the world and products distributed throughout New Zealand. To reduce their dependence on fossil fuels and metals the company have developed programmes to reduce the purchase of imported products and to minimise the impacts associated with the company's transportation. Products continue to be packaged in glass bottles and jars in preference to plastic alternatives.

The main initiatives undertaken include:

Running a GreenFleet, (a sustainable transport programme administered by the Sustainable Business Network), to reduce the impact associated with running a small vehicle fleet of 3 trucks and 5 cars.

Phoenix has:

- A Transport Policy, which includes a vehicle code of conduct for staff and for scheduling in regular vehicle checks;
- A system for carefully planning trips; Investigated new ways of selling to minimise fuel use;
- Annual native tree planting programmes to offset the carbon emissions associated with each vehicle.
- Reduced Auckland fleet from 4 vans to 3 trucks, which has enabled us to carry more stock and reduce the amount of trips back to the factory.
- Encouraged staff to carpool, cycle, walk or use public transport to and from work. Have provided bikes for staff members who wish to use this form of transport.
- All our trucks fill up at Gull to ensure the use of low sulphur diesel.

Purchasing locally made products and ingredients over imported alternatives.

Phoenix has:

- Reduced the importation of stylish glass bottles and jars from Portugal, now purchasing standard models produced in New Zealand or Australia;
- Continued to encourage the growth of certified organic produce in New Zealand to reduce their dependence on imported produce.

Avoid using products made from fossil fuel (e.g. most plastics):

Phoenix has:

- Chosen to use glass bottles and jars, thus also avoiding the problems associated with chemical leaching and contamination of the product.

Avoid Persistent Chemicals (System Condition Two)

Phoenix purchases produce from growers around the world, with a preference for locally grown. The company has a commitment to organics thus avoiding the impacts associated with pesticide and other chemical use on conventionally-grown crops. Phoenix continues to use a small quantity of chemicals for cleaning equipment.

To minimise the use of persistent chemicals Phoenix has:

Adopted BioGro certification and only purchase organically certified products or those that meet the standards required for BioGro Certification.

Phoenix has:

- Committed to producing an organically certified product range to reduce the chemical use associated with conventional growing practices
- Encouraged local growers to become BioGro certified to enable future purchase from these local growers
- Is a founding member of the Waitakere/Rodney District Council Organic Cluster. A group of businesses and growers committed to promoting organic in our region.

Conducted an audit of all cleaners and chemicals.

Phoenix has:

- Reduced the number of chemicals used on site and now have only one chemical supplier.
- Developed good information on the environmental and health effects associated with all chemicals used and have worked with our chemical supplier to reduce those effects.

Conducted a survey of their suppliers and drawn up a Purchasing Policy which:

- Encourages suppliers to support our efforts to Green our Fleets.
- Requires BioGro certified product suppliers to provide up-to-date copies of their certification.
- Requests suppliers to provide assurance that all products supplied are free from genetically modified ingredients (no GMOs or 'GE free').
- Requests support in reducing waste by providing returnable or recyclable packaging.

Protect Natural Ecosystems (System Condition Three)

Phoenix impacts on the natural ecosystems throughout their product life cycle, (e.g. through growing of produce, transportation, manufacture, sale, use and disposal).

To minimise the impact the company has on natural ecosystems Phoenix has:

- Committed to organics. This protects and enhances the environment by working with nature rather than against it.
- Participated in regular native tree-planting programmes to help absorb carbon dioxide emissions from vehicles as well as provide natural habitat for native flora and fauna.

In addition Phoenix has:

- Reduced its impacts on stormwater systems by cleaning cars at 'Wash-world'.
- Convert rain water to be used for pasteurisation, toilet system and gardens.
- Labelled all stormwater drains on site to prevent staff or visitors inadvertently putting wastes into the drains and therefore into local streams or harbours.
- Taken a clear stand on promoting a 'GE free' New Zealand
- Incorporated comprehensive native plantings around the new factory to encourage insect and bird life (and provide a nice relaxing place for staff to enjoy).
- Have worked with Unitec horticulture students to design a new garden, based around permaculture principles, to provide a lovely place for staff to relax and to act as a learning area for staff. (we are yet to finalise the details on this)

Use Resources Efficiently and Fairly: Meet Human Needs (System Condition Four)

Phoenix has been running a Cleaner Production Programme since 1996 to improve resource efficiency. Until the adoption of the TNS framework this programme focused only on the resource use during the manufacturing process. The programme has expanded into broader areas through the implementation of The Natural Step framework, and the BioGro programmes. The company recognises a role for educating customers on sustainable lifestyles through their website and marketing materials.

In terms of resource efficiency this means:

- Less potential for waste or recalls through better quality management systems
- Reduction of resource use by: lagging pipes, better housekeeping practices, composting organic waste, recycling and reusing of packaging.
- Reduction of packaging waste by working with customers to return Phoenix packaging for reuse or recycling.
- Designed the new premises to incorporate some sustainable building criteria including; water and energy efficiency measures.
- Continue research into viable systems for collection and refilling of bottles and jars.

Source: www.phoenixorganics.co.nz

So we have to go through those for all the major decisions," Brown said.

Phoenix was also constrained in how far it could unilaterally take its sustainability program. The company would prefer glass bottles that were returnable and refillable, but the only provider of glass bottles in New Zealand—ACI - did not make refillable glass. On its own, Phoenix was not big enough to influence that market dynamic, but it was an active participant in the local organic cluster of many small enterprises.

The company's sustainability ethic also limited its product options. Bottled water would seem to have been a natural for Phoenix, but most water was sold in plastic. Brown also pointed out that there should have been no reason for people in New Zealand to be drinking bottled water. "The fact that our rivers have become polluted or that people are not feeling confident about drinking water out of the tap is really a worry," she said. Instead of joining the rush to make a profit from bottled water, the Phoenix philosophy suggested that New Zealand should look seriously at how to restore people's confidence in drinking tap water.

Another critical issue for the company was genetic engineering (GE). The company had a clear stand promoting a 'GE free' New Zealand (see Appendix 1 for more information on GE). "Not only is there a question over the damage to our natural ecosystems, but there seems to me a strong economic case for [New Zealand] remaining GE free," Morrison said.

Morrison also suggested that Phoenix was targeted more by competitors eager to tarnish its environmental good guy image. "The whole sustainability thing is interesting because you go down that track and you start talking about what good business is about etc. from a sustainable perspective, and then you're opening yourself up to criticism. People are just desperate to knock you down."

Despite the challenges, Phoenix's directors clearly saw its social and environmental sustainability image as a winning combination and the company had collected a number of awards for its sustainable business practices. "The fact that they're doing all this sustainability stuff keeps this loyal customer base going. It makes it very difficult for other companies to copy because the company brand is so interlinked with the owners, and their beliefs systems, and their value base," Brown said.

Mapping the Beverage Landscape

Phoenix was one of only six companies in the organic beverage market and the only player producing substantive volume.[8] But it was selling in a market where not everyone was concerned whether their drinks were organic or not. So, the wider non-alcoholic beverage industry whose players were arguably less environmentally and socially concerned made for a very competitive landscape. Exhibit 3 below shows the size of the main categories in the non-alcoholic beverage market in New Zealand. The carbonated beverages category was the single biggest category and incorporated typical soft drinks such as colas. New Age Beverages included energy drinks such as Red Bull that were characterized by the addition of energy enhancing ingredients and water-soluble vitamins. Fruit juice and drinks was the second largest category in New Zealand and included both fruit juice based beverages as well as water based beverages with fruit juice added (fruit drinks). As fruit drinks can be carbonated or still, this was the category that

EXHIBIT 3 Grocery Sales by Category

Category	Leading Brands	2004 (NZ$Million)	2003 (NZ$Million)
Carbonated Beverages	Coca-Cola, Fanta	209.8	199.9
New Age Beverages	V, Red Bull	31.7	27.0
Fruit Juice & Drinks	Fresh-up, Keri	131.3	124.0
Non-Carbonated Mineral Water	Mizone, h2go	23.0	20.4

Source: Grocers' Review, September 2004 (www.grocersreview.co.nz/archives/sep04_3.htm)

Phoenix Organic was included in. Bottled water sales had only recently begun to take off in New Zealand and are shown in the non-carbonated mineral water category.

Per capita consumption of soft drinks (carbonated beverages) in New Zealand was high by world standards at 360 bottles per year (although lower than the U.S. at 450). However, the market was considered mature and had been growing at 4–5 percent annually.[9] Coca-Cola New Zealand had dominated soft drinks since coming to New Zealand in 1939 and in 2004 continued to sell the majority of soft drinks in New Zealand (77.6 percent share of supermarket sales),[10] including the top six brands. Private label soft drinks had eaten into the virtual monopoly of Coca-Cola in recent years, while Pepsi had remained a minor player in New Zealand with less than 10 percent market share.

Coca-Cola was also active in other non-alcoholic beverage segments beyond soft drinks. The 2002 acquisition of Rio Beverages had gained Coca-Cola access to New Zealand's second largest juice company. Key brands from the acquisition—Keri and Robinsons - accounted for 20 percent of Coca-Cola's New Zealand production in 2004. Coca-Cola had 18.3 percent market share of the fruit juice category sold through supermarkets.[11] The largest juice company in New Zealand was Frucor—itself acquired by the French multinational Groupe Danone in January 2002. Frucor's origins dated back to the 1961 launch of Fresh-Up under the old Apple and Pear Marketing Board. In 1988, Frucor had been spun-off from the Marketing Board and in 1999 Frucor had acquired the Pepsi bottling business in New Zealand from Lion Nathan. Exhibit 4 below compares Phoenix with Coca-Cola and Frucor in terms of New Zealand staff, advertising and brands as well as global sales.

Both Frucor and Coca-Cola had brands in other segments such as bottled water and energy drinks. Bottled water continued a recent trend of strong growth (13.7 percent) in 2004. Energy drinks were the fastest growing (24 percent) beverage segment in New Zealand with Frucor's V brand being market leader in Australasia.[12] Coca-Cola's new regional managing director, George Adams, saw real growth potential in both water and juice: "New Zealand is a very small bottled-water consumer because no one has taken the market and built it, no one has told consumers it tastes better than tap water, that it is treated and convenient. The juice business is low due to a reasonably underdeveloped market, which needs a big player with serious distribution money to grow it. We want to lift juice—it is a market which responds to innovation in packaging and flavors. Over the next two years we will bring more innovation to the business."[13] Frucor had a stronger reputation for innovation stemming from its introduction of V and Mizone.

Coca-Cola planned growth in soft drinks from a strategy of 'expandable consumption'—based on research that showed it didn't seem to matter how many bottles were bought, it all got drunk. "If soft drinks are in the home they will be used, so we are constantly widening our distribution to have the product within an arm's length of desire," argued George Adams, "Seventy percent of product is bought on impulse. It's all about . . . understanding placement and making it easy for people to buy."[14]

EXHIBIT 4 Phoenix versus Large Competitors in New Zealand, 2003

Company	Staff	Advertising (NZ$000)	Key NZ Brands	Corporate Global Sales (NZ$m)
Phoenix	25	40	Phoenix	6.5
Frucor	500	13,619	V, Fresh Up, G Force, Mizone, Evian, Pepsi	25,265
Coca-Cola	1000	28,298	Coca-Cola, Fanta, Sprite, L&P, Pump, Keri, Powerade	33,500

Sources: Phoenix, Coca-Cola, Frucor, Groupe Danone, Neilson Media research

Aside from Coca-Cola and Frucor, other competitors with Phoenix included Arano, Juice Express and Charlies in juices. The overlap with Phoenix was not that large and Phoenix had co-operated with Arano in the past, with Phoenix supplying carbonated drinks and Arano supplying juices to specific events. The closest competitor to Phoenix in terms of products and style was probably San Pellegrino. Having already established a high-end position in Australia, San Pellegrino had made in-roads into the café and restaurant market in New Zealand. San Pellegrino offered a collection of lightly carbonated flavored mineral waters produced in Italy.

The Australian non-alcoholic beverages market was similar to New Zealand in both preferences and trends. Key differences were in terms of size—where the Australian market was approximately five times as large—and in terms of a larger number of competitors.

Future Challenges . . .

Ironically, Phoenix's successes had started to work against it in some segments of the market. Although in 2004 it was not a big problem, there were some very top end cafés that would not take the Phoenix brand because it was getting more commonplace, a trend Phoenix needed to watch closely. The company was also attracting more attention from the big players in the New Zealand beverage industry, which was one of the reasons Phoenix was looking so closely at its Australian options. To continue operating only in New Zealand and maintain historical growth levels, Harris said Phoenix would have to find ways to take the Phoenix Organic brand bigger, which would mean selling cheaper or launching other products. Either option would likely draw fire from bigger competitors like Coca-Cola and Frucor.

The company was leery about going head-to-head with the really big players. "Going directly against Coke or Frucor is inherently stupid in my opinion," Harris said. He found the Phoenix niche a safer scene. "There are certain rules for survival in this game and a lot of them are around understanding your market, understanding your niche. Once you get that down, you know your niche, then you can see what your tolerance is for other decisions."

The recent growth trends augured well for Phoenix's immediate future; however Morrison was aware of the risks. "We've still got to be realistic.

We're not a huge company and we're still vulnerable. Something might happen that could pull us down." One risk he saw was the danger of growing too big and losing the focus on sustainability. "I believe that there are some significant issues related to sustainability for businesses that get beyond a certain point." The strong relationships with staff, suppliers and customers that Morrison credits as the key to Phoenix's success was much more difficult to maintain the bigger an organization becomes, particularly if growth was occurring beyond the domestic market. Being a public advocate for sustainability didn't worry Morrison. He was committed to the idea and believed there was much work to be done in convincing others to take up what he saw as a necessary but ongoing challenge, even for businesses like his own.

. . . and Opportunities

To maintain growth, Phoenix was hoping to get its products into more service stations and more distant overseas markets such as Japan and Malaysia. But the biggest growth could come from supermarkets and Australia. "With our brand and our type of product, after the service stations, my view has been that we need more export business. We need Australia," Harris said.

In terms of new products, the Phoenix team accepted that Phoenix was going to remain a beverage company. But within that frame there was plenty of room for innovation. Hot drinks were one possibility, Harris pointed out. "The trade we work with deals in hot and cold beverage, and we want to be meaningful and useful to our trade, and give our salespeople a year round opportunity." The company was already marketing "the Chai experience." Chai is a creamy, milky, spicy tea—and Harris was enthusiastic about its potential. "We're talking about students . . . we're talking about people who haven't become coffee fanatics yet. They're looking for something that maybe isn't the mainstream, that isn't like everyone else." Phoenix wanted to increase its focus on organics, but knew that could prove difficult in a number of ways.

Not surprisingly, the founders had considered the what-if scenario of a buyout by a larger corporation. Morrison was unenthusiastic, acknowledging the hard work done by Phoenix in establishing the organic beverage niche. What if organics became much more popular? Would one of the big players suddenly become very interested? Morrison did not dismiss the possibility entirely but saw a danger that public companies and shareholders would be completely focused on the financial bottom line. Plus, Morrison still maintained his enthusiasm for the job, "I don't think we're halfway through the journey and I'm very keen to see us grow. I find it very stimulating and exciting and get a huge amount of my personal needs met out of business."

End Note

The authors do not have access to quantitative information on the industry, and the company was unwilling to provide financial information, thus a comprehensive financial analysis can not be conducted.

Notes

1. All currency is in New Zealand dollars. In early January 2005, the exchange rate was $1NZ = $.70 US.
2. Ginger Fizz refers to the brand and the product name. Half of each brew was strained through muslin, lemon juice, brown sugar, powdered ginger and water. The remaining half was fed with brown sugar and water for the following weeks' production. The brew was left to settle and then bottles were capped and left to ferment until the desired carbonation was achieved.
3. Phoenix Organic is both the company name and the brand, although on products that are not organic, the brand Phoenix is used.
4. Feijoa is a small, green fruit grown on trees. The fruit has a sweet, almost bubble-gum like flavor.
5. The global awareness of food safety issues and the impact on New Zealand organic companies is documented on the website of The Organic Products Exporters of New Zealand Inc at: www.organicsnewzealand.org.nz.
6. GreenFleet is a practical program developed by the Sustainable Business Network which enables New Zealand businesses to do something towards reducing the impacts of their vehicle fleet on the environment and people.
7. Porter, M. & van der Linde, C. (1995). Green and competitive: Ending the stalemate. *Harvard Business Review*, 73(5), 120–129.
8. www.organicsnewzealand.org.nz
9. Kennedy, G. (2004, February 5) 'Kiwi's thirsty enough?' *National Business Review*, p. 28.
10. www.grocersreview.co.nz/archives/sep04_3.htm
11. Ibid.
12. Grocers' Review, September 2004 (www.grocersreview.co.nz/archives/sep04_3.htm)
13. Kennedy, G. (2004, February 5) 'Kiwi's thirsty enough?' *National Business Review*, p. 28.
14. Ibid.

Appendix 1 Background Information on Organic, Natural and GE-Free

What Is Organic?

In very general terms, organic means that a product has been produced without using artificial chemicals. BioGro defines organic produce as:

> Grown naturally without the routine use of synthetic agricultural chemicals such as fungicides, herbicides, insecticides, growth regulators, and soluble fertilizers; processed with nil or minimal use of synthetic additives like stabilizers, emulsifiers, antioxidants, preservatives, colors, and flavor enhancers; much more than spray-free or residue-free because it is produced under positive agri-ecological management systems which work in harmony with nature (www.BioGro.co.nz).

There are a number of different bodies, national (New Zealand) and international, that provide organic certification to ensure products marked "organic" have been produced in accordance with certain standards. Exhibit 1 shows that some of Phoenix's products were certified organic by BioGro, which is accredited by the International Federation of Organic Agriculture Movements (IFOAM). BioGro is one of 30 international organic certification agencies accredited by IFOAM. Certified organic producers can use the organic logo and are allocated a unique customer number to enable product traceability throughout the supply chain. The certification by BioGro enabled Phoenix to sell its products internationally with an organic label signifying certification.

What Is the Difference between "Natural" and "Organic" Produce?

IFOAM declares the difference between natural and organic as:

> Organic agriculture is based upon a systematic approach and standards that can be verified and are recognized internationally. Natural foods, on the other hand, have no legal definition or recognition, and are not based on a systematic approach. While natural products

may generally be minimally processed, there are no requirements to provide proof, leaving open the possibility for fraud and misuse of the term (http://www.ifoam.org).

What Is the Connection Among "Natural," "Organic" and "GE-Free?"

According to IFOAM, the absence of genetic engineering is a requirement for organic certification, however there is no such requirement for natural foods.

New Zealand had a moratorium on commercial releases of genetic engineering until 2003 when the ban was lifted. Applications for the release of genetically modified material was considered on a case by case basis by the Environmental Risk Management Authority, the government agency established to protect the New Zealand environment from potential hazards. In 2004, there had been no GE release applications to the New Zealand government.

The GE-Free/monarch butterfly symbol, shown on Exhibit 1, implies an association with the non-profit organisation GE-Free New Zealand in food and environment (Rage Inc.). GE-Free New Zealand promotes making the New Zealand environment and food free of genetically engineered organisms http://www.gefree.org.nz/about.htm. Members are concerned about negative human and environmental health implications of GE. In addition, businesses belonging to the group saw the ability to offer GE-free products as a source of international competitive advantage through a differentiation strategy, charging a premium for GE-free products. As a small island nation, New Zealand had, it was felt by GE-Free members, a unique opportunity to remain a GE-free country.

Appendix 2 Background on Sustainability

Sustainability visibly entered the public arena with the release of the (1987) World Commission on Environment and Development's (Brundtland) report entitled *Our Common Future*. The report gives a commonly accepted definition of sustainable development as development "which meets the needs of the present without compromising the ability of future generations to meet their own needs."[a] However, there are many different definitions of sustainability, sustainable business and sustainable development (e.g. www.sustainableliving.org/appen-a.htm lists 57 differing definitions of sustainable development). The consequence of this ambiguity is that sustainability has become a contested concept invoked to support numerous political and social agendas including that of business.

The business case for sustainable development is based on doing good for the environment and society in so far as it does good for the business. However, many critics believe that this approach is insufficient to broad based achievement of ecological and societal sustainability.

Elkington (1997) translated sustainability in the business context to mean that business has more than an economic bottom-line, but rather a triple-bottom line of economic, social and environmental performance. However, there is not one internationally accepted set of sustainability protocols. For businesses interested in becoming less unsustainable, there are a wide variety of frameworks and tools available, as well as consultants and business associations to assist and advise. But many of these offer only incremental change to business as usual.

Phoenix implemented the Natural Step framework, which is more radical and challenging in its requirements for fundamental change. The Natural Step (http://www.naturalstep.org.nz) uses a science-based, systems framework to help businesses, organizations, and communities understand and move towards sustainability. The Natural Step's upstream approach means it addresses problems at the source and turns them into opportunities for innovation.

In 2004, Chris Morrison was the Chair of the Sustainable Business Network (SBN). SBN members agree to work towards:

- **Economic Prosperity**—to undertake best business management so as to support long-term economic growth for New Zealand.
- **Environmental Quality**—to go beyond compliance through the adoption of proactive strategies which restore and enhance the environment in which we live, work and play.
- **Social Equity**—to see NZ business operating as a good corporate citizen and encouraging respect and dignity to

all stakeholders by developing mutually beneficial partnerships with local community stakeholders.

- **Corporate Governance & Ethics**—to conduct business in an ethical manner and to seek to do business with companies which adopt the same principles (www.sustainable.org.nz).

Some companies are releasing sustainability or triple bottom line reports to communicate to stakeholders progress towards sustainability goals. The Global Reporting Initiative is an international collaboration associated with the United Nations whose mission is to develop and disseminate globally applicable sustainability reporting guidelines. These guidelines are for voluntary use by organizations for reporting on the economic, environmental, and social dimensions of their activities, products, and services (www.globalreporting.org).

Note

a. World Commission on Environment and Development (1987) *Our Common Future*, Oxford: Oxford University Press, p. 43.

Traditional Case 11: Chipco International: "We Didn't Create the Problem, but We Have to Survive It."

This case was prepared by Thomas C. Leach, University of New England, and is intended to be used as a basis for class discussion. The views represented here are those of the case author and do not necessarily reflect the views of the Society for Case Research. The author's views are based on his professional judgment. Copyright © 2003 by the Business Case Journal and the author. No part of this work may be reproduced or used in any form or by any means without a written permission of the Society for Case Research.

On May 31, 1996, John Kendall, owner and chief executive officer of Chipco International, was settling into a long flight to Sydney Harbor Casino, Sydney, Australia. Kendall's company manufactured gaming chips for the international gaming (casino) industry and was located in Raymond, Maine, 20 miles from Portland. Normally, Kendall looked forward to the trips to the various casinos around the world, often located in luxurious resort destinations. The visits centered on business, but usually allowed for a little recreation time, too. This trip was different. Kendall wasn't looking forward to a meeting with Mr. Edwards, the general manager of Sydney Harbor Casino, one of Chipco's largest accounts. Kendall had to explain Chipco's recall of 362,000 recently produced gaming chips, valued at approximately $181,000 with an additional $10,000 in shipping charges. Kendall also had to convince Mr. Edwards that the problem was not anything Chipco had done or could have done. Kendall needed to reassure Edwards that Chipco would honor its warranties and correct the problems that caused a worldwide chip recall. He also had to restore trust in Chipco as an industry leader in casino gaming chips.

The competitive atmosphere in the casino industry had intensified after the news of Chipco's product failure spread. Some casinos dropped Chipco and bought competitive, low-tech products. Competitor sales representatives contributed to the intense atmosphere by emphasizing the qualities of their more basic transaction pieces, price and durability. The industry increasingly became price driven and questioned the durability of Chipco products.

At this time the estimated overall cost of the total recall was approaching $600,000. This was significant when compared to Chipco's annual sales in 1995 of $3,001,653. Adding to the severity of the problem was the calling of Chipco's bank loan of $227,000 on May 10. The $600,000 problem alone exceeded the company's net worth of $457,000 and that forced the bankers' action. Kendall was aware and fearful that in addition to the damage to customer relations and a growing cash flow problem, he was faced with a problem so severe that his company was facing possible bankruptcy with company-wide repercussions.

Industry Background

In the early 1960s, commercial gaming was minimal. Lotteries had been made illegal throughout the country, since before the turn of the century (Clotfelter and Cook, 1989). Casinos, off track betting, bookmaking, and sport wagering were illegal in the United States except in Nevada (Rose, 1991). The only legal gambling was horse racing and bingo. Horse racing gambling was restricted to wagers made at the track, with live racing in approximately 30 states. Bingo was usually offered by churches and fraternal organizations and was justified as socialization and fund raising for good causes. Even social gambling, at-home poker, was illegal in many states (Ciaffone, 1991). The laws regulating gaming began to change in the 1970s and casino gaming has become a growing industry in the United States for over the past 30 years. In 1969, the Nevada Corporate Gaming Act was passed, which allowed publicly traded corporations to obtain gaming licenses. Soon afterward major hospitality and entertainment firms entered the industry, including MGM, Hilton, Holiday Inn, and Ramada. In 1976, New Jersey allowed legalized gaming in Atlantic City, making it the second state in the country to have legalized gaming. By the mid-1980s, Atlantic City had 12 casinos in operation. Their revenues, as measured by winnings, briefly surpassed Las Vegas. In 1998, Las Vegas regained its dominance with gaming revenues of $5.5 billion compared to Atlantic City's $4 billion. New Jersey shaped its casino industry differently than Nevada. It required a specific size and space criteria, which limited investors to organizations that were able to secure large amounts of financial capital. This resulted in an oligopolistic environment. Nevada erected relatively few barriers to firms wishing to enter the industry. However, due to economies of scale, the industry there evolved into an oligopoly, even though there still remained numerous smaller casinos. By the late 1990s, 27 states had some form of gaming. Riverboat casinos were legalized in Illinois, Mississippi, Louisiana, Missouri, and Indiana. New Orleans (1992) and Detroit (1996) legalized land-based casinos. Locations such as former mining towns in the western United States, destination resorts, and Indian reservations offered gambling throughout the United States. A 1995 survey by the *Casino Journal* showed that 53.7 percent of all Americans and 66 percent of those between 18 and 25 approved of casino gaming. Money won by casinos had also grown dramatically. In 1970, owners of Nevada casinos had gross winnings of $540 million. By 1997, gross revenues by casinos across the United States had grown to $25 billion (Christiansen, 1998). Refer to Exhibit 1 for the gross revenues by sector of the industry for the years 1982 and 1997.

Legalized gaming in the United Kingdom occurred in 1968 and casinos first appeared in 1972 in Australia. Canada's first casinos were temporary in nature and benefited nonprofit enterprises such as the Calgary Stampede and Edmonton's Klondike Days. Over time the charitable casinos became permanent and regulations limiting casinos were relaxed (Eadington, 1999) with regulatory authorities established at the provincial level in the 1990s. In 1995, annual global sales were 25 million chips and Chipco had sold 24 per cent of this amount in the previous two years (Chipco interview).

Industry Licensing. The industry was carefully regulated, since gaming chips were money for the casinos. All supplier companies were scrutinized to assure that there was no illegal money or illegal contacts of any kind related to any manufacturer. Chip manufacturers were literally mints for the casinos, since the chips were purchased by gaming patrons from the casinos and used for betting. In the United States, chip manufacturers were required to obtain licenses from gaming commissions of states where gaming was legal and were physically audited with frequent plant visits. Investigation agents of the 30 state gaming commissions conducted the audits that included inventory control systems, chip distribution and manufacturing processes, and records to assure that the chips were not overproduced and would not be unscrupulously redeemed for cash. Another part of the scrutiny was to audit the financial condition

| EXHIBIT 1 | Gross Revenues by Sector,a U.S. Commercial Gaming Industries, 1982 and 1997 (millions of 1997 dollars) | | |

Average Sector	1982	1997	Growth Rate
Parimutuel[b]	$ 4,644	$ 3,811	−1.31%
Lotteries[c]	$ 3,609	$16,567	10.69%
Casinos[d]	$ 6,985	$20,528	7.45%
Bookmaking	$ 43	$ 96	5.46%
Card rooms	$ 83	$ 700	15.26%
Bingo, charitable	$ 1,956	$ 2,430	1.46%
Indian gaming	$ 0	$ 6,678	
Total	$17,320	$50,810	7.45%

a. Revenues retained by operators after payment of prizes.
b. Includes horse racing, dog racing and jai alai.
c. Includes video lottery terminals.
d. Excludes Native American casinos, but includes non-casino devices.

Source: Christiansen (1998, pg11).

of chip manufacturers; if a manufacturer fell into bankruptcy it would lose its license. Suppliers with sales of greater than $100,000 to chip manufacturers were also audited, having their physical property and accounting records carefully checked. Chip manufacturers that passed the audits were initially given licenses good for three years. At the end of that period, manufacturers were audited again in order to have their licenses renewed. After several renewals, the gaming investigators usually issued licenses for a five-year period. Further, any company that underwent any type of reorganization or other significant event, for instance, shareholder changes of greater than 10 percent of ownership, would be reviewed. If any suspicious issues were found a manufacturer's license to supply chips could be suspended. New manufacturers needed to obtain a license in order to sell chips to casinos, a process that could take up to two years.

Competitive Situation. There were four major gaming chip and accessory companies that served the worldwide gaming industry. The chips served as the money of casinos and were purchased by gamblers from casinos and used as betting tokens or transaction pieces, as the trade termed them, at the various gaming tables and slot machines. The quality of chips was a significant issue for casinos. They represented a sizeable investment and long-lasting chips saved the casinos money over time, since they would not need replacing as often. The casinos were at risk of having chips counterfeited and then redeemed for cash. Aesthetically attractive transaction pieces produced additional, albeit small, income because customers frequently kept a few chips as souvenirs of their vacation to the casino. The casino floor managers were usually the chip-buying decision makers. They placed emphasis on price and quality, as measured by the chips' durability, and tended to buy from only one chip manufacturer, since they wanted to keep the look of their chips consistent throughout the casino. Security features and the aesthetics of the transaction pieces were less important than price for most buyers, but if a given chip's durability was believed equal to others, then aesthetics and security features played a significant role in the final purchase decision.

Paul-Son Gaming Corporation, headquartered in Las Vegas, Nevada, was the leading manufacturer and supplier of casino table game equipment in the United States with 48 percent of the global round style chip, which was the preferred style of chip in the United States, Canada, and Asia. The European casinos tended to use square chips, normally called plaques. Paul-Son chips were made of clay and compression molded in Mexico, using an older manufacturing technology. The company's product list included casino chips, table games layouts, playing cards, dice, gaming furniture, and miscellaneous table accessories such as chip trays, drop boxes, and dealer shoes. It also sold its products for personal use, where state and local laws allowed. Casino gaming chips were generally priced between $.60 and $.80 per chip.

Chipco International was the second largest round chip producer with 24 percent of the global market. As mentioned above, Chipco was the leader in technologically advanced transaction pieces, with invisible security and casino chip inventory control benefits. Its chips had never been counterfeited or replicated. Its Pro-Tec™ series sold from $.50 to $.80 per chip.

The third largest casino supply company was Bud Jones Company, Inc., of Las Vegas, Nevada. Bud Jones had been a family-owned company since its inception in 1965 and represented around 20 percent of the round chip global market. It supplied a full line of casino supplies including dice, chips, cards, tables, wheels, and various miscellaneous supplies. Its chips were made of plastic and used an inlaid coin to give the chip the weight normally expected in a chip. Bud Jones chip prices were below Chipco's at $.35 to $.45 each and did not have the technological options that Chipco offered. Further, it did not offer the same degree of design variety as Chipco.

Bourgogne & Grasset of France was the fourth largest casino supply company in the world and represented only 8 percent of round chip global sales. The firm was the leader in Europe where square plaques were traditionally used and continued to dominate the market. There were other chip producers but they catered to the non-casino market of individuals and private organizations.

Company Overview

Prior to June 15, 1985, when John Kendall bought the Burt Company, he was an experienced trouble-shooter for a venture capital firm's underperforming investments for three years. Kendall had always been entrepreneurial, having built Portland's first indoor tennis facility, the Tennis Racket, in the early 1970s. After he sold that business he and his brother Bill founded a payment and transfer services technology company called Time Share Incorporated. This business was a precursor to electronic funds transfer, as it enabled banks, investment companies, and Texaco and Mobile oil companies to move money electronically. The company was later sold to McDouglas Inc.

Kendall had been looking for a business to buy when the Burt Company was brought to his attention. Kendall, along with a few family investors, bought the company from members of the Burt family after the death of Alonzo Burt at age 89. John was the major shareholder while his father Richard, brother Thomas (who joined the company in January 1995 and worked in manufacturing) and uncle William Poole held minor ownership positions. The Burt Company had been founded in 1895 as the Portland Billiard Ball Company and in the 1920s poker chips were added to the product line. The chips were made out of clay using a compression molding process, as were the billiard balls.

Modernization. From the 1920s to the mid-1980s, the Burt Company earnings fluctuated between profit and loss. At the time of purchase the company was losing $30,000 per month; however, the firm had a significant manufacturing capacity with compression molding capabilities, laminating, grinding equipment, and punch presses. The company also had 22 distributors around the world selling its clay-based poker chips. However, the manufacturing processes were antiquated and inefficient.

From 1985 until the 1990s, Kendall overhauled and modernized the Burt Company's products and operations, and increased its number of gaming jurisdictions. He purchased graphic art software, several Apple MacIntosh computers, and added research and development capability. He acquired accounting software and related items that allowed the company to upgrade its accounting function from a basic bookkeeping operation. From an accounting perspective, these activities were shown under the General and Administrative Expense line item of the earnings statement and the Equipment accounts of the balance sheets (see Exhibits 2a and 2b). It cost Chipco $120,000 per year to maintain its 30 gaming

jurisdictions. Some licenses were included with the purchase of Burt Company; others were acquired after Kendall purchased the company. The annual cost was for all of the expenses for the licensing audits that were required during a year. The fees were paid to the investigator agents of the state gaming commissions. The company was profitable in the early 1990s, with 1993 being a particularly good year. Kendall believed that the company was in a position for sustained growth, so in 1994 and 1995 Kendall continued the modernizing process and expanded Chipco's infrastructure and overhead. In 1995, Chipco acquired printing equipment that enabled it to produce its own printed materials.

Kendall had an innovative attitude about business and was the conceptual leader of the company's research and development (R&D) and its small staff (see the organizational chart, Figure 1). It was not unusual for him to think of several innovative solutions for a given problem. Since he knew that counterfeiting was a serious problem for the industry, Kendall envisioned a chip that would have invisible security measures and unique decorative designs to thwart would-be counterfeiters. He outsourced the refinement of his technological ideas and ultimately was able to obtain a special resin formula, created by G.E. Plastics of Pittsfield, Massachusetts. The resin had the properties necessary to accept infrared and ultraviolet bar coding and PIN numbers and would be durable.

Burt Company introduced the Pro-Tec™ chip in 1987. The new chips had the features Kendall envisioned, infrared spectrum and ultraviolet bar coding of PIN numbers. Along with the new product introduction, the company name was changed to Chipco International as a way of emphasizing the company's changes. Kendall was proud of the fact that Chipco was the most technologically advanced producer and that it had a comprehensive warranty covering its products. In addition to the security benefits, casino inventory control could be improved by requesting ultraviolet serial numbering and/or PIN numbers. Further, on the Pro-Tec™ series, chips had intricate edge designs that incorporated wording, denomination, and graphics. Pro-Tec™ chips had never been replicated or counterfeited. In addition, Chipco's technological advantage enabled it to use full-color photographs of entertainers, monuments, trademark signage, or

Chipco International, LTD. Balance Sheet (December 31, 1993, 1994, and 1995)

Assets

	1993	1994	1995
Current Assets:			
Cash	$8,857	$40,510	$46,327
Accounts receivable	$435,472	$175,526	$90,006
Inventory	$217,813	$344,546	$412,701
Prepaid expenses	$43,493	$61,766	$68,146
Due from employees	–	$61,610	$105,177
Total Current Assets	$705,635	$683,958	$722,357
Property, plant, equipment:			
Machinery and equipment	$212,762	$298,871	$445,291
Office equipment	$85,197	$120,600	$136,830
Leasehold improvements	$93,911	$111,079	$114,574
Automobiles	$32,186	$32,186	$32,186
	$424,056	$562,736	$728,881
Less accumulated depreciation	$127,339	$118,134	$196,587
Net property, plant, equip.	296,717	444,598*	532,294
Other assets:			
Due from officers	–	–	$111,175
Intangible assets, net of amortization	$40,565	$24,766	$15,904
Research and develop., net of amort.	$44,342	–	–
Note receivable from related co.	$40,649	$48,830	$91,878
Note receivable from stockholder	$64,206	–	–
Deposits on equipment	$3,000	$6,000	$24,500
Total other assets	$192,762	$80,596*	$243,457
Total Assets	$1,195,114	$1,209,152	$1,498,108

Liabilities and Stockholders' Equity

	1993	1994	1995
Current Liabilities:			
Line of credit	–	$100,000	$75,000
Current portion of long-term debt	$42,030	$94,109	$93,352
Accounts payable	$360,672	$264,147	$452,507
Accrued expenses	$17,216	$27,707	$87,727
Customers' deposits	$250,604	$141,735	$179,770
Due to officer	–	$100	–
Total current liabilities	$670,522	$627,798	$888,356
Long-term debt, excluding current portion	$65,984	$170,546	$127,919
Total Liabilities	736,506	798,344	1,016,275
Stockholders' equity:			
Common stock, $1 par value.			
Authorized 100,000 Shares, issued and outstanding shs.:	$1,196	$1,196	$1,196
Additional paid-in capital	$104,909	$104,909	$104,909
Retained earnings	$352,503	$304,703	$375,728
Total stockholders' equity	458,608	410,808	481,833
Liabilities and Owners' Equity	$1,195,114	$1,209,152	$1,498,108

* differences due to rounding
Source: Chipco Doc.

2b Chipco International, LTD. Statement of Earnings and Retained Earnings (Years Ended December 31, 1993, 1994, and 1995)

	1993	1994	1995
Sales	$2,798,950	$3,033,654	$3,001,653
Cost of Goods Sold	$1,645,275	$1,811,355	$1,530,908
Gross Profit	$1,153,675	$1,222,299	$1,470,745
General and Administrative Expenses (Includes Salaries Expense)	$829,697	$1,156,653	$1,357,919
Operating Income	$323,978	$65,646	$112,826
Other Income (Expense):			
Interest Income	$5,168	$2,464	$14,814
Interest Expense	$(9,890)	$(15,617)	$(40,207)
Other Income	$5,000	$11,300	$13,384
	$278	$(1,853)	$(12,009)
Net Earnings	324,256	63,793	100,817
Retained Earnings, beginning of year	28,247	376,428	304,703
Distribution to Stockholders	–	(135,518)	(29,728)
Retained Earnings, end of year	$352,503	$304,703	$375,792

FIGURE **1** Organizational Chart

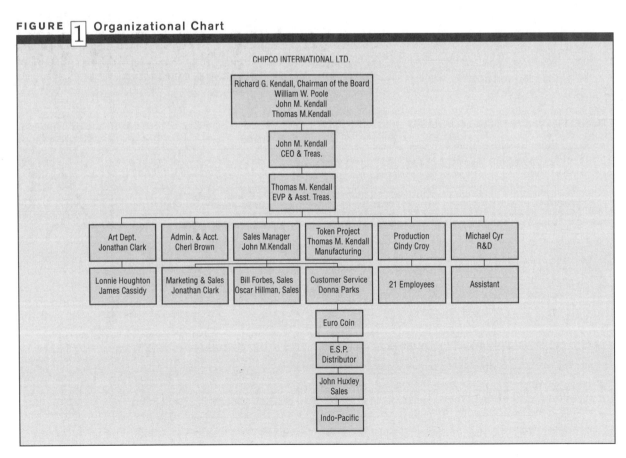

any visual or picture a customer might choose to have on its chips. Further, the intricacy and beauty of the chips resulted in some of them being kept as souvenirs, netting casinos an additional, albeit small, profit. Prices for the Pro-Tec™ series ranged from $.50 to $.80 per chip.

Chipco produced lower-priced chips, as well. The Unicorn™ Series was stocked in 13 colors. These chips were popular for various promotions such as 'Casino Nights' and 'Charity Gaming' events many organizations commonly held. All Chipco chips were washable and durable. Chipco also produced automated chip sorting and washing machines. In Europe, Chipco had only limited sales of the traditional square plaques.

Supply and Manufacturing. The supplier that Kendall chose for the Pro-Tec™ chip resin had served Chipco with resin for its lower grade chip, the Unicorn™, for two years before the new chip had been developed. Kendall trusted the company and felt comfortable in expanding the supply relationship. Kendall gave the supply company the special resin formula with specific grades of ingredients. He did not negotiate a specific agreement saying that notification was necessary for any change in the formula, because he believed that it was understood that there would be no change to the formula. A lab-tested sampling of the resin showed that the original formula was being used.

The purchase order form used by Kendall did not include terms and conditions wording. The supplier, on the other hand, had numerous terms and conditions on the back of its invoice. If any issues arose about a shipment they had to be notified within 10 days, or the shipment would be considered accepted.

Supply management and manufacturing were logistically simple, with Chipco using one supplier for all of its resin. The resin was drop-shipped to the carefully selected contracted injection molding company. Kendall used a subcontractor for injection molding of the chips to a firm that met his requirements, since this process was a commodity industry and a less expensive alternative for Chipco. The molded chips were then safety packed and shipped back to Chipco. Upon receiving the chips they were visually inspected before the infrared and ultraviolet bar coding, PIN numbers, special

edge designs, and other decorative touches were added by Chipco. These manufacturing processes were unique and gave Chipco control over its trade secrets. The finished chips were then inspected and sent out after a quality check through Chipco's channels to its customers.

Proprietary Information. Kendall had resin formulas and manufacturing processes that could have been patented, but he chose not to do so in order to keep his proprietary knowledge secret. Patents give inventors 20 years of protection from competition on the patented items, but the patented items become public information, as they are registered and on file at the U.S. Patent and Trademark Office. There exists a risk to inventors with patents that their ideas could be understood by individuals and provide insights for competitive products and processes. The invisible security process of the Pro-Tec™ chip was technically complex, but viewed simplistically it involved four keys: the chemical formula of the resin that accepts the invisible bar coding; the finish manufacturing process of the chip; the energy source activation of a reader; and the return signal recognition of the energy source by the reader. Kendall controlled all of the technological details for the keys. The chemicals used in the secret resin formula were not available commercially, but had to be created using ingredients that originated in a rare earth chemical family. G. E. Plastics, the developer of the formula, coded it and filed it in a separate place not in its Customer Service Bank. He also had an agreement with the resin supplier not to divulge any of the resin's secret properties.

Marketing. Before the resin problem, Chipco's promotional program consisted of personal selling, advertising; and trade show attendance. From 1985 to 1995, Chipco had gained brand equity in the industry due to the awareness of the technological advantages of the Pro-Tec™ chip. Chipco was the second largest chip manufacturer in the world and had been growing by approximately 15 percent each year for the past five years. Chipco had been profitable with its new Pro-Tec™ chip since 1992, five years after its introduction. The sales force consisted of five individuals who maintained personal relationships with their customers. They made sales calls and attended the four major gaming industry trade shows: two shows in Las Vegas, one in London, and one in Mississippi. The sales force covered the global gaming industry and was organized regionally, with the greatest concentration in the United States. This resulted in the reps traveling about one week per month. The reps used the phone and written communiqués to supplement their activities, along with company brochures. In January 1995, Richard Kendall contributed printing equipment from his printing business. This equipment enabled Chipco to reduce its costs of various printed materials. The company did not have an internet web site. Chipco was a member of the two trade associations: the World Gaming Congress and the American Gaming Association. The firm advertised in the two trade journals, the *Casino Journal* and the *Casino Executive*, at a cost of $19,000 per year.

The distribution channel was direct from Chipco to casinos in North America through the company's marketing representatives. It also sold to resellers that combined the chips with various casino products, dice, furniture, etc. Distributors were used outside of North America with all shipments made using insured UPS and armored car deliveries.

Kendall believed that trust in Chipco by his customers and employees was essential for long-term relationships. He often told his salespeople, "If you lie to the customer even once, they'll never buy from us again. We must honor our commitments. Gaming is a people business."

Human Resources. Chipco did not have a formal written mission statement, but Kendall believed in honest and fair dealings with all stakeholders. Chipco offered 37 employees safe jobs, paid its employees well in terms of area wages, and provided good health benefits. Chipco paid 100 percent of major medical insurance coverage, with a $1,000 deductible per person. The high deductible policy allowed for cost-effective rates to Chipco. Chipco then paid the first $600 of any employee health problem coming from a fund of $600 per employee. Any unused medical funds were given to the employees as a bonus at the end of the year. Chipco funded the program by adding $600 per week during the year until the needed amount was fully contributed. Kendall supplied the company kitchen with food and snacks, at no charge to employees. Kendall believed in open communications with his staff and was available to hear employee concerns. Additionally, Chipco allowed a liberal vacation benefit that was better than other employers in the area.

The Problem

The chip defect first occurred in July 1995 when the Casino Nova Scotia in Halifax, Nova Scotia, reported to Chipco that some of its new chips had broken. Kendall responded quickly by replacing the broken chips and assuring the casino that Chipco would make good on its warranty. Later, during the summer of 1995, other casinos reported to Chipco that their chips had broken, worn thin, and faded. Thin chips resulted in operational failures at casinos because count errors had occurred. In some cases, 21 chips were given to patrons instead of 20. This caused the cash cages to be short and resulted in immediate losses to the casinos.

Kendall replaced all of the defective chips as they were reported, but wasn't certain of the cause of the problem. He thought that the problem could have been related to the finish manufacturing processes done at the Chipco facility. Kendall carefully examined his operations but couldn't find the problem.

By September, Kendall's anxiety concerning the disaster was growing. He had informed his directors of the problem, as he believed in being forthright. During the third week of the month, he attended the World Gaming Expo, the industry's major trade show. Rather than socializing with his customers he was "assaulted" by some of them, as he explained to a close associate. Several customers had brought failed chips to his booth to show him. He assured them that he would honor the Chipco's warranty, replace the failed chips, and "make whole" the situation by bearing all of the costs associated with replacing the defective chips.

On November 2, 1995, Kendall contacted the resin supplier to probe into the problem but didn't receive a definitive answer as to why the chips had failed. It wasn't until late in November that the resin supplier admitted that it had changed a grade level of one of the raw materials of the resin formula that Chipco had given to the supplier. The supplier made the change as a cost savings, believing that it would not have any negative consequences. The change did, however, result in the product failures.

Kendall demanded that the original formula be used. Further, Kendall asked that the supplier support the replacement program, "to make whole the problem." The supplier agreed to work with Chipco. Unfortunately two of the supplier's chemists had left the company, which made it difficult to precisely reformulate the original resin. Meanwhile, the replacement chips had been made of the resin formula that caused the problems.

In December 1995, Kendall began his search for alternate resin suppliers. He soon contacted Hoerst-Celanese, a large German petrol-chemical company, and the LNP Company, located in Extin, Pennsylvania. By April 1996, the samples that he had requested from both companies had been received and tested. Both companies' samples had passed the lab tests.

By mid-April 1996, the number of flawed chips was estimated to be 750,000, worth approximately $400,000, but the exact number distributed could not be estimated because it was not known exactly when the supplier changed the resin formula. At this point, the resin supplier reneged on its agreement to support the replacement program, viewing it as a problem without an end. Kendall was now without support to recall all chips that had been produced with the changed resin formula.

Toward the end of April, Kendall changed his resin supplier to LNP. They had been more aggressive in their bidding than Hoerst-Celanese and agreed to supply the resin at a lower price. The new resin was shipped by the end of the month.

On April 30, 1996, Kendall voluntarily met with his bankers to explain the problem, which he estimated at a cost $600,000. (Refer to Exhibits 2a and 2b for a review of Chipco's financial statements). The bankers seemed understanding and told Kendall to put together a plan and return in two weeks. Kendall was optimistic that the bank would accept the plan and work with him.

Within a few days after the bank meeting, Kendall had called a company-wide meeting to inform his employees of the recall and to let them ask questions. Kendall had followed what he believed was good human resource management by always being honest and fair with his workers. Kendall praised his staff for their hard work in the past and asked that they stay with him in this difficult time. He mentioned that there would likely be overtime work ahead as replacement chips must be produced. Kendall received words of understanding about the situation and angry comments toward the supplier.

Three of five salespeople quit almost immediately after learning about the recall. They felt that their lives would be miserable when they called on their customers and their incomes would suffer since their compensation was about 70 percent salary and 30 percent commission. The decrease in payroll somewhat eased the cash flow problem that was to unfold, since each representative was paid on average $60,000 per year. However, the loss of 60 percent of the sales staff left a void in Chipco's market coverage. Most of his 37 employees stayed with the company initially, but a couple of people eventually left Chipco several months later, for what they believed were more secure jobs.

On May 10, 1996, the bank called a second meeting. Three bank personnel attended, one of whom Kendall did not know. The third person turned out to be the bank's attorney. He read a lengthy, legalistic document. Kendall presented his crisis management plan and was expecting the bank to go along with him. Instead, Kendall listened to what was the calling-in of Chipco's outstanding debt of $227,000. Kendall was given ten days to deliver the funds to the bank, or Chipco's assets would be seized and the business would be shut down. The bankers felt that with a net worth of $457,000 and the $600,000 problem Chipco was insolvent and they said, "you're bankrupt, you can't make it, so we're calling the loan." After hearing the bankers Kendall said, "I'm bankrupt only if I stop operating, if I don't stop operating then I can cover the losses as we move forward, by cycling in those that we have to replace each month. But you calling the loan have greatly contributed to the other guy winning and I won't survive the event. This is the worst day of my life." He left the meeting thinking, "We did nothing (wrong). We didn't create the problem, but we have to survive it."

By the end of the ten-day period, Kendall was able to meet the bank's demand through funds from all of his personal savings, savings for his children's college educations, life insurance policies cash values, mortgages on his home, and loans from family and friends. Cash flow became critical for Kendall, since there was absolutely no extra cash available and no line of bank credit.

At the end of May, Kendall and his attorneys launched a legal action against the supplier. The attorneys, understanding the financial pressures on Chipco, agreed to receive their fees after the case had been resolved. Kendall knew he had a case, but was not sure how long it would take for a ruling to resolve the matter. If the court ruled in Chipco's favor, would the decision be appealed?

Surviving. As of May 1996, Kendall had replaced failed chips as they were reported. He had met some customers at trade shows and at their casinos, primarily in the U.S. He now was on a global tour of casinos serviced by distributors. The problem had become progressively worse and now had reached true crisis proportions with the bank having called in his loans. Kendall knew that his company's financial condition was significantly weakened. The total stockholders' equity in December prior to the crisis was $481,833. Kendall estimated the cost of the recall and replacement at $600,000. The company was insolvent. A common strategy for insolvent companies is to use the Chapter 11 option of the Bankruptcy Law[1] In this type of bankruptcy, a company would be reorganized, with a court-appointed executor and a time limit to develop a recovery plan, before debt payments would be required.

A bankruptcy proceeding would invalidate a chip producer's license. Bankrupting Chipco and immediately starting a new company also was not an alternative, since it would take two years to obtain new chip manufacturer's licenses. When discussing the problems facing the company with close associates, Kendall often said, "I'm bankrupt only if I stop operating," but to keep the company operating would require carefully crafted survival strategies and day-to-day cash flow monitoring.

Before meeting with his customers, Kendall knew he needed consistent customer relations and marketing strategy to cope with his crisis. He had solid relationships with his customers and Kendall knew that this trust was crucial if the company were to survive. Should he attempt to reduce the cost of the chips? Should he cut advertising? Should he skip a trade show or two? Should he cut prices? A price reduction, Kendall thought, would in some way reduce the cost of the recall. If he cut prices, by how much should they be reduced? Would price increases later, after the problem was corrected, create another problem? Kendall had to move ahead swiftly and address numerous issues to save his company.

In addition to the original resin supplier, there were other supply companies. Kendall struggled over how to handle their concerns as they learned of the problem. Chipco was not the same credit risk that it was before the problem erupted. Should he be straight- forward and tell suppliers exactly what had happened? How could he respond to them if Chipco was placed on a cash-on-delivery (C.O.D.) basis? Chipco had about 15 suppliers where a current debt existed of between $10,000 and $60,000. How could he keep these companies from forcing Chipco into bankruptcy? How could he work with smaller supply accounts?

Kendall needed a cash flow strategy to keep Chipco from toppling over the "financial cliff," a phrase he used often. He needed to finance the costs of the recall and replacement of chips and be prepared for a possible drop in sales volume. Normally, all sales were shipped to customers with invoices to follow, net 30 days. Would Kendall be able to continue allowing credit? Would customers balk at a request for cash C.O.D. or prepayment? Would even suggesting such terms further exacerbate Chipco's weakened relations with its customers?

Kendall wondered how he should respond to his employees as the crisis unfolded. How could he keep his staff from deserting? Should he tell them the whole story or just parts as events unfolded? How should Kendall respond to employees that may seek alternative employment? Could he ask them to work overtime if normal production schedules weren't sufficient to meet replacement schedules? Should he freeze wages and if so, when and how could they be adjusted at a later date? Was there any way to raise morale of his staff? Kendall had to develop a strategy that would enable him to keep his employees and pay them weekly.

While these problems needed immediate attention, Kendall knew that his operating systems cost precious cash to operate. Was there anything that could be done to reduce costs in the plant or overall operations?

As the flight to Sydney Harbor Casino progressed, Kendall's mind wandered over the multiple issues facing him. He had to create a comprehensive survival strategy to save his company and he had to craft it soon.

Note

1. The most common type of bankruptcy is Chapter 7. This type of proceeding turns over all of the debtor's property that is not exempt and has equity to a trustee for a court-administered sale. The proceeds are distributed to the company's creditors. In a Chapter 13 bankruptcy a company continues to pay off debts under an installment plan administered by a trustee. The third form of bankruptcy is Chapter 11, which is designed to allow a company to reorganize and continue operating with certain court protection from creditors, while it attempts to develop a plan to pay the creditors. (Maine State Bar Association, 2001)

References

Casino Executive by Ascend Media Gaming Group. 11600 W. College Blvd., Overland Park, Kansas 66210.

Casino Journal by Ascend Media Gaming Group. 11600 W. College Blvd., Overland Park, Kansas 66210.

Ciaffone, Bob. 1991. A comparative study of state laws on social gambling. *Gambling and Public Policy: International Perspectives.* Eadington, William R. and Judy A. Cornelius, eds. Reno: Institute for the Study of Gambling and Commercial Gaming, University of Nevada, pp. 183 to 204.

Chipco International, company documents & interviews. 1281 Roosevelt Ave.,

Raymond, Maine 04071. August 2000—May 2002.

Christiansen, Eugene. 1998. The United States 1997 gross annual wager.

Supplement to *International Gaming and Wagering Business Magazine.* August.

Clotfelter, Charles and Philip Cook. 1989. Selling Hope: State Lotteries in America. Cambridge: *Harvard University Press.*

Eadington, William. 1999, Summer. The economics of casino gambling.

Journal of Economic Perspectives. 173 to 192.

Maine State Bar Association. 2001. Basic fact about bankruptcy in the state of Maine.

Rose, I. Nelson. 1991. The rise and fall of the third wave: gambling will be outlawed in forty years. *Gambling and Public Policy: International Perspectives.* Eadington, William R. And Judy A. Cornelius, eds. Reno: Institute for the Study of Gambling and Commercial Gaming, University of Nevada, pp. 65–86.

Underwood, Elaine. 1995. Casino gambling's new deal. *Brandweek* Apr. 10 p. 21–4.

Traditional Case 12: Dixie Chicks: Heading Home or Moving On? Controversy and Strategic Positioning in the Music Business

This case was prepared by Kelley A. Still and Clifton D. Petty, both of Drury University. It is intended to be used for class discussion. The views presented here are those of the case authors and do not necessarily reflect the views of the Society for Case Research. The authors' views are based on their own professional judgment. Copyright © 2006 by the Society for Case Research and the authors. No part of this work may be used or reproduced in any form or by any means without a written permission of the Society for Case Research.

Three women wait to take the stage at the famed Shepherd's Bush Empire in London, England. This is one of the most storied venues of rock and roll, a concert hall that has featured classic performances by the Rolling Stones and The Who. The crowd is chanting, and the lead singer begins to ascend the stage. She and her fellow band members are dressed in the standard trappings of rock and roll performers.

It is March 10, 2003. And this is the moment before everything changes for this famous trio. These three women rising to take the stage at Shepherd's Bush are no typical rockers. They are country music's hottest band, the Dixie Chicks. In January, they played one of music's most coveted gigs—singing the National Anthem at the Super Bowl. Barely a month later, the Dixie Chicks collected three Grammy awards. Their latest album, *Home*, is number one on the charts. In the week following the Grammy awards, sales of *Home* spiked 60 percent to 202,530 units.[1] They are at the peak of country music success.

But beyond their success as country performers, the Dixie Chicks are a type of very rare bird indeed. They are a crossover act, attracting both country and pop fans. They follow in footsteps that only a few—Elvis Presley, Garth Brooks, Shania Twain–performers have successfully maneuvered. As they have done for countless nights over the past few years, the celebrities known as the Dixie Chicks take the stage to a thunderous welcome.

Back in Natalie Maines' hometown of Austin, Texas, it is a cool spring day. Country radio station FM 101 (KASE) airs a typical country playlist,

including a healthy offering of the Dixie Chicks' latest hit singles. The Texas country music faithful listen and hum along. None of these fans in Austin or London could know it at the time, but by morning they will be choosing sides. And by morning the Dixie Chicks will face both a firestorm of controversy and enormous uncertainty about the future of their audience.

The Dixie Chicks' Climb to Fame

The Dixie Chicks' success did not arrive overnight. The beginnings of the band can be traced to the early classical training of sisters Martie and Emily Erwin. Born in Dallas, Texas, Martie and Emily were early recruits to lessons on multiple instruments. With their parents as overseers, Martie and Emily became accomplished musicians and by 1984 were touring Texas with a bluegrass band. By 1989, they were performing on the sidewalks in Dallas with two singer girlfriends. They called themselves the Dixie Chicks, a name drawn from a line in a song by the rock band Little Feat. By 1993, the Dixie Chicks had three albums under their belt and were well respected for their traditional country/bluegrass sound. Despite some initial success, the Dixie Chicks felt misunderstood by the music industry. At the time, they considered themselves most effective in concert, and felt that record labels didn't "get" them and wanted them to be something they were not.[2] Their future seemed uncertain when one singer left in 1992 and Laura Lynch left the group in 1995.

After the departures of their two fellow band members, Martie and Emily asked Natalie Maines to join them as lead singer in 1995. The sisters had met Natalie through her father, Lloyd, a respected musician who had played steel guitar for some of the band's early recordings. Maines was a solid musician in her own right, and like the Erwin sisters she was a music student. She had studied music at Berklee School of Music in Boston, and graduated from the commercial music program at South Plains College, a two-year college in Texas.[3] Their first album with Maines, *Wide Open Spaces*, sold 6 million copies and won them a Best New Artist Grammy.

In 1999, it appeared that the band was trying to make the crossover into mainstream pop music. The Dixie Chicks joined the Lillith Fair, a music tour conceived by Sarah MacLachlan to promote women in music. They brought country music to the Lillith Fair tour, and brought the band exposure to audiences that did not typically listen to country music. Their marketing appeared to be pushing them mainstream, but, ironically, their music was moving the other way. The Lillith Fair was great publicity for their next album, *Fly*, which returned to a stronger bluegrass and Texas country music sound. The fiddle and banjo instrumentals were more evident than they had been in the *Wide Open Spaces* album. Pressured to water down the fiddle for VH1 play, the Dixie Chicks refused. They asserted that they took this stand to protect their sound and to avoid "selling out" to appeal to everyone.[4]

After *Fly* was released, the Dixie Chicks did an 85-city tour in 2000. Many of the venues they played had as many as 20,000 seats. They insisted on input on every aspect of the tour, including a very theatrical-feeling set design. According to Martie (Erwin) Seidel, "Do it our way" was the Dixie Chicks motto. They grossed $40 million from *Fly* tour and capped off 2000 with a prime-time NBC special.[5]

The Dixie Chicks took an artistic and peforming break in 2001. Additionally, they put real teeth behind their motto of "Do it our way" and sued their record label for underpayment of royalties and requested to be released from their contract. If the band had successfully broken their contract in court, they might have changed the recording industry forever.[6] Instead, the two parties settled and the band gained more artistic and marketing control. The success of the first two albums, *Wide Open Spaces* and *Fly* (20 million copies), had given the band new negotiating leverage with Sony.

The Dixie Chicks began work on the album *Home* before the resolution of their litigation with Sony. They financed the production, chose to produce it in Texas rather than Nashville, and co-produced it with Lloyd Maines, Natalie's father. The band even went so far as to shop the album around to other record companies before settling with Sony.[7] The Dixie Chicks' settlement with Sony provided them with the unusual provision of their own Sony subsidiary, Open Wide Records, which released *Home*.

The musical direction taken by *Home* was a more acoustical, bluegrass sound. This surprised many critics and fans, who generally expect a group to become more "slick" and "polished" with each round of success. The homey roots may have reflected the band's personal lives in this period, as the break from tour provided more time at home with family. The band may have been responding to some critics as well. Maines reportedly wanted to show that she could sing without shouting and the sisters wanted to explore more instrumentation. Apparently the band knew that they might be taking new risks with their existing fan base.

With a clear management situation and a new album, the Dixie Chicks mounted a major tour in 2002. The tour included 52 performances, most at major arena venues. Once again they broke with tradition by declaring an "on-sale" date for the entire tour. This was counter to accepted practice in the country music industry, which normally works about four weeks out with ticket sales. The Dixie Chicks also seemed very unconcerned about what artists were playing what dates close to their dates and locations.[8]

Igniting Controversy

Betty Clarke, a music critic for *The Guardian*, was assigned the Dixie Chicks' concert at Shepherd's Bush on March 10, 2003. Clarke's review described the bands' outfits as "more New York than Nashville." She highlighted the Dixie Chicks' recent run of success, and their feisty nature. The review included some positive statements about their music: "Bluegrass' charm lies in its rawness, but the Dixie Chicks have polished the mountain sound and made it palatable for a new audience."

But a single quote from this review made history.[9]

Just so you know, we're ashamed the president of the United States is from Texas. (Natalie Maines, Dixie Chicks lead singer, March 10, 2003)

Maines' "President Bush" comment quickly lit up international news wires. The spring of 2003 was a time of remarkable international tension. The world's attention was focused on the crisis swirling around Iraq, the latest crescendo in the escalating war on terrorism.

The War on Terrorism. Following the terrorist attacks on the World Trade Center buildings on September 11, 2001, President Bush declared a "war on terrorism."

The United States issued an ultimatum to Afghanistan's Taliban leaders on September 16, 2001. The Taliban refused to give up the alleged mastermind of the September 11 attack, Osama Bin Laden, and on October 7, 2001 the United States attacked Afghanistan. Although Bin Laden eluded capture, the operation was generally considered a success. The first major operation of the war on terrorism was over.

Waves of "high alert" terrorist warnings came and went in the United States in the months following the war in Afghanistan. U.S. agents and military personnel continued the hunt for Bin Laden. Near misses were reported, but Bin Laden was never located. And his elusiveness fueled increasing concerns about international terror networks.

The attention of the White House shifted to Iraqi leader Saddam Hussein. Hussein had never fully complied with United Nation's resolutions passed in the aftermath of the first Gulf War (1990/1991). In addition, the Bush administration argued that large-scale terror attacks carried fingerprints of support from states. The administration gave increasing attention to the list of states alleged to sponsor terrorism. In his State of the Union Speech on January 29, 2002, President Bush named Iran, Iraq, and North Korea as an "axis of evil," and chief among the state sponsors of terrorism.

President Bush's "axis of evil" speech fueled heated debate and controversy. The United Nations took up the issues raised by the speech, and over time attention focused squarely on Iraq. While many argued that North Korea or Iran posed greater or more immediate threats, President Bush argued that Iraq was both an immediate threat and an illegitimate regime. In pressing the case, he highlighted Iraq's long and consistent history of violating or ignoring U.N. resolutions and sanctions. British Prime Minister Tony Blair resolutely supported the U.S. position. But many European leaders, chiefly French President Jacques Chirac and German Chancellor Gerhard Schroder, vigorously opposed the U.S.

position on Iraq. They argued for more weapons inspections, and against the use of force to enforce prior resolutions.

Early in 2003, the debate on Iraq boiled over into acrimony and bitter debate. The "inspections" faction, led by France, blocked all U.S. attempts to gain UN resolution supporting the application of force (as called for in the resolutions) to enforce Gulf War and Post 9/11 resolutions on Iraq. Frustrated at the United Nations, the U.S., Great Britain and Spain formed a "coalition of the willing" and proceeded with war plans.

Backlash. By the time Natalie Maines made her President Bush comment, a war with Iraq seemed imminent. Although President Bush had approval ratings in the 60 to 65 percent range, his position on Iraq was controversial. Anti-war demonstrations were held in major cities, and several public figures spoke out in opposition to the war policy. Prime Minister Blair was a more controversial figure, and the British public was more strongly opposed to the war with Iraq. Several large anti-war demonstrations were held in London in February and March of 2003.

The Dixie Chicks entered this international controversy near the zenith of tension and debate. Their March 10 concert in Shepherd's Bush preceded the beginning of the war in Iraq by one week.

Reactions to the President Bush comment were swift and intense. Cumulus Media instructed all of its 42 country stations to stop playing the group's music until further notice.[10] Clear Channel, the owners of FM 101 (KASE) in Austin, also pulled the band from their playlist nationwide.

Maines' "President Bush" comment made headlines across the United States, and country music fans began expressing their displeasure through calls to local radio stations. Stations that attempted to keep the Dixie Chicks on their playlist were bombarded with calls of protest. According to USA Today, Houston station KKBQ-FM had been airing the Dixie Chicks hit single, "Travelin' Soldier," an average of 12 times a day. KKBQ polled listeners after the President Bush comment. By a 3-1 margin, listeners voted to halt the play of Dixie Chicks music, and KKBQ complied.[11] Sales of the Dixie Chicks latest album, titled *Home,* declined by more than 40 percent in the week following the comment.[12]

In some cities, events were held to denounce the band and destroy their CDs. A local radio station in Bossier City, Louisiana, sponsored a "Chick Bash." A few hundred protestors attended the gathering, and expressed support for President Bush and nearby Barksdale Air Force Base. They also expressed their displeasure with the *Dixie Chicks* by running over their CDs with a tractor.[13] A Kansas City station offered receptacles for disposal of Dixie Chicks CDs.[14]

On March 14, the band issued a statement from Natalie Maines of the Dixie Chicks:

As a concerned American citizen, I apologize to President Bush because my remark was disrespectful. I feel that whoever holds that office should be treated with the utmost respect. We are currently in Europe and witnessing a huge anti-American sentiment as a result of the perceived rush to war. While war may remain a viable option, as a mother, I just want to see every possible alternative exhausted before children and American soldiers' lives are lost. I love my country. I am a proud American.[15]

This statement did little to quell the mounting controversy. One week later, on the night of March 19, President Bush announced the beginning of "Operation Iraqi Freedom." The war had begun.

Country music has a long tradition of closing ranks to support the United States in wartime. In an interview with CMT.com, Billboard country charts editor Wade Jensen observed: "I think this is new territory, and it's very, very sensitive and very emotional. It's particularly sensitive in the country format because we're really where patriotism lives. Country is the format that expects patriotism. But at this time in the nation's history, there's a lot of confusion over just what patriotism is and what it constitutes."[16]

Others were less conflicted. Shortly after the Dixie Chicks issued their apology statement, the South Carolina House of Representatives passed a resolution calling for the Dixie Chicks to apologize directly to South Carolinians, and requesting that the trio play a free concert for troops and military families in the state. The opening of the Dixie Chicks' United States tour was scheduled to begin in South Carolina on May 1.

On April 25, 2003, President Bush was interviewed by Tom Brokaw of NBC. Brokaw asked the president about his reaction to the comments made by Dixie Chick Natalie Maines. President Bush responded:

They can say what they want to say. And . . . they shouldn't have their feelings hurt just because some people don't want to buy their records when they speak out. You know, freedom is a two-way street.[17]

The Dixie Chicks Respond

In a startling twist, the Dixie Chicks posed nude on the cover of the May edition of *Entertainment* magazine. The photo included various conflicting labels written on their bodies, including "Traitors," "Saddam's angels," and "Proud Americans." Reuters reported that the trio posed nude "in response to the controversy created by pro-war advocates over Maines' remark at a concert in London on March 10 that they were ashamed President George W. Bush was from their home state of Texas."[18]

On April 24, 2003, the group appeared on *Primetime Thursday* for an interview with Diane Sawyer. The title of this interview segment was "Landslide: The Dixie Chicks," a play on their recent hit remake of the Fleetwood Mac song "Landslide." In one line of conversation, Diane Sawyer pressed the trio about the "mistake":

Diane Sawyer: (Voice over): Her statement talked about her frustration over the war. And apologized to the President. But it only added fuel to the fire.

Natalie Maines: People who are on our side think I was pressured. They like to believe that I was made to apologize, you know, because they liked me until I apologized. And then the people who didn't like me thought that it was written by someone else and couldn't give me credit for my own apology. And neither of those is true.

Emily Robison: We do make mistakes, as we all have, you know.

Diane Sawyer: But you haven't told me what the mistake was.

Natalie Maines: I think it came down to that it was a foreign country. And it was that it was an off-the-cuff statement. And the way I said it was disrespectful. The wording I used, the way I said it. That was disrespectful.

Diane Sawyer: I hear something not quite, what, wholehearted.

Natalie Maines: Really?

Diane Sawyer: When you talk about apologizing for what you said about the President.

Natalie Maines: I understand what you're saying. And I might be doing that. But it's not, it's not because it's not genuine. It's because I'm on guard now. But I feel regrettable. I feel regret for, you know the choice of words. For the non-choice of words. Am I sorry I said that? Yes. Am I sorry I spoke out? No. Am I sorry that I asked questions that I just don't follow? No.

And this brief exchange near the end of the interview:

Diane Sawyer: "If the President's watching tonight?"

Natalie Maines: "We hope not, don't we?"

Diane Sawyer: "Want to say something?"

Natalie Maines: "Your show's not long enough."[19]

The Dixie Chicks opened their U.S. tour in Greensboro, South Carolina on May 1, 2003. They offered those attending the concert an opening segment to "boo" if they wanted. Few did, and the Dixie Chicks launched into their show. They did not apologize to South Carolina, or meet the other requests of the South Carolina legislature.

The Dixie Chicks tour had sold $45 million in tickets in January 2003, before the controversy erupted. The tour was originally headlined as "Lipton Tea Presents the Dixie Chicks Top of the World Tour." But in early May, *USA Today* reported that Lipton had retreated from key aspects of the promotional arrangement.[20] According to this report: "Unilever, which owns the Lipton brand, and Pepsi, which markets Lipton tea drinks, jointly announced the concert sponsorship and sweepstakes with much fanfare in February." Original plans called for Lipton to include pictures of the Dixie Chicks on packages of Lipton products beginning in May 2003. But Lipton scrapped these promotions and cancelled plans for a sweepstakes linked to the Dixie Chicks.

Courtesy of the Red, White and Blue. As the Dixie Chicks responded to mounting controversy, patriotic songs flew up the country music chart. "Have you Forgotten?," a post 911 anthem by Darryl Worley, climbed to number one after only five weeks on the chart.[21] Lee Greenwood's 1984 release, "God Bless the USA," received strong airplay and returned to the country charts.

Some of the music also underscored support for the military. Two examples included the Clint Black release "I Raq and Roll," and Toby Keith's "Courtesy of the Red, White and Blue." A few of these songs also expressed empathy and support for President Bush. The Warren Brothers' song, "Hey Mr. President," entered the charts at number 47 in the week of March 31, 2003, the highest-debuting single of that week.[22]

Clint Black's "I Raq and Roll" included the following lyrics:

> You can wave your signs in protest
> Against America taking stands
> The stands America's taken
> Are the reason that you can…[23]

This patriotic sweep also rekindled a simmering feud between the Dixie Chicks and Toby Keith. Months before the "Courtesy of the Red, White and Blue" climbed the charts, *Country Weekly* quoted Maines' offering an opinion of the song: "I hate it. It's ignorant and it makes country music sound ignorant." Toby Keith responded: "You've got to be in my league as a songwriter before I'll even respond to you. If she had written some songs like me, then we'd talk about the inside of the song."[24] The dispute intensified through the period of controversy, with Keith allegedly including images of Natalie Maines with Saddam Hussein in his concert shows. When the Dixie Chicks appeared in a live performance via satellite for the 2003 CMA Awards program, Maines wore a shirt with initials widely interpreted as a derogatory message for Toby Keith. The CMA Awards program aired on May 21, 2003. By this time, country fans were weighing in and taking sides. Toby Keith won Entertainer of the Year that night, and received more nominations (eight) than any other performer. The Dixie Chicks were nominated for three awards, but failed to collect on any of their nominations.

Trends in the U.S. Music Market

Musical Genres. The U.S. music industry crested at just over US$14 billion in sales in 1999. Since 1999, the U.S. market has mirrored the international pattern of declining sales. Total U.S. music sales dropped roughly 10 percent in 2002, to $12.8 billion (see Figure 1).

In addition to the decline in overall sales, consumer preferences for musical genres and sales channels have shifted in the 1993/2002 period (see Figure 2).

FIGURE 1 Total Annual U.S. Music Sales: 1993 to 2002

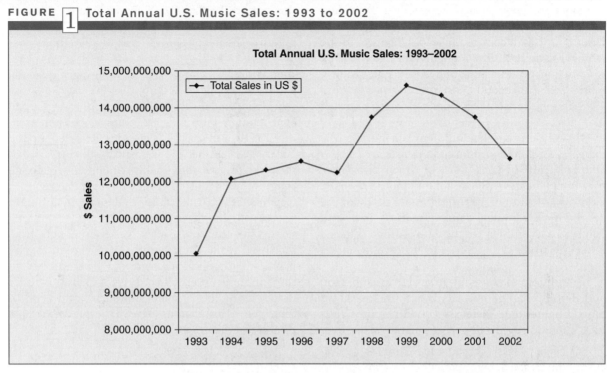

FIGURE 2 Trends in U.S. Music Consumers by Genre

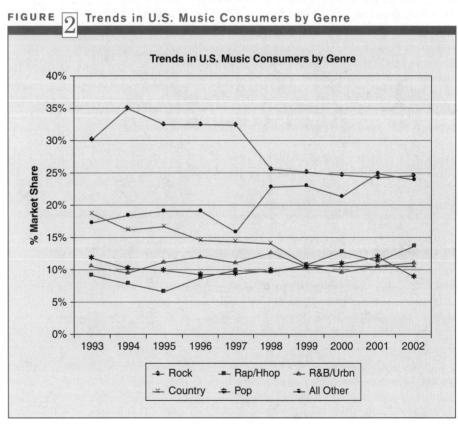

475

Only two major musical genres have generated growth in recent years—Rap/Hip Hop, and R&B/Urban. Although rock music leads all genres in the United States, its 24.7 percent market share in 2002 is far below the 1994 peak of 35.1 percent. Country music was the second most popular genre until 1998. But in the 1999/2002 period, country music's market share slid 24 percent.[25]

Pop music is the leading genre in most music markets. The two exceptions to this rule are Ireland and the United States, both of which favor rock over pop.[26] In the U.S. market, pop music reversed a downward slide in 1997. Beginning in 1998, the genre enjoyed gradual gains in market share. But 2002 was a tough year for the genre, which suffered a decline from 12.1 percent to 9 percent market share.

In addition to the shift toward Rap/Hip Hop and R&B/Urban genres, the U.S. music market is more fragmented. Various secondary genres (all) have gained roughly 50 percent market share over the period 1997/2002. The dominance of rock music has slipped steadily since the late 1990s, and together the major genres have "flat lined."

Demographics. The U.S. market has aged over the 1993 to 2002 period. Only the 45+ category rose sharply in the late 1990s, claiming just over 25 percent market share in 2002. Sales to consumers in the 15/19 and 20/24 categories declined in the late 1990s. This decline is particularly worrisome as these two groups traditionally combined to generate roughly half of all U.S. music sales (see Figure 3).

Since 1995, U.S. music sales to males have decreased from 53 percent to 49.4 percent of total sales. Over the same period, sales to females have increased from 47 percent to 50.6 percent of the market. This gender pattern may be connected to shifts in genre preference. Both rock and country draw slightly larger male audiences, and each of these genres lost market share in the late 1995/2002 period (see Figure 4).

FIGURE 3 Age Distribution in U.S. Music Market: 1993 to 2002

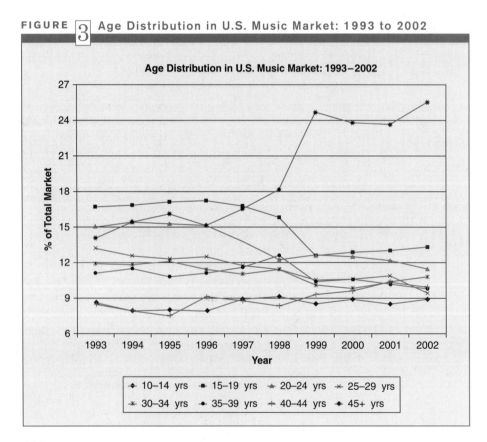

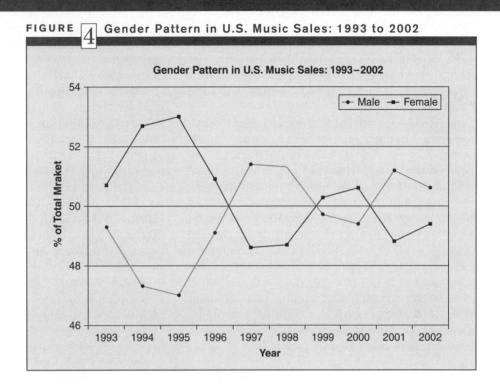

FIGURE 4 Gender Pattern in U.S. Music Sales: 1993 to 2002

Country Music and Country Crossovers

Down, but Certainly Not Out. Although country music has lost U.S. market share in recent years, the genre remains a potent force. In 2001, Airplay Monitors reported 5 country stars among its lists of Most-Played List in all formats—Faith Hill (1), Tim McGraw (3), George Strait (6), Alan Jackson (7), and Garth Brooks (9).[27] The American Music Awards have also showcased the influence of the genre. In 2001, Faith Hill won both Favorite Female Pop/Rock Artist, as well as two awards specific to country music (Favorite Female Country Artist, and Favorite Country Album). Garth Brooks received the special Award of Merit at the 2002 American Music Awards.

Perhaps the clearest example of the reach of country music is the meteoric rise of Shania Twain. Twain joins Whitney Houston and Mariah Carey as the only single performers to achieve back-to-back albums with sales above 10 million. Her album *Come on Over* is the best-selling album ever by a female solo artist, and fourth on the all time "single CD" best selling albums list behind Fleetwood Mac's *Rumours*, Led Zeppelin's *Led Zeppelin IV*, Michael Jackson's *Thriller*, and the Eagle's *Greatest Hits*.[28]

From Hillbilly to Mainstream. The music known today as "country" traces its roots to the "back home" folk music of the 1920s. At a time of rapid urbanization, the early forms of country music filled a longing for the country life. This early folk music gave way to the honky-tonk era of Hank Williams in the middle of the century. Around the same time, such "white hat" traditionalists as Roy Rogers and Dale Evans provided musical backdrop for the heyday of cowboy movie popularity.

The rather wide-ranging forms of honky-tonk, western swing and cowboy movie music gave way in the 1950s to the "Nashville sound," perhaps best exemplified by Chet Atkins, Eddy Arnold, and Patsy Cline. This smoother and better orchestrated form of music generated record sales and fueled the careers of such second-generation stars as Charley Pride, Crystal Gale, Anne Murray and Glen Campbell.

In the 1960s, a return to the rowdier days of honky-tonk was fueled by balladeers such as Merle Haggard, Waylon Jennings, Willie Nelson and

Johnny Cash. These artists incorporated rock elements with blues and modern honky-tonk lyrics. The results spawned some new attention and notoriety for the country music form, and also fostered several later stars such as Hank Williams Jr., and Mickey Gilley.

The new popularity of country and country-rock drove the brief but intense "Urban Cowboy" movement. The John Travolta movie by this name was the peak of the country-chic fad. Partially in reaction to this movement, a new wave of traditional country emerged in the late 1980s. Artists such as Clint Black, Randy Travis and George Strait hearkened back to the cowboy and folk heritage of mainstream country music. These "New Traditionalists"[29] were enormously successful. Garth Brooks, one of the most successful country crossover artists of all time, drew upon both the New Traditionalist and Outlaw bases to create an explosive blend of traditional country-rock. This formula yielded Brooks both crossover appeal and celebrity status.[29]

The Era of Crossover. The most recent eras of county music have differed from previous ones in the potential for a country music artist to attract a crossover audience. To build their audience, artists must typically establish their identity and credibility within a particular musical genre. The dress, style of music, and other trappings tend to "place" musicians in their home genre. In rare cases, an artist is able to bring together an audience across musical lines. To cross over two or more genres is not only rare, but enormously valuable. Given established fan loyalties to other performers, the mainstream country fan base is not large enough to support record sales in the heights achieved by Shania Twain, Faith Hill, and more recently, the Dixie Chicks. Successfully crossing genres both differentiates a particular artist, and sends their sales potential skyward.

The first country crossover success was Eddie Arnold.[30] Arnold crossed over in country and pop in the late 1950s. Over the succeeding decades a few other country artists have managed to straddle two genres. Most notable among these 1960 to 1980 crossover successes were Kenny Rogers, Barbara Mandrell, Emmylou Harris, Willie Nelson, and the group Alabama. Despite these notable successes, true crossover status during this period was rare and mostly fleeting. Maintaining a strong identity

and audience appeal across genres proved enormously difficult. The "where are they now?" games are filled with artists who created a one-hit crossover single or album.

Enter Garth Brooks. Garth Brooks exploded onto the country music scene in the late 1980s. His arrival ushered in a new era of country music crossover opportunities. Together with the groundwork laid by earlier country-rock and country-pop crossovers, the Garth Brooks phenomena widened the audience base for country music. It also redefined country music concert success. In 1993, Garth Brooks sold out Texas Stadium in 92 minutes, selling over 65,000 tickets. Responding to the ticket-buying frenzy, he performed two subsequent shows in this venue, each selling out within 92 minutes.[31] *Rolling Stone* commented: "If Garth's sales have propelled country music into the American mainstream, he has achieved them by exploding country stereotypes. While his songs strive for the intimacy of feeling and literary finesse of singer-songwriters like James Taylor and Dan Fogelberg, his shows are raucous rock-outs."[32] Over 5 million concert goers saw Garth Brooks over his three-year World Tour in the late 1990s. The tour grossed more than $105 million. Total country music concert receipts were $150 million in 1998, up 23 percent from 1997.[33]

The country audience also became more diverse. Throughout the 1990s, country music made gains among younger listeners, women, and international audiences. By the year 2000, approximately one-third of the country music audience was under the age of 34. Women composed 54 percent of the country audience in 2000, compared to roughly 50 percent for music overall.[34] Despite its traditional hard luck themes, the family incomes of this audience are slightly higher than the national average. In 1999, 75 percent of the country audience owned their own homes and 53 percent had household incomes exceeding $50,000.[35]

Although the U.S. market remains home base, country music has made inroads in global markets. Of the 36 million copies of *Come on Over* sold by Shania Twain by early 2002, roughly 17 million were sold outside the United States. This album was also certified platinum in Germany in 2000, 15x platinum in Australia, and was ranked the top-selling album in the United Kingdom in 1999.[36]

Shania Twain was not the only female country artist to emerge as a crossover star in the late 1990s. LeAnn Rimes' crossover single "How do I Live" remained number one on the Billboard Pop Chart for a record 32 weeks, and achieved 3x platinum sales. This single also set the record for endurance on Billboard's Top Country Chart, at more than 200 weeks. Deana Carter's debut album, *Did I shave my legs for this?* went gold in 6 weeks, and platinum in 3 months. And finally, the established star Faith Hill rose to celebrity status. In 1999, Faith Hill appeared in the VH1 Divas '99 concert, and in 2001 she sang the theme song "There You'll Be" in the Oscar-nominated theme to the movie *Pearl Harbor*.[37]

But perhaps the most talked-about new arrivals in female country circles were the Dixie Chicks. Since the release of *Wide Open Spaces* in 1998, the trio has sold 25 million albums, and won seven Grammy awards. Like Garth Brooks, the Dixie Chicks seemed to have arrived in the right place at the right time. Female country singers were dominating the charts in the late 1990s, and a few were achieving huge crossover success. Before March 10, 2003, it seemed that the Dixie Chicks were destined for reaching the same lofty heights as Garth and Shania.

Crossroads

After March 10, 2003, the Dixie Chicks faced a much more uncertain future. Country radio has the greatest reach of any musical genre. In the weeks following Maines' President Bush comment, the Dixie Chicks were dropped from most country radio playlists. Although they have returned to the airwaves in many markets, their airplay ratings remain far below the heady days of 2002. Will the country audience return? Should the Dixie Chicks take steps to reposition themselves in the country market?

Like other crossover acts before them, the Dixie Chicks success was fueled by working at least two audiences at any given time. In addition to their huge country base, the band had cultivated a pop music following. Should the Dixie Chicks now take a turn toward the pop audience? How would the Dixie Chicks position themselves more deeply in the pop side of the market, and what would such a transition require?

Controversy is certainly nothing new to the music business. The music industry is a vibrant and volatile blend of art and business. But on March 10, 2002, the Dixie Chicks ignited a controversy of presidential proportions. At the time, they occupied a strong competitive position across country and pop categories. It is certainly possible that, like many other controversies, this one will fade like a fast moving thunderstorm. Perhaps the Dixie Chicks will weather the storm and regain their prior position. But whether short or long, mild or severe, this controversy requires strategic response. As in any controversy, the ground underneath all participants in this market has rumbled and shifted. Some, such as Toby Keith, appear to have already benefited from these changes. What strategy should the Dixie Chicks pursue post-controversy? What strategic adjustments should the band make in the shorter term, and what market position should they aim for in the longer term?

The Dixie Chicks have long claimed the motto "Do it our way." It seems a fitting motto for a band whose name became instantly synonymous with large-scale controversy. And now this controversial group must seek its home amidst the turbulence.

Notes

1. *"Dixie Chicks* see sales slump," *World Entertainment News Network,* 3/30/03,
2. Orr, Charlene & Melinda Newman, "Continental Drift," *Billboard,* 6/4/94, 24.
3. Hellinger, Jeremy & Chris Rose, "Feather Friend," *People,* 9/28/98, 167/168.
4. Flippo, Chet, "Dixie Chicks see a Mainstream Crossover in Lillith Tour," *Billboard,* 5/8/99, 30–31.
5. Waddell, Ray, "For a Monument's *Dixie Chicks*, the Motto is 'Do it Our Way,'" *Billboard,* 12/9/2000.
6. Spong, John, "Cheap! Cheap!" *Texas Monthly,* January 2002.
7. Tyrangiel, Josh, "Dixie Divas," *Time,* 8/26/02.
8. Waddell, Ray, "Can marketplace handle busy Country tour lineup," *Billboard,* 3/15/03.
9. Betty Clarke, "The Dixie Chicks, Shepherd's Bush Empire, London," *The Guardian,* 3/12/03.
10. "Anti-Bush remark hits band CD sales," *Guardian Newspapers,* 3/19/03.
11. Cited in "Anti-Bush remark hits band CD sales," *Guardian Newspapers,* 3/19/03.
12. "Dixie Chicks see sales slump," *World Entertainment News Network,* 3/30/03,
13. "CDs smashed to protest Dixie Chicks," *Louisiana Gannett News,* 3/17/03.
14. "Upset about Bush remarks, radio stations dump Dixie Chicks," Click2Houston.com, 3/14/03.

15. "Statement from Natalie Maines of the Dixie Chicks," Dixie Chicks website, 3/14/03.
16. Calvin Gilbert, "Country radio still weighing Chicks controversy," CMT.com, 3/17/03.
17. Maria Recio, "Dixie Chicks free to speak, Bush tells NBC's Brokaw," *Star-Telegram Washington Bureau*, 4/26/03.
18. "Dixie Chicks pose nude in response to critics," Reuters (NY), 4/25/03.
19. "Landslide: The Dixie Chicks," Transcript of *Prime Time* interview with Diane Sawyer, 4/24/03, 11, 19/20.
20. Theresa Howard, "Lipton ices some Chicks promos," *USA Today*, 5/1/03.
21. Calvin Gilbert, "Singles chart salutes Darryl Worley," CMT. com, 3/31/03.
22. Gilbert, "Darryl Worley," CMT.com, 3/31/03.
23. "I Raq and Roll," Words and Music by Clint Black and Hayden Nicholas, www.clintblack.com/songlyrics.html.
24. Chris Neal, "Smackdown! The recent feud between Toby Keith and Dixie Chick Natalie Maines continues country's long line of fussin' and fightin'" *Country Weekly Online*, 11/29/02.
25. "2002 Consumer Profile," *The Recording Industry Association of America (RIAA)*.
26. "The World Sales 2002 Report," *IFPI*, 4/9/03.
27. "2002 Consumer Profile," *The Recording Industry Association of America (RIAA)*.
28. Richard Skanse, "Shania Twain reaches a record sales peak," Rolling Stone.com, 3/16/2000.
29. Historical overview drawn from BBC Music, "A quick guide to country," 6/18/03.
30. BBC Music, "A quick guide to country," 6/18/03.
31. Roughstock, "Garth Brooks: Career Chronology 1989/1998."
32. "The Cat in the Hat: Garth Brooks," *Rolling Stone Magazine*, 4/1/93.
33. 1999 Country Music Industry Overview, CMAWorld.com.
34. 2000 MRI Country Listener Analysis, CMAWorld.com.
35. 1999 MRI Country Music Listener Analysis, CMAWorld. com.
36. 2000 Country Music Industry Overview, CMAWorld.com.
37. Allison Stewart, "Deana Carter: Artist Focus," and Michael McCall, "Faith Hill: Artist Focus," Launch.Yahoo.com.

A

acquisition A form of a merger whereby one firm purchases another, often with a combination of cash and stock.

adaptive culture A culture whereby members of an organization are willing and eager to embrace any change that is consistent with the core values.

agency problem A situation in which a firm's top managers (i.e., the "agents" of the firm's owners) do not act in the best interests of the shareholders.

B

backward integration A firm's acquisition of its suppliers.

balanced scorecard An approach to measuring performance based on an array of quantitative and qualitative factors, such as return on assets, market share, customer loyalty and satisfaction, speed, and innovation.

barriers to entry Obstacles to entering an industry, including economies of scale, brand identity and product differentiation, capital requirements, switching costs, access to distribution channels, cost disadvantages independent of size, and government policy.

BCG growth-share matrix A corporate portfolio framework developed by the Boston Consulting Group that categorizes a firm's business units by the market share that the firm holds and the growth rate of the firm's respective markets.

best practices Processes or activities that have been successful in other firms.

brand manager The project manager in Proctor & Gamble's version of the matrix structure.

business model The economic mechanism by which a business hopes to sell its goods or services and generate a profit.

business process reengineering The application of technology and creativity in an effort to eliminate unnecessary operations or drastically improve those that are not performing well.

business unit An organizational entity with its own unique mission, set of competitors, and industry.

business web A system of internetworked, fluid, specialized businesses that come together to create value for customers.

business-to-business (B2B) The segment of electronic commerce whereby businesses utilize the Internet to solicit transactions from each other.

business-to-consumer (B2C) The segment of electronic commerce whereby businesses utilize the Internet to solicit transactions from consumers, also known as *e-tailing*.

business-to-government (B2G) The segment of electronic commerce whereby businesses utilize the Internet to solicit transactions from government entities.

C

capital-labor substitution An organization's ability to substitute labor for capital or vice versa as production increases.

centralization An organizational decision-making approach whereby most strategic and operating decisions are made by managers at the top of the organization structure (at corporate headquarters).

CEO duality A situation in which the CEO also serves as the chair of the board.

clicks and bricks The simultaneous application of both electronic ("clicks") and traditional ("bricks") forms of commerce.

commoditization The increasing difficulty that firms have distinguishing their products and services from those of their rivals.

comparative advantage The idea that certain products may be produced more cheaply or at a higher quality in particular countries, due to advantages in labor costs or technology.

competitive advantage A state whereby a business unit's successful strategies cannot be easily duplicated by its competitors.

competitive benchmarking The process of measuring a firm's performance against that of the top performers, usually in the same industry.

conglomerate unrelated diversification A form of diversification in which a firm acquires a business to reduce cyclical fluctuations in cash flows or revenues.

consumer-to-business (C2B) The segment of electronic commerce whereby consumers utilize the Internet to solicit transactions from businesses.

consumer-to-consumer (C2C) The segment of electronic commerce whereby consumers utilize the Internet to solicit transactions from each other.

contingency theory A view which states that the most profitable firms are likely to be the ones that develop the best fit with their environment.

core competencies The firm's key capabilities and collective learning skills that are fundamental to its strategy, performance, and long-term profitability.

corporate governance The board of directors, institutional investors, and blockholders who monitor firm strategies to ensure managerial responsiveness.

corporate profile Identification of the industry(ies) in which a firm operates.

corporate-level strategy The strategy that top management formulates for the overall company.

corporate restructuring A change in the organization's structure to improve efficiency and firm performance.

creative destruction A process whereby managers consciously and constantly destroy the old by recombining its elements into new forms.

crisis management The process of planning for and implementing the response to a wide range of negative events that could severely affect an organization.

crisis management team A cross-functional group of individuals within the organization who have been designated to develop and plan for worst-case scenarios and define standard operating procedures that should be implemented prior to any crisis event.

crisis Any substantial disruption in operations that physically affects an organization, its basic assumptions, or its core activities.

481

critical success factors (CSFs) Factors that are generally prerequisites for success among most or all competitors within a given industry.

culture A society's generally accepted values, traditions, and patterns of behavior.

D

decentralization An organizational decision-making approach in which most strategic and operating decisions are made by managers at the business unit level.

differentiation strategy A generic business unit strategy in which a larger business produces and markets to the entire industry products or services that can be readily distinguished from those of its competitors.

distinctive competence Unique resources, skills, and capabilities that enable a firm to distinguish itself from its competitors and create competitive advantage.

diversification The process of acquiring companies to increase a firm's size.

diversity The extent to which individuals within an organization are different; what constitutes "different" is often debated, however.

divestment A corporate-level retrenchment strategy in which a firm sells one or more of its business units.

downsizing A means of organizational restructuring that eliminates one or more hierarchical levels from the organization and pushes decision making downward in the organization.

E

economies of scale The decline in unit costs of a product or service that occurs as the absolute volume of production increases.

emotional intelligence One's collection of psychological attributes, such as motivation, empathy, self-awareness, and social skills.

employee stock ownership plan (ESOP) A formal program that transfers shares of stock to a company's employees.

environmental scanning The systematic collection and analysis of information about relevant macroenvironmental trends.

e-tailing Another term for *business-to-consumer (B2C)*.

exit barriers Economic, strategic, or emotional obstacles to leaving an industry.

experience curve The reduction in per unit costs that occurs as an organization gains experience producing a product or service.

external growth A corporate-level growth strategy whereby a firm acquires other companies.

F

first-mover advantages Benefits derived from being the first firm to offer a new or modified product or service.

flat organization An organization characterized by relatively few hierarchical levels and a wide span of control.

focus-differentiation strategy A generic business unit strategy in which a smaller business produces highly differentiated products or services for the specialized needs of a market niche.

focus–low-cost strategy A generic business unit strategy in which a smaller business keeps overall costs low while producing no-frills products or services for a market niche with elastic demand.

focus–low-cost/differentiation strategy A generic business unit strategy in which a smaller business produces highly differentiated products or services for the specialized needs of a select group of customers while keeping its costs low.

formal organization The official structure of relationships and procedures used to manage organizational activity.

forward integration A firm's acquisition of one or more of its buyers.

functional strategies The strategies pursued by each functional area of a business unit, such as marketing, finance, or production.

functional structure A form of organizational structure whereby each subunit of the organization engages in firm-wide activities related to a particular function, such as marketing, human resources, finance, or production.

G

gap analysis Identifying the distance between a firm's current position and its desired position with regard to an internal weakness. All things equal, it is desirable to take action to close the gap, especially when the gap leaves a firm vulnerable to external threats in its environment.

generic strategies Strategies that can be adopted by business units to guide their organizations.

geographic divisional structure A form of organizational structure in which jobs and activities are grouped on the basis of geographic location (e.g., Northeast region, Midwest region, and West region).

goals Desired general ends toward which efforts are directed.

gross domestic product (GDP) The value of a nation's annual total production of goods and services.

growth strategy A corporate-level strategy designed to increase profits, sales, and/or market share.

H

horizontal growth An increase in the breadth of an organization's structure.

horizontal related diversification A form of diversification in which a firm acquires a business outside its present scope of operation but with similar or related core competencies.

horizontal related integration A form of acquisition in which a firm expands by acquiring other companies in its same line of business.

horizontal structure An organizational structure with fewer hierarchies designed to improve efficiency by reducing layers in the bureaucracy.

human capital The sum of the capabilities of individuals in an organization.

human resources The experience, capabilities, knowledge, skills, and judgment of the firm's employees.

I

industrial organization (IO) A view based in microeconomic theory which states that firm profitability is most closely associated with industry structure.

industry life cycle The stages (introduction, growth, shakeout, maturity, and decline) through which industries are believed to pass.

industry A group of competitors that produces similar products or services.

inert culture A conservative culture that encourages maintenance of existing resources.

informal organization Interpersonal norms, behaviors, and expectations that evolve when individuals and groups come into contact with one another.

information asymmetry When one party has information that another does not.

information symmetry When all parties to a transaction share the same information concerning that transaction.

innovation Developing something new.

integrative social contracts view of ethics Perspective suggesting that decisions should be based on existing norms of behavior, including cultural, community, or industry factors.

intended strategy The original strategy top management plans and intends to implement.

internal growth A corporate-level growth strategy in which a firm expands by internally increasing its size and sales rather than by acquiring other companies.

international franchising A form of licensing in which a local franchisee pays a franchiser in another country for the right to use the franchiser's brand names, promotions, materials, and procedures.

international licensing An arrangement whereby a foreign licensee purchases the rights to produce a company's products and/or use its technology in the licensee's country for a negotiated fee structure.

intrapreneurship The creation of new business ventures within an existing firm.

J

justice view of ethics Perspective suggesting that all decisions will be made in accordance with preestablished rules or guidelines.

just-in-time (JIT) inventory system An inventory system, popularized by the Japanese, in which suppliers deliver parts just at the time they are needed by the buying organization to use in its production process.

K

knowledge management People and their skills and abilities (i.e., knowledge capital) represent the only resource that cannot readily be reproduced by a firm's competitors. Knowledge capital must be effectively leveraged if high-performing firms are to remain as such over the long term.

L

leadership style The consistent pattern of behavior that a leader exhibits in the process of governing and making decisions.

leadership The capacity to secure the cooperation of others in accomplishing organizational goals.

learning The increased efficiency that occurs when an employee performs a task repeatedly.

leveraged buyout (LBO) A takeover in which the acquiring party borrows funds to purchase a firm.

liquidation A corporate-level retrenchment strategy in which a firm terminates one or more of its business units by the sale of their assets.

low-cost strategy A generic business unit strategy in which a larger business produces, at the lowest cost possible, no-frills products and services industry-wide for a large market with a relatively elastic demand.

low-cost–differentiation strategy A generic business unit strategy in which a larger business unit maintains low costs while producing distinct products or services industry-wide for a large market with a relatively inelastic demand.

M

macroenvironment The general environment that affects all business firms in an industry, which includes political-legal, economic, social, and technological forces.

managerial ethics An individual's responsibility to make business decisions that are legal, honest, moral, and fair.

market share The percentage of total market sales attributed to one competitor (i.e., firm sales divided by total market sales).

mass customization The ability to individualize product and service offerings to meet specific buyer needs.

matrix structure A form of organizational structure that combines the functional and product divisional structures.

merger A corporate-level growth strategy in which a firm combines with another firm through an exchange of stock.

mission The reason for an organization's existence. The mission statement is a broadly defined but enduring statement of purpose that identifies the scope of an organization's operations and its offerings to the various stakeholders.

multiple strategies A strategic alternative for a larger business unit in which the organization simultaneously employs more than one of the generic business strategies.

O

objectives Specific, verifiable, and often quantified versions of a goal.

offshoring Relocating some or all of a firm's manufacturing or other business processes to another country to reduce costs.

organizational culture The shared values and patterns of belief and behavior that are accepted and practiced by the members of a particular organization.

organizational resources The firm's systems and processes, including its strategies at various levels, structure, and culture.

organizational structure The formal means by which work is coordinated in an organization.

outsourcing Contracting out firm's noncore, nonrevenue-producing activities to other organizations primarily to reduce costs.

P

partnership A contractual relationship with an enterprise outside the organization.

PEST An acronym referring to the analysis of the four macroenvironmental forces political-legal, economic, social, and technological.

physical resources An organization's plant and equipment, geographic locations, access to raw materials, distribution network, and technology.

PIMS (profit impact of market strategy) program A database that contains quantitative and qualitative information on the performance of more than 5,000 business units.

process innovations A business unit's activities that increase the efficiency of operations and distribution.

process R&D Research and development activities that seek to reduce the costs of operations and make them more efficient.

product divisional structure A form of organizational structure whereby the organization's activities are divided into self-contained entities, each responsible for producing, distributing, and selling its own products.

product innovations A business unit's activities that enhance the differentiation of its products or services.

product/service R&D Research and development activities directed toward improvements or innovations in the quality or uniqueness of a company's outputs.

profit center A well-defined organizational unit headed by a manager accountable for its revenues and expenditures.

Q

quality The features and characteristics of a product or service that allow it to satisfy stated or implied needs.

R

realized strategy The strategy top management actually implements.

recession A decline in a nation's GDP for two or more consecutive quarters.

relative market share A firm's share of industry sales when only the firm and its key competitors are considered (i.e., firm sales divided by sales of the key firms in the industry).

religious view of ethics Perspective that evaluates organizational decisions on the basis of personal or religious convictions.

resource-based theory The perspective that views performance primarily as a function of a firm's ability to utilize its resources.

retrenchment strategy A corporate-level strategy designed to reduce the size of the firm.

rights view of ethics Perspective that evaluates organizational decisions on the extent to which they protect individual rights.

S

self-interest view of ethics Perspective suggesting the benefits of the decision maker should be the primary consideration when weighing a decision.

self-reference criterion The unconscious reference to one's own cultural values as a standard of judgment.

simple structure An organizational form whereby each employee often performs multiple tasks, and the owner-manager is involved in all aspects of the business.

social responsibility The expectation that business firms should serve both society and the financial interests of shareholders.

societal values Concepts and beliefs that members of a society tend to hold in high esteem.

span of control The number of employees reporting directly to a given manager.

stability strategy A corporate-level strategy intended to maintain a firm's present size and current lines of business.

stakeholders Individuals or groups who are affected by or can influence an organization's operations.

strategic alliances A corporate-level growth strategy in which two or more firms agree to share the costs, risks, and benefits associated with pursuing new business opportunities. Strategic alliances are often referred to as partnerships.

strategic capabilities The mechanism through which individuals in an organization coordinate efforts along one or more resources to solve a particular problem.

strategic control The process of determining the extent to which an organization's strategies are successful in attaining its goals and objectives.

strategic group A select group of direct competitors who have similar strategic profiles.

strategic leadership Creating the vision and mission for the firm, developing strategies, and empowering individuals throughout the organization to put those strategies into action.

strategic management The continuous process of determining the mission and goals of an organization within the context of its external environment and its internal strengths and weaknesses, formulating and implementing strategies, and exerting strategic control to ensure that the organization's strategies are successful in attaining its goals.

strategy Top management's plans to attain outcomes consistent with the organization's mission and goals.

strong culture A culture characterized by deeply rooted values and ways of thinking that regulate firm behavior.

structural innovations Modifying the structure of the organization and/or the business model to improve competitiveness.

subculture A culture within a broader culture.

substitute products Alternative offerings produced by firms in another industry that satisfy similar consumer needs.

sustainable strategic management (SSM) Strategies and related processes that promote superior performance from both market and environmental perspectives.

sustained competitive advantage A firm's ability to enjoy strategic benefits over time.

SW/OT matrix A tool for generating alternative courses of action by identifying relevant combinations of internal characteristics (i.e., strengths and weaknesses) and external forces (i.e., opportunities and threats).

switching costs One-time costs that buyers of an industry's outputs incur as they switch from one company's products or services to another's.

SWOT analysis An analysis intended to match the firm's strengths and weaknesses (the *S* and *W* in the acronym) with the opportunities and threats (the *O* and *T*) posed by the environment.

synergy When the combination of two firms results in higher efficiency and effectiveness that would otherwise be achieved by the two firms separately.

T

takeover The purchase of a controlling quantity of shares in a firm by an individual, a group of investors, or another organization. Takeovers may be friendly or unfriendly.

tall organization An organization characterized by many hierarchical levels and a narrow span of control.

top management team A team of top-level executives, headed by the CEO, all of whom play instrumental roles in the strategic management process.

total quality management (TQM) A broad-based program designed to improve product and service quality and to increase customer satisfaction by incorporating a holistic commitment to quality, as seen through the eyes of the customer.

transactional leadership The capacity to motivate followers by exchanging rewards for performance.

transformational leadership The capacity to motivate followers by inspiring involvement and participation in a mission.

turnaround A corporate-level retrenchment strategy intended to transform the firm into a leaner and more effective business by reducing costs and rethinking the firm's product lines and target markets.

U

utilitarian view of ethics Perspective suggesting that anticipated outcomes and consequences should be the only considerations when evaluating an ethical dilemma.

V

value chain A useful tool for analyzing a firm's strengths and weaknesses and understanding how they might translate into competitive advantage or disadvantage. The value chain describes the activities that comprise the economic performance and capabilities of the firm.

value innovations Modifying products, services, and activities in order to maximize the value delivered to customers.

vertical growth An increase in the length of the organization's hierarchical chain of command.

vertical integration A form of integration in which a firm expands by acquiring a company in the distribution channel.

W

weak culture A culture that lacks values and ways of thinking that are widely accepted by members of the organization.

World Wide Web (WWW) The vast assortment of computers on the Internet that support hypertext.